DIVE ATLAS
OF THE WORLD

AN ILLUSTRATED REFERENCE TO THE BEST SITES

DIVE ATLAS
OF THE WORLD
AN ILLUSTRATED REFERENCE TO THE BEST SITES

GENERAL EDITOR
JACK JACKSON

The Lyons Press
Guilford, Connecticut
An imprint of The Globe Pequot Press

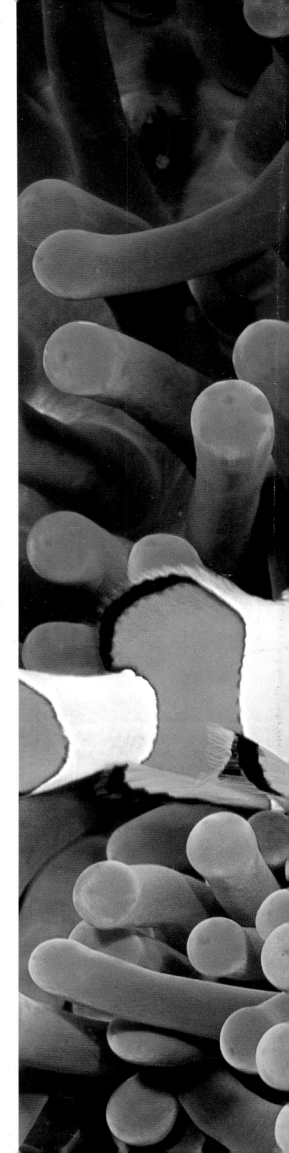

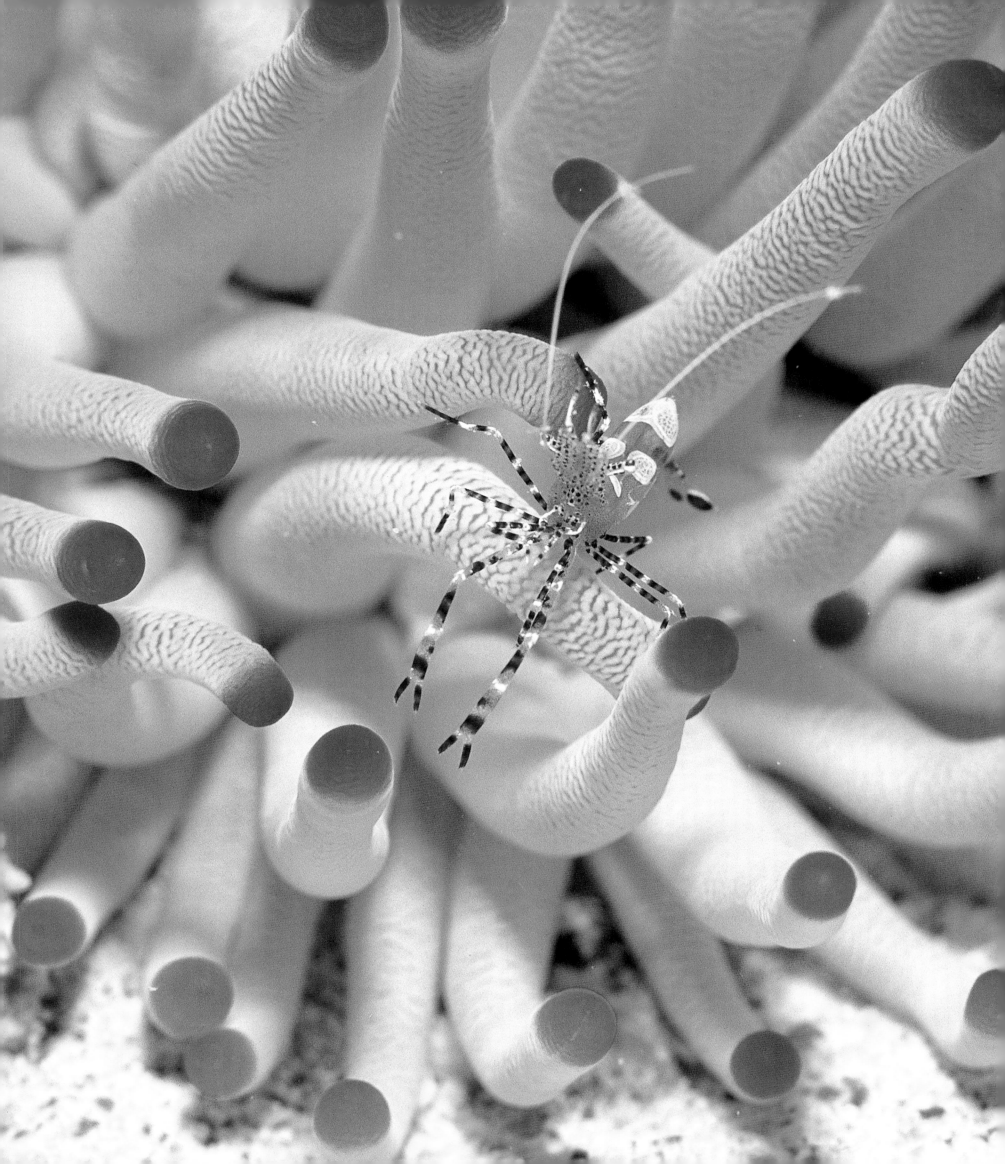

First published in 2003 in the U.S. by The Lyons Press
First published in 2003 in the U.K. by New Holland Publishers

Copyright © 2003 New Holland Publishers (UK) Ltd
Copyright © 2003 in text: individual authors
Copyright © 2003 in maps: New Holland Publishers (UK) Ltd
Copyright © 2003 in photographs: individual photographers and/or their
agents as listed on page 300

The Lyons Press is an imprint of The Globe Pequot Press

ISBN 1-59228-206-7

Library of Congress Cataloging-in-Publication Data is available on file.

Although the publishers have made every effort to ensure that information contained in this book was meticulously researched and correct at the time of going to press, they accept no responsibility for any inaccuracies, loss, injury or inconvenience sustained by any person using this book as reference.

Reproduction by Hirt & Carter (Pty) Ltd, Cape Town

Printed and bound in Singapore by Tien Wah Press (Pte) Ltd

HALF TITLE *An aerial view of Green Island, Great Barrier Reef.*
FULL TITLE *A pair of Clown Anemonefish (Amphiprion percula)
among the tentacles of their host anemone. Sulawesi, Indonesia.*
LEFT *Cleaner shrimp on anemone, Caribbean.*

CONTENTS

DIVE ATLAS OF THE WORLD

DIVE ATLAS OF THE WORLD

INTRODUCTION

by Jack Jackson

TROPICAL ISLANDS, BEACHES, TURQUOISE SEAS AND COLOURFUL reefs attract non-divers, divers and snorkellers alike, but experienced divers also enjoy deep walls in open sea, interaction with marine animals, the bounty of cold waters and the atmosphere of shipwrecks.

Remaining shallow maximizes divers' time in the water, but some divers favour short deep 'bounces', hoping to encounter sharks. While most divers prefer relaxing dives, some seek heart-thumping, shark feeding-frenzies or the adrenaline rush of high-voltage drift dives. Some divers prefer clear, warm water while others are happy with limited visibility or cold water. Wreck fanatics often ignore everything else. Whatever type of diving is preferred, most training agencies will offer a speciality course on how to enjoy it safely. Remember that deep dives, cold water and strong currents are physically demanding and conditions can change quickly, so always be prepared to abort a dive.

We have chosen popular sites for each region, with a good range of underwater environments and geographical coverage. Our criteria included quality, quantity, beauty and uniqueness of marine life, accessibility and the requirement of only a reasonable degree of physical fitness. The selection offered here celebrates the underwater world while appealing to a broad spectrum of active and armchair divers.

The book is organized according to oceans and regions within those oceans, beginning with the Atlantic and working west to east and north to south. Practical information is given in the directory appendix.

ABOVE *The Red-tipped Sea Star* (Fromia monilis) *is one of the commonest species of* Fromia *in the western Pacific and one of the most striking.*

There is considerable diversity among diving destinations. Most temperate and warm water species or seawater and freshwater species do not mix. Where regions become isolated, either permanently or temporarily such as when ice ages lowered sea levels and cut off the Red Sea, Gulf of Aden and the Arabian Gulf from the Indian Ocean, some species evolve in isolation and become endemic to those regions. Coral reefs harbour many colourful species. Nutrient-rich, cold waters offer abundant marine life that is often larger and longer-living than its tropical counterpart. Some regions have large tidal ranges. Under ice, over rock or coral and over deep water visibility can be exceptional, but where there is a large tidal flow, a sandy or muddy bottom or a plankton bloom, visibility can be awful.

Most coral reef life evolved in what is now the region bordered by the Philippines, Malaysia and Papua New Guinea and then spread out to colonize other regions. The Atlantic Ocean formed late in geological time and, early in its development, was cut off from the Pacific by North and South America fusing together. The connecting ridges in the eastern Caribbean also prevent the interchange of deep water from the Atlantic into the Caribbean. Partly as a result of being cut off on west and east, the Caribbean has fewer marine species than the Indo-Pacific.

Many Caribbean countries have sophisticated ambience, extensive facilities, maximum water clarity, habituated animal encounters and often current-free diving, a package that is particularly attractive to divers on vacation. The Indo-Pacific has the greatest species diversity, though the high level of plankton that feeds this profusion of life often degrades visibility. Some Pacific areas have strong currents and one tide each day much stronger than the other.

SHORE DIVING

Entering the water from a beach or jetty is relatively simple, but climbing over slippery rocks in full diving gear can be difficult. When entering from the rocks of a slope or wall, divers will require knowledge of the local tides because low water could result in a large drop into the water and a height too great for divers to be able to exit the water. There may be long swims across fringing reefs and photographers have extra problems with grit. Shore diving is cheaper than day-boat diving, but most of the accessible sites are not as good as those on offshore reefs.

DAY-BOAT DIVING

Day boats leave the shore for near-shore dive sites once or twice a day (few operators offer three per day). Night dives are optional. Frequently, equipment needs to be carried to and from the beach or jetty. As with any form of boat diving someone must be delegated to ensure that everyone who should be on board is on board when it departs and, most importantly, when it leaves the dive site.

In the case of an inflatable or small tender, divers will embark already kitted-up, except for fins. On larger boats divers will kit up about 15 minutes from the dive site.

Shore and day-boat diving are preferred by those who cannot sleep on a moving boat or are accompanied by non-diving partners or families and those with an interest in the local nightlife.

LIVE-ABOARD BOAT DIVING

With live-aboard diving there is less carrying of heavy equipment, no swimming over fringing reefs, biting insects are left behind when you leave port and sailing overnight maximizes the diving time on remote offshore sites. There are fewer restrictions on night dives and divers get three to five dives each day instead of heading back to shore after two dives. Photographers do not have to worry about sand damaging O-rings and have more time to sort out cameras between dives.

On the minus side, narrow boats and those that are high in the water roll about with the slightest swell or chop, some people cannot sleep on a moving boat and rough seas can be frightening. Live-aboards appear expensive, but you get more dives for your money and all food is included. You need to pack warmer clothing for the cooler conditions at sea.

While live-aboards may offer five dives per day, divers also have to think about tides, currents, personal nitrogen-loading, and the visibility on ebb tides can be poor. It is better to take fewer (quality) dives each day than five dives, of which some may be mediocre.

Most divers do not like to have large numbers of people in the water at the same time. Larger live-aboard boats should either have two tenders serving two separate dive sites, or have a rota system whereby only half of their clients are in the water at any one time.

There have been cases of live-aboard boats leaving divers in the water and sailing off without them, so make sure that the boat you use has a foolproof diver check-in and check-out system.

REEF DIVING, DROP-OFFS AND WALLS

Reefs may have several distinct profiles. The top of the reef is likely to be a coral garden with smaller species of fish and crustaceans. Slopes or drop-offs have larger gorgonias and larger fish in shoals. Walls combine the above and have larger pelagic species, especially when over deep water. A wall is near-vertical and may be overhanging or undercut, while drop-offs are steep slopes of 60–85°.

Inshore fringing reefs tend to have poor visibility due to pollution from construction, domestic or industrial waste or mud carried down rivers, but they are good study areas as they harbour immature species.

Where offshore reefs have lagoons, these are convenient for safe anchorage, muck diving and snorkelling, but many prefer the better diving outside the reef. Channels into lagoons are good places to dive when the current is running, because the nutrients it carries attract smaller fish, which in turn attract larger predators. Where one side of a reef is longer or more contorted than the other side, the current is slowed down more on that side. When the currents meet again at points on the lee end of the reef they are travelling at different speeds, producing whirlpools and upwellings full of nutrients that attract large shoals of fish. In turn these fish attract sharks and other predators. If you can find shelter from the current, these points are great places to dive.

DIVING IN FRESHWATER

The main difference between diving in seawater and diving in freshwater is that freshwater is less buoyant and there are few freshwater sites that are charted. Some freshwater sites will be at a high enough altitude to require the use of special dive tables and corrections to the measured depths. Heavy rain can reduce freshwater visibility to zero.

In some areas lakes are fed by hot springs and can get very hot!

Diving in lakes or flooded quarries is relatively easy, but diving in rivers can be difficult if they are fast flowing. In general the current will be slower near the riverbank due to the friction of the water against the bank, but you must always consider where you can exit the river before you enter it. Hooks can be used to pull yourself along the river bottom against the current.

Freshwater and brackish-water sites, particularly lakes, quarries, dams, canals and slow-flowing rivers, often carry infections such as Weil's disease (Leptospirosis) and, in countries where it is endemic, Bilharzia (Schistosomiasis).

Some reefs are submerged and can only be found by a knowledgeable boat skipper or Global Positioning System. Divers have to descend quickly to the lee of the reef for shelter from the current before they get swept off. However, such reefs usually have top diving and pelagics.

DRIFT-DIVING

Drift-diving can vary from pleasantly drifting in a gentle current to high-voltage rushes as divers are swept along walls and gullies. The main concerns are good boat cover and becoming separated from diving buddies. Divers not using surface marker buoys should carry a delayed deployment surface marker buoy or, better still, a high-visibility rescue tube or collapsible flag, which can be raised above the swell.

Insist that the chase-boat crew follow the surface marker buoy or divers' bubbles and do not go to sleep or have loud music preventing them from hearing divers' whistles when they surface. Power whistles are better at attracting the boat cover than manual whistles and an old CD can be used as a heliograph.

Buddies, and preferably the whole group, should enter the water together so that they do not get separated on the surface and they should try to keep together underwater. If divers do get separated from their boat cover, it is wise to tie a buddy line between each other, inflate the BCDs (Buoyancy Compensator Device) and conserve air. It is usually best to retain weight belts unless buoyancy is a problem; in certain circumstances it may be better to jettison the scuba cylinders.

Divers wanting to fin ashore while wearing a normal BCD rather than wings will find it less tiring to fin on their backs. At the shore, untie the buddy line before trying to swim through surf or breakers.

WRECK AND CAVE DIVING

When diving in enclosed overhead environments, it is not easy to reach the surface in the event of equipment failure.

Any level of diver can enjoy diving around a wreck, but penetrating large wrecks is advanced diving and novice divers should only attempt it when accompanied by an instructor. Plan dives to coincide with slack water and wear gloves for protection from sharp metal. Carry a sharp knife and a suitable monofilament line cutter or shears for cutting fishing line and nets. Have a good dive-light and carry another as backup. Make sure that equipment is streamlined against the diver's body where it cannot snag.

Divers should tie off a guideline before penetration and feed it out as they go, tie back any doors or hatches, so that they

cannot close in a current. Remember that exhaust bubbles disturb sediment, as do fins and hands. Leave plenty of air to get out of the wreck and back to the surface.

Cavern diving, where divers are always within sight of daylight, is not difficult. However, cave diving, beyond any source of daylight, requires a safety guideline so that the divers can find their way back to safety in zero visibility. They will also need separate backup sources of light and breathing-gasses. Most important is the rule of thirds: divers turn around when one-third of their breathing gas is used up, leaving one-third to find their way out and one-third for emergencies. Apart from exhaust bubbles disturbing sediment as they strike the roof, divers can minimize the disturbance of sediment by learning to use gentle, shallow fin-strokes.

NIGHT DIVING

For night dives, divers should choose a shallow dive with easy marks for navigation, with which they have already familiarized themselves in daylight. The easiest night dives are along reef edges, where divers can swim out along the face at one depth and return along it at a shallower depth. If there is a current divers should set out against it and return with it.

Avoid dive lights that are too powerful and carry a spare as a backup, but spend some time with your lights switched off. When your eyes are accustomed to the dark, wave your arms about and you will notice phosphorescent plankton and, in caves, you may spot the biolumines-cence of flashlightfish.

TEMPERATE WATERS VERSUS TROPICAL WATERS

Many divers do most of their diving in temperate waters. Shipwrecks are the most popular sites, but the marine life can be just as interesting as

---

ICE DIVING

Always be prepared for equipment failure – even weightbelt buckles have failed. Although the water temperature cannot fall below –1.8°C (28.7°F), or it would be frozen solid, wind-chill can make air temperature many degrees colder. A full-face mask makes it difficult to access a backup regulator. Each diver should have two separate regulators, either on separate scuba cylinders or on a single one with a V-manifold. Cylinders should be filled with air that is as dry as possible. Cylinders and regulators should be stored out of the wind in a dry place until entering the water. Regulator first stages should be environmentally sealed against the ingress of water and not breathed through until both first and second stages are submerged to avoid condensation freezing the regulator. Divers should each be attached to a line strong enough for hauling them to the surface. Each line should be tied off securely and attended by someone doing nothing else, feeling for an agreed series of rope signals from the diver. Erratic pulls, unreadable pulls or no response, should be treated as an emergency and the diver pulled up.

Diving under ice is a surreal experience. The ice forms amazing shapes and at high latitudes the animals exhibit gigantism.

in tropical waters. In general the visibility and surface conditions will not be that good. By contrast, when diving in the warm, clear water of the tropics, surrounded by colourful marine life, divers are likely to be more relaxed. The main danger with such clear water is that you are likely to dive deep without realizing it. Many of the more popular diving holiday destinations are in areas where tides and currents are minimal and sea conditions usually calm.

It is wise to wear thin exposure suits against creatures that sting, but the best chance of ruining your holiday comes from sunburn or insect bites when you are not diving.

ARCHAEOLOGICAL DIVING

Archaeological diving is usually restricted to academics but there are times when they are grateful for amateur help and some of the finds in the Egyptian Mediterranean are now open to guided diving tours. Where such sites are close to a port there will be sewage and industrial pollution in the water and oil on the surface. Divers should take a course of broad-spectrum antibiotic as a prophylactic against intestinal infections. Diesel oil on the surface causes skin-burns and degrades exposure-suit materials, so wash all equipment (and yourself) with freshwater immediately after immersion.

UNDERWATER VISIBILITY

In mid-oceanic waters the vertical visibility can reach 100m (328ft), but horizontal visibility greater than 50m (165ft) is mythical. Coastal waters are affected by rain, run-off, disturbed bottom sediment, agricultural, industrial and domestic pollution, landfill, quarrying, volcanic eruptions and plankton blooms, so the visibility is less. Water clarity is better over deep water or a solid bottom. Ebb tides lower water clarity by carrying sediment off beaches and reefs; visibility usually improves on a flood tide. Care with buoyancy will prevent divers from disturbing the bottom sediment.

Heavy rain and wind reduce visibility if bad weather causes freshwater and saltwater to mix or if it sets off a plankton bloom. Offshore waters appear blue, but the decaying organic matter in coastal waters is yellow, so some of the blue is filtered out and the waters look green. Local mineral deposits or mining are also factors that can affect the colour of the water.

REPETITIVE DIVES

For surface intervals greater than 16 hours, divers can assume that there is no excess nitrogen remaining and can therefore treat the next dive as if it were the first. A second dive in less than a 16-hour period must be classed as a repetitive dive. The possible depths and times can be calculated from a dive planner, dive tables or shown by a diving computer. Divers performing repetitive dives over several days should take a complete day off after four days to allow the nitrogen remaining in the body tissues to dissipate completely.

ABOVE *Wrecks are perfect sheltering places for shoals of tiny fry and larger juvenile fish. This is the wreck of the* Nebo *at Aliwal Shoal.*

DECOMPRESSION DIVES

Decompression dives are not recommended for recreational divers and most American recreational dive planners do not allow for them, although European dive tables do. There may be times when, for whatever reason, divers exceed the no-stop dive time limit at a given depth and then have to make stops on the ascent, long enough to let excess nitrogen diffuse out of their body tissues (decompression stops).

Different training agencies recommend different depths and times for these stops, though the deeper ones are more easily maintained in a swell. If the divers have not been very deep and not for too long, then one stop will be sufficient, usually at a depth of between 3m (10ft) and 6m (20ft). If the divers have been relatively deep or exceeded the no-stop time for longer, they will have to make additional stops at greater depths and then a longer one between 3m (10ft) and 6m (20ft). Special tables are available for diving at altitude or on Enriched Air Nitrox.

FINISHING A DIVE

Divers should finish all dives, whether decompression or not, with a five-minute safety stop at 3–6m (10–20ft). It can be difficult to hold a stop at 3m (10ft) in a swell. It is easier to hold 5m (16ft), which allows leeway if the swell causes you to ascend a little.

ALTITUDE AND FLYING AFTER DIVING

When diving at altitude, divers must use tables or computers designed for altitude diving. The reduced pressure in aeroplanes at height can cause large bubbles to form, causing decompression sickness in divers who fly before their body has had enough time to release most of the accumulated nitrogen. Even worse, high-flying aircraft cabins have been known to depressurize in flight. Divers intending to fly should allow at least 24 hours after diving.

CLIMATE CHANGE

Scientists disagree over the rate and likely extent of change resulting from global warming. Similar events have occurred throughout history and some glaciers are currently expanding. In Antarctica the Ross Ice Shelf has grown several kilometres (miles) in the last two decades. However, most glaciers are receding and large amounts of polar ice are melting. The resulting increase in sea levels threatens the existence of low-lying islands such as the Maldives and increases the risk of flooding on the lower sides of regions such as the UK.

THE EL NIÑO-SOUTHERN OSCILLATION PHENOMENON (ENSO) AND LA NIÑA

El Niño conditions can result in strange weather patterns in some diving areas. Warm water means that many sharks descend to deeper, colder water, but most importantly, animals that have symbiotic algae may expel them as in coral bleaching.

In normal years, the upwelling cold water in the trade-wind belts off the west coast of South America leads to rich fishing and causes the overlying air to cool below the temperature at which water vapour condenses (dew point), producing fog. However, sea-surface temperature changes in the equatorial Pacific sometimes produce a major climatic disturbance known as El Niño, Spanish for The Boy Child, because

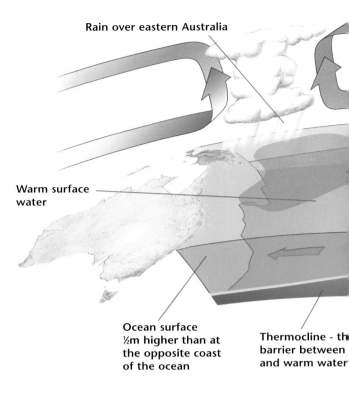

Rain over eastern Australia

Warm surface water

Ocean surface ½m higher than at the opposite coast of the ocean

Thermocline - the barrier between and warm water

BLEACHING

Bleaching occurs when corals, anemones, clams and some other animals like sponges, expel their symbiotic algae (zooxanthellae) or the pigments of those algae. This is thought to occur due to higher temperatures and excess ultraviolet light penetration due to failed monsoons, very calm seas or lack of cloud cover. Some bleaching may be a seasonal event in the Indo-Pacific and the Caribbean, when full recovery is normal. If the water temperatures quickly return to normal then the animals recover, otherwise they die. Bleaching is most pronounced in water less than 15m (50ft) deep and particularly affects fast-growing species such as Acropora. Slower growing massive species like *Porites* also bleach, but are more likely to recover in a couple of months.

Bleaching was particularly far-reaching during the 1997/8 El Niño-Southern Oscillation Phenomenon, with areas such as Bahrain, the Maldives, Sri Lanka, Singapore, and parts of Madagascar and Tanzania being seriously affected. Scientists recently found that after having expelled one type of Zooxanthellae, some corals can take up other types that are better suited to the higher temperatures, thus enabling them to survive as long as temperatures do not get too high.

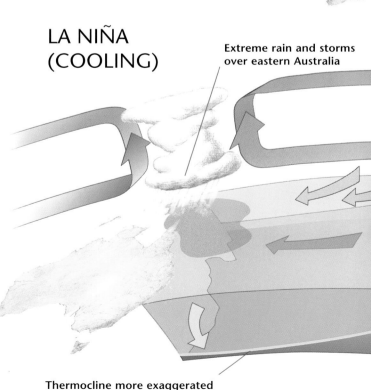

LA NIÑA (COOLING)

Extreme rain and storms over eastern Australia

Thermocline more exaggerated than during normal conditions

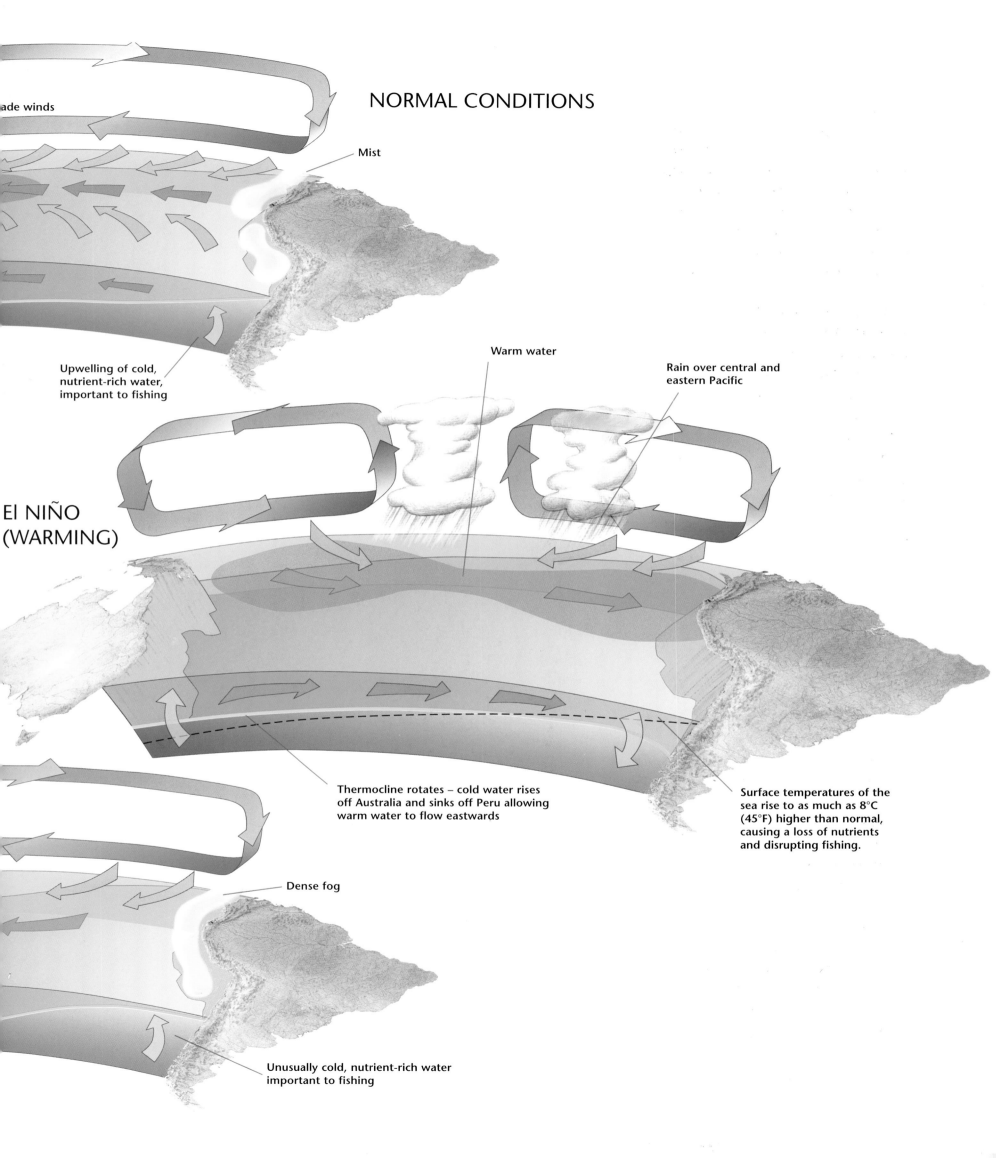

NORMAL CONDITIONS

ade winds

Mist

Warm water

Rain over central and
eastern Pacific

Upwelling of cold,
nutrient-rich water,
important to fishing

El NIÑO
(WARMING)

Thermocline rotates – cold water rises
off Australia and sinks off Peru allowing
warm water to flow eastwards

Surface temperatures of the
sea rise to as much as 8°C
(45°F) higher than normal,
causing a loss of nutrients
and disrupting fishing.

Dense fog

Unusually cold, nutrient-rich water
important to fishing

GENERAL INTRODUCTION

Peruvian fishermen noticed that it often began around Christmas. During an El Niño/Southern Oscillation Phenomenon, a weakening of the easterly trade winds in the Central Pacific means that warm surface water is no longer pushed west to allow for a cold, nutrient-rich upwelling off the coasts of Peru and Ecuador. The warmer sea-surface temperature transforms the coastal climate from arid to wet and causes the huge fish stocks, normally associated with the nutrient-rich cold water, to migrate away. The phenomenon is normally accompanied by a change in atmospheric circulation, called the Southern Oscillation. It is associated with changes in precipitation in regions of North America, Africa, and the western Pacific, droughts and bush fires in Australia and droughts in southeastern Asia, India and southern Africa. It is one of the main causes of change in the world's climate, and the 1997/8 event was the worst on record. The sea-surface temperatures in most tropical seas were particularly high, resulting in large-scale coral bleaching, particularly in Bahrain and the Maldives. Nearly every region on earth felt El Niño's effect in some way.

El Niño is called a warm event. La Niña, which means The Little Girl is called a cold event. (The phenomenon is also known as Viejo, the Spanish word for old.) The opposite of El Niño, with unusually cold surface temperatures in the Eastern Tropical Pacific, it usually, but not always, follows an El Niño and did so in 1998. The effects on global climate are the opposite to those of El Niño.

WEATHER, CURRENTS AND TIDES

In regions where there is a distinct summer and winter, many divers would normally avoid diving at offshore sites in winter. Some areas have distinct seasons of travelling storms of great violence that form over warm oceans when several thunderstorms release heat. These tropical cyclones are known as hurricanes in the North Atlantic and eastern North Pacific, and as typhoons in the western North Pacific. The winds of these systems revolve around a centre of low pressure, 'the eye,' in an anticlockwise direction in the northern hemisphere and in a clockwise direction in the southern hemisphere.

Tropical cyclones are a phenomenon of the tropical oceans. They originate in two distinct latitude zones, between 4° and 22° South and between 4° and 35° North. They are absent in the equatorial zone between 4° South and 4° North. Most tropical cyclones are spawned on the poleward side of the area known as the intertropical convergence zone (ITCZ).

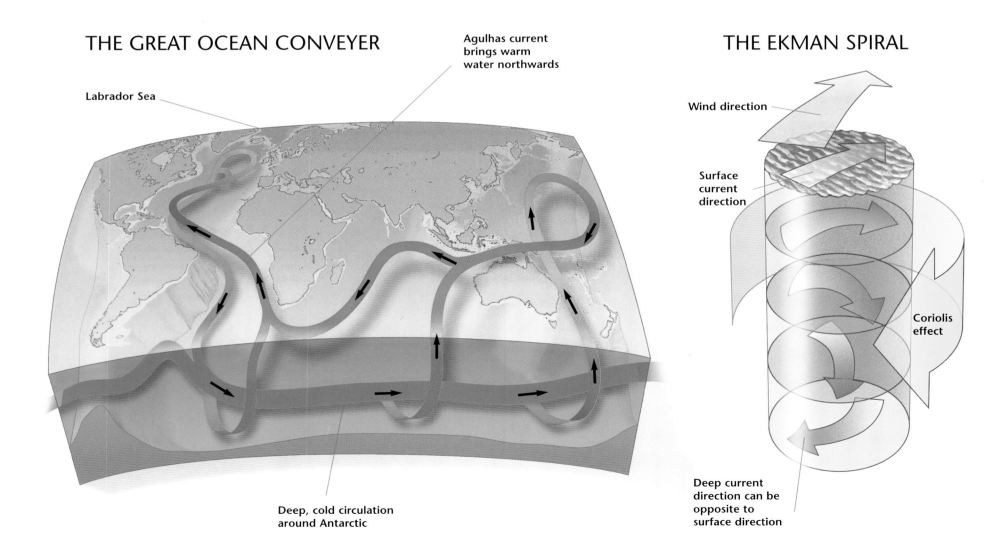

THE GREAT OCEAN CONVEYER

Agulhas current brings warm water northwards

Labrador Sea

Deep, cold circulation around Antarctic

THE EKMAN SPIRAL

Wind direction

Surface current direction

Coriolis effect

Deep current direction can be opposite to surface direction

Monsoon winds are primarily caused by the difference between temperatures over large landmasses and adjacent large oceans, notably Arabia, Asia, Australia, and the Indian subcontinent. Seasonal changes in temperature are large over land, but small over oceans. A monsoon wind blows from cold to warm regions and, in summer, from the sea towards land carrying humid air from the ocean. In winter it blows from the land toward the sea. As a consequence, where monsoons occur, one side of a landmass may get heavy rain and not be divable at one time of year and the opposite side of that landmass at another.

Some regions are known for consistently bad tropical cyclones or monsoons at certain times of year and the resorts shut down for that period. Regions where these events only occasionally cause problems, tend to stay open during the bad weather season, while offering cheaper rates. Divers who book resorts in these regions at this cheaper time of year should be aware that their holiday could be ruined.

Although not necessarily of tropical cyclone strength, bad weather can occur anywhere at any time of year. However, diving can be quite pleasant during inclement weather, if divers jump into the water and quickly descend below the swell. The real problems are in getting the boat out to the site and, worse, getting out of the water into a boat in a heavy swell.

MAJOR CURRENTS

Although local currents vary during the day due to winds, upwellings, downwellings and the heat of the sun, there are more consistent current patterns in the world's oceans that affect the climate, conditions for diving and which migratory species can be found at a given time in a normal year.

Ocean currents are horizontal and vertical circulation systems of ocean waters that are produced by the earth's rotation, gravity, wind friction, and the variations in water density that result from differences in temperature and salinity.

For instance, the currents that form the Gulf Stream bring warm waters northward, affecting the climates and waters of the Bahamas, Bermuda, eastern North America, the British Isles and the Atlantic coast of Norway. This leads to tropical species off Bermuda and some surprising species such as Ocean Sunfish and Leatherback Turtles visiting the west coast of the UK. Similarly, part of the South Equatorial Current that flows towards East Africa joins the Agulhas Current and relatively warm water flows southward at high speed along the east coast of South Africa. However, when this current is reversed, cold water flows north, bringing with it huge quantities of sardines, which in turn attract large predators.

THE TIDE CYCLE

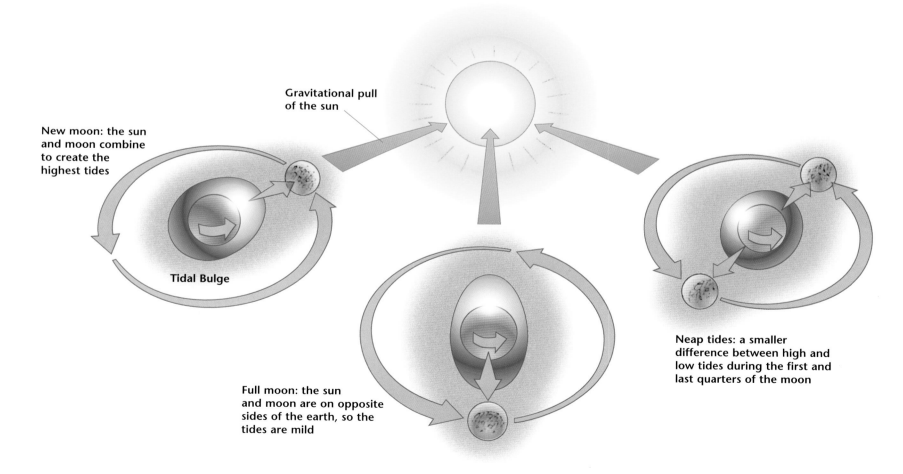

Gravitational pull of the sun

New moon: the sun and moon combine to create the highest tides

Tidal Bulge

Full moon: the sun and moon are on opposite sides of the earth, so the tides are mild

Neap tides: a smaller difference between high and low tides during the first and last quarters of the moon

GENERAL INTRODUCTION

ABOVE *The Lionfish (*Pterois miles*) is the Indian Ocean relative of the Pacific's* Pterois volitans. *They are often treated as a single species.*

ABOVE *Tube worms burrow into sediment or live coral. They retract instantly into their tubes if a shadow passes over them.*

ABOVE *The Red Sea Bannerfish (*Heniochus intermedius*) is endemic to the Red Sea. Juveniles form shoals, but adults are solitary or in pairs.*

TIDES

Tides are primarily caused by the combined effects of the centrifugal force of the spinning earth and gravitational attraction between the moon and the earth. The sun, despite its huge size, is so far away that its effect on the tides is only about half that of the moon. The cycle of one tide, to go from high water to low water and back to high water again, usually takes roughly 12 hours (semidiurnal). In some parts of the world it may take roughly 24 hours (diurnal), depending on whether the sun or the moon is dominant. Some areas experience a mixture of both diurnal and semidiurnal tides. The normal tidal day is 24 hours and 50 minutes. Around some islands and reefs you may, effectively, get four tides per day if the flow along one side of the obstacle is longer than along the other.

Spring tides, those of maximum range and flow, occur twice a month at, or near, a new or full moon. Equinoctial spring tides, those that are of greater than average range and flow, occur near the equinoxes in March and September, at new and full moon. Neap tides, those of minimum range and least flow, occur twice a month at or near the first and last quarters of the moon. These are best for wreck diving and photography. The word spring (an outflow of water) and the word neap (Anglo-Saxon for scanty) are both from Old English. Local tide tables enable divers to calculate incoming flood tides, (sea level rising), outflowing ebb tides (sea level falling) and slack water, the time of least flow when tides are changing from flood to ebb or vice versa.

The shape of the shoreline has an effect on the height of the tide. Where stretches of water are enclosed by a shoreline with a funnel shape, tides are amplified as the funnel narrows. The upper parts of Nova Scotia's Bay of Fundy have the world's highest tidal range – 16m (52ft).

THE MARINE ENVIRONMENT

Viewed from space the oceans dominate the earth, covering 70 per cent of our planet. They provide us with food, a large area for recreation and they regulate the climate. Mankind has treated the oceans as a rubbish pit for centuries. However, modern agricultural and industrial pollution is much more damaging and is accompanied by prodigious overfishing, often by detrimental methods. The combined effect has been threefold: huge plankton blooms (that suffocate organisms below), damaged reefs and depleted fish stocks. Ships taking on seawater as ballast in one region and discharging it in another, and aquariums emptying exotic fauna and flora into seas where they have no natural predators, have severely upset the ecology, often with disastrous results. We are slowly learning that there is a limit to the way in which we can treat the oceans.

Storm-driven wave action will occasionally damage coral reefs. However, some human activities, such as blast and cyanide fishing, coral mining, landfill, dredging, siltation caused by dredging or logging, and the indiscriminate collection of corals to sell as curios, are just as destructive. Similarly, overfishing depletes fish life, upsets the food chain and, in the case of herbivorous fish, leads to the corals becoming overgrown with algae. Corals found deep down in temperate waters are also being damaged by destructive fishing methods.

As diving becomes more popular, environmentalists are becoming increasingly concerned by the damage done by careless divers to live corals. Some diving operators in warm waters have banned the use of gloves, except on wrecks, in an effort to stop divers from holding on to live coral. If divers have to settle on the seabed to practise diving exercises or adjust equipment, they should do so only on dead sand to avoid killing live coral.

The growing awareness of environmental issues has given rise to ecotourism – tourism with an ecological conscience. Ecotourism is often summed up as 'take nothing but photographs, leave nothing but footprints,' but even footprints, as indeed any form of touching, is a problem for corals. It may be better to manage tourism, and the tourists themselves, in such a way as to be ecologically sustainable. The capital investment necessary to develop ecotourism is minimal, much-needed employment becomes available to the local population and in the long term the profits exceed those of logging or overfishing.

Although many divers, dive operators and diving resorts lead the field in protecting marine ecosystems, we all require somewhere to eat and sleep. If a small resort is built without a waste-treatment system, the nearby reefs may not be damaged irreparably. However, if those same reefs attract increasing numbers of tourists and more resorts, then controls on the resorts, visiting divers from nearby areas, and visiting live-aboard boats, become necessary.

Coral reefs are not the only places affected by divers, but that is where concentrations of divers are found. There is also concern over some divers' behaviour in places where annual congregations of larger animals occur, but this can be controlled by educating divers and operators.

It has been suggested that in a few cases environmentalists have gone too far. If rules in one area are too strict, divers and snorkellers will lose interest in that area and either give up entirely or go elsewhere. Either way, if divers and snorkellers are not around regularly to keep an eye on the animals or coral reef, and the local people do not gain employment from tourism, there is more chance of unscrupulous fishermen wiping out the animals or using damaging fishing methods on reefs.

ECO-FRIENDLY DIVING

Ecological sustainability of the marine environment depends as much on individual divers as on dive operators and resorts.

- Do not touch living marine animals or organisms with either your body or your diving equipment.
- Control your fins. Their size and the force produced by the fin-stroke can damage large areas of coral. Do not use deep fin-strokes next to the reef, the surge of water can disturb delicate organisms.
- Master good buoyancy control. Much damage is caused by divers descending too rapidly or crashing into corals while trying to adjust their buoyancy. Be properly weighted and if you have not dived for a while, practise your skills where you can do no damage.
- Do not kick up sand. Clouds of sand settling on the reef can smother corals. Snorkellers should be careful not to kick up sand when treading water in shallow reef areas.
- Do not stand on corals. Living coral polyps are easily damaged by the slightest touch. Similarly, never pose for pictures or stand inside giant basket or barrel sponges.
- Do not collect or purchase shells, corals, sea stars, turtle shells or any other marine souvenirs.
- If you are out of control and about to collide with the reef, steady yourself with your fingertips on a part of the reef that is already dead or covered in algae. If you need to adjust your diving equipment or mask, try to do so in a sandy area away from the reef.
- On any excursion, whether with an operator or privately organized, make sure you take your garbage back for proper disposal on land.
- Take care in underwater caverns and caves. Avoid several people

ABOVE *The endearing Dusky Anemonefish or Clownfish* (Amphiprion melanopus) *in a* Heteractus crispa *anemone at Pulau Redang.*

ABOVE *A colourful Gorgonian with its polyps retracted on the reef edge at Calusa Island in the Philippines Sulu Sea.*

ABOVE *Close-up of a Humphead or Napoleon Wrasse* (Cheilinus undulatus) *at Taytay Bay, Philippines. One of the largest of reef fish.*

crowding into a cave, and do not stay too long, because your air bubbles collect in pockets under the roof of the cave and delicate creatures living there 'suffocate' in air.

- Before booking a dive trip on a boat, ask about the company's environmental policy – particularly on the discharge of sewage and anchoring. Avoid boats, both live-aboard and day, that cause unnecessary anchor damage, have bad oil leaks, or discharge untreated sewage near reefs.

- Do not participate in spear-fishing for sport, selectively killing the larger fish upsets the chain of reproduction. If you are living on a boat and relying on spear-fishing for food, make sure you are familiar with all local fish and game regulations and obtain any necessary licenses.

- Do not move marine organisms around to photograph or play with them. In particular, do not hitch rides on turtles, Manta Rays or Whale Sharks, since it causes them considerable stress.

THE ETHICS OF FEEDING

Conservationists argue that feeding fish alters their natural feeding behaviour, affects their health, makes them dependent on divers and could attract more dangerous predators. They have a point with regard to feeding Humphead (Napoleon) Wrasse with eggs or any fish with food that is not part of its natural diet, but others argue that feeding does not alter long-term behaviour. Most animals are opportunistic feeders, not averse to carrion and the amount of food that divers introduce is minimal so the fish do not become reliant on it. At the Cayman Island's Stingray City, where the rays are fed many times each day, the rays are still observed feeding naturally and at shark feeds a few dominant animals take most of the food, while most sharks present go without. More importantly, the quantity of divers these events attract, causes

ABOVE *Typical view of a northern Red Sea reef. Colourful anthias forage over a mixture of soft and stony corals on Jackson Reef in the Strait of Tiran.*

governments to realize that the animals are worth more when kept alive for tourism than wiped out by fishermen. It is estimated that half the diving/snorkelling dollars spent in Grand Cayman are on the stingray feeds and that in the Bahamas shark-feeds bring in over $60 million a year.

However, things must be placed into perspective. Sharks have attacked in areas where no feeding occurs and without obvious reason. When wearing light-coloured fins, I have had them bitten by large groupers and sharks at dive sites where no feeding had ever taken place. Possibly, the larger fish considered the fins to be smaller, prey-sized fish. A large barracuda has also attacked me in water with poor visibility. I was wielding a camera at the time so a glint of sun on the lens may have looked like the flash of a small silver fish. I know two divers who have been bitten by sharks while swimming too close to bait-balls that the sharks were feeding on. Several well-known operators have been badly bitten by groupers or moray eels that they fed regularly, but at the time of the respective incidents they were feeding another fish. Several people have suffered small grazes at organized shark feeds in the Bahamas.

Even where hundreds of non-cage shark feeds are performed yearly with hand-feeding and/or large amounts of bait, there have been few injuries and those that did occur were mostly to those doing the hand-feeding. When sharks attack spear-fisherman, they are usually carrying dead, or worse still, struggling-while-they-die fish. Eventually, by the law of averages a tourist will suffer a serious injury or die during a feeding operation. However, the incident-rate is well within the range of adventure sports in general and much safer than mountaineering, skiing or snowboarding. Many more people are killed by bee-stings.

There are many locations where fish feeding is restricted or prohibited. Recently the anti-feeding lobby in Florida, backed by spear-fishermen and commercial fishermen, managed to have fish-feeding banned. Media frenzy claimed that more shark attacks than usual had occurred locally, but this was not true. The rule-makers ignored the fact that currents had driven fish-shoals inshore; that people were filmed swimming among shoals of fish on which sharks were preying; and that a myriad of commercial fishermen were chumming the water, catching, killing and cleaning fish right off the tourist beaches. Florida now has a situation where dive operators are not allowed to use chumsickles (large blocks of frozen fish parts) to attract sharks, yet spear-fishermen and commercial fishermen are still permitted to use this baiting technique to attract sharks and other marine animals.

With reference to feeding sharks, some species are more belligerent than others, and Grey Reef Sharks can be more so in some areas than in others. Having regularly organized shark feeds in the Red Sea since the early 1980s, my feeling is that many operators use too much bait. A couple of 25cm (10in) fish hidden in the coral are enough to keep the sharks interested for 20 minutes. It is also better not to hand-feed, even with chain-mail gloves, as this gives the sharks the impression that man supplies the food and could result in sharks harassing divers who are not involved in feeding.

The case of researcher Erich Ritter being bitten by an adult Bull Shark at Walkers Cay, Bahamas, while being filmed for the Discovery Channel's *Shark Week* series, will not help the pro-feeding lobby. However, those who regularly dive with sharks believe that if done in a responsible manner, shark dives are reasonably safe. We are privileged to have close encounters with wildlife underwater, often within arm's length. Not everyone wants to get this close to a shark, but there have been many instances where other animals such as large barracuda, large groupers, Moray Eels and even Titan (Moustache) or Yellowmargin Triggerfish have either bitten or butted divers in situations not connected to feeding. Feeding fish is an emotive issue – you will have to make up your own mind.

DIVING WITH GASES OTHER THAN NORMAL AIR
ENRICHED AIR NITROX

The term Nitrox is commonly applied to oxygen-enriched air. By increasing the percentage of oxygen, and thus decreasing the percentage of nitrogen, divers will absorb less nitrogen during a dive and have less to eliminate during the ascent.

Diving on Nitrox can be treated in several ways. By calculating dive-plans from Nitrox tables, divers will have longer no-decompression stop times at their maximum depth. If calculating dive-plans from air tables, they will have an extra safety factor. If divers go into decompression, it will be shorter if calculated from Nitrox tables, but have a greater safety factor if calculated from air tables. Many divers feel less fatigued after diving on Enriched Air Nitrox, though there is no scientific proof of this, and many experience a lower rate of gas consumption.

Another way in which Nitrox can be used to divers' advantage is that divers, who have been deep while breathing air or other gas mixtures, can shorten their decompression times at shallow depths by changing to a mixture containing 50–80 per cent oxygen. This mixture enables faster elimination of excess nitrogen (if using air) or helium (if using mixed gases). However, due to oxygen toxicity, the depths to which divers can descend depend on the percentage of oxygen in the Nitrox mix used. The higher the percentage of oxygen, the shallower will be the maximum depth to which they can go. Divers should not descend to depths where the partial pressure of oxygen exceeds 1.4ata. Atmospheres absolute (ata) is the sum of atmospheric pressure and the hydrostatic pressure – the total weight of water and air above us.

There may be circumstances when a diver breathing Enriched Air Nitrox has to go deeper than oxygen toxicity allows on that particular Nitrox mixture. In this situation, if the diver has a separate small cylinder of normal air fitted with its own regulator, it is possible to switch to breathing from this cylinder for a brief foray deeper than the depth allowed on the Nitrox mixture. The diver can then switch back to breathing Enriched Air Nitrox after returning to a depth where oxygen toxicity is no longer a problem.

OPEN-CIRCUIT SCUBA

1	Gas supply cylinder
2	On/off valve
3	First-stage regulator
4	Second-stage regulator
5	Pressure gauge

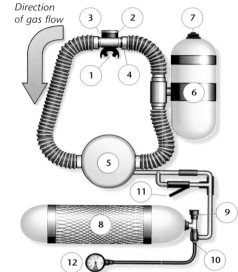

Direction of gas flow

SEMI-CLOSED REBREATHER

1	Mouthpiece
2	Mouthpiece shutoff
3	Downstream check-valve
4	Upstream check-valve
5	CO_2 absorbent canister
6	Counterlung
7	Overpressure release-valve
8	Supply gas supply cylinder
9	Supply gas on/off valve
10	Supply gas regulator
11	Manual supply gas bypass
12	Supply gas pressure gauge

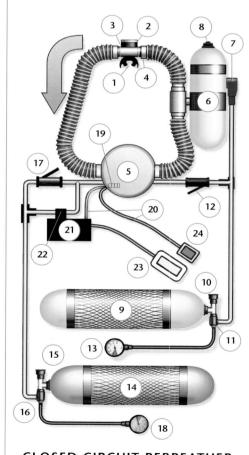

CLOSED-CIRCUIT REBREATHER

1	Mouthpiece
2	Mouthpiece shutoff
3	Downstream check-valve
4	Upstream check-valve
5	CO_2 absorbent canister
6	Counterlung
7	Diluent addition valve
8	Overpressure release-valve
9	Diluent supply cylinder
10	Diluent on/off valve
11	Diluent regulator
12	Manual diluent bypass
13	Diluent pressure gauge
14	Oxygen supply cylinder
15	Oxygen on/off valve
16	Oxygen regulator
17	Manual oxygen bypass
18	Oxygen pressure gauge
19	Oxygen sensors
20	Oxygen sensor cable
21	Main electronics
22	Oxygen solenoid valve
23	Primary display
24	Secondary display

Another problem with oxygen breathed at higher than normal partial pressures, is that when used over long periods it affects the central nervous system. Divers must be careful not to exceed the recommended oxygen tolerance units (OTUs), particularly on repetitive dives.

High concentrations of oxygen cause combustion on contact with oils and greases. Scuba cylinders and their valves come in contact with pure oxygen during filling, so they must be scrupulously clean. Standard regulators should be suitable for Nitrox mixtures of less than 40 per cent oxygen, but for higher concentrations, their O-rings must be replaced with ones that do not require lubricants.

HELIOX AND TRIMIX

For deeper diving, one must lower the oxygen content to reduce oxygen toxicity as well as reducing the nitrogen content. This is done by replacing some of the nitrogen with helium (Trimix) or all the nitrogen with helium (Heliox). Helium has the advantage of reducing problems with Nitrogen Narcosis, but gives no advantage with decompression times. It is a lighter element than nitrogen and more of it is absorbed by the body, which then has to be eliminated on ascent. It also conducts heat away from the body more quickly during respiration.

As divers go deeper they must reduce the oxygen content still further. There is almost an optimum mix for each depth. Divers use a 'travel-mix' suitable for breathing from the surface down to a calculated depth and then switch over to a 'bottom-mix' with an even lower oxygen content. However, bottom-mixes have too low an oxygen content to be breathed safely at shallower depths. During ascent, there will be a depth at which the divers must switch back to the travel-mix; shallow decompression stops will be shorter if they switch to mixes high in oxygen when close to the surface. Deep dives using Heliox or Trimix involve several clearly-marked cylinders of different gas mixtures and the diver has to identify the correct regulator attached to the correct cylinder, for each phase of the dive. This has led to the development of modern rebreathers, in which the gas mixture can be modified as one changes depth.

REBREATHERS

The acronym SCUBA stands for Self-Contained Underwater Breathing Apparatus. With traditional SCUBA we waste most of the oxygen we breathe by exhaling into the water. This is termed an open-circuit system. Some companies have modernized, closed or semi-closed circuit scuba equipment for recreational use and these are termed rebreathers. When using rebreathers, divers breathe a gas mixture containing oxygen and when they exhale, the carbon dioxide in their exhaled gases is chemically removed by passing the gases through Soda-Lime. The Soda-Lime is referred to as a scrubber. Some additional oxygen is added to the cleaned, exhaled gases and that mixture is breathed again, hence the name rebreather. The closed-circuit system does not dump any gas into the water until the diver ascends, while the semi-closed circuit system only dumps a small portion of each exhalation. In this way divers get long diving times out of a relatively small amount of breathing gas.

Rebreathers can be based on Nitrox or, for deeper diving, Trimix or Heliox. They require considerable maintenance and a constant eye must be kept on gauges to ensure that everything is working correctly.

TRAVELLING TO DIVE

The terrorist attacks on the USA of 11 September 2001 has changed security measures for air travel, with underwater photographers and divers being the hardest hit. Many airlines no longer allow carry-on baggage even when items could be damaged in the hold.

Apart from ensuring that you have all the necessary paperwork, passport, visa, vaccinations/health certificates, travel and diving insurance, prescription medications and C-card, the most important part of travelling to dive is to have these and other essentials such as cameras, film, diving computers, prescription masks and spectacles in your carry-on baggage. Airlines are notorious for losing or delaying baggage.

Your passport should be valid for six months longer than the expected duration of the trip and have at least six empty pages. If you carry local banknotes, these should be clean and unmarked. Have photocopies of all paperwork, passport photographs for local permits and your driving license if intending to hire a vehicle.

Keeping diving equipment within most airlines' check-in baggage limit of 20kg (44 lb) is a problem. Some airlines will allow an extra 10kg (22 lb) for divers on presentation of a C-card. American airlines have more sensible baggage limits based on size.

ABOVE *Divers pass the entrance of a cavern in the Amirantes in the Indian Ocean. Black corals are often found in the dim light under overhangs.*

DIVE PLANNING – 'PLAN THE DIVE AND DIVE THE PLAN'

All dives should be planned. The leader of the dive should give a detailed briefing that covers the expected time in the water, what the current is doing, what should be seen on the dive, what depth divers should expect to dive to and when they should ascend.

However, divers should also take into account their own health and fitness, and normal rate of air consumption. They should consider the depths and times of their last few dives, the surface intervals between them and the time that has elapsed since the last dive. There is now some debate over whether the first dive of the day should always be the deepest and all other dives on the same day progressively shallower, but it is best to keep to the standard practice.

Diving bags or rucksacks are preferred for easy stowage by live-aboard boat skippers, but they attract attention as containing expensive equipment and do not stand up well to airport baggage handlers. Pelican cases are also prime targets for airport thieves. Shabby cases are a better option.

Check out what equipment is available for rent at your destination so that you can minimize your checked baggage. However, remember that at Third World destinations rental equipment may be in poor condition and fins and wet suits are often too small for large Caucasians.

TRAVELLING DIVER'S CHECK LIST
- Clothes and wash kit for surface use
- Mask, snorkel and fins (either full-foot or adjustable with bootees)
- Regulator with contents gauge (manometer) and alternate air supply
- Buoyancy Compensator Device (stabilizing jacket)
- Weight belt and weights if not provided by the operator
- Compass
- Diving knife and shears for cutting monofilament line (some airlines no longer allow diving knives to be carried even in checked baggage)
- Diving computer, preferably with watch, depth gauge and tables
- Wet suit, Lycra skin or dry suit
- Delayed deployment or other surface marker buoy or flag
- Whistle or powered whistle
- An old CD for use as a heliograph
- Waterproof light
- Diving log book
- Mask anti-misting solution (liquid detergent works just as well!)
- Slate and pencil or other form of underwater communication
- Swimming costume and sunglasses
- Spare prescription spectacles if worn
- Wet bag for diving gear

- Dry bag or case for paperwork, cameras, medications, wash kit etc.
- First aid kit
- Towel if not supplied at destination

SPARES KIT
- Mask and mask straps, fin straps and knife straps
- O-rings, including a few for cylinder/regulator fitting
- Any necessary tools for small repairs, and batteries

Regulators travel best when disassembled, and you may need special tools to re-assemble them. Diving computers and depth gauges should travel as hand baggage on aircraft or in a pressure-proof container.

TRAVELLING DIVER'S MEDICATIONS

A minor ear or sinus infection can ruin a diving holiday, especially in a remote area or on a live-aboard boat. Being prepared can save your vacation. Many divers travelling to a live-aboard boat assume that they do not require antimalarial prophylactics because they will spend most of their time at sea where mosquitoes do not exist. However, it only needs one mosquito bite in an airport and there is always the chance of aircraft or boats being delayed, forcing extra time at risk on land.

The correct malaria prophylactic should be taken where necessary and most divers carry decongestants, drops that dry out the ears, antihistamine cream, sunburn lotion, lip-salve, anti-diarrhoea medicine, rehydration salts, antibiotics, seasickness remedies and insect repellents.

Masks that keep ears dry are now available.

Remember that most decongestants and seasickness remedies can make you drowsy and should not be taken before diving.

ABOVE *Squirrelfish (Sargocentron Spp) of different species form loose aggregations in protective crevices during the day and feed at night.*

THE ATLANTIC OCEAN

by Jack Jackson

THE ATLANTIC IS THE SECOND LARGEST of the world's oceans. The boundaries defining its northern limits are not universally accepted, but the two most common latitudinal boundaries are 65° North and the Arctic Circle – 66° 32' North. The western boundary is the Americas and the eastern boundary is Europe and Africa. To the south the most widely accepted limit between the Atlantic and the Pacific oceans is the Drake Passage. Between the Atlantic and Indian oceans it is the 20° meridian East through Cape Agulhas at the southern end of Africa.

With an area of about 82,000,000 sq km (31,660,000 sq miles) without its attendant seas and 106,460,000 sq km (41,100,000 sq miles) with them, the Atlantic covers one-fifth of the earth's surface and has the largest river drainage of the world's oceans.

CONDITIONS AND COASTAL HABITATS

In the north there are temperate waters and some unusual conditions caused by the warm Gulf Stream. There is temperate water diving off eastern North America, while Bermuda, Florida, the Bahamas and the countries at the northern end of South America are Caribbean-like. Brazil's coastline has conditions from Caribbean-like to temperate. Argentina has a long temperate coastline and large mammals including some unique Orcas that hunt at the edge of the beach.

Europe has lots of temperate water diving. Islands off the west coast of Africa have Mediterranean conditions when the weather is fine. Central west Africa has the wettest climate in Africa and large river outlets give murky waters. Near the coast divers have died of dysentery carried in river run-off, but diving is safer at islands well offshore such as Principe. Namibia's coast is cold and murky, so most diving is done in inland sinkholes. There is diving off the Atlantic coast of South Africa. The remote islands of Ascension, Saint Helena, Tristan da Cunha, and the Falklands have good temperate water diving.

Most islands are in the Caribbean. The British Isles, Falkland Islands and Newfoundland are continental. Iceland, the Azores, Ascension, Saint Helena, Tristan da Cunha, the South Sandwich Islands, the West Indies and Bermuda are exposed tops of submarine ridges. The Canaries, Cape Verde and Madeira rise from the continental margins of Africa while the Bahamas are coral islands lying on the Blake Plateau.

ABOVE *Whale watching has become a popular pastime in the Atlantic, often bringing in a considerable income from tourism. Whales are identified by markings and scars on their tails.*

KEY TO MAPS

1. USA - East Coast p29
2. Bermuda p30
3. United Kingdom p32
4. Scotland - Scapa Flow p34
5. Scotland - St Abbs and Eyemouth Marine Reserve p35
6. South Ireland p36
7. South Africa - Cape Peninsula p38
8. South Africa - Mossel Bay to Plettenberg Bay p41

ATLANTIC OCEAN

ABOVE *Off South Africa, Great White Sharks are observed from the safety of a steel cage. They are drawn closer with chunks of fish or meat.*

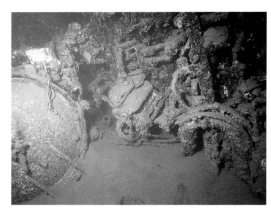

ABOVE *Shipwrecks are a major draw off the East Coast of North America. This is the torpedo room of the German submarine U–352.*

ABOVE *Cuckoo Wrasse* (Labrus bimaculatus) *are among the more colourful fish of the Eastern Atlantic. They live up to 17 years.*

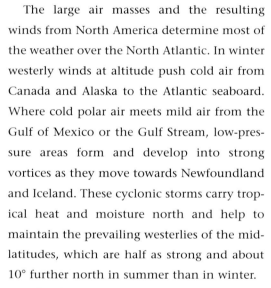

The large air masses and the resulting winds from North America determine most of the weather over the North Atlantic. In winter westerly winds at altitude push cold air from Canada and Alaska to the Atlantic seaboard. Where cold polar air meets mild air from the Gulf of Mexico or the Gulf Stream, low-pressure areas form and develop into strong vortices as they move towards Newfoundland and Iceland. These cyclonic storms carry tropical heat and moisture north and help to maintain the prevailing westerlies of the mid-latitudes, which are half as strong and about 10° further north in summer than in winter.

Iceland is normally dominated by low pressure, but in some winters high pressure systems prevail and storms leaving the North American coast are blocked and diverted to the Azores. Warm maritime air that normally gives Europe relatively mild winters is replaced by cold air from the European Arctic and Siberia.

HURRICANES

Between 15° and 30° North, high pressure prevails so the weather is usually fine. South of this, the northeast trade winds blow steadily. However, during late summer and early autumn, large amounts of heat are released when vapour rises from the warm ocean and then condenses as heavy showers. This can develop into tropical-storm vortices called hurricanes, which often move clockwise around the North Atlantic high-pressure belt and into the prevailing westerlies, ending up around Iceland. Occasionally they reach the British Isles and even the Azores.

Fog banks off the Grand Bank in summer are due to moisture in warm air from the continent and the Gulf Stream condensing as it flows over the cold Labrador Current.

WINDS AND TIDES

In the South Atlantic a belt of westerlies extends from roughly 40° South almost to Antarctica. The South Atlantic high-pressure region is centred around 30°S. Wind rotation around the high-pressure region is opposite to that in the northern hemisphere because of the effect of the earth's rotation (Coriolis Effect). This circulation gives the southeast trade winds on the northern side of the high-pressure region, which meet the northeast trade winds in the intertropical convergence zone (the doldrums), around the equator.

The weather is usually fine in the latitudes of high pressure. The great storms of the southern hemisphere westerlies are due to the temperature contrast between the Antarctic continent and the adjacent open ocean.

Tides in the Atlantic are mostly semi-diurnal. Labrador, some areas of the Mediterranean, Gulf of Mexico, Caribbean, the southeastern coast of Brazil and Tierra del Fuego have mixed tides. Purely diurnal tides occur in parts of the Gulf of Mexico. Tidal ranges vary from less than 1m (40in) in the Gulf of Mexico, Caribbean, and Mediterranean to 16m (52ft) in Canada's Bay of Fundy.

OCEAN TOPOGRAPHY

The shape of the Atlantic coastline of the Americas fits closely that of Europe and Africa. Between the two, the S-shaped Mid-Atlantic Ridge also fits. Crustal material on either side of the ridge is younger than that on the seafloor to either side. This indicates an uprising of material from the earth's mantle onto the crest of the ridge as the seafloor spreads.

The Mid-Atlantic Ridge is a mountain range and fault zone extending the length of the Atlantic. The Atlantic basin is widening, causing the flanks of the ridge to build up from accumulating lava. In places the ridge reaches the surface as volcanic islands. Ancient volcanoes, singly or in rows, rise as seamounts, islands and, occasionally, guyots. Moving away from the Mid-Atlantic Ridge towards the continents, there are abyssal plains followed by undulating continental rises. The Romanche furrow, near the equator, is a deep break in the ridge, which allows deep water to flow freely between east and west.

The average depth of the Atlantic is 3300m (10,925ft) and maximum depth 8380m (27,493ft) in the Puerto Rico Trench in the North Atlantic.

The North and South Atlantic central waters make up the surface waters of the Atlantic. The sub-Antarctic intermediate water drops to depths of 1000m (3300ft), the North Atlantic deep water reaches depths of around 4000m (13,200ft) and the Antarctic bottom water fills ocean basins at depths beyond that. The North Atlantic's deep and bottom water consists of surface water sinking between Iceland and Greenland and in the Labrador Sea, which then spreads south. At 1000–2000m (3300–6500ft) water flowing out from the Mediterranean gradually loses salinity while spreading as far south as latitude 40° South.

In the Antarctic, bottom water is so cold that it is denser than the North Atlantic Deep Water and flows as far north as latitude 40° North. Surface water sinking at the Antarctic Convergence spreads north, crosses the equator and can be traced as far as 20° North. Large quantities of the Antarctic Bottom Water and Intermediate Water mix with the North Atlantic Deep Water, return to the south, and produce nutrient-rich upwellings at latitudes 50–60° South, accounting for the high productivity of Antarctic waters.

The Atlantic's deep and bottom waters have sunk from the surface, where they became saturated with oxygen by contact with the air. Their circulation is quite rapid so they sustain their high oxygen content.

Due to the earth's rotation (Coriolis Effect) the currents of the North Atlantic move clockwise and those of the South Atlantic counterclockwise.

NORTH ATLANTIC CURRENTS

The trade winds maintain a current from east to west with much of the water continuing into the Caribbean and through the Yucatán Strait into the Gulf of Mexico. It flows out through the Florida Straits as the warm Florida Current and, reinforced by water from the Antilles Current, forms the Gulf Stream. The Gulf Stream follows the American coast as far north as Cape Hatteras, continues away from the coast, and turns east to the south of Newfoundland's Grand Bank. Branches of warm water then turn south to form part of the anticyclonic gyre circulating around the Sargasso Sea. Colder water continues toward Europe as the North Atlantic Current.

The Canary Current branches south from the North Atlantic Current and flows southwest along the west coast of northwest Africa where cold water upwellings caused by offshore winds produce rich fishing grounds. This water continues west across the southern part of the North Atlantic as part of the warm North Equatorial Current, which on reaching the West Indies turns northwest as the Antilles Current.

ABOVE *The Spanish luxury liner* Cristóbal Colón *ran aground north of Bermuda in 1936. She was salvaged and used for bombing practice.*

SOUTH ATLANTIC

In the South Atlantic the southeast trade winds maintain the South Equatorial Current. While flowing west this current divides into two branches. One continues into the northern hemisphere and enters the Caribbean and the other turns south as the Brazil Current, a weaker counterpart of the Gulf Stream. Squeezed between the equatorial currents, the Equatorial Countercurrent flows east and combines with a warm, south-flowing extension of the Canary Current to become the Guinea Current. South of the South Atlantic high-pressure region, the Brazil Current flows east and becomes the South Atlantic Current which, on reaching the African coast, turns towards the equator as the Benguela Current. The Benguela Current also has nutrient-rich cold water upwellings near the coast. Further south the east-flowing Antarctic Circumpolar Current enters the Atlantic Ocean through the Drake Passage. One branch flows north along the east coast of Argentina as the Falkland Current, another helps to form the Benguela Current, while most water continues into the Indian Ocean.

In addition to pollution and overfishing the Atlantic has more than its fair share of industrial complexes discharging toxic chemicals, which tend to accumulate in higher organisms, making them a threat to marine life and humans.

ICEBERGS AND THE OCEANS

The North Atlantic Ocean has some of the world's busiest shipping lanes, so the northern lanes are patrolled for icebergs. They are common in Davis Strait, Denmark Strait, and the northwestern Atlantic Ocean from February to August. They have been seen as far south as Bermuda and the Madeira Islands.

In the southern hemisphere some icebergs drift north of latitude 42° South in the Atlantic Ocean, compared with a limit of latitude 56° South in the Pacific Ocean.

In the Indian Ocean, in the southern hemisphere, icebergs and pack ice are found south of latitude 65° South throughout the year and they can be found as far north as latitude 45° South.

The North Pacific Ocean does not experience much pack ice or icebergs. The Bering Sea is clear during the northern summer, but in winter and spring pack ice reaches as far south as latitude 40° North. In the South Pacific most icebergs are concentrated south of latitude 56° South.

EAST COAST USA

by Jack Jackson

STRETCHING OVER A VAST AREA FROM THE Canadian border to Florida, the East Coast of the US is one of the most active scuba diving areas. Often bathed by the clear, warm waters of the Gulf Stream, the marine life is good with tropical species found much further north than normal. There are shipwrecks from many eras: Spanish galleons, centuries of buccaneers, warships and commercial vessels of all ages. They were sunk in natural disasters, by poor navigation and various accidents, in acts of war, in explosives testing and some were environmentally cleaned and sunk to serve as artificial reefs. During World War II, in 1942, the commander of Germany's U-boat fleet, Admiral Karl Donitz, sent five U-boats to attack shipping off the East Coast in what was termed *Paukenschlag* or Operation Drumroll. The US was not prepared for this onslaught and German U-boats sank nearly 300 vessels, while suffering few casualties themselves.

TOP LEFT *The Florida Keys are a group of coral and limestone islands connected by 42 bridges for over 300km (186 miles).*
TOP RIGHT *Famous for its shipwrecks, Bermuda consists of seven main islands and over 170 named islets and rocks.*
RIGHT *Chinaware, prized by divers over the years, lies in the mud and debris of the first class dining room of the* Andrea Doria.

For deep dives, such as on the *Andrea Doria*, it will be necessary to dive with gases other than normal air (*see page 20*).

Many of the wrecks are well offshore or in deep water. Surface conditions can be rough and the currents strong. For years, experienced divers regularly endured nitrogen narcosis while diving much deeper wrecks than they should have done on air. These divers and the cave diving community in Florida were at the forefront in developing what we now know as technical diving.

In addition to lobsters, barracuda, jacks, spadefish, groupers and dense shoals of bait fish or silversides, many of the wrecks also attract sharks, from lone Bull Sharks to small shoals of Raggedtooth (Sand Tiger) Sharks in

October and November. Divers can even dive with sharks a few hours from New York City. Over 80km (50 miles) offshore from Rhode Island, boats search out eddies of the Gulf Stream and chum the water. Blue Sharks are common. The shark cage is floated on the surface, so divers require extra weight to minimize being tossed around by wave action.

1 ANDREA DORIA

The 212m (697ft) luxury liner SS *Andrea Doria* was the flagship of the Italian Line. In dense fog 72km (45 miles) south of Nantucket, at 23:22 on 25 July 1956, the Swedish American Line's *MV Stockholm* powered into her starboard side. The *Andrea Doria* took 11 hours to sink and, although it happened near

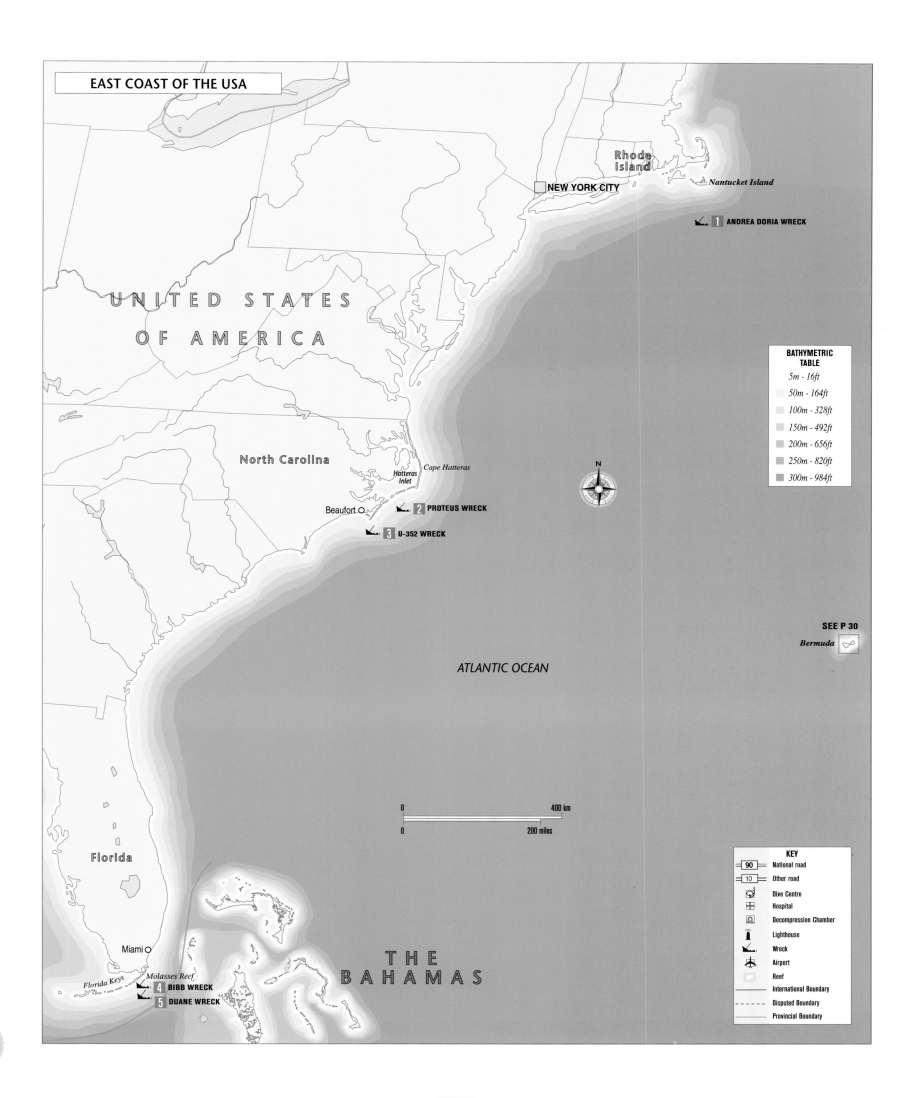

EAST COAST OF THE USA

Rhode Island

NEW YORK CITY

Nantucket Island

1 ANDREA DORIA WRECK

UNITED STATES OF AMERICA

North Carolina

Hatteras Inlet

Cape Hatteras

Beaufort

2 PROTEUS WRECK

3 U-352 WRECK

N

ATLANTIC OCEAN

SEE P 30

Bermuda

Florida

Miami

Molasses Reef

Florida Keys

4 BIBB WRECK

5 DUANE WRECK

THE BAHAMAS

BATHYMETRIC TABLE

5m - 16ft
50m - 164ft
100m - 328ft
150m - 492ft
200m - 656ft
250m - 820ft
300m - 984ft

0 — 400 km

0 — 200 miles

KEY

90	National road
10	Other road
	Dive Centre
	Hospital
	Decompression Chamber
	Lighthouse
	Wreck
	Airport
	Reef
	International Boundary
	Disputed Boundary
	Provincial Boundary

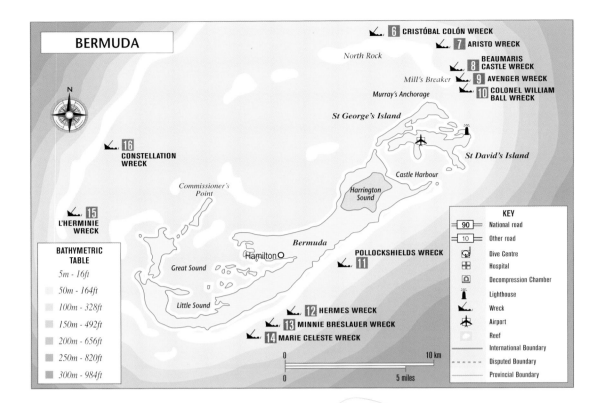

Map: **BERMUDA**

North Rock

6 CRISTÓBAL COLÓN WRECK
7 ARISTO WRECK
8 BEAUMARIS CASTLE WRECK
Mill's Breaker **9 AVENGER WRECK**
Murray's Anchorage **10 COLONEL WILLIAM BALL WRECK**

St George's Island

16 CONSTELLATION WRECK

St David's Island

Castle Harbour

Commissioner's Point

Harrington Sound

15 L'HERMINIE WRECK

BATHYMETRIC TABLE
5m - 16ft
50m - 164ft
100m - 328ft
150m - 492ft
200m - 656ft
250m - 820ft
300m - 984ft

Great Sound

Little Sound

Bermuda

Hamilton

POLLOCKSHIELDS WRECK 11

KEY
90 National road
10 Other road
Dive Centre
Hospital
Decompression Chamber
Lighthouse
Wreck
Airport
Reef
International Boundary
Disputed Boundary
Provincial Boundary

12 HERMES WRECK
13 MINNIE BRESLAUER WRECK
14 MARIE CELESTE WRECK

0   10 km
0   5 miles

---

enough to New York for an efficient rescue, 46 of the 1706 passengers and crew on board the *Andrea Doria* and five of the *Stockholm's* crew were killed. The *Stockholm* managed to limp into port.

Today, the *Andrea Doria* lies on her starboard side in 73m (240ft) of water with unpredictable ocean currents kicking up the silt to give poor visibility. On the ship, summertime water temperature is around 7°C (45°F). Most divers penetrate the ship looking for china. The *Andrea Doria* has exerted its attraction on scuba divers from the moment it sank. It is not the deepest wreck, nor the largest, but it has mystique and has become known as the American divers' premier challenge – the Mount Everest of wreck diving.

② *PROTEUS*

Off the coast of North Carolina, aptly named 'the graveyard of the Atlantic' for the hundreds of ships that have sunk there, over 100 wrecks are on the regular itineraries of diving charter vessels. Located in the Gulf Stream, the diving conditions are easier than those further north and in the late summer months the water temperatures are warm enough to find tropical species such as angelfish and butterflyfish.

One of the most popular wrecks in the area is the *Proteus*, a 125m (406ft) steamship that sank after a collision with the *SS Cushing* 40km (25 miles) south of Hatteras Inlet on 19 August 1918. Today she lies in 39m (125ft) of water with the stern mostly intact, listing to port and rising 15m (50ft) from the bottom. The animal life includes large stingrays and Cobia. Large shoals of Raggedtooth Sharks gather on the stern and bow in October and November. The current ranges from slight to very strong and the visibility is mostly better than 18m (60ft).

③ *U-352*

Southwest of the *Proteus*, and south of *Beaufort*, the *U-352* was a 67m (218ft) type VII-C German submarine sunk by depth charges from the United States Coast Guard cutter *Icarus* on 9 May 1942. She lies at 35m (115ft) with a heavy list to starboard. A relatively small wreck that can be navigated easily, most of the outer casing has corroded away, exposing the pressure hull. Animal life is good, visibility is generally better than 15m (50ft) and the currents slight.

④ *BIBB* AND ⑤ *DUANE*

Novice divers and experienced deepwater wreck divers alike are attracted to the Florida Keys by the combination of clear, warm

waters, reefs in marine sanctuaries and wrecks. The United States Coastguard cutters *Bibb* and *Duane* were stripped of armament, their hatches removed, partly sealed and 'environmentally cleaned' before being sunk as artificial reefs just south of Molasses Reef on 27 November 1987. Unfortunately, some divers have damaged or removed the barriers, allowing creatures such as turtles, and inexperienced divers, to penetrate areas where they can become trapped.

The 100m (327ft) vessels are buoyed, so divers descend the shotlines to the buoys. Due to the Gulf Stream, visibility is often over 30m (100ft), but the current is usually very strong. Although they are sister ships, they are two completely different dives. The *Bibb* lies on her starboard side in 40m (130ft) of water with the port gunwale railing at 29m (95ft). As a result she is less frequently visited by divers and in better condition than the *Duane*. The hull is encrusted with corals and Goliath Groupers, Cobia, barracuda, amberjacks and turtles are common. The *Bibb* is popular with technical divers.

One of the most spectacular dives in the Florida Keys, the *Duane* sits upright at 28m (90ft) with her crow's nest reaching nearly 18m (60ft) from the surface. She lies 0.8km (half a mile) south of the *Bibb*. Barracuda, angelfish, butterflyfish, jacks, grunts, snappers, wrasse, turtles, sharks and even Manta Rays have been seen.

BERMUDA

Bermuda is in the path of the Gulf Stream so, despite its relatively northern location 970km (600 miles) off the coast of North Carolina, it has the northernmost coral reef system in the world. Much of the marine flora and fauna is that found in the Caribbean, including angelfish, butterflyfish, Goliath Groupers, Eagle Rays, parrotfish, stony corals and gorgonias. The good visibility in summer, shallow-water reefs and a number of underwater caverns make it a popular destination for scuba divers, but the numerous wrecks are the main attraction.

Lying on top of a seamount, Bermuda's treacherous shallow reefs have over 350 registered wrecks dating back to the 15th Century: wooden vessels from early explorers including Spanish treasure galleons; majestic tall ships; iron-hulled freighters; and cruise liners. The list of wrecks include the *Constellation*, which inspired Peter Benchley's novel *The Deep*. Often dubbed the Shipwreck Capital of the Atlantic, treasure hunters found several wrecks with cargoes that included gold and jewellery and thus the name, Bermuda's Golden Circle was coined.

6 CRISTÓBAL COLÓN

Taking some of the popular Bermuda wrecks in a clockwise direction around the ring, the largest is the *Cristóbal Colón*, a 150m (500ft) Spanish luxury steam liner that ran aground 13km (8 miles) north of Bermuda at North Rock on 25 October 1936. She was easily looted and salvaged and during the Second World War, US Navy aircraft pilots used her for target practice, blowing most of her to pieces and finally breaking her back across the reef. Broken in two and divided by the reef, the *Cristóbal Colón*'s wreckage is spread over a large area, ranging in depth from 5m (16ft) at the bow to 25m (80ft) at the semi-intact stern. A huge wreck site that takes several dives to cover, like most of Bermuda's wrecks she is relatively shallow and the marine life includes stony and gorgonian corals, wrasse, snappers, barracuda and schools of chromis. Turtles pass by and large groupers hide in the hull. Propellers, turbines, drive shafts, boilers, evidence of cruise liner luxury and even unexploded artillery shells litter the ocean floor in a tangled mass.

7 ARISTO

The *Aristo* was a 75m (250ft) Norwegian freighter whose captain mistook the *Cristóbal Colón* for a ship under way, altered course to follow her and ran aground in 1937. She was towed off the reef, but soon sank and now sits bow and stern intact at 15m (50ft). The bow rises to within 5½m (18ft) of the surface.

8 BEAUMARIS CASTLE,
9 AVENGER,
10 COLONEL WILLIAM BALL

These three wrecks all ran into Mill's Breaker, northeast of St George. The 60m (200ft) iron-hulled English sailing vessel *Beaumaris Castle* ran aground in April 1873. The most intact of the three, her bow is at 12m (40ft). *The Avenger* was a wooden brigantine wrecked in February 1894 and the *Colonel William Ball* was a 40m (130ft) luxury yacht that sank in 1943.

11 POLLOCKSHIELDS

The 99m (323ft) English cargo vessel *Pollockshields* ran into a storm on 2 September 1915 and struck the reef five days later. She was later blown up and scattered wreckage is found at 5–12m (16–40ft).

12 HERMES

One of the most popular wrecks, the *Hermes* was a 50m (165ft) American freighter sold to a Philippine company and abandoned in Bermuda. She was eventually seized by the government and sunk by local dive operators as an artificial reef in 1985. She now lies fully intact and penetrable in 25m (80ft) of water with her mast around 9m (30ft).

13 MINNIE BRESLAUER

A 90m (300ft) English steel-hulled freighter on her maiden voyage, the *Minnie Breslauer* hit the reef on 1 January 1873 and sank during the attempted rescue. Today she lies at 12–20m (40–65ft) deep.

14 MARIE CELESTE

The 69m (225ft) *Marie Celeste* was a side-wheeled paddle steamer used as a blockade runner during the American Civil War. Cruising at speed under a Bermudan pilot, she hit the reef 0n 26 September 1864. Today her remains lie in 17m (55ft) of water.

15 L'HERMINIE

L'Herminie was a 90m (300ft) French frigate sunk on her way home from Cuba on 3 December 1838. The wreck has mostly rotted away, but 59 cannons are spread over a wide area in 9m (30ft) of water.

16 CONSTELLATION

The 60m (192ft) four-masted wooden schooner *Constellation* sank on 31 July 1943 after striking either the northwest reef or the wreck of the *Montana*. Carrying cosmetics, haberdashery, bags of cement, 700 cases of Scotch whisky and drugs, she inspired Peter Benchley's novel *The Deep* and the film of the same name. Today she lies broken-up in 9m (30ft) of water with the top of the cement cargo reaching 2½m (8ft) from the surface.

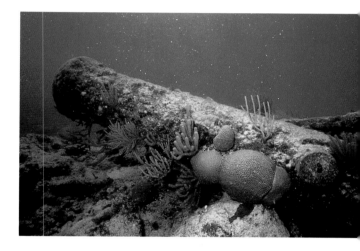

TOP *Very little is left of the structure of L'Herminie, but there are 59 cannons strewn over a wide area in 9m (30ft) of water.*

ABOVE *The* Constellation, *which was carrying cement, drugs, cosmetics and haberdashery, inspired Peter Benchley's novel* The Deep.

UNITED KINGDOM

Introduction by Jack Jackson

THE UK MAY NOT BE VERY LARGE AND ITS temperate waters are often murky, but it has plenty of interesting dive sites, a large number of shipwrecks and many divers who are keen to dive on them. In places with good conditions for bottom-dwelling organisms, sites are as colourful as their tropical counterparts. Beach dives, rocky gullies full of anemones, sea fans, crustaceans and nudibranchs, natural reefs, shoals of fish, kelp, seals, Fin and Minke Whales, Pilot Whales and other dolphins, various sharks and sea horses are all found in British waters.

To the west the warm Gulf Stream brings some surprising visitors including Ocean Sunfish and Leatherback Turtles. The whole western half of the UK sees basking sharks in spring and summer and sometimes these attract orcas. Ships pumping out ballast taken on in other climates and a slight warming of the waters has also enabled divers to find creatures that were not common here in the recent past.

TOP LEFT *Europe's most popular wreck diving destination, Scapa Flow, is a sheltered, open lagoon encircled by the Orkney Islands.*

TOP RIGHT *The Churchill Barriers were constructed after the german submarine U-47 sneaked past Scapa Flow's blockships and sank HMS Royal Oak.*

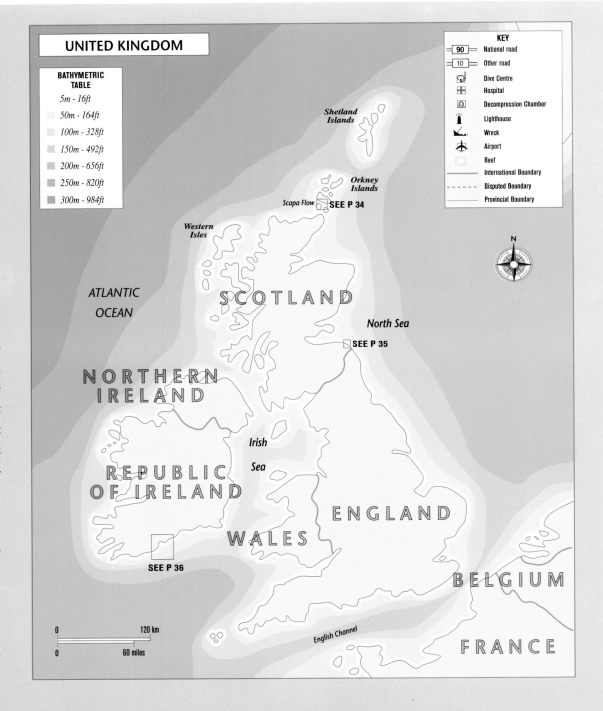

UNITED KINGDOM

BATHYMETRIC TABLE
5m - 16ft
50m - 164ft
100m - 328ft
150m - 492ft
200m - 656ft
250m - 820ft
300m - 984ft

KEY
90 National road
10 Other road
Dive Centre
Hospital
Decompression Chamber
Lighthouse
Wreck
Airport
Reef
International Boundary
Disputed Boundary
Provincial Boundary

Shetland Islands
Orkney Islands
Scapa Flow SEE P 34
Western Isles
ATLANTIC OCEAN
SCOTLAND
North Sea
SEE P 35
NORTHERN IRELAND
Irish Sea
REPUBLIC OF IRELAND
ENGLAND
WALES
SEE P 36
BELGIUM
English Channel
FRANCE

0   120 km
0   60 miles

Deep, cold water coral species are found off northern and western coasts and a reef built up by honeycomb worms has been found at 25m (80ft) off Dorset.

Wrecks are probably the most popular sites for those who dive in UK waters. With its rich maritime history of trade and war, the area is littered with thousands of wrecks dating from Tudor times through to the present day. During rough weather there is inland freshwater diving, particularly in winter.

SCOTLAND
by Lawson Wood

Diving in Scotland is known for its clear water, abundant marine life and historic shipwrecks. Dives range from the easy, steep muddy slopes of the southern sea lochs to vertical and underhanging walls. Sea caves and underwater caverns sculpt the western and northern isles. Many of the islands and sea lochs offer challenging drift dives in formidable tidal streams. Most of the diving is done by boat, visiting offshore wrecks, reefs and shoals hitherto unknown to subaquatic exploration. For the most part – with the exception of a few popular wrecks – much of the diving can still be considered exploratory diving.

With an average tidal range of around 5m (16ft), and buoyed by the Gulf Stream, a large amount of water moves along some 10,000km (6000 miles) of coastline around hundreds of named islands and thousands of lonely, rocky stacks and reefs.

Most of the dives are far from convenient car parks, launching sites or towns and require considerable planning and backup. For that reason the bulk of the diving is carried out around a number of well-established commercial centres that have the combination of a good road and rail network, accommodation, slipways, air compressors and dive boats. Most coastal towns have dive clubs or at least dive club members. With these dive clubs you will experience more of the varied diving to be found. Over 60 per cent of all British diving takes place in Scottish waters.

ORKNEY ISLANDS – SCAPA FLOW

I am not the first to think the Orkney Islands are magical. Witness the standing stones and stone rings dotted all over the islands. Scapa Flow is the largest sheltered natural harbour in Europe and this is where the Home Fleet made its Atlantic base during the last two major world conflicts.

Considered impregnable, the Bay of Scapa Flow, covering some 310 sq km (120 sq miles), is sheltered by a ring of protective islands. Situated 25km (15 miles) north of the Scottish mainland, access is by daily car ferry from Scrabster or by regular flight to Kirkwall airport from Edinburgh and Aberdeen.

A prime target for aerial or naval attack, a system of defence was installed in the form of anti aircraft gun emplacements, submarine netting, vigilant patrols and the now-famous blockships. This is also where one of the

ABOVE *A shipwreck at Scapa Flow. Wherever the interior of a wreck is open to passing current, it quickly becomes covered in marine life.*

largest concentrations of shipwrecks in the world is found – the scuttled German High Seas Fleet, dating from 1919.

Most diving concentrates on the sunken German fleet, but the blockships lie in clearer water at the entrance to Burra Sound. The central location of the German fleet means there is little water movement, which is fine for scuba diving, but also tends to trap particulate matter in the water column, resulting in poor visibility. This reduces the awe of these massive ships as you can only see small sections at a time and it takes many dives to explore each shipwreck safely. However, there are many other shipwrecks and remains of the already salvaged fleet, such as gun batteries, so the diving does not have to be restricted to the High Seas Fleet ships. There is also the wreckage of a WWII German ship, the *F2* [4], a salvage barge nearby at Lyness and older ships such as *HMS Roedean* [5].

RESTRICTIONS ON DIVING ON MARITIME WAR GRAVES

There is a small minority of divers who cannot resist disturbing wrecks and the temptation of removing brass and other artefacts. Diving on deep wrecks has been facilitated by the introduction of technical diving for recreational divers and this has worried those still living who are connected with many who lost their lives in this century's maritime military conflicts and disasters. In an effort to give greater protection to maritime war graves and military wrecks against trophy hunting, 16 wrecks have been designated Controlled Sites – where no diving is allowed without a special permit.

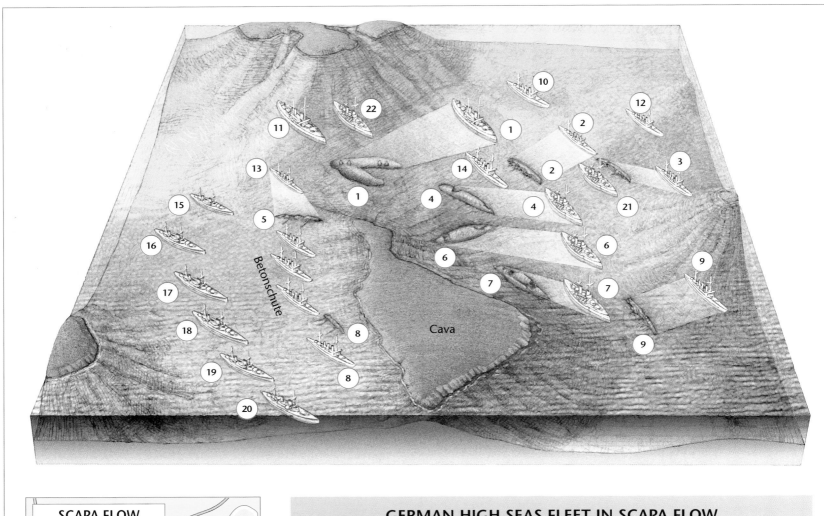

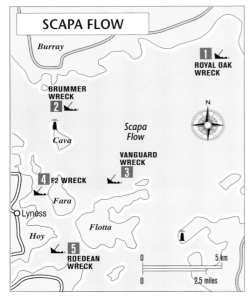

GERMAN HIGH SEAS FLEET IN SCAPA FLOW

1. SMS Bayern
2. SMS Brummer
3. SMS Köln
4. SMS Kronprinz Wilhelm
5. SMS Karlsruhe
6. SMS Markgraf
7. SMS König
8. SMS S36
9. SMS Dresden
10. SMS Emden
11. SMS Baden

12. SMS Frankfurt
13. SMS König Albert
14. SMS Grosser K
15. SMS Kaiseren
16. Derfflinger
17. Hindenburg
18. SMS Von der Tann
19. SMS Moltke
20. SMS Seydlitz
21. SMS Bremse
22. F der G

In June 1919 the interned German navy scuttled its High Seas Fleet to prevent the ships from falling into Allied hands. Most of them have subsequently been salvaged. The presumed position of each ship in June 1919 is shown in white.

Whatever your preferences, German High Seas Fleet has mystique and historical importance. The wrecks are an important part of the Orkneys' naval heritage, having played such a significant part in its history. These ships are fortunately protected now. Their watery grave is no longer such a mystery to us, yet it is deep enough to deter those who take these ancient warhorses less seriously. The ships themselves are disintegrating at an alarming rate; bad visibility and wreckage can result in getting snagged if you are not careful; and the depth limitations are such that many divers each year succumb to decompression sickness (the bends). This results from staying too deep for too long and not taking enough time to return to the surface. The diving on the ships is perhaps some of the most advanced in Europe and only properly trained divers should attempt the German Fleet.

This deep, formidable, cold, natural harbour has served the warring nations' fleets for centuries. At present there are remains of three German battleships, four light cruisers, five torpedo boats (destroyers), a WW2 destroyer (*F2*), two submarines, 27 large sections of remains and salvage equipment, 16 known British wrecks, 32 blockships and two battleships (the **Vanguard** 3 and the **Royal Oak** 1), with a further 54 sections of unidentified wreckage.

2 THE GERMAN LIGHT CRUISER *BRUMMER*

The *Brummer* (a German light cruiser) was scuttled in 1919 at 58° 53' 50"N, 03° 09' 07"W. Built in the Vulcan shipyard at Stettin on the Baltic coast in 1914, she carried 360 mines and

had a top speed of 34 knots. She displaced 4000 tons and was 138m (460ft) long.

The *Brummer* is just one of four German light cruisers that were scuttled under the orders of Admiral Ludwig von Reuter in 1919. Through the descending gloom, the graceful arch of the sharp bows comes into view. Dropping to the stony seabed divers can gaze upwards in awe at this massive ship lying on her starboard side. The hull is festooned in Plumose Anemones (*Metridium senile*) and feather stars (*Antedon bifida*). From here divers swim along the now-vertical decking, past the forward 150mm (5.9in) gun and approach the

superstructure, which has mostly collapsed. The central section of the ship was blasted apart by salvage divers. The stern, however, where the other 150mm (5.9in) gun can be found, is mainly intact. Maximum depth is 36m (120ft) and divers return to surface by the mooring buoy line.

Conditions vary tremendously during the season. Visibility is generally poor and it is dark on the seabed. In the centre of Scapa Flow lights should always be used. Work-up dives should be undertaken before doing the deeper battleships. Photographers prefer the blockships at the entrance to Burra Sound,

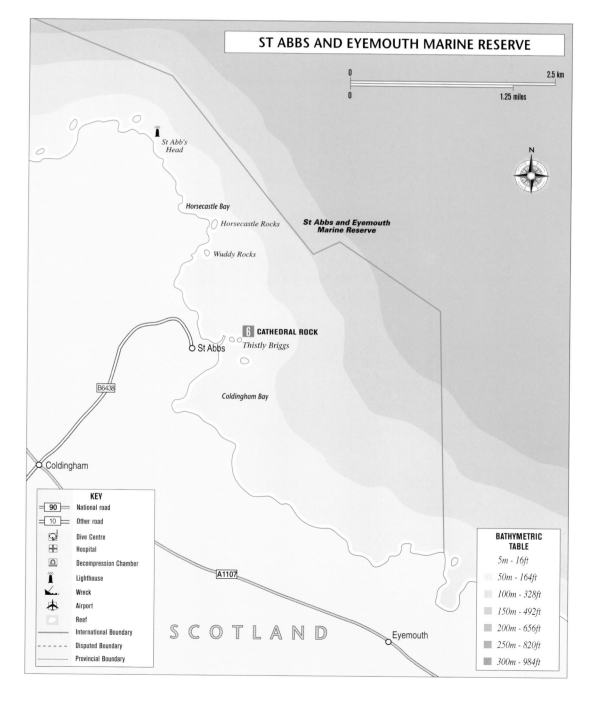

ST ABBS AND EYEMOUTH MARINE RESERVE

0 — 2.5 km
0 — 1.25 miles

N

St Abb's Head

Horsecastle Bay

Horsecastle Rocks

St Abbs and Eyemouth Marine Reserve

Wuddy Rocks

6 CATHEDRAL ROCK
Thistly Briggs

St Abbs

B6438

Coldingham Bay

Coldingham

KEY

90	National road
10	Other road
	Dive Centre
	Hospital
	Decompression Chamber
	Lighthouse
	Wreck
	Airport
	Reef
	International Boundary
- - -	Disputed Boundary
	Provincial Boundary

A1107

S C O T L A N D   Eyemouth

BATHYMETRIC TABLE

	5m - 16ft
	50m - 164ft
	100m - 328ft
	150m - 492ft
	200m - 656ft
	250m - 820ft
	300m - 984ft

TOP *European wax anemones, also known as snakelocks anemones (here* Anemonia sulcata*) live symbiotically with spider crabs, gobies and periclimenes shrimps.*

ABOVE *Due to strong current, visibility at the Gobernador Bories is good.*

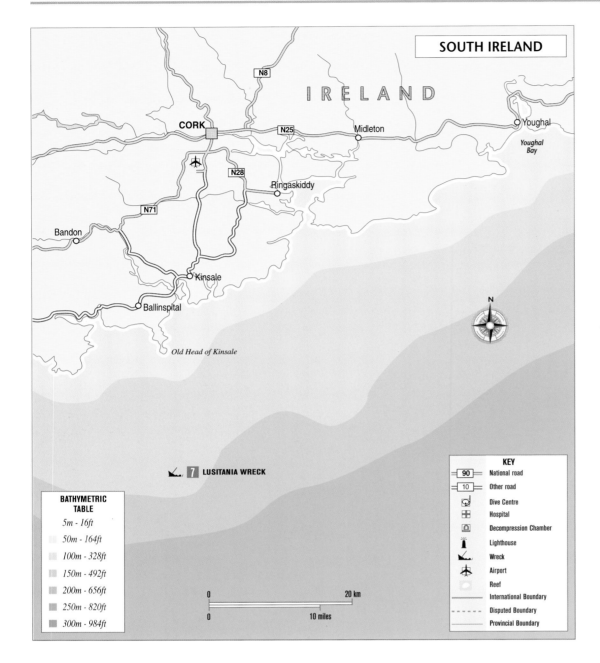

SOUTH IRELAND

IRELAND

CORK

N8

N25 · Midleton

Youghal

Youghal Bay

N28

Ringaskiddy

N71

Bandon

Kinsale

Ballinspital

Old Head of Kinsale

N

7 LUSITANIA WRECK

BATHYMETRIC TABLE

5m - 16ft
50m - 164ft
100m - 328ft
150m - 492ft
200m - 656ft
250m - 820ft
300m - 984ft

	KEY
90	National road
10	Other road
	Dive Centre
	Hospital
	Decompression Chamber
	Lighthouse
	Wreck
	Airport
	Reef
	International Boundary
	Disputed Boundary
	Provincial Boundary

0 — 20 km
0 — 10 miles

LEFT *Royal Navy Divers and a few civilians perform an annual memorial dive on the War Grave of* HMS Royal Oak *and replace the flag.*

where the average depth is half that of the German warships; there is much more light; more interesting marine growth; and the water is much clearer as the tidal race at Burra Sound sweeps away all sedimentation particles. However, this also limits diving time on these wrecks and even that only at slack tide.

On the night of 14 October 1939, 20 years after the German Fleet was scuttled, the 188 metre (600ft) battleship *Royal Oak* was lying at anchor in the sheltered bay of Scapa Flow in the Orkney Islands. Her duties were to protect Kirkwall and the British fleet from aerial attack. Scapa Flow was considered impenetrable because of the narrow passages between the reefs and islands. Attack was considered

likely only from the skies. However, nobody told this to Günther Prien, commander of the *U–47*. He stealthily approached Scapa Flow, in what is considered by many to be one of the bravest feats in naval history and, at the dead of night, sank the *Royal Oak*. The *Royal Oak* is now a designated war grave and protected by law. Diving on her is strictly forbidden. As a result, she is the ship most divers want to visit.

TOP TEN TIPS TO DIVING AT SCAPA FLOW

Most of the diving in Scapa Flow is potentially dangerous and virtually all the German Fleet wrecks should be treated as decompression dives. Not only does this put undue stress on the diver, it considerably reduces

the time to be spent in the water and the ultimate enjoyment of the wrecks. Most divers are attracted to the 'technical' side of deep diving. However, the larger battleships are not only in very deep water, they are all upside down, boring and, unless you want to spend your entire dive on the underside of a ship's hull, they can be dangerous to explore any further.

- Attend a deep diving course with a recognized training agency.
- Buy and learn how to use, not only a computer, but also standard air decompression tables – and never trust either.
- Never use your computer 'to its limit', always stay within the safety margin.
- Increase depth slowly for acclimatization.
- Recognize symptoms of nitrogen narcosis.
- When symptoms of narcosis appear, ascend immediately until symptoms are relieved.
- Dive only with experienced deep divers.
- Be Safe; do not put yourself or others at risk.
- Plan your dive and dive your plan accordingly, with no open-water decompression stops, use the wreck marker buoy lines for ascent and descent.
- Always obey the dive boat captain.

⑥ CATHEDRAL ROCK
ST ABBS AND EYEMOUTH MARINE RESERVE

Cathedral Rock is at Lat 550 53' 55"N and Long 020 07' 29"W. Better still, invest in Ordnance Survey Pathfinder 423 Map sheet NT 86 / 96 G.R. 922 673. Admiralty chart No.160.

At the opposite end of Scotland, on the extreme southeast coast, is Scotland's only marine reserve, founded by Lawson Wood. First discovered in the 1950s, Cathedral Rock is the most popular dive site within the St Abbs and Eyemouth Voluntary Marine Nature Reserve and possibly one of the most dived in the whole of the British Isles.

Many divers often fail to find the site, relying on poor information, inadequate navigational skills or, more often than not, are just enjoying themselves so much off St Abbs harbour wall, that they never get as far as Cathedral Rock. The rock is part of the reef which runs perpendicular to the corner of St Abbs harbour wall, known locally as Thistly Briggs. The rock is never visible, even at the lowest of tides and many divers mistake a reef close by for Cathedral Rock. Underwater, the wall falls away and is deeply undercut with eroded horizontal strata lines, now filled with squat lobsters and Leopard Spotted Gobies. Comprising two chambers, the top tunnel is known as the Keyhole. Although it is easily negotiated, exhaust air can become trapped and kill marine life, therefore it is best not to linger in this area. The lower tunnel archway is massive, of double-decker bus proportions, with a stony bottom directly under the arch and a tumble of boulders on each side. The walls and the roof of the arches are festooned with a dwarf species of the Plumose Anemone (*Metridium senile*) as well as sponges, soft corals (Dead Men's Fingers), mussels and hydroids. Small schools of pollack are often herded into this natural arena by predatory cod. For Photographers there are panoramic vistas of the archways, diver portraits, diver interaction shots and the staggering amount of macro work on nudibranchs, crabs and molluscs.

⑦ THE WRECK OF THE LUSITANIA
by Jack Jackson

The 232m (762ft) Cunard luxury liner *RMS Lusitania* was the largest and fastest vessel of her time plying the Atlantic route. She was torpedoed 19km (12 miles) south of Ireland's Old Head of Kinsale by the German submarine *U-20* at 02:10 hours on 7 May 1915 and sank in 18 minutes. More than 1200 of the 1257 passengers and 702 crew died. The fact that she was a passenger ship and that the dead included 123 Americans, 291 women and 94 children, had much to do with America entering World War I in 1917.

The wreck was first dived in 1935 by Jim Jarrett using a forerunner of the armoured one-atmosphere diving suit. The Royal Navy dived her in 1954 and in the late 1960s. In the early 1970s John Light, an American naval diver who then owned the wreck,

dived her several times with limited bottom times. In 1982, using Heliox and a diving bell, her anchors and three propellers were recovered. In 1993 the locator of the *Titanic*, Robert Ballard, surveyed her with submersibles and Remotely Operated Vehicles.

The first visit by recreational technical divers was in 1994 when eight Britons, led by Polly Tapson, were joined by deep-wreck diving expert Gary Gentile and three of his friends from the East Coast of America. The *Lusitania* was dived again in 1995, 1999 and in 2001 by a Starfish Enterprise team led by Mark Jones. They worked with current owner Gregg Bemis on an archaeological survey as a precursor to raising and conserving artefacts. The wreck lies on her starboard side with the bow in good condition and draped in lost trawl nets. The stern is still recognizable as part of the ship but the middle section is badly broken up.

ARGON

Technical divers using dry suits often use argon gas for suit-inflation to help maintain body temperature. Denser than air and much denser than helium, argon acts as a better insulator for retaining body heat, while inflating the suit enough to eliminate body-squeezes.

The argon is carried in a separate small cylinder, but it is particularly important to make sure that only the correct inflation hose is connected between the cylinder and the dry suit so that the gas cannot be breathed by mistake. Some divers use a standard regulator, which still has a regulator second stage attached, as well as a suit-inflation hose. The argon cylinder does not contain any oxygen, so if the diver switched to the wrong second stage by mistake, the result would be fatal.

TOP *Ceramic floor tiles in one of the bathrooms of the* RMS Lusitania.
ABOVE *A close-up of a porthole among the wreckage of the* RMS Lusitania.

SOUTH AFRICA

by Chris Fallows

SINCE THE MID-1990S SOUTH AFRICA HAS become renowned for Great White Shark viewing and diving. All the diving activities, which are conducted from the safety of a steel cage, are practised along the Cape south and southwest coasts. The Cape coast has a Mediterranean climate with winter rain from May to August and daily air temperatures of 15–20°C (60–68°F). In summer, November to March, the average air temperatures are 25–30°C (77–86°F). During the shark season (when the sharks congregate around the seal colonies), from April to October, the water temperatures are around 12–16°C (54–61°F), making at least a 5mm wet suit necessary. Charter boats are launched from three different sites on trips to see Great White Sharks. Each of these offers a different viewing opportunity.

Great White Sharks (*Carcharodon carcharias*) are magnificent predators that often occur around huge colonies of Cape Fur Seal (*Arctocephalus pusillus pusillus*) and this is where

TOP LEFT *Mossel Bay is home to an offshore seal colony, which attracts Great Whites at certain times of the year for good cage diving.*

TOP RIGHT *African Black Footed Penguins are among many bird species on the islands off the Cape coast. These birds occasionally fall prey to a hungry Great White, but not often.*

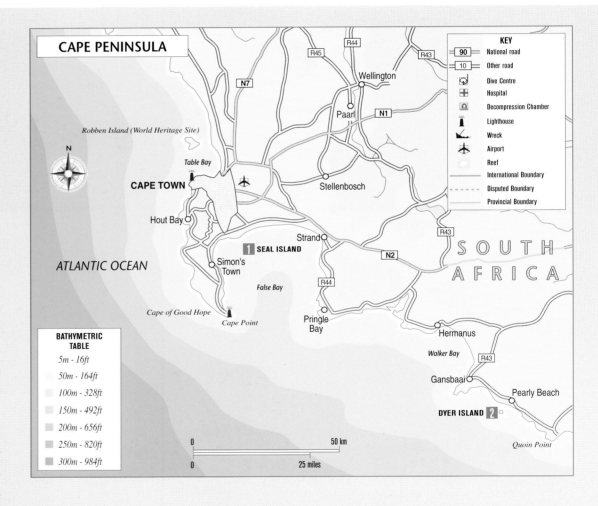

CAPE PENINSULA

Robben Island (World Heritage Site)

Table Bay

CAPE TOWN

Hout Bay

ATLANTIC OCEAN

Wellington

Paarl

Stellenbosch

Strand

1 SEAL ISLAND

Simon's Town

False Bay

Cape of Good Hope

Cape Point

Pringle Bay

Hermanus

Walker Bay

Gansbaai

Pearly Beach

DYER ISLAND 2

Quoin Point

S O U T H A F R I C A

KEY

90	National road
10	Other road
	Dive Centre
	Hospital
	Decompression Chamber
	Lighthouse
	Wreck
	Airport
	Reef
	International Boundary
	Disputed Boundary
	Provincial Boundary

BATHYMETRIC TABLE

5m - 16ft
50m - 164ft
100m - 328ft
150m - 492ft
200m - 656ft
250m - 820ft
300m - 984ft

50 km
25 miles

various charter companies offer opportunities to view these super sharks. While waiting for the sharks it is also very enjoyable to watch the delightful antics of these seals as they cavort in and out of the water.

1 SEAL ISLAND

Seal Island in False Bay has become famous because the Great Whites here leap clear of

the surface of the water (breaching) on a regular basis in pursuit of the seals that come and go from the 64,000-strong colony. The operation in this area specializes in viewing natural behaviour with very little chumming, while much time is spent observing the aerial hunting of the Great Whites in the morning and in the evening. Their hunting behaviour is spectacular, as these marine leviathans, often weighing over 1000kg (2200 lb), leap as much as 3m (10ft) into the air. This phenomenon has attracted *National Geographic, Discovery,* BBC and others to film at this location.

This area is recommended for anyone with an interest in observing the Great Whites in the most spectacular display of their natural behaviour when feeding.

Tours to Seal Island depart from the old British Naval port of Simon's Town, which boasts a resident colony of African Penguins (*Sphenicus demersus*), and which is only 35 minutes' travel from South Africa's mother city, Cape Town. Charters are run from two high-powered 8m (25ft) catamarans specifically designed for photography and close encounters, and the boat trip out to the island takes around 25 minutes.

Diving around Seal Island can be very good at times even though this activity is overshadowed by the surface spectacle. Visibility can be around 15m (50ft), but the average is 8m (25ft). Water temperatures are around 15°C (60°F) and the dives are conducted from a steel cage, which is floated on the surface. This area's other claim to fame is the size of the Great Whites that have frequented the island over the years. Two of them, dubbed Hercules and Submarine, are both over 6m (20ft), although the latter has not been seen for some years. The average size of the sharks is around 3.5m (11ft).

GANSBAAI

Another Great White Shark dive site is Gansbaai, two hours' drive east of Cape Town. This is the most commercial area for viewing these sharks and there are many operators offering trips. It is the area where commercial cage diving began in South Africa in 1991. Most boats launch from the quaint harbour of Kleinbaai and head out to Dyer Island, which lies about 20 minutes offshore. The launch can be an adventure in itself, because open ocean waves often break across your path just outside the harbour.

Between **Dyer Island** 2 and Geyser Rock lies a channel known as shark alley. The

TOP *Cape Fur Seals are the preferred winter prey of the Great Whites patrolling these waters in search of marine mammals. Large bull seals can weigh over 300kg and are themselves formidable predators.*
ABOVE *Although it is still possible to free-dive with other species of shark such as the Zambezi (Bull) Shark, it is now illegal to do so with the Great White.*

boats anchor in the 5m (16ft) deep channel and wait for the patrolling sharks. Geyser Rock has about 50,000 seals which, like at Seal Island, attract the Great Whites. The average visibility is also around 8m (25ft), while on exceptional days it is up to 15m (50ft) and more.

Dyer Island also has a multitude of bird species, including the rare Leach's Storm Petrel. Water temperatures are usually around 15°C (60°F), but occasionally can be lower. Dyer Island operations focus solely on diving, as very little breaching or predation is seen here and all the operators carry cages and diving gear. For those interested purely in observing Great Whites underwater, Dyer Island should be first choice. The sharks in this area are around 3.5m (11ft) on average, but larger ones often put in an appearance. Dyer Island is also famous for a couple of operators who free-dive with the sharks, although this practice is not recommended and is, in fact, illegal.

3 MOSSEL BAY

Mossel Bay, about 400km (250 miles) east of Cape Town, has a small Cape Fur Seal colony numbering around 6000 animals. Here, like at Seal Island in False Bay, there is only one operator. Diving is done from a large yacht and the cage is attached directly to the boat. This set-up allows snorkellers the opportunity to view the sharks, making it the only operation in South Africa where you can snorkel in a cage.

Mossel Bay has large numbers of Great Whites earlier in the season than the other two areas. They often arrive in March and occasionally even in February. The launch

ABOVE LEFT *Breaching Great Whites are the reason Seal Island has attracted film crews from all over the world. These spectacular bursts last only a split second, but the memory lasts forever.*

LEFT *After the initial strike the seal is quickly consumed. Great White Sharks are the apex predators around the Cape coast.*

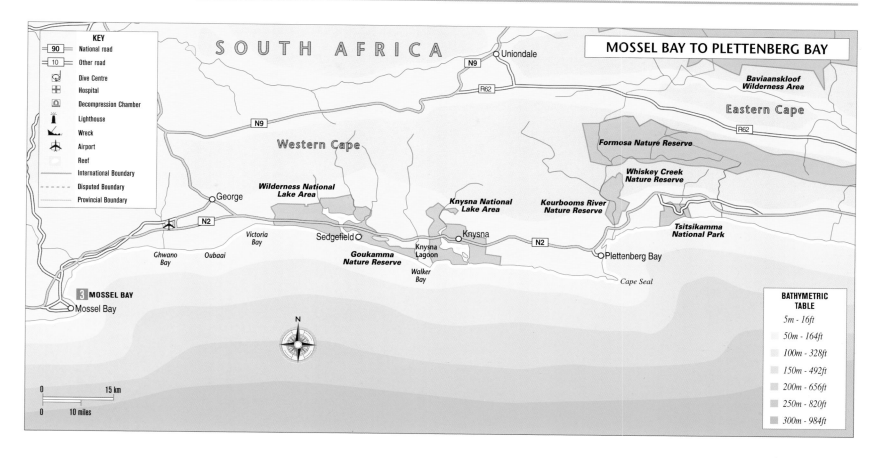

MOSSEL BAY TO PLETTENBERG BAY

KEY

90	National road
10	Other road
	Dive Centre
	Hospital
	Decompression Chamber
	Lighthouse
	Wreck
	Airport
	Reef
	International Boundary
	Disputed Boundary
	Provincial Boundary

BATHYMETRIC TABLE

5m - 16ft
50m - 164ft
100m - 328ft
150m - 492ft
200m - 656ft
250m - 820ft
300m - 984ft

site is only 10 minutes' sail from where the shark viewing and baiting (chumming) takes place. The water is generally warmer in this area, averaging around 17–18°C (63–65°F) during the shark season. Blue, warm, open-ocean water sometimes sweeps into the bay, making for a great dive. Breaches and predation are also observed in Mossel Bay. The scenic Garden Route, which really starts from here, makes this site a worthwhile visit for anyone with time to spend in South Africa.

When planning a trip to South Africa to dive with Great Whites, it is advisable to make contact with the operator of your choice and find out if they are in fact seeing Great Whites shortly before your intended stay. These animals are free to come and go as they please and it is a long way to travel to be disappointed. If you are fortunate enough to have a good encounter with these majestic, super predators, you will never forget the experience. Divers may be the first people to develop affection for these majestic animals.

South Africa is the best location for a chance to see Great Whites and, considering the country's marine and terrestrial diversity, it is an outdoor explorer's Utopia.

ABOVE *Although diving with Great Whites is the star attraction, Blue and Mako Shark diving 50km (30 miles) off Seal Island is for the purist. Sharks are attracted with the use of sound devices.*

FRANCE

Cannes
Marseille
Toulon
Cape Antibes
Cape Juan
Porquerolles
Côte D'Azur

Golfe du Lion

Banyuls-sur-mer
Cerbère-Banyuls Nature Reserve

FRANCE

Seine
Paris

②

Barcelona

Costa Brava

①

Mediterranean Sea

0   200 km
0   100 miles

ROMANIA

Lyon

Rhône

CROATIA

Gulf of Venice

Bucharest

BULGARIA

Banyuls-sur-mer
Marseille
Cannes
Ligurian Sea
ITALY
Adriatic Sea

Golfe du Lion
Corsica
VATICAN CITY
Rome

ALBANIA

Bosphorus Strait
Istanbul
Sea of Marmara

Barcelona
Costa Brava

SPAIN

Strait of Bonifacio

Tyrrhenian Basin
Tyrrhenian Sea

Aegean Sea

GREECE

Golfo de Valencia
Balearic Basin
Balearic Islands
Menorca
Sardinia

Golfo di Taranto
Euboea

Mallorca
Golfo di Cagliari
Strait of Messina
Athens

Palermo
Sicily
Strait of Sicily
Ionian Sea

Rhodes

Algiers
MALTA ④
⑤ ③
Medina Bank
Crete

Tunis
Mediterranean

ALGERIA

Gulf of Gabès

TUNISIA

Gulf of Sidra (Khalij Surt)

Tripoli

PORTUGAL

SPAIN

Golfo de Valencia

LIBYA

GIBRALTAR
Strait of Gibraltar
Alborán Basin

ATLANTIC OCEAN
Tangier

ALGERIA

0   200 km
0   100 miles

MOROCCO

ARCTIC OCEAN

N

North America
Europe
Asia

Mediterranean Sea

KEY TO MAPS

① Spain - Medas Islands p46

② Spain - Central Costa Brava p48

③ Malta p51

④ Gozo p53

⑤ Comino p54

Tropic of Cancer
ATLANTIC OCEAN
Africa
Equator
INDIAN OCEAN

Tropic of Capricorn
South America

PACIFIC OCEAN

0   400 km
0   200 miles

UKRAINE

Sea of
Azov

45°N

Black Sea

Ankara
○

TURKEY

Adana
○

CYPRUS

SYRIA

LEBANON

○Beirut

e a

ISRAEL
○Jerusalem

○Alexandria
Cairo

Suez Canal

30°N

Nile

Red Sea

EGYPT

Tropic of Cancer   23°30'N

THE
MEDITERRANEAN

by Jack Jackson

ALMOST LANDLOCKED, THE MEDITERRANEAN SEA LIES between Africa and Eurasia, exhibiting evidence of a complex geological history. Elongated from west to east, in the west the Mediterranean extends to the Strait of Gibraltar between Spain and Morocco, only 13km (8 miles) wide at its narrowest point and its only connection with the Atlantic Ocean. To the east it is bordered by the shores of Turkey, Syria, Lebanon and Israel. Nearly 4000km (2500 miles) wide, including the Sea of Marmara, it occupies an area of approximately 2,510,000 sq km (970,000 sq miles).

To the northeast the Mediterranean Sea connects with the Black Sea through the Dardanelles, the Sea of Marmara, and the Bosphorus Strait. To the southeast the Suez Canal, an artificial waterway across the Isthmus of Suez, connects with the Red Sea.

Diving in the Mediterranean has considerable variety. Seismic action, uneven deposition of river sediments, some of which were remelted, and uneven erosion together with the movements of the sea and the emergence and submergence of the land have resulted in a variety of coastlines. The northern shores of the eastern Mediterranean are complex and have variable fold mountains. The north coast of Africa bordering the eastern Mediterranean is low-lying and uniform except for the Cyrenaica highlands east of the Gulf of Sidra in Libya. Diving is popular everywhere with the local inhabitants, but there are some areas where only local nationals are allowed to dive and others that do not attract visiting divers. At Gibraltar and the marine reserves and Balearic Islands of Spain, the marine life is still good, but diving resorts on the Mediterranean coast of Morocco have not proved popular. The Mediterranean coast of France has good wrecks. Corsica and Sardinia have everything from wrecks to caverns. Algeria would have good diving but has never developed it; Tunisia has and its diving is quite good. The Tyrrhenian and Adriatic coasts and Sicily are popular and have plenty of wrecks. Malta, Gozo and Comino are particularly popular with UK clients and the government has scuttled six ships for divers. While not a problem for divers, Great White Sharks have been seen in Sardinia, Tunisia, Malta, Sicily and the mouth of the Adriatic. Greece and Turkey limit the areas where foreigners are allowed to dive to protect ancient shipwrecks, although Turkey has just opened some of these areas. Libya, Syria and Lebanon have never developed their diving. Cyprus has good diving, Israel limits access to its Mediterranean underwater archaeological sites, but Egypt has opened up the recent finds near Alexandria.

ABOVE *The Bryozoan colony (Myriapora truncata) is called False Coral because its colour and shape are similar to that of Red Coral. When dead, it loses the colour whereas true Red Coral remains red.*

Much of the Mediterranean coastline has rugged hills rising sharply from the water, but Egypt and Libya have plains lying next to the sea. The largest island is Sicily while in decreasing size other large islands include Sardinia, Cyprus, Corsica and Crete. There are myriads of smaller islands and those of the Aegean are so numerous that the name Archipelago was formerly applied to the Aegean Sea. These islands have frequent earthquakes.

The large volume of warm water gives the surrounding land a subtropical climate known as a Mediterranean climate, even when it occurs elsewhere. Most Mediterranean countries have hot, dry summers and mild, wet winters. In summer, the temperature may reach 27° (80°F) while in winter it rarely drops below 4°C (39°F). Egypt and Libya have tropical climates. Off the coast of Libya, the Gulf of Sidra can reach 31°C (88°F) in August.

WINDS AND RAINFALL

Airflow into the Mediterranean Sea is mainly through breaks in the mountain ranges. The cold, dry, northwesterly mistral passes through the Alps-Pyrenees gap. The strong northeasterly bora passes through the Trieste gap. The cold easterly levanter and the westerly vendaval pass through the Strait of Gibraltar. Hot, dry southeasterly winds, known locally as the sirocco, ghibli or khamsin, frequently blow into the Mediterranean from the Arabian Peninsula and the Sahara desert when low-pressure zones cross the sea in late winter and early spring. These winds reduce the heat of the surface water by evaporative cooling. This is enough to increase its density so that it sinks and increases the salinity of incoming Atlantic surface water.

The distribution and quantity of rainfall is variable and unpredictable. Maximum rainfall is found in mountainous coastal areas. The Dalmatian coast of Croatia can get 2540mm (100 in) per year, while the north African coast from Gabès in Tunisia to Egypt gets less than 250mm (10in). Overall, the loss of water by evaporation is three times the combination of rainfall and river drainage into the sea.

TIDES

Most regions of the Mediterranean have semidiurnal tides. The average tidal range is only about 300mm (12 in), but the change in water level caused by strong winds can be four times greater. However, the Gulf of Gabès off Tunisia has a range of nearly 2m (6½ft). The Atlantic affects tides in the Strait of Gibraltar, but its influence declines further east. A strong current flows into the Mediterranean from the Black Sea.

The tides are significant in the Aegean Sea where the Euripus Phenomenon (violent currents, variable in speed and direction) is named after the tide of the strait lying between continental Greece and the island of Euboea (Évvoia). These currents are mainly influenced by the winds.

SEAFLOOR TOPOGRAPHY

A submarine ridge with a sill depth of about 365m (1200ft) between the African coast and the island of Sicily divides the Mediterranean Sea into western and eastern sections. The sea has an average depth of 1501m (4926ft). The eastern basin is the deeper than the western one, reaching a maximum depth of 5093m (16,302ft) in the Hellenic Trough between Greece and Italy.

The western section is characterized by broad, smooth, abyssal plains and is further subdivided into three main basins. The Alborán Basin is east of Gibraltar, between the coasts of Spain and Morocco. The Balearic Basin, sometimes called the Algerian or Algero-Provençal Basin, is east of the Alborán Basin and west of Sardinia and Corsica, extending from the coast of Algeria to the coast of France. The Tyrrhenian Basin, covered by the Tyrrhenian Sea, lies between

DENSITY CURRENTS

Density currents are currents that move by the force of gravity acting on small density differences caused by variations in salinity or temperature. The surface layer, which is disturbed by the waves, is there because it is less dense than the deeper waters due to being warmer or less saline. The oceans are composed of layers of water that have distinctive chemical and physical properties, which move more-or-less independently of each other and which do not lose their individuality by mixing even after they have flowed for hundreds of kilometres (miles) from their point of origin.

The water from the Mediterranean Sea flowing through the Strait of Gibraltar into the Atlantic Ocean is an example of this type of density current or stratified flow. The Mediterranean is enclosed in a basin that is relatively small compared with the ocean basins and, because it is located in a relatively dry climate, evaporation exceeds the supply of fresh water from river drainage. The result is that the Mediterranean Sea contains water that is both warmer and more saline than normal deep-sea water. Overall the Mediterranean water is denser than the water in the upper parts of the North Atlantic. This difference in density causes the lighter Atlantic water to flow into the Mediterranean in the top 200m (660ft) of the Strait of Gibraltar and the denser Mediterranean water to flow out into the Atlantic between 200m (660ft) and the top of the sill separating the Mediterranean from the Atlantic at a depth of 320m (1050ft). Because the strait is relatively narrow, both inflow and outflow achieve quite high speeds. Near the surface the inflow may reach speeds of 2m (6½ft) per second, and the outflow 1m (40in) per second. A result of the high current speeds in the strait is a considerable amount of mixing, which reduces the salinity of the outflowing Mediterranean water, which sinks until it encounters colder, denser Atlantic water, where it then spreads out.

Italy and the islands of Sardinia and Corsica.

In contrast, the Mediterranean's eastern section is dominated by the Mediterranean Ridge system and is further subdivided into two main basins. The Ionian Basin, the area known as the Ionian Sea, lies to the south of Italy and Greece. A submarine ridge between Libya's Cyrenaica and the western end of Crete separates the Ionian Basin from the Levantine Basin to the south of Anatolia (Turkey). The island of Crete separates the Levantine Basin from the Aegean Sea. The Aegean is that part of the Mediterranean Sea lying north of Crete, bounded on the west and north by the coast of Greece; and on the east by the coast of Turkey. The Aegean Sea contains the many islands of the Grecian Archipelago. To the northwest of the main body of the Mediterranean lies the Adriatic Sea, which is bounded by Italy to the west and north; and by Croatia, Bosnia-Herzegovina, Serbia and Albania to the east.

Modern studies suggest that the structure and present form of this tectonically active basin and its bordering mountain system have been determined by the convergence and recession of the continental plates of Eurasia and Africa squeezing and stretching the Earth's crust. As they drifted apart, Eurasia turned clockwise and Sardinia, Corsica and Africa turned anticlockwise, opening a waterway to the ocean at the western end of the sea. There were many alternating phases of flooding and evaporation. Geological data suggests that there are currently at least six main areas of collision between Africa and Eurasia, resulting in volcanism, mountain building, and land submergence. Earthquakes occur frequently throughout the region, especially in Greece and western Turkey. Volcanic action formed many of the islands in the Mediterranean Sea and volcanoes, including Mount Etna, Stromboli, and Vesuvius, still erupt in the region.

SURFACE CIRCULATION AND TIDES

Mediterranean surface circulation basically consists of separate anticlockwise movements of the water in the western and eastern basins, but many small eddies and other local currents occur because of the complexity of the northern coastline and the many islands. Although only significant in the Gulf of Gabès and the northern Adriatic, tides add complications to the currents in narrow channels such as the Strait of Messina.

Historically, large seasonal variations were caused by the flooding of the Nile, which reduced the salinity of coastal waters of the southeastern Mediterranean and increased the stratification and productivity of these waters. This influence ended with the completion of the Aswan High Dam. The amount of Red Sea water passing through the Suez Canal into the Mediterranean is negligible.

The opening of the Suez Canal turned the Mediterranean into one of the world's busiest shipping lanes and it became heavily polluted with oil, agricultural run-off, industrial pollutants and sewage, even spreading typhoid and infectious hepatitis. Eventually the United Nations Environment Program (UNEP) sponsored the Barcelona Convention for the Protection of the Mediterranean Sea Against Pollution, calling on all Mediterranean countries to clean things up. Recently there have been spills of toxic chemicals, leaks from offshore oil installations and a virulent alien alga discharged from an aquarium, but generally things are much improved.

TOP RIGHT *Blackfaced Blenny (*Tripterigion delaisi*). Territorial males have black heads where the coloration does not extend to the pectoral fins, and yellow bodies.*

MIDDLE RIGHT *Found in much of the Atlantic Ocean, including the Mediterranean, Salema or Saupe (*Sarpa salpa*) usually congregate on rocky or sandy seabeds with lots of vegetation.*

RIGHT *Wide-eyed Flounders (*Bothus podas*) lie camouflaged on sandy bottoms where they feed on small fish and invertebrates. Both eyes are on the left side, with the lower eye forward.*

SPAIN AND FRANCE

by Lawson Wood

THE MEDITERRANEAN, WHERE THE FIRST sport diving took place, has received a bad press over the years. Population and industrial growth has resulted in vastly increased pollution levels. Much of the original coastline has been changed irrevocably by marinas, harbours and housing developments. Monaco has now lost some 75 per cent of its original coastline. The Mediterranean Sea is undoubtedly one of the world's most threatened seas, due to the increased demand on its natural resources and pollution from homes, industry and intensive agriculture. Fortunately, the influx of fresh seawater from the Atlantic has managed to slow the deterioration.

While small areas such as the waters around Venice and the northern Adriatic, sections of the Greek coast and parts of Tunisia are under increased threat due to the pressures of tourism, this is usually on a seasonal, temporary basis and the marine life does regenerate itself. However, there is now

TOP LEFT *L'Estartit, is the staging port for all sub aquatic activities to the Medas Islands. There are also several diving schools.*

TOP RIGHT *The Medas Islands became a marine preserve in 1983 and are renowned for the large number of friendly groupers, sea bream and colourful Gorgonian Sea Fans.*

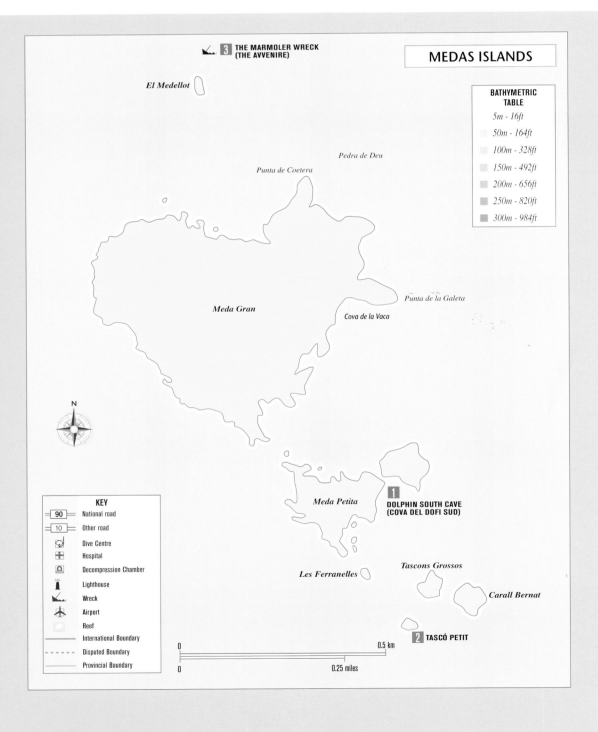

MEDAS ISLANDS

3 THE MARMOLER WRECK (THE AVVENIRE)

El Medellot

Pedra de Deu

Punta de Coetera

BATHYMETRIC TABLE

5m - 16ft
50m - 164ft
100m - 328ft
150m - 492ft
200m - 656ft
250m - 820ft
300m - 984ft

Meda Gran

Punta de la Galeta

Cova de la Vaca

N

Meda Petita

1 DOLPHIN SOUTH CAVE (COVA DEL DOFI SUD)

KEY

90	National road
10	Other road
	Dive Centre
	Hospital
	Decompression Chamber
	Lighthouse
	Wreck
	Airport
	Reef
	International Boundary
	Disputed Boundary
	Provincial Boundary

Les Ferranelles

Tascons Grossos

Carall Bernat

2 TASCÓ PETIT

0   0.5 km

0   0.25 miles

a new threat: the introduction of alien species of algae to this enclosed sea as well as commercial fishing.

There are protected areas around the shores of the Mediterranean, but enforcement is difficult, particularly when it involves huge factory ships. Most countries now accept that a successful tourist industry relies on strict conservation policies. For this industry to succeed and prosper, tourists also have to be made aware of the impact they have on small areas. Membership of conservation agencies is an important step towards understanding and protection of marine habitats.

The **South of France** is still very popular with divers, despite the effects of the 'killer algae' *Caulerpa taxifolia*, which has overrun many coastal reefs. There are a number of marine parks along the southern French coast, starting with the nature reserve of Cerbère-Banyuls just north of the Spanish Border. Similar to the geology of Estartit, with many sea caves, the reserve is supported by the Arago Oceanographical Laboratory located at Banyuls-sur-mer to the north. The reserve is noted for its dead men's fingers and precious Red Corals. Near Toulon, the island of Porquerolles is administered by the French National Trust and has many interesting wrecks nearby. The Côte D'Azur has excellent diving around the offshore islands near Cannes, Cape Juan and Cape Antibes with some superb walls and interesting topography.

Much of the **southern Spanish coast** is similar in topography and species diversity to Gibraltar. As you travel northeast towards the French coast there are a number of protected areas, with good diving and excellent marine life to be found at Al Muñequa and Fuengirola. The most famous of the protected areas is the Medas Islands off the coast near the resort of Estartit. These small rocky islands have been protected since the early 1980s and have huge concentrations of fish, including grouper, sea bass, bream, sardines and mullet.

MEDAS ISLANDS

Travelling south from the border of France into the Costa Brava region of Spain, the coastline rises perceptibly with huge limestone massifs eroded over aeons into a picturesque coastline dotted with islands, subterranean seamounts and carved with thousands of caves, many only accessible from underwater.

The largest group of islands is the Medas group, only a kilometre (⅔ mile) east of the deep-water marina of Estartit. The Medas Island group was declared a national marine park in 1983. The islands are known for the profusion of marine life due to the upwelling of a cold water stream from the central Mediterranean combining with organic material from the River Ter and the wide river deltas along the south coast of France. It was important to protect the islands from large-scale commercial fishing and drastic steps were taken in the early 1980s. After initial opposition, fishermen are now happy with

ABOVE *Red Dead Men's Fingers soft corals (Alcyonium spp.) can be found covering large areas of the lower rocky cliffs, in shaded areas which are swept daily by the nutrient-rich waters of the northern Mediterranean.*

ABOVE *Active predators at night, common octopus (Octopus vulgaris) are a common find along all the rocky shorelines. Their lairs are easy to find by the shells (remains of their dinners) scattered around the entrance.*

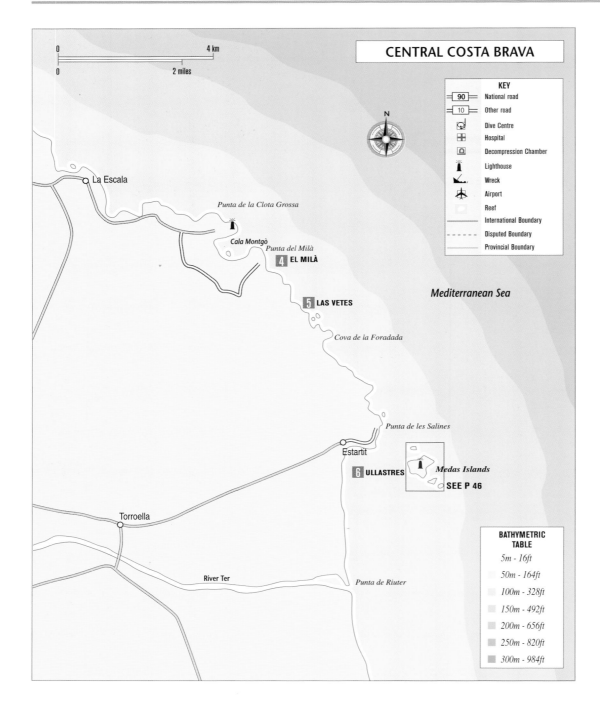

CENTRAL COSTA BRAVA

KEY

90	National road
10	Other road
	Dive Centre
	Hospital
	Decompression Chamber
	Lighthouse
	Wreck
	Airport
	Reef
	International Boundary
	Disputed Boundary
	Provincial Boundary

La Escala

Punta de la Clota Grossa

Cala Montgò
Punta del Milà
4 EL MILÀ

5 LAS VETES

Mediterranean Sea

Cova de la Foradada

Punta de les Salines

Estartit

6 ULLASTRES *Medas Islands*
SEE P 46

Torroella

River Ter *Punta de Riuter*

BATHYMETRIC TABLE

5m - 16ft
50m - 164ft
100m - 328ft
150m - 492ft
200m - 656ft
250m - 820ft
300m - 984ft

their yields on the perimeter of the marine park and the upsurge in tourism boat traffic.

The islands are known for the huge numbers of fish at all depths, with anchovies and sprats feeding on the surface, Bogue and chromis in the mid-water column hunted by sea bass, jacks, Dentex and, at the top of this small food chain, large grouper and barracuda. The Medas group has average depths of 10–25m (33–80ft) with many vertical and underhanging walls covered in brilliant yellow cup corals, colourful sea fans, Golden Zoanthids, anthias (*Anthias anthias*) and nudibranchs by the score. However, most divers come back year after year for the cave systems, many of which cut all the way through the islands with small chambers and air vents.

1 DOLPHIN SOUTH CAVE

The largest cave system under Meda Petita, known as Cova del Dofi Sud (Dolphin South Cave) is very complex and there is a small, stylized statue of a dolphin at the main entrance. From there a series of shafts and tunnels traverse the island. Spiny lobster, precious Red Coral, golden cup corals, colourful sponges and sea squirts adorn the walls everywhere. A delightful surprise is the number of friendly groupers, weighing 45kg (100lb) and more, which come directly up to you.

2 TASCÓ PETIT

One of the smaller rocky islets is Tascó Petit, located to the west of Carall Bernat in the southern group. Here huge limestone boulders have created narrow canyons covered in brilliant purple and yellow Gorgonian Sea Fans. Scores of bream and wrasse in at least half a dozen varieties vie for feeding space around the ledges and the macro aspects of the marine life here are perfect for underwater photographers.

LEFT *Armed with a mouth full of razor sharp teeth, the lizardfish (Synodus saurus) await their prey either partly hidden in the sand or perched on algae-covered boulders.*

3 THE MARMOLER

To the north of the Medas Islands, lying in 42m (138ft), is the wreck of the *Avvenire*. Known locally as the Marmoler (due to the cargo of marble it was carrying), she sank in 1971 after hitting the coastline. Tide and current carried her to her present position, sitting upright on a sandy plain. Visibility is generally poor and the thermoclines inhibit most divers, with the temperature dropping by as much as 7°C (45°F). The wreck is quite intact and an oasis for fish life, but can be dangerous due to all the netting that drapes the decks.

COSTA BRAVA

4 EL MILÀ AND 5 LAS VETES

Further along this northern stretch of coastline are two superb cave and cavern systems. These are El Milà and the massive Las Vetes. Again, these caves are quite complex and should only be dived with an experienced local guide. Las Vetes is particularly convoluted, with many side passages and narrow dead ends. El Milà is easier with its two long caverns. Ancient stalagmites can be seen underwater and still-forming stalactites are evident in the numerous air chambers. During the summer months the air in one chamber is filled with the sight and smell of thousands of bats. The walls play host to a huge variety of sponges and other colourful invertebrates including the now-rare precious Red Coral.

6 ULLASTRES

To the south of Estartit, and about 45 minutes travel time by dive boat, is a series of offshore seamounts called Ullastres, which rise from 65m (213ft) to around 5m (16ft). The water is always much clearer to the south, well away from any river estuaries. These seamounts are covered in colourful Gorgonian Sea Fans and surrounded by schools of various types of fish, each in their allocated feeding zones. It is amazing to watch the interaction of fish species and the ever-present predators such as Almaco Jacks, Dentex and barracuda.

While the Mediterranean is inevitably exposed to the problems of an enclosed sea,

the far-sightedness of the Catalan Government in protecting their islands and coastline has paid off handsomely with a sustainable ecosystem for good catches of fish and, of course, the pleasure of visiting divers. Estartit and the Medas Islands should be on everyone's diving list.

TOP *The distinctively coloured Spotted Doris (Discodoris atromaculata) can be found feeding on sponges at the entrance to deeper caves and in shaded areas.*

ABOVE *Triplefin Blennies (Tripterygion spp.) only grow to 5cm (2 in) long and can be found at shallow reefs.*

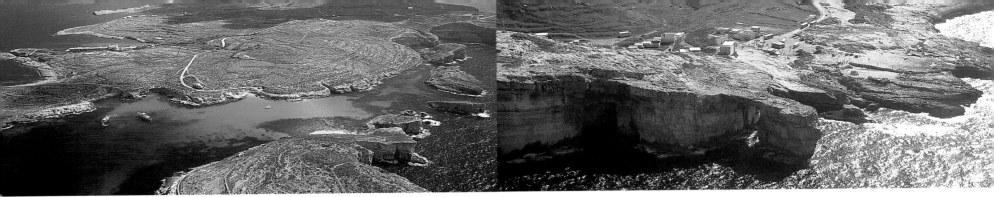

MALTESE ARCHIPELAGO

by Lawson Wood

THE MALTESE ARCHIPELAGO LIES IN THE central, southern Mediterranean Sea 96km (60 miles) south of Sicily and 467km (290 miles) from the African coast. The Republic of Malta consists of three main islands, Malta, Gozo and Comino, and they are steeped in history. Their language, a curious mixture of Arabic and Latin known as Malti, derives from the various conquests of the islands by the Phoenicians, Carthaginians, Greeks, Romans, Arabs, Normans, Spanish, French and the Knights of St John.

The islands were the most popular overseas diving destination before the Red Sea opened to mass tourism, and remain favourites of German, Dutch and Italian as well as British divers, with some 40,000 visiting each year. There is no limit to the number or type of dives to be undertaken around the islands. A vast number of submarine caves and caverns are to be found here too.

There is little conservation legislation on the islands, other than those rules imposed by

TOP LEFT *The Blue Lagoon at Comino is sheltered, with numerous caves. It is often the first point of entry for many people snorkelling in the Maltese Islands.*
TOP RIGHT *Dwejra Point on Gozo is a shore diving location. The six dive sites offer spectacular underwater topography and marine life.*

the diving industry partners. However, a new conservation policy is gaining strength, spearheaded by local groups and dive centres. One of the first areas to be protected will be Cirkewwa on Malta, and a number of the new wrecks will also be subjected to fishing restrictions. Malta's climate has to be the best in Europe. In summer the sun blazes in cloudless blue skies, and because these islands are further south than parts of the North African coast, temperatures are high.

MALTA

Malta is the largest of the three islands at 246 sq km (95 sq miles), and is characterized by steep cliffs in the south, deeply indented northern shores and the sheltered areas around the Grand Harbour of Valletta. Cirkewwa, also known as Marfa Point, is next to the ferry terminal for Gozo and is a magnet for dive training and for more experienced divers who want to dive the wreck of the *Rozi*.

The islands were awarded the George Cross for their diligence in the face of the enemy during World War II. Valletta Harbour has six divable wreck sites, including *HMS Maori* and the Carolita barge. Other accessible wrecks are the **Tent Peg Wreck** [12], mv *Odile*, **HMS Jersey** [9], the **Blenheim bomber** [7] and the latest addition, the tanker **Um El Faroud** [6] and cargo ship **Imperial Eagle** [13].

[1] THE TUGBOAT *ROZI*

The *Rozi* was sunk deliberately in 1992 for divers and sits upright on sand at 36m (120ft). It is home to thousands of chromis, bream and sand smelt. Nearby, the Posidonia seagrass beds contain cuttlefish and pipefish.

[2] MARFA CENTRAL (THE TRAINING POOL)

With access from the car park down a concrete ramp to the water's edge and 1m (3ft) of water, this is perfect for trainees, with a rocky seabed of varying depths and a small shelf and mini-wall that eventually drops to 18m (59ft). An excellent night dive, the site is highly regarded for its octopuses, moray eels, shrimps, crabs and golden cup corals.

[3] ANCHOR BAY

This lies down the steeply cut road to the small pier opposite Popeye Village. The diving is best out of the bay and around the corner to the left. A massive boulder next to the wall marks the entrance of the cave and has a base of rounded stones. You will find lots of brittle stars and cave shrimps here.

[4] MTAHLEB

This is an unspoiled dive site due to the conditions on the shore before you get to the water. Its all right clambering down 300m (984ft) of rugged headland, but it is another

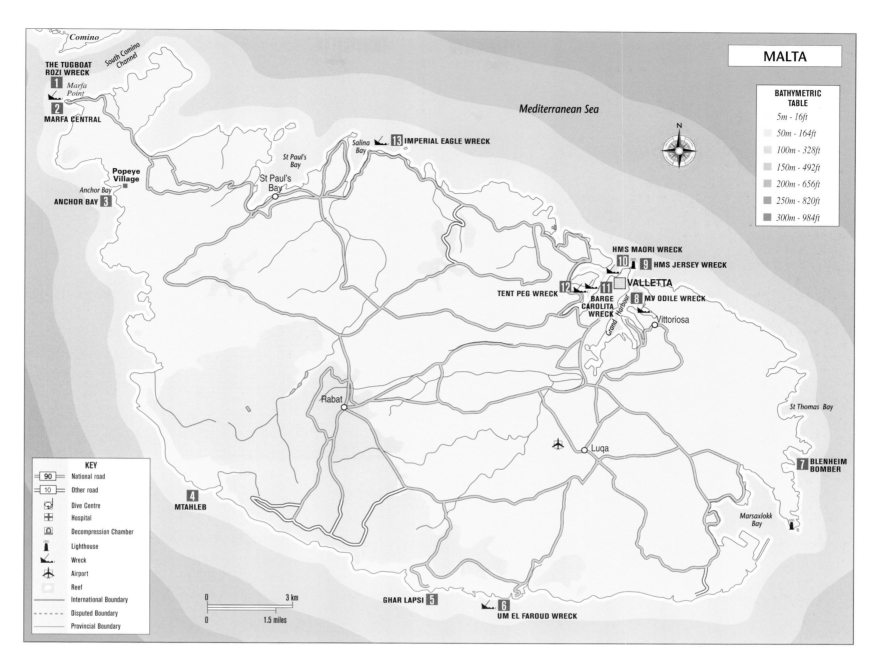

MALTA

BATHYMETRIC TABLE

5m - 16ft
50m - 164ft
100m - 328ft
150m - 492ft
200m - 656ft
250m - 820ft
300m - 984ft

Comino
South Comino Channel
THE TUGBOAT ROZI WRECK 1 Marfa Point
2
MARFA CENTRAL
Mediterranean Sea
13 **IMPERIAL EAGLE WRECK** Salina Bay
St Paul's Bay
Popeye Village
St Paul's Bay
Anchor Bay
ANCHOR BAY 3
HMS MAORI WRECK
10 9 **HMS JERSEY WRECK**
TENT PEG WRECK 12 11 **VALLETTA**
BARGE CAROLITA WRECK 8 **MV ODILE WRECK**
Grand Harbour
Vittoriosa
Rabat
St Thomas Bay
Luqa
7 **BLENHEIM BOMBER**
4 **MTAHLEB**
Marsaxlokk Bay
GHAR LAPSI 5
6
UM EL FAROUD WRECK

KEY
90 National road
10 Other road
Dive Centre
Hospital
Decompression Chamber
Lighthouse
Wreck
Airport
Reef
International Boundary
Disputed Boundary
Provincial Boundary

0   3 km
0   1.5 miles

matter climbing back up after a deep dive! The vertical walls, ledges, caves and caverns are home to large numbers of wrasse, parrotfish, chromis (*Chromis chromis*) and grouper.

5 GHAR LAPSI

This is a safe, shallow cave that runs through the headland. It starts in about 3m (10ft) and comes out on a convoluted wall at 6m (20ft), with a large pile of algae-covered boulders at the entrance. It is near the

RIGHT *The wreck of the Rozi off Cirkewwa Point sits intact and upright on sand in 36m (120ft). She is always surrounded by large schools of Bogue, chromis, picarel and sand smelt.*

recently sunk **Um El Faroud** 6, a tanker that sits in 36m (120ft). This huge ship is a ten-minute swim offshore, but can be reached from the shore entry point for the Blue Grotto, or as a boat dive.

8 *MV ODILE*

First thought to be the wreck of *HMS Abingdon*, this is in fact an Italian steam freighter, bombed during the war and salvaged in the 1970s. Fairly well broken up, she faces northwest and lies on her port side, covering quite a large area. She is difficult to find without local knowledge because of poor underwater visibility. Penetration is possible for experienced divers with suitable equipment.

10 *HMS MAORI*

This ship was launched in 1937 and saw considerable action in the Mediterranean, being ultimately responsible for the sinking of the *Bismarck*. During a massive aerial bombardment in February 1942, she sank quickly from a direct hit. The bows and the entire stern are gone. Part of the bridge is accessible above the muddy seabed of the harbour, but divers should beware the numerous live shells sticking out of the wreckage and mud.

11 BARGE *CAROLITA* (CORAL)

Struck by torpedo in April 1942, the *Carolita* sank immediately and now rests against the shore opposite the old naval hospital. Her bow is in 6m (20ft) and her stern at 22m (72ft). Access into this flat barge is fairly restricted, but you can examine the engine room from the damaged stern.

TOP LEFT *Cardinal fish (*Apogon imberbis*) are found in groups under overhangs and cave entrances during the day.*
CENTRE LEFT *Small caves, tunnels and caverns are common all over the archipelago, covered in algae, corals and sponges.*
LEFT *Though common around the islands, the camouflage techniques of the sea horse (*Hippocampus ramulosus*) makes it hard to find.*

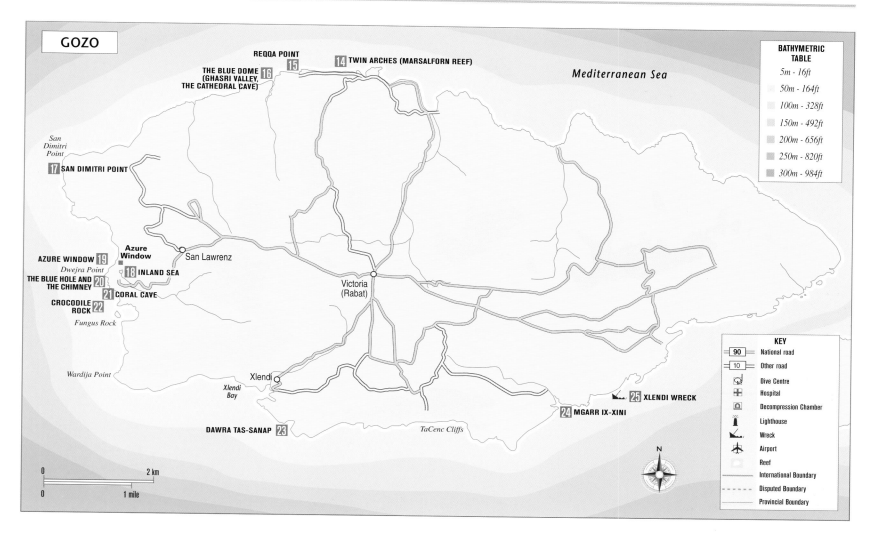

GOZO

Much of the best diving in the Maltese islands is done off Gozo, and day-trip cars and dive-centre vehicles cross regularly on the ferry from Malta. At just over a quarter the size of Malta, it has 43km (27 miles) of coastline and is so popular because much of the diving is done from shore. Like Malta, the northern coast is gently sloping, but here it drops vertically, in many places to more than 60m (200ft). To the south of the island, huge vertical cliffs, make boat diving more appropriate.

To the west, at Dwejra Point, is an area considered to be one of the natural wonders of the Mediterranean. Several fantastic sites can be found within a small area, all accessible from the large car park. Dominated by the spectacular natural arch called the Azure Window, its caves and caverns are among the most scenic dives I have encountered. To the southwest and south the landmass rears up vertically, with only a few entry points except at Xlendi Bay. From St Andrew's Divers

Cove, much of this coastline is covered by dive boats, which give the only access to the caves below these awesome ramparts, particularly towards the incredible Ta' Cenc Cliffs. In winter, periodic rains can reduce the visibility in the natural inlet at Xlendi Bay, but the boat dives are still superb. The former ferry boat *Xlendi* 25 is an accessible wreck on the southeast of Gozo.

14 TWIN ARCHES (MARSALFORN REEF)

There is prolific fish life around this underwater rocky spur, which has two large archways cut into the cliff. The first, smaller one starts at 20m (65ft), and directly underneath is a larger one that stretches to the seabed at 45m (150ft). This is best done as a boat dive to avoid a lengthy swim out.

15 REQQA POINT

This headland is very exposed and the entry can be rather difficult over sharp, fossilized rock. A vertical wall drops away to the east (or

right) and you can find a shaft that drops through the reef from 6m (20ft) to 16m (52ft). This site is also popular with fishermen.

16 THE BLUE DOME (GHASRI VALLEY, THE CATHEDRAL CAVE)

The Blue Dome at the mouth of Ghasri Valley is best done as a boat dive. The cave is along the right-hand wall, with entry in only 5m (16ft). Inside, the huge roof reflects the outside light, creating the blue-dome effect. Perfect for photography, the cave walls and rocky floor are filled with marine life, including pen shells and sea horses.

17 SAN DIMITRI POINT

This site on Gozo's most westerly point has a shallow reef that juts out from the headland, where the dive boat can anchor in 6m (20ft). It is done as a deep dive, and includes the thrill of diving with a large school of barracuda. The reef has vertical walls and some interesting potholes carved out by tidal forces.

18 INLAND SEA

The Inland Sea at Dwejra Point is a sheltered lagoon, offering easy access from a small jetty. Pleasure boats use this route to the open sea, so watch out. Passing through a massive fissure in the rock, divers enter a canyon that runs through to open water. First descend to 6m (20ft) and gradually to 25m (80ft) below the cliffs at the seaward side, where the drop continues to more than 60m (200ft). The vertical and underhanging walls are covered with marine life, and the view out to sea is breathtaking.

19 AZURE WINDOW

The site gets its name from the underwater view as you look up towards the natural arch above the surface. It reflects the azure-blue colour as if you were looking through a massive window. The seabed under the arch is covered in large boulders 18m (60ft) below, all covered in an algal fuzz that is home to large numbers of wrasse, bream and Spiny Sea Stars. Entry is from The Blue Hole nearby.

20 THE BLUE HOLE AND THE CHIMNEY

Not a true blue hole (as found in the Bahamas), this one is carved from fossilized rock over generations of winter storms. The outer wall has created a sheltered entry site for divers, who drop down and exit under a huge archway. There is a cave at the bottom left-hand corner near the archway which is home to some interesting tubeworms and anthias. The wall leading to the western headland is vertical and sea horses are found here. Further towards the corner, a thin fissure leads up to a colourful, narrow chimney.

21 CORAL CAVE

Entry is by taking a giant stride off the fossilized rocky shoreline, directly over this semicircular cavern, which has a sandy bottom 30m (100ft) below. Breathtaking in scale, the walls are covered in delicate hydroids and bryozoans that resemble true corals. Framed by fish, the vertical wall to the right (or north) eventually leads you around to the top side of the Chimney, then on to the Blue Hole, where the best exit is.

22 CROCODILE ROCK

A shallow platform of ancient seabed separates Crocodile Rock from Dwejra Point, and this is where a dive boat can anchor safely in 7m (23ft). Reminiscent of Shark Reef in the Red Sea, it is a natural amphitheatre with near-vertical sides. It drops away below you and the dive is conducted around the outer wall, where large shoals of Salema or Saupe are always encountered. This site is also known for its grouper, but then you must dive fairly deep to see them.

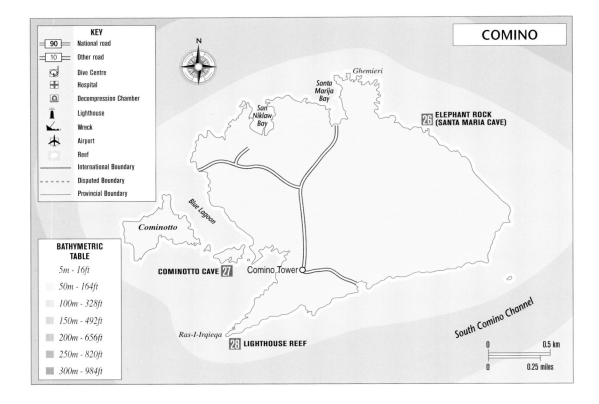

LEFT *Streaked Gurnard* (Trigloporus lastoviza) *occur on most sandy areas, often coming close to shore in search of food.*

23 DAWRA TAS-SANAP

Just around the corner from Xlendi Bay, and only done as a boat dive, this site features a huge natural arch with encrusted boulders at its base. On the southern wall there is a large cavern in 18m (60ft). Follow the vertical wall on your left to a sheltered bay where nudibranchs and spiny lobsters are to be found.

24 MGARR IX-XINI

This is another safe and easy shore dive, with access directly from the shore in front of the car park. The sandy seabed is popular with photographers seeking Flying Gurnards, flounders and cuttlefish. The wall on the right leads to the entry point at Ta' Cenc, and there are a number of caves on the way.

COMINO

Once a pirate's haven, Comino is dominated by a square tower built in 1618 to protect the Comino channel from raiders. The smallest inhabited island in the archipelago at 3 sq km (1 sq mile), it lies midway between Malta and Gozo. The Blue Lagoon here gets hundreds of snorkelling and diving visitors whenever sea conditions allow the crossing.

26 ELEPHANT ROCK
(SANTA MARIA CAVE)

This is a large cave and cavern system that runs more than 30m (100ft) through the headland to connect with another cave. At this junction a shaft opens to the sky, increasing the pleasure of the dive. The site is popular with fish-feeders and the fish are friendly.

27 COMINOTTO CAVE

Often blown out due to the surge, which has created an interesting cavern with a chimney

TOP RIGHT *Known as the Sea Rose, the colourful algae* Peyssonnelia squamaria *prefers low light and is found at cave entrances.*

RIGHT *It is only in the female stage that the Mediterranean Parrotfish* (Sparisoma cretense) *displays such colourful markings.*

at the far end, this cave has walls pockmarked by small sea urchins, snails and corals. There is a lot of sea grass at the entrance, and cuttlefish are common.

28 LIGHTHOUSE REEF

To the southwest of the island, a small navigational light marks one of its best dive sites. A chimney drops through the reef from 6m (20ft) to 18m (60ft) and big boulders have created numerous swim-throughs. The dive boat anchors on the old limestone shelf next to the chimney entrance. The sides are rather rough, because of the ancient skeletons of tubeworms and corals, so care should be taken. On exiting the cave at the bottom of the reef, groupers and numerous wrasse can be seen among the boulders. Large sea stars are everywhere and sea horses have also been found here.

THE RED SEA

Introduction by Jack Jackson

KEY TO MAPS

1. Israel p60
2. Jordan p63
3. Gulf of Aqaba (Eilat) p65
4. Northern Egypt p66
5. Port Safâga to El Quseir p68
6. Southern Egypt p70
7. North Sudan p73
8. South Sudan p75
9. Suākin Reefs Detail p77

30°N

30°E

THE RED SEA IS A LONG, NARROW STRIP OF water which extends from the Gulf of Suez in the north-northwest to Bāb-el-Mandeb (the gate of tears) in the south-southeast. At its southern end it joins the main Indian Ocean via the Gulf of Aden. Covering an area of 438,000 sq km (169,000 sq miles) it is the northern end of the rift valley and is still evolving as the African and Arabian tectonic plates move apart at a rate of just over one centimetre (half an inch) per year.

The seafloor of the Red Sea has two principal features: a broad, smooth continental shelf and a deep axial trough, which is further split by an even deeper trough some 25km (15 miles) wide.

Volcanic activity where the seafloor is spreading, isolated topographic depressions filled with geothermal brines in the central and northern Red Sea and evaporation due to high temperatures and low rainfall have produced some of the hottest and most saline seawater in the world. This has led to prolific coral growth much further north than would normally occur, a rich ecosystem that has over several hundred species of coral and almost as many fish and invertebrates as Australia's Great Barrier Reef.

Only 350km (217 miles) east-west at its widest point and less than 160km (100 miles) wide in places, there are almost no tides. Currents are mainly the result of density gradients in the water column. The maximum tidal range in the north reaches 0.9m (3ft) on spring tides, but in the central Red Sea there is hardly any tidal movement at all. For much of the year the prevailing winds are from the northwest and in the central Red Sea wind-driven seasonal changes and evaporation in summer have the most effect on the water level.

It is one of the deepest seas in the world with depths reaching 3040m (9974ft). Between Port Sudan and Jeddah brine pools have been measured with a salinity of over 250 parts per thousand and a temperature of 60°C (140°F). This suggests that the brine is hotter than 100°C (212°F) when extruded.

The land next to the Red Sea is generally mountainous with a low, sandy plain, the Tihama, to the shore. The Sinai Peninsula separates the Gulf of Aqaba and the Gulf of Suez, which is connected to the Mediterranean Sea by the Suez Canal. The Strait of Tiran is the approach to the Gulf of Aqaba and the Strait of Gubal is the approach to the Gulf of Suez. Both experience heavy shipping traffic in tricky waters. As a result shipwrecks are common. The Gulf of Aqaba averages 1700m (5500ft) deep with drop-offs that descend to the seabed. The Gulf of Suez, with an average depth of 60m (200ft), has many islands in the Strait of Gubal, which also has active oilfields.

ABOVE Dendronephthya *Soft Tree Corals swell up to their full glory in strong currents, extending fully to maximize their chances of capturing plankton in the passing current.*

23°30'N   Tropic of Cancer

15°N

0   400 km

0   200 miles

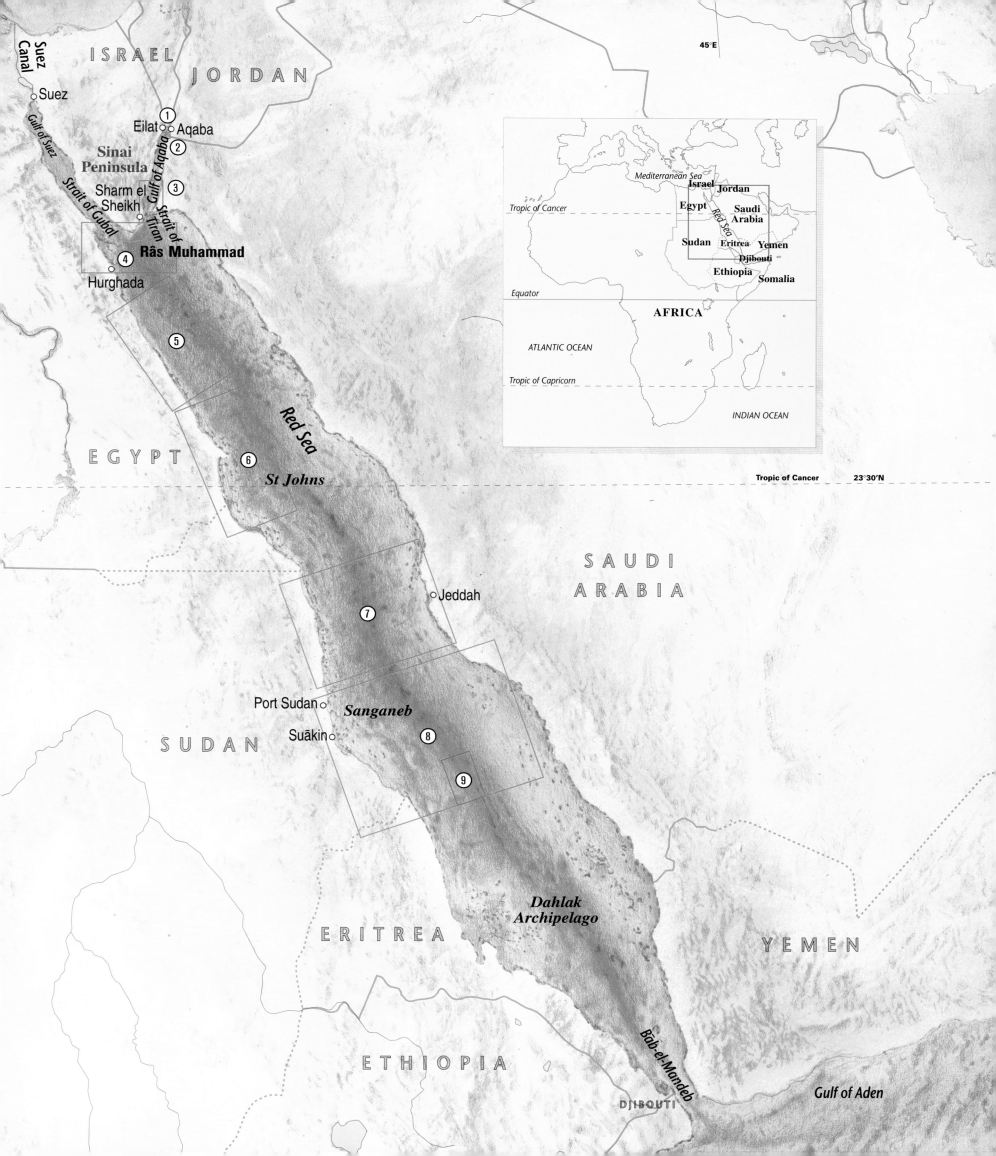

ISRAEL

JORDAN

Suez Canal

Suez

Gulf of Suez

① Eilat ○ Aqaba ○

Sinai Peninsula

② Gulf of Aqaba

Sharm el Sheikh

③ Strait of Tiran

Strait of Gubal

④ **Râs Muhammad**

Hurghada ○

⑤

EGYPT

Red Sea

⑥ *St Johns*

Tropic of Cancer   23°30'N

SAUDI

ARABIA

○ Jeddah

⑦

Port Sudan ○

Suākin ○ *Sanganeb*

⑧

SUDAN

⑨

Dahlak Archipelago

ERITREA

YEMEN

Bâb-el-Mandeb

ETHIOPIA

DJIBOUTI

Gulf of Aden

45°E

Mediterranean Sea

Israel Jordan

Egypt   Saudi Arabia

Tropic of Cancer

Sudan   Eritrea   Yemen

Djibouti

Ethiopia   Somalia

Red Sea

AFRICA

ATLANTIC OCEAN

Equator

Tropic of Capricorn

INDIAN OCEAN

CENTRAL RED SEA

From Hurghada to Port Sudan on the west, and Jeddah on the eastern side, the general topography is of shallow, shelving fringing reefs, inshore islands with sheltered diving, and offshore reefs that descend into the depths. Boats plying these passages often come to grief. Further offshore, islands and reefs rise from deep water to the surface as walls or drop-offs.

The diving is well documented except for that in Saudi Arabia, which until recently was open only to Saudi Arabian nationals, scientists and foreigners with work permits. Tourist divers can now obtain packages to Saudi Arabia through sponsorship by local dive operators. The diving is good, though several areas along the coast have suffered sedimentation and blasting from construction and spear-fishing by guest workers from the Far East. Parts of Saudi Arabia are well protected and home to the largest number of Dugongs left in the Red Sea.

While Egyptian diving gets better as you go south, Sudanese waters north of Port Sudan have the best diving and largest species diversity of the Red Sea. Isolated coral atolls and pinnacles rise steeply to the surface from deep water, giving great wall diving among healthy corals, good visibility and large fish, including shoals of Bumphead Parrotfish.

SOUTHERN RED SEA

The Red Sea's topography changes south of Port Sudan. The water becomes progressively shallower and often has a boulder-strewn sandy bottom with coral outcrops, where there is no drop-off or wall diving. Reduced visibility makes the fish harder to see and the corals are less prolific due to sedimentation. The seabed is actually rising, making the water even shallower and warmer. As well as the usual fish and invertebrate species common in the Red Sea there are beds of sea grass where one can still find Dugongs.

Eritrea has a longer Red Sea coastline than Sudan and more than 350 islands. Over 200 of these are in the Dahlak Archipelago, though only four are inhabited. This archipelago was a marine park during Ethiopian rule and it is still strictly controlled. Some islets still contain antipersonnel mines, so it is inadvisable to venture ashore without a guide.

In Yemen, Djibouti and the straits of Bāb-el-Mandeb, where the Indian Ocean sweeps into and out of the Red Sea, the visibility varies with plankton blooms, but the marine life is profuse and often shows subtle differences from that further north. The seabed becomes more volcanic, and the area around the Bāb-el-Mandeb is known for currents and big fish. Baleen Whales are sighted in March and April and Whale Sharks are found in June. A very large nudibranch, similar to a Spanish Dancer nudibranch, but with four gills rather than six, is found at the volcanic islands known as the Seven Brothers (Les Sept Frères), also known as Les Isles du Sebbah or Sawabi.

WEATHER

Weather throughout the Red Sea is mainly hot and sunny, though in winter it can be cold at sea. Temperatures vary along its length. Egypt, Israel and Jordan vary from below freezing in the desert in winter to 45°C (113°F) in summer. From southern Egypt southwards, winter temperatures only drop to 20°C (68°F) at sea and rise to a humid 47°C (117°F) at sea, or a dry 50°C (122°F) in the desert in summer. Mountainous areas can experience brief periods of torrential rain. To the north there is

WHY THE 'RED' SEA?

The name Red Sea was handed down through history and we are not sure how it originated. There are various theories: the red rock of the mountains that surround it; the deep red sunsets; extensive blooms of the algae *Trichodesmium erythraeum*, which turn the sea reddish-brown when they die; and the historical name the Hebrews gave to the people of the trade routes south of Israel, who lived among red rocks, the Edomites, derived from the Hebrew word for red.

When the Greeks began documenting the then-known world, the land of the Edomites became the land of the Erythraen people after *erythros*, the Greek word for red. Later, when the Egyptians expanded south, their southernmost colonization was called Erythraea, modern day Eritrea. The Romans carried on the tradition by using the name Mare Rubrum.

LEFT *Dust in the atmosphere produces deep red sunsets along the Red Sea. These Sudanese shellfishermen, sheltering in the lagoon at Sha'b Rumi, are preparing for evening prayer.*

little rain or coastal cultivation. Most of the rain drains into the desert, but in Sudan, Eritrea and Yemen, the normally dry riverbeds (wadies) can briefly turn into raging torrents.

Seasonal winds affect some regions' weather and have much to do with uncomfortably short seas. In the north, one such wind, the Khamsin, blows hot, dry air from the south or southwest (the Northern Sahara desert) between February and May and often brings sandstorms. The name, Khamsin, is derived from the Arabic word for fifty, because it can last up to 50 days. In August, the torrential rains in the Ethiopian highlands that fill the Blue Nile and cause the Nile in Egypt to flood, extend to southern Sudan and cause haboobs. The prevailing north winds become squalls of Force 8 or more from the southeast through west. Sandstorms, even well out to sea, reduce visibility to a few metres.

MARINE LIFE

Sometimes called God's Other World, the Red Sea is famous for its marine life. North of Port Sudan, luxurious growths of stony and soft corals abound with dark magenta species of *Dendronephthya* Soft Tree Corals. In the far north the reef fish are so used to divers that they almost pose for them. The sharks that made Râs Muhammad famous are still there, but there are so many divers nowadays that they remain deep during the day. Whale Sharks are often found in the Gulf of Aqaba.

All along the Red Sea, huge shoals of fish gather to spawn in the spring and shoals of different species of dolphin occur close to reefs where they can shelter in rough weather. As you go south, shoals of reef fish become more frequent and the offshore reefs teem with sharks. In Sudan, north of Port Sudan, pelagics become common – Manta Rays, Marlin, Sailfish, tuna, Doublespotted Queenfish or Leatherback (*Scomberoides lysan*), known locally as Shirwi, and huge shoals of migrating Pilot Whales. Massive groupers can still be found on offshore reefs. There are no sea snakes, but snake eels are found at Sanganeb and become more common as you go south.

South of Suākin you can see whales blowing on the surface in the distance. Closer to the Gulf of Aden there are more pelagics, including Spanish Mackerel. The stony corals are not too good, but soft corals flexing in the current shake off the sediment, and muck diving (*see p197*) is rewarding.

Despite being connected to the Indian Ocean, the Red Sea has only one species of clownfish, the Twobar Anemonefish. Species endemic to the Red Sea and nearby areas include the Yellowbar (Map) Angelfish, Arabian Angelfish and the Masked Butterflyfish, also known as the Lemon or Golden Butterflyfish.

ENVIRONMENT

What little industrial pollution occurs in the Red Sea comes from shipwrecks, a few oilfields in northern Egypt and ports that are widely strung out along its length. Construction at Sharm el Sheikh and Hurghada has been responsible for sedimentation, sewage and indiscriminate anchoring on coral reefs, but these problems are now being addressed. Due to the number of reefs, commercial fishing is not a large industry, although sharks are targeted at the southern end where sun-dried shark meat was a major food source for the poor long before shark fins became valuable exports for sharkfin soup. There have been a few incidents of armed piracy on the Yemen side of the Bāb-el-Mandeb and also off Yemen and Somalia in the Gulf of Aden.

DIVING THE RED SEA

Recreational Red Sea diving began as land-based diving in Israel, northern Egypt, Sudan and what was then Ethiopia. Temperatures on land made winter preferable. Some northern areas have become package holiday destinations for sunseeking vacationers during winter. However, winter water temperatures in the north can be cold enough to warrant diving in a dry-suit and it can be cold in the wind out to sea. In summer it is hot on land, and water temperatures are more pleasant. Made famous by Hans Hass and Jacques Cousteau, the Red Sea can now be enjoyed by all.

TOP *The Yellowbar Angelfish (*Pomacanthus maculosus*) is endemic to the Red Sea, Gulf of Aden, Gulf of Oman, Arabian Gulf and East Africa. Juveniles of this species have a completely different colour pattern.*

ABOVE Dendronephthya *Soft Tree Corals vary in colour from deep magenta, through red, orange and yellow to white.*

ISRAEL & JORDAN

by Jack Jackson

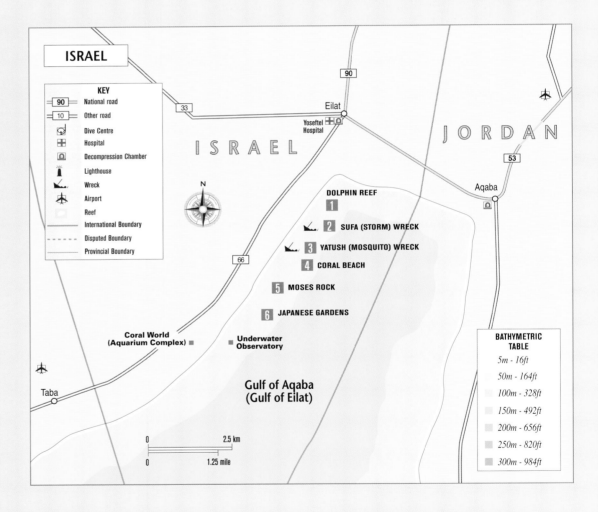

SITUATED ALONGSIDE EACH OTHER AT THE top of what the charts call the Gulf of Aqaba, but the Israelis call the Gulf of Eilat, the waters of Israel and Jordan are sheltered and almost invariably calm. Visibility is often spoilt near the ports. Most dive sites are accessible from shore, though diving from boats is necessary for one site in Israel and is becoming popular in Jordan. The two countries cooperate in running marine parks, and dive operators in Israel and Jordan run safaris that cover sites in both countries. The weather allows for diving all year round, though the water is colder than that off the southern Sinai. There can be heavy rain and even snow for a few days in winter.

The tiny region of Israel bordering the Gulf was one of the first areas to offer diving tourism in the Red Sea. It went on to become the diving classroom of the world, with many competing dive schools and a high standard of tuition. Each of its dive sites is different, ranging from shallow coral gardens to drift dives, wall dives, multilevel dives, wreck diving and night diving. There is almost no current and some areas have sea grasses. More importantly, the fish are very tame – a bonus for photographers. Dolphin Reef is undoubtedly the top diving and snorkelling attraction.

Reefs along Eilat's 7km (4-mile) coastline are among the most heavily dived in the world, with about 250,000 dives each year,

most of them by relatively inexperienced divers. Signs of wear and tear have begun to show, so strict laws have been passed that state how close divers may get to coral.

Between Israel and Saudi Arabia, Jordan has 27km (17 miles) of coastline but has not seen the pressure of diver numbers experienced by Israel. There is some damage to the marine

TOP LEFT *The main base for diving in Jordanian waters, Aqaba is near the ancient site of Petra, 'the rose-red city half as old as time' and the 'Lawrence of Arabia' scenery of Wadi Rum.*

TOP RIGHT *Eilat's aquarium complex has a jetty out to its famous underwater observatory in the Gulf of Aqaba (Eilat). The yellow submarine takes passengers on underwater excursions.*

ABOVE *Lone Bottlenose Dolphins* (Tursiops truncatus) *are the species of dolphins most likely to seek out interaction with divers, snorkellers and swimmers. However, lone males can become aggressive.*

environment around the port in the north, but south of this the reefs are in good condition. Among many good dive sites, two artificial reefs, the *Cedar Pride* and the Russian Tank, are popular.

There are not that many dive operators in Aqaba, but they cannot agree on the names of many dive sites. They use different names and some sites are divided into two, each with a different name.

ISRAEL
☐ DOLPHIN REEF

Dolphin Reef, which has an area of 10,000 sq m (107,000 sq ft) averaging 12m (40ft) deep, is fully enclosed with buoyed nets. It is situated 1km (0.6 miles) south of Eilat and is home to a group of Bottlenose Dolphins (*Tursiops truncatus*). The dolphins often jump the net to freedom, returning later with fresh propeller scars on their backs. The enclosure contains a wooden wreck and reef fish, including Cobia and large, habituated stingrays rescued from fishermen. Sea lions from an adjacent, smaller enclosure regularly jump the net to join in the fun.

A member of the staff must accompany all participants. Snorkellers enter the enclosure over the net, but divers enter through a sliding curtain facing the shore at the bottom. The dolphins sense the noise of this curtain being opened and immediately appear at high speed with lots of clicking and shrieking. Once they have done a quick inspection of the newcomers, and searched the accompanying staff for titbits of food, they go back to their boisterous play, occasionally preying on reef fish hiding in the sand. On the first dive of the day the sand has not yet been stirred up and the dolphins, having had no human contact overnight, tend to be more curious.

☐ SUFA (STORM)

The scuttled 46m (150ft) Israeli missile boat *Sufa* (Storm) lies 2km (1 mile) south of Dolphin Reef, 300m (330yd) north of Aqua-Sport dive centre. She lies upright in 30m (100ft), with the top of the mast at 15m (50ft). Dangerous areas have been sealed off. The bridge, missile launcher and engine are accessible and corals, particularly soft corals, are beginning to colonize the wreck.

☐ YATUSH (MOSQUITO)

Immediately in front of the Aqua-Sport dive centre, 400m (440yd) south of the *Sufa* wreck, is the small *Yatush* (Mosquito) gunboat wreck. She is lying at an angle at the bottom of a drop-off with the stern in 33m (110ft) of water and the bow in 25m (80ft). The boat's aluminium construction means that corals have been slower to settle and grow, but the fish life is good and includes fair-sized groupers.

☐ CORAL BEACH

Coral Beach, 200m (656ft) south of the *Yatush* wreck, slopes gently to 10m (33ft) before dropping more steeply to 40m (130ft). Entry is at the north edge of the nature reserve fence. The topography is coral patches on sand and the fish life is surprisingly good.

☐ MOSES ROCK

Just south of Coral Beach, also in the nature reserve, Moses Rock is one of the best-known sites at Eilat. A large coral head in 9m (30ft) of water near the drop-off, it is a microcosm of Eilat's prolific reef life and popular with photographers. Divers searching hard will find almost everything here, including different species of moray eels. The gentle slope down to the coral head is good snorkelling and there are many sponges and anemones further out.

☐ JAPANESE GARDENS

Near the Underwater Observatory, south of Coral Beach, the Japanese Gardens are considered to be one of Eilat's best dive sites and are now only accessible by dive boat. There is the usual gently sloping reef to 10–15m (33–50ft), then a steeper drop-off to beyond 40m (130ft), with pagoda-like *Acropora* table corals, soft corals and prolific fish life benefiting from nature reserve regulations. There is a limit on the number of divers allowed here at any one time and they should be careful of the yellow submarine that works from beside the observatory. Barracuda, jacks, stingrays and turtles are common. There are crocodile-fish and frogfish. Anthias, called goldfish in Israel, hover over stony corals.

JORDAN

⁷ THE POWER STATION

Just south of Aqaba, the Power Station has a gentle slope of sand and stony coral to 15m (50ft), then a drop to a narrow ledge at 40m (130ft), before dropping into the depths where pelagic fish abound. Shore divers enter the water at the northern end, but boat divers can moor closer to the southern end where, at 25m (80ft), anemones grow on the branches of black corals. Barracuda and Humphead (Napoleon) Wrasse cruise the drop-off, while in the shallows are anthias, angelfish, butterflyfish, parrotfish and moray eels.

⁸ FIRST BAY

Opposite the Club Murjan Dive Centre, at First Bay, the reef slopes gently to 15m (50ft) and then more steeply, but the 6–8m (20–25ft) range is best. A garden of *Acropora* and *Porites* corals almost reaches the surface and the fish life is good. South of the coral garden Cazar Reef has black corals and macro fish life including frogfish and pipefish.

⁹ ABDULLAH REEF AND ¹⁰ BLACK ROCK

South of First Bay and Cazar Reef, offshore of the government camp site, Prince (now King) Abdullah (Abdallah) Reef and Black Rock offer good diving. The camp site controls entry, so many dive operators ignore this area.

King Abdullah Reef slopes gently as sand with coral patches to beyond 30m (100ft), with moray eels, angelfish, butterflyfish, goatfish, triggerfish, anthias, Bluespotted Ribbontail Rays and Clown Coris (*Coris aygula*). At the southern edge of the government camp site, Black Rock is a similar slope with the added attraction of the chance to see turtles.

¹¹ CEDAR PRIDE

A little more than 2km (1 mile) south of the container port, 4km (2 miles) north of the Royal Diving Centre, the 74m (243ft) freighter *Cedar Pride* was cleaned up and purposely sunk for divers in November 1985. She now lies on her port side at 25m (80ft), across two raised sections of the seabed so that there is a swim-through between them under the wreck at 27m (89ft). There are lots of colourful soft corals draped around the wreck, prolific fish life including Humphead (Napoleon) Wrasse, large snappers and groupers and sea horses. Some penetration is not too difficult for experienced divers. The wreck is too large to fully appreciate in one dive and is an excellent night dive. South of the *Cedar Pride*, **Hussein Reef** ¹² has another gently sloping profile broken by coral heads with abundant fish life.

GORGONIAN SEA FANS

About 3km (2 miles) north of the Royal Diving Centre there are several dive sites close together. **Gorgonian I** ¹³ is named after the huge solitary Gorgonian Sea Fan at 16m (52ft). South of Gorgonian I, **Gorgonian II** ¹⁴ has two Gorgonian Sea Fans, one at 20m (65ft) and the other at 30m (100ft). To the west of Gorgonian II, Seven Sisters are seven coral pinnacles at 8–9m (25–30ft). To the south, **Oliver's Canyon** ¹⁵ is a canyon leading to a drop-off at 40m (130ft). The shallows have the shell of a **Russian Tank** ¹⁶ purposely sunk and prepared for divers. All these sites have excellent fish life including anthias, angelfish, parrotfish, moray eels, frogfish, crocodilefish, scorpionfish, Lyretail Groupers and stonefish, shoals of squid and many invertebrates including nudibranchs. Even turtles can be seen.

TOP *Mushroom Coral colonies, in the adult form, are not attached to any substrate so they are usually found below the depth of any strong wave action.*

CENTRE *Tasselled Scorpionfish (Scorpaenopsis oxycephalus) change their colour to be camouflaged against the substrate so that they can lie in wait for passing prey.*

BOTTOM *Manta Rays (Manta birostris) are a common sight throughout the Red Sea. On clear, sunny days they are often seen feeding on the surface when the plankton rises in the afternoon.*

There are several dive sites in Big Bay. **Blue Coral** 17, 2km (1 mile) north of the Royal Diving Centre, is named after a species of blue-tinged lacy coral found there. The reef slopes beyond 40m (130ft), but most of the interest is much shallower with good stony and soft corals. South of Blue Coral, **Moon Valley** 18 is a gentle undulating slope interspersed with valleys of sand, hence the name. The best corals are in the deeper water. Sometimes called **Long Swim** 19, the distance from Moon Valley to the Royal Diving Centre is 700m (770yd). Although patchy, the coral is generally in good condition and the fish life good. The reef drops below 30m (100ft), but most divers stay shallow because of the distance they have to cover. There are moray eels, parrotfish, many species of wrasse, pufferfish, lionfish, scorpionfish, stonefish and shoals of fusiliers.

20 THE AQUARIUM

The northern house reef at the Royal Diving Centre is called The Aquarium. The reef descends to 37m (120ft) with good marine life, including table corals draped with soft corals and great fish life. South of the jetty The (Coral) **Gardens** 21 have stronger currents than those usually found in Jordanian waters. The gently sloping reef of sand with coral heads descending to 25m (80ft) is populated with pipefish, sea horses and shoals of Red Sea Bannerfish and anthias, while black coral are found deeper down.

22 SAUDI BORDER

Approximately 300m (330yd) north of the Saudi Arabian border, 4km (2.5 miles) south of the Royal Diving Centre, the dive site called Saudi Border is one of the most popular in Jordan. The reef slopes to 12m (40ft) and then descends over a steep drop-off to more than 40m (130ft). The corals are spectacular. Divers can expect to see large Humphead (Napoleon) Wrasse and turtles, which are common. Whitetip Reef Sharks are seen occasionally and Manta Rays appear in the spring. The drop-off is nearly 850m (930yd) long.

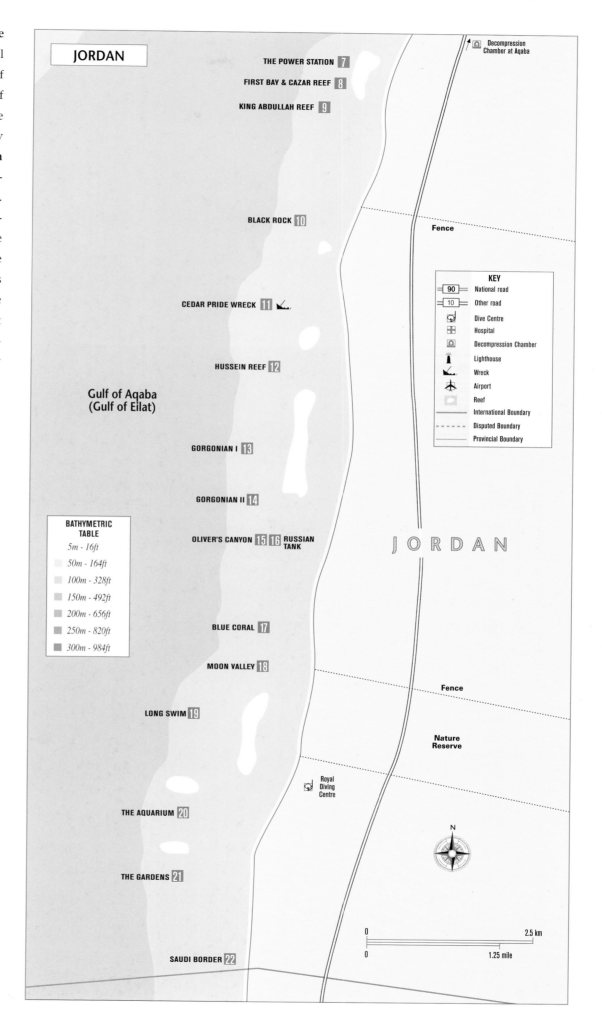

JORDAN

THE POWER STATION 7

FIRST BAY & CAZAR REEF 8

KING ABDULLAH REEF 9

BLACK ROCK 10

Fence

Decompression Chamber at Aqaba

CEDAR PRIDE WRECK 11

Gulf of Aqaba (Gulf of Eilat)

HUSSEIN REEF 12

GORGONIAN I 13

GORGONIAN II 14

OLIVER'S CANYON 15 16 RUSSIAN TANK

JORDAN

BLUE CORAL 17

MOON VALLEY 18

LONG SWIM 19

THE AQUARIUM 20

THE GARDENS 21

SAUDI BORDER 22

Royal Diving Centre

Fence

Nature Reserve

N

BATHYMETRIC TABLE

5m - 16ft
50m - 164ft
100m - 328ft
150m - 492ft
200m - 656ft
250m - 820ft
300m - 984ft

KEY

90	National road
10	Other road
	Dive Centre
	Hospital
	Decompression Chamber
	Lighthouse
	Wreck
	Airport
	Reef
	International Boundary
	Disputed Boundary
	Provincial Boundary

0 — 2.5 km
0 — 1.25 mile

NORTH EGYPT

by Jack Jackson

WITH GOVERNMENT HELP NORTHERN EGYPT has been developed extensively as a winter-sun destination for European holiday-makers with conveniently located airports and cheap charter flights. Initially, enterprising operators bought blocks of tickets for these flights and sold them on to divers. Nowadays divers have become a major source of revenue, and civil strife in nearby regions has forced prices down even further. As a result, northern Egypt has become the cheapest and busiest package diving destination in the world. However, while temperatures on land are more comfortable in winter, those diving on offshore reefs will find the temperatures more comfortable and the wind less of a problem in summer.

This region consists of the Gulf of Aqaba, which connects with the main Red Sea through the Strait of Tiran, and the coastlines, islands and reefs either side of the Strait of Gubal in the Gulf of Suez. It is part of the great geological fault known as the East African Rift Valley System. The movement of Africa away from Arabia began some 55 million years ago and the Gulf of Suez, which is 24–36km (15–35 miles) wide and shallow, opened up about 30 million years ago. However, the Gulf of Aqaba, which is 24km (15 miles) wide and 1676m (5500ft) deep, is only 3 to 4 million years old and is still parting at around 15mm (0.6in) per year.

The Gulf of Aqaba lies in a pronounced cleft between hills rising abruptly to about 600m (2000ft). Navigation is difficult at the narrow entrance of the Strait of Tiran where four reefs – Jackson, Woodhouse, Thomas and Gordon – rise out of the depths between the east coast of the Sinai Peninsula and Tīrān Island, causing strong currents. The area is also subject to sudden squalls.

Linked to the Mediterranean Sea since 1869 by the Suez Canal, the Gulf of Suez is one of the world's most important shipping routes. Shipwrecks have occurred along the southern approaches to the Suez Canal ever since it was constructed, but the majority of ship and aircraft wrecks date from World War II when ships at anchor, waiting to proceed north through the canal, were attacked by German aircraft based in the Mediterranean. Poor navigation, bad weather and insurance fraud have resulted in more shipwrecks since then.

Winds and currents in the Egyptian section of the Gulf of Aqaba can be strong and if the surface current is running in the opposite direction to that of the wind, the waves can be large. However, because of the depth, bad weather does not have much effect on visibility, which remains good. The landmass of the Sinai Peninsula shelters the dive sites on the coast of Southern Sinai and those north of the Strait of Gubal. The wind usually blows from the north and strong currents flow either way, but generally one side of the Sinai Peninsula will have diving conditions that are acceptable. Nevertheless, the Gulf of Suez is shallow and sandy, so inclement weather can reduce visibility drastically. The Strait of Gubal itself and the sites south and west of it are exposed to the full force of the prevailing winds.

Water temperatures in winter can be cold and, due to the wind-chill factor after a dive in a wet suit, some divers prefer dry suits. There are restrictions on sport diving in the Gulf of Suez due to numerous oilfields.

Along the northern part of the Egyptian Gulf of Aqaba, the diving is a slightly upmarket version of what it was like in the 1970s, with the advantage of avoiding the crowds further south. The sites from the Israeli border to Nuweiba and Dahab are treated as shore dives; some require access by four-wheel drive vehicle and in a few instances camels are used, though this is just for the experience and not

TOP LEFT *The arid, rocky coastline of Râs Muhammad is in stark contrast to the colourful world beneath the surface of the sea. Sharks are still found here, but are now accustomed to divers and stay deep.*
TOP RIGHT *Bluff Point on Sha'b 'Ali has a solar-powered navigation light. Live-aboard boats such as the S/Y Poolster can hang off from the point in the wind.*

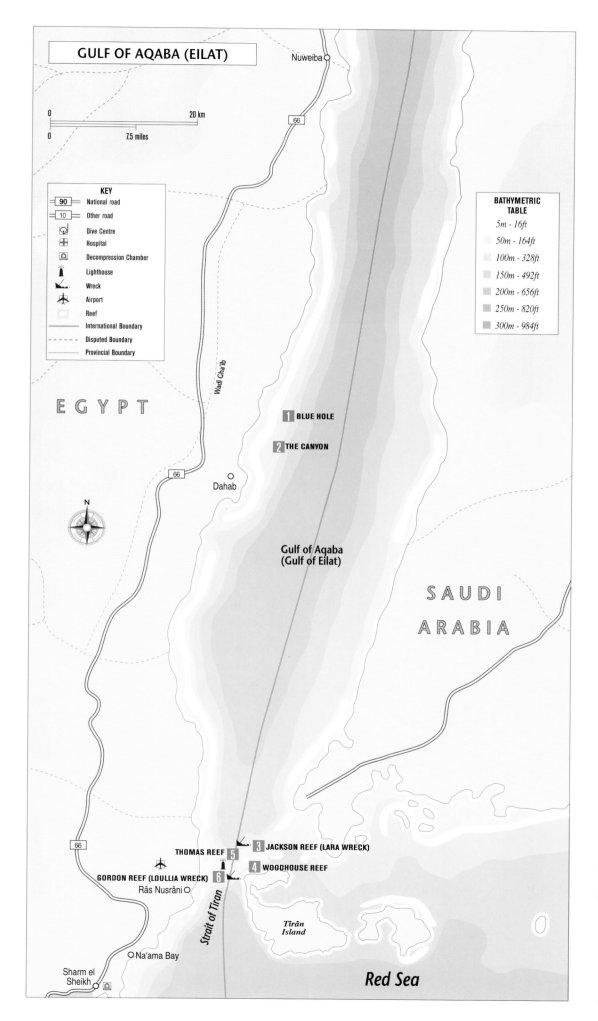

GULF OF AQABA (EILAT)

Nuweiba

KEY

90	National road
10	Other road
	Dive Centre
	Hospital
	Decompression Chamber
	Lighthouse
	Wreck
	Airport
	Reef
	International Boundary
	Disputed Boundary
	Provincial Boundary

BATHYMETRIC TABLE

5m - 16ft
50m - 164ft
100m - 328ft
150m - 492ft
200m - 656ft
250m - 820ft
300m - 984ft

E G Y P T

Wadi Gha'ib

N

1 BLUE HOLE

2 THE CANYON

Dahab

Gulf of Aqaba
(Gulf of Eilat)

S A U D I

A R A B I A

THOMAS REEF **5** **3** JACKSON REEF (LARA WRECK)

4 WOODHOUSE REEF

GORDON REEF (LOULLIA WRECK) **6**

Râs Nusrâni

Strait of Tiran

Tîrân
Island

Na'ama Bay

Sharm el
Sheikh

Red Sea

essential. Shore diving is partly necessary due to the difficulty in anchoring boats along an oft-sheer north-south coastline in the prevailing north winds. Underwater there is a mixture of sandy slopes, drop-offs and coral gardens with plenty of reef fish. There are few pelagic species along the shore, but species as large as Whale Sharks pass by offshore and have been seen as far north as Jordan.

Nuweiba has become a busy port with top quality hotels and resorts strung out along the coast. Further south Dahab still has its sleepy, hippy ambience that attracts independent travellers, but there are top quality hotels and dive packages for those who want them.

Near the southern tip of the Sinai Peninsula, the coast from Râs Nusrâni through Na'ama Bay (Merset et 'At) and the once sleepy little port of Sharm el Sheikh has seen massive development. Sand and cement blown into the water from building construction has smothered some of the nearby corals. Some of the easier dive sites are suffering as a result of their accessibility to novice divers.

ABOVE *Due to strong currents, the reefs in the Strait of Tiran are very healthy. Stony and soft corals attract reef and pelagic fish, including the Anthias (Fairy Basslets) seen here.*

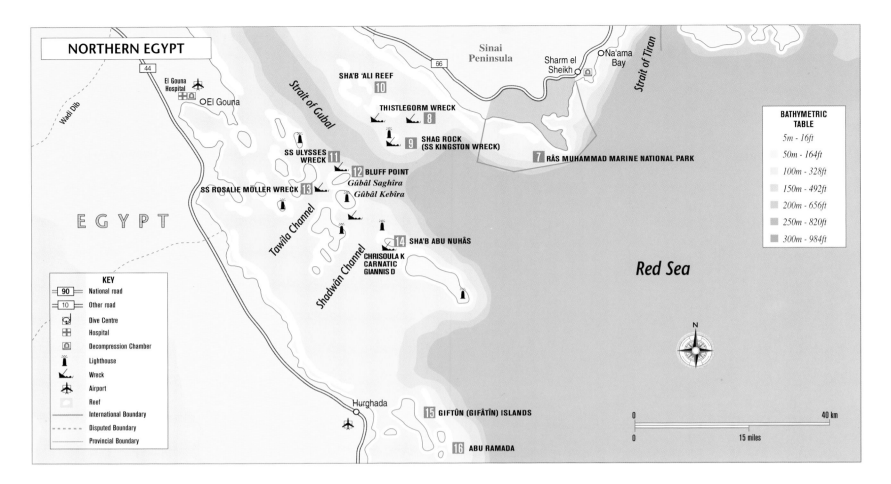

NORTHERN EGYPT

KEY

90	National road
10	Other road
	Dive Centre
	Hospital
	Decompression Chamber
	Lighthouse
	Wreck
	Airport
	Reef
	International Boundary
	Disputed Boundary
	Provincial Boundary

BATHYMETRIC TABLE

	5m - 16ft
	50m - 164ft
	100m - 328ft
	150m - 492ft
	200m - 656ft
	250m - 820ft
	300m - 984ft

However, in general the better dive sites accessed from here are very good. Shore diving used to be popular here, but nowadays fleets of day boats head out for nearby dive sites every morning, while live-aboard boats head further afield. Good at any time of year with lots of pelagic species in the spring and early summer, the diving on the reefs in the Strait of Tiran and Râs Muhammad Marine National Park is exceptional as large shoals of fish gather to spawn. The sharks that attracted divers in the 1970s are still there, but they have become accustomed to divers and are no longer curious about them. Whitetip Reef Sharks are common and if divers pick a site with strong currents and go deep in the early morning, larger sharks such as Grey Reef and Hammerhead Sharks are usually found. Along the inshore reefs west of Râs Muhammad there are regular sightings of Variegated (Leopard) Sharks.

In good weather, day boats and live-aboard boats from Na'ama Bay and Sharm el Sheikh sail as far northwest as Shag Rock and Sha'b 'Ali for excellent reefs and wrecks. Live-aboard

boats cross the Strait of Gubal to join those from El Gouna and Hurghada operating in the Tawîla and Shadwân channels and on the many wrecks at Sha'b Abu Nuhâs.

On the main Egyptian coast, Hurghada has seen the worst of resort development, with little or no town planning and too many winter-sun and dive resorts packed closely together. El Gouna 20km (12 miles) to the north has been developed more aesthetically. Most of the dive sites are more than 30 minutes offshore, but the area is heavily dived. In 1992 local operators formed the Hurghada Environmental Protection and Conservation Agency (HEPCA). With help in funding from USAID, the Egyptian Environmental Affairs Agency and the Red Sea Governorate, HEPCA has been fixing mooring buoys to all dive sites in order to reduce anchor damage.

As the dive sites south and west of the Strait of Gubal get the full force of the prevailing northerly winds on windy days, sailing in the smaller day boats can be rough. Local operators tend to look at the weather each morning before deciding which dive sites to visit.

NORTHERN SINAI – DAHAB

At Dahab the best-known site is **Blue Hole** [1], 8km (5 miles) to the north. The sloping reef outside has good stony corals and fish life, but the vertical shaft known as the Blue Hole is notorious for divers coming to grief by descending too deep. The best dive is **The Canyon** [2], just north of the town, with shoals of Sweepers milling around inside and outside a narrow cleft, which goes down from 20m (65ft) to 30m (100ft).

SOUTHERN SINAI

Dividing the Strait of Tiran northeast of Râs Nusrâni, the offshore reefs of Jackson, Woodhouse, Thomas and Gordon rise from deep water with strong currents, excellent diving and several wrecks to the west. **Jackson Reef** [3] has the high-and-dry wreck of the *Lara* and probably has the best diving of the four. With stunning walls and prolific marine life, it is treated as a drift dive. **Woodhouse** [4] has no shelter and can only be dived in good weather. **Thomas Reef** [5] is spectacular and **Gordon** [6] has the high-and-dry wreck of the

ABOVE *Twobar Anemonefish (Amphiprion bicinctus), also known as clownfish, and Threespot Dascyllus (Dascyllus trimaculatus), also known as Domino Damselfish, often share large anemones.*

ABOVE *The wreck of the barge at Bluff Point is regularly used for both day and night dives by divers on live-aboard boats. The area offers comfortable, sheltered anchorage.*

Loullia and a sheltered plateau from 10m (33ft) to 24m (79ft) at the southern end.

There are a number of wrecks at **Rás Muhammad Marine National Park** [7] and the Strait of Gubal. West-southwest of the **Thistlegorm** [8], **Shag Rock** [9] at the southern end of **Sha'b 'Ali** [10] has the high-and-dry wreck of a fishing boat. On the western side is the *SS Kingston*. A World War II Dornier bomber lies at 27m (90ft) to the northeast.

GÛBÂL ISLANDS

Across the Strait of Gubal, the two Gûbâl Islands and Sha'b Gûbâl have at least five wrecks. **Bluff Point** [12], the northeast point of Gûbâl Saghîra (little Gûbâl), shelters an overnight anchorage for live-aboards with the remnants of a barge at 12m (40ft) suitable for night dives. Northeast of Sha'b Gûbâl, the stern wreckage of **SS Ulysses** [11] is at 28m

(92ft). West of Gûbâl Kebîra (Large Gûbâl), in the Tawîla Channel, the World War II wreck of the **SS Rosalie Möller** [13] sits upright on the sand with her bow at 39m (130ft) and her rudder at 45m (150ft). With strong currents, poor visibility and the depth she should only be dived in good weather.

[14] SHA'B ABU NUHÂS

North of Shaker Island (Shadwân), close to the main shipping lane, the treacherous reef of Sha'b Abu Nuhâs is famous for having the largest grouping of shipwrecks at divable depths on a single reef in the Red Sea.

There are at least seven wrecks, some piled on top of one another, so that it is difficult to separate them out and there is confusion over the exact identity of some wreckage. Some of the wrecks are due to navigational errors or bad weather. Others, however, are probably

insurance frauds because their listed cargo is missing. Along the northwest face, the *Giannis D* is near the western corner, the *Carnatic* is near the centre, while near the eastern corner the *Chrisoula K* is next to the earlier wreck of the *Marcus* and further to the east is the wreck of the *Olden*. In contrast to the other wrecks in this locality, the *Carnatic* has over 100 years of coral growth.

EL GOUNA AND HURGHADA

Most of El Gouna's and Hurghada's dive sites are accessed by boat, with the nearby reefs of the **Giftûn (Gifâtîn) Islands** [15] and **Abu Ramada** [16] providing most of them. All are now marine parks. Live-aboards access reefs and islands south of the Strait of Gubal and the Offshore Marine Park Islands, The Brothers, Dædalus, Gezîret Zabargad and Rocky Islet, from here.

SOUTH EGYPT

by Jack Jackson

THE SOUTH EGYPTIAN RED SEA HAS A wonderful collection of coral reefs in warm water with great visibility, but the offshore reefs can have strong currents. There has been very little coral bleaching. As one heads south from Port Safâga the fringing and near-shore reefs have not suffered the construction sediment or diver pressure that has occurred further north. The diving is as good as it was at Sharm el Sheikh in the early 1970s, with healthy corals, big fish and shoals of pelagics and brightly coloured reef fish. Whale Sharks swim by frequently and sharks and dolphins are relatively common, particularly around offshore reefs. Turtles can be found anywhere and even nest on quiet beaches such as those at Gezîret Zabargad.

The fringing reefs tend to be coral, sloping down to sand. Where coral pinnacles rise from the seabed some have sea-grass beds where Dugongs have been seen. The offshore reefs, whose drop-offs rise from deep water,

ABOVE LEFT *The top of Dœdalus Reef from the top of the British-built lighthouse, showing the jetty used to transport supplies and a live-aboard boat hanging off in the wind.*

ABOVE RIGHT *The British-built lighthouse at Dœdalus Reef, showing the railway lines on the jetty that are used to convey supplies on a trolley. The jetty is in a poor state of repair.*

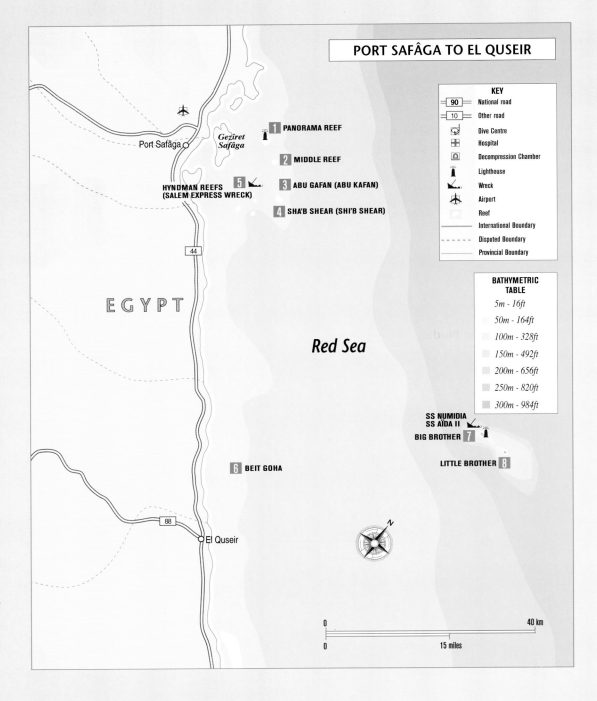

obstruct strong currents causing nutrient-rich upwellings that feed a luxuriant marine life and this attracts pelagic fish.

Off Port Safâga the reefs seaward of Gezîret Safâga (Safâga Island) are exposed to the full force of the prevailing wind, so day boats only dive on them in good weather, but live-aboard boats dive them regularly. In strong winds, smaller boats find shelter along the fringing reefs. This area can be cold in winter.

Until recently the area south of El Quseir was only accessible to divers on live-aboard boats or from a few eco-camps around Marsa 'Alam. Now there are hotels and resorts all along the new asphalt road to Marsa Wadi Lahami. Fortunately, they are well strung out. An airport has been built north of Marsa 'Alam. There is almost 100km (62 miles) of divable fringing reef and in good weather day boats from the operations furthest north can reach the sharks at Elphinstone Reef and those furthest south can cover Fury Shoal.

Well offshore are the reefs of The Brothers Islands, Dædalus, Gezîret Zabargad, Rocky Islet and Saint John. Mostly marine parks, these live-aboard-only destinations have the best diving in Egypt. For weather reasons, trips are only offered in summer and even then some may be cancelled for safety reasons. There are strict controls on charters. There are supposed to be controls on the number of boats with permits to visit The Brothers at any one time, but some boats have had to cut short their visits because all the fixed moorings were in use.

Easily dived shipwrecks have been found off Hyndman reefs, Abu Galawa, The Big Brother Island and Gezîret Zabargad. More are regularly found. Most operators offer Nitrox or recreational technical diving.

☐ PANORAMA REEF

East-northeast of Port Safâga, 8km (5 miles) east of Gezîret Safâga (Safâga Island), Panorama Reef is a large circular reef with walls dropping to over 200m (656ft). Its dive sites are as good as the best at Râs Muhammad. There are several around the reef with caves and overhangs, stony corals, *Dendronephthya* Soft Tree Corals, Black Coral, sharks, turtles, dolphins, and Egyptian reef fish (there are small differences in the fish life between Egypt and Sudan, more noticeable in Yemen and Djibouti). The East Face has Gorgonian Sea Fans and a huge Anemone City with clownfish.

☑ MIDDLE REEF

East-southeast of Port Safâga, Middle Reef is another with brilliant diving. The northern end slopes to 30m (100ft) and then drops into the depths as a wall. The east side has some anchor damage, but like the west side, has *Acropora, Porites* and lettuce corals, while the south side has caves, tunnels and gullies. Fish life includes sharks, jacks, groupers, Humphead (Napoleon) Wrasse and sweetlips.

☒ ABU GAFAN (ABU KAFAN)

South of Middle Reef, east-southeast of Port Safâga, is Abu Gafan (Abu Kafan) which has possibly the best diving off Safâga. A narrow, 300m (980ft) reef, with walls dropping below 100m (330ft) and plateaus at the north and south ends, it has great stony and soft corals, turtles and reef fish. It is normal to judge the current, enter the water on the side with the current and swim round the reef to be picked up on the lee side. Keep an eye on the open water for dolphins and hammerhead sharks.

☓ SHA'B SHEAR (SHI'B SHEAR)

East of Hyndman Reefs, southeast of Port Safâga, Sha'b Shear (Shi'b Shear) is an elongated reef with a shallow lagoon at its south side and coral gardens on its east and west ends. *Acropora* corals, *Porites* corals, fire corals, Gorgonian Sea Fans and *Dendronephthya* Soft Tree Corals abound. Turtles, jacks, groupers, tuna, fusiliers, goatfish, snappers, parrotfish, triggerfish, rabbitfish, surgeonfish, angelfish, soldierfish, squirrelfish, bigeyes, butterflyfish and Bluespotted Ribbontail Rays are common.

☖ HYNDMAN REEFS

There are several sites on Hyndman Reefs. Just south of the largest of these is the wreck of the

TOP *The S-insignia on one of the funnels of the Salem Express, which sank with great loss of life on Hyndman Reefs. The ship was en route from Jeddah to Port Safâga and had almost reached its destination when it struck the reef.*

ABOVE *Endemic to the Red Sea, the exquisite Butterflyfish (Chaetodon austriacus), which can grow to a size of 13cm (5in), is one of several that have an eye hidden in a mask, as well as stripes, to confuse predators.*

ABOVE *The wreck of the tug* Tienstin *on Sha'b Abu Galawa has some amazing stony coral growth for the time that she has been underwater. Part of the wreck can be snorkelled.*

Salem Express. The 115m (377ft) roll-on/roll-off ferry hit a small reef and sank quickly with great loss of life in December 1991. She now lies on her starboard side in 30m (100ft) of water with her port side at 12m (40ft). The authorities have sealed the ship's interior, but there are personal effects scattered everywhere. The wreck is better lit in the mornings.

⑥ BEIT GOHA

Beit Goha, 20km (12 miles) north of El Quseir, is one of the plethora of good shore dives in this region. Generally an elaborate coral garden at around 10m (33ft), it drops to 30m (100ft) on the seaward side of the reef.

THE BROTHERS (EL AKHAWEIN)

The Brothers (El Akhawein), 52km (32 miles) east-northeast of El Quseir, are two isolated islands rising out of deep water. **Big Brother** ⑦ has a lighthouse at the centre of the southwest face and is only about 400m (1310ft) long, but it dwarfs **Little Brother** ⑧ a kilometre (half a mile) to the southeast. As part of the Offshore Marine Park islands only the fixed moorings can be used. Big Brother offers excellent wall diving along the southern side of the reef, with strong currents promoting the growth of spectacular soft corals and frequent sightings of big pelagics. It also has two wrecks at its northern tip. The 173m (568ft) *SS Numidia*, which sank in 1901, lies at the northernmost tip, starting at 9m (30ft) with the stern lying at 80m (260ft). Only 100m (330ft) south of the *Numidia* lies the 75m (250ft) *SS Aida II*, which sank in 1957. The bow section is unrecognizable, but the stern lies from 30m (100ft) to 65m (210ft) and the rest is scattered over the reef. The strong currents have produced great soft corals on these wrecks, while at Little Brother they have produced some of the most colourful *Dendronephthya* Soft Tree Corals in the Red Sea. The Brothers attract several species of sharks, including Scalloped Hammerheads, Silvertip and Oceanic Whitetip.

⑨ ELPHINSTONE REEF (SHA'B ABU HAMRA)

Elphinstone Reef (Sha'b Abu Hamra) is an elongated reef in the middle of nowhere, 9km (6 miles) off the coast below Marsa Abu Dabbâb, with sharks all around it. The plateau at 20–25m (65–80ft) on the south point has Scalloped Hammerhead Sharks and Oceanic Whitetip Sharks. Down in the depths of nitrogen narcosis a legend has grown around a rectangular section of reef that some claim to be a sarcophagus and subsequently dubbed The Tomb of the Pharaoh.

⑩ DÆDALUS REEF (ABU EL KÎZÂN)

Dædalus Reef (Abu el Kîzân) is another isolated reef rising from deep water, 160km (100 miles) south-southeast of The Brothers, 83km (51 miles) off Marsa 'Alam. It has a lighthouse and is famous for sharks, especially Thresher Sharks. The north side has the region's best selection of pelagic fish and the reef has more of the colourful reef fish than The Brothers. Unique to Dædalus Reef are inquisitive cornetfish and a cave at 18m (60ft) on the southwest corner with aggressive lionfish.

Either side of Marsa 'Alam there are 100km (62 miles) of fringing reef with an underwater topography of coral and coral pinnacles sloping down to sand at 30–40m (100–130ft). Two such reefs are in front of the Kahramana Resort Hotel at Blondie Beach north of Marsa 'Alam, and Sha'b Marsa 'Alam itself.

⑪ SHA'B SHARM

Off El Sharm, 16km (10 miles) north of Gezîrat Wadi Gimâl, Sha'b Sharm is one of many good inshore sites in the area. A horseshoe-shaped seamount with steep drop-offs, the most popular site is at the southern end where a gentle slope descends from 15m (50ft) to 30m (100ft) before dropping into the depths. There can be a strong current.

⑫ FURY SHOAL

Fury Shoal is an expanse of reefs 17km (11 miles) north-northwest of Râs Banâs. The largest of these is often called Dolphin Reef. In general there is good diving everywhere, many shoals of reef fish, lone Whitetip Sharks and huge anemones. The reef's outer edge has a reputation for dolphins and larger sharks. Part of Fury Shoal, Abu Galawa has the wreck of the tugboat *Tienstin* leaning on the south side of the reef at its western end. Listing to starboard, the bow of the wreck is on the reef and breaks the surface while the stern is on sand at 18m (60ft). The western-style toilet and the holds harbour shoals of sweepers. The propeller is still attached and the hull has a prolific growth of stony and soft coral, including some large *Porites*.

13 GEZÎRET ZABARGAD

Situated 46km (28 miles) southeast of Râs Banâs, the larger island of Gezîret Zabargad, with its 234m (770ft) peak, was called Topazos in ancient times and more recently Saint John's Island. It is no longer inhabited, but its olivine mines were excavated for 3500 years. Live-aboard boats use the island as an overnight anchorage for forays to Rocky Islet. The island is a ship graveyard with the *Neptuna*, a Swiss-run diving live-aboard that sank in April 1981, an unidentified Russian freighter on the western side of the south bay and the *Maidan*, a British steamship that sank in 1923.

14 ROCKY ISLET

Rocky Islet, consisting of steep, bare rock rising from very deep water about 6km (3 miles) southeast of Gezîret Zabargad, has a reputation for sharks and large pelagics. The northern face is open to the full force of the prevailing wind, so divers are dropped here, then swim east round to the calmer waters of the south face to be picked up. The narrow sandy shelf that surrounds the islet is widest at its eastern end where, at 25m (80ft) on the southeast corner, it has become the place for observing sharks among a wide selection of pelagics.

15 SAINT JOHN'S REEF

Just north of the Sudanese border, 26km (16 miles) southwest of Rocky Islet, Saint John's Reef covers a huge area with many coral heads that are separate dive sites. Some have plateaus as shallow as 8m (25ft) while others slope below 70m (230ft) with stony corals, soft corals, Gorgonian Sea Fans and Sea Whips, shoals of barracuda, tuna, batfish, sweetlips, snappers and jacks and the ever-present sharks.

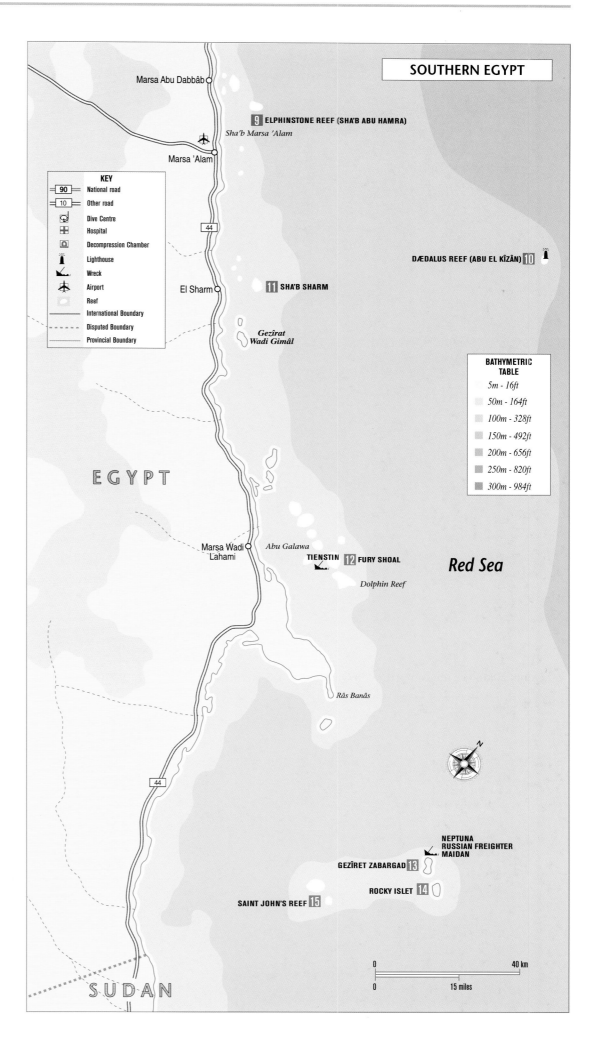

SUDAN

by Jack Jackson

THE SUDANESE RED SEA HAS A COLLECTION of healthy coral reefs, many of which rise steeply from deep water. The water is warm, visibility is great and there has been very little coral bleaching. Sudanese waters are currently difficult to reach due to unreliable flights, minimal infrastructure and political unease. Sites north of Port Sudan have the best diving and largest species diversity in the Red Sea.

Sudan was one of the first countries to ban spear-fishing and there are so many shallow reefs that large-scale commercial fishing has never been practical except for prawns in the sandy areas south of Port Sudan. Sudan has the deepest and warmest waters found anywhere in the Red Sea, with depths reaching over 3000m (9800ft) between Port Sudan and Jeddah. Isolated coral atolls and pinnacles rise vertically from very deep water to touch the surface, giving great wall diving among prolific marine life, healthy corals, good visibility and large fish, including shoals of Bumphead Parrotfish, which are rarely found north of the Sudanese/Egyptian border.

Four dive sites – the South Point of Sha'b Rumi, the North and Southwest Points of Sanganeb and the *Umbria* wreck – are among the finest in the world, but your dive guide must know where to enter the water for the best results. It is equally important to begin diving early in the morning. Winter winds can be strong. The summer, while hot on land, is comfortable, if humid, offshore. August is best avoided as heavy rain in the nearby Ethiopian highlands produces south winds and haboobs. These are violent squalls of Force 8 or more with dense sandstorms that, even well offshore, can reduce above-water visibility to a few metres in minutes.

Nowadays, most tourist diving in the Sudan is offshore by live-aboard boat. The boats working from Port Sudan are mostly Italian, but not exclusively so. Before booking a Sudanese diving vacation it is imperative to talk to someone who has been there for the purpose of diving, because some operators' advertising material contains charts, facts and local names that are incorrect. Wrong information and impossible itineraries are signs that they do not know the area.

South of Port Sudan the sea becomes progressively more shallow with a sandy bottom, so the diving is not as good. There are hundreds of sites in the Suākin Group, including North Jumna Shoal, Hindi Gider, Sha'b 'Anbar, Masamirit and Karam Masamirit.

Slightly less popular are Pfeiffer Reef and Qita el Bannā in the north and in the south, Protector Reef, Dahrat Ghab and Dahrat 'Abīd, which have high-and-dry wrecks and Preserver Reef, which does not. There are Tiger Sharks off the entrance to Port Sudan and huge ones on Green Reef. For the adventurous, the effort to reach Sudanese diving is worth it.

☐1 ELBA REEF

On the Egyptian/Sudanese political boundary 18km (11 miles) east-northeast of Marsa Umbeila, Elba Reef has the *Levanso* (*Levanzo*) wreck. The shallow parts of the wreck are easily dived, but the drop-off continues well beyond 50m (165ft) with lots of big fish and sharks.

☐2 PFEIFFER REEF

Situated 15km (9 miles) southeast of Marsa Halaka, Pfeiffer Reef slopes to a plateau at 40m (130ft) before dropping off into the depths. As with every other deep reef in this region, there are sharks deeper down. East of Muhammad Qōl, Mesharifa has Manta Rays gathering to mate in August.

☐3 ABINGTON, ☐4 ANGAROSH AND ☐5 MERLO REEFS

About 22km (14 miles) southeast of Râs Abu Shagara, Abington, Angarosh and Merlo Reefs teem with inquisitive sharks among the prolific marine life.

TOP LEFT *The small boat jetty, inner lagoon and the top of the reef at Sanganeb – one of the favourite sites of underwater film pioneer Hans Hass.*

TOP RIGHT *Traditional Egyptian cargo boats, called* sambuks, *in Port Sudan harbour. Sharks are found at the entrance to the harbour and nearby Wingate Reef shelters the* Umbria *wreck.*

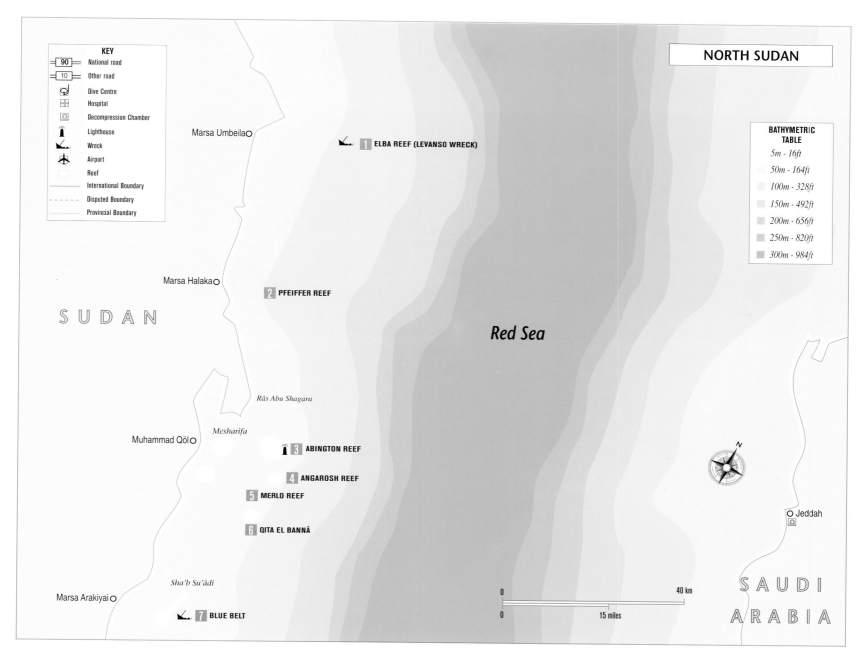

KEY

	National road
	Other road
	Dive Centre
	Hospital
	Decompression Chamber
	Lighthouse
	Wreck
	Airport
	Reef
	International Boundary
	Disputed Boundary
	Provincial Boundary

NORTH SUDAN

BATHYMETRIC TABLE

5m - 16ft
50m - 164ft
100m - 328ft
150m - 492ft
200m - 656ft
250m - 820ft
300m - 984ft

Marsa Umbeila

1 ELBA REEF (LEVANSO WRECK)

S U D A N

Marsa Halaka

2 PFEIFFER REEF

Red Sea

Râs Abu Shagara

Mesharifa

Muhammad Qōl

3 ABINGTON REEF

4 ANGAROSH REEF

5 MERLO REEF

6 QITA EL BANNĀ

Sha'b Su'ādi

Marsa Arakiyai

7 BLUE BELT

0   40 km

0   15 miles

Jeddah

S A U D I

A R A B I A

6 QITA EL BANNĀ

Qita el Bannā, 18km (11 miles) south-southwest of Angarosh, is similar to Abington, Angarosh and Merlo Reefs, with sheer walls, great corals, teeming fish and plenty of sharks. Most of the diving is deep, but there are good shallow areas.

7 *BLUE BELT*

There are numerous reefs in this area, but the reefs near Marsa 'Arūs (Arous) and Port Sudan are most popular because they can be reached by inflatable as well as live-aboard boats. East of Marsa Arakiyai, 65km (40 miles) north of Port Sudan, lies the large reef of Sha'b Su'ādi where the main attraction is the wreck of the 2545-tonne freighter *Blue Belt*. Wrongly called

the *Blue Bell* in some guides, the *Blue Belt* went aground on Sha'b Su'ādi in December 1977 and when two tugs from Port Sudan pulled her off too energetically, she overturned and sank. Carrying Toyota vehicles and spares, she is known locally as the Toyota wreck. Today she lies upside down with the top of the bow on sand at 15m (50ft) and the rest of the ship over the drop-off descending steeply into the depths at 65m. Penetration requires care

RIGHT *One of the Toyota trucks that spilled from the deck of the* Blue Belt *as she turned over. Pulled over and sunk in December 1977, she is known locally as the Toyota wreck.*

because the vessel is upside down, which forces divers to go deep again at the end of the dive to get back out. Vehicles spilled from the deck onto sand at 15m (50ft) make a good dive. Much of the shallow stony coral has been killed by fuel oil leaking from the ship.

SHA'B RUMI (ROMAN REEF)

East of Marsa 'Arūs, 40km (25 miles) north-northeast of Port Sudan, Sha'b Rumi (Roman Reef) is a large reef with its longest sides parallel to the prevailing north-to-south current. On the west side there are two entrances to its lagoon and, lying on a ledge at 9m (30ft) just outside the southern entrance, are the remains of Jacques-Yves Cousteau's **Conshelf II** [8] experiment of 1963 (*see p78*). The largest of the remains is the onion-shaped submersible hangar. Its portholes have gone, but the roof holds an air pocket of divers' exhaust gases in which they can converse. East of the hangar lie the cables that ran to the utility ship *Rosaldo* in

the lagoon and just to the north of the hangar is the tool shed. Further north, abreast of the lagoon entrance, three multicoloured fish pens covered in *Dendronephthya* Soft Tree Corals move around in rough seas, while over the drop-off a shark cage is the only remnant of the deep habitat at 27m (89ft).

Inconsiderate divers have broken off some of the table corals on the hangar, but the site is still full of nostalgia and makes an excellent night dive. The memorial casket under the submarine hangar has an inscription dedicated to a German diver who died here in 1973. The narrow lagoon entrance leads to safe anchorage and the best time to dive the site is very early morning. Sharks are rare, except deep over the drop-off, but turtles and dolphins are common.

With the eastern side of Sha'b Rumi more contorted than on the west, the current is slowed down more. When the currents meet off the narrow **South Point** [9], they are

travelling at different speeds, producing whirlpools and upwellings full of nutrients that attract large shoals of fish. These in turn attract large numbers of sharks. In the shelter of the wall, over a sandy plateau sloping from 20m (66ft) to 36m (118ft), the marine life is prolific, with massive shoals of fish, and there can be 50 sharks circling in the early morning. Large Silvertip Sharks, aggressive Silky Sharks, Grey Reef and smaller Whitetip Reef Sharks are common, while Scalloped Hammerhead Sharks shoal over the drop-off. A German film crew placed the tiny shark cage here in 1975.

SANGANEB

About 30km (20 miles) northeast of Port Sudan, and marked by a lighthouse at its southern end, the large atoll of Sanganeb is famous for a profusion of 23 top dive sites. The **North Point** [10] is exposed to the prevailing north winds and currents, so it can only be dived in good weather and is best dived in

ABOVE *Endemic to the Red Sea and the western Gulf of Aden, Red Sea Bannerfish* (Heniochus intermedius) *shoal as juveniles and sometimes as adults. This shoal is on Sha'b Rumi Reef.*

ABOVE *This 3m (10ft) coral pinnacle on the southwest plateau of Sanganeb has colourful* Dendronephthya *Soft Tree Corals. The anthias (fairy basslets) are resident, while the Emperor Angelfish* (Pomacanthus imperator) *is just passing.*

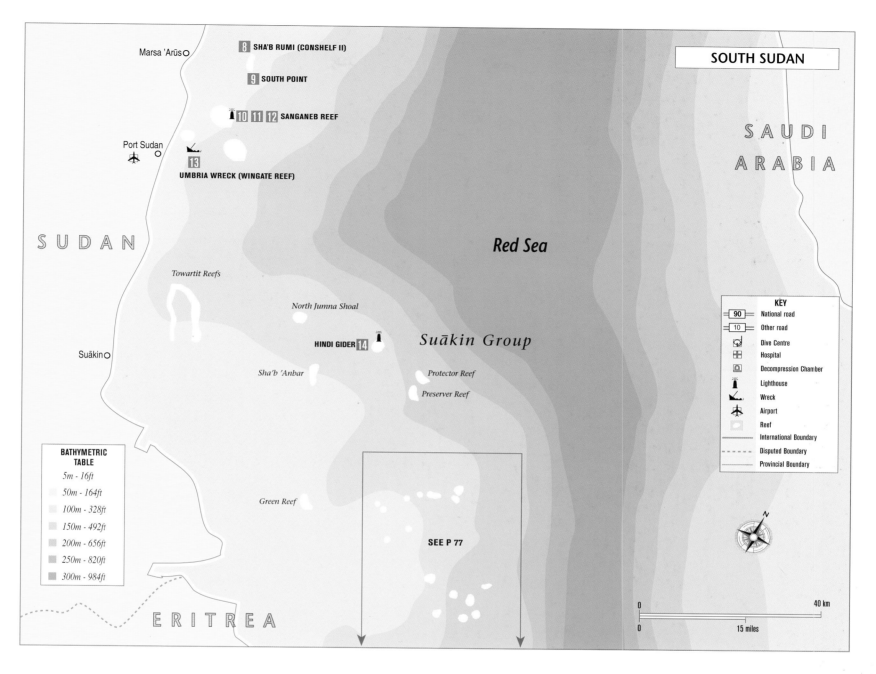

the early morning when it is calm. The point drops off in steps with a healthy reef table at 5m (16ft); a sandy platform pointing north with a raised lip at 20m (65ft); and a much larger sandy plateau protruding 100m (330ft) further north and shelving from 50m to 60m (165ft to 200ft). The platform with the raised lip often has a Manta Ray. The upper reef table is carpeted with stony corals, soft corals and gorgonians, while the reef fish are dense and varied. The deeper plateau has large numbers of pelagics, including a huge shoal of barracuda circling in a tightly-knit ball, and shoals of Scalloped Hammerhead Sharks. In the early morning Grey Reef Sharks are found resting on the sand. Visibility is good enough

for divers to observe these creatures from the outer reef wall, without having to go deep.

On the east side of the North Point there is an obvious separate large coral head and south of it there are two very deep wrecks. The shallowest of these is a large old wooden vessel covered in whip corals, but its highest point is at 70m (230ft). Some 20m (65ft) north of the coral head, divers can descend to a small sloping shelf at 45m (150ft), which overlooks a gully to the east. Grey Reef Sharks, Whitetip Reef Sharks and shoals of over 40 Scalloped Hammerhead Sharks cruise this gully. In April shoals of Blackspotted Grunts congregate here in small caves. Many liveaboards avoid this dive because they cannot

anchor, but some hold off the reef and others make the long journey from the lagoons by inflatable. On a good day this is possibly the best dive in the world.

Sanganeb's **East Face** 11 is several kilometres long and has to be treated as several north-south drift dives. A sheer wall throughout its length, it drops vertically to 90m (300ft) before shelving off into the depths. There are signs of at least two large wrecks having dragged along it. Opposite Sanganeb's outer lagoon there is a large anchor and wreckage, and opposite the inner lagoon there are the metallic remains – engine, gearbox and tanks – of a wooden wreck. It lies at 10m (33ft) within a curve in the reef that gives shelter from the

ABOVE *A diver surveys the captain's bathroom on the* Umbria. *Scuttled in 1940 and lying in sheltered water inside Wingate Reefs, this well-lit wreck has abundant marine life and is very popular with underwater photographers.*

current. It is possible for clever coxwains to anchor small boats here. Being beside a large area of deep water, this face combines the best of reef life with pelagic creatures: stonefish, Torpedo (Electric) Rays, snake eels, surgeonfish, angelfish and butterflyfish are found in the shallows. Sharks, including Variegated (Leopard) Sharks, inhabit the deeper water while sailfish, turtles, Manta Rays, Bottlenose Dolphins and pilot whales regularly pass by.

The remains of a wooden live-aboard lie near where most live-aboard boats anchor in the outer lagoon. Named either *White Elephant* or *Saida III*, depending on whether the Austrian/Italian owner was chartering or smuggling, it slowly sank where it was after the owner had mysteriously disappeared. Now it makes a good night dive.

People often camp around the lighthouse from where they can dive the south wall, which is about a kilometre (half a mile) long and 70m (230ft) deep, or the Southwest Point from the south jetty. At night Spiny Lobsters, Spanish Dancer Nudibranchs, Sea Hares, Banded Coral Shrimps, snake eels, octopuses, Basket Stars and Tun Shells are on show. This end of the reef is sheltered from all but August's south winds, and when winter's north winds are very strong, shoals of up to nine Manta Rays congregate here.

At the **Southwest Point** [12] the upper reef wall has prolific marine life, including shoals of Sailfin Surgeonfish, unicornfish and barracuda, shoals of Blackspotted Grunts congregate around the caverns in April. Below the reef wall, a wide sandy plateau slopes gently from 20m to 36m (65ft to 118ft), while protruding southwest for 100m (330ft). On the south and west of this plateau the drop-off descends at around 60–70° into deep water so divers can peer over the edge at the sharks below. But to the north there is only a slope. Grey Reef and Scalloped Hammerhead sharks

patrol the southern edge of this plateau, lone Silvertip or Tiger Sharks are sometimes encountered and Leopard (Variegated) Sharks have been seen where it joins the south wall.

Every combination of Red Sea pelagic and reef fish is found among the stony corals, soft corals, Gorgonian Sea Fans and Sea Whips on the plateau including Bluespotted Ribbontail Rays, large Humphead (Napoleon) Wrasse and many huge Brownmarbled Groupers.

[13] *UMBRIA* WRECK

At the northern end of the main ship's anchorage for Port Sudan, the 155m (509ft) cargo/passenger vessel *Umbria* is sheltered by Wingate Reefs and can be dived in any weather. There is no current, but lots of light, great visibility and prolific marine life. Scuttled at anchor in June 1940, she was first dived recreationally by Hans Hass in 1949. The *Umbria* lies at an angle on her port side, with her starboard davits breaking the surface. The port propeller is buried in the coral, but the starboard propeller is in clear water at 15m (50ft). The stern rests on coral at 20m (65ft), while the bow rests on sand at 36m (120ft). Most of the ship is easily penetrated. The holds are open and ordnance, wine bottles, batteries and Kilner jars are scattered around. Many sacks are no longer supported so divers require good buoyancy control to avoid dislodging them. Entering the engine room and kitchen are more difficult, and care should be taken not to disturb the silt. The engines are intact and an outboard motor is clamped to the engine room wall. It is one of the world's best dives and one of the most photogenic wrecks.

Around the ship's anchorage, Wingate Reefs are in shallow water, but have good marine life including Tiger Sharks, Blacktip Reef Sharks, dolphins and congregations of Manta Rays during the worst winter winds.

SOUTH SUĀKIN GROUP

South of Port Sudan, Towartit Reefs and some of the hundreds of low-lying islets and reefs in the Suākin Group south-southeast of Port Sudan (including North Jumna Shoal, Hindi

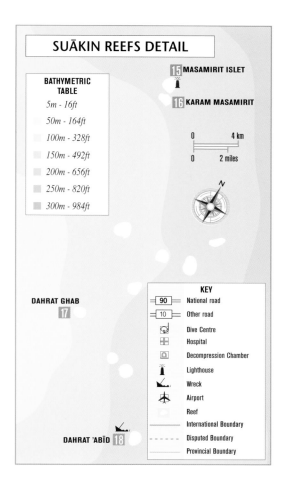

SUĀKIN REEFS DETAIL

BATHYMETRIC TABLE
5m - 16ft
50m - 164ft
100m - 328ft
150m - 492ft
200m - 656ft
250m - 820ft
300m - 984ft

15 MASAMIRIT ISLET

16 KARAM MASAMIRIT

0 — 4 km
0 — 2 miles

N

DAHRAT GHAB
17

KEY	
90	National road
10	Other road
	Dive Centre
	Hospital
	Decompression Chamber
	Lighthouse
	Wreck
	Airport
	Reef
	International Boundary
	Disputed Boundary
	Provincial Boundary

DAHRAT 'ABĪD 18

Gider, Sha'b 'Anbar and Masamirit), tend to be popular with Italian live-aboard boats and form a sheltered anchorage for local fishermen. Over relatively shallow water, with slopes rather than drop-offs, the marine life is just as good as that further north, but visibility is relatively poor. Lone Grey Reef Sharks, Whitetip Reef Sharks, Nurse Sharks and Variegated (Leopard) Sharks are common; large Tiger Sharks and whales are seen.

Between Port Sudan and Suākin many of the reefs near the shore were used as sheltered anchorages for ships waiting to enter Port Sudan Harbour. Unfortunately they were damaged by bored ship's crews ripping up tons of stony coral with crowbars.

North Jumna Shoal (the most northerly islet in the Suākin Group), Hindi Gider and Sha'b 'Anbar (east-southeast of Port Sudan) have quite good fish life. **Hindi Gider** 14 (known locally as Hind Kadam) is an islet with a sand cay 55km (34 miles) east-northeast of Suākin harbour. It has an automatic navigational light and huge Osprey nests. The depths drop well beyond 50m (165ft).

About 16km (10 miles) south-southeast of Hindi Gider, Protector Reef is a large reef with a rusting wreck on its northern fringe and a gentle slope down to a drop-off at 20m (65ft) at the southern end. A little south-southwest of Protector Reef, Preserver Reef has a steep drop-off at its southern end.

15 MASAMIRIT ISLET

Masamirit Islet, 174km (108 miles) southeast of Port Sudan, has a steep drop-off on the east side. There is a plateau at 25–30m (80–100ft) at its northern end. This plateau has many coral heads and it is a good place from which divers can observe the deeper reef life swimming by below.

16 KARAM MASAMIRIT

Just southeast of Masamirit, Karam Masamirit has deeper drop-offs. The north and south ends slope down to the edges of these drop-offs at around 25m (80ft), where divers can again peer over the edge at the pelagics, including sharks, below. Eagle Rays and Humphead (Napoleon) Wrasse are quite common.

ABOVE *Grey Reef Sharks (Carcharhinus ambly-rhynchos) are the commonest sharks in Sudanese waters. At one time the name Blacktail Shark (C. wheeleri) was used in the northern Red Sea, but they are now considered Grey Reef Sharks.*

17 DAHRAT GHAB

About 28km (17 miles) south-southeast of Masamirit, Dahrat Ghab, is another islet fringed by a good reef. But the southern tip probably has the best diving with a separate ridge from 22m (72ft) from where divers can look over the drop-off.

18 DAHRAT 'ABĪD

The southernmost islet in the Suākin Group, Dahrat 'Abīd, has the remains of a wreck on top of the reef and shoals of reef fish. In the shallows there are good soft corals. The depths provide good opportunities for divers to see pelagics swimming past, including Grey Reef Sharks, Whitetip Reef Sharks, Thresher Sharks and Silvertip Sharks. This is the last reef to have a reasonable drop-off as boats go south.

CONSHELF II

An artist's reconstruction of Jacques-Yves Cousteau's Conshelf II experiment of 1963 at Sha'b Rumi, an attempt at establishing a scientific colony on the continental shelf. A 24m (80ft) bridge was built from the support ship Rosaldo anchored in the lagoon, across Roman Reef to the jumping-off ladder above the sunken village. The upper level carried pedestrians and the lower carried power cables, compressed air hoses, television and phone lines. The Starfish House cutaway shows the crew's sleeping quarters, the laboratory and the central living area with a bank of television monitors and a kitchen. One of the divers is shown handling Claude, the parrot, which they tried unsuccessfully to interest in the parrotfish in the window. The Diving Saucer Hangar had an open entry port below, the water kept out by air compressed to 2 atmospheres. An overhead four-ton winch lifted the Diving Saucer into the hangar. A removable plywood floor was placed over the 3m (10ft) hatch for the mechanics to walk on. Between the hangar and Starfish House the cook is depicted feeding the triggerfish that had become habituated and could be attracted by tapping on the Starfish House window. The fish was able to identify the cook from among identically clad divers. Next to him is a fish pen, one of five geodesic cages of metal frame and varicoloured Plexiglas where specimens, captured unharmed in the divers' hands, were kept. In the Wet (tool) Shed they stored submarine scooters, fish traps, geological tools, builder's supplies and anything else that water could not damage. Fish were trapped and placed in water-filled plastic bags, with a shot of compressed air from the diver's mouthpiece to buoy the bag. The bags were tied to the Wet Shed to be sorted later and transported to the Oceanographic Institute in Monaco. Deep Cabin was moored against a coral escarpment. Communication cables connected it to Starfish House from where the occupants could be monitored via television. It was occupied for a week by two 'oceanauts' who lived in a room 2m (7ft) across, pressurized to 3½ atmospheres. The open hatch was protected by a shark-proof grille. Divers also explored in the Diving Saucer.

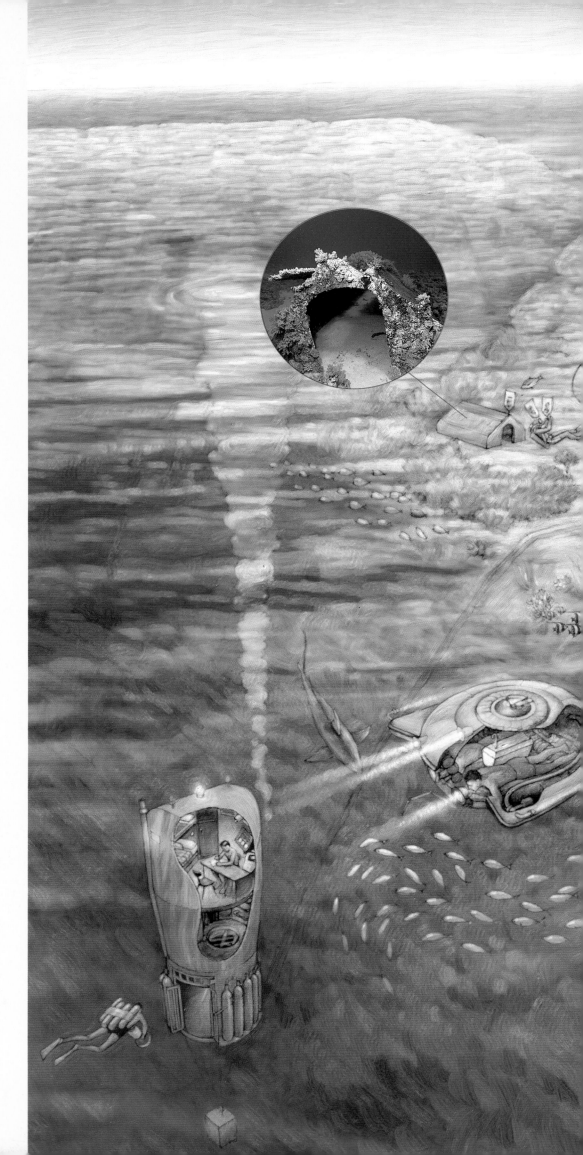

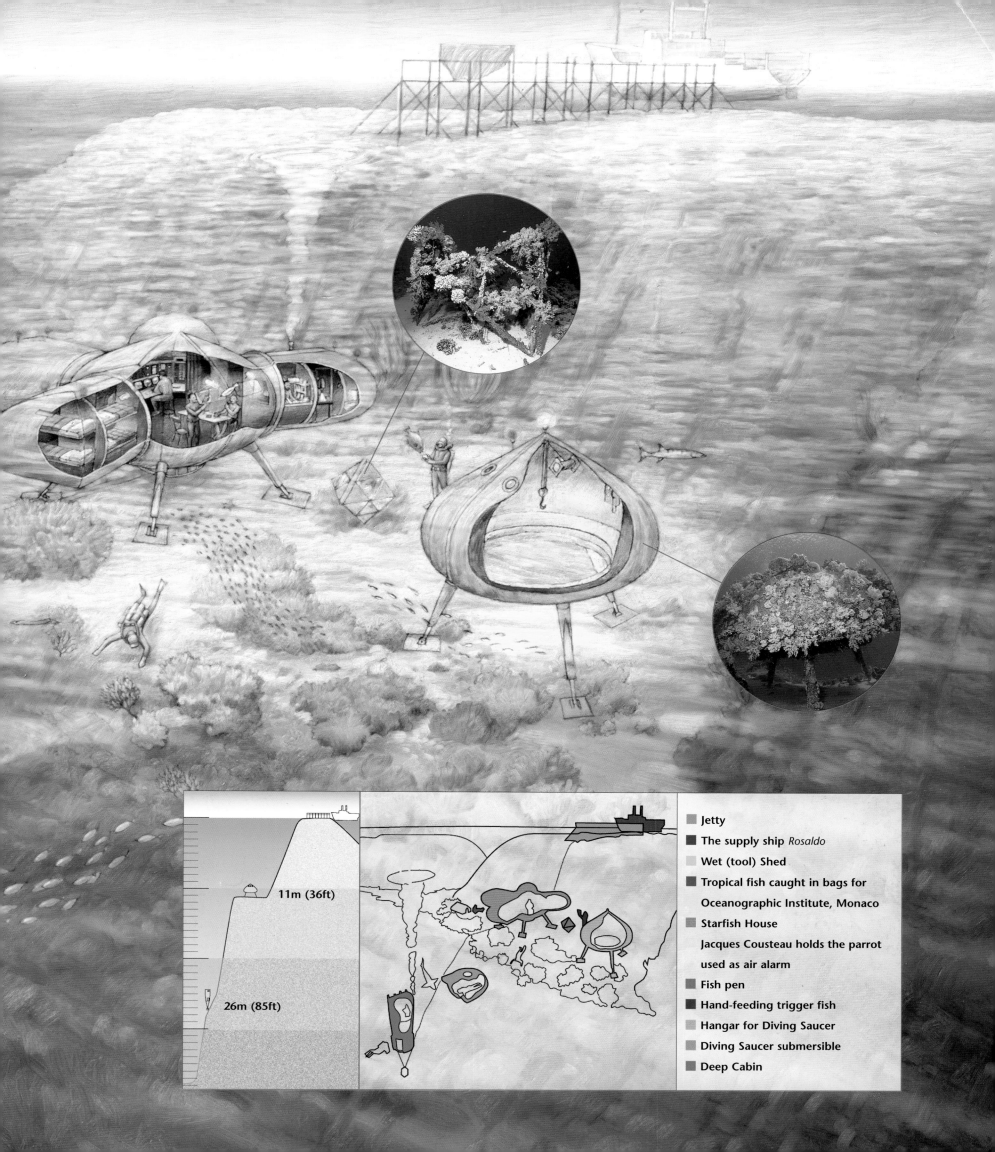

11m (36ft)

26m (85ft)

Jetty

The supply ship *Rosaldo*

Wet (tool) Shed

Tropical fish caught in bags for
Oceanographic Institute, Monaco

Starfish House
Jacques Cousteau holds the parrot
used as air alarm

Fish pen

Hand-feeding trigger fish

Hangar for Diving Saucer

Diving Saucer submersible

Deep Cabin

THE
INDIAN OCEAN

Introduction by Jack Jackson

THE INDIAN OCEAN IS THE THIRD-LARGEST BODY OF WATER in the world after the Pacific and Atlantic Oceans. It covers roughly 20 per cent of the earth's water surface and is the youngest and physically most complex of the three major oceans. No natural boundary separates the Indian Ocean from the Atlantic, Antarctic and Pacific Oceans. The 20° meridian east of Greenwich, through Cape Agulhas at the southern end of Africa, is used to denote separation from the Atlantic Ocean south of Africa and the 147° meridian east of Greenwich, separates it from the Pacific Ocean south of Australia. The northeastern border is difficult to define. The one most commonly accepted runs northwest across the Timor Sea from Australia's Cape Londonderry, along the southern shores of the Lesser Sunda Islands and the island of Java, and then across the Sunda Strait to the shores of Sumatra. Between Sumatra and the Malay Peninsula the boundary is usually drawn across the Singapore Strait. The Antarctic Ocean, often called the Southern Ocean, includes all oceanic areas surrounding Antarctica, south of latitude 55° south.

Including the Gulf of Aqaba, the Red Sea, the Arabian (Persian) Gulf, the Gulf of Oman, the Arabian Sea, the Bay of Bengal, the Strait of Malacca, the Great Australian Bight and the Bass Straight, the Indian Ocean covers an area of 73,556,000 sq km (28,400,000 sq miles).

Bordered in the north by southern Asia, in the west by the Arabian Peninsula and Africa, in the east by the Malay Peninsula, Indonesia and Australia and in the south by Antarctica, the Indian Ocean is extremely varied in its coastal habitat, reef development and species diversity.

In the north, the Gulf of Aqaba and the Red Sea are more saline and warmer than one would expect from their geographical position. Volcanic activity at the seafloor increases the water temperature and the desert coastline has no large river systems flowing out. This has led to healthy reef development and good species diversity.

During ice ages, lower sea levels isolated the Arabian (Persian) Gulf, Gulf of Aden and the Red Sea from the Indian Ocean, precluding the interchange of species and allowing some 15 per cent of the species here to evolve endemically. Even when the ice melted and sea levels rose again, the

ABOVE *Powder-blue Surgeonfish* (Acanthurus leucosternon) *sometimes occur in large feeding aggregations that can overwhelm any territorial damselfish guarding their 'private' algae.*

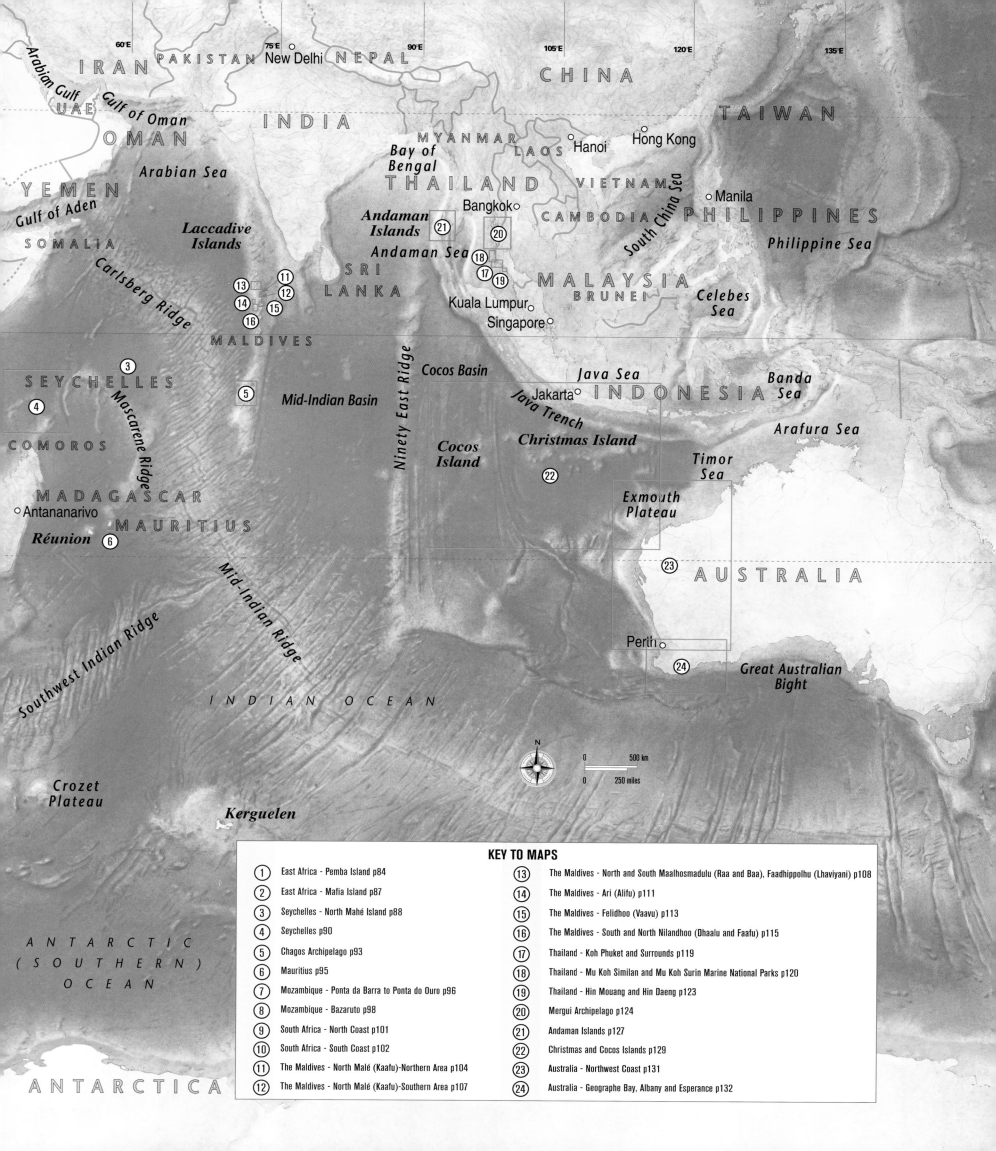

60°E 75°E 90°E 105°E 120°E 135°E

IRAN
PAKISTAN
New Delhi NEPAL
CHINA

Arabian Gulf
UAE
Gulf of Oman
OMAN
INDIA
TAIWAN

YEMEN
Arabian Sea
MYANMAR
Hanoi
Hong Kong

Gulf of Aden
Bay of Bengal
LAOS

SOMALIA
Laccadive Islands
THAILAND
VIETNAM
Manila

Bangkok
CAMBODIA
PHILIPPINES

Carlsberg Ridge
Andaman Islands ㉑
⑳
South China Sea
Philippine Sea

⑬ ⑪
⑫
SRI LANKA
Andaman Sea ⑱
⑰ ⑲
MALAYSIA
Celebes Sea

⑭ ⑮
BRUNEI

⑯
MALDIVES
Kuala Lumpur

③
Singapore

④
Mid-Indian Basin
⑤
Cocos Basin
Java Sea
INDONESIA
Banda Sea

SEYCHELLES
Mascarene Ridge
Ninety East Ridge
Jakarta
Java Trench

COMOROS
Cocos Island
Christmas Island
Arafura Sea

MADAGASCAR
Antananarivo
MAURITIUS
㉒
Timor Sea

Réunion ⑥
Exmouth Plateau

Mid-Indian Ridge
㉓
AUSTRALIA

Southwest Indian Ridge
INDIAN OCEAN
Perth
㉔
Great Australian Bight

Crozet Plateau

Kerguelen

ANTARCTIC (SOUTHERN) OCEAN

N
0 ——— 500 km
0 ——— 250 miles

ANTARCTICA

KEY TO MAPS

INDIAN OCEAN

ABOVE *Indian Ocean Oriental Sweetlips (Plectorhinchus vittatus) can be found singly, but they often also occur in large shoals.*

sandy bottom and upwelling along the coast of Somalia limited the development of reefs and reef species there. This lower species diversity reinforces the isolation of reef species to the north. In the Arabian Gulf, the sandy bottom, upwelling and extremes of winter and summer temperatures inhibit reef growth. The result is that species diversity is lower than in the Red Sea and the Gulf of Aqaba, but there is still a high degree of endemism.

The coast of Pakistan has low winter temperatures. Most of the coast from India to Myanmar (Burma) has massive seasonal outflows of sediment-laden freshwater from large river systems. Reef development along these coasts is limited. The Andaman Sea, southern Myanmar and western Thailand have huge granite boulders and small reefs. Northwest Malaysia has a few reefs and good species diversity, but suffers from agricultural run-off. The Strait of Malacca has agricultural run-off and heavy shipping movements. A restricted water mass, the run-off also lowers its salinity, but the few small reefs found in the Strait of Malacca have good species diversity. Indonesia has some of the best coral and species diversity in the world. The west and south coasts of Australia are not as good as the Great Barrier Reef in the Pacific, but there is fine diving all the way round to the Bass Strait and Tasmania where the water is cold enough for kelp.

Some of the islands off southwest India, Sri Lanka, the Maldives, East Africa, Comoros and Madagascar have suffered recent coral bleaching, but there is still good species diversity. The islands on the Mascarene Ridge, Mauritius, Réunion, Rodrigues and the Seychelles, have less species diversity, but a degree of endemism. The east African coast has coral reefs as far south as Durban. Juvenile tropical inshore fish may be swept seasonally by the current as far south as the Cape of Good Hope. Mozambique and South Africa's coastline ranges from coral reefs to waters as cold and rough as that of Europe.

The Indian Ocean has the fewest seas. To the northwest are the Red Sea, Arabian Gulf, gulfs of Aden and Oman and the Arabian Sea. To the northeast are the Andaman Sea and the Bay of Bengal. The Great Australian Bight is off the southern coast of Australia. The Indian Ocean only goes as far north as the Red Sea – it cannot reach a temperate or cold region. It has fewer islands. Madagascar is the world's fourth-largest island and Sumatra is the fifth. The Seychelles, Socotra, and Sri Lanka are continental fragments, while all other islands are volcanic. It is the only ocean whose surface circulation lacks symmetry and, in the north, reverses semiannually.

The semiannual reversals of wind direction, known as monsoons from the Arabic word *mausim* for season, vary in their date of onset and intensity. Monsoon dynamics are modulated by the El Niño/Southern Oscillation Phenomenon of the South Pacific and cyclones that form over the open ocean.

During the northern winter, from November to April, high atmospheric pressure develops over India due to the cold, falling air. This combines with the low-pressure system north of Australia to cause the northeast monsoon and the northeast-to-southwest

RIGHT The old Greek freighter Paraportiani *sank in a storm at the southern end of Pemba in the late 1960s. Lying in shallow water she is well colonized with marine growth.*

winds and currents that bring a wet season to southern Indonesia and northern Australia. These winds generate the North Equatorial Current, which carries water towards the coast of Africa.

In the northern summer, from May to October, low atmospheric pressure develops over Asia from hot, rising air. This results in the southwest monsoon and southwest-to-northeast winds. The southwest monsoon brings heavy rain to the Indian subcontinent and a wet season in south Asia.

In the southern hemisphere, the winds are generally milder, but summer storms near Mauritius can be severe. Trade winds drive a broad, circular system of currents (a gyre) of warm water anticlockwise. The South Equatorial current carries water towards Africa, where the portion not connected with the monsoon wind system curls south below Madagascar and reinforces the Agulhas Current. In winter this combined southward flowing current can reach speeds of 180km (112 miles) per day along the edge of South Africa's continental shelf. At this speed it can more than double the height of waves travelling north from storms in the Antarctic Ocean and divers have to put up with a high-voltage, camera-damaging experience as their boats are launched through the surf.

Tropical cyclones occur during May/June and October/November in the northern Indian Ocean and January/February in the south. When the monsoon winds change, cyclones sometimes strike the shores of the Arabian Sea and the Bay of Bengal.

Sailing ships plying the important India and southeast Asia trade route made full use of the monsoon trade winds. They made the eastward journey with the winds of the south-west monsoon and used the winds of the northeast monsoon for their return between November and March. Nowadays, ships have a shorter passage through the Suez Canal.

All three types of tides are found in the Indian Ocean, but semidiurnal tides are the most common, prevailing in east Africa as far north as the equator and in the Bay of Bengal. Tide types are mixed in the Arabian Sea and the inner part of the Arabian Gulf. Southwest Australia, the coast of Thailand in the Andaman Sea and the south shore of the central Arabian Gulf have small areas of diurnal tides. Tidal ranges vary considerably – Mauritius has a tidal range of only 50cm (20in) on springs, while Australia's Port Hedland has 600cm (19ft), and Rangoon, 520cm (17ft).

The average depth of the Indian Ocean is 3890m (12,760ft). Its deepest point, in the Sunda Deep off the southern coast of Java,

Indonesia, in the Java Trench, is 7450m (24,442 feet). This is thought to mark the line of subduction where the Australian Plate goes below the Eurasian Plate. The related volcanic activity is high. The eruption of Krakatoa in 1883 was heard as far away as Australia.

The African, Indian, and Antarctic tectonic plates diverge in the Indian Ocean as the mid-oceanic ridge. Shaped like an inverted Y, the stem runs north and then west as the Carlsberg Ridge to join the rift system of the Red Sea. One arm extends around southern Africa to connect with the Mid-Atlantic Ridge, while the other extends south around Australia to connect with the East Pacific Rise. This underwater chain of mountains represents strong volcanic activity. At the Red Sea the northern part of Africa is moving apart from Arabia. In geological time it will probably become wide enough to be an ocean.

All bottom water originates from outside the Indian Ocean's boundaries. Below the surface currents, deep water movement is sluggish. The highly saline water from the Arabian Gulf and the Red Sea sinks below the fresher surface water to form the North Indian High Salinity Intermediate Water between 610m (2000ft) and 1000m (3300ft). This layer spreads east into the Bay of Bengal and as far south as Madagascar and Sumatra. Below this,

ABOVE *Some* Turbinaria *species of stony corals have highly convoluted growth to collect the maximum amount of sunlight.*

the Antarctic Intermediate Water continues to 1500m (5000ft). A current from the north Atlantic, the North Atlantic Deep Water, flows between 1500 (5000ft) and 3050m (10,000ft) and below 3050m (10,000ft) the Antarctic Bottom Water comes from the Weddell Sea. These cold layers flow slowly northward from the Antarctic Circumpolar Region, becoming extremely low in oxygen in the north.

The Indian Ocean is nearly as good as the Pacific Ocean for species diversity, but overfishing is a problem. Destructive fishing methods have ruined coral reefs in places. Indonesia, whose reefs straddle the Indian and Pacific Oceans, has the greatest share of coral reefs in the world (18 per cent) of which 82 per cent are under threat. Diver numbers and indiscriminate anchoring have damaged some areas, but are now being addressed.

Cultivation, hunting and guano mining on land used to be the main threats to the environment. Nowadays agricultural, domestic and industrial waste flowing into nearshore waters, oil spills from normal tanker operations and occasional large-scale tanker catastrophes are the major problems.

LEFT *Anthias, mostly* Pseudanthias *species, are known as Fairy Basslets or Goldies in some countries. Usually small and brightly coloured, they feed on zooplankton above reefs.*

EAST AFRICA

by Mark and Charlotte Durham

VAST AREAS OF FRINGING CORAL REEF HUG the East African coastline and the shores of the nearby islands. Stretching south from the equator these impressive formations provide shelter and food to over 3000 species of marine plants and animals.

Like many of the coral corners of the world, a combination of the 1997/8 El Niño/Southern Oscillation Phenomenon and the over-harvesting of marine life has taken its toll. Turtles in Kenya are still under threat from local traditions and encroaching tourism, and blast-fishing continues to decimate the fish population in parts of Tanzania. Fortunately, through natural rehabilitation, local conservation efforts and national marine park protection, recovery is under way.

Two out of three 'spice islands' lying off the Tanzanian coast merit the 'good diving' label. Pemba, in the north, offers dramatic vertical coral cliffs bustling with life, strong ocean currents, big pelagic species, and can have 30m (100ft) visibility. Mafia Island Marine Park in

TOP LEFT *The sight of a traditional dhow sailing across the deep waters of the Pemba Channel. A living reminder of Pemba's past.*

TOP RIGHT *An idyllic tropical setting for Pemba's first marine reserve, Mesali Island is situated on the west coast, surrounded by colourful coral reefs that sustain a diverse ecosystem.*

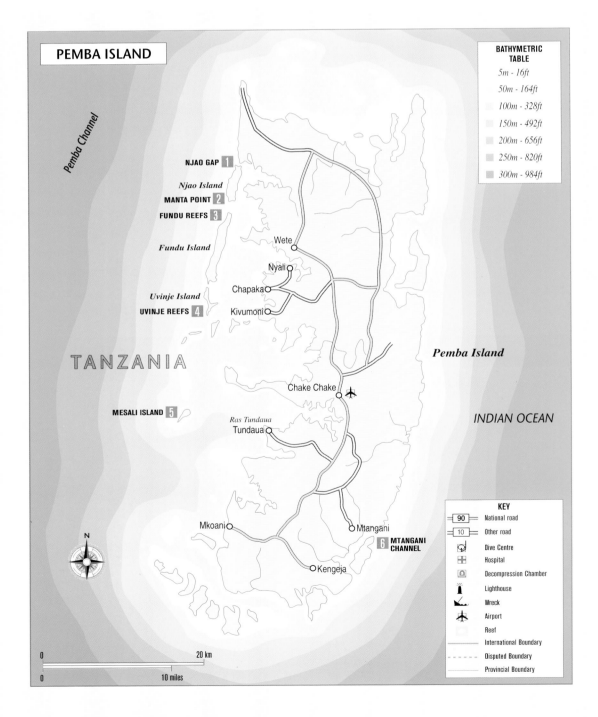

PEMBA ISLAND

BATHYMETRIC TABLE
5m - 16ft
50m - 164ft
100m - 328ft
150m - 492ft
200m - 656ft
250m - 820ft
300m - 984ft

Pemba Channel

NJAO GAP 1
Njao Island
MANTA POINT 2
FUNDU REEFS 3
Wete
Fundu Island
Nyali
Chapaka
Uvinje Island
UVINJE REEFS 4
Kivumoni

TANZANIA

Pemba Island

Chake Chake

MESALI ISLAND 5

INDIAN OCEAN

Ras Tundaua
Tundaua

Mkoani
Mtangani
6 MTANGANI CHANNEL
Kengeja

KEY
90 | National road
10 | Other road
Dive Centre
Hospital
Decompression Chamber
Lighthouse
Wreck
Airport
Reef
International Boundary
Disputed Boundary
Provincial Boundary

N

0 _____ 20 km
0 _____ 10 miles

the south boasts great species abundance and diversity, good visibility and exciting tidal challenges. Between them lies the popular tourist spot, Zanzibar Island, offering excellent diving around Mnemba Atoll in the north. However, for diving it does not rival the splendour or diversity of the Pemba or Mafia reefs.

PEMBA ISLAND

Pemba, the lush emerald isle off East Africa, is separated from the mainland by the seemingly bottomless blue Pemba Channel. When Cousteau visited this area with the *Calypso* in 1967, he recorded that the divers discovered a treasure trove of marine life. Still occasionally true today, this channel is characterized by superb visibility, sometimes more than 50m (165ft), and big fish, such as sharks, barracuda, tuna, Manta Rays and Whale Sharks. Live corals in Pemba have been recorded to depths of 64m (210ft), covering between 21 and 60 per cent of the island's coastline.

Guidebooks claim that the best diving is on the west coast of Pemba. Names such as **Njao**

RIGHT *Banded Pipefish* (Syngnathidae) *share the sea horse's unusual habit of the male carrying the fertilized eggs until they hatch.*

Gap 1, **Manta Point** 2, **Fundu** 3 and **Uvinje** 4 reefs and **Mesali Island** 5 roll off the tongues of seasoned Pemban divers – and for good reason. Here you can drift along dramatic cliff walls that stretch down to the blue depths. These walls are alive with huge Gorgonian Sea Fans and colourful corals. Reminiscent of the Red Sea, the reefs dance with an array of tropical marine life, some species being exclusive to these shores. Yellow-edged Chromis (*Chromis pembae*), a small rare chromis damselfish, is named after the island.

Night diving provides an opportunity to watch the mesmerising spectacle of a Spanish Dancer (*Hexabranchus sanguineus*) as it undulates bright red and white through the black water.

Pemba's wilder east coast has recently started to attract the thrill-seekers. Less protected from the elements, the east coast

offers adrenaline-filled diving and a good chance to see the big stuff. Live-aboards can anchor in the **Mtangani Channel** 6 where still waters reflect the mangrove roots and coconut palms lining peaceful shores. For

ABOVE *A diver looking through the* Paraportiani *wreck at a stingray feeling through the sand for a meal.*

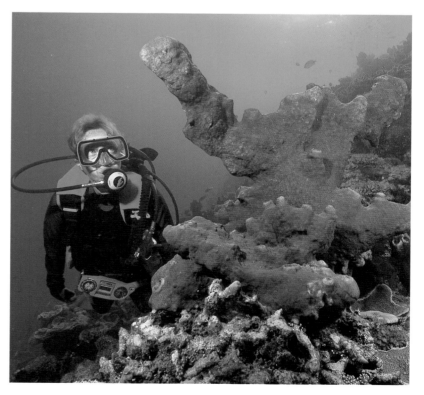

ABOVE *Diver inspecting a coral outcrop* (Montipora efflorescens) *on the upper reef slopes of Pemba Channel.*

INDIAN OCEAN

the experienced only, dives here are rapid, deep, blue-water drifts involving free descents without reference. Concentration is key, firstly on maintaining a constant depth while being swept up, down, and sideways by unpredictable currents and secondly on the surrounding blue. Drop in either a few hundred metres north or south of the channel, depending on which way the tide is flowing, and simply drift back past the channel entrance, zigzagging towards and away from the reef. You are searching for hammerheads (*Sphyrnidae*), marlin, Sailfish, Wahoo (*Acanthocybium solandri*), barracuda, tuna and kingfish (jacks and trevallies). As always, it is the chance of what you might see that is so exciting, rather than what you can expect to see. Keep constant vigil on depth and time, as the currents become dangerously strong, especially up and downward currents near the channel entrance. Take your time to observe the bizarre forms of the plankton drifting in the surface currents. The rewards are great, but diving on the east coast is not for the faint-hearted, and should only be done with an experienced guide and realistic dive plan.

MAFIA ISLAND

Mafia Island has been described as 'a shallow Pemba with more fish.' Certainly, the diving depth rarely exceeds 30m (100ft) and the profusion and diversity of the fish and plant life is extensive with over 400 species of fish and 50 different types of coral now recorded. The widespread and varied reefs in the southeastern region around **Chole Bay** [7] were declared Tanzania's first national marine park in 1995 and remain in good condition today despite the marine threats of recent years. Although the coral bleaching seriously affected Mafia's staghorn (*Acropora*)-dominated reefs, the remaining reefs were left surprisingly unharmed. Continuing on this positive note, the Green and Hawksbill Turtles still breed here successfully and blast-fishing has hardly touched Mafia's shores.

The beautiful coral gardens, walls, pinnacles and caverns around Chole Bay provide a rich feasting ground for clouds of damselfish, fusiliers, anthias (Fairy Basslets), butterfly and angelfish and every other imaginable Indian Ocean reef fish. An exceptional variety of nudibranchs and flatworms add to the carnival of tropical colour on these reefs. The constant ebb and flow of the tides carry the larger shoals of groupers, turtles and pelagic fish in and out of the bay and provides some exciting diving through a natural opening in the reef known locally as Kinasi Pass.

Kinasi Pass [8] can be treacherous on an ebb tide, but during slack/flood tides it is

TOP *The Regal Angelfish* (Pygoplites diacanthus) *is one of the most colourful of the angelfish family. Usually solitary or in pairs, they can be found swimming in and out of protective crevices.*
ABOVE *A typical macro subject for muck divers, the Emperor shrimp* (Periclimenes imperator) *lives commensally on several hosts such as Spanish Dancer nudibranch or, as here, on a sea cucumber.*

RIGHT *Mafia Island offers shallow yet spectacular diving and is home to a profusion of diverse plant and fish life. Over 400 species of fish and 50 different types of coral have been recorded.*

southern Mafia's premier site. The caverns, small walls and overhangs house a multitude of juvenile barracuda (*Sphyraenida*) and a variety of jacks and trevallies (*Carangidae*), larger game fish and Potato Grouper (Cod) (*Epinephelus tukula*) plus an expanse of dense, unspoiled sponges and corals. The dive starts at the ancient *Porites* spire The Pinnacle, where huge moray eels (*Muraenidae*) and giant batfish (*Ephippidae*) reside. The dive drifts westwards to the wall between 18m and 26m (60ft and 85ft), where fish feed on the flood tide. Fringing reefs lie north and south of The Pass, boasting pristine stands of blue-tipped Staghorn (*Acropora*) and large table corals. Lyretail (Lunartail) Groupers (*Variola louti*) and parrotfish (*Scaridae*) are often seen among the turtles and rays.

Dindini Wall 9 is one of the many spectacular dives in the archipelago outside Chole Bay. Sponges and corals adorn the upper section of the wall with Gorgonian Sea Fans and Whip Corals (*Gorgonacea*) on the lower section. The caves, caverns and overhangs harbour Humphead (Napoleon) Wrasse (*Cheilinus undulatus*) and groupers. This reef is close to a big drop-off so look into the blue for Sailfish, very large tuna and dolphins.

In recent years, the reefs further away from the southeast of Mafia Island have been explored and documented and are now visited by dive centres and passing live-aboard boats. New and less accessible sites are always a thrilling temptation for adventure seekers. Lying offshore from Ras Mkumbi in the north, **The Lighthouse** 10 consists of a variety of small walls, coral gardens and overhangs. A naturalist's heaven, they are frequented by large turtles and less common species such as Longnose Butterflyfish (*Forcipiger flavissimus*). Sailfish and Giant Trevally visit the more exposed reefs.

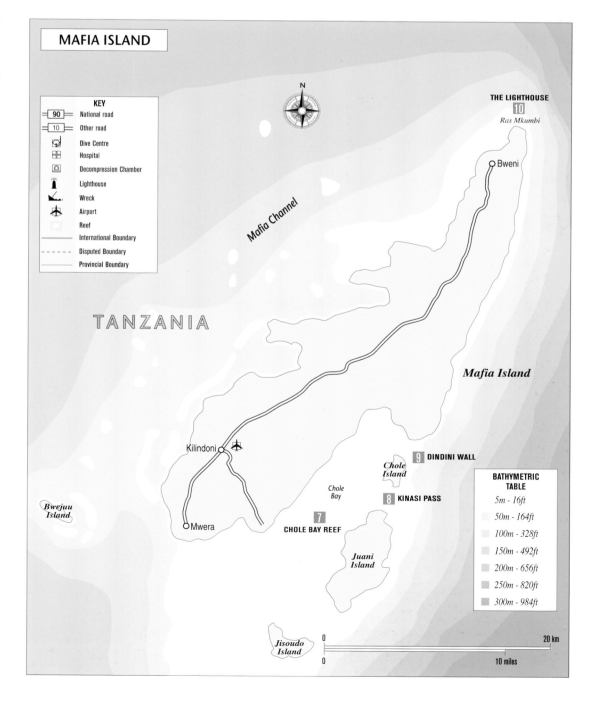

MAFIA ISLAND

KEY

90	National road
10	Other road
	Dive Centre
	Hospital
	Decompression Chamber
	Lighthouse
	Wreck
	Airport
	Reef
	International Boundary
	Disputed Boundary
	Provincial Boundary

THE LIGHTHOUSE 10
Ras Mkumbi

Bweni

Mafia Channel

TANZANIA

Mafia Island

Kilindoni

9 **DINDINI WALL**

Chole Island

Chole Bay

8 **KINASI PASS**

7 **CHOLE BAY REEF**

Bwejuu Island

Mwera

Juani Island

BATHYMETRIC TABLE

5m - 16ft	
50m - 164ft	
100m - 328ft	
150m - 492ft	
200m - 656ft	
250m - 820ft	
300m - 984ft	

Jisoudo Island

0 — 20 km
0 — 10 miles

SEYCHELLES

by Lawson Wood

THE NAME ALONE CONJURES UP IMAGES OF palm-fringed, white, sandy beaches, crystal clear waters, coral-fringed atolls and brightly coloured tropical fish. Those images become reality when you touch down on Mahé, the main island in the Seychelles archipelago just 4° South of the equator.

The Seychelles archipelago is what remained when Africa split away from India in the Pre-Cambrian period over 650 million years ago. Consisting almost entirely of granite, the main islands have little or no fringing reef for protection. Bird Island is the only true coral island in the northern group. All the other groups are coralline atolls, including the Amirantes, Farquar and, of course, one of the the largest coral atolls in the world, Aldabra.

The Islands' geographical position has also led to a varied and chequered past. The locals, or Seychellois, are a mixture of Indian, European, Asian and African descendants. The origins are so varied that all classification was abandoned in 1911. This amazing racial mix

TOP LEFT *The general profile of the main Seychelles Islands is of granite boulders which usually continue underwater where low encrusting corals and sponges are found.*

TOP RIGHT *The marina at Victoria, capital of the Seychelles. The crystal clear waters are a natural breeding ground for many species of fish.*

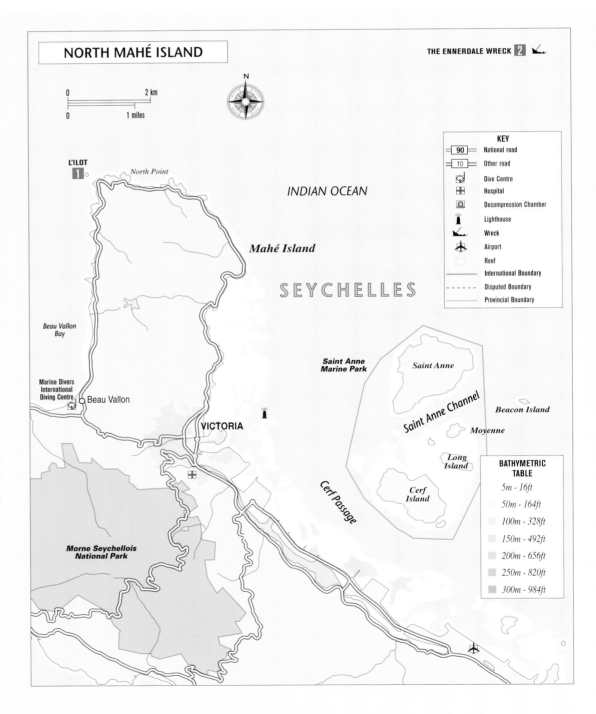

also accounts for the relaxed, hospitable atmosphere, where even language takes a side step from French, English and Creole, which is the language of the local people, of the market place and of the kitchens.

The islands have been visited over the centuries for victualling by Arab traders and pirates. It was not until 1770, when the first French colonists settled with their African slaves, that man started to make an impression on the islands. The French were succeeded by the British, who made the Seychelles a separate crown colony in 1903. It finally became an autonomous nation in 1977 after a coup by France-Albert René. The Republic of Seychelles is today an independent, non-aligned country with a combination of ethnic affinities that have resulted in a culture that is unmistakably Seychellois.

Nestled in the Indian Ocean, the Seychelles escaped human habitation until the early 18th century. Their oceanic isolation accounted for a vast number of rare species of animals and plants amid lush vegetation. Many endemic birds thrive on several of the isolated islands. This island group is an oasis for marine life with over 900 species of fish recorded. While El Niño had a devastating effect on the inshore coral reefs, the offshore and granite boulder communities have

recovered well. Interestingly, the upwelling also brought an increase in fish numbers at shallower reefs and this more than compensated for poorer quality corals.

The subtropical Vallée de Mai on Praslin has been hailed as the original Garden of Eden. The valley is a World Heritage Site and known for its many ancient forest specimens including the coco de mer tree. At up to 22kg (48lb), the coco de mer nut is the biggest seed in the world. Going to Praslin's sister island La Digue is like stepping back in time. Transport is by bicycle or oxcart. The island is instantly recognizable from advertising campaigns and is home to a population of giant turtles. These photogenic islands have massive granite boulders and palm trees hanging over the edge of the crystal clear blue sea. The islands off Praslin, and in particular South Felicité, all offer diving that includes encounters with sharks, turtles and Bumphead Parrotfish.

1 L'ILOT

This tiny cluster of granite boulders topped by palm trees is located on the exposed tip of Beau Vallon Bay at North Point. Susceptible to strong currents due to the confluence of tidal streams, the site can only be dived at slack water, but this jumble of rocks are

bursting with marine life. The exposed surfaces have only small clusters of soft corals and are mainly overrun by rock oysters and mussels. In sheltered sections golden cup corals predominate. Small gorgonias and sea fans can be found in deeper waters. When the tides and weather conditions are right, L'Ilot is particularly popular at night for its large numbers of Spanish Dancer nudibranchs, lobsters and sleeping parrotfish. Between the small island and the mainland the current is usually quite strong, but with care this small cluster of boulders in the centre yields one of the highest densities of life I have seen anywhere. Small Peppered Moray Eels vie for space among thousands of Durban Hinge-beak shrimps, so densely packed that the young often sit on the heads of the adults. L'Ilot is also near the St Anne Marine Park where encounters with Whale Sharks are common.

2 THE *ENNERDALE*

The *Ennerdale* wreck is a former British Royal Navy Fleet Auxiliary motor tanker, owned by the Anglo-Norness Shipping Co. Ltd. Built in Kiel by Lieler Howaldtswerke A.G. in 1963, she was chartered to the Royal Fleet Auxiliary (RFA) in 1967. The 216m (710ft), 29,189 tonne *Ennerdale* had a beam of 30m (100ft), a top speed of 29km/h (16 knots) and was loaded with 41,500 tonnes of refined furnace oil and gasoil to supply HM Frigate *Andromeda*. Interestingly, the ship's company were awarded the Wilkinson Sword of Peace for rescuing staff of the weather station at Gough Island in severe weather. The *Ennerdale*'s service with the RFA lasted only three years. She sank on 1 June 1970 on a sandbank after striking an uncharted rock seven miles from Port Victoria (lat 04°29'36"N, long 55°31'22"E), badly holing her starboard side.

The *Ennerdale*'s 18 British officers and 42 Seychellois seamen all abandoned safely. The wreck, considered a navigation hazard, was demolished and is now lying in three sections in 30m (100ft) of water. Dives tend to be around the stern where the ship is mostly

RIGHT *Zebra flatworms are colourful coral reef foragers only 2¾cm (1 in) long. Grazing on algae, which grows around the rim of hard corals, they move with impunity over stinging coral cells.*

INDIAN OCEAN

intact, with the wheelhouse and propeller readily accessible. The main part of the superstructure is quite open and undergoing colonization by soft and hard corals, with fire coral in abundance on some of the upper sections. As you descend to the ship, the water column soon becomes crowded with large schools of Longfin Batfish (*Platax teira*) which will follow you about on the entire dive.

The bows tend to have a congregation of stingrays and small Whitetip Reef Sharks, but these head off into the blue as soon as you approach them. The tangled superstructure is quite interesting and, being quite open, allows for relatively safe exploration. Due to the depth limitations of the wreck, it is better to swim back towards the stern where it is home to numerous moray eels,

schools of batfish and Golden-lined Snapper (*Lutjanus boutton*) vying for attention. The underside of the hull is covered in large mussels and oysters.

3 SOUTH FELICITÉ

The southern, outer wall of Felicité has a deeply scoured granite cliff, with gullies and canyons cut into the steeply sloping wall.

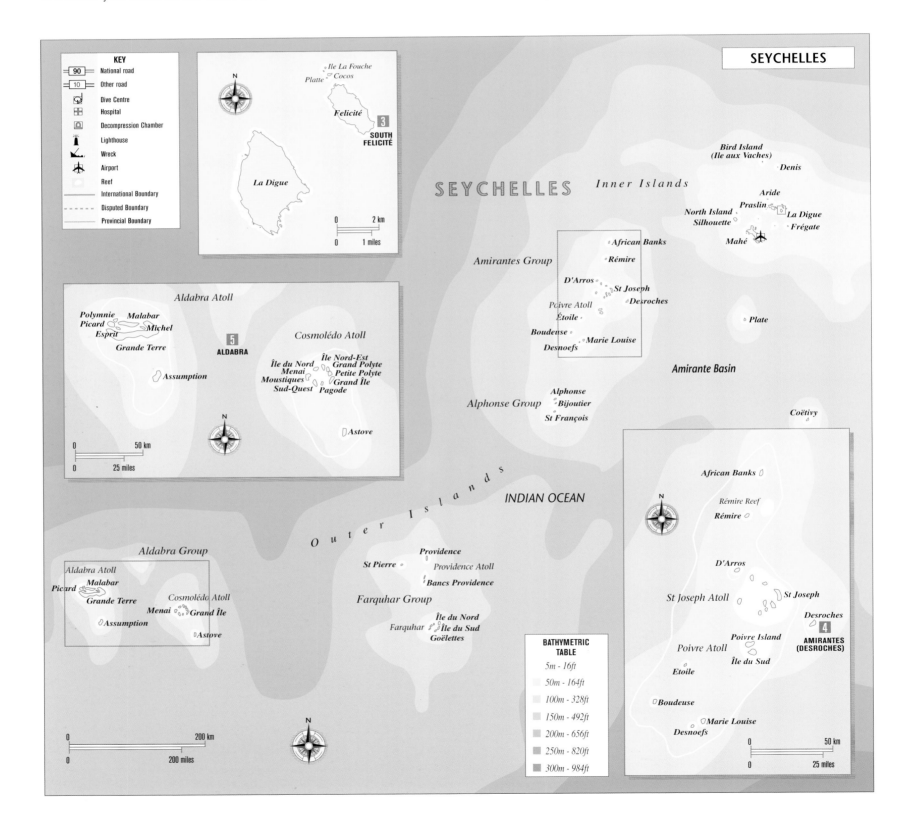

With a maximum depth of only 15m (50ft), the site is ideal for extended dives. There is oceanic surge on this exposed headland, so dives are only done in near-perfect conditions. The main attraction of this site is the chance to dive with Grey and Whitetip Reef and Nurse Sharks, as there are always five to eight of these. Unfazed by divers, they hunt in the shallow waters for reef fish and will come quite close. Turtles are also common.

4 AMIRANTES

The Admiral's Islands, as they were formerly known, are a group of 17 coral cays, islets and atolls. The largest island, Desroches, is on the southern side of a huge submerged atoll. All diving is off Desroches, unless you are on the only live-aboard dive boat in the area. Centuries of winds and waves have sculpted the reef crest of Desroches into a series of caves, caverns, overhangs, gullies and canyons. Divers enter these caverns on the reef crest, drop into the main cavern beside schools of batfish, Bengal snapper and sleeping Nurse Sharks, then negotiate the wide entrance and passageway to the outer reef where brilliant red Gorgonian Sea Fans with Longnose Hawkfish can be found. Several species of clownfish and pufferfish are all common in the area and while the outer wall can be somewhat barren, the wave-sculpted gullies are crammed with marine life.

5 ALDABRA

Aldabra is a UNESCO World Heritage Site. Located 1150km (715 miles) southwest of Mahé, the Aldabra group could be the most pristine islands in the Indian Ocean. Apart from seasonal nature wardens on the main atoll, there is now no human habitation. Only private charter yachts, a live-aboard dive boat and passing cruisers ever come this way. One of the best dives is through the main channel on the flooding tide where divers are swept into the main lagoon, passing schools of Eagle Rays, stingrays, groups of sharks and large groupers, all tempted into the channel by passing prey.

WHALE SHARKS

Nothing quite prepares you for that massive rush of adrenaline as you slip over the side of a boat into the water and see a monster of the deep, with gigantic shark fins, seemingly rushing straight at you, mouth agape. Reason tells you that this shark is a plankton eater, but your instinctive, primeval reactions tell you that this is most definitely a shark and the scientists could be wrong.

The Whale Shark (*Rhincodon typus*) is the largest fish in the sea and eats the smallest of creatures, having a diet almost exclusively of plankton, that life-giving soup of the oceans. Very much a shark in shape, but reaching whale-like proportions, the fish has tough skin, gills and a vertical tail, which it moves from side to side for propulsion. As the largest of the shark family it is also the largest fish and the largest cold-blooded animal in the world. By comparison, whales are warm-blooded, air-breathing mammals with skin, hairs and a large horizontal tail, which is moved up and down for propulsion.

My first encounter with a Whale Shark was with one of a large feeding-group that congregates each year in the St Anne Marine National Park off the island of Mahé, east of Victoria, capital of the Seychelles. When approached by snorkellers and divers, the sharks may stop in mid water and 'stand' on their tails. Never hold onto any of the fins or try to ride them. They will react as if being attacked from the rear and a 20-ton shark putting on a burst of speed is a formidable creature and can swat you aside like a tiny, irrelevant piece of flotsam.

The Shark Research Institute gave us specific instructions on how to interact with the Whale Sharks without frightening or harming the creatures. When the shark is still or moving slowly in the water, you can swim towards the head, allowing the shark to take a good look at you. If the shark decides to allow you to swim close enough, then you can gently stroke the top of its head. The Whale Shark appears to enjoy this sensation (as if we were giant cleaner fish) and will rise slowly to the surface to allow for greater interaction. The thrill of swimming with the largest fish in the sea is an unforgettable and humbling experience. We soon learned about the speed of the creatures as we tried to keep up with them. We saw the interaction of hundreds of remoras, cobia, juvenile Golden Trevally and thousands of other jacks swarming around the Whale Sharks feeding on the soup of stinging plankton and *Ctenophores* (thank goodness for full wet suits). We quickly appreciated how insignificant we were compared to these gentle giants who wander the oceans. And then the sharks stopped just long enough to let us catch up with them and allow us the privilege of scratching the tops of their heads.

Back on the boat, breathless with nervous excitement, eyes gleaming, smiles from ear to ear, someone looked at me and said 'did that really happen?' I could only smile in return as I rapidly rewound my film to be ready for another experience of a lifetime.

THE CHAGOS ARCHIPELAGO

by R Charles Anderson

CHAGOS, AN ISOLATED GROUP OF ATOLLS and reefs, lies 480km (300 miles) south of the Maldives in the central Indian Ocean. This is one of the world's least accessible places.

The archipelago consists of five atolls and 10 reefs and submerged shoals. There are about 50 islands, which in general appearance are similar to those of the Maldives. There is a US military base on the southernmost atoll, Diego Garcia. The other islands are uninhabited. Because of the military presence, the whole archipelago is off limits to visitors.

The French and the British laid rival claim to the islands in the 18th century, with the French establishing coconut plantations on several of the islands. However, the capture of Mauritius (from where the French had administered the Chagos) in 1810, left the islands firmly in British control, a position that was ratified by the Treaty of Paris in 1814. The Chagos has remained a British possession to this day, and is now known officially as the British Indian Ocean Territory.

TOP LEFT *The northeastern part of Peros Banhos Atoll. Most of these islands have been declared nature reserves to protect the breeding grounds of seabirds.*
TOP RIGHT *Going ashore in Salomon Atoll. It is a popular anchorage for yachts and there can be up to 20 at a time.*

In 1966 a 50-year agreement was signed between the UK and the USA, granting the USA use of the islands for defence purposes. Under this agreement the coconut plantations were closed and the workers forcibly deported to Mauritius in 1970. In December 2000, after an appeal to the High Court in London, the displaced islanders, or *ilois*, won the right to return to the Chagos.

The British government is currently investigating the feasibility of re-establishing settlements in the Chagos; and options for viable commercial activities. One possibility is diving tourism. Until that happens, commercial dive charters remain banned. To dive in the Chagos you will have to join an authorized scientific expedition, or travel there by private yacht. Divers who do manage to find their way to the Chagos will find the diving very similar to that in the Maldives. However, there are a few fascinating differences. For one, the Maldives lacks the submerged 'offshore' reefs that are so common in the Chagos. Also, the Chagos is home to a few marine animals found nowhere else in the world, for example the Chagos Anemonefish, (*Amphiprion chagosensis*).

As with the Maldives, the entire Chagos is one enormous dive site. To choose just a handful of spots is almost impossible, so I have tried to pick a variety of different dive types, from each of the three main atolls.

While it is possible to dive from the beach of some islands, you really need a boat to get around the atolls and to make these dives.

1 THE PASS (SALOMON ATOLL)

Salomon is a small atoll, only 8km (5 miles) long, but it is almost entirely enclosed. As a result it offers particularly safe anchorage and is the favourite of visiting yachtsmen. The single entrance channel on the northern side is wide, but shallow – only 6–8m (20–25ft) deep. This channel offers some great diving. A flood tide brings clear water from outside, and a modicum of safety too, since the current will carry you into the atoll and not out into the ocean if you miss your boat cover. At the outer edge of the channel, the reef drops away steeply to great depths. Near the edge are superb *Acropora* table corals, which further down the slope are replaced by beautiful sea fans. Look out here for the Chagos Anemonefish, which prefer reef slopes to shallower reef flats. This is also a likely place for sharks.

2 MAPOU GARDEN (PEROS BANHOS ATOLL)

This small sheltered reef lies on the inside of Île Mapou, inside the northwestern corner of Peros Banhos Atoll. Here a calm shallow embayment, no more than 8m (26ft) deep, offers extended bottom times among rich corals interspersed with white sandy patches. This is ideal territory for the macro photographer hunting obscure wrasse and gobies, and also for searching out nudibranchs and flatworms. This is a particularly good site to visit for a second dive, after a deep dive on the outer reef, or if conditions are too rough on the outside.

3 VIENNA ROCK (PEROS BANHOS ATOLL)

In the southwestern corner of Peros Banhos Atoll is Île Vache Marine. On the northern side of this small island is a superb dive site, called Vienna Rock. It could be dived from the beach, but a small boat makes access much easier. Vienna Rock is a coral rock pinnacle reaching up from about 15m (50ft) to 8m 25ft) and it is plastered with marine life. Thick growths of gorgonias sprout from the walls, and in their shade a rich carpet of sponges and ascidians provides a rich hunting ground for the macro photographer. Further out, the sandy bottom slopes slowly down, providing a home for many other fascinating creatures.

4 MIDDLE BROTHER (GREAT CHAGOS BANK)

The Great Chagos Bank is a vast maze of submerged coral reefs. The Three Brothers is a group of four (yes, four) small islands on the western side of the bank. Because the atoll rim of the Great Chagos Bank is not complete, big ocean swells crash in on the Three Brothers from all sides, even on calm days. Depending on conditions at the time, there may not be a sheltered side on which to anchor. One possible anchorage is on the extreme southeastern side of the reef of Middle Brother. This will put you right next to a rich coral wall and over a flat sand and coral reef step in 18m (60ft). Getting in could not be simpler – jump straight off the boat into a coral-lined swimming pool with more than 30m (100ft) visibility. There are great stony corals, including a dense patch of *Heliopora* corals on the main reef slope, as well as some unusual sponges. Several different species of parrotfish, numerous jacks, emperors and goatfish, and many others can be seen.

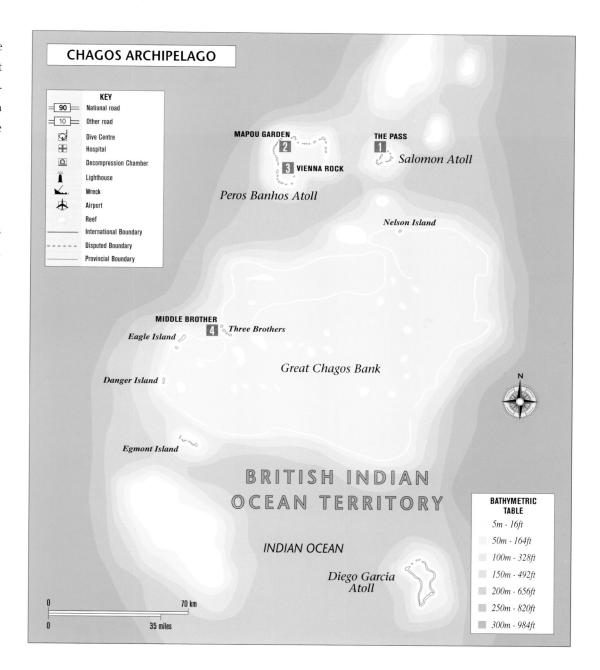

CHAGOS ARCHIPELAGO

KEY
90 National road
10 Other road
Dive Centre
Hospital
Decompression Chamber
Lighthouse
Wreck
Airport
Reef
International Boundary
Disputed Boundary
Provincial Boundary

MAPOU GARDEN 2
3 VIENNA ROCK
THE PASS 1
Salomon Atoll
Peros Banhos Atoll
Nelson Island

MIDDLE BROTHER
4 *Three Brothers*
Eagle Island
Great Chagos Bank
Danger Island
N
Egmont Island
BRITISH INDIAN OCEAN TERRITORY

BATHYMETRIC TABLE
5m - 16ft
50m - 164ft
100m - 328ft
150m - 492ft
200m - 656ft
250m - 820ft
300m - 984ft

INDIAN OCEAN
Diego Garcia Atoll

0 ———— 70 km
0 ———— 35 miles

ABOVE *A diver takes a closer look at the north side of the Vienna Rock, in Peros Banhos Atoll. This side is festooned with Gorgonian Sea Fans.*

MAURITIUS

by Alan Mountain

ALTHOUGH IT IS SOMETIMES COMPARED unfavourably with the Seychelles, the Maldives and Kenya, Mauritius is an exciting place to dive. Here it is possible to play with Spotted Eagle Rays (*Aetobatus narinari*), watch sharks hunt their prey, swim through forests of gorgonias – some over 2m (7ft) in height – see walking Filament-finned Scorpionfish (*Inimicus filamentosus*), also known as Dragon scorpionfish and Indian Walkman, flex their beautiful wings when they feel threatened. Pass through lobster-filled chimneys and canyons. You can feel the power and purpose of tuna (*Thunnus* sp. and *Katsuwonus pelamis*), Wahoo (*Acanthocybium solandri*) and even marlin (*Makaira* sp.). The quiet diffidence of shoals of jacks and trevallies (*Carangoides* sp.), as they briefly encircle you and then move off, leaves you wondering whether their curiosity was satisfied.

There is, however, another dimension to diving in Mauritius. The island has some of the most relaxed and amiable dive centres in

TOP LEFT Île aux Bénitiers offers good snorkelling in the translucent waters of the coral lagoon that encapsulate the Le Morne coastline.
TOP RIGHT The Mahébourg coastline offers the romance of a tropical island basking in a giant basin of warm turquoise waters, where divers can also try other forms of watersport.

the world that are nevertheless professionally operated to a high standard. Here you are not a number, or just another diver waiting in a queue to be whisked off to a dive site and taken down by a divemaster who has become an automaton. In Mauritius the natural hospitality of the people comes bubbling through and you are soon made to feel as if you are diving with 'buddies' whom you have known all your life. The dive centres, most of which are hotel-based, normally operate a six-day week with a morning dive at 09:30 and an afternoon dive at 13:30 (depending on demand) and so it is possible for suitably qualified divers to arrange a dive at a time and place of their choice.

Mauritius is a small island and so access by road to dive sites in different parts of the island is relatively easy. With the exception of the south coast, where the coral reefs are less developed, Mauritius offers interesting dive sites right around the island. The most popular are those along the west and north coasts.

SOUTHWEST REGION

The southwest region stretches from south of the Le Morne Peninsula up to Black River. The underwater topography is made up of a sandy floor dotted with coral patches and rocky outcrops encrusted with corals. An interesting feature is that nearly 60 percent of the corals in this subregion display their polyps in day-

light while sifting the water for zooplankton, which creates interesting opportunities for macrophotography.

WEST COAST

Off the west coast the best diving is to be found from Black River up to just north of Flic en Flac. Diving takes place in a fairly concentrated area characterized by a series of more-or-less parallel terraces. These are made up of boulders interspersed with small caves, larger caverns, archways, chimneys and tunnels – leading to a sharp drop-off where some dives extend down to 60m (200ft). Top sites include **Couline Bambou** [1], **Cathedral** [2] and **Shark Place** [3].

NORTH OF THE ISLAND

In the north of the island, the best diving takes place between Pointe aux Piments in the south and Pointe l'Hortal in the north with the offshore islands of Grand Baie offering some excellent sites to experienced divers. This part of the island is popular with holiday-makers, offering long, uninterrupted white beaches in the west and the tourist bustle around Grand Baie in the north. In the west the sea bottom is sandy and most diving is done either on rocky outcrops or along the barrier reef and on the drop-off. In the north the bottom is made up of a volcanic shelf that extends from the main island to the offshore

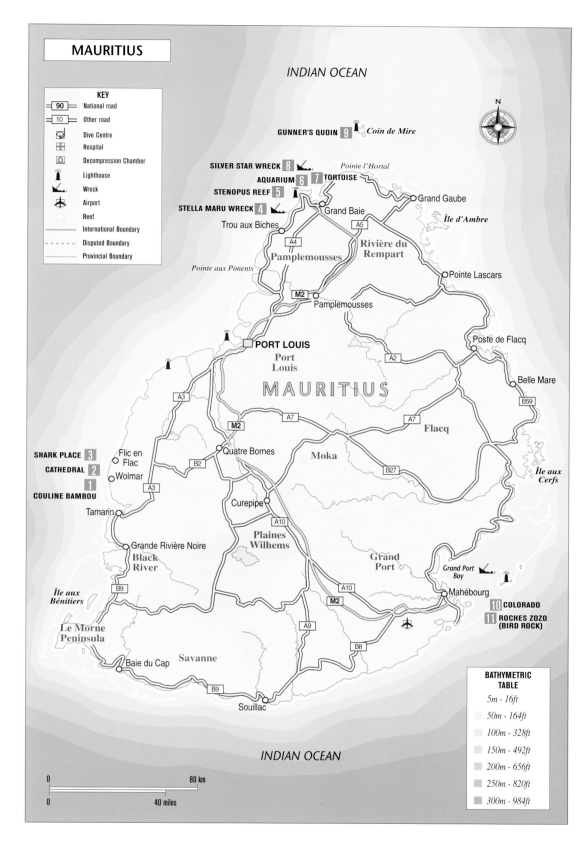

MAURITIUS

KEY

90	National road
10	Other road
	Dive Centre
	Hospital
	Decompression Chamber
	Lighthouse
	Wreck
	Airport
	Reef
——	International Boundary
- - -	Disputed Boundary
·····	Provincial Boundary

INDIAN OCEAN

N

GUNNER'S QUOIN 9 — Coin de Mire

SILVER STAR WRECK 8 — Pointe l'Hortal
AQUARIUM 6 7 TORTOISE
STENOPUS REEF 5
STELLA MARU WRECK 4 — Grand Baie
Trou aux Biches — Grand Gaube — Île d'Ambre

A5
A4
Pamplemousses — Rivière du Rempart
Pointe aux Piments — Pointe Lascars

M2
Pamplemousses

PORT LOUIS
Port Louis — Poste de Flacq
A2
MAURITIUS — Belle Mare
B59
A3
A7 — A7 — Flacq
M2
SHARK PLACE 3 — Flic en Flac — Quatre Bornes — Moka — B27 — Île aux Cerfs
CATHEDRAL 2 — B2
1 — Wolmar
COULINE BAMBOU — A3
Tamarin — Curepipe — A10
Plaines Wilhems — Grand Port
Grande Rivière Noire — Grand Port Bay
Black River — Mahébourg
Île aux Bénitiers — B9 — A10 — 10 COLORADO
M2 — 11 ROCHES ZOZO (BIRD ROCK)
Le Morne Peninsula — A9
Savanne — B8
Baie du Cap
B9
Souillac

INDIAN OCEAN

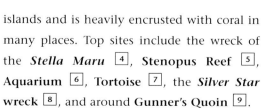

0 — 80 km
0 — 40 miles

BATHYMETRIC TABLE
5m - 16ft
50m - 164ft
100m - 328ft
150m - 492ft
200m - 656ft
250m - 820ft
300m - 984ft

islands and is heavily encrusted with coral in many places. Top sites include the wreck of the **Stella Maru** 4, **Stenopus Reef** 5, **Aquarium** 6, **Tortoise** 7, the **Silver Star wreck** 8, and around **Gunner's Quoin** 9.

The north of the island is well protected from the prevailing southeasterly winds, which makes year-round diving possible.

EAST

There are some exciting dives in the east, but they are weather dependent. In the south some of the best diving can be done off Mahébourg, the top sites being **Colorado** 10, a mini grand canyon of the sea, and **Roches Zozo** 11 (Bird Rock), which features tunnels, canyons and a huge arch.

TOP *Squirrelfish* (Sargocentron caudimaculatum) *are common on outer reef slopes.*

CENTRE The Stella Maru *was purposely sunk in the 1980s and is still largely intact. It is one of the top sites north of the island.*

ABOVE *Queen Coris* (Coris frerei) *is an uncommon wrasse with strikingly different colour phases. It is often seen on its own.*

MOZAMBIQUE

by Stefania Lamberti

LONG PROTECTED FROM OVER-EXPLOITATION by Mozambique's civil war, the reefs along this 2500-km (1550-mile) sweep of southeast African coastline have been lying forgotten and untouched. Although the land was pillaged and the abandoned tourist resorts raided by refugees, the offshore reefs thrived and developed into magnificent underwater wonderlands. Situated between the equatorial tropical and the South African subtropical zone, the reefs have escaped the dangerous rise in temperature that has caused widespread coral bleaching. These pristine reefs are a showpiece of untouched marine environments.

PONTA DO OURO

This thriving border town, just a hop across the border from South Africa, was a popular holiday destination many years ago, before the war ravaged the country. It was reopened in 1994 and, although it is a growing commercial centre with a bank, a few restaurants,

TOP LEFT *Ponta do Ouro has been accessible to divers since 1994 and has grown from war-ravaged village to bustling diving destination.*

TOP RIGHT *The Inhambane estuary forms an enormous, calm, clearwater lagoon with mangroves, small islands and sandy coves where pansy shells lie just below the sand.*

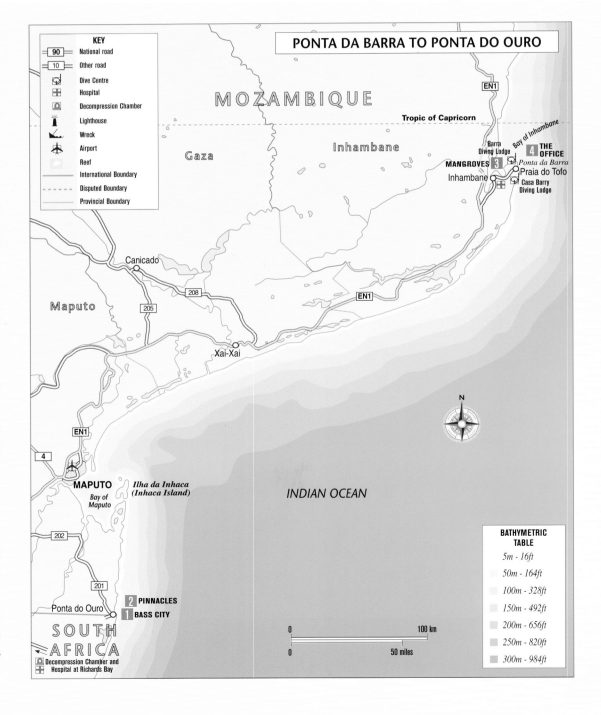

PONTA DA BARRA TO PONTA DO OURO

KEY
90 National road
10 Other road
Dive Centre
Hospital
Decompression Chamber
Lighthouse
Wreck
Airport
Reef
International Boundary
Disputed Boundary
Provincial Boundary

MOZAMBIQUE

Tropic of Capricorn

Gaza

Inhambane

EN1

Bay of Inhambane

Barra Diving Lodge

4 THE OFFICE

MANGROVES 3

Ponta da Barra

Praia do Tofo

Inhambane

Casa Barry Diving Lodge

Canicado

208
205

Maputo

EN1

Xai-Xai

N

EN1

4

MAPUTO
Bay of Maputo

*Ilha da Inhaca
(Inhaca Island)*

INDIAN OCEAN

202

201

Ponta do Ouro

2 PINNACLES
1 BASS CITY

SOUTH
AFRICA

Decompression Chamber and
Hospital at Richards Bay

0 ——— 100 km
0 ——— 50 miles

BATHYMETRIC TABLE
5m - 16ft
50m - 164ft
100m - 328ft
150m - 492ft
200m - 656ft
250m - 820ft
300m - 984ft

renovated hotels, bed-and-breakfast establishments and a large campsite, it is still a rustic, seaside village on the never-ending beach that frames the eastern shore of Africa. It has become one of Mozambique's most accessible and most popular dive destinations. About 33 reefs line the coast, each different in topography, nature and character, each offering a unique underwater experience. All the sites are accessible by boat from the beach of Ponta do Ouro and the smaller one of Ponta Malongane. After the dive, during the boat ride back to shore, there is a chance of seeing a Whale Shark or the resident pod of dolphins.

1 BASS CITY

Five coral outcrops at a depth of 25m (80ft) form the domain of a stocky Potato Grouper (or bass) and his harem of healthy females. Although he fiercely protects his kingdom from strangers, Bert (as he has been affectionately called), welcomes divers. Curious and quite nosy he might single out a diver and try to bite shiny gadgets such as torches, watches and cameras. Bert has an entourage of juvenile Golden Trevally pilot fish who use his bulk for protection while darting out to catch crustaceans and molluscs buried in the sand.

The five outcrops are covered in sponges and algae that sway gently in the swell. Among them moray eels take shelter in the fissures, often accompanied by cleaner shrimps. Thousands of sweepers and small-fry hover in dense clouds for protection, but they become easy prey for the fast-moving groupers. Where the reef meets the sandy floor lionfish lie motionless, waiting for unsuspecting prey to venture too close. Beneath a thin layer of sand, stingrays and electric rays wait for their chance to pounce.

2 PINNACLES

Pinnacles is 4km (2½ miles) offshore and 12km (7½ miles) from Ponta do Ouro. It is a dive suitable only for experienced divers as it reaches a depth of 40m (130ft). Although this reef is rich in corals, Gorgonian Sea Fans, colourful schools of snappers and shimmering

shoals of game fish, they are not the reason for the popularity of this dive site. Divers come to pinnacles to see sharks: Bull, Silvertip, Blacktip and the occasional Tiger.

The depth only allows for a short dive and all too soon it is time to abandon the ocean floor, but the underwater pageant follows divers to the surface. Schools of game fish come and go in the blue, the sharks may

TOP *The Tomato Grouper (Cephalopholis sonnerati) has a sturdy body and a large caudal fin which helps it lunge at prey from its hiding place.*
ABOVE *The Variegated (Leopard or Zebra) Shark (Stegostoma fasciatum) is one of the more docile inhabitants of the reefs. The body and tail are adapted to a life on the seafloor. It feeds on molluscs and crustaceans which it can crush in its powerful jaws.*

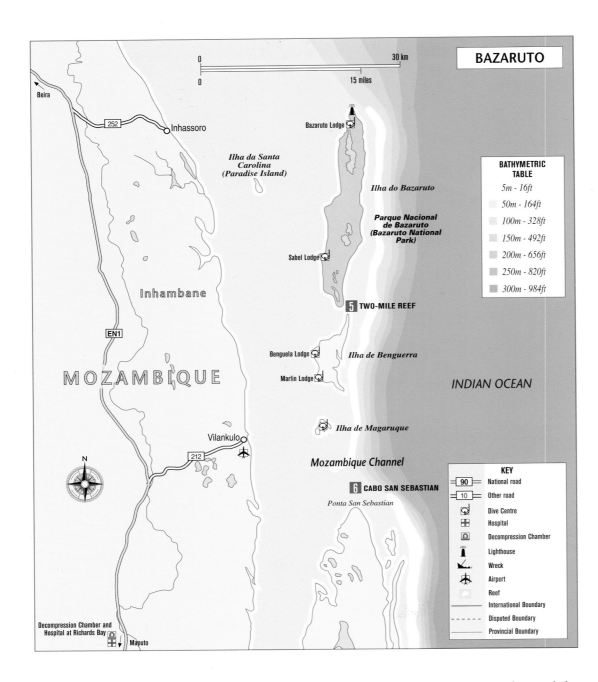

to dive here is at the end of the high tide when the flood tide brings clear water and the water flow slows before turning to rush out to sea again. Extremely rare Dugongs have been seen swimming along the channels.

4 THE OFFICE

About 15km (9½ miles) offshore, where the ocean floor reaches a depth of 25m (80ft), the reef forms an intricate ledge covered in a tapestry of corals, algae and sponges. Pelagics such as jacks regularly use this as a feeding site. Mantas hover in platoons waiting to be cleaned and graceful devilrays swarm in the blue above. This is the haunt of harems of Potato Groupers and lonely Leopard Sharks.

BAZARUTO ARCHIPELAGO

The sands of Africa's east coast rise and fall beneath the shallows of the Indian Ocean, forming undulating turquoise channels interspersed with sinuous islands. For early mariners these islands held the promise of slaves, pearls and spices, but today, for the dive adventurer, the reefs hold a natural treasure rich in marine life.

The Bazaruto Archipelago lies halfway between Mozambique's two main cities: Maputo (the capital) in the south and Beira in the north. The five islands that make up this group – Santa Carolina (or Paradise Island), Bazaruto, Benguerra, Magaruque and the tiny Bangué, were orphaned from the mainland some 30,000 years ago when the rising sea level filled the shallows between the African mainland and the sand dunes that lined the shore. Beyond these shifting dunes, submerged sandbanks solidified into sandstone and over time the tidal waters of the Indian Ocean carved an intricate maze of caves and gullies, which formed the substructure of the archipelago's tropical reefs. These reefs lie parallel to the line of islands and stretch from 20km (12½ miles) north of Santa Carolina to Cabo San Sebastian, a promontory south of the islands. All reefs are accessible by boat from Bazaruto and Benguerra.

follow the divers for a while and for the lucky few a marlin or Sailfish may make a fleeting, but breathtaking, appearance.

PONTA DA BARRA

The wild shores of central Mozambique have a magical aura. It looks as if time stopped here during the war, and never resumed ticking again, leaving the town of Inhambane and its surrounds in a strange juxtaposition of old Portuguese and local vernacular. This quiet enclave of expansive mangroves, low-lying islands and protected bays was only discovered in the late 1400s by Portuguese explorers. Today the only visitors are tourists, divers and backpackers looking for a quiet retreat where idyllic beaches

are framed by swaying coconut palms and the azure sea holds pristine, wild reefs inhabited by an unbelievable number of marine creatures. This is Mozambique's secret treasure.

3 MANGROVES

Great tidal movements change the sheltered area of the Bay of Inhambane from a marshy swamp to an intricate maze of quiet channels lined by mangrove trees. Many species of reef fish spend the early part of their lives here, hiding among the roots of the trees. Brittle stars, segmented worms and cowrie shells find shelter from the pounding ocean. Plants and animals here have adapted to cope with this alternating dry and wet world. The best time

ABOVE *Crown of Thorns Starfish* (Acanthaster planci) *is a reef predator that feed on stony coral polyps. They can destroy patches of reef.*

ABOVE *The Honeycomb Moray Eel* (Gymnothorax favagineus) *can grow to 1½m (5ft) long. It emerges at night to hunt octopuses.*

ABOVE *Gorgonian Dwarf or Whip Coral Goby* (Bryaninops yongei). *Only 3cm (1 in) long, it lives on sea whips at 15–40m (50–130ft).*

5 TWO-MILE REEF

Between the islands of Bazaruto and Benguerra, the top of the reef lies exposed during low tide to the waves of the ocean. Tidal movements between the open ocean and the shallows between the islands and the mainland can cause surge and varied visibility. The flood tide brings clear water and a procession of enormous schools of game fish like barracuda and trevallies.

The caves and gullies of the reef hide a variety of inhabitants: the juveniles hide from predators, the nocturnal fish such as the bigeyes, rest up till nightfall and several sharks take a rest. Whitetip Reef Sharks and Tawny Nurse Sharks have developed the skill of actively pumping water over their gills while at rest and breathing in their sleep.

RIGHT *The red colour and large eyes of the Bigeyes* (family Priacanthidae) *show their nocturnal lifestyle. By day they hide in caves.*

6 CABO SAN SEBASTIAN

The most stunning of the Archipelago's dive sites is Cabo San Sebastian – a reef that can be located only with GPS receivers. Earlier, only sport fishermen, who told larger-than-life stories about shoals of fish so huge that the waters boiled, frequented this spot. When divers first ventured to Cabo they found the fishermen's tales to be true. Huge schools of gamefish crowd the waters from the surface down to the reef, 30m (100ft) below. Potato Groupers of more than a metre (a yard) in length protect their harems, Grey Reef Sharks patrol the edges of the reef and huge turtles rest in the caves while mantas hover over the reef waiting to be cleaned.

SOUTH AFRICA

by Judy and Bruce Mann

SODWANA BAY

THIS WORLD HERITAGE SITE IS HOME TO a colony of coelacanths just a few hundred metres out to sea. Situated on the east coast of South Africa, about 300km (186 miles) north of Durban in the Greater St Lucia Wetland Park, Sodwana Bay is an eco-tourism destination offering interest both above and below the water. There are over 340 species of bird and large mammals including elephant, buffalo and rhino. A relatively safe launch from Jesser Point takes divers to a number of reef complexes that run parallel to the shoreline about one kilometre (half a mile) offshore. In the subtropical climate water temperatures vary from 21°(70°) to 28°C (82°F). Underwater visibility ranges from 10m (33ft) to 30m (100ft). Although diving is best from April to June, Sodwana Bay is usually good for diving at any time of the year.

The enormous biodiversity of the area is the result of being in the transition zone between the warm tropical north and the cooler subtropical south. The Agulhas current, usually a few kilometres offshore, brings warm tropical water southwards. This warming effect allows many tropical species to survive this far south. Hundreds of species of invertebrates have been identified and there are probably more awaiting discovery. Over 400 bony and 25 cartilaginous fish species are known to occur in the area. A group of coelacanths was recently discovered at a depth of about 100m (330ft) in Jesser Canyon off Jesser Point. These living fossils have remained relatively unchanged for over 300 million years and are related to the ancestors of the first terrestrial vertebrates.

1 TWO-MILE REEF

Two-Mile Reef, named for the distance from the launch site at Jesser Point, is particularly suitable for novice divers. Descending to the reef that varies in depth from 12m (40ft) to over 18m (60ft), a diver is likely to encounter huge shoals of zebrafish (*Diplodus cervinus hottentotus*), Humpback Snappers (*Lutjanus gibbus*), or Dusky Sweetlips (*Plectorhinchus chubbi*). They hang in columns in the water, parting and closing around divers. Once on the reef, divers can explore a range of caves and overhangs, as well as some low relief, flatter areas. The sand next to the reef should not be ignored, as this is the home of cuttlefish, rapidly changing their colour, tiny Fire Dartfish (Red Fire Gobies) (*Nemateleotris magnifica*) and Blue-streak Gobies (*Valenciennea strigata*). This is a popular night dive because it is close to shore and the launch is easy. The reef changes completely at night as the night shift emerges to take over from the diurnal species. Coral polyps extend their delicate tentacles in an astounding array of colours, and squirrelfish (*Sargocentron* spp.) emerge cautiously from the crevices in which they hide during the day.

2 FIVE-MILE REEF

For the more experienced diver, Five-Mile Reef is a little further from the launch site. Whale Sharks, turtles and dolphins and even the occasional Humpback Whale can be seen on the boat ride out to the reef. Humpback Whales migrate to breed off southern Mozambique during autumn and return to their Antarctic feeding grounds in spring, passing Sodwana Bay twice each year.

Ranging in depth from 15m (50ft) to 24m (79ft), the reef is a series of gullies, caves and overhangs. The tiny, brightly coloured nudibranchs (sea slugs), crabs, fan worms, snails, sea stars and tiny fish are usually well camouflaged. The more northerly sites, such as **Seven-Mile** 3 and **Nine-Mile** 4 reefs, offer a similar variety of fish and invertebrates, diversity of stony and soft corals and near-pristine reefs.

TOP LEFT *This aerial view of the Jesser Point area clearly shows the launch site, as well as the estuary and beach.*

TOP RIGHT *Sport divers gather for a pre-dive briefing before an exciting boat trip and spectacular dive on the Aliwal Shoal off Umkomaas, KwaZulu-Natal.*

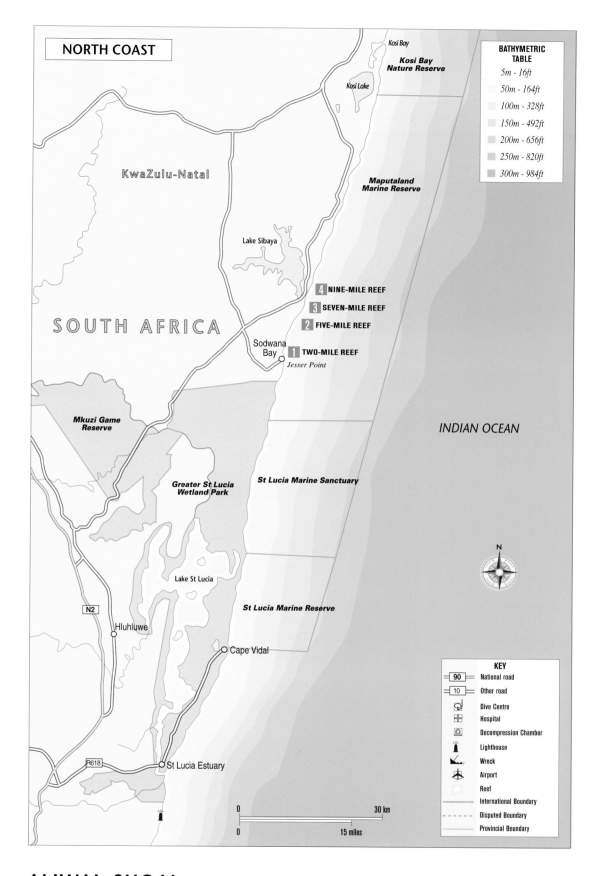

NORTH COAST

Kosi Bay

Kosi Bay
Nature Reserve

Kosi Lake

KwaZulu-Natal

Lake Sibaya

Maputaland
Marine Reserve

4 NINE-MILE REEF

3 SEVEN-MILE REEF

SOUTH AFRICA

2 FIVE-MILE REEF

Sodwana
Bay

1 TWO-MILE REEF

Jesser Point

Mkuzi Game
Reserve

INDIAN OCEAN

Greater St Lucia
Wetland Park

St Lucia Marine Sanctuary

Lake St Lucia

St Lucia Marine Reserve

N2

Hluhluwe

Cape Vidal

R618

St Lucia Estuary

	BATHYMETRIC TABLE
	5m - 16ft
	50m - 164ft
	100m - 328ft
	150m - 492ft
	200m - 656ft
	250m - 820ft
	300m - 984ft

KEY

90 National road
10 Other road
Dive Centre
Hospital
Decompression Chamber
Lighthouse
Wreck
Airport
Reef
International Boundary
Disputed Boundary
Provincial Boundary

0 — 30 km

0 — 15 miles

associated with inshore waters during the summer months. Depths range from 5m (16ft) to 35m (115ft), depending on the area, and visibility varies from 5m (16ft) to 25m (80ft), while the water temperature ranges from 18°C (65°F) to 24°C (75°C).

The boat ride to the reef can be exciting as the launch at the mouth of the Mkomazi River is tricky, requiring a skipper with nerves of steel and divers who can hold on tight. Currents usually prevail on the reef, so that long drift dives are often the order of the day. The caves and overhangs of the reef are best explored on calm days with little surge.

The reef has a wide variety of filter-feeding invertebrates such as large sponges in varying

TOP *Tiger rockcod or Striped-fin Grouper (Epinephelus posteli) waits in ambush for passing prey on a reef at Sodwana Bay.*

ABOVE *A hermit crab (Aniculus maximus) peers out of its home – a disused whelk shell. These animals grow out of their 'borrowed' homes and need to move into larger shells periodically.*

ALIWAL SHOAL

Situated on the KwaZulu-Natal south coast about 50km (30 miles) south of Durban, the small town of Umkomaas is home to a range of dive resorts and schools. A range of dive experiences are available, including shallow dives, shark dives and wreck dives. Aliwal

Shoal is about 4km (2½ miles) long, about 300m (330yd) wide and lies parallel to the shore. The shoal is an ancient sand dune that has been consolidated into beach rock. The shoal is about 5km (3 miles) offshore, washed by the clean, warm waters of the Agulhas current and is seldom influenced by the turbidity

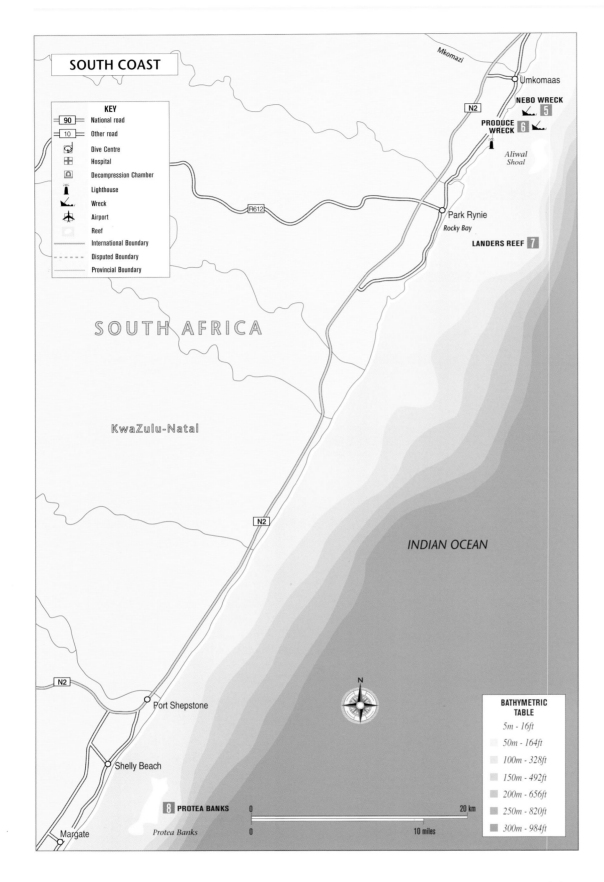

SOUTH COAST

KEY

90	National road
10	Other road
	Dive Centre
	Hospital
	Decompression Chamber
	Lighthouse
	Wreck
	Airport
	Reef
	International Boundary
	Disputed Boundary
	Provincial Boundary

Mkomazi

Umkomaas

N2

NEBO WRECK 5

PRODUCE WRECK 6

Aliwal Shoal

R612

Park Rynie

Rocky Bay

LANDERS REEF 7

S O U T H   A F R I C A

KwaZulu-Natal

N2

INDIAN OCEAN

N

Port Shepstone

BATHYMETRIC TABLE

	5m - 16ft
	50m - 164ft
	100m - 328ft
	150m - 492ft
	200m - 656ft
	250m - 820ft
	300m - 984ft

Shelly Beach

8 **PROTEA BANKS**

Margate

Protea Banks

0   20 km

0   10 miles

(*Sparidae*) such as the Slinger (*Chrysoblephus puniceus*) and the Englishman (*C. anglicus*). Silver gamefish such as Eastern Little Tuna (*Euthynnus affinis*), Pickhandle Barracuda (*Sphyraena jello*) and kingfish (*Caranx* spp.) are often seen circling above the reef. Dolphins and turtles may also be seen. The reef is also home to a range of colourful tropical and sub-tropical fish such as butterflyfish (*Chaetodon* spp.) and angelfish (*Pomacanthus* spp.).

Aliwal shoal is famous for its shark dives. Each year between June and September hundreds of Raggedtooth Sharks (*Carcharius taurus*), also known as Grey Nurse or Sand Tiger Sharks, gather as part of an annual northward breeding migration from the Eastern Cape towards the warm waters off northern KwaZulu-Natal and southern Mozambique. The fierce appearance of these sharks belies their rather timid nature. Their pointed, sharp teeth are designed for grasping fish and squid, and they prefer prey that they can swallow whole. They seldom attack humans unless provoked. Divers should, however, treat all sharks with respect and observe the appropriate protocols. Tiger sharks (*Galeocerdo cuvieri*) are also seen occasionally on Aliwal Shoal.

WRECKS OF THE *NEBO* AND THE *PRODUCE*

Near Aliwal Shoal, the wreck of the *Nebo* 5, which sank in 1884, and the *Produce* 6, which sank in 1974, both lie at a maximum depth of 30m (100ft). The *Produce* is rather unstable and occasionally leaks oil, while the *Nebo* is largely intact. Both wrecks are home to some very large Giant Groupers (*E. lanceolatus*) and moray eels (*Gymnothorax* spp.), while large kob (*Argyrosomus japonicus*) are often seen on the sand near the wrecks.

7 LANDERS REEF

Slightly south of Aliwal Shoal, Landers Reef is reached via the launch site at Rocky Bay. Hundreds of bright orange and red anthias dart above the fields of red and pink *Dendronephthya* Soft Tree corals that cover much of the

shapes, colonial and solitary ascidians, tunicates, and feather stars, as well as red algae. Enormous, branched, black corals wave in the deeper areas. Bright orange *Dendrophyllia* corals are common in low light areas under overhangs and in caves. A limited number of other species of stony and soft corals also

abound on the reef. The variety of bony fish is also good and over 300 different species have been identified, some of which are endemic and found nowhere else in the world. Enormous Potato Groupers (*Epinephelus tukula*) and Giant Groupers (*E. lanceolatus*) are found on the reef, as are endemic seabreams

ABOVE *The mystique of wreck diving on the* Produce, *home to a wide variety of marine life which can easily be seen on a short dive.*

ABOVE *Lyretail Anthias or Goldies (*Pseudanthias squamipinnis*) hover over a colourful reef.*

reef. The anthias live in small groups of females controlled by one large, dominant male. If the male dies, the most dominant female will, over a period of weeks, change sex and become the dominant male, complete with colour change, an increase in size and a more dominant attitude. The reef also has some fine specimens of the giant green tree corals (*Tubastrea micranthus*) and smooth-horned corals (*Stylophora* spp.).

Because of its marine biodiversity, there are plans to establish Aliwal Shoal as a marine protected area and it may become a no-take zone. This should allow the recovery of a number of larger reef fish species.

8 PROTEA BANKS

The Protea Banks offer exciting dives for the more experienced diver. Situated between the KwaZulu-Natal south coast towns of Margate and Shelly Beach, about 100km (62 miles) south of Durban, these reefs are reached from the launch site at Shelly Beach. The reefs are well known to local skiboat fishermen, who make use of every opportunity to fish the area. Similar to Aliwal Shoal, this site also forms part of an extensive, consolidated dune cordon, that lies about 8km (5 miles) offshore. Much of the reef lies at depths greater than 35m (115ft). However, there are a number of

high points on the reef that rise to between 25m (80ft) and 30m (100ft), which are more accessible to divers. Visibility on the reef is usually good and varies from 8m (25ft) to 30m (100ft). The Protea Banks usually have a strong north-to-south current flowing over the reef, which means that drift dives are often the only way to see it. Drifting past the kaleidoscopic reef, alive with brightly coloured fish, divers are swept through a marine world of unforgettable images. Only experienced divers should attempt this dive because of the depths and strong currents.

The Protea Banks are famous for their shark dives, where a wide variety of sharks, including Bull or Zambezi Sharks (*Carcharhinus leucas*), Tiger Sharks (*Galeocerdo cuvieri*), hammerhead sharks (*Sphyrna* spp.) and Raggedtooth Sharks (*Carcharius taurus*) occur at different times of the year. Great White Sharks (*Carcharodon carcharius*) and Shortfin Mako Sharks (*Isurus oxyrinchus*) are also occasionally seen, especially during the winter months when large shoals of sardines (*Sardinops sagax*) make their annual northward migration. Care should be taken when diving with these potentially dangerous animals and the appropriate diving protocols should be observed. This will help to ensure that the sharks are not disturbed and that

later groups of divers will also have the opportunity to see the animals. Another feature of the area is the large number of gamefish such as yellowfin tuna (*Thunnus albacares*), Spanish Mackerel (*Scomberomorus commerson*), Bigeye Trevallies (*Caranx sexfasciatus*) and barracudas (*Sphyraena* spp.). These spectacular, fast-moving creatures are frequently seen during descents, ascents, or during decompression stops.

The reef has a variety of soft and stony corals – notably the smooth-horned stony coral (*Stylophora* spp.) and various gorgonian species. Leafy sponges also abound. The rare deepwater One-stripe Anthias (*Pseudanthias fasciatus*) occurs on the northern pinnacles. There are always shoals of reef fish such as Redtooth Triggerfish (*Odonus niger*), Natal Fingerfin (*Chirodactylus jessicalenorum*) and African Butterflyfish (*Chaetodon dolosus*) in the vicinity of the southern pinnacles, while on the southern, flatter areas of the reef, Giant or White-spotted Guitarfish (*Rhynchobatus djiddensis*) are common.

As with Aliwal Shoal, the exceptional biodiversity of the region requires protection. Experienced divers have the opportunity to view a pristine area that few others are privileged to see. They also have the responsibility to ensure that it remains untouched for generations of divers to come.

THE MALDIVES

by Sam Harwood

ANYONE WHO HAS VISITED THE MALDIVES will remember the breathtaking sight as the aircraft makes its descent to the international airport. The coral reefs that comprise the North Malé Atoll are clearly visible; on one side of the reefs the ocean is a deep, inky blue while on the other side the waters of the lagoons are turquoise. The atoll is peppered with sandbars and islands surrounded by reefs.

North Malé Atoll and South Malé Atoll form one large administrative district, also known by its alternative Dhivehi name, Kaafu. The capital city, Malé, and the airport are both in the southeastern corner of this atoll. In spite of the fact that over the past 10 years these centres have become extremely busy, it is only necessary to travel a few kilometres (miles) to escape the hustle and bustle to enjoy peace and tranquillity as well as some fine diving.

North Malé Atoll offers an exciting mixture of channel and *thila* (a reef formation) diving.

TOP LEFT *A tropical island surrounded by sandbars, showing the breathtaking shades of blue and turquoise typical of the Maldives.*

TOP RIGHT *Island and reef. The archipelago offers an exciting mixture of channel and* thila *diving. The best sites are exposed to strong currents, which deter the less experienced.*

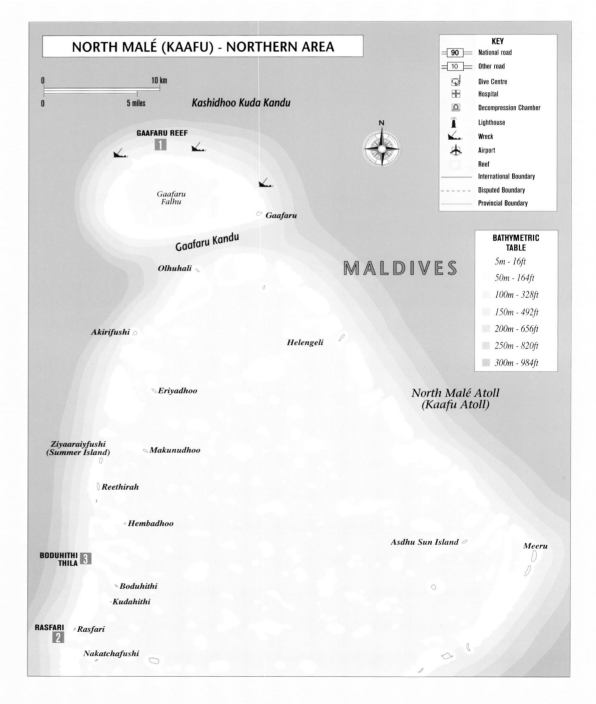

Because of its proximity to the capital and the concentration of resort islands in the southern area, the dive sites can be extremely crowded at certain times of the year. However, the best sites are exposed to strong currents, which tend to deter the less experienced, which has helped to ensure the survival of the reefs of the area.

A deep channel, Vaadhoo Kandu, separates North Malé Atoll from South Malé Atoll and this narrow ocean pass acts as a funnel for the prevailing currents. From December to April, in the northeast monsoon season, clean oceanic waters flow into the atoll and visibility is often excellent. During this same season, many of the channels on the western side are the favourite haunts of Manta Rays (*Manta birostris*) and Whale Shark (*Rhincodon typus*). From May to December, in the southwest monsoon season, the opposite applies, although Manta Rays and Whale sharks can still be found on the eastern side.

The inner ring reefs have been depleted by earlier coral mining for building purposes, but the Maldivian government has now introduced laws to control this practice.

NORTH MALÉ ATOLL (KAAFU) NORTHERN AREA

Although this region is quite close to the international airport, it is surprisingly quiet and offers some fascinating diving. At least seven wrecks can be found on the **Gaafaru Reef** [1], which is separated from the rest of the atoll by the 3km (2-mile) wide Gaafaru Kandu (channel). Many other ships have come to grief on this reef, but years of relentless pounding by the ocean swells have by now obliterated all evidence of their sad fate.

There are ten resort islands in this section of the atoll, most of which are small and were among the first to be established as tourist islands. Among the few uninhabited islands, **Rasfari** [2], on the exposed west side of the atoll, offers some exciting and challenging diving. During the northeast monsoon, between December and April,

visibility tends to deteriorate on the western side of the atoll, but the average visibility of this region is 20–25m (65–80ft).

RASFARI

Rasfari is an ocean reef off an uninhabited island. The site is exposed to south and northwesterly winds, but sheltered during the northeast monsoon. Large ocean swells can build up and currents are moderate to strong.

The reef slopes gently down to a plateau with an average depth of 20–30m (65–100ft), then drops off into the ocean depths. A small *thila*, with a reef top at 25m (80ft), sits in the centre of this plateau and divers can make their descent onto the main reef, then swim some 70m (230ft) over the plateau and onto the top of this *thila*. The currents around the *thila* can be strong, and reaching the peak can be quite difficult, but efforts to do so will be rewarded by sightings of many large fish. At times, as many as 25 Grey Reef Sharks (*Carcharhinus amblyrhynchos*) can be seen gathering, as well as Spotted Eagle Rays (*Aetobatus narinari*), Giant Reef Rays (*Taeniura melanospilos*) and some Great Barracuda (*Sphyraena barracuda*). Having explored the *thila*, divers can drift on the current back to the main reef. The diving is so exciting and there is so much to see that divers have to be careful not to get carried away and forget to check air consumption and decompression.

This is a protected marine area, which means that the removal of any natural object or live animal is forbidden, as is any activity that could damage the area or its marine life.

The resort islands near this dive site are Nakatchafushi, which is 15 minutes away by *dhoni* (ferry), Kudahithi (25 minutes), Boduhithi (35 minutes), Hembadhoo (60 minutes) and Ihuru (60 minutes).

[3] BODUHITHI THILA

Boduhithi Thila sits in the middle of the Boduhithi channel. During the northeast monsoon it is a sheltered site, but for the rest of the year it is exposed and currents can be very strong.

TOP AND ABOVE *Wreck of the* Maldives Victory, *a 3500-tonne, 110m (360ft) cargo ship lying parallel to the reef of Hulhule Airport Island. The midships mast stands intact, reaching to 12m (40ft), where a shotline is attached. The diver is looking out from the bridge.*

INDIAN OCEAN

During the sheltered northeast monsoon period the channel acts like a funnel for the currents flowing out of the atoll. When this outflow hits the ocean it creates an upwelling of plankton-rich waters over the *thila*. Consequently, this is a wonderful place to watch Manta Rays (*Manta birostris*) congregating in large numbers to feed. Whale Sharks (*Rhincodon typus*) also gather here, scooping the plankton into their cavernous open mouths like giant vacuum cleaners.

The coral heads in the southeast corner attract a variety of reef life, while in the current Whitetip Reef Shark (*Triaenodon obesus*) and Longfin Batfish (*Platax teira*) can be seen schooling in large numbers. Divers jumping in at this point can explore caves and overhangs as they drift along the reef. Where the ocean meets the southwest corner, mantas can often be seen hovering above, while they are being cleaned by small fish. The site is also excellent for snorkelling, because the Manta Rays often echelon-feed in formation on the surface.

This site is within easy reach of nearly all resorts in North Malé Atoll and can be quite busy during the northeast monsoon season.

NORTH MALÉ ATOLL SOUTHERN AREA

The capital island of Malé and the international airport are both situated in the southern section of North Malé Atoll, which makes it a busy part of the country. There are not many uninhabited islands, but as many as 17 resort islands in this area. Their easy access from the airport, usually by high-speed boats, has made them a very popular tourist destination. Some have conference rooms, freshwater swimming pools and restaurants offering a wide choice of international cuisine. Other large islands, such as Meeru and Lohifushi, offer simple accommodation, an informal atmosphere and an excellent selection of sporting activities such as catamaran sailing and tennis. There are some much smaller and quieter islands in the region where guests can enjoy a more relaxed style of holiday.

There are six protected marine areas in this southern section of North Malé Atoll – Hans Hass Place, Lion's Head, Kuda Haa, Banana Reef, HP Reef and Paradise Rock.

④ GIRIFUSHI THILA (HP REEF)

HP Reef sits on the western arm of North Malé Atoll, just off the main reef of Himmafushi Island. The wind blowing against the direction of the tide can result in short, choppy seas. Strong currents in the channel can cause surface eddies. Yet this is one of the best dives in the Maldives. However, it must be said that to enjoy this site, divers must be confident in strong currents and it is not suitable for beginners or snorkellers. The visibility is generally good, averaging 30m (100ft). The *thila* is made up of enormous boulders, piled up to create a superb collection of caves, crevices and overhangs. Blue, yellow and orange *Dendronephthya* Soft Tree Corals and Gorgonian Sea Fans line the walls of a stunning vertical tunnel, that is formed where the reef drops from the top at 12m (40ft) to a depth of 25m (80ft).

The currents flowing in and out of the atoll wash the *thila*, thus providing perfect conditions for both reef and pelagic fish. Divers can enjoy the sight of large schools of Grey Reef Sharks (*Carcharhinus amblyrhynchos),* Spotted Eagle Rays (*Aetobatus narinari*) and Great Barracuda (*Sphyraena barracuda*) swimming by.

Girifushi is a protected marine area and also an army training camp where rifle practice sometimes takes place. When an exercise is planned, a red flag is flown from the island and diving in the channel is forbidden. Many resort centres within the atoll bring divers to this site.

⑤ LANKANFINOLHU FARU (MANTA POINT)

Manta Point, on the western seaway of North Malé Atoll and in the southeast corner of Lankanfinolhu Reef, is one of the most popular dive sites in the Maldives. It is within easy reach of both North and South Malé atolls. From May to December, in the

ABOVE *When young, Three-spot Dascyllus Damselfish* (Dascyllus trimaculatus*) live in a commensal relationship with a large anemone. This one is outside the anemone's skirt.*

southwest monsoon season, a large number of Manta Rays gather here for cleaning.

The top of the reef is at 12m (40ft) and slopes gently down to 40m (130ft). The current along the reef can be very strong and there is often a heavy swell and surge, which can make it a difficult dive for novices and snorkellers. The *Porites* corals are home to a myriad of cleaner fish and the Manta Rays sail in and hover over the coral heads, while these busy little cleaner fish set to work. Divers need to be patient and position themselves close to, but not on, the coral heads and, provided discretion prevails, the mantas will carry on with their cleaning rituals despite the spectators. Any attempt to touch the mantas will scare the whole group away from the area.

In addition to the mantas, divers can see huge schools of Zaiser's Bigeyes (*Priacanthus hamrur*), Indian Ocean Oriental Sweetlips (*Plectorhinchus vittatus*) and Napolean or Humphead Wrasse (*Cheilinus undulatus*). In addition, there are often large numbers of turtles and various species of moray eels (of the family *Muraenidae)* swimming around the area and hiding in the many caves on the western point of the reef.

Divers are advised to swim away from the reef on surfacing, because the swell around the reef can be difficult for boat captains to manoeuvre safely while people are climbing back on board.

The site is visited by most of the resorts in the southern part of North Malé Atoll and from South Malé Atoll.

6 OCCABOLI THILA (BARRACUDA GIRI)

Occaboli *thila* is found east of Bandos Resort Island, in the Bodu Kalhi channel. It is sheltered at most times of the year, but the wind blowing over the tide can stir up some choppy seas and currents can be very strong. It sits well inside the atoll so that visibility is not always of the best, but the wide variety of fish life make it a site worth visiting.

There are two parts to the dive – the main reef, which is 200m (660ft) around, with an

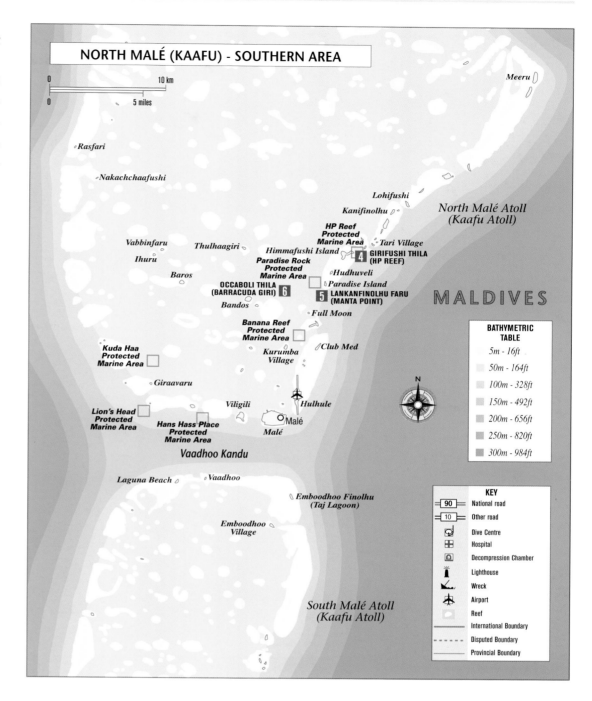

average depth of 10m (33ft), and a small, narrow *thila*, which lies 50m (165ft) off the southeastern corner. From May to November, during the southwest monsoon, Manta Rays can be seen hovering over the coral heads of the main reef, awaiting their turn to be cleaned. Anemones live on top of the reef with their symbiotic clownfish (*Amphiprion*, a subspecies of *Pomacentridae).*

The small *thila*, which forms the second part of the dive, is about 75m (250ft) long and only a few metres (yards) wide at the top, with one end rising to 12m (40ft) and the other to 18m (60ft). At some time in the past a coral rock has broken away and the resultant

OCEANS AND SEAS

Oceans contain many seas and gulfs. Common usage has made the terms 'oceans' and 'seas' interchangeable, but technically seas are subdivisions of oceans. The International Hydrographic Bureau, the agency responsible for world standardization and cooperation in the measurement and description of the physical features of the oceans, recognizes 54 different seas.

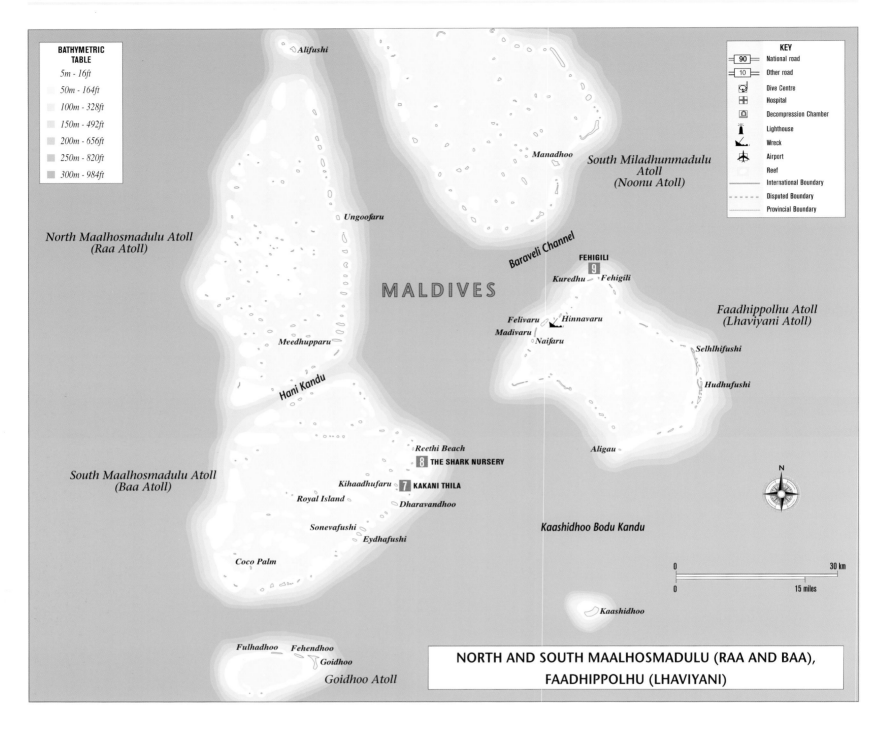

BATHYMETRIC TABLE

5m - 16ft
50m - 164ft
100m - 328ft
150m - 492ft
200m - 656ft
250m - 820ft
300m - 984ft

KEY

90	National road
10	Other road
	Dive Centre
	Hospital
	Decompression Chamber
	Lighthouse
	Wreck
	Airport
	Reef
	International Boundary
	Disputed Boundary
	Provincial Boundary

Alifushi

Manadhoo

South Miladhunmadulu Atoll (Noonu Atoll)

North Maalhosmadulu Atoll (Raa Atoll)

Ungoofaru

MALDIVES

Baraveli Channel

FEHIGILI 9
Kuredhu · Fehigili

Felivaru · Hinnavaru
Madivaru
Naifaru

Faadhippolhu Atoll (Lhaviyani Atoll)

Selhlhifushi

Hudhufushi

Meedhupparu

Hani Kandu

Reethi Beach
8 THE SHARK NURSERY

Aligau

South Maalhosmadulu Atoll (Baa Atoll)

Kihaadhufaru 7 KAKANI THILA
Royal Island
Sonevafushi
Dharavandhoo
Eydhafushi

Kaashidhoo Bodu Kandu

Coco Palm

N

0 ————— 30 km
0 ————— 15 miles

Kaashidhoo

Fulhadhoo Fehendhoo
Goidhoo
Goidhoo Atoll

NORTH AND SOUTH MAALHOSMADULU (RAA AND BAA), FAADHIPPOLHU (LHAVIYANI)

canyon between *thila* and reef is covered in corals. When the current flows into this canyon, schools of fusiliers can be seen swarming into the gap, making it a popular hunting ground for Bigeye Trevallies. The canyon is also home to a family of Humphead (Napoleon) Wrasse.

NORTH AND SOUTH MAALHOSMADULU ATOLL (BAA AND RAA)

For many years the Maalhosmadulu atolls were undeveloped and the only visitors came on safari boats. In 1995 a luxury island resort was opened in South Maalhosmadulu (Baa), followed by four more. In addition, there are 10 fishing islands and some 38 beautiful uninhabited islands, some of which are used for growing fruit and coconuts.

The best diving in South Maalhosmadulu is found on the many *thilas* inside the fringing reefs of the atoll. The channels are quite wide and therefore do not attract the wide variety of marine species that can be found on the *thilas*. Due to the width of the channels and the shelter provided by two nearby atolls, currents in this region are not as strong as elsewhere in the Maldives.

Between December and May the water is calm and visibility usually very good. During the rest of the year the seas can be rough and visibility tends to be reduced. However, during May, June and July a large number of Manta Rays (*Manta birostris*) and Whale Shark (*Rhincodon typus*) can be found here and this is an excellent time to observe these fascinating marine creatures.

North Maalhosmadulu Atoll (Raa) has only recently been opened to tourists, so there is a wealth of diving to be explored. Judging by the topography, the dive sites would be similar to those of South Maalhosmadulu.

7 KAKANI THILA

Kakani *thila* lies 500m (1640ft) northeast of the resort island of Kihaadhufaru on the east side of the atoll. The *thila* is 150m (500ft) long and 50m (165ft) wide, with a reef top at 10m (33ft). On the north side the seabed drops over a step midway along the reef, descending sharply from 30m (100ft) to more than 60m (200ft). Along the ridge there are caves and overhangs which are home to large schools of Indian Ocean Oriental Sweetlips (*Plectorhinchus vittatus*), Bluefin Trevally (*Caranx melampygus*), barracuda and Napoleon Wrasse (*cheilinus undulatus*). The whole area is covered in orange and yellow *Dendronephthya* Soft Three Corals that are a feature of this particular region. There are also many large caves on the vertical face of the *thila*, making this an exciting dive with bountiful fish life and stunning topography.

Dive boats from all the resorts in South Maalhosmadulu visit this site.

8 THE SHARK NURSERY

This site derives its name from the number of sharks that can be seen here. It is one of the best sites in the atoll to see Whitetip and Grey Reef Sharks, including many juveniles. Situated 3km (2 miles) to the northwest of the uninhabited island of Dharavandhoo, it is a favourite site with the five resort islands in the atoll.

The site also offers excellent opportunities to see stingrays. Because the site is well inside the atoll, the water is calm, although the ocean currents still flow through the Dharavandhoo channel. Divers should jump in on the main reef and descend onto the branch of coral that projects from the basin off the main reef. From here, provided divers do not invade their space, the sharks can be observed as they school and rest on the sand floor.

FAADHIPPOLHU ATOLL (LHAVIYANI)

Faadhippolhu atoll lies 120km (75 miles) from the capital, Malé. Although it is one of the smaller atolls, only 37km (23 miles) wide and 35km (20 miles) long, it has a population of 8000. The Felivaru Tuna Fish Canning Factory, which was opened as a joint venture between a Japanese company and the Maldivian government in the late 1970s, employs around 200 staff, most of whom live on the two nearby islands of Hinnavaru (population 2500) and Naifaru (population 3000). However, the government has set up schemes to encourage inhabitants to move to the nearby island of Madivaru to ease the overcrowding. There are three other inhabited islands on the west side of the atoll and another on the east. There are also many large islands with dense vegetation, most of which are situated on the outer rim of the atoll. In total, there are 50 uninhabited islands and five resorts in this atoll at present, but with the pressure of increased tourism to the Maldives, it is quite likely that the government will allocate other uninhabited islands in the atoll for development as resorts. Kuredhu Island Resort is one of the largest in the Maldives.

The atoll offers a great variety of excellent dive sites, with coral reefs, narrow channels and wrecks near the island of Felivaru. Around the southeast corner there is a very long reef – from Selhlhifushi in the north down to Aligau in the south. This causes the water in the southeastern part of the atoll to flow less freely than in the northern part; consequently there is less destructive wave action and the *giris* (submerged reefs) and patch reefs inside the southern part of the atoll are in perfect condition. Inevitably, the gentler currents mean that there are fewer chances to see the large pelagic fish, but these can be seen in the narrow channels of the north.

9 FEHIGILI

Fehigili is on the eastern side of the northernmost tip of the atoll and currents here can be very strong and the sea very choppy. This makes it unsuitable for inexperienced divers and quite uncomfortable for anyone suffering from seasickness. Once on the reef, the fish

ABOVE *Collare Butterflyfish (Chaetodon collare) are often found in pairs and groups. Their natural diet consists mainly of coral polyps.*

life is amazing and there are good opportunities for photographers in the basin at the corner on the ocean side, where the schooling fish seem to be friendly and large.

The inside reef of the Fehigili channel consists of a series of steps, each one about 10m (33ft), descending eventually to the ocean drop-off at 40m (130ft). Where the steps meet the corner of the reef there are caves and overhangs full of *Dendronephthya* Soft Tree Corals and huge schools of soldierfish (*Myripristis* spp.), squirrelfish (*Sargocentron* spp.), Harlequin Sweetlips (*Plectorhinchus chaetodonoides*) and many other varieties.

Divers can descend a little deeper to the atoll plate at 35m (115ft), where a huge overhang is adorned with *Dendronephthya* Soft Tree Coral and bright orange *Tubastrea* corals. This protected area is a good place to see schooling barracuda, trevallies, tuna and other fish coming in from the ocean.

ARI (ALIFU)

Some of the best sites in the Maldives are in Ari Atoll, about 60km (37 miles) west of Malé and separated from North Malé Atoll by the Alihuras Channel. It is one of the largest atolls in the archipelago, measuring about 80km (50 miles) long and about 30km (20 miles) wide.

There are many resort islands spread over the length and breadth of this huge atoll, ranging from very small, exclusive places with just 50 beds to Kuramathi, the largest resort in the Maldives, with 508 beds. The complex area of reef formations provides every type of dive imaginable, making this an ideal destination for experienced and novice divers and snorkellers. The area is dotted with numerous *thilas* where the shallow reeftops provide good light for coral growth. The sides are often sheer, dropping away to around 30m (100ft), interspersed with intriguing caves and overhangs, sheltering a wide variety of reef and pelagic fish. Most sites are small enough to be explored in a single dive.

From December to April there are some really exciting manta points, where divers can sit in shallow water and watch these awesome creatures as they hover around the cleaning stations. It is not unusual for Whale Sharks (*Rhincodon typus*) to be in the same area. In the southwest season, from May to November, the population of Grey Reef Sharks (*Carcharhinus amblyrhynchos*) appears to increase. This could be due to the slightly cooler water at this time of the year. Manta Rays are not quite so common in the area during this season, but encounters with the Whale Sharks are often reported.

ARI ATOLL – SOUTHERN AREA

There are ten fishing islands in the south of this large atoll, one of which, Mahibadhoo, is

ABOVE *Diver over a coral reef. Tiered coral heads like these may be hundreds, if not thousands, of years old. Coral is characterized by its skeleton and often named for its shape.*

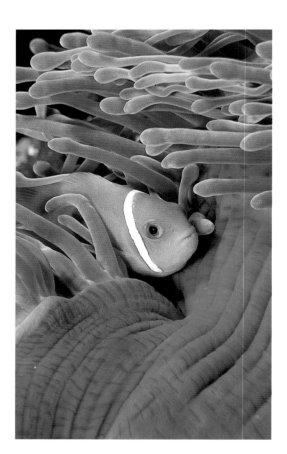

ABOVE *The Maldives anemonefish or clownfish* (Amphiprion nigripes) *gains protection by retreating among its host's tentacles. The host is* exclusively Heteractis magnifica.

ABOVE *Schooling bannerfish* (Heniochus diphreutes), *a type of butterflyfish, is often considered to be indicative of healthy reefs. They occur primarily along outer reef slopes.*

the administrative capital. In addition, there are 16 resort islands and 11 uninhabited islands, some of the latter being little more than a sand bar, while others are quite large, with rich vegetation.

10 KUDARAH THILA

Kudarah Thila is situated just one kilometre (half a mile) southeast of Kudarah Resort Island. The topography is quite complex and spring tides can bring extremely strong currents, making it unsuitable for novice divers.

The *thila* is divided into four large coral heads resting on a plateau and rising from 40m (130ft) to 12m (40ft). The entire *thila* is no more than 100m (330ft) in diameter and can be encompassed in a single dive. Each coral head is undercut from 15m (50ft) to 25m (80ft) with superb caves full of corals, Gorgonian Sea Fans and Whip Corals. A swim-through archway in the southwest corner leads into the centre well of four pinnacles, where there are deep ravines harbouring a stunning amount of marine life. The hollow centre of the *thila* goes down to 20m (65ft) and thousands of Bluelined Snappers (*Lutjanus kasmira*) school in the gullies, shadowed by yellow trumpetfish (*Aulostomus chinensis*). Grey and Whitetip Reef Sharks can be seen on the points of the current.

Divers must be careful not to go into decompression on this dive, because there are no shallow points on the reef at which to carry out stops.

This is a protected marine area. Many resorts in Ari Atoll visit this site by *dhoni* (ferry) but the nearest resort islands are Kudarah and Vakarufalhi (10 minutes) and Machchafushi (20 minutes).

11 HUKURUELHI FARU (MADIVARU)

Hukuruelhi Faru, or Madivaru, is on the south side of Rangali channel. *Faru* is the Dhivehi name for a circular reef that is exposed to the ocean and rises up from the ocean floor, while *madi* means ray, so it is not surprising that, in the northeast season, this has superb manta

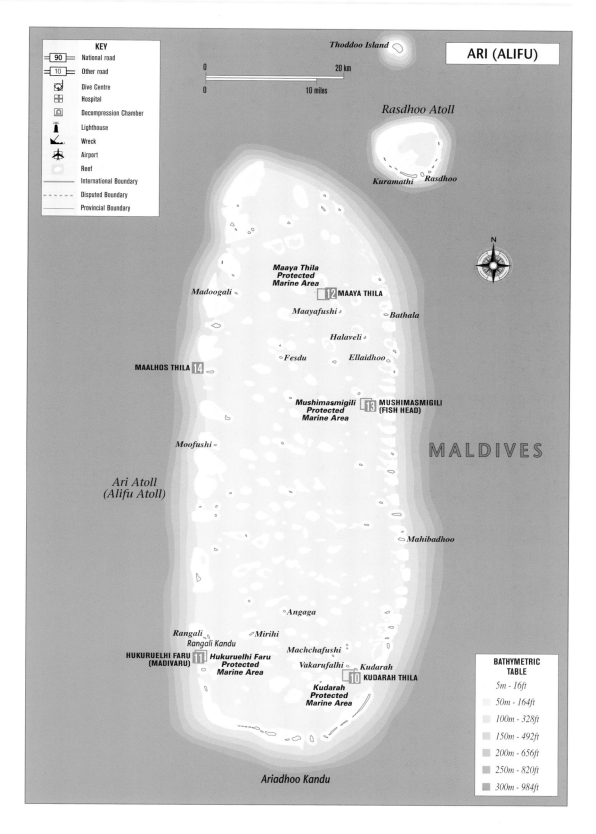

cleaning stations. The reef slopes down gently from the top at 8m (25ft) to the ocean bed at 30m (100ft). The manta cleaning stations are spread all along this reef, but they are at their most active midway along the northern side. Here a deep basin, almost 100m (330ft) across, has formed in the coral and the mantas are attracted by the waters that eddy here as the currents flow out of the atoll.

To the east of the basin the reef drops steeply to the sand floor at 30m (100ft). About 25m (80ft) down this wall is a large cave, which runs along the reef for 200m (656ft). To appreciate the splendour of this site, divers should stay low on the reef and keep as still as possible. Patience will be rewarded when the mantas come in to hover like spaceships, awaiting their turn at the cleaning stations.

ABOVE *Manta Ray (Manta birostris) with wrasse cleaner fish. Manta Rays frequently glide into cleaning stations all over Ari Atoll. These harmless filter-feeders can grow to 6½m (22ft) wide.*

ABOVE *A diver hovering over a mixture of stony and soft corals that is common where the currents are strong when the tide is in full flow. The brightly coloured soft corals swell up to their full glory in strong currents.*

This site has been designated a protected marine area by the Maldivian government. Many resorts in Ari Atoll offer day excursions to this site during the manta season.

ARI ATOLL – NORTHERN AREA

There are seven inhabited islands in this region. Thoddoo Island, at the far north of the area, is an important fishing island and famous for the *bandiyaa*, a dance performed by a group of local girls. It is a large island in the middle of the ocean pass. Visitors are welcome, but only small fishing boats are able to anchor off its shores. The island of Rasdhoo is not a resort island, but it is located next to the large island of Kuramathi, on which there are three individual resorts. Consequently, Rasdhoo now has over 30 tourist shops and provides the hub for air transfer services to the Kuramathi resorts. Altogether, there are 11 resorts and about 13 uninhabited islands in this northern part of the atoll.

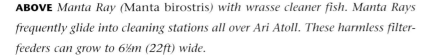

12 MAAYA THILA

Situated just 3km (2 miles) northwest of Maayafushi Resort Island, Maaya Thila is one of the best-known dives in the Maldives, with an amazing variety of marine life – Grey and Whitetip Reef Sharks, turtles, stonefish, frogfish, Longfin Batfish (*Platax teira*) and many other species. This site can be very busy, but it has been given the status of a protected marine area, which will help to conserve its marine life.

The *thila* is small enough, at 30m (100ft) in diameter, to swim around in one dive, but as always, the underwater activity is concentrated around the point of the current. The top of the *thila* is at 8m (25ft) and at the edge due north of this point there is a large overhang full of bright orange *Tubastrea* corals. A large satellite rock can be seen off this point and is well worth visiting. The top of the rock, at 15m (50ft), is covered in corals, while the vertical sides drop down to the atoll plate at 40m (130ft). Grey Reef Sharks (*Carcharhinus amblyrhynchos*) can frequently patrol the

channel between this rock and the *thila*, while Whitetip Reef Sharks (*Triaenodon obesus*) can often be seen resting on the sand.

To the south of the *thila* there is another, smaller satellite rock, which also merits investigation, although the coral growth on this side of the *thila* is not as beautiful as that on the northern side. This is an excellent site for night diving.

Because this site is so well known, it is visited from many resorts within Ari Atoll.

13 MUSHIMASMIGILI (FISH HEAD)

Mushimasmigili is an uninhabited island and this site can be found just 4km (2½ miles) to the south. *Mushimas* is the Dhivehi word for 'little fish' and the site is named after the small brown fusiliers which can be seen in their thousands on the *thila*. This protected marine area is also home to a resident school of Grey Reef Sharks (*Carcharhinus amblyrhynchos*), which often pass quite close to the divers and there is usually a family of

Humphead (Napoleon) Wrasse (*Cheilinus undulatus*). The top of this small *thila* is at 10m (33ft). It is oval in shape and about 100m (330ft) long and 60m (200ft) wide. The southern side drops down in two steps, from 8m (25ft) to 20m (65ft) and down again to the atoll plate at 42m (138ft). At the southeast corner a large overhang, known as The Fish Head, projects from the *thila*. This provides shelter for a huge school of thousands of Blue-lined Snappers (*Lutjanus kasmira*). The drop on the north and west side is steeper and at 20m (65ft) the reef is undercut with an overhang that curls around a large part of the *thila*.

This is an excellent dive for all standards of diver and offers the opportunity to observe a wide variety of marine life. It is popular with most resorts in Ari Atoll and some resorts in both North and South Malé Atoll run day excursions here.

14 MAALHOS THILA

Located in the north channel of the fishing island Maalhos, this *thila* is exposed from May to November and conditions can be difficult. At all times of the year the currents over this area can be fierce and not suitable for inexperienced divers. However, this 200m (660ft) long *thila* is one of the most beautiful and colourful in the Maldives, with stunning corals adorning the many caves and overhangs that run the length of the site. Reef fish abound in hundreds, with great schools of Bluelined Snappers (*Lutjanus kasmira*), soldierfish (*Myripristis* spp.*)*, Moorish Idols (*Zanclus cornutus*) and Indian Ocean Oriental Sweetlips (*Plectorhinchus vittatus*). There are several large coral heads on the ocean side of the *thila* where divers can see Great Barracuda (*Sphyraena barracuda*), Spotted Eagle Rays (*Aetobatus narinari*) and Whitetip Reef Sharks (*Triaenodon obesus*). The shallowest point of the *thila* is 10m (33ft), so decompression diving should be avoided.

Day excursions are made from resorts on the east side of Ari Atoll. The nearest resort islands are Fesdu (45 minutes), Moofushi and Madoogali (both 50 minutes).

FELIDHOO ATOLL (VAAVU)

Felidhoo atoll and next-door Mulaku (Meemu) atoll are quiet in terms of tourist resorts and fishing islands. It is only recently that the government agreed to the opening of the first two resorts in Mulaku. However, the boot-shaped atoll of Felidhoo has been a great favourite with safari boat operators for some time because it offers many excellent dive sites as well as being a very beautiful area of the country.

Fulidhoo in the north, Thinadhoo, Felidhoo and Keyodhoo on the east and Rakeedhoo in the south are all locally inhabited islands, where the locals rely heavily on tuna fishing for their livelihood. There are also a number of uninhabited islands. Fotteyo, the largest of these, is the easternmost point of the Maldives archipelago. Bodumohoraa and Hulidhoo are both idyllic tropical islands with superb beaches, ideal for snorkellers, while Kudiboli, a small uninhabited island on the west side, has safe anchorage for safari boats. To the south of

the main atoll sits Vattaru Falhu. A *falhu* is a shallow reef rising up from the atoll floor and forming a crescent facing the inside of the atoll. Vattaru circles the island of Vattaruhuraa, which has dense vegetation and no beaches. The shallow fringing reef makes access extremely difficult.

There are only two resort islands in Felidhoo atoll, Alimathaa and Dhiggiri, both of which are beautiful, with excellent diving.

The many channels which break the outer rim of this atoll offer some exciting diving, although dives tend to be deeper than the *thila* diving that is normally found in the northern atolls and success tends to depend on currents. The reefs on both the east and west sides drop down to great depths, rather than shelving out at around 40m (130ft) as is more usual for the Maldives.

From December to April clear blue oceanic water flows in through the narrow channels, bringing in large numbers of pelagic species and Grey Reef Sharks. On the western side of the atoll Manta Rays and Whale Sharks can be found feeding on the plankton-rich waters

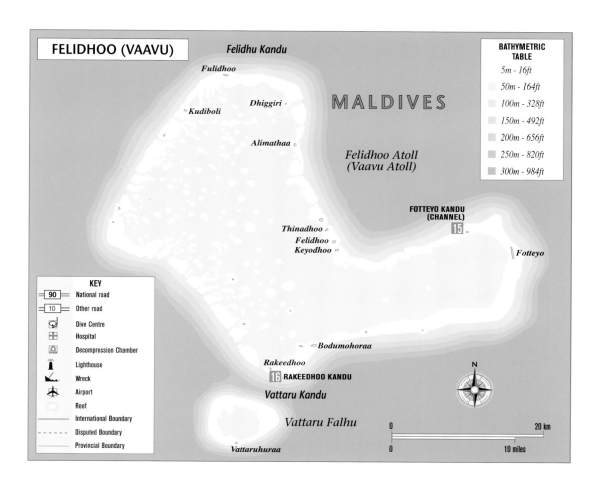

flowing out into the ocean, particularly during the season of the southwest monsoon. However, seas can be rough at this time of the year, so diving the channels can be difficult.

15 FOTTEYO KANDU (CHANNEL)

Fotteyo Kandu is the first channel to the west of the uninhabited island of Fotteyo, which sits on the north fringing reef of the atoll. It is a beautiful dive site and worthy of several visits, for there is so much to see. A vertical wall on the fringing reef causes a funnel effect with the water that is flowing into the channel and this is what attracts the great variety of marine life.

Fotteyo Kandu is about 200m (656ft) wide and is split into two narrow passes by a *thila*, which shallows to within 3m (10ft) of the surface. The west pass is around 100m (330ft) wide, the east pass much narrower, about 30m (100ft). The average depth of the channel is 20m (65ft) until it drops off vertically into the ocean, descending many hundreds of metres. Spotted Eagle Rays (*Aetobatus narinari*) frequently hang in the currents that flow through this narrow passage. In the western pass, there is a catacomb of caves in the wall

of the ocean drop-off, spreading from 20m (65ft) down to a depth of 50m (165ft). The roofs of these caves and overhangs are festooned with corals. The area abounds with reef fish. Divers can drift over the sandy floor of the channel where they will find triggerfish – this has been dubbed triggerfish alley – and dolphins can often be seen and heard swimming through the channel.

The water is generally calm except when the wind is against the tide, when big overfalls can build up. Also, the currents into and out of the channel can be very strong. This is a popular site and many resort islands run day excursions to here for divers.

16 RAKEEDHOO KANDU

There are two dives, one on each side of the Rakeedhoo channel. Rakeedhoo is the southernmost point of Felidhoo atoll and there is a huge flow of water in and out of the channel. It is quite narrow, but just too wide and too deep to cross, and conflicting currents can create turbulent water and overfalls across the entrance. However, the dives on each corner of this channel are wonderful.

On the eastern side are vertical walls peppered with numerous caves at depths of between 20m (65ft) and 40m (130ft). Here Giant Reef Rays (*Taeniura melanospilos*) lurk, while large groupers (*Epinephelus* spp.), turtles and families of Humphead (Napoleon) Wrasse live on the top of the reef. This is a splendid drift dive from the outer fringing reef into the channel. In good conditions it is an excellent site for snorkelling.

On the west side of the channel the floor slopes quickly down to the atoll plate before meeting the ocean drop-off at 30m (100ft). Here again, there are many large caves lined with corals, Gorgonian Sea Fans and Whip Corals. It is possible in the right conditions to

BELOW LEFT *Diver and mature Humphead (Napoleon) Wrasse (*Cheilinus undulatus*). One of the largest fish on the reef, they occur singly or in small groups feeding on molluscs and other well-armoured invertebrates.*

BELOW *Bigeyes and snappers often share the same sheltered caves and crevices during the day and disperse to feed at night.*

hang in the ocean at a depth of 35m (115ft) and gaze up at these caves – the contrast of the deep blue water beneath and the bright colours in the caves make a stunning sight. This is a good site for seeing big pelagics and a school of Bigeye Trevallies can often be seen in the channel.

Although Alimathaa and Dhiggiri are the only resort islands in this atoll, other resorts run day excursions to Rakeedhoo Kandu.

SOUTH AND NORTH NILANDHOO ATOLL (DHAALU AND FAAFU)

These two atolls, opened to tourists in 1997, lie just south of Ari Atoll. South Nilandhoo is 150km (95 miles) from Malé and has two resort islands, the small and very pretty island of Velavaru, and the larger Vilu Reef. In the smaller North Nilandhoo atoll, only one island has been developed as a resort. This is Filitheyo, which has an accessible house reef and a high standard of accommodation.

In South Nilandhoo there are eight fishing islands and over 38 uninhabited islands. The island of Ribudhoo is famous for the beautiful jewellery made by the locals. North Nilandhoo is smaller, with just five inhabited and 18 uninhabited islands.

The region has considerable historical significance. The famous anthropologist Thor Heyerdahl excavated several sites here and discovered evidence of seven Hindu temples on the island of Nilandhoo. This island is also home to a mosque dating back to the 12th Century, which was built with stones from the ancient Hindu temples. This mosque is one of the oldest and most revered in the Maldives.

Diving in both atolls is exciting and varied and suitable for divers of all levels of experience. The small number of resorts in the atolls means that all sites are relatively quiet and that fish abound. There are two known wrecks off the island of Kudahuvadhoo in South Nilandhoo atoll. The *Liffey* foundered in 1879 and the smaller *Utheema I* went down in 1960.

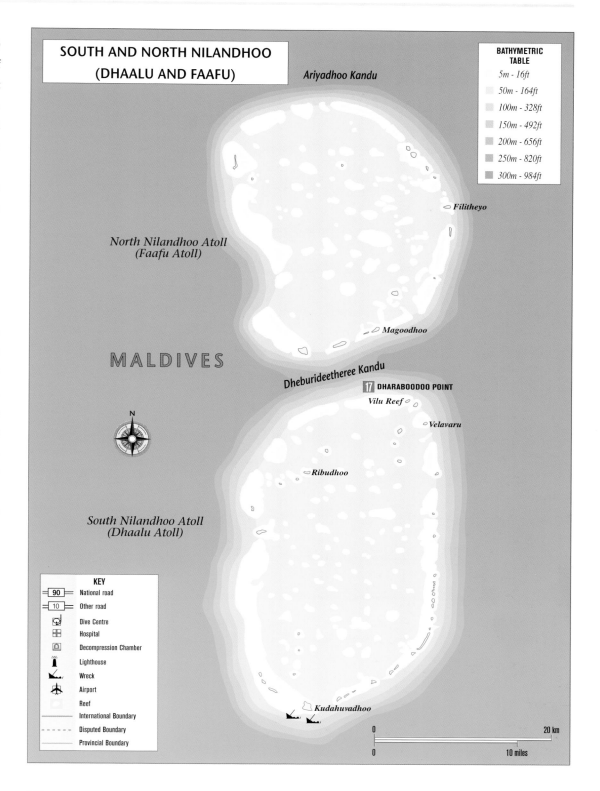

17 DHARABOODOO POINT

Dharaboodoo point lies off the east of the island's house reef. The site is best dived between May and December on flood tides. Five large coral outcrops have broken away from the main reef and now lie in the channel. Currents sweep through the passage that these coral blocks have formed with the wall of the reef, making it attractive to a multitude of schooling fish, while corals adorn the whole area.

Where the house reef has collapsed, there are huge caves and overhangs from the surface down to 35m (115ft). The reef is home to huge schools of fusiliers, snappers and groupers.

Filitheyo resort and safari boats are the only means of access to this site, so it is quiet. Because it is relatively new, the fish are also less used to divers and tend to be more shy than elsewhere in the Maldives. It is a wonderful site and well worth a visit, especially in the southwest monsoon season.

ATOLL FORMATION

An atoll starts to form when a volcano rises above the sea. Stony corals, marine animals which secrete calcium carbonate to form a skeleton, begin growing near the ocean's surface to form a fringing reef around the volcano. When the volcano subsides, the coral continues to grow upwards and outwards to form a barrier reef enclosing a shallow lagoon. Eventually the island formed by the volcano sinks, leaving a ring-shaped reef, or atoll. If the island sinks faster than the coral can grow, then you are left with a seamount below the surface of the sea.

A reef is made up of many layers of coral, with the top layer of live coral colonies growing on the calcified remains of dead coral. Stormy seas break off chunks of coral, which crumble to form sand.

ABOVE *Urchins, like the one in the foreground, are a problem for swimmers. They are rarely poisonous, but the spines break off under the skin and the irritation can last for weeks. Like the sea stars, they can move with the aid of their tube-feet.*

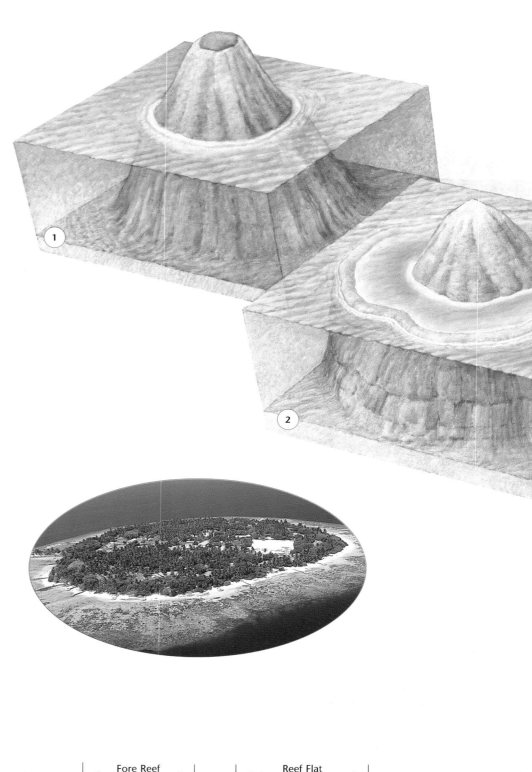

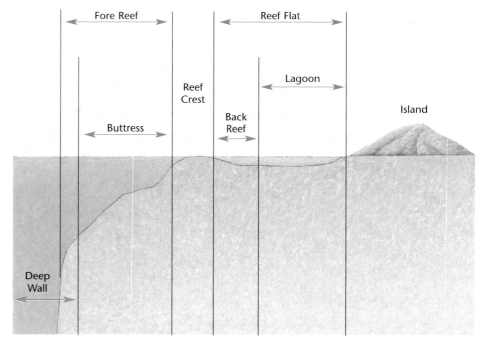

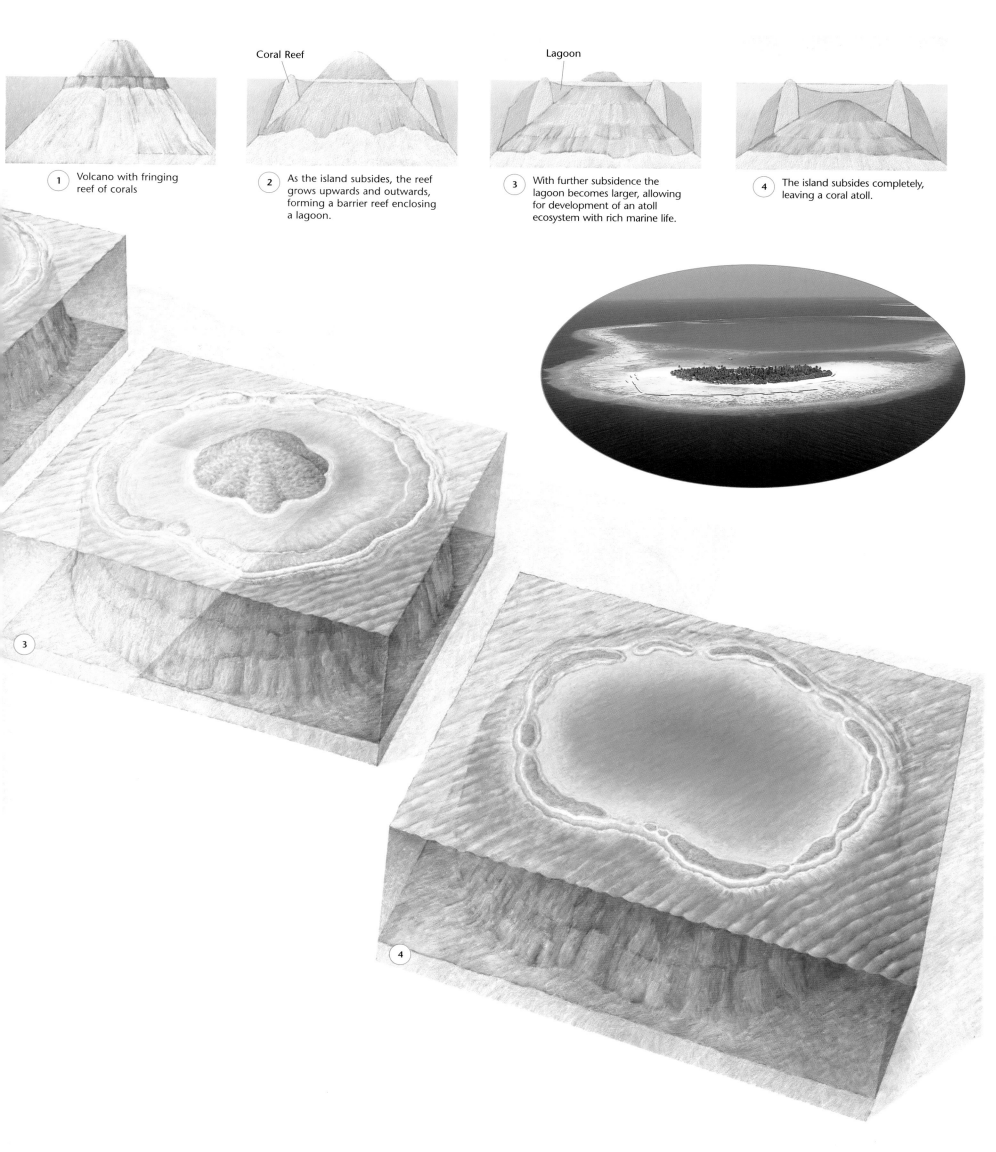

1 Volcano with fringing reef of corals

Coral Reef

2 As the island subsides, the reef grows upwards and outwards, forming a barrier reef enclosing a lagoon.

Lagoon

3 With further subsidence the lagoon becomes larger, allowing for development of an atoll ecosystem with rich marine life.

4 The island subsides completely, leaving a coral atoll.

ANDAMAN SEA

by Paul Lees

THAILAND SITS RIGHT IN THE HEART OF Southeast Asia, making it convenient for international trading and as a base for travel throughout the region. Whereas the country's northern region is covered with undulating hills and mountains, the south is adorned with splendid palm-fringed beaches and tropical islands. The largest and best known of the islands, Koh Phuket, has been attracting international visitors for many years, and a steady growth has resulted in tourist services spreading further afield. A number of neighbouring islands are now also enjoying a brisk tourist trade. To the east, the Phi Phi Island group have upgraded their amenities from that of stand-alone, coconut-palm huts to air-conditioned accommodation with restaurants and tourist services. Beyond these islands the world-class beaches in Krabi Province are slowly following a similar route. Further south, however, the island of Koh Lanta seems to be quite content with its more undeveloped beaches and adequate accommodation.

TOP LEFT *The narrow isthmus of Koh Phi Phi Don, the only inhabited island in the Phi Phi group, is where the accommodation is.*

TOP RIGHT *Koh Bangu, commonly referred to as Island Number Nine, is the northernmost in the Mu Koh Similan Marine National Park. Its northern shoreline has protected anchorages.*

All these destinations proffer scuba diving services in some form or another; all offer diver education and trips to the best sites – be they daily or multiday live-aboard excursions.

KOH PHUKET AS A BASE

Koh Phuket (Phuket Island) remains one of the top tourist destinations in the region with countless activities and attractions. The island's western coast is broken by a number of beaches; and these are the main tourist centres offering all amenities and scuba diving facilities. Diving education classes for beginners up to instructor are all regularly scheduled. Dive trips to all the local sites and live-aboard excursions to those further afield are readily available. Phuket also serves as a connecting point for travel to more southern destinations such as Krabi, Koh Phi Phi and Koh Lanta.

Day trips – local diving

Several diving destinations to the southeast of the island are worth visiting; namely Shark Point Marine Sanctuary and the Phi Phi island group. The two islands of Koh Phi Phi Don and Ley rise majestically above the water 48km (30 miles) southeast of Phuket, and are contained in Had Nopparat Marine National Park. The smaller, more rugged island of Koh Phi Phi Ley remains uninhabited, whereas the larger island is now a bustling holiday resort.

On the northwest coast of Koh Phi Phi Ley is the tiny bay of **Ao Nui** 4 . A rocky outcrop in the centre of the bay, with relatively shallow waters around its eastern face, affords good snorkelling. There are many corals and reef fish among small boulders and rocks encrusted with patches of sponges. The outcrop's outer wall is pitted with holes and tunnels, providing lairs to a variety of moray eels. Indian Ocean Lionfish, Bluering and Emperor Angelfish all flit around a narrow crevice, the inside of which is littered with small corals and sea fans. Off the two southern prongs of Phi Phi Don, **Hin Phae** 5 and **Hin Dot** 6 are good snorkelling and diving destinations. Invertebrates abound. The occasional Painted Rock Lobster and smaller reef crabs mingle with busy Cleaner and Hinge-beak Shrimps as they tend to a number of reef dwellers. The deeper sections have numerous oysters and clams clinging to, and embedded in, the rocky surfaces. Common reef octopuses secrete themselves against the scattered rocks and lunge at unsuspecting blennies that leave the security of their tiny burrows. Barracuda and other pelagics are also fairly common passers-by. Further south are two rocky karsts separated by a narrow channel. Both **Koh Bida Nai** 7 (inner) and **Koh Bida Nok** 8 (outer) are great destinations for observing small marine creatures around walls, fringing reefs and scattered boulders.

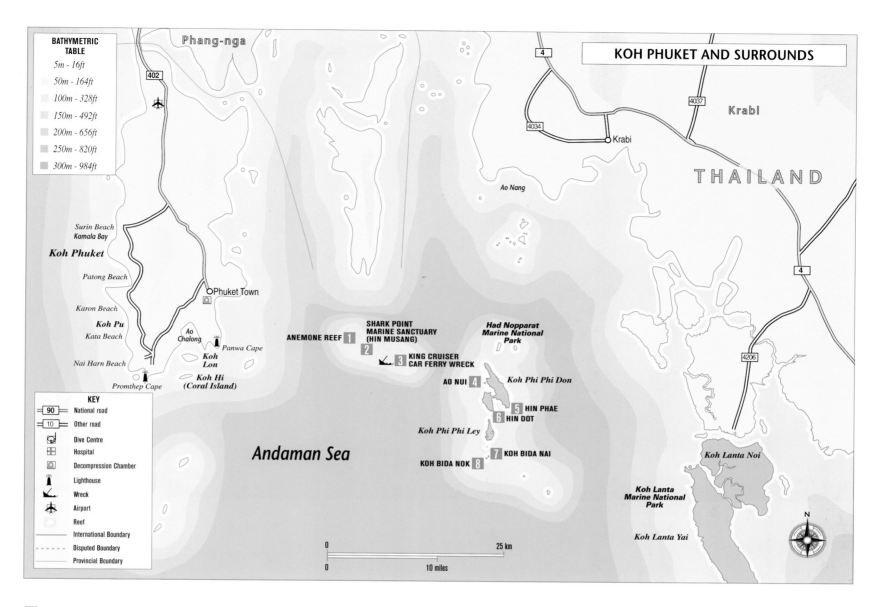

BATHYMETRIC TABLE
5m - 16ft
50m - 164ft
100m - 328ft
150m - 492ft
200m - 656ft
250m - 820ft
300m - 984ft

KEY
90 National road
10 Other road
Dive Centre
Hospital
Decompression Chamber
Lighthouse
Wreck
Airport
Reef
International Boundary
Disputed Boundary
Provincial Boundary

Phang-nga

Krabi

THAILAND

Ao Nang

Surin Beach
Kamala Bay
Koh Phuket
Patong Beach
Phuket Town
Karon Beach
Koh Pu
Kata Beach
Ao Chalong
Panwa Cape
Koh Lon
Nai Harn Beach
Koh Hi (Coral Island)
Promthep Cape

ANEMONE REEF 1
SHARK POINT MARINE SANCTUARY (HIN MUSANG) 2
KING CRUISER CAR FERRY WRECK 3

Had Nopparat Marine National Park

AO NUI 4
Koh Phi Phi Don
HIN PHAE 5
HIN DOT 6
Koh Phi Phi Ley
KOH BIDA NAI 7
KOH BIDA NOK 8

Koh Lanta Noi

Koh Lanta Marine National Park

Koh Lanta Yai

Andaman Sea

0   25 km
0   10 miles

N

2 Shark Point Marine Sanctuary (Hin Musang)

In 1992, two popular scuba diving sites became part of a marine sanctuary. A third site was added to the list in 1997. Hin Musang, locally referred to as Shark Point, consists of three submerged pinnacles lying north-to-south. Between them they have a high proportion of stony and soft corals at all depths. All manner of reef residents animate the otherwise fixed patterns of colour. Leopard Sharks are the main attraction here, and divers can observe these harmless bottom feeders at close hand. The site also features many cleaning stations hosted by a multitude of cleaning fish and shrimps, whose regular customers include a variety of snappers, jacks, trevally, mackerel and the occasional barracuda. Although the diving all around this site is impressive, the most concentrated presence of marine life is found at the southernmost pinnacle. This is a community all on its own with sea horses, Ghost Pipefish, damsels, wrasse, parrotfish, octopuses and a host of invertebrates.

Although the submerged pinnacle known as **Anemone Reef** 1 is now half its original size, the upper part of the pinnacle is once again covered in sea anemones hosted by numerous species of clownfish, and closer inspection reveals even more symbiotic residents: tiny anemone crabs and clear Cleaner shrimps, only visible by their translucent internal organs. Below these, enormous, healthy, Gorgonian Sea Fans form a backdrop to hovering prides of Indian Ocean Lionfish and large clusters of radiant soft tree corals.

The sanctuary's third and most recent site was the cause of halving Anemone Reef. The *King Cruiser Car Ferry* 3 now sits in 32m

(109ft) of water. The structure attracts a high diversity of marine life and the formation of an artificial reef is well under way. Daylight penetrates most of the wreck, but there are still a number of areas that would be better explored with the aid of an artificial light source. Divers intending to explore the murky interior should be aware that the once-proud vessel's ceilings are no longer strong.

LIVE-ABOARD EXCURSIONS TO SITES FURTHER AFIELD

Mu Koh Similan Marine National Park

This, Thailand's most talked about diving destination, rises above the Andaman Sea 92km (57 miles) northwest of Phuket, and was declared a marine national park in 1982. The surrounding 128 sq km (49 sq miles) were also included. With the exception of unnamed island number five, the islands are categorized

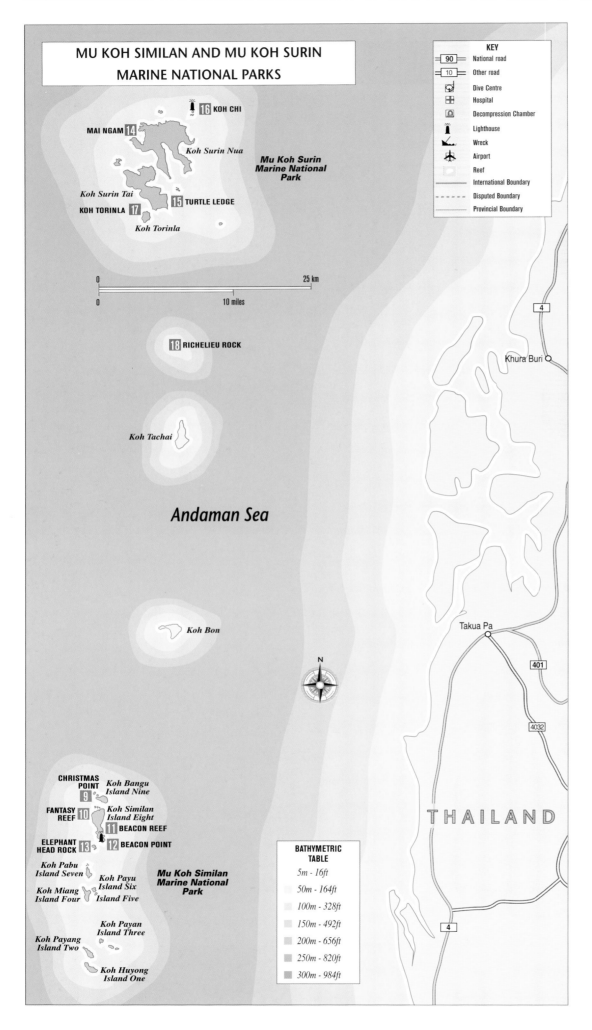

MU KOH SIMILAN AND MU KOH SURIN MARINE NATIONAL PARKS

KEY

90	National road
10	Other road
	Dive Centre
	Hospital
	Decompression Chamber
	Lighthouse
	Wreck
	Airport
	Reef
	International Boundary
	Disputed Boundary
	Provincial Boundary

16 KOH CHI

MAI NGAM 14

Koh Surin Nua

Mu Koh Surin Marine National Park

Koh Surin Tai

KOH TORINLA 17 **15 TURTLE LEDGE**

Koh Torinla

0 ———————— 25 km

0 ———————— 10 miles

18 RICHELIEU ROCK

Koh Tachai

Andaman Sea

Koh Bon

N

CHRISTMAS POINT 9 *Koh Bangu Island Nine*

FANTASY REEF 10 *Koh Similan Island Eight*

11 BEACON REEF

ELEPHANT HEAD ROCK 13 **12 BEACON POINT**

Koh Pabu Island Seven

Koh Payu Island Six

Koh Miang Island Four *Island Five*

Mu Koh Similan Marine National Park

Koh Payan Island Three

Koh Payang Island Two

Koh Huyong Island One

BATHYMETRIC TABLE

5m - 16ft	
50m - 164ft	
100m - 328ft	
150m - 492ft	
200m - 656ft	
250m - 820ft	
300m - 984ft	

4

Khura Buri

Takua Pa

401

4032

THAILAND

4

---

by name and number, ascending northwards. The Royal Forestry Department has installed two offices and the duty rangers are the only permanent residents on any of the islands, although the Royal Thai Navy temporarily act as protector of a turtle rehabilitation project on Koh Huyong (island one).

The topography of the east and west coasts are in complete contrast. The former experiences milder weather conditions and has sheltered coastlines with sandy beaches underlined by gently sloping reefs. The more exposed west coast features weather-beaten boulders rising from the seabed, crowned by leaning trees, forced over by the heavy monsoon winds. These configurations continue beneath the water line. The western coastlines are typified by giant boulders tumbling down to the seabed; adjoining gaps are swept free of sand and coral fragments by strong currents during the harsher months, which clear the way for exciting tunnels, arches, caverns and crevices, all awaiting exploration, whereas other, more scattered, pinnacles and plateaus act as submerged auditoriums for pelagic enthusiasts.

There are over 200 recorded species of stony corals alone, along with an equally large, although not as apparent, variety of soft corals. Visibility sometimes tops the 30m (100ft) mark. There is, however, a drop during the country's hottest months, when a rise in water temperature often results in a plankton bloom. This, in turn, increases the spectrum of marine life, which attracts pelagic visitors. Tuna, barracuda, jacks and trevallies are accompanied by Manta and Eagle Rays and the odd Whale Shark.

There is world-class diving to be found all around the archipelago. Starting off the northwest coast of Koh Bangu, island nine, the first site is **Christmas Point** 9 .

Boulders of various shapes and sizes fringe the island's northern shoreline in depths averaging 25m (80ft), increasing in size and depth towards the north. Their upper slopes are punctuated by *Dendronephthya* Soft Tree Corals, which also fringe small rocky overhangs. Wide areas between the rocks are shared by varying amounts of stony corals, the most common being broad plate corals. The narrow gaps and steps act as cleaning stations for Giant Morays who are tended to by shrimps. Oriental sweetlips enjoy a similar service from cleanerfish and V-shaped squadrons can be seen patiently awaiting their turn around the site. The western quadrant of the site features a couple of wedge-shaped archways leading through an enormous rocky centrepiece. Passing through these dramatically alters the seascape and the feel of the dive. They also act as escape routes if the current suddenly picks up, which tends to happen here.

A matrix of submerged boulders rise from the seabed around 50m (165ft) from the northwestern coastline of Koh Similan (island eight), spreading out towards the west. These scattered plateaus have several names, the most common of which is **Fantasy Reef** ⑩. The site was declared out-of-bounds between

2000 and 2003 to allow the corals time to recover from diver damage, although the damage was more likely to have been caused by fishing nets. The site comprises extensive rocky mounds, connected by wide gullies to other solitary pinnacles marking out the perimeter. The higher rocky platforms sit 14m (45ft) below the surface, while others drop to below 40m (130ft). Large crevices split the otherwise unbroken surfaces in leaf-vein formations, the main arteries of which are flanked by impressive gorgonias. The adjoining thoroughfares are used as ambushes and lairs by a variety of reef fish and Giant Moray Eels. The diversity of marine life in every part of this site is outstanding. A variety of triggerfish mingle with schools of parrotfish, Coral Groupers, lionfish and sweetlips.

The bottom composition is fragmented coral substrate. This is the home of the tiny, but magnificent Ribbon Eel. Both the blue-bodied adults and black juveniles are seen frequently. The best way to locate these eels is

by looking out for Purple Fire Gobies (Decorated Dartfish) that hover slightly above the bottom; the eels are never far away.

Fringing the island's opposite coast is **Beacon Reef** ⑪, the longest continuous coral structure in the island group. The reef flat sits in an average of 5m (16ft) and comprises many examples of Brain corals, heavily punctuated by clusters of Staghorn, all rich with colourful reef fish such as damsels, wrasse, parrot and surgeonfish. The coral formations remain constant over the southern section of the reef, with examples increasing in size with depth as they appear on the reef slopes. Stony leaf corals such as Lettuce Corals mix with a variety of horizontal plates. The fish life is similar to that found in shallower water, although the presence is higher and examples larger. It is not uncommon to see small Whitetip Reef Sharks swagger by over the sands in the depths. The sandy bottom begins where the reef leaves off in around the 28m (92ft) mark and slowly tapers away into the

ABOVE *In Orangestriped Triggerfish (*Balistapus undulatus*) mature males lose most of the orange lines over the snout.*

ABOVE *The* Lutjanidae *family, more commonly known as snappers, are frequently seen in the Indian Ocean.*

ABOVE *This Tiger Tail Sea Horse (*Hippocampus comes*) can be found by peering into dark recesses and under ledges.*

abyss. The shallower part of this area is liberally punctuated by a chain of bommies covered in soft coral, whose colourful presence is further enriched by orange and blue encrusting sponges and multicoloured feather stars. The reef's southern tip is referred to as **Beacon Point** 12, and is popular for observing stingrays gliding over the seabed and also in the shallow waters. There have been more encounters with Manta and Eagle Rays here than anywhere else in the marine national park.

To the immediate southwest, **Elephant Head Rock** 13 is a cluster of weather-beaten boulders, the larger and southernmost of which resembles a swimming elephant's head: hence the name. The underwater terrain is breathtaking. The dive takes you around boulders, many with a circumference in excess of 30m (100ft), creating narrow passages and alleyways. The outer surfaces of these underwater monoliths are occasionally highlighted by an encrusting sponge, but inside the passageways most of the upper surfaces are covered with colourful soft corals. The seabed drops to beyond 30m (100ft) to the east of the main and largest structure, which is also a good place for nudibranch spotting.

Mu Koh Surin Marine National Park

This park, consisting of granite islands and two rocky outcrops, covers an area of 135 sq km (52 sq miles). The largest island, Koh Surin Nua has an area of 19 sq km (7 sq miles), and to the immediate southwest its neighbour, Koh Surin Tai, covers 12 sq km (5 sq miles). These two islands are covered with primary evergreen forest, fringed with mangrove forests occasionally broken by beaches. There are only three locations inhabited by humans on the northern island: the park headquarters on the western shoreline, a small fishing community, and a Chao Ley (sea gypsy) village on the southern coast.

The coral formations here are predominantly fringing reefs in that they circumscribe, at least in part, small islets, rocky outcroppings and submerged pinnacles. Koh Surin Nua boasts several interesting locations such as **Mai Ngam** 14 on the western coast, where one can catch glimpses of Green and Hawksbill Turtles as they come ashore to start the arduous task of laying their eggs.

Of the Koh Surin Tai sites, **Turtle Ledge** 15, is the most impressive and named for the frequent sightings of turtles, in particular the Hawksbill, although there are other visitors, including triggerfish, snappers and sweetlips. The higher portions of the reef slope have many examples of sea anemones, and False Clown or Ocellated Anemonefish. In other areas, clusters of Stag and Elkhorn Corals climb over Giant clams, this particular species being the largest of the giant clam family.

To the northeast of the islands, **Koh Chi** 16 is among the best locations to observe large visiting pelagics such as Great Barracuda, Dogtooth Tuna, Threadfin Trevally and Bigeye Trevallies. It is also a good place for observing turtles on their way to and from Koh Surin Nua – even the rarely seen Leatherback has been spotted here in recent years.

The reef at **Koh Torinla** 17 extends for around one kilometre (⅔ mile), at which many species of marine life have to date been identified, 15 of which were different species of sea slug, or nudibranch. Coral Groupers shelter beneath many corals, and many members of the *chromis* family dart among large tables of staghorns. There are many shelves of rocks at varying depths, all with different features. The shallower ones host hermit crabs, cleaner shrimps and colourful feather stars.

About 14km (9 miles) to the east of the two Surin Islands lies the area's star attraction: **Richelieu Rock** 18. This five-pronged series

LEFT *Gorgonian Sea Fans are found at right angles to strong currents, predominantly in deeper water. These expansive coral structures attract all manner of marine creatures.*

of pinnacles attracts so many Whale Sharks with such regularity that some consider them to be residents. But even if visitors are unlucky enough to miss them, there is a wealth of other creatures to see. Three southern pinnacles sit in 22m (72ft) and feature large numbers of orange Gorgonian Sea Fans, immediately beneath many-hued soft corals. Scorpionfish, stonefish, moray eels, long spined sea urchins, shrimps, crabs and colourful nudibranchs can always be found among the rocky crevices. The radiant *hermatypic* corals also harbour a wide diversity of marine life: common residents include Schooling Bannerfish, Blackspot and Humpback Snappers, Indian Ocean and Spotfin Lionfish, Moorish idols and Titan triggerfish.

Since this is the only food source in the immediate area, it is a first-class location for spotting large pelagics, with plenty of species to choose from: Rainbow Runners, Great Barracuda, trevallies, tuna and jacks. The seabed here consists of sand mixed with fragmented coral substrate and is home to a variety of molluscs, including some large squid, octopuses and a variety of gastropods, mainly Lister's conch. However, the nocturnally active Cone and Mitre shells are also in abundance. Other attractions of the deep include Guitarfish with their half-shark half-ray body and, on a much smaller scale, the Tiger Tail Sea Horse. Above these, many clumps of *Tubastrea* corals have fallen prey to Golden Wendletrap Snails, their skeletal remains left to act as egg hatcheries.

THE DEEP SOUTH

In the deep south, again on the live-aboard circuit, are the two attractions of Hin Daeng and Hin Mouang.

The numbers and health of both reef inhabitants and pelagics here are exceptional. Open-ocean fish are often found in strong water movement, because it stimulates their desire to hunt. Large schools come in to feed, Dogtooth Tuna, Rainbow Runners, Longfin Great, Chevron and Yellowtail Barracuda, Trevally and other jacks are almost resident.

HIN MOUANG [19]

The name of this submerged mountain means Purple Rock and refers to the rich garden of purple sea anemones carpeting the top of the most prominent pinnacle which sits in about 16m (52ft). The southernmost configuration begins as a sheer wall which descends to a narrow platform at about 40m (130ft) before it plummets further, to more than 70m (230ft).

There are a number of narrow valleys breaking the otherwise solid infrastructure, which are almost obscured by *Dendronephthya* Soft Tree Corals and Gorgonian Sea Fans.

There is a prominent cavern, about 50m (165ft) wide, almost midway in the length of the structure. However, it does not cut through the rock as do the smaller examples,

Lastly, a much larger visitor, the enormous Whale Shark, provides welcome encounters. This is onother of the top destinations in Southeast Asia for encounters with this gentle giant. Another of the ocean's graceful creatures, the Manta Ray, is also a frequent visitor.

HIN DAENG [20]

Unlike its close neighbour, Hin Daeng, or Red Rock, does break the water's surface; but only at low tide. This rock is named after the red *Dendronephthya* Soft Tree Corals which adorn its upper slopes and walls. The drop continues but breaks off halfway and changes course along its length, splitting the infrastructure. This rocky blockade provides great shelter in adverse currents, and because of the diversity and colour of the marine life found in the gorge, it is also one of the highlights of the site. At night Painted Rock Lobsters look like a regimental guard along narrow shelves and tunnels in the walls, and the eyes of cleaner shrimps and minute reef crabs reflect the light in the form of tiny red dots. On a larger, and more obvious scale, Giant Morays cause a temporary increase in divers' air consumption as they abandon their lairs for the night to participate, along with the motionless scorpionfish, in their own particular style of nocturnal hunting.

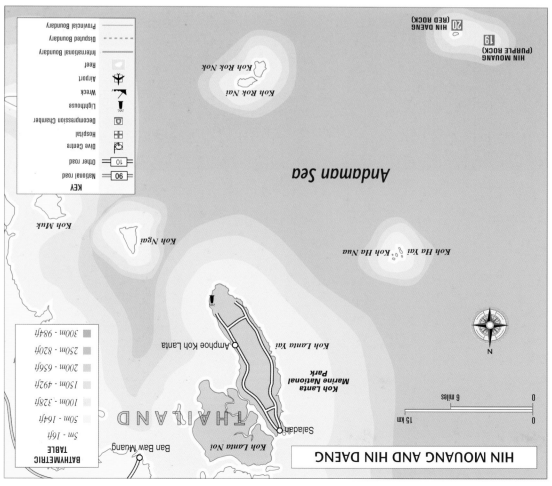

HIN MOUANG AND HIN DAENG

Andaman Sea

THAILAND

Koh Lanta Noi
Koh Lanta Yai
Amphoe Koh Lanta
Saladan
Ban Baw Muang
Koh Muk
Koh Ngai
Koh Ha Yai
Koh Ha Nua
Koh Lanta Marine National Park
Koh Rok Nai
Koh Rok Nok
HIN MOUANG (PURPLE ROCK) 19
HIN DAENG (RED ROCK) 20

N

0   15 km
0   6 miles

BATHYMETRIC TABLE

	5m - 16ft
	50m - 164ft
	100m - 328ft
	150m - 492ft
	200m - 656ft
	250m - 820ft
	300m - 984ft

KEY

96	National road
10	Other road
	Dive Centre
	Hospital
	Decompression Chamber
	Lighthouse
	Wreck
	Airport
	Reef
	International Boundary
	Disputed Boundary
	Provincial Boundary

here has always looked rugged. Not every-where underwater is a kaleidoscope of colour – in most cases you have to look for it. Unfortunately, this undeserved bad press has deterred many a diver from visiting the area. Don't be put off by rumour, it would be such a shame to miss this site out.

MERGUI ARCHIPELAGO MYANMAR (BURMA)

Described as one of the most scenic and charming island groups in Southeast Asia, the Mergui Archipelago comprises no less than 804 islands, islets and rocky outcrops. The dive sites here differ from those off Western Thailand in that coral representation is more sporadic and not as colourful. The underwater terrain is a lot more rugged and visibility tends to be slightly less. However, the area has two draw cards: firstly, there's the big fish, namely sharks, rays and a wealth of pelagics; and secondly, a handful of the sites are teeming with minute reef inhabitants.

[21] BLACK ROCK

About halfway up the archipelago, a solitary craggy outcrop sits proud of the water by some 20m (65ft), spreading more than five times that, from east to west. The southern side of the rock drops off to varying depths and at different angles. In places it is sheer, in others it drops down ledges and over enormous boulders. The southwestern end of the site features a series of granite plateaus sloping away slightly from the main rock. Their surfaces are almost completely obscured by low-lying pink and white bushes of Dendrophthya soft corals, among which chains of scorpionfish, and Common Reef Octopus, lie incognito. On a smaller scale, but with a slightly more obvious presence, are a host of tiny hawkfish and blennies, all flitting around nervously. The outer faces of these plateaus descend below 40m (130ft) and these deeper waters are the preferred location for sighting Grey Reef Sharks as they circle round, gradually approaching a wide gully that separates this colourful area from the main rocky

as a series of walls with intermittent shelves, all decorated with varying amounts of coral heads, sea whips and carpet anemones. The diversity of everyday marine life is grand and ranges from tiny invertebrates to intimidating Grey Reef Sharks in the depths. The latter are actually quite timid and often flee at the exhalation of divers' bubbles. Other shark encounters here include Variegated (Leopard), which are usually around the southern section of the site. This area comprises two elevated ridges divided by a steep slope of small corals and more rocks; rather like a giant horse-shoe. The inner section is great for spotting an unusual selection of marine life, with no particular pattern to it. There are cuttlefish

and Common Reef Octopus, lionfish and scorpionfish, the odd stonefish, also morays, mantis shrimps and sea kraits (snakes). Schools of various snappers are also present, but they tend to pass by. The Leopard sharks seem to be content with chasing after one another, cat-and-mouse style around and between small jutting pinnacles. Although surrounded by pinnacles rather than sand dunes, the centre section of this site is a bit like an oasis, in that it provides shelter for many temporary inhabitants. Stingrays, Coral Groupers and pufferfish all take advantage.

Claims that this area is being destroyed by blast fishing is spread by inexperienced observers, who don't realize that the terrain

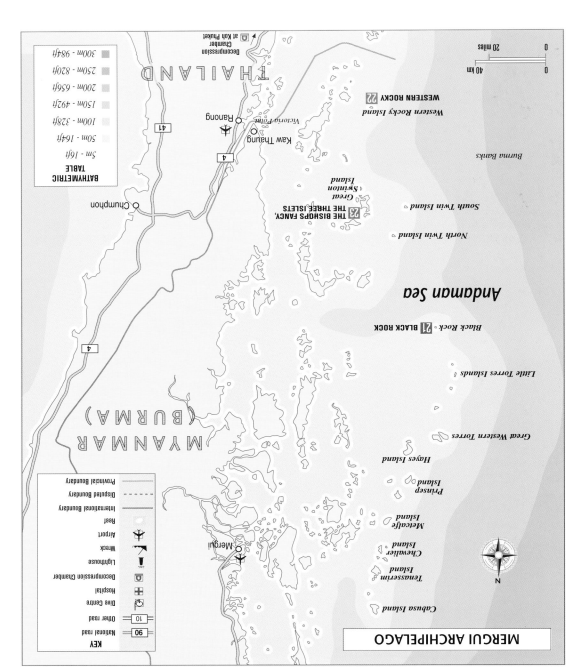

MERGUI ARCHIPELAGO

INDIAN OCEAN

TOP RIGHT *During the male Pharaoh Cuttlefish (Sepia pharaonis) uses a modified arm to place packets of sperm into a pouch beneath the female's mouth.*

RIGHT *Roving Coralgrouper (Plectropomus pessuliferus) are often seen waiting their turn at one of the cleaning stations around coral reefs.*

22 WESTERN ROCKY

The southernmost destination, it lies some 82km (51 miles) southwest of Kaw Thaung on Victoria Point. Above the water, it looks like a collection of rocky pillars in varying sizes. This site differs from others in the area in that the reefs are separated – either to fringe the larger of the outcrops individually, or to connect the adjoining smaller ones. On the rocks, Banded Sea Kraits twist by sea anemones tended to by porcelain crabs, shrimps and a selection of anemonefish, while deeper down large cowries punctuate Gorgonian Sea Fans. In the wide ravines below, among the coral substrate seabed, Ribbon Eels mingle with burrowing prawn gobies and pistol shrimps which, in turn, are passed over by groups of amorous cuttlefish in their search for partners. The biggest rocky structure features a couple of caves, the largest of which has an

structure. Sometimes other sharks grace the waters with their presence, including the majestic Whale Shark.

Close inspection of the main structure reveals the likes of almost transparent shrimps, minute coral snails and Crinoid crabs, surreal nudibranchs and a mixture of cephalopods (octopus and squid) with colours adjusted to blend in with their backgrounds.

The layout of the opposing reef differs in that it descends more gradually over a jumble of rocks of varying sizes, reaching a more steady depth at about 30m (100ft) where it meets the sandy seabed. Banded Sea Kraits and a variety of moray eels meander around the gaps in search of food and use the many dark recesses, not only as lairs, but as places to get tended to by cleaning invertebrates.

23 THE BISHOPS FANCY, THE THREE ISLETS

Three unnamed rocky outcrops lie immediately north of Great Swinton Island. The largest, central, outcrop features small creatures and large predators. The average depth is 20m (65ft) and in places it is deeper than 30m (100ft). Beneath the islet is split in two from west to east by a canyon, which becomes narrower as you pass through it. The western end is marked by a large solitary rock with prominent ripples in the sand to each side. Behind this rock the gorge twists to the entrance in the southern wall next to a splendid rocky archway covered in corals. The entrance can be found in around 20m (65ft) and it continues as a tunnel with walls and ceiling frequently broken by crevices. There are shelves full of Painted Rock Lobsters; their eyes reflecting the diver's artificial light. After a relatively short distance the tunnel dips to the right, into a small bowl formation. This occasionally hosts an irritable 2m (6ft) Nurse Shark. The tunnel has two exits. The larger, preferred one, is to the right. The other exit is a lot smaller and often blocked by a number of Nurse Sharks. The other cave is smaller and not nearly as exciting, although at the entrance there are at least three anglerfish as well as lion, scorpion and stonefish, and is worth checking out.

right and then follows through an archway highlighted by orange and yellow encrusting sponges. Beyond the arch is a small hole in the rocky floor, only large enough for a single diver to drop into. This opens into a small, low cave. It is very dark, but torchlight often reveals as many as five sleeping Nurse Sharks, some of them stacked. Returning to the underwater canyon can be an adventure as this is where Grey Reef Sharks and stingrays can be seen swimming nose to tail. Unfortunately, they are fairly nervous creatures and don't hang around for very long.

Exiting the crevice brings you to an area teeming with tiny invertebrates and curious marine life – perfect for macro enthusiasts. Shrimps, eels and even sea horses are all regular sightings, along with ghost pipefish (frogfish) and the not-so-commonplace basket star.

INDIA – ANDAMAN AND NICOBAR ISLANDS

The Andaman and Nicobar archipelagos comprise 572 islands nestled in the Bay of Bengal. They are also collectively referred to as Little India, although the islands are more commonly recognized as two separate groups. The Andaman Islands cover an area of about 352km (219 miles) top to bottom by 51km (32 miles) across. This narrow archipelago comprises five main islands: North, Middle, South and Great Andaman (the latter being the combination of Baratang and Rutland Islands). Port Blair on South Andaman is the islands' capital and administrative centre.

To the east of the main island chain lies the uninhabited volcanic mound of Barren Island, the only active volcano in the Indian territories. Beyond this, heading further north is the Special Armoured Post (SAP) at Narcondam Island, which oversees the northern approaches. Both are favoured diving destinations. While cruising between these islands, sightings of dolphins, flying fish and even the rare Dugong are possible.

To date world-class diving sites have been discovered to the north and south of the island groups, particularly along the islands' eastern coastlines and offshore islands. That is not to say that there are no prime sites around the opposite coastlines; these remain to be discovered during future exploration. The diversity of marine life and the corals found so far in this area is well represented and occur through a range of depths, with the deeper waters experiencing the higher proportion of enormous Gorgonian Sea Fans and bursts of radiant Dendronephthya Soft Tree Corals. There are high-voltage dives along sheer walls and around submerged pinnacles and plateaus. Equally enjoyable is a healthy supply of fringing and offshore reefs. Colourful reef fish abound as do invertebrates and a selection of turtles, a high proportion of which are familiar sights at a network of cleaning stations. Some of these serve large customers such as Great Barracuda and a variety of large rays, including Manta and Eagle. Large pelagics are plentiful, as are a variety of sharks such as, in order of frequency: Blacktip and Whitetip, Grey Reef, Silvertip, and hammerhead. Narcondam Island also has its own attraction for the occasional Whale Shark.

24 BARREN ISLAND

Barren Island is located some 137km (85 miles) northeast of Port Blair. The sloping sides of blackened rocks, rolling ash and hardened lava flow right down and beyond the water's edge at this 305m (1000ft) high conical island. Due to the heavy volcanic soil, the visibility underwater is usually good. Depths vary enormously. Walls and slopes drop to 40m (130ft) and may level out briefly before plummeting back down to beyond 600m (1970ft). Looking down it is common to see reef sharks and the odd Silvertip on patrol.

The diving here is in complete contrast to other sites in the area. It follows sheer walls, occasionally broken by steep, undulating hills of volcanic soil. Directly off the northwestern point of the island the seascape drops in places to 80m (260ft), levels out to form a wide canyon and then climbs back over a narrow crest to around 40m (130ft). The outer wall of the crest then drops to beyond 120m (400ft). This location is an enjoyable dive, but corals only have an erratic presence, as do bushes of white stinging hydroids. The almost slate-like walls and deep ledges are adequately represented in the world of colour, courtesy of feather stars and orange and blue sponges.

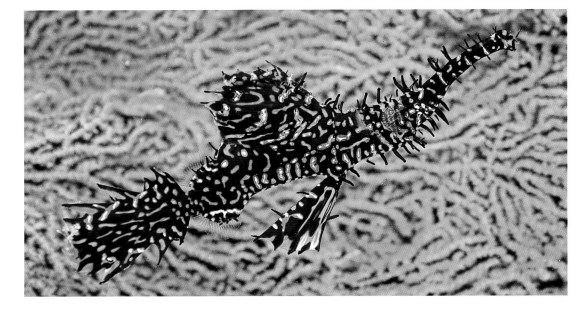

LEFT *Harlequin Ghost Pipefish (Solenostomus paradoxus) give birth to hundreds of minute, perfectly formed offspring, which are nursed in the male's pouch.*

The majority of reef fish here tend to be either angel or butterfly fish, which seem to be in their juvenile stage.

The ashen slopes dissecting the drop-offs are punctuated by a variety of gobies, including the magnificent Purple Fire Gobies (Decorated Dartfish). A great selection of nudibranchs brightens the many dark rocks in the soil. The depths of this underwater canyon are almost constantly patrolled by large sharks, including Blacktip, Whitetip and Grey Reef and Silvertips. Large schools of pelagics rise from the abyss in search of prey, and there are regular sightings of Dogtooth Tuna, Giant and Chevron Barracuda and Rainbow Runners.

NARCONDAM ISLAND

This lush rainforest-covered island lies some 259km (161 miles) east of Port Blair. This island acts as the northern gateway to the archipelago. It offers a few dive sites, one of which is **Lighthouse Point** 25, although the lighthouse is actually a warning beacon on the northwestern point of the island. It has an average depth of around 25m (80ft) and a maximum depth of 40m (130ft). The formation underwater is, apart from the dead trees, similar to that on the surface, in that it continues to taper off in the same direction until it reaches an area of enormous geometric boulders at 32m (105ft). Their cheek-by-jowl formation is highlighted by clumps of soft corals and large Gorgonian Sea Fans; there is also a fair representation of other marine life milling about, particularly small reef sharks, unicornfish and sweetlips. Drifting back into the shallows takes you over terraces of plate corals and rocks blanketed with encrusting sponges – a great place for nudibranch enthusiasts.

There's a small Rocky outcrop in the bay to the south of the SAP Lookout Post. Called **The Estate** 26, it is a series of enormous, craggy, towering rocks. The dive takes you around and through cavernous alleyways, which separate these submerged tower blocks, with patches of encrusting sponges

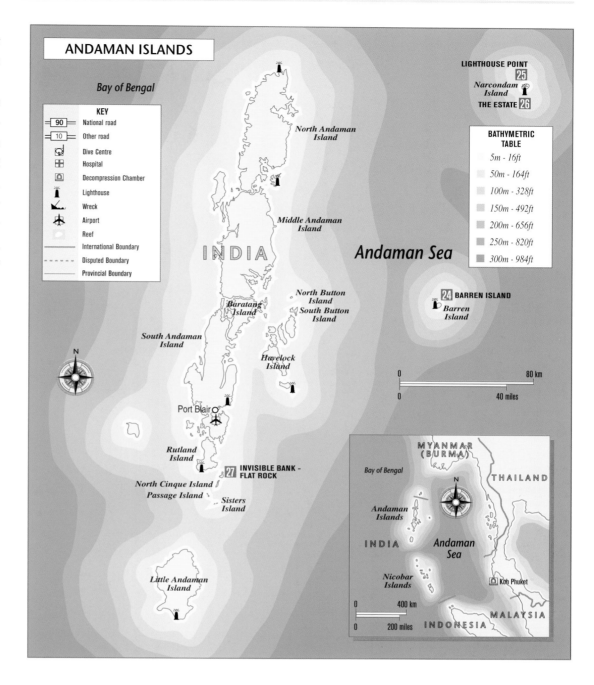

and the occasional splash of *Dendronephthya* Soft Tree Corals brightening up the otherwise stony faces. The fish life in the depths is big and includes a group of resident Malabar Grouper and intimidating shoals of oversized tuna. There is plenty of smaller stuff to see here, such as Purple Fire Gobies, Oriental Sweetlips, Indian Ocean Lionfish, fairy basslets and the odd moray, the shallows are a good place for nudibranchs.

27 INVISIBLE BANK, FLAT ROCK

Flat Rock lies dangerously, depending on the tide level, slightly above or below the water line at the southern end of Invisible Bank, about 100km (62 miles) to the southeast of

Port Blair. The average depth here is 12m (40ft) with the waters around the Bank dropping down to below 35m (115ft). Invisible Bank itself is an extensive rocky plateau featuring few live corals, except in some sheltered areas. Marine life is good, but scattered. Flat Rock, however, is a different scenario. Again, there are few corals, but the topography is dramatic, with scattered rocks over a sandy bottom, and the concentration of fish can be remarkable. The reef life is especially noteworthy, with schools of unicorns, surgeons, trigger, grouper and sweetlips. Grey and Whitetip Reef Sharks are usually patrolling, as are pelagics such as mackerel, tuna, barracuda and trevally.

WESTERN AUSTRALIA

by Ann Storrie

NEARLY ONE THIRD OF AUSTRALIA'S 20,000KM (12,000 mile) coastline is along the state of Western Australia. This area ranges from the tropical coral reefs off the Kimberly coast, to the temperate granite and limestone habitats southwest of the state. Tropical waters surround the Christmas and Cocos Islands and a band of oceanic atolls, including the Rowley Shoals, Scott Reef and Seringapatam Reef. These areas are remote and provide pristine and exciting tropical diving.

Further south, the waters of Ningaloo Reef near Exmouth support a wonderful mix of tropical and temperate life. Ningaloo is the longest fringing reef in the world and provides many safe, sheltered lagoons for snorkelling and diving. The area is also renowned for the annual migration of Whale Sharks that congregate to feed on plankton after the corals spawn in March.

The southwest of Western Australia has delightful, temperate marine environments. Limestone and granite pinnacles, caves, ledges

TOP LEFT *The Ningaloo Reef is the longest fringing reef in the world and provides many beautiful, safe bays and dive sites.*

TOP RIGHT *Esperance is well endowed with picturesque bays and islands. Enormous granite boulders also provide spectacular underwater scenery with temperate water invertebrates.*

and overhangs brim with invertebrates, the colour of which rivals that of the tropical coral reefs. There are marine parks right on Perth's (the capital city's) doorstep, which serve to protect marine life while allowing people to indulge in many of their favourite activities such as fishing and collecting crays (*Panulirus cygnus*). Some of the best sites are just a stone's throw from the main swimming beaches of Perth, and Rottnest Island, which lies 18km (11 miles) off the coast.

Wrecks also feature along the Western Australian coastline. There are still 17th Century vessels to be discovered, and many old ships are regularly dived along the coast. Not content with these, Western Australia has scuttled two Australian navy warships, *HMAS Swan*, which is now a major dive attraction in Geographe Bay, and *HMAS Perth* on the south coast at Albany.

For a real adrenaline rush, try a cage dive with great white sharks off the Neptune Islands in South Australia. Colonies of New Zealand fur seals and Australian sea lions provide a banquet for the great whites and, often, good shark sightings for the divers.

With increasing tourism, the dive industry in Australia has become very efficient. Diving can be arranged on arrival for most areas along the coast, although some of the remote areas, such as the Rowley Shoals and Scott Reef, require prior preparation and planning.

CHRISTMAS AND COCOS ISLANDS

Christmas and Cocos Islands are some of the remotest and least known of Australia's island territories. They are situated over 2600km (1616 miles) from Perth and only 360km (224 miles) and 1000km (621 miles) from Jakarta respectively. Christmas Island is a volcanic atoll renowned for its lush tropical rain forest with magnificent bird life, and the annual red crab migration. Its topography is spectacular and the sites are nearly all deep wall dives with many caves, overhangs and spectacular coral growth. Sites worth diving are: **The Grotto** [1], **Northeast Point** [2], **Flying Fish Cove (and Cantelievers)** [3], **Thundercliffe Cave** [4], **West White Beach** [5], **Boat Cave** [6], and **Pig Rock (Egeria Point)** [7].

Cocos Island is a true coral atoll, and drew the attention of Charles Darwin in 1836. It was here that Darwin formulated his theories on coral atoll formation. Cocos is renowned for its large pelagic fish, reef sharks, Manta Rays, giant Humphead (Napoleon) Wrasse, turtles, and a variety of different dive sites within a relatively small area. There are walls and small drop-offs, a huge expanse of *Turbinaria* coral that forms an enormous 'cabbage patch,' large plate corals that slope from the surface to about 25m (80ft) and safe snorkelling and diving in the lagoon. Sites worth diving are: **Garden of Eden** [8], **Cologne Gardens** [9],

Cabbage Patch [10], The Towers [11], Two Trees [12], The Atrium [13], Govie House [14], East White Beach [15], Spanish Eyes [16], Prison Gardens [17], Lion Cave [18], and Manta Ray Corner [19].

As is common on isolated atolls, many marine species have proliferated on Christmas and Cocos Islands, while others have not yet colonized the areas. The absence of Coral Groupers, Humbug Damsels and dragonets is countered by the abundance of other groupers, wrasse, damselfish, gobies, butterflyfish, surgeonfish, blennies and cardinalfish. Many of these species thrive in above-average numbers compared with other Indo-Pacific localities.

At both islands, access to various dive sites depends on the weather. The climate is tropical. During the summer months, the northwesterly winds may inhibit diving on those sides of the islands, but diving on the east coasts can usually be arranged at this time. The water temperature averages 28°C (82°F) and visibility on the walls is generally 30–50m (100–165ft). During summer, in the cyclone season, visibility may be less, and a day or two's diving may be lost if a cyclone passes nearby.

ROWLEY SHOALS, SCOTT AND SERINGAPATAM REEFS

The Rowley Shoals are some of the best examples of shelf atolls in Australian waters. They formed over 10 million years ago when the western continental shelf subsided. As the land submerged, the corals grew upwards to form three oval-shaped atolls, 30–40km (20–25 miles) apart, and approximately 280km (174 miles) from the Western Australian mainland. Each atoll consists of a rim of reef surrounding a large lagoon. They rise from over 400m (1312ft) of water, and their western sides all drop off extremely steeply.

When the first surveys of marine life were conducted at the Rowley Shoals in 1982 and 1983, the Western Australian Museum added over 340 new species of fish to Western Australian records. One of the most impressive species of these fish is the huge Potato

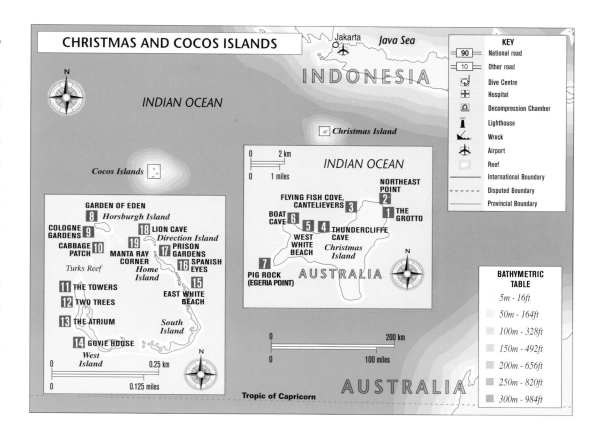

ABOVE *Western Australia's northern atolls (excluding the Rowley Shoals) support the largest sea snake population in the world. These are Turtle-headed Sea Snakes.*

INDIAN OCEAN

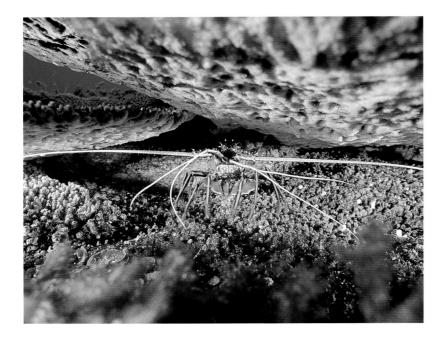

ABOVE *Western Rock Lobsters (crayfish). On every dive around Rottnest you can see their antennae waving from under limestone ledges.*

ABOVE *Rarely seen by divers, both the tropical and temperate water species of Blue Ringed Octopus have an extremely toxic venom.*

Grouper (*Epinephelus tukula*). These fearless, inquisitive monsters often approach divers and even taste outstretched hands and fins. Huge clams, spider shells, cowries, colourful anemones with associated anemonefish, damsels and striking Yellowstriped Anthias all crowd among prolific coral growths at depths of less than 5m (16ft) on top of the reef. Shallow bommies within the lagoons support enough life to entertain a diver for hours, while the outer reef drop-offs are simply breathtaking. The entire surface of the coral foundation is covered with living stony corals, soft corals, anemones, ascidians, hydroids and sponges. Reef fish from nearly every family are found, and large schools of trevally, bream, snapper, tuna, mackerel and bonito are often sighted. Reef sharks and Manta Rays are also common. Sites worth diving are: **Lively** [25], **West Wall** [26], **North Wall** [27], **Mermaid Channel** [28], **Cod Hole** [29], **Southeast Wall** [30], **Jimmy Goes to China** [31], **Blue Lagoon** [32], **Clerke Reef Channel** [33] and **Southeast Wall** [34].

Scott Reef and Seringapatam lie about 400km (250 miles) north of the Rowley Shoals. The diving and marine life here are similar to the Rowley Shoals, with one important exception. Sea snakes are in abundance at these more northerly atolls which boast the largest sea snake population in the world. Surprisingly, the snakes have not yet populated the Rowley Shoals. If you are looking for snakes, at Scott Reef and Seringapatam you may find up to 20 snakes on each dive. Beautiful, inquisitive, and sometimes extremely friendly, snakes of several species may follow divers during most of their time underwater. Provided the snakes are not antagonized, they are rarely a problem. It is a wonderful experience to glide gently through the calm waters of the lagoons and watch the sea snakes gently winding their way through the branches of staghorn corals where they poke into crevices for prey. Sites worth diving are: **Seringapatam** [20], **Northeast Wall – North Reef** [21], **Southeast Wall – North Reef** [22], **Sandy Islet** [23] and **South Reef** [24].

Visibility of over 40m (130ft) is normal during winter and early spring at the Rowley Shoals, Scott and Seringapatam Reefs, although water temperature may be a little cooler than expected for a tropical reef environment. Underwater temperatures of 29–30°C (84–86°F) do occur, but 25–26°C (77–80°F) is not uncommon. In August and September, when the winds are still and the land temperature a pleasant 30°C (86°F), there is nothing better than to relax after a day's diving in a motionless boat, watching the most magnificent sunset reflected in the mirror of the lagoons. The waters of these atolls are pristine and one of the relatively untouched diving frontiers of the world.

NINGALOO REEF AND CORAL BAY

The Ningaloo Reef is one of Australia's most important tracts of reef. It extends for approximately 260km (162 miles) from the northwest cape at Exmouth to just south of Coral Bay. The reef ranges from 7km (4½ miles) off the coast to less than 200m (656ft) from shore. It is the longest fringing reef in the world and many of its beautiful lagoons provide some of the easiest and most delightful snorkelling and shallow diving in Australia.

Ningaloo is best known for its regular visits by Whale Sharks. It is here that these magnificent fish can be predictably found and studied. The Whale Shark is the largest cold-blooded animal in the world, and the largest fish. It grows to over 12m (40ft) and can have a mouth 1m (3ft) wide. Yet it is a harmless filter feeder. The sharks come to Ningaloo every March and usually stay until June. This coincides with the annual coral spawn on the reef that turns the sea into plankton soup. However, despite the plankton, visibility is often 20–30m (65–100ft). Charter boats employ spotter planes to guide them to the Whale Sharks, and sometimes seven or eight sharks can be seen in one day.

To swim with a Whale Shark is an awesome experience. The gigantic mouth is held wide open as it feeds and you can see it gulp an enormous quantity of water and plankton. The head is usually surrounded by small pilot fish, including juvenile Golden Trevally, while remoras are often stuck to its ventral surface. Other large fish, such as cobia, are sometimes seen swimming close by.

There is of course more to Ningaloo than Whale Sharks. This area is home to over 500 species of fish, 250 known species of corals and about 600 species of molluscs. Green, Loggerhead and Hawksbill Turtles are prevalent. Green Turtles, in particular, have extensive nesting sites along this coast. Manta Rays are common and occasionally large shoals can be seen feeding on the plankton.

Sites worth diving are: **Navy Pier** 35, **Cod Spot** 36, **Northwest Ridge** 37, **Blizzard Ridge** 38, **Turtle Mound** 39, **Turquoise Bay** 40, **Coral Bay** 41.

Whale-watching tours are organized between August and October when Humpback Whales migrate down the coast. They calve in the tropical waters and meander back close to the coast on their way to the southern regions for summer. Schools of dolphins are often sighted and Dugongs feed in the shallow sea grasses along the coast.

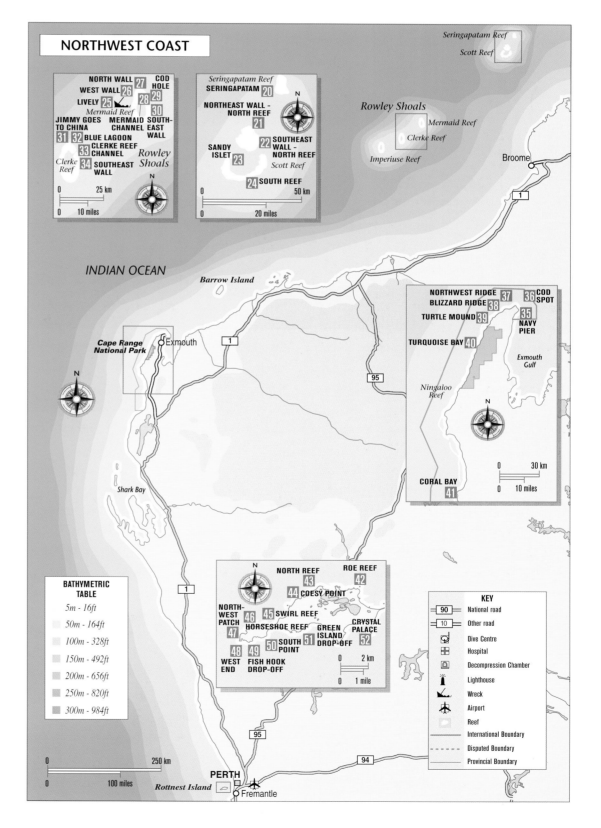

ABOVE *Feather stars like to perch as high as they can to obtain the best vantage point for trapping passing plankton, while shoals of tiny juvenile fish swirl around.*

INDIAN OCEAN

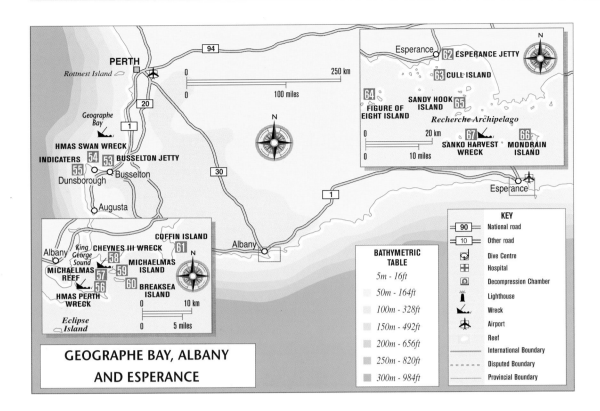

GEOGRAPHE BAY, ALBANY AND ESPERANCE

KEY

90	National road
10	Other road
	Dive Centre
	Hospital
	Decompression Chamber
	Lighthouse
	Wreck
	Airport
	Reef
	International Boundary
	Disputed Boundary
	Provincial Boundary

BATHYMETRIC TABLE

	5m - 16ft
	50m - 164ft
	100m - 328ft
	150m - 492ft
	200m - 656ft
	250m - 820ft
	300m - 984ft

ROTTNEST ISLAND

In 1696 when Dutch navigator Willem de Vlamingh visited a small island 18km (11 miles) off the coast of Fremantle in Western Australia, he wrote in his log: 'Here it seems that nature has spared nothing to render this isle delightful above all other islands I have ever seen.' The commander named this island after the small rat-like marsupials that scurried through the scrub (*rott* being Dutch for rat). We now call the island Rottnest, and the 'rats' Quokkas.

Quokkas (*Setonix brachyurus*) are still abundant on Rottnest, and the scenery is as beautiful as De Vlamingh described it three centuries ago. Although it is only 10km (6 miles) long and 4km (2½ miles) at its widest point, Rottnest is a haven of flora and fauna. This A-class reserve is regarded as one of Perth's top tourist venues and the favourite holiday playground for the city's residents.

The colourful, vibrant marine life inhabits limestone reefs that provide interesting caves, crevices, pinnacles and overhangs to explore. The area supports many tropical species of reef fish and corals that would not normally live so far south. The reason for their presence is a warm band of water, the Leeuwin current, that circles down from the tropics and

moderates the water temperatures offshore. In some of the island's sheltered bays, stony corals such as *Pocillopora* proliferate, and vivid tropical coralfish and butterflyfish can be found flitting through the kelp.

Temperate water reef fish are abundant. Western King Wrasse, Blackspot Pigfish, leatherjackets, blue devils, scalyfins, Breaksea Cod, Woodward's Pomfreds, sweep, morwongs, moonlighters, bullseyes, old wives and Eastern Talma (or truncate coralfish) are just a sample of the species that you can see on one dive. Large sponges and colourful gorgonias grow on the deeper reefs surrounding the island, while rock lobsters, cuttlefish, octopuses and wobbegong sharks are prevalent under ledges and in the caves and crevices of the weathered limestone.

Rottnest is also a graveyard of many old ships that struck reefs around the island. An iron steamer, the *Macedon*, and an iron sailing ship, the *Denton Holme*, both struck Kingston Reef in the late 19th Century. They lie just offshore from the main settlement. The *Macedon*'s hull is still clearly defined and provides added interest among the caves and colourful ledges of Kingston Reef.

With its wrecks, caves, and vibrant marine life, Rottnest does not need sheer walls and

deep diving to be impressive. The terrain is more subtle and the marine life more cryptic. Divers who are prepared to think small and look closely under the ledges and on the roofs of caves, will be rewarded by the wonderful colours and numbers of creatures that are compacted into every crevice of limestone.

Sites worth diving are: **Roe Reef** [42], **North Reef** [43], **Coesy Point** [44], **Swirl Reef** [45], **Horseshoe Reef** [46], **Northwest Patch** [47], **West End** [48], **Fish Hook Drop-off** [49], **South Point** [50], **Green Island Drof-off** [51], **Crystal Palace** [52].

GEOGRAPHE BAY – HMAS SWAN AND BUSSELTON JETTY

Beautiful Geographe Bay lies 300km (186 miles) south of Perth in Western Australia. The towns of Busselton and Dunsborough are tourist meccas, close to the southwest wineries, natural forests, limestone cave systems, sandy, white, safe beaches, and natural and artificial reefs that offer some of the best diving and snorkelling in the state. One of the highlights is **Busselton Jetty** [53]. Nearly 2km (1¼ mile) long, it is the longest wooden jetty in the southern hemisphere. During summer and autumn, the end of this jetty offers one of the safest and prettiest dives in the world. The timbers (some that have been laid for over a century) are coated with an extraordinary array of soft corals, ascidians, sponges, bryozoans and other encrusting invertebrates, while enormous schools of herring, Yellowtail Scad and Long-finned Pike swirl around the piles. Graceful old wives, Truncate Coralfish (Eastern Talma), leatherjackets, pufferfish and bullseyes live under the jetty, picking food from the piles or from among the rubble on the seabed under the decking.

An underwater observatory has been constructed close to the end of the jetty to allow non-divers to view this wonderland. There is a permanent camera mounted underwater to allow Internet viewing of the underwater scenery, and an interpretive centre at the start of the jetty provides information on the area, souvenirs, and a wonderful underwater photographic display. A small train takes visitors and divers as far as the observatory. Steps to the waterline allow easy entry and exit for divers. Shops at Busselton take regular dive charters to the end of the jetty.

Geographe Bay has many beautiful natural reefs and is the site of Western Australia's first artificial naval wreck dive. In 1997, **HMAS Swan** 54 was scuttled a few kilometres out from Dunsborough. It is 113m (371ft) long, 13m (41ft) wide and 23m (75ft) high. Most of the ship is accessible to divers, although cave diving qualifications are recommended to penetrate the hull. The magazine room, the galley, toilets and crew's quarters all contribute to the excitement of diving the vessel, but you don't have to enter these areas to enjoy the dive. The navigation tower looms up to within 7m (23ft) of the surface, and on a clear day, you can see the whole outline of the HMAS Swan from your dive boat. The bridge is easily accessible, and is now shared by divers, invertebrates and hundreds of fish that have made the Swan their home.

On the western side of Cape Naturaliste there are many other interesting dive sites, including the **Indicators** 55 near Canal Rocks.

THE SOUTH COAST ALBANY AND ESPERANCE

Albany is a picturesque town that overlooks the beautiful Princess Royal Harbour in King George Sound. Small islands and a southern headland shelter it from the sometimes fierce storms travelling north from the Antarctic Ocean. Many dive sites on the islands are spectacular with deep canyons and walls. Once past the surface layer of kelp, these granite outcrops are covered in invertebrates including enormous black corals, gorgonias and bright pink soft tree corals. Sponges and ascidians encrust the surfaces of the rocks and many well-camouflaged fish such as Harlequin Fish, sea perch and scorpionfish are found resting on the ledges among the colourful invertebrates.

In 2001, Albany became the home of the largest prepared naval dive wreck/artificial

reef in the southern hemisphere. The **HMAS Perth** 56 was scuttled in just over 30m (100ft) of water within King George Sound. She is 133m (436ft) long, with a beam of 14m (45ft). The top of the tower stands about 3m (10ft) above the water level and is adorned with the mandatory navigational lights. Within 12 months of sinking, the hull was being covered by several species of invertebrates and the fish life was increasing. Other popular dive sites are: **Michaelmas Reef** 57, **Cheynes III Wreck** 58, **Michaelmas Island** 59, **Breaksea Island** 60 and **Coffin Island** 61.

Esperance lies approximately 480km (298 miles) east of Albany and is situated on the shores of a delightful heart-shaped bay. Beyond this bay, over 100 granite islands make up the Recherche Archipelago that stretches along the coast over an area of nearly 4000 sq km (1544 sq miles). Many of its islands are nature reserves and the region is becoming a popular destination for ecotourism. The magnificent underwater landscapes of sheer granite walls, caves and ledges are a diver's delight. Colourful sponge gardens are a feature of this area. Huge orange, yellow, red and purple sponges sit on ledges in the depths down to 60m (200ft) and provide interesting habitats

ABOVE *Large schools of bullseyes hover around and inside* HMAS Swan. *Within 12 months of sinking, more than 60 species of fish were recorded here.*

for thousands of other invertebrates and fish. Majestic big fish such as Western Blue Groper (a wrasse) and Queen Snapper are common in the Recherche Archipelago. Large leatherjackets, sweep, wrasse, boarfish, truncate coralfish and old wives also abound. Popular sites are: **Esperance Jetty** 62, **Cull Island** 63, **Figure of Eight Island** 64, **Sandy Hook Island** 65, and **Mondrain Island** 66

A particularly good site to see these fish is on a very interesting wreck dive off Esperance. In 1991 the **Sanko Harvest** 67, a bulk cargo ship carrying phosphate, hit an uncharted reef while taking a shortcut through the Recherche Archipelago. It threatened an environmental disaster, with over 30,000 tonnes of phosphate and 300 tonnes of oil spilling into the ocean. A well-organised clean-up operation, however, saved much of the wildlife and quickly cleaned up the beaches. The site is now an extremely interesting dive that has been turned into an asset by the wildlife that it threatened at first.

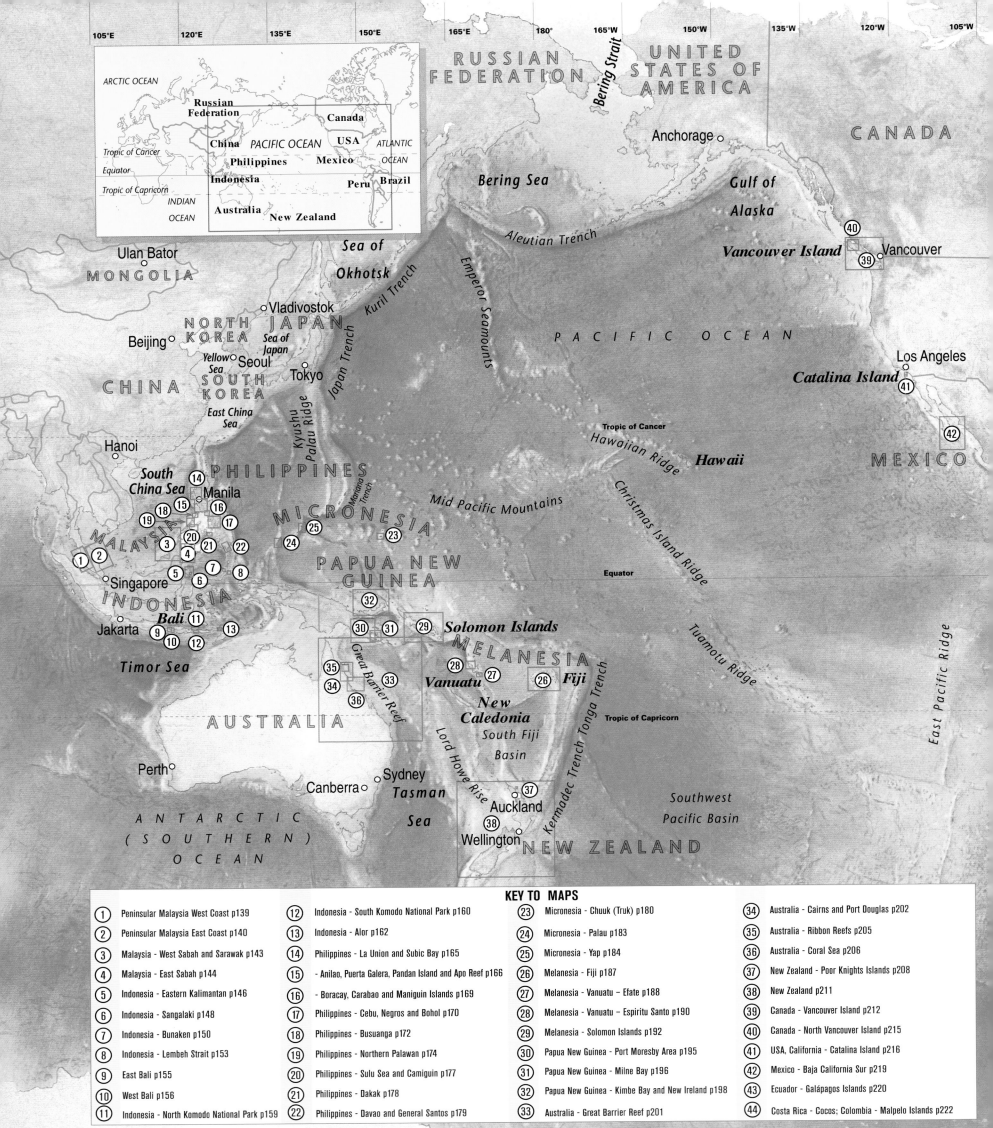

KEY TO MAPS

1. Peninsular Malaysia West Coast p139
2. Peninsular Malaysia East Coast p140
3. Malaysia - West Sabah and Sarawak p143
4. Malaysia - East Sabah p144
5. Indonesia - Eastern Kalimantan p146
6. Indonesia - Sangalaki p148
7. Indonesia - Bunaken p150
8. Indonesia - Lembeh Strait p153
9. East Bali p155
10. West Bali p156
11. Indonesia - North Komodo National Park p159

12. Indonesia - South Komodo National Park p160
13. Indonesia - Alor p162
14. Philippines - La Union and Subic Bay p165
15. - Anilao, Puerta Galera, Pandan Island and Apo Reef p166
16. - Boracay, Carabao and Maniguin Islands p169
17. Philippines - Cebu, Negros and Bohol p170
18. Philippines - Busuanga p172
19. Philippines - Northern Palawan p174
20. Philippines - Sulu Sea and Camiguin p177
21. Philippines - Dakak p178
22. Philippines - Davao and General Santos p179

23. Micronesia - Chuuk (Truk) p180
24. Micronesia - Palau p183
25. Micronesia - Yap p184
26. Melanesia - Fiji p187
27. Melanesia - Vanuatu - Efate p188
28. Melanesia - Vanuatu - Espiritu Santo p190
29. Melanesia - Solomon Islands p192
30. Papua New Guinea - Port Moresby Area p195
31. Papua New Guinea - Milne Bay p196
32. Papua New Guinea - Kimbe Bay and New Ireland p198
33. Australia - Great Barrier Reef p201

34. Australia - Cairns and Port Douglas p202
35. Australia - Ribbon Reefs p205
36. Australia - Coral Sea p206
37. New Zealand - Poor Knights Islands p208
38. New Zealand p211
39. Canada - Vancouver Island p212
40. Canada - North Vancouver Island p215
41. USA, California - Catalina Island p216
42. Mexico - Baja California Sur p219
43. Ecuador - Galápagos Islands p220
44. Costa Rica - Cocos; Colombia - Malpelo Islands p222

THE PACIFIC OCEAN

by Jack Jackson

BY FAR THE LARGEST OF THE WORLD'S OCEANS, the Pacific stretches from the Arctic to the Antarctic and lies between Asia and Australia in the west and the Americas in the east, roughly one-third of the earth's surface and double the area of the Atlantic Ocean.

The Pacific meets the Arctic at the Bering Strait and the Atlantic in the Drake Passage between South America's Tierra del Fuego and Antarctica's Graham Land. The border with the Indian Ocean is considered to run northwest across the Timor Sea from Australia's Cape Londonderry, along the southern shores of the Lesser Sunda Islands and the island of Java, and then across the Sunda Strait to the shores of Sumatra. Between Sumatra and the Malay Peninsula the boundary is usually drawn across the Singapore Strait. To the south of Australia the boundary extends across the Bass Strait and from Tasmania to the Antarctic Ocean, which commences at latitude 55° South.

The Pacific covers 165,250,000 sq km (63,800,000 sq miles) – more than the total land surface of the earth. Covering such a vast area with a wide variation in temperatures and conditions, the Pacific is extremely varied in its coastal and island habitat and has great species diversity. Although there is diving in the colder waters of China and Japan, by far the most diving in the world is done on the coral reefs and islands in the tropical Pacific from Taiwan to Hawaii in the north to Australia's Great Barrier Reef and Oceania in the south. Further south, along the Australian coast, conditions change to temperate waters and species that continue to New Zealand.

In the north, cold water, strong tidal currents and upwellings in summer bring nutrient-laden waters to fish and crustaceans, many of which are larger than their tropical counterparts. The Californian coast is a temperate-water diving region, while offshore of southern California there is cage diving for Blue and Mako Sharks. Grey Whales breed on the ocean side of the Baja Peninsula in winter. On the Farallon Islands researchers study Great White Sharks. The Gulf of California (Sea of Cortés) was once a paradise for migrating marine mammals. However, it has been damaged by overfishing, despite marine reserves. Before divers discovered Cocos and Malpelo islands, the seamounts of the Sea of Cortés were the places for shoaling hammerheads, but few are left now.

ABOVE *A Hawksbill turtle (*Eretmochelys imbricata*) on the deck of the* Yongala *wreck. They are one of the smallest of marine turtles, reaching a maximum length of 84cm (33in).*

PACIFIC OCEAN

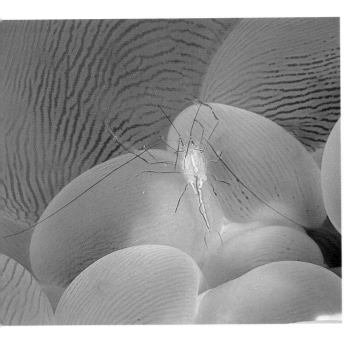

ABOVE *A commensal shrimp living on a host Bubble (Grape) Coral (*Plerogyra*), which can sting soft human skin.*

In addition to the Pacific coasts of Mexico, Costa Rica and Panama, the most popular diving in this region is at Cocos, Malpelo and the Galápagos Islands. Panama's Golfo de Chiriqui claims the most extensive coralline reefs of the Central American Pacific and Ecuador's Isla de la Plata for the South American Pacific. There is diving in Peru and Chile, even on volcanic Easter Island (Isla de Pascua), one of the most isolated islands in the world.

The western Pacific includes the Bering Sea, Sea of Okhotsk, Sea of Japan, Yellow Sea, East China Sea and South China Sea. The major rivers of eastern Asia, whose basins contain over a quarter of the world's population, drain into the Pacific by way of these marginal seas.

Most islands lie between the tropics of Cancer and Capricorn and in the western Pacific. Taiwan, the Philippines, Borneo, Indonesia, New Guinea and New Zealand are continental. The volcanic Hawaiian archipelago consists of around 2000 islands, but the term Hawaiian Islands usually refers to those at its eastern end. Micronesia, lies mainly north of the equator and west of the 180° meridian east of Greenwich. Melanesia is south of Micronesia, and Polynesia is to the east.

Further east, Cocos and Malpelo Islands are close to the equator and the Galápagos Islands are on it, but cold currents affect the marine life. All are volcanic, with a small amount of coral that suffered in the 1997/8 El Niño.

The pressure systems of the Pacific closely follow the planetary system, where the patterns of air pressure and wind result from the earth's rotation (Coriolis Force) and the inclination of its axis towards the sun. In general the atmospheric circulation in one hemisphere mirrors that in the other. The huge amount of open water influences pressure and wind patterns over it. The climate in the southern and eastern Pacific, where the trade winds and westerlies are steady, is the most regular on the planet. However, in the northern Pacific it is more variable – the cold winters of the east coast of Russia contrast sharply with milder winters in British Columbia.

The Pacific's trade winds are most prominent over the northeast and southeast Pacific between the latitudes of 30°N and 40°S. The angle of the earth's rotation on its axis and its revolution around the sun limits the seasonal shifting of the Pacific trade wind belts to about 5° of latitude. The easterly winds along the equator form the intertropical airflow and tend to be strongest in the eastern Pacific. In the equatorial region, the trade winds of the northern and southern hemispheres converge, giving rise to the doldrums.

Although the climatic conditions of the trade wind belts are generally uniform, storms

known as typhoons in the western Pacific do originate there. The ideal conditions for their development occur between the parallels of 5° and 25° north in late summer when the temperature of surface water is at least 27°C (80°F).

Within the belts of westerly winds, cold easterly winds from the polar regions meet the warm westerly winds of the middle latitudes producing travelling depressions. Their region of convergence, the polar front, is most evident in winter when the contrast in temperature and humidity is greatest. Westerlies in the southern hemisphere are strong and the gales accompanying their depressions gave rise to the name Roaring Forties after the latitude where they commonly occur.

In the western Pacific, monsoons, which are caused by land-sea temperature differences, replace the planetary system.

All three types of tide occur. At some places in the South Pacific the oscillation period follows the sun. Instead of getting later each day by about 50 minutes, tides in places such as Tahiti are about the same for several days in succession. Mixed tides occur along the Pacific coast of North America. Diurnal tides occur in the Gulfs of Tonkin and Thailand, the Java Sea, and Bismarck and Solomon seas. In general, tidal ranges in the Pacific are small, but the upper reaches of the Gulf of California and Korea Bay have ranges of more than 10m (33ft).

The average depth is 4280m (14,040ft) and the Mariana Trench is 11,034m (36,201ft) – the deepest of any ocean.

ABU SAYYAF

The southwesternmost islands of the Philippines are hide-outs for a dissident Muslim faction loosely termed Abu Sayyaf. Now advised and assisted by Osama Bin Laden's Al-Qa'eda (Qa'ida) terrorist organization, Abu Sayyaf has recently become more active and taken tourists hostage in Malaysia and southern Palawan. Until the Philippines armed forces have gained control of this group, divers should avoid Basilan Island and the Filipino islands to its southwest and take government advice over the far west of Mindanao.

The security at all resorts and airstrips has been increased and Club Noah Isabelle has even set up its own radar defence system and regularly patrols the fish sanctuary.

Pacific Ocean **136** Introduction

ABOVE *A Potato Grouper (*Epinephelus tukula*). Known in Australia as a Potato Cod, it is the joint second-largest grouper.*

ABOVE *Masters of camouflage, Harlequin Ghost Pipefish (*Solenostomus paradoxus*) hide among gorgonias, weeds or crinoids.*

ABOVE *A* Chromodoris willani *nudibranch off Sumilon Island, Philippines. This species feeds on sponges on exposed reefs and slopes.*

Seismically active over much of its area, the zone that surrounds the Pacific from New Zealand to southern Chile is known as the Ring of Fire. The geological history of the western Pacific basin is not fully understood. Some fragments of oceanic crust have escaped remelting and now lie against the coasts of Japan, California and South America, but much of the original structure has been destroyed by subsequent volcanic activity.

The eastern Pacific basin is simpler. West of the American continent, at the East Pacific Rise, the crust being pulled towards the western Pacific is separating at 16.5cm (6.5in) a year, the fastest in the world. A branch of this rise is opening the Gulf of California and two less active ridges branch eastward from it. They are the Galápagos Spreading Center near the equator and the Chile Rise in the southeast. Also in the eastern Pacific are the east-west fracture zones and submerged volcanoes, some of which have merged, like the Cocos Ridge. The Pacific has many flat-topped seamounts (guyots) rarely found in other oceans.

The most important influence on the vertical circulation of the Pacific is the dense, cold water from the Antarctic, which sinks and then spreads northward to form the bottom layer of the greater part of the ocean. Deep-water circulation is also influenced by the sinking surface water at zones of convergence, which sink to about 90m (300ft) before spreading laterally. To compensate, other water rises (upwelling) at zones of divergence, particularly along the coasts of the Americas.

Pacific trade winds drive surface waters west to form the North and South Equatorial currents. Between them is the Equatorial Countercurrent from the Philippines to Ecuador. Most of the North Equatorial Current turns north near the Philippines to form the warm Kuroshio (Japan) Current. East of Japan the Kuroshio swings east to form the Kuroshio Extension, which further east becomes the North Pacific Current. The cold, southeast-flowing California Current forms the eastern section of the returning branch of the North Equatorial Current.

Most of the South Equatorial Current divides into three branches while flowing west. The two westernmost branches turn south off Australia's east coast to form the East Australian Current, which becomes the Tasman Current, turns back to the northeast and disperses west of New Zealand. The easternmost branch flows to the south, roughly along the 180° meridian, turning east as the warm South Pacific Current at 50° south. Between 80° and 90° west it turns north and then west as the Mentor Current before returning to the South Equatorial Current.

One branch of the cold Antarctic Circumpolar Current becomes the Humboldt (Peru) Current, whose nutrient-rich upwellings produce prolific fishing grounds.

The north Pacific's currents and freshwater run-off are ideal for bottom-living species. The cold-water coasts of America have vast kelp beds harbouring a marine diversity almost as good as on coral reefs. Whales make long migrations from cold-water feeding to warm-water breeding and calving grounds.

Nutrient-rich upwellings support some of the world's largest fisheries off Japan and Peru and the western Pacific has the richest and most extensive coral reefs of any ocean and a great variety of pelagic species.

The Pacific suffers from the same problems of pollution, sedimentation and destructive fishing as any of the big three oceans, but overfishing is the largest threat of all.

MALAYSIA

by Jack Jackson

MALAYSIA HAS A COLLECTION OF HEALTHY coral reefs or boulders covered in coral in Peninsular Malaysia and coral reefs in East Malaysia. The water is always warm, but the visibility can vary from medium to good. There has been some coral bleaching on very shallow reefs. The number of diving operators has increased on Pulau Perhentian Besar and Kecil, Pulau Redang, Pulau Aur and Pulau Tenggol. Pulau Lang Tengah has become a mainstream diving destination while on Pulau Tioman standards have risen.

Layang Layang, called The Jewel of the Borneo Banks, has expanded considerably. There are many good reefs in this area, but a quality resort and the presence of the Malaysian Navy make Layang Layang popular.

Off Sabah's west coast, shipwrecks are the main interest off Labuan, operators are offering diving off Sarawak and newer sites are becoming popular at Pulau Mantanani and north of Kudat. Whale Sharks pass along the west coast between January and April.

Off Sabah's east coast the diving resorts on Pulau Mabul and Pulau Kapalai were developed as a way of having more luxurious accommodation than could be constructed on Pulau Sipadan for ecological reasons. However, the surge of interest in muck diving has made them diving destinations in their own right. There are several other good diving destinations in the Semporna area and north of

Sandakan, Pulau Lankayan is one of the latest, there is even a good chance of sighting a Dugong. Whale Sharks pass by in April.

There is little need for Nitrox or recreational technical diving in Malaysia, but the training is available and deep wrecks are now within the realms of technical divers. As a result, the British government has declared *HMS Prince of Wales* and *HMS Repulse* as Protected Places – diving is only permitted on a do-not-touch basis.

PENINSULAR MALAYSIA

Where and when you dive in Peninsular Malaysia depends on the monsoon, although the start and end of monsoon seasons can vary by a few weeks. In general the west coast experiences the southwest monsoon from April to October and is drier from November to March. The east coast is drier from April till October and experiences the northwest monsoon from November till March and this is wet enough to close northern resorts. Whale Sharks and Manta Rays are regularly seen at all east coast sites and most of the dive sites are buoyed to prevent anchor damage.

THE WEST COAST AND THE STRAIT OF MALACCA

The west coast of Peninsular Malaysia is much more developed and industrialized than the east coast. The narrow Malacca Strait drains

agricultural run-off from rivers in Malaysia, Thailand and Indonesia and has heavy shipping movements. Unable to clear itself easily, the visibility is normally poor.

Off the coast of Kedah, the Payar Marine Park consists of the main island of **Pulau Payar** 3, the smaller islands of **Pulau Kaca** 2 and **Pulau Lembu** 1 to its east-northeast, and the two large rock outcrops making up **Pulau Segantang** 4 13km (8 miles) to the west-southwest. Pulau Payar has one of the few coral reef areas on the west coast and, together with Pulau Redang on the east coast, has been a focus of WWF's marine park studies. First gazetted a fisheries protected area in 1985, the marine life is abundant.

Further south, off the coast at Lumut, in the strait of Malacca, **Pulau Pangkor** 5, **Pulau Pangkor Laut** 6 and the **Sembilan group** 7 also have diving in sheltered waters that are conveniently close to Kuala Lumpur.

TOP LEFT *Empty beaches, clear turquoise seas and wonderful scenery exemplify Pulau Redang. The surrounding seas have the finest coral in Peninsular Malaysia and have been extensively studied by the WWF.*

TOP RIGHT *A fishing boat converted into a ferry leaves Pulau Perhentian Besar, the largest of the Perhentian Islands. Empty beaches and interesting jungle walks also make it the most popular.*

THE EAST COAST
TERENGGANU MARINE PARKS

The Terengganu parks consist of the Perhentian islands, Pulau Lang Tengah, Pulau Redang, Pulau Kapas and Pulau Tenggol.

The Perhentian islands, 20km (12 miles) off Kuala Besut, consist of **Pulau Perhentian Besar** 9 and **Pulau Perhentian Kecil** 8, with several small islets and exposed rocks to the northwest. The diving off the two main islands consists of rocks sloping to sand, with shoals of fusiliers, snappers and jacks, stingrays and various species of pufferfish. The sand has many varieties of invertebrates and occasionally sea snakes.

The best diving is at the isolated rock outcrops, jumbles of large volcanic boulders down to 30m (100ft), forming caves, crevices and swim-throughs. Below the tide-line these boulders are covered with soft corals and anemones. Below 7m (23ft) they have black corals, Gorgonian Sea Fans, *Tubastrea* corals, unusually large *Dendronephthya* Soft Tree Corals, Harp Corals and cowrie, murex and volute shells. Deeper down, stony corals, barrel sponges covered in Alabaster Sea Cucumbers and nudibranchs abound with Spanish Dancers out in daylight. The pelagic fish life is good and the reef fish prolific, including Bumphead Parrotfish, small Whitetip and Blacktip Reef Sharks and stingrays, while dolphins, including Pilot Whales, are seen in July and August.

ABOVE *A sea star at Pulau Perhentian. They usually have five arms, but often more. Many have the ability to grow a new arm if one is damaged, and a severed arm can grow a complete new body.*

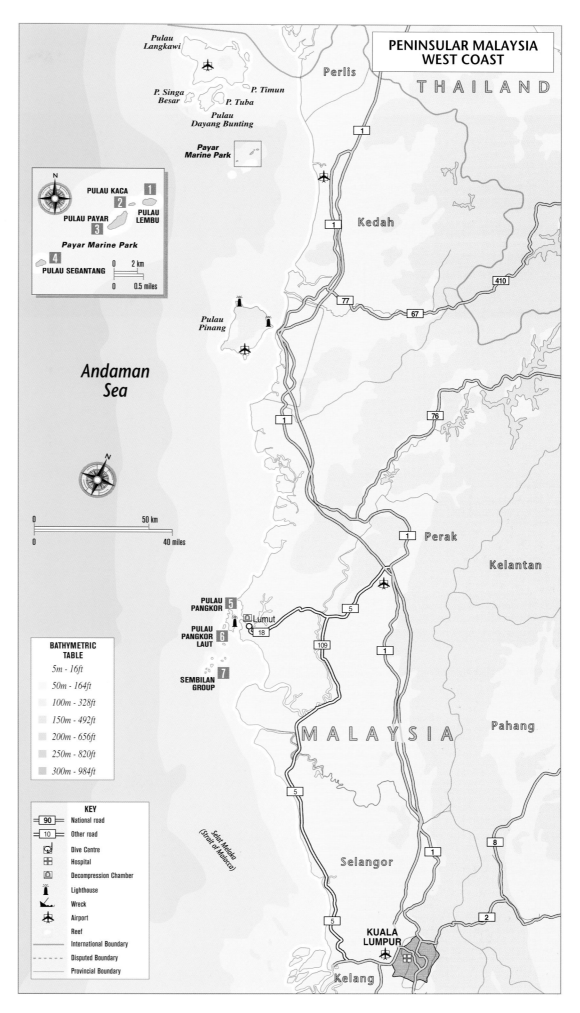

PENINSULAR MALAYSIA
WEST COAST

Andaman
Sea

BATHYMETRIC TABLE

5m - 16ft

50m - 164ft

100m - 328ft

150m - 492ft

200m - 656ft

250m - 820ft

300m - 984ft

KEY

90	National road
10	Other road
	Dive Centre
	Hospital
	Decompression Chamber
	Lighthouse
	Wreck
	Airport
	Reef
	International Boundary
	Disputed Boundary
	Provincial Boundary

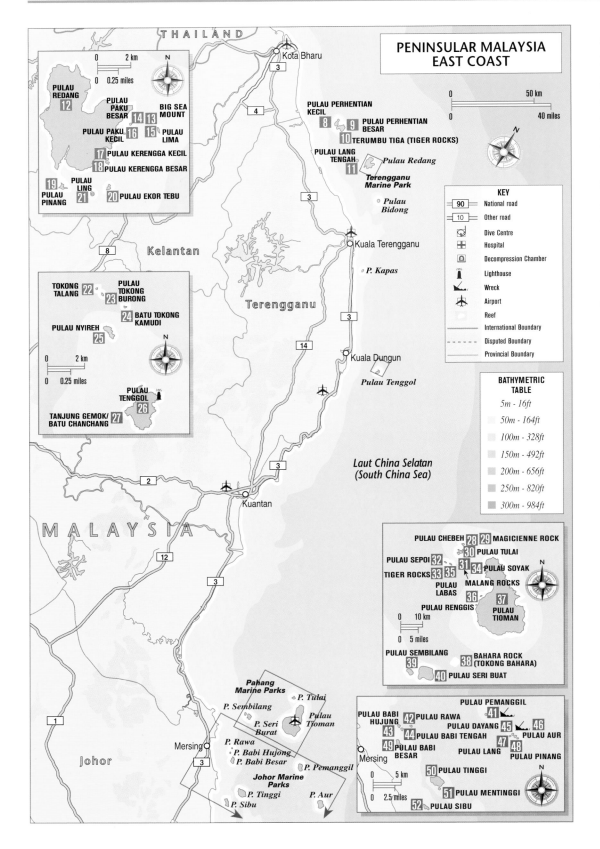

PENINSULAR MALAYSIA EAST COAST

rabbitfish, many different varieties of pufferfish, lionfish, surgeonfish, cardinalfish, lizardfish, hawkfish and shoals of sweetlips, snappers, shrimpfish and fusiliers. **Pulau Lang Tengah** [11], 10km (6 miles) from Pulau Redang has similar diving.

The Pulau Redang Archipelago, 45km (28 miles) northeast of Kuala Terengganu consists of nine islands. The two largest are **Pulau Redang** [12] and **Pulau Pinang** [19]. The other seven islets are **Pulau Kerengga Besar** [18], **Pulau Kerengga Kecil** [17], **Pulau Paku Besar** [14], **Pulau Paku Kecil** [16], **Pulau Ekor Tebu** [20], **Pulau Ling** [21] and **Pulau Lima** [15]. Prohibited fisheries waters since 1983, and a marine park since 1985, it has the best coral reefs and the most intensively studied reefs in Peninsular Malaysia.

The east side of Pulau Redang has sandy beaches, while the west side has stony beaches. The most extensive reefs, down to 25m (80ft), are around the small islets and are most diverse on their deeper north and east sides. The coral gardens are dominated by staghorn, table and boulder corals. The steep cliffs have soft corals and encrusting corals on the granite. Hawksbill and Green Turtles nest along the west coast of Pulau Redang.

Most dives are jumbles of boulders covered in stony corals. The sites around Pulau Lima have some of the most spectacular diving off Peninsular Malaysia. **Big Sea Mount** [13], 50m (165ft) north of Pulau Lima, has a jumble of boulders rising from 30m (100ft) to within 10m (33ft) of the surface. The top is covered in stony, leathery, soft and encrusting corals, tunicates and sponges, Gorgonian Sea Fans and anemones with clownfish. The seaward slope continues beyond 40m (130ft) with *Tubastrea micranthus* corals and large *Dendronephthya* Soft Tree Corals. Fish life is prolific and includes Eagle Rays.

The Pulau Tenggol group, with its main island of **Pulau Tenggol** [26], is about 29km (18 miles) from Kuala Dungun. The smaller **Pulau Nyireh** [25] is to the north-northwest. The islets and rocks of **Batu Tokong Kamudi** [24], **Pulau Tokong Burong** [23] and

Terumbu Tiga (Tiger Rocks) [10], just south of Pasir Tinggi, at the centre of the east coast of Pulau Perhentian Besar, is one of the best dives. There are large boulders down to sand at around 18–20m (60–65ft), with caves and tunnels to swim through. The upper rocks are carpeted with leathery soft corals and small *Dendronephthya* Soft Tree Corals. Deeper rocks

are covered in black corals, bubble corals, Gorgonian Sea Fans, stinging hydroids, Harp Corals and anemones with clownfish. On the sand there are large barrel sponges covered in Alabaster Sea Cucumbers, many species of sea stars, cushion stars, sea cucumbers and black sea urchins. Fish life includes Bumphead and other parrotfish, angelfish, butterflyfish,

Tokong Talang  are to the north of Pulau Nyireh, while Batu Tong Daik is south-south-west of Pulau Tenggol. In general these islands have steep cliffs descending into deeper water than most of Peninsular Malaysia's east coast. The underwater boulders are covered with stony, soft and encrusting corals and sponges. Visibility is good and the currents strong. Nurse Sharks, reef sharks, large tuna, groupers and Eagle Rays are common.

The west side of Pulau Nyireh is particularly rich with large shoals of Bumphead Parrotfish, barracuda, tuna, jacks and snappers, while the drift from **Batu Chanchang** 27 to Tanjung Gemok is probably the best dive in the area for prolific fish life over rock outcrops on sand. There is an old 20m (65ft) wreck lying at 7m (23ft) about one kilometre (half a mile) north of Kuala Dungun.

EAST COAST
PAHANG MARINE PARKS

Pahang Marine Parks consist of the large island of **Pulau Tioman** 37 and the smaller islands of **Pulau Renggis** 36, **Pulau Sepoi** 32, **Pulau Labas** 35, **Pulau Soyak** 34, **Pulau Chebeh** 28, **Pulau Tulai** 30, **Pulau Sembilang** 39 and **Pulau Seri Buat** 40. Pulau Tioman is 56km (35 miles) from Mersing. It has coral reefs and sandy beaches along its west coast, but the best diving is around the smaller islands and rocks 13km (8 miles) to the northwest. The east coast is too exposed for coral growth apart from a few encrusting species and soft corals.

Again, most of the dive sites are jumbles of boulders dropping to various depths between 12m (40ft) and 30m (100ft), covered in stony corals, black corals, *Tubastrea* corals and *Dendronephthya* Soft Tree Corals. The prolific fish life includes Leopard (Variegated) Sharks, Humphead (Napoleon) Wrasse, lots of small shoaling fish and their predators and many species of butterflyfish and angelfish including the Yellowmask (Blue-face) Angelfish (*Pomacanthus xanthometopon*) and the rarer Bluering Angelfish (*Pomacanthus annularis*).

Magicienne Rock 29 lies north-northwest of the northern end of Pulau Tioman. It is a pinnacle that rises to within 8m (25ft) of the surface. Colourful corals and sponges in strong currents attract pelagic and reef fish. **Malang Rocks** 31, west of the northern end of Pulau Tioman is a pretty, shallow dive around volcanic boulders with large patches of lettuce

TOP *Red Feather Stars (*Himerometra robustipinna), *Stony Cup Corals (*Tubastrea micranthus) *and* Dendronepthya *Soft Tree Corals form a colourful carpet on the volcanic boulders off the east coast of Peninsular Malaysia.*

ABOVE *Christmas Tree Worms (*Spirobranchus giganteus) *and Sea Squirts (*Atriolum robustum) *are further colourful animals.*

TOP *These colourful Squat Lobsters (Lauriea siagiani) are usually found in the central cavity of barrel sponges. Covered in white and pink bristles, these animals are a brilliant pink with purple stripes on their carapace. The chelipeds have sharp spines and purple spots.*

ABOVE *A Gorgonian Dwarf Goby or Seawhip Goby (Bryaninops yongei) hides on a Gorgonian Whip Coral. This muck-diving subject reaches a maximum length of 4cm (1½in) and lives and spawns on Gorgonias.*

corals, sponges and big *Dendronephthya* Soft Tree Corals. There are invertebrates, occasional Variegated (Leopard) Sharks and shoals of barracuda and trevallies in the open water.

The best dive off Pulau Tioman is **Tiger Rocks** [33]. A jumble of volcanic boulders rise to within 10m (33ft) of the surface with swimthroughs teeming with shoals of fish, including barracuda, rainbow runners, tuna, batfish, trevallies and countless colourful reef fish and turtles. West of the southwest corner of Pulau Tioman, **Bahara Rock** (Tokong Bahara) [38] has a mini drop-off down to 18m (60ft) with some different corals and many pelagic species as well as most of the local reef fish. This area is not dived often, so on a calm day you can find plenty of marine life here.

EAST COAST
JOHOR MARINE PARKS

The marine parks of Johor are situated around the islands of **Pulau Rawa** [42], **Pulau Babi Hujung** [43], **Pulau Babi Tengah** [44], **Pulau Babi Besar** [49], **Pulau Tinggi** [50], **Pulau Mentinggi** [51] and **Pulau Sibu** [52]. The diving on these islands is not that good, but 65km (40 miles) off the coast at Mersing, there is excellent diving around **Pulau Aur** [46] and the three smaller islands of **Pulau Dayang** [45], **Pulau Lang** [47] and **Pulau Pinang** [48]. **Pulau Pemanggil** [41], 15km (9 miles) northwest of Pulau Aur, is also good. Well offshore and with deeper and clearer water, sightings of large pelagic species are common, shoals of hammerhead sharks, lone Whale Sharks and Manta Rays and lobsters and octopuses can still be found. At the southeast of Pulau Aur, pinnacles rise to within 10m (33ft) of the surface and **Pulau Pinang** [48] has good wall diving down to 60m (200ft) with caves and overhangs.

The beach opposite Pulau Pinang on **Pulau Aur** [46] and the beaches on the north side of **Pulau Dayang** [45] slope gently down with coral heads, staghorn and table corals. A sea mount called Rayner's Rock is northeast of Pulau Dayang and there is some deep wreck diving for technical divers.

SABAH AND SARAWAK
SOUTH CHINA SEA
TERUMBU LAYANG LAYANG

Diving at Layang Layang, 306km (190 miles) northwest of Borneo's Kota Kinabalu, is like diving a remote reef from a live-aboard, but without the rocking boat. The dive sites with strong currents are very good. There is good muck diving with sea horses and ghost pipefish in the lagoon, but this is a waste of time with such good visibility outside the reef. Most sites are treated as drift dives and there is a chance of seeing larger sharks on any dive outside the lagoon. The Scalloped Hammerhead Sharks are usually deeper down, but there is always the chance of one or two appearing at 10m (33ft).

Off the northern edge of the atoll are **Wrasse Strip** [53], **Crack Reef** [54] and **Navigator Lane** [55]. A gentle shelf with a rich growth of healthy stony and soft corals, gorgonians, sponges and clownfish in anemones, the best diving is from the surface to 20m (65ft) with Blacktip Sharks in the open and Whitetip Reef Sharks resting in crevices. A steeper slope goes down to 50m (165ft) and then it drops to the depths. There are giant clams; turtles are common, while Manta Rays and other fish gather at cleaning stations.

Around the East Point, **Gorgonian Forest** [56], **The Point** [57], **Dogtooth Lair** [58] and **Wreck Point** [59] are spectacular because of the strong currents. It starts with a gentle slope to 30m (100ft), flattening out as a terrace before plunging to the depths, where small crevices and terraces shelter reef fish. Out in the blue large Dogtooth Tuna, barracuda, Humphead (Napoleon) Wrasse, Bigeye Trevallies, and Scalloped Hammerhead, Grey Reef and Whitetip Reef Sharks abound.

WEST COAST
SABAH

Off the northern point of Sabah there is exploratory diving out of Kudat, while 35km (29 miles) offshore from Kota Belud, **Pulau Mantanani Besar** [60] and the smaller island of Pulau Lungisan have wrecks including the

Nittetsu Maru and *Eiko Maru* in deep water. The Tunku Abdul Rahman Marine Park, 3–8km (2–5 miles) off Kota Kinabalu, incorporates five islands: **Pulau Gaya** 61, **Pulau Sapi** 62, **Pulau Manukan** 64, **Pulau Mamutik** 66 and **Pulau Sulug** 65. The coral reefs are generally shallow and have seen some blast fishing, but where they are still intact there is a profusion of colourful stony corals. Whale Sharks are seen here from January to April. The north and west shores have been ravaged by monsoon weather resulting in rocky cliffs and banks of rubble, but the eastern and southern shores have beaches slowly shelving to coral reefs. Large areas of staghorn, *Acropora* table and lettuce corals and smaller areas of boulder, mushroom, whip and bubble corals and large brown vase sponges. The fish life is limited to the smaller reef fish.

Among the best dives is **Mid Reef** 63, directly east of the east point of Pulau Manukan. It slopes gently from 6m (20ft) to 20m (65ft) with good stony corals, encrusting corals and vase sponges, but few soft corals. The invertebrates include turtles, Christmas tree, flat and fan worms, nudibranchs, sea squirts, sea stars, sea cucumbers and sea urchins. The fish life includes barracuda, groupers, lionfish, scorpionfish, stonefish and shoals of catfish. Most anemones do not have clownfish.

Now made famous by a reality television show, **Pulau Tiga** 69 and the two smaller islands of **Pulau Kalampunian Damit** 67 and **Pulau Kalampunian Besar** 68 were gazetted as The Pulau Tiga National Park in 1978. The main island, 48km (30 miles) southwest of Kota Kinabalu, has active mud volcanoes, which last erupted in a big way in 1941. The reefs of the smaller islands and the north side of Pulau Tiga are heavily blast-fished, but there are two good dive sites either end of Picnic Bay to the south of Pulau Tiga. Most of the stony corals are damaged, but small soft corals and other invertebrates thrive. This park is noted for having more gorgonias, including and whip corals than can normally be found on the west coast of Sabah.

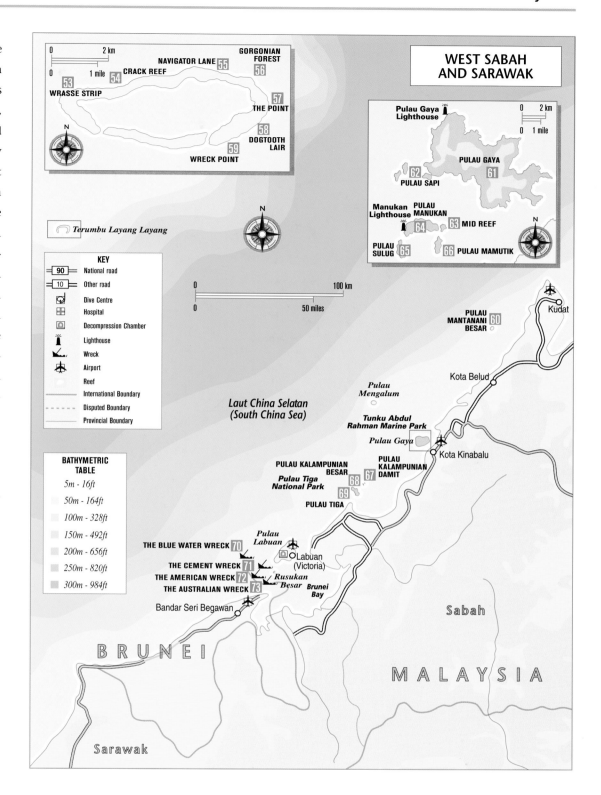

WEST COAST LABUAN

At the northern mouth of Brunei Bay, just 8km (5 miles) off mainland Sabah, and 115km (71 miles) south of Kota Kinabalu, the reefs of Pulau Labuan are too near the outlets of sediment-laden rivers to be good for diving. However, there are four good shipwrecks. All the wrecks experience strong surface currents, but in each case divers can quickly descend to the lee of the wreck.

The Blue Water Wreck 70 30km (20 miles) directly west of Labuan island, is the 80m (260ft) Philippine stern trawler *MV Mabini Padre*, which sank in November 1981. The ship is lying on her port side at 35m (115ft) with the starboard side at 24m (79ft). The fish life is quite good but the coral is poor.

The Cement Wreck 71, 20km (12 miles) south-southwest of the Labuan Marina, is the 92m (302ft) Japanese freighter *Tung Hwang*, which foundered in September 1980. Easy to

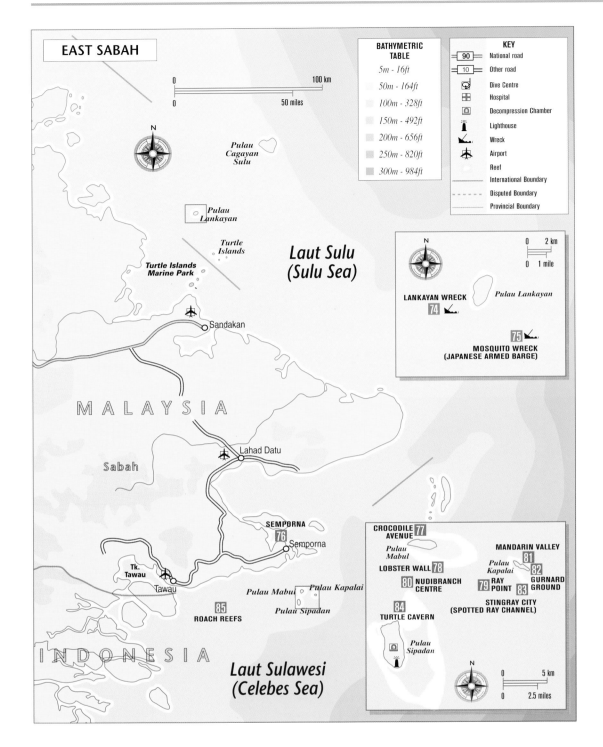

EAST SABAH

BATHYMETRIC TABLE
5m - 16ft
50m - 164ft
100m - 328ft
150m - 492ft
200m - 656ft
250m - 820ft
300m - 984ft

KEY
90 National road
10 Other road
Dive Centre
Hospital
Decompression Chamber
Lighthouse
Wreck
Airport
Reef
International Boundary
Disputed Boundary
Provincial Boundary

Pulau Cagayan Sulu

Pulau Lankayan

Turtle Islands

Turtle Islands Marine Park

Sandakan

Laut Sulu (Sulu Sea)

LANKAYAN WRECK 74 *Pulau Lankayan*

75 MOSQUITO WRECK (JAPANESE ARMED BARGE)

MALAYSIA

Lahad Datu

Sabah

SEMPORNA 76 Semporna

Tk. Tawau

Tawau

Pulau Mabul *Pulau Kapalai*

85 ROACH REEFS *Pulau Sipadan*

INDONESIA

Laut Sulawesi (Celebes Sea)

CROCODILE AVENUE 77

Pulau Mabul

LOBSTER WALL 78

80 NUDIBRANCH CENTRE

MANDARIN VALLEY

Pulau Kapalai 81

82

79 RAY POINT 83 GURNARD GROUND

STINGRAY CITY (SPOTTED RAY CHANNEL)

84 TURTLE CAVERN

Pulau Sipadan

---

penetrate, she lies upright on the bottom at 30m (100ft) with some broken masts rising to 8m (25ft). The main deck is at 19m (62ft). This wreck has extremely colourful soft corals, sponges and feather stars carpeting the entire superstructure, and the fish life is prolific. The visibility is usually better than that on the other Labuan wrecks, but there are several fishing nets that have snagged on the wreck.

The American Wreck 72, 24km (15 miles) southwest of Labuan Marina, southwest of the island of Rusukan Besar, has been identified as the US Navy's 56m (184ft) Admiral Class mine

hunter, *USS Salute*, which was sunk by a Japanese mine in June 1945. She now lies at 30m (100ft), broken in half and folded back on herself with the bow lying on top of the stern. The fish life is good but there are few corals.

The Australian Wreck 73, 23km (14 miles) southwest of Labuan Marina, southwest of the island of Rusukan Besar, has now been identified as the 85m (280ft) Dutch Steamship *SS De Klerk*. This passenger/freighter was scuttled in Singapore, but salvaged by the Japanese and added to their fleet as the *Imabari Maru*. Now lying at a fifty

degree angle on its port side at 33m (110ft), with the starboard side at 21m (69ft), the wreck has abundant marine life.

WEST COAST
SARAWAK

South of Labuan, Sarawak has good diving, including shipwrecks, when far enough offshore to be clear of the river sediments.

EAST COAST

The latest diving destination to be developed on the east coast is Pulau Lankayan, northeast of Sandakan. Declared a marine conservation area in 2000, uninhabited and protected from blast-fishing for the ten years before it was developed, the island is a macro photographers paradise. It also gets larger creatures, including Whale Sharks in April and the occasional Dugong. Recent research found less than five per cent of coral bleaching; healthy corals recolonizing the area; high biodiversity; and many of the commercial species that are harvested on other reefs are plentiful. A mixture of sandy areas on gentle slopes with sponges, gorgonians and coral heads, there can be strong surface currents. There are many pelagics and the smaller subjects include decorator and spider crabs, nudibranchs, porcelain crabs, gobies, jawfish, Ghost Pipefish, mandarinfish, Blue-ringed Octopus, Mimic Octopus, Bamboo Sharks and frogfish. There are two wrecks. The **Lankayan Wreck** 74 is an ocean-going fishing vessel caught poaching and purposely sunk here in 23m (76ft) of water. The other is the wreck of a Japanese armed barge (**Mosquito Wreck**) 75 that was sunk during World War II.

Situated within easy diving-boat distance of Pulau Sipadan, the diving resorts on Pulau Mabul and Pulau Kapalai were originally developed as a way of having more luxurious accommodation than could be constructed on Pulau Sipadan for ecological and political reasons. However, divers soon realized that there was good muck diving. Being on the edge of the continental shelf, they are not surrounded by deep water.

South of Semporna and just north of Pulau Sipadan, Pulau Mabul lies on the northern end of a large reef. The diving is mainly sand and coral rubble, but every hole is inhabited with Ghost Pipefish, frogfish, gobies, shrimps, mandarinfish, crocodilefish, Flamboyant Cuttlefish, cowfish and nudibranchs.

The best dives include **Ray Point** 79, a succession of terraces down to 14m (45ft) on the southwest side of the reef with better corals and fish life. **Lobster Wall** 78 and **Nudibranch Centre** 80 northwest of Lobster Wall, descend below 50m (165ft) on the west side of the reef. **Crocodile Avenue** 77, a shallow dive northwest of the Smart jetty, could be the benchmark for muck diving.

Only 15 minutes from Pulau Sipadan, between Pulau Sipadan and Pulau Mabul, Pulau Kapalai has been the local divers' macrophotography destination for two decades. The island is eroded so that only a sandbar is visible at low tide and the resort is built on stilts above the sea. A weak current produces better visibility and the site has all the species found at Pulau Mabul including Blue-ringed Octopuses, dragonets, mating Mandarinfish, frogfish, jawfish and Flamboyant Cuttlefish.

Mandarin Valley, 81 the resort's jetty on the north side of the reef and **Gurnard Ground,** 82 north of the northeast point of the reef, are similar dives down to 20m (65ft). There are also Humphead (Napoleon) Wrasse and Mandarin Valley even has Bumphead Parrotfish. On the west side of the reef, **Stingray City** (Spotted Ray Channel) 83 drops only to 13m (43ft), but its fish life includes Bluespotted Ribbontail Rays.

The cream of Malaysian diving, and among the best in the world, the Pulau Sipadan Marine Reserve is just south of Pulau Kapalai, 35km (20 miles) south of Semporna. Malaysia's only volcanic island, it is perched atop a volcanic seamount rising from 600m (1969ft), 10km (6 miles) south of the continental shelf. The island was declared a bird sanctuary in 1933 and re-gazetted in 1963.

Underwater, Pulau Sipadan has almost everything that exists in the Indo-Pacific. The coral and fish life is prolific. The coral cover of the shallow areas is in excellent condition, with large areas of staghorn, table, plate, lettuce and boulder corals, encrusting corals, bubble corals and mushroom corals. Lying among the stony corals are large soft corals, vase and barrel sponges and true giant clams.

The drop-offs and walls also have *Tubastrea* species, Gorgonian Sea Fans and black corals. The water teems with fish, including a huge shoal of Bumphead Parrotfish, but the big draw is the countless Green and Hawksbill Turtles that nest there.

The beach in front of Borneo Divers and Pulau Sipadan Resort is one of the top beach and night dives in the world, as the wall is just a few swimming-strokes away. East of the jetty, **Turtle Cavern** 84 is now limited to divers accompanied by a local divemaster, due to a number of fatalities.

There are other sites off southeast Sabah including **Roach Reefs** 85 off Tawau, **Semporna** 76 itself and the islands of the proposed Semporna Marine Park.

The long-running dispute over the ownership of Pulau Sipadan between Malaysia and Indonesia was resolved on 17 December 2002 when the International Court of Justice in The Hague ruled 16 to 1 in favour of Malaysia.

ABOVE *A favourite nesting site for Green and the occasional Hawksbill Turtle, the waters of Pulau Sipadan teem with turtles, so accustomed to divers that they ignore them. This juvenile is resting on the coral for a nap during the day.*

ABOVE *Originally named* Chromodoris bullocki, *these colourful nudibranchs have recently been renamed* Hypselodoris bullocki. *They can be found in many colour variations from the Maldives to tropical Australia.*

INDONESIA

Introduction by Jack Jackson

ALTHOUGH NOT THE EASIEST OF DESTINATIONS to get to, the thriving, pristine reefs of the islands in the Celebes Sea off Berau on Kalimantan's east coast are among the best of Indonesian diving. The Island of Sangalaki and its surrounding reefs are protected as a marine park. The main dive sites are located around Pulau Derawan, Pulau Samama, Pulau Maratua, Pulau Kakaban and Pulau Sangalaki with pelagic species particularly abundant at the latter three. Shoals of tuna, trevallies, barracuda, Eagle Rays, Scalloped Hammerhead Sharks and Grey and Whitetip Reef Sharks frequent these waters. Pulau Sangalaki is particularly known for its inquisitive Manta Rays, some of which have wingspans exceeding 5m (16ft). Others are unusual in that they are totally black.

The most unusual dive here is a brackish lake on Pulau Kakaban. It is similar to the lakes at Palau, except that the jellyfish were not damaged by the 1997/8 El Niño Southern Oscillation Phenomenon. Prehistoric uplifting

TOP LEFT *The Lembeh Strait is critter heaven for muck divers. The style of diving is to fin slowly and look down.*
TOP RIGHT *A dive boat negotiates the channel cut through the fringing reef while leaving Pulau Sangalaki for a dive. All dives are outside the fringing reef.*

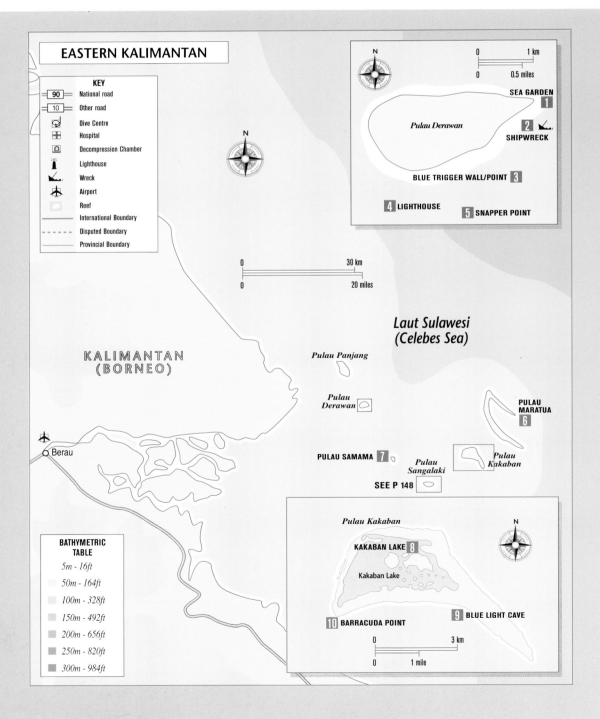

trapped a lake of seawater that gradually became less saline due to rain, forcing marine life to adapt to the changed environment. The lake is populated by at least four species of non-stinging jellyfish. Three species of *Halimeda* green algae cover the lake bottom. Mangrove roots coexist with tunicates, sponges, tube worms, bivalves, crustaceans, anemones and several species of gobies.

Pulau Kakaban, 190km (120 miles) south of Pulau Sipadan, was the first to attract interest when Borneo divers surveyed it, but mangrove swamps made it unsuitable for resort development. However, further research found Pulau Sangalaki to be similar, so Pulau Sangalaki Resort was developed.

PULAU SANGALAKI

There is a tidal range of 2.5m (8ft) at Pulau Sangalaki and the reefs extend 600–1000m (1970–3280ft), continuing as gentle slopes. A small-boat channel is cut through the outer reef and all diving is drift diving from small boats. When the tide is in, divers can board the dive boat at the beach, but by the time they return from that dive the dive boat will ground some 150m (500ft) out, leaving all personnel to walk in. Similarly, all personnel will have to walk out to the boat for the next dive, but by the time the boat returns the tide will allow the boat right up to the main beach again. This walking is no hardship, as resort staff will help divers carry their equipment.

PULAU DERAWAN

Since Pulau Sangalaki Resort was established, another resort has been set up 50 minutes north-north-west on the larger inhabited island of Pulau Derawan, which has both freshwater and a jetty. The diving at Pulau Derawan is similar to that on Pulau Mabul in nearby east Sabah and particularly good for macrophotography. During the day, most divers concentrate on Pulau Sangalaki, Pulau Kakaban, Pulau Maratua and Pulau Samama.

The visibility in this area is affected by heavy rain on the mainland increasing the river run-off. Pulau Sangalaki usually has

ABOVE *The Sea Star* (Choriaster granulatus) *is stouter than most Sea Stars that have separate arms and appears to scavenge on coral polyps and other invertebrates. The one shown here is apparently arched over a piece of stony coral. It is also called a Thick-arm Starfish.*

better visibility than Pulau Samama or Pulau Derawan because it is further offshore. Pulau Kakaban and Pulau Maratua tend to have better visibility than Sangalaki because they are even further out.

Although Pulau Derawan suffers reduced visibility, it has diverse marine life and is good for small critters and night diving. The dive sites cover reef slopes with a variety of corals including one new to science, and appropriately called *Acropora derawanensis*, walls and caves. Green Turtles (*Chelonia mydas*), Whitetip Reef, Variegated (Leopard) and Nurse Sharks, shoaling barracuda, Humphead (Napoleon) Wrasse, cuttlefish, Spanish Mackerel (*Scomberomorus commersoni*), jacks, batfish and colourful reef fish are common.

Some of the best diving is in 5–15m (16–50ft) of water at the end of Pulau Derawan's 200m (656ft) jetty on the southeast face. It has clownfish, lionfish, scorpionfish, crocodilefish, batfish, pufferfish, anthias, turtles and macro subjects such as pipefish, seahorses, mantis shrimps, decorator crabs, seahorses and nudibranchs.

Lying 200m (656ft) offshore, northeast of the jetty, **The Shipwreck** ⊡ is a burnt-out hulk at 27m (88ft) on sand that harbours countless small organisms. At **Blue Trigger Wall** ⊡, blue juvenile Redtooth Triggerfish (*Odonus niger*) peer out of holes at around 18m (60ft). Blue Trigger Point has Gorgonian Sea Fans, black corals and soft corals. Off the northeast point, **Sea Garden** ⊡ has healthy corals at 10m (33ft) and there are many species of flatworms, nudibranchs, ribbon eels, gobies and blennies. **Snapper Point** ⊡ and **Lighthouse** ⊡ are similar to Blue Trigger Wall/Point.

⊡ PULAU MARATUA

One hour northeast of Pulau Sangalaki, Pulau Maratua is a large island with a lagoon. The island circles part of the lagoon, the rest is fringing reef. The lagoon is 100–400m (330–1300ft) wide and it fills and drains through a single channel, creating a very strong tidal flow. The surrounding walls are covered with stony and soft corals and have several dive sites, but it is the channel into and out of the lagoon that is the main focus of divers' attention as the tides produce amazing drift dives twice a day. The pelagic and reef fish life is prolific. A swirling mass of barracuda, shoals of snapper, Dogtooth Tuna, Spanish Mackerel, jacks and surgeonfish, Scalloped Hammerhead, Nurse, Grey Reef and Whitetip Reef Sharks, Manta Rays, Eagle Rays and huge groupers. The currents can be strong and up and down-currents are common. Most dive operators put divers into the water on a flood tide, not only for better visibility, but also to avoid the possibility of divers being swept into the open sea. Sometimes the currents are not too bad, but in general it is not wise to carry a large housed camera.

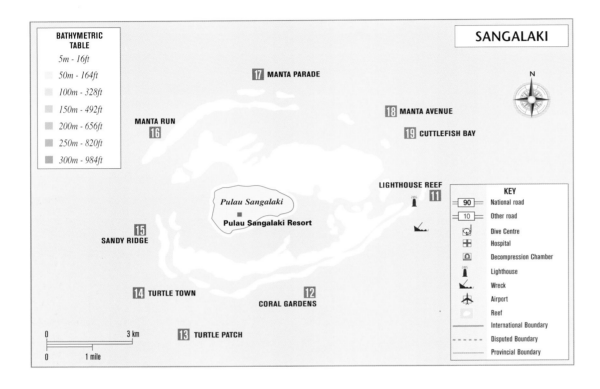

ABOVE *The magenta patch on male Squarespot Anthiases (*Pseudanthias pleurotaenia*) seems to glow, giving rise to their alternative common name of Mirror Basslets.*

☐ PULAU SAMAMA

Pulau Samama, 15 minutes northwest of Pulau Sangalaki, has mangroves open to the sea, so the water around the tangled root system is much clearer than you would normally expect, giving access to the interesting small creatures which inhabit them. Away from the mangroves, the reef is great for muck diving and macrophotography among good corals, with lots of nudibranchs, flatworms, pipefish, gobies and blennies, Warty (Clown) Frogfish (*Antennarius maculatus*) and other species of frogfish.

PULAU KAKABAN

About 20–25 minutes east-northeast of Pulau Sangalaki, Pulau Kakaban rises steeply with walls to 240m (790ft), visited by many pelagic species. These current-swept walls, decorated with Gorgonian Sea Fans, soft corals and twisted barrel sponges, give high-voltage drift dives. The currents can be strong with upwelling and downwelling, and sometimes reversing direction, but they produce prolific fish life. At **Barracuda (the southwest) Point** ☐ these currents bring shoals of barracuda, jacks, surgeonfish, snappers, trevallies and Grey Reef, Whitetip Reef and Variegated (Leopard) Sharks and Scalloped Hammerhead Sharks. A grab line has been secured at 24m (79ft) across a relatively flat area on the up-current side of the point to help divers ascend to the calmer shallows.

On the wall, **Blue Light Cave** ☐ is a deep cave which should only be attempted by experienced divers and accompanied by a local divemaster. The system starts on the top of the wall at one metre (40 inches) at high tide and descends via a narrow, vertical chimney to the roof of a large, dark chamber at about 21m (70ft). Divers swim out along the ceiling of that chamber towards the wall until they can finally see the light from outside. The exit is a long vertical crack in the wall, which is about 2m (7ft) wide at the top, and it gets wider and wider as it goes down. Divers usually exit onto the wall at about 40m (130ft).

ABOVE *A Pink Anemonefish* (Amphiprion perideraion) *in a large Anemone* (Heteractis magnifica) *at Pulau Sangalaki. Anemonefish, popularly referred to as clownfish, live in symbiosis with anemones without being stung.*

ABOVE *A cuttlefish* (Sepia pharaonis) *laying eggs among the coral at Pulau Sangalaki. Cuttlefish are not fish, but molluscs, related to squid and octopuses. They can give a display of intricate colour patterns that change continuously.*

Kakaban Lake 8 covers almost the entire island. The 20-minute hike into the interior is on a relatively easy trail starting near the centre of the southern bay. However, it has sharp and slippery rocks so wear sensible footwear and have mosquito repellent as the trek is through rainforest. Most of the lake is only 3–5m (10–16ft) deep so most people snorkel in it. As well as the jellyfish, there are white anemones that eat small jellyfish and the mangroves along the edge of the lake have lots of interesting sponges attached to them.

PULAU SANGALAKI

Pulau Sangalaki is known for its Manta Rays and turtles. A shallow lagoon surrounds the island and the reefs begin well out to sea. With so much reef, there is a large diversity of marine life and since the area is a protected marine park, the reefs are in good condition. The reefs slope gently with many of the sites having a maximum depth of less than 20m (65ft). There are over 500 species of stony and soft corals and a profusion of invertebrate and

fish life. On almost every dive there are Manta Rays, cuttlefish, Eagle Rays, stingrays, batfish, barracuda, many species of grouper including Barramundi Cod (Humpback Grouper, *Cromileptes altivelis*) and Coral Trout. Orangestriped and Titan Triggerfish, squirrelfish, surgeonfish and many species of angelfish and butterflyfish abound, but there are few parrotfish. There are many species of pufferfish, sweetlips, hawkfish, bream, damselfish, anthias, chromis and moray eels. **Sandy Ridge** 15 has garden eels. There are small sharks and shoals of fusiliers, snappers, catfish and jacks. Large barrel sponges and true giant clams are found on the sand. Lettuce coral is interspersed with boulder coral, smaller fields of soft corals, many tube sponges and isolated Gorgonian Sea Fans carpet the seabed.

The currents vary from medium to strong. The speed and direction of drift will depend on the direction of the tide at the time of the dive. Snorkelling is the best way to interact with the Manta Rays, who then keep on coming back out of curiosity.

Just west of the small boat channel, **Coral Gardens** 12 is a mix of stony and soft corals shelving out gradually to 27m (90ft) and then becoming flat sand. It is possible to drift from Coral Gardens, through **Turtle Town** 14 to **Sandy Ridge** 15 over an undulating stony coral bottom with vast fields of lettuce coral. The maximum depth is 28m (92ft).

Turtles shelter under overhangs formed by large boulder corals at 12m (40ft) at **Turtle Patch** 13. Turtle Town has gullies and small ridges on stony coral in all directions with lots of turtles at 15m (50ft). At the northwest to west area of the reef, the drift from **Manta Run** 16 to Sandy Ridge is over undulating sand with coral heads at 28m (92ft), where more than 20 Manta Rays repeatedly swim closely overhead. **Manta Parade** 17 has a flat sandy bottom, interspersed with small coral heads at 15m (50ft), where Manta Rays parade up and down. The drift from **Manta Avenue** 18 through **Cuttlefish Bay** 19 to **Lighthouse Reef** 11 covers the northeast area of the reef over a gentle slope from 16m (52ft) to 5m (16ft).

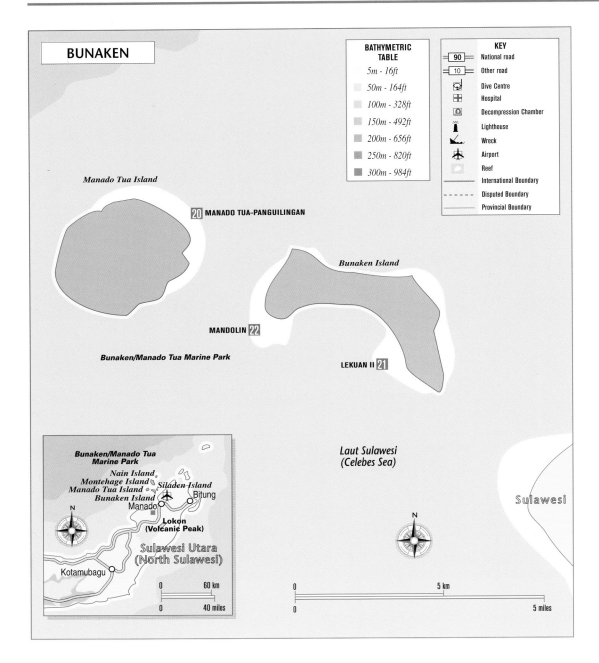

BUNAKEN

BATHYMETRIC TABLE
- 5m - 16ft
- 50m - 164ft
- 100m - 328ft
- 150m - 492ft
- 200m - 656ft
- 250m - 820ft
- 300m - 984ft

KEY
- 90 National road
- 10 Other road
- Dive Centre
- Hospital
- Decompression Chamber
- Lighthouse
- Wreck
- Airport
- Reef
- International Boundary
- Disputed Boundary
- Provincial Boundary

Manado Tua Island

20 MANADO TUA-PANGUILINGAN

Bunaken Island

MANDOLIN 22

Bunaken/Manado Tua Marine Park

LEKUAN II 21

Laut Sulawesi (Celebes Sea)

Bunaken/Manado Tua Marine Park
- Nain Island
- Montehage Island
- Manado Tua Island
- Bunaken Island
- Siladen Island
- Bitung
- Manado
- Lokon (Volcanic Peak)
- *Sulawesi Utara (North Sulawesi)*
- Kotamubagu

Sulawesi

| 0 | 60 km |
| 0 | 40 miles |

| 0 | 5 km |
| 0 | 5 miles |

NORTH SULAWESI
by Michael Aw

North Sulawesi, the narrow jagged peninsula forming the northern arm of the island, has a population and geography unlike anywhere else in the archipelago. Its marine environment is acclaimed internationally as one of the richest in the world. Shaped like a distended spider, Sulawesi is split into an assortment of four peninsulas. These peninsulas, divided by deep, contoured gulfs, are so completely separate from each other that the earliest Portuguese explorers thought that Sulawesi was a group of individual islands rather than a single landmass.

The longest and thinnest peninsula is Sulawesi Utara, or North Sulawesi. Due to the isolation of this strip of land from the rest of Sulawesi, the local Minahasa people are more attuned to the outside world than to the rest of Indonesia. The geographical proximity of the Philippines, only a few hundred kilometres north, has had a great influence on the area, resulting in many linguistic and cultural links. The peninsula itself is mountainous and volcanic, lushly covered with a variety of vegetation. Lying on a major fault-line of the famous Ring of Fire, North Sulawesi is peppered with volcanic peaks – some of them, like the 1584m (5197ft) Lokon near Manado, still active. As befits an area with such an abundance of coastline, the inhabitants of North Sulawesi take pride in their seas. The peninsula is fringed by extensive coral reefs, but those found at Bunaken/Manado Tua Marine Park at the extreme northwest tip of the peninsula are very rich and diverse.

The geographical crossroads of intercontinental currents of the Indian and Pacific oceans, led scientists to conclude that Sulawesi region is part of the heartland of marine biodiversity. In 1990, a marine scientist from the University of Guam documented over 150 genera of hard corals around Bunaken Island, the principal island of the marine park. Cumulative surveys document that 3000 species of fish are found in Indonesia, compared with more than 2000 in the Philippines and just over 1300 in Palau. As the distance away from Sulawesi increases, the number of species decrease with a species low of 125 at Easter Island, far east of New Zealand. In the early 90s, coral scientists confirmed that most of the reefs in North Sulawesi comprised over 90 per cent live corals, a high percentage relative to reefs elsewhere in the world. Research published by Dr Allan White in 1992 indicates that the number of endemic species here exceed those of the Philippines and Great Barrier Reef systems.

Diving in North Sulawesi centres around Manado, the provincial capital and the closest population centre to the renowned Bunaken/Manado Tua Marine Park. Since the inception of direct flights from Singapore dive centres and resorts mushroomed from three in 1992 to over 15 operating along the coastline and on Bunaken Island itself. The international airport is within easy driving distance from the city centre.

On the southeastern tip of the peninsula near Bitung, the strait between the mainland and Lembeh Island is known to be refuge for rare and weird marine critters. Lembeh Strait is the Mecca for the intrepid diver, attracting the Who's Who in underwater photographers from all over the world. The Sangihe and Talaud Islands, far to the north, are also known for their excellent diving, which can at present only be accessed by live-aboards leaving from Manado.

BUNAKEN

Bunaken Manado Tua Marine Park comprises a group of five islands: Bunaken, Siladen, Nain, Montehage and Manado Tua, surrounded by an area of 75,265 ha (186,000 acres) of water. Separated from the mainland by an oceanic trench in excess of 1400m (4600ft) deep, frequent upwellings from the deep, and environs, bring rich nutrients for phytoplanktons (plants) to grow. These in turn provide for zooplanktons, which contain many offspring from the animal, pelagic and coral reef realms. All islands are fringed by a shallow reef zone, with a depth ranging from 1m (3ft) – some exposed at low tide – to 7m (23ft) before edging out to plummet down vertical walls to a ledge at about 60m (200ft).

The five islands in the park are distinctly different. Bunaken, the principal Island, has a deep, calm bay that shelters prolific coral formations; the composition of fauna on the reef flat, edge and wall of this bay is extraordinary and has become the signature dive site for tourists visiting Manado. Curators of Vancouver Aquarium were so impressed that they made a showcase tank in their tropical gallery based on the walls of Bunaken. Along the western side of Bunaken, facing Manado Tua, is a 3km (2-mile) wall, plummeting straight to over 90m (300ft). Large volumes of water swish back and forth through this channel, drawing in pelagics to feed on the reef. Eagle Rays, Rainbow Runners, trevallies and tuna patrol along the steep wall. Here the crucible of creation spellbinds the intrepid visitor with the myriad of life among giant sponges, multicoloured pink, green and gold fans and whip corals. It is not unusual to see a shoal of Pyramid Butterflyfish envelope a diver like a locust plague within seconds. The soft coral formations that surround a huge cavern are among the most awe-inspiring in the world.

Shaped like a cylindrical cone that characterizes volcanoes, Manado Tua seems to rise out from the sea and is the highest island in the reserve. Though inhabited, wild black apes still roam the lush vegetation typical of tropical rainforest, which shroud the island almost in its entirety. Surrounding the island is a narrow fringing reef that plummets to several hundred metres. Oceanographers using satellite imagery recently found an oceanic trough just off the northeast corner of Manado Tua. Here large schools of barracudas, trevallies, Blacktip Sharks and Dogtooth Tunas sometimes come out of the dark blue depths. Along the wall reside huge barrel sponges. Once common, but now seldom seen among the corridors of overhangs and caverns are huge Napoleon Wrasse.

Siladen is a small, round island to the east of Bunaken; largely owned by a local scholar, John Rihasia, who proposed the theory that the people of the South Pacific such as Fiji and the Solomons are descendants of people from North Sulawesi. Swift currents constantly sweep the southwestern wall, supporting a terrain of giant coral trees and sponges. Garden and Ribbon Eels are found in phenomenal numbers on the reef flat.

North of Bunaken is Montehage, the biggest island of the five, surrounded by an extensive mangrove and fringing reef. The northwestern wall also plummets steeply and is subjected to the strong oceanic currents.

ABOVE *Soft coral on the west side of Bunaken Island, where the reef wall drops steeply to a ledge at 40m (130ft) before plummeting to abyssal depth. At 30m (100ft), stony coral coverage diminishes and soft corals cover caverns and overhangs. This area is the most colourful of Bunaken Marine Park.*

ABOVE *Crinoids are prolific on reef slopes and walls where they feed in passing currents. The are common in Bunaken's reefs.*

Schooling hammerheads in deeper water and huge schools of barracudas are predictably found on this site. Endless meadows of stony corals, the best that I have ever seen in Asia, are found on the reef slope of Nain, the island furthest away from the mainland. A fringing reef surrounds an aqua-blue lagoon filled with an amazing diversity of invertebrate fauna.

The variety of life and dramatic seascapes of the marine park impresses and fascinates even well-travelled divers. Shoals of bright blue fusiliers, tuna and Black Snappers, clownfish playing in the anemones, colourful parrotfish,

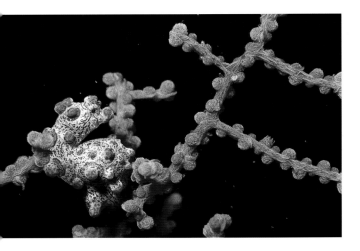

TOP *Bargibant's Pygmy seahorse* (Hippocampus bargibanti) *escaped notice until recently because of its size, between 3mm (⅛in) and 1cm (⅜in).*

ABOVE *During the day lionfish can be found hanging out beneath caverns and crevices, but at night they move out on top of the reefs to feed on passing fish.*

Butterflyfish, batfish, blue starfish, the occasional sea snake, Napoleon Wrasse, ferns and feathery fans, giant clams, bright orange and red corals and fluorescent yellow sponges are all part of this magical kingdom of nature.

BEST DIVE SITES
BUNAKEN MANADO TUA MARINE PARK
20 **Manado Tua – Panguilingan**

Situated on the northeast corner of the extinct volcano Manado-Tua, this is the most exhilarating dive in the marine park. While schools of barracuda and other pelagics hang out in the blue, Bigeye Trevallies intermittently dash in to prey upon unsuspecting fish.

The steep reef falls quickly to 32m (105ft), where a wall begins. This wall is completely covered with prolific coral trees, sea fans, oversized dinnerplate-shaped sponges and coral colonies. Jacks, Eagle Rays, tunas, Rainbow Runners and Whitetip Reef Sharks are often encountered off the wall or on the coral-covered slope. Soft corals, anemones, whip corals, and sponges are plentiful on shallow reef. Blue water and swift fish action in fast currents are the elements of this site.

21 Bunaken: Lekuan II

This is the signature dive of the marine park. It is located on the south coast of Bunaken, towards Depan Kampung. The reef flat is exposed at low tide, but the deep, vertical wall plummets straight down to over 40m (130ft). This is one of three sites, known collectively as Lekuan, along this outcrop of Bunaken's fringing reef. The shallow reeftop is perfect for snorkellers. Further down, caverns, canyons, fissures and inlets split the wall. On the reef edge, thousands of Fairy Basslets rise and fall among *Acropora* formations and Pyramid Butterflyfish feast in the blue water.

Like the majority of south Bunaken sites, the site has extensive coverage of stony and soft corals. Sponges, in barrel and pipe forms, abound, as well as numerous large and small gorgonias. This is a good spot for big fish, with larger reef species and pelagics schooling off the reef-face in respectable numbers. A

small school of Bumphead Parrotfish is often seen grazing on the meadow of stony corals.

There are many species of jacks and trevallies in particular, especially Golden and Bigeye Trevally. Snappers, in Red and Midnight varieties, are also numerous. There are unicornfish and surgeonfish, though less abundant. Giant Groupers and large Longnosed Butterflyfish are common. *Teira* Batfish, trumpetfish, filefish, huge pufferfish and porcupinefish abound. Big Yellowfin Tuna and the more common Dogtooth Tuna can often be seen in the blue, as can Great and Barred Barracuda. Sharks are less frequent, but Whitetip, Blacktip and Grey Reefs can be seen.

22 Bunaken: Mandolin

On the southwest coast of Bunaken that faces Manado Tua, the reef wall is almost vertical and falls precipitously to over 60m (200 ft). A very wide, flat reeftop extends 200–300m (656–984ft) from shore, providing a lifetime of entertainment for snorkellers. A few lucky ones have swum alongside dolphins and orcas. The reef flat is covered in a profusion of soft corals and stony-coral colonies in various forms. While Gorgonian Sea Fans and Sea Whips reach out from the wall to filter-feed, constant strong currents also bring in some big pelagics and schooling species. Large schools of trevallies, big barracudas and swarms of snappers, unicornfish and surgeonfish are all common. There are often tuna off the reef, including monster Dogtooth weighing close to 100kg (220 lb). Giant Groupers and other species of grouper are all well represented, and there are some big Longnose and other emperor varieties. The site is home to huge numbers of Pyramid Butterflyfish, in denser concentrations than anywhere else in Indonesia; other butterflyfish species are common here. Regal, Emperor and Blue-faced Angelfish are plentiful. The site has triggerfish, particularly the big Clown variety and some very nice Picassos. Big Whitetip Reef Sharks, Banded Sea Snakes of about 1m (40in), moray eels, smaller tuna of about 90cm (3ft) and turtles are often seen.

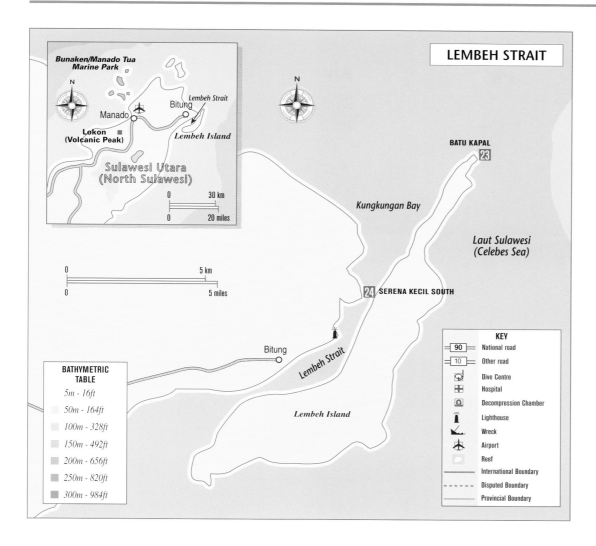

ABOVE *Resembling sedentary sponges, frogfish have a large mouth, relative to their size, and an abdomen that can expand to engulf prey twice their size. Masters of camouflage, they appear in red, pink, yellow, maroon and blue at Lembeh Strait.*

LEMBEH STRAIT

The more than 40 dive sites along the 16km (10-mile) Lembeh Strait are mostly patch reefs on a sandy slope. It is the universe of the weird and wonderful. Though there are decent coral meadows on the northern end of the strait, the focus is on muck diving; peeling back layers of life to reveal shy critters such as the Mimic Octopus, the Flamboyant Cuttlefish, Harlequin Shrimp, Wonderpus and skeleton shrimps. The assemblage of extraordinary fish at Lembeh is impressive. Although water temperatures are comparatively cold for the tropics, the sheltered conditions make diving possible all year round.

ᕮᓚ Batu Kapal

In terms of fish life, this is one of the best in North Sulawesi. Situated at the north end of the Sulawesi–Lembeh channel, Batu Kapal is a deep dive on a large rock off the Lembeh coast. The dive begins at 24m (80ft), the foot of the Batu Kapal itself, and follows a submerged ridge running northeast to a large pinnacle at 36m (120ft). The area has many outcrops and pinnacles, but the main attraction is the ridge, which provides a current shelter harbouring big pelagics.

The site has an exceptional variety of good coral cover, with a preponderance of soft and plate corals. Fish include big schools of jacks and trevallies, Dogtooth Tuna, schooling barracuda, Grey and Whitetip Reef Sharks and the occasional Whale Shark, along with a good assortment of the normal reef species. When the current is running, the fish mêlée around this rock is electrifying.

ᕮᓔ Serena Kecil South

Located on the south side of Serena Kecil, this site is the twilight zone of weird and rare critters. It yields more nocturnal life per square metre than just about any other site in Indonesia. It is a shallow, sloping reef, bottoming out at just 18m (60ft), composed of an assortment of coral heads and outcrops. There are sandy areas between some of the larger coral patches, and all the heads and outcrops are contoured, offering plenty of hidy-holes to explore. Slow, gradual progress yields the best results – lots of small attractions might escape attention when moving too fast.

Octocorals, bubble corals, anemones, cabbage corals and sea whips are common. There are the usual reef-fish species, but the nocturnal residents are special – common among them are: Shortfin (Dwarf) Lionfish, Leaf and Bearded Scorpionfish, as well as Decorator, Anemone, Sponge and Hermit Crabs (among many other small and medium crabs). The many lobsters include very large Slipper Lobsters. There are Slate Pencil Urchins; moray eels on feeding forays; sleeping parrotfish; many nudibranchs and flatworms, including some small Spanish Dancers. There are Bluespotted Stingrays and Whitetip Reef Sharks off the reef; and beautiful juvenile Pinnate Batfish. Frogfish and Pygmy sea horses can also be found nearby.

BALI

by Michael Aw

BALI IS RECOGNIZED AS ONE OF ASIA'S MOST magical islands – every year thousands of people flock to the beaches of its south coast, and a well-established tourist industry has sprung up to cater for this influx. The beaches, the lush tropical landscape of the island's interior and the rich cultural traditions of the Balinese people are all great attractions. The over one million visitors per year has caused many experienced divers to snub Bali for off-the-beaten-track destinations. Nevertheless, the quality and excitement of the dive sites off Bali are some of the best in the world.

Amid the cornucopia of lush coral reef lives an equally diverse fish population. All the classic reef fish are here in force: parrotfish, Moorish Idols, angelfish, groupers, frogfish, wrasses, eels, lionfish, to name a few. Tulamben Bay on the northeastern coast offers an experience that is almost like diving into a living encyclopedia. Robert Myers, a leading ichthyologist from Guam, recorded 649 fish species in just six days in the Tulamben Bay

TOP LEFT *Secret Bay, off Gilimanuk, is the only refuge for many young marine animals from the strong currents in the narrow Bali Strait.*
TOP RIGHT *Tulamben Bay is calm and sheltered, fringed with coconut palms and set against Mt Agung, the highest mountain in Bali. It harbours some of the best dive sites of Indonesia.*

area. *National Geographic* photographer, David Doubilet, was so impressed with Tulamben that he returned twice to photograph the habitats and diversity of benthic life for three weeks on each visit in 1996.

Bali's fish population is not limited to reef-dwellers. Fed by the rich upwellings of the Indian Ocean, Bali's waters are home to a wide variety of pelagics – tuna, mackerel, jacks and bonito, as well as barracuda and several species of shark. Rays are common at many sites, especially around Nusa Penida, whose environs are particularly rich in big deep-water fish. Many species of marine mammal are found off the island's coasts, including dolphin, Bryde's whale and manatees, although these are admittedly very rare.

Located in the Lesser Sundas, Bali is midway along Indonesia's southernmost chain of islands between Java and Lombok. The island's south coast touches the easternmost edge of the Indian Ocean, while the north coast looks onto the Java Sea. The islands of Penida, Lembongan and Cenida lie in a tightly-packed group just off the southeast coast of Bali. The Bandung Strait not only separates these islands from mainland Bali, but is also part of the Wallace line, an imaginary border that separates the flora and fauna of Southeast Asia and Australasia. As such, the natural environment here is distinctly different from Bali and Java. Impressive cliffs rising

up to 200m (656ft) show distinct strata lines. The dry weather conditions have resulted in bizarre, arid landscapes.

While at the narrowest point of the channel Bali is a mere 11km (7 miles) away, it is in every sense as far as one can be from the real world. This region is constantly flushed by huge volumes of water between the Indian Ocean and Java Sea. Deep, icy, ocean upwellings, downwellings and fast currents replenish the reef systems with rich nutrients. Diving can be treacherous for the inexperienced, but a serious jolt of adrenaline for the well prepared. One of the best dive sites in Bali, Jurassic Point, is described by a dive operator as: 'a place that can be the best, worst or last dive you will ever have.' When in the right mix, diving Lembongan and Penida is almost surreal. On the far northwestern tip of the island lies Pulau Menjangan, which in 1978 became Bali's first internationally known dive location. The island is part of the Bali Barat National Park and offers some of the best wall dives in Indonesia.

The five main areas for diving in Bali are Nusa Dua and Sanur; Padang Bai and Candidasa; Nusa Penida; Tulamben and Menjangan. Each area is unique and offers suitable conditions for both beginners and seasoned divers. One of the best ways to dive the best of Bali is to join a Bali 'safari package' with one of the leading dive operators.

1 *LIBERTY* WRECK, TULAMBEN

Lying just 30m (100ft) offshore at Tulamben, northeast Bali, is the wreck of *USAT Liberty*. This impressive 100m (328ft) remnant of World War II was built in 1915 and torpedoed on 11 January 1942 about 15km (9 miles) southwest of Lombok by a Japanese submarine. She was taken in tow by the two destroyers *HNLMS Van Ghent* and *USS Paul Jones*. She was perilously taking on water and, in an effort to salvage the cargo, she was successfully beached on the shores of Tulamben. Since ships are made for a life at sea, the violent eruption of 1963 toppled and pushed the vessel back into the water to lie almost parallel to shore. Today, she is Indonesia's diving mascot. The hull is badly broken up, with the stern lying towards the beach and the bow pointing towards the depths. The wreck is not intact enough to speak of actually penetrating it, but parts of the hold are whole, and there are numerous overhanging sections and swim-throughs which give the sensation of being inside the old ship. The metal of the hull is now completely encrusted by coral, but many details can still be made out, including the bow gun.

However, it is neither the structure nor history that attracts divers from all over the world, but the density and quality of marine life found on her. The vessel celebrates the richness of Indonesia's marine biodiversity, although the ease of diving, and lying at a depth of between 5 and 30m (16 and 98ft), has a lot to do with the wreck's popularity. The most obvious attraction on the wreck is the sheer number and variety of fish. Sergeant-major Damselfish, Crescent Wrasse and unicornfish often swim right up to divers to inquire about a free feed. The bigger fish,

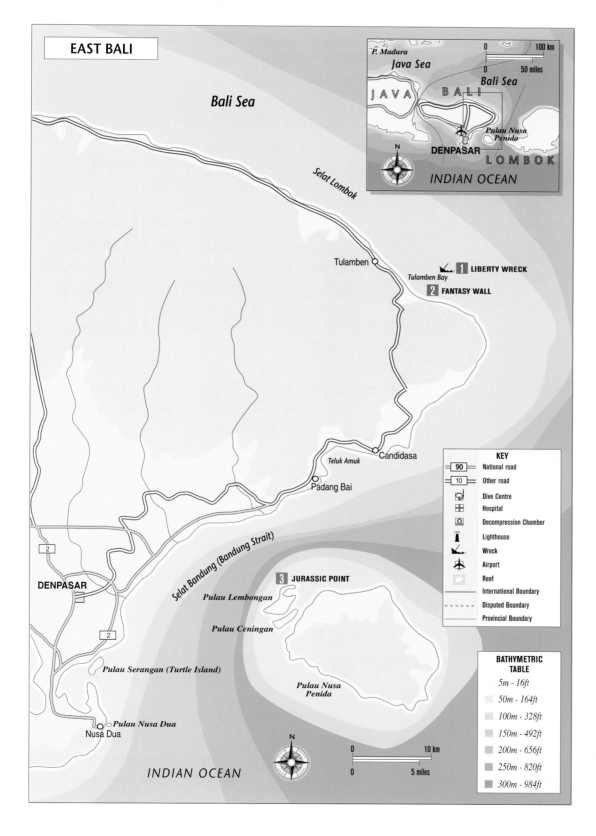

EAST BALI

Bali Sea

Selat Lombok

Tulamben

Tulamben Bay

1 LIBERTY WRECK

2 FANTASY WALL

Teluk Amuk Candidasa

Padang Bai

DENPASAR

Selat Bandung (Bandung Strait)

3 JURASSIC POINT

Pulau Lembongan

Pulau Ceningan

Pulau Serangan (Turtle Island)

Pulau Nusa Penida

Pulau Nusa Dua
Nusa Dua

INDIAN OCEAN

P. Madura
Java Sea
Bali Sea
JAVA   BALI
Pulau Nusa Penida
DENPASAR
LOMBOK
INDIAN OCEAN

KEY

90	National road
10	Other road
	Dive Centre
	Hospital
	Decompression Chamber
	Lighthouse
	Wreck
	Airport
	Reef
	International Boundary
	Disputed Boundary
	Provincial Boundary

BATHYMETRIC TABLE

	5m - 16ft
	50m - 164ft
	100m - 328ft
	150m - 492ft
	200m - 656ft
	250m - 820ft
	300m - 984ft

ABOVE *Just off the beach of Tulamben are two resident schools of Bigeye Jacks, one adult and one juvenile, that often swirl around divers.*

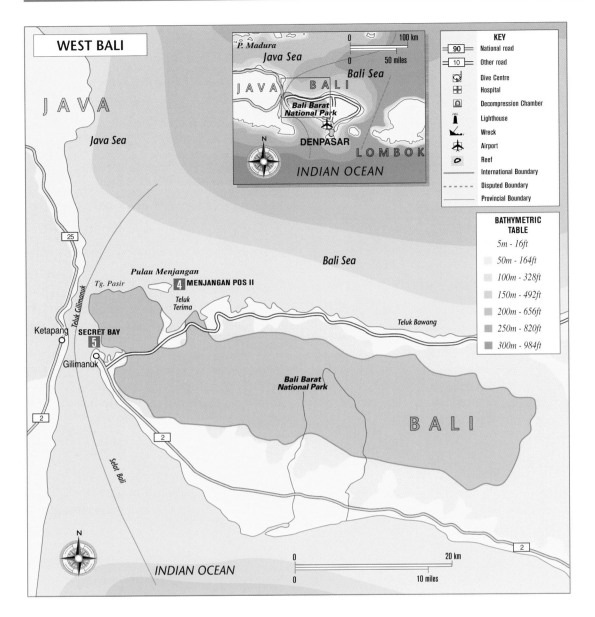

ABOVE *Snorkellers have much to see in this part of the world, considered the heartland of biodiversity where the species of the vast Pacific Ocean meet those of the Indian Ocean.*

such as Bumphead Parrotfish, Napoleon Wrasse, Oriental Sweetlips, rabbitfish, Coral Trout and other groupers, sometimes hover in mid-water, making great subjects for fish portraits. Although only a few table-sized stony corals are found on the outer edge, the superstructure is heavily colonized by soft corals, Gorgonian Sea Fans, tall black and green coral trees, stinging hydrozoans and colourful sponges. The gun is still intact on the stern at 28m (92ft), completely encrusted with sessile animals and sea fans. At 30m (100ft), the reef is covered with red sea whips, huge barrel sponges and numerous species of gobies. Even snorkellers can enjoy themselves on the wreck – the bow is a mere 30m (100ft) swim from shore, heavily encrusted with sponges, sea squirts and a haven of friendly fish.

② FANTASY WALL – TULAMBEN BAY

On the eastern end of Tulamben Bay, beneath the temple, a wall plummets from near-surface to beyond 60m (200ft). This is the benchmark of wall diving. The wall is completely covered with huge barrel sponges, coral trees, oversized Gorgonian Sea Fans, one of which is prominently positioned on a ledge at 30m (100ft), over 3m (10ft) in height and adorned with Longnose Hawkfish and bright yellow damselfish. Within numerous caverns and crevices are thorny oysters, *Tubastrea* corals, crabs, and shrimps sharing home with squirrelfish, Coral Trout, blennies and scorpionfish. Among fish experts, this wall is famous for harbouring hard-to-find and hard-to-photograph species, including the Comet (*Calloplesiops altivelis*), a fish with elaborate finnage and a false eyespot. Mola Mola, hammerhead sharks and Whale Sharks have been sighted near this location.

A night dive is essential for the surrealistic experience that it offers. You need to descend to 30m (100ft), face the wall, switch off your torch and watch. Millions of tiny green bulbs will suddenly appear, as if by magic, to perform a show of twinkling zigzagging lights. These are the flashlightfish, the nocturnal fish with a bioluminescent organ beneath each eye.

3 JURASSIC POINT – LEMBONGAN ISLAND

Jurassic Point is where Mola Mola, or Sunfish, are predictably found between August and November. The reef terrace begins at 10m (33ft), precipitously drops to 25–30m (80–100ft), followed by a gentle slope to 600m (1970ft). Pinnacles and rocky outcrops are found at 30m (100ft). Once off the reef terrace, the structure is similar to the odd terrain on the surface, but covered with a never-ending meadow of multicoloured, soft, stumpy corals. The abundance of reef life supports many big groupers, sharks, tunas, Eagle Rays and hundreds of Blotched Fantail Rays, which sometimes congregate to mate among the ledges and crevices. Because of the narrow channel, pelagics cruise close to the wall, well within range of the divers also passing with the swift current. The biggest attraction of this site is the Mola Mola that makes frequent appearances at depths of 20–40m (65–130ft) when in season. These 3–4m (10–13ft) oddballs of the sea are shaped like a flying saucer with two wings in the wrong places. Two huge fins, one on the top and one on the bottom, a disc-shaped gelatinous body, big bulbous eyes and a tiny mouth give them an appearance of being uncoordinated; a creature evolved from a bad joke. Mola Mola, or Ocean Sunfish, belong to the family of Molidae and they are totally oceanic with a diet of jellyfish and plankton. Mola Mola are surreal, big and appear deceivingly slow, which tempts closer investigation, but any awkward grasp by the observer will cause them to vanish in a flash. Swimming with Mola Mola is a surrealistic experience, which can be repeated without fear of boredom.

4 MENJANGAN POS II – NORTHWEST BALI

At the Southeast corner of Pulau Menjangan, eastward around the coast, is the signature dive site of the nature reserve. It offers spectacular coral growth and fish life in astounding numbers along a sharply angled wall. Starting with a steep slope, the wall approaches the near-vertical in many places, where there is more variety to the reef profile, with plenty of nooks and crannies, cavelets and fissures. Coral growth is extraordinary, as good as anything you'll find in the Indo-Pacific waters. Stony corals are extensive, but the soft corals outshine the stony varieties; barrel and other sponges are common all over the slope. Large numbers of red and yellow gorgonias are scattered around the reef-face.

As in all Menjangan dive sites, this dive is the best representation for the vast numbers and diverse make-up of the fish population. From tiny basslets and dottybacks to huge cruising tuna, this site has them all. Surgeonfish and unicornfish of many types are prevalent, particularly the Bluespine Unicornfish. There are several varieties of triggerfish, and both Pinnate and Teira Batfish. Big Star and Spotted Trunkfish (Black Boxfish) and several other types of boxfish make their cumbersome way along the reef, among clouds of butterflyfish and stately, regal-looking lionfish. Rabbitfish are plentiful, angelfish more so, and the entire reef-face is dotted with nudibranchs that seem to glow with colour.

5 SECRET BAY – MENJANGAN

Across the road from Gilimanuk, the ferry crossing point to Java, is the road to the entry point to the twilight zone of diving in Indonesia. Secret Bay is an easy shore dive, but water temperature is usually cold due to the nearby deep-water cold currents directed into the bay by regular upwelling and tidal change. Nutrient-rich colder water blends with the sea grass mangrove environment, making this a special nursery for both Pacific and Indian Ocean animals. Many species found here are endemic to the site, rare or non-existent in other parts of Bali or even the rest of Indonesia. The site is different to any other in Bali, mostly shallow to no more than 6m (20ft), and a black, sandy bottom covered with loose seaweed and sargassum. Once beneath the surface the trained observer will find critter heaven: sea horses, Common Lionfish (Turkeyfish), Ghost Pipefish, Spiny Leaf fish (Spiny Waspfish), snake eels, stonefish, nudibranchs, gobies, dragonets, sea urchins, exotic species of cardinal fish and anglerfish (frogfish). The latter is particularly abundant and diverse in the bay – four different species are found here, including the Spot-fin, Sargassum, the Painted and a species currently awaiting scientific description. Especially during low tide, visibility and density of rare critters will redefine the meaning of muck diving for the macrophotographer. It is also seventh heaven for the marine naturalist.

TOP *Sea turtles are on the brink of extinction worldwide, mostly due to human activities such as poaching and habitat destruction.*

ABOVE *Tube anemones such as this one are scattered across the vast black sand slope. These and other critters are more visible against the black sand in clear water.*

KOMODO AND ALOR

by Michael Aw

KOMODO

THERE IS SOMETHING ABOUT KOMODO THAT is rather unearthly; this group of islands with savannah landscape, resembling a wilderness that seems to belong to another place and time. Though it is only 370km (230 miles) east of Bali, between the islands of Sumbawa and Flores, Komodo is untypical of the tropical isles of the Indonesian archipelago. The arid weather conditions distinctive of the area, which has an annual rainfall of about 800mm (30in), support a dramatically desolate setting of harsh, undulating terrain punctuated at random with Lontar palms. The huge volume of water that washes back and forth between the Indian Ocean and Flores Sea amid uncountable shelters, bays, and islets makes this location perfect for the intrepid diver.

The islands are the habitat of the *Varanus komodoensis,* a giant, primeval monitor lizard that walks and grunts aggressively like a dinosaur. The Komodo Dragon is the largest

TOP LEFT AND RIGHT *Although Komodo is in the centre of the Indonesian archipelago, the islands between Sumbawa and Flores are very different to the other tropical islands of Indonesia. The low annual rainfall of about 800mm (30in) has resulted in a dramatically desolate setting of harsh terrain, dotted with Lontar palms.*

lizard in the world and when a Dutch aviator reported his sightings in the early 1900s of 4m (13ft) dragons roaming in Jurassic-like countryside, his story was probably considered the product of a silly explorer's imagination. It wasn't until another Dutchman, this time a military officer, Van Steyne, brought two cadavers to the Bogor Zoological Gardens in 1912, that the curator, PO Ouwens, formally described the animal as *Varanus komodoensis*. Today there may be as few as 3000 of these prehistoric monitor lizards remaining in the wild. Because they exist nowhere else, scientists began to lobby for their protection as far back as 1915. In 1977 the Komodo Island and environs were listed in the UNESCO Man and Biosphere (MAB). This is a worldwide programme designed to conserve the remaining diversity of plants, animals and microorganisms that make up our living biosphere.

Encouraged by the listing, the local municipality inaugurated Komodo National Park in 1980 to protect the area's biological diversity, particularly the habitat of the last of the dragons. In all, the park has a total land area of 75,000ha (185,325 acres) and encompasses a number of environs including islets, bays, mangrove swamps and islands. The largest island is Komodo with 34,000ha (84,014 acres), followed by Rinca with 20,000 ha (49,420 acres), Padar, Nusa Kode, Motang,

numerous smaller islands, and the Wae Wuul sanctuary on Flores. A total of 112,500ha (277,988 acres) of the surrounding waters is also under the jurisdiction of the park rangers. The landscape stirs the imagination with its exotic hillsides covered by dry savannah and pockets of thorny green vegetation contrasting starkly with the brilliant white sandy beaches and blue waters surging over coral reefs.

Extensive research suggests that reefs around here are among the most productive in the world due to upwelling and a high degree of oxygenation from strong tidal currents that flow through the Sape Straits. Beneath Komodo lie some of the last pristine coral reefs, which by themselves are the richest on the planet.

Marine naturalists have compared diving these waters to being in the middle of the wildebeest migration in the Serengeti. The marine biodiversity encompasses an unimaginable variety of invertebrates, over 1000 species of fish and 250 species of reef-building corals with new ones constantly being discovered. In 1991, Komodo National Park was inscribed on the World Heritage List.

Though Komodo is renowned for swift currents and pelagic fish life that can leave one in awe, there are many sheltered bays, submerged reefs and calm reef slopes endowed with pristine coral coverage, rare critters and zillions of ornamental reef fishes. One such

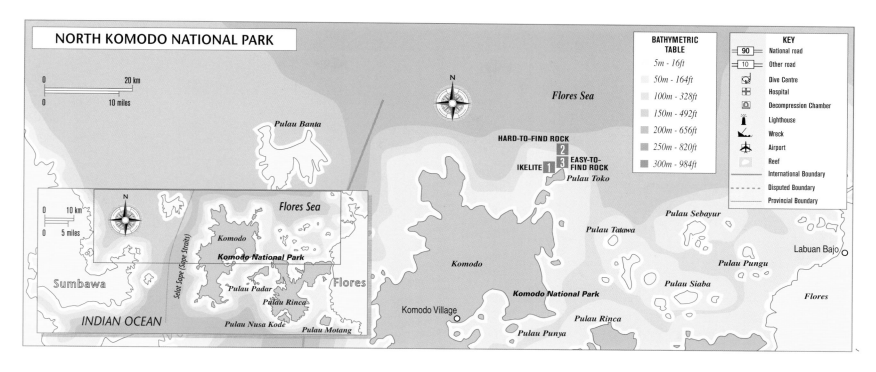

NORTH KOMODO NATIONAL PARK

BATHYMETRIC TABLE

5m - 16ft
50m - 164ft
100m - 328ft
150m - 492ft
200m - 656ft
250m - 820ft
300m - 984ft

KEY

90 National road
10 Other road
Dive Centre
Hospital
Decompression Chamber
Lighthouse
Wreck
Airport
Reef
International Boundary
Disputed Boundary
Provincial Boundary

Pulau Banta

Flores Sea

HARD-TO-FIND ROCK

2

IKELITE 1 3 EASY-TO-FIND ROCK

Pulau Toko

Pulau Sebayur

Pulau Tatawa

Labuan Bajo

Komodo

Pulau Pungu

Komodo National Park

Pulau Siaba

Flores

Komodo Village

Pulau Rinca

Pulau Punya

Flores Sea

Komodo

Komodo National Park

Sumbawa

Pulau Padar

Flores

Pulau Rinca

INDIAN OCEAN

Pulau Nusa Kode

Pulau Motang

dive is in a sheltered bay called Big Fat Rock where hundreds of batfish are predictably found. Schools of barracuda are also found hanging out on the ocean side of the rock and groups of Spotted Sweetlips in large numbers are found at 30m (100ft). Corals and sponges cling to every square inch, others thrive in symbiotic or parasitic relationships. Swarming on every ledge and crevice are hundreds of angelfish and butterflyfish. Damsels frolic in an *Acropora* coral at 10m (33ft). It is one of those splendid sites that one can return to again and again. But be warned: some sites are not for the faint-hearted. They have rapid currents, up and down, in eddies, and six-knot drifts are not uncommon. Diving in such conditions demand a higher level of alertness and preparation.

One of the inconveniences of diving Komodo is that the water temperature varies from 30°C (86°F) in the north to a chilly 19°C (66°F) in South Komodo. Expect 25–30m (80–100ft) visibility when diving the north, but moving south the azure water gradually surrenders to the nutrient-rich water of the Antarctic Ocean. Frequent upwellings make the water colder, and green, so that visibility sometimes drops to a mere 5m (16ft). But it is all worth it; the rich cold water yields an assemblage of critters that become the signature of Komodo diving. One such place is

Cannibal Rock, another rock that falls steeply to 25m (80ft). Gorgonian Sea Fans, organ pipe corals, black coral trees, orange sponges and carpets of red, blue, green and yellow feather stars festoon the slope and hundreds of tapestries of ornamental reef fish swarm in the water column. At 20m (66ft) the rock is surrounded by a garden of sponges and tall coral trees; snow white coral trees adorned with Long-nose Hawkfish. Sea Apples and a bright red sedentary cucumber are found in abundance on the reef slope. While orange, blue, yellow and white frogfish and Ghost Pipefish merge with the rich foliage, multicoloured nudibranchs, feather stars, tunicates, soft corals, anemones and sponges are common. Though some dive sites in North Komodo are accessible by day trip from Labuan Bajo on the island of Flores, the best way to explore Komodo is by one of the diving-dedicated live-aboard vessels operating from Bali.

1 IKELITE REEF

Located near the edge of Pulau Toko, Ikelite Reef is a rock that rises like a mountain from 50m (165ft) to near-surface. Fish life and coral life here is spellbinding, with schools of resident barracuda, sweetlips and jacks. To fish ecologists, this site is a well-known grouper aggregation and breeding spot. By nature's biological clock, groupers come here from

miles around to 'stir the pudding' and make baby groupers. Possibly they congregate here to procreate because two merging currents create a 'washing machine on rinse cycle' effect that most efficiently disperses their sperm and eggs. Most of the time, a manta or two can be seen gliding here, as well as some

ABOVE *Immune to the stinging cells of the anemone, this tiny clownfish will probably live out its life within this anemone.*

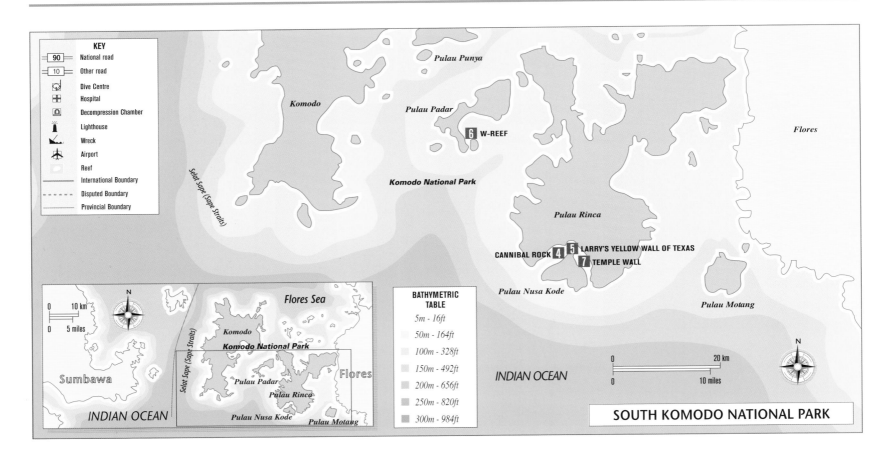

SOUTH KOMODO NATIONAL PARK

rare scorpionfish, including beautiful yellow Leaf Scorpionfish. Dolphins usually hang out just out of visibility range, which is often a respectable 25m (80ft), and beyond.

HARD-TO-FIND ROCK 2 AND EASY-TO-FIND ROCK 3

Hard-to-Find Rock (HTF) and Easy-to-Find Rock (ETF) are close to Pulau Toko. They offer similar marine life and bottom contours. Only one rock is exposed, making it easy to find and the other is submerged, even at low tide, making it hard to find. It was at HTF rock that pygmy sea horses were first discovered in Indonesia. And, yes, they are still there. Also, there are some brilliant pink/purplish Leaf Scorpionfish on HTF Rock. Most of the time, there are resident schools of big spadefish hanging around both sites. A good-sized school of barracuda usually hangs out around

30m (98ft) on the west side of ETF Rock. Typical of submerged reef in North Komodo, the reef's edge falls from about 5m (16ft) to 45m (148ft). It is entirely overgrown by encrusting sponges, tunicates, sea whips, and coral colonies. This is also a spawning site for Napoleon Wrasse, Blotched Fantail Rays and sweetlips. On the seaward side, Whale Sharks and mantas are frequently sighted.

4 CANNIBAL ROCK

Located off Rinca Island, one of Komodo National Park's most spectacular landscapes, Cannibal Rock has been described by well-travelled divers as one of the top five dive sites in the world. There are meadows of multi-coloured feather stars that harbour frogfish, cuttlefish, snails and many rare nudibranchs. Cannibal Rock has an abundance of little gems of the sea from 5m (16ft) to beyond 35m

TOP LEFT *Sea Apples, bright red sedentary sea cucumbers found only in colder tropical waters, are abundant in South Komodo. A relative of the sea star, this attractive species of sea cucumber feeds by trapping food in the passing current with its waving tentacles.*

LEFT *Longnose Hawkfish (Oxycirrhites typus) can be found among the black coral trees of Komodo at depths of 15m (50ft) to 30m (100ft).*

ABOVE *Cannibal Rock, South Komodo, falls steeply to 25m (80m), decorated with Gorgonian Sea Fans, corals, sponges, carpets of feather stars and swarms of ornamental reef fishes.*

(115ft). There are Ghost Pipefish, fire urchins complete with Coleman Shrimps, zebra crabs, yellow, white, and pink pygmy sea horses (*Hippocampus bargabanti*), mobula rays, Manta Rays and oversized Spanish Dancers.

5 LARRY'S YELLOW WALL OF TEXAS

Situated on the south side of Rinca, this site is called the Yellow Wall of Texas because of the rich foliage of yellow soft corals, yellow encrusting sponges, and yellow frogfish. It seems like just about everything here has some yellow somewhere on it, making it a truly beautiful site. The wall is nearly vertical and falls straight to over 50m (165ft). At around 35m (115ft) the wall curves into a spectacular overhang, covered from floor to wall with lush invertebrate and fish life.

The shallow slope of this site is dotted with big barrel sponges and they are home to the little fuzzy and purple Sangian crab with blood-red eyes. The Yellow Wall of Texas goes on and on, sometimes punctuated for a short distance by areas of coral slope. Currents are not much of a problem here. Spanish Dancers are almost always found, but mostly during night dives. Because it is in the strait between Rinca and Nusa Kode, The Yellow Wall of Texas is always protected from any weather from any direction.

Criniods and crinoid critters, frogfish, emperor shrimp, whip coral shrimp, sleeping sharks, orangutan crabs and jacks are easily found. The display of colours is a delight for professional photographers. Though subject to swell and tidal currents, Yellow Wall of Texas is easily accessible at any time of year.

6 W–REEF

W-Reef consists of a series of pinnacles located near Padar Island. The shallowest reef starts at about 4m (13ft) from the surface and the deepest at around 25m (80ft). It derives its name from a series of rocks that form a big underwater W. Giant Dogtooth Tuna, mobula and Manta Rays are frequently seen here. Nudibranchs are found in large numbers, frogfish abound and the sea fans are home to pygmy sea horses. A small cave next to the sea horses is reputed to have the biggest congregation of moray eels on the planet resting alongside Nurse Sharks. W–Reef is known to have something for everybody – from strange, minute critters to big pelagics lurking in the depths off the wall. The site is notorious for strong currents, thus the best time to dive here is when the moon is around half full. At full or new moon (at spring and neap tides) the currents are difficult to manage.

7 TEMPLE WALL

The long swim-through at a depth of 30m (100ft) at The Temple Wall off Rinca passes through an interesting rock formation. The wall is completely covered with colourful soft corals and splashed with multicoloured crinoids. A resident school of sweetlips hangs out in the dramatic structure of basalt rock platforms creating the feeling that one is diving in a temple. The wall is a kaleidoscope of orange cup corals and purple, pink, red and yellow ascidians. The site is subject to strong swells.

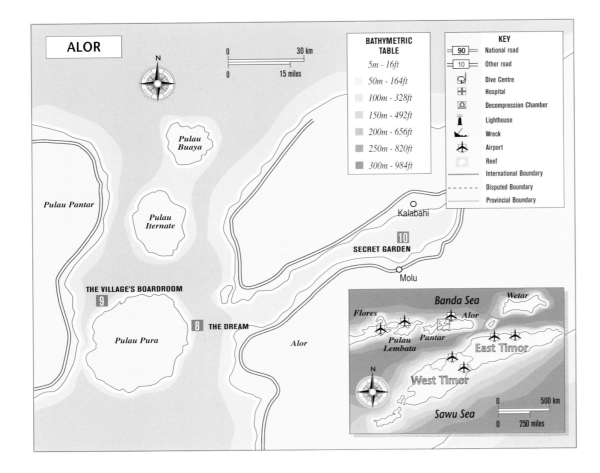

ALOR

The Alor group of islands, lying less than 50km (30 miles) north of central Timor, is one of Indonesia's least explored areas. The arid, rugged, mountainous terrain makes travel in its interior difficult. This natural barrier has isolated the island's many tribes and ethnic groups, not only from the outside world, but even from neighbouring communities. The population of only 100,000 is split into more than 50 separate tribal communities, each with its own language.

Luckily the island's coastline is more accessible, with motorized vessels bypassing the difficulties of overland travel. The coastline offers sparkling beaches and huge swathes of reef waiting to be discovered. Tidal forces push vast quantities of water back and forth through the narrow straight between Alor and its neighbouring island, Painter, to the west. Jagged coastlines and tiny islets, which dot the channel, make navigation perilous. The ever-changing and unpredictable currents also make diving here rather demanding. The deep, cold, nutrient-rich waters running beneath the Sawu Sea collide with tropical waters from the Banda Sea, resulting in thermoclines and plankton blooms which sometimes limit underwater visibility. However, these same conditions also provide a haven for marine life, which is the richest and healthiest in the Indonesian archipelago.

There are three distinct terrain types for exploration: the submerged sea ridges, outer fringing reefs, slopes and walls, and the brackish bay-water environment. While a respectable number of robust Grey Reef Sharks are often found patrolling deep reefs, schools of Dogtooth Tuna and Rainbow Runners, massive curtains of Golden Trevallies, Spanish Mackerel, and surgeonfish swarm the submerged and fringing reefs. Parades of Bumphead Parrotfish gnaw corals and encrusting algae, while vast numbers of smaller ornamental reef fish flutter in the currents, all but obscuring the corals on the reef's walls and plateaus. Often, it is necessary to swim through schools of barracuda

ABOVE *Current beneath The Dream is so strong that even big fish seem daunted. The unpredictability of the currents further taxes divers' skills to the limit.*

just to see the sharks. Big pelagics, magnificent walls covered with lush soft coral, Gorgonian Sea Fans in a variety of colours, and friendly octopuses can be seen on almost every dive. Three dive sites are benchmarks of diving adventures in Indonesia – Secret Garden, the Dream, and the Village's Boardroom are located around three islands lying between Alor and Pantar: Pulau Buaya, Ternate and Pura.

8 THE DREAM

The Dream is not for the neophyte diver or the faint-hearted. The submerged reef systems in the channel between Pura and Alor are like obstacles in a pinball machine as huge volumes of water flow through the gaps and currents of up to six knots are generated in unpredictable directions. Even the big fish seem daunted by the current. On two occasions we were careened to The Abyss, a sheer wall, by downcurrent. We briefly converged with tuna, dolphin fish, sharks and trevally, and realized we were about to be sucked out to the blue by another current. We climbed, hand over hand, from 60m towards shallower water, while fellow divers were being plucked off the wall one after the other by the surges of passing current.

Diving pioneer Karl Muller rated this, say local dive operators, among the top five dives of his long and varied career. Sharks (including abundant Grey Reefs), Dogtooth Tuna, Yellowtail and Great Barracuda appear in phenomenal numbers, and in sizes ranging from good-sized juveniles to the biggest adults. They come in close to check out divers, perhaps encouraged by the dense swarms of schooling fish on the reef – snappers, Blue Triggerfish, unicornfish, surgeonfish and fusiliers – sometimes there seems to be more fish than water.

Napoleon Wrasse, rays and the mother (or father) of all Giant Groupers, at least 2m (6ft) long and as bulky as a small car, are also often seen here. The reef is densely covered with sponges, barnacles and corals – particularly *Tubastrea* corals. However, the strength of the constant current forces coral to grow tight in against the reef. Coral growths at the reef-face don't stand out more than 20cm (8in), but at this site the stunted growth continues down the slope for at least as far as the edge of visibility at 70m (230ft). By virtue of the reef profile, this site is only for experienced divers.

9 THE VILLAGE'S BOARDROOM

Situated on the northwest coast of Pura, a steep wall falls to a depth of beyond 70m (230ft). The wall is punctuated with caves and overhangs, with a concentration of shallow caves in the 10–18m (33–60ft) range containing some spectacular virgin coral growth. The boulder slope closest to the coast on the inner side of the wall is entirely overgrown with coral, and there are large barrel sponges all over the site. The corals are predominantly soft species, particularly in the caves and overhangs. The reef fish population is rich and diverse; all the normal small species are well represented, but the larger schooling species are the most profuse, with dense schools of fusiliers, surgeonfish, jacks and Black Snappers all commonly found. Big sweetlips are also around in noticeable concentrations and sharks, including Whitetip Reef, are widespread.

However, the attraction of the Boardroom is really the people who live in the bay. Each day, when the spirit moves them, the village people convene in this small bay; adults and children alike play, swim and free-dive among the coral reefs that have sustained these families for generations. They have a childlike innocence, which they share easily with visiting divers. It is not uncommon to find a few of them free-diving to pose for underwater photographers in full scuba equipment.

10 SECRET GARDEN

Three coconut palms hang over this site on the dark stretch of water of Kalabahi Bay on the island of Alor. From about 15m (50ft) below the surface to a depth of below 30m (100ft) the area is covered by a forest of gold, white, green and black coral trees, barrel sponges, red soft coral trees, staghorn corals and encrusting

ABOVE *Flame files shells are found only in the inner recesses of caverns, cracks and dark places. The red membrane seems to shimmer rhythmically when illuminated by divers' lights.*

sessile animals. While tidal currents bring in huge amounts of plankton-rich water to sustain the enormous density of filter feeders, larvae take up residence on this already overcrowded suburb, settling for 'apartment-dwelling in an urban high-rise society'.

Beneath the fronds of the three palm trees, the strangest and the oddest critters, rare in other coral reefs of the world, are common. Associates of both large and small animals occupy every space conceivable – anemones hosting clownfish, porcelain crabs and transparent shrimps, feather stars with fascinating residents of clingfish, shrimps and squat lobsters, allied cowries on every branch of gorgonian coral, and territorial gobies on whip coral. Reportedly, David Doubilet, the world's most celebrated *National Geographic* underwater photographer, once visited Alor and dived this reef twice a day for ten days.

PHILIPPINES

by Jack Jackson

THE PHILIPPINES HAS A GLORIOUS COLLECTION of coral reefs, many with strong currents and pelagics. Warm water and great visibility is the norm. It lies in a region where scientists believe that most of the Pacific's marine organisms evolved. There has been some coral bleaching on very shallow reefs. Some of the reefs damaged by man are recovering after the banning of destructive fishing methods.

Most reefs have better conditions than would normally qualify as muck diving. With keen observation and concentration it is possible to find unusual creatures. However, because there is such good diving nearby, these macro diving opportunities had previously been overlooked. Pygmy sea horses, Flying Gurnards, Harlequin Ghost Pipefish, Clown Frogfish and Harlequin shrimps can be seen at Puerto Galera, Malapascua and Anilao. Shipwrecks are the main features of Subic Bay and the area off Busuanga/Coron. Whale Sharks can appear almost everywhere in season.

TOP LEFT *The main beach and wooden chalets at Club Noah Isabelle. It is the only habitation on Apulit Island in Palawan's Taytay Bay, where fishing is now banned and large fish are common.*
TOP RIGHT *Outrigger boats called* bancas *across Alona Beach – typical of the larger ones used on diving safaris to various destinations.*

Pandan Island, a marine reserve off Sablayan on the west side of Mindoro Island, has diving from shallow coral gardens to deep drop-offs. It is only 32km (21 miles), or 90 minutes away from Apo Reef (not to be confused with Apo Island off Negros Island). Once the Philippines' most famous diving destination, Apo Reef is slowly recovering from blast fishing. The strong currents ensure that there are many sharks, turtles and Manta Rays.

WWF-Philippines is studying Dugongs at Club Paradise on Dimakya Island north of Busuanga and they are also found off northern Palawan. Boracay and the multitude of resorts both sleepy and sophisticated on and off Negros, Cebu and Bohol have everything divers appreciate. Malapascua Island, a new sleepy destination off the northern tip of Cebu, is known for Manta Rays, between June and January, and Thresher Sharks all year round at what is believed to be a cleaning station. A good all-round site, like many others in the Philippines, it is gaining a reputation for macrophotography.

Northern Palawan has two top quality ecoresorts, El Nido on the west and Club Noah Isabelle on the east. Club Noah Isabelle, on Apulit Island is in a no-fishing area in Taytay Bay. It is not yet in the mainstream of Philippine diving, but due to fishing restrictions it has many impressively large Humphead (Napoleon) Wrasse, groupers and trevallies.

At Moalboal the body-shell of a kit-plane has been deliberately sunk for divers, just west of Copton Point.

Southern Leyte has just about everything around Tancaan Point and Limasawa Island. However, some dives have depths and currents best suited to experienced divers. Vast coral gardens and plenty of fish, turtles and sea snakes make this a popular area.

Liloan Point, Santander, at the southern end of Cebu is a favourite with Japanese divers where the currents enable lengthy drift dives and produce Whitetip Reef Sharks. Offshore, Sumilon Island and Siquijor Island are attracting divers again. Sumilon has interesting walls and lots of fish, while Siquijor has large basket sponges, healthy stony corals and it teems with fish. Apo Island, between Siquijor and Negros, is a marine sanctuary that is fully protected once more. Whitetip Reef Sharks, Bumphead Parrotfish, trevallies, Picasso Triggerfish, turtles, Manta Rays, a large Anemone City and seeded giant clams are just a few of the treats found here.

The remote reefs in the Sulu Sea such as Tubbataha Reefs, offer superb diving, strong currents and a multitude of reef and pelagic species including Guitar Sharks and Manta Rays. The dark volcanic sand of Camiguin Island belies a beautiful island with great variety of diving including turtles and rare Clown Groupers. At the northern tip of Mindanao's

Zamboanga del Norte, Dakak is one of the most beautiful resorts in the Philippines, but it is suffering due to concerns about Abu Sayyaf terrorist activity. On the east side of Mindanao Island, the Gulf of Davao southeast of Davao City has two sunken World War II Japanese shipwrecks in the waters in front of Pearl Farm Resort. The waters south of Pearl Farm Resort together with Sarangani Bay south of General Santos City have some of the best coral gardens in the world, but parts of Sarangani Bay are being spoilt by sediment from commercial fish farming. In the far southwest of the Philippines, the Sulu Archipelago has good diving among reefs damaged by blast fishing, but at present the Abu Sayyaf terrorist activity puts them out of bounds to tourists. The islands off Jolo have the best diving in this region, including the wreck of a Chinese junk that has been salvaged of its porcelain, while reefs around Tawi-Tawi have the most coral damage.

Nitrox and recreational technical diving are now available from the larger dive centres.

NORTH PHILIPPINES DIVE SITES

The poor relation of Philippine diving for visitors, the island of Luzon is highly regarded by local divers. North of Manila, La Union at the northern end of the Lingayen Gulf, is a thriving tourist resort. The departure of the American forces from Subic Bay means that its wrecks are now open to divers. South of Manila, Anilao is a good diving destination in its own right as well as being good for muck and macro diving.

LA UNION

The main interests at La Union are the American M10A1E tanks that were dumped near **Fagg Reef** ☐1, 4km (2 miles) offshore, north of Poro Point at the end of World War II. Three are together at 40m (130ft) and another is roughly 20m (65ft) to the east.

Other popular sites include **Caves** ☐4 on Research Reef and **VOA** ☐2 (the reef by the Voice of America relay station). **Robert's**

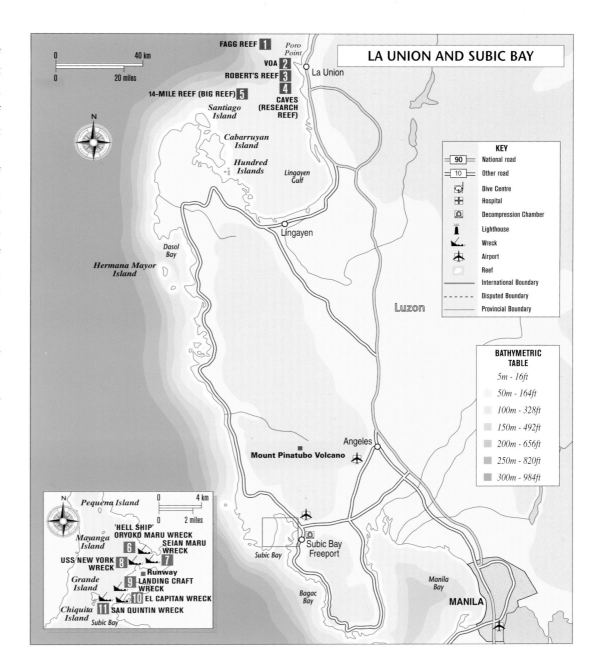

Reef ☐3 runs out from the point south of VOA. **14-Mile Reef (Big Reef)** ☐5 has almost everything because of the strong currents.

SUBIC BAY

Despite the poor visibility often produced by typhoon rains and siltation from the eruption of Mount Pinatubo, Subic Bay is sheltered enough to be dived in any weather. Though murky outside, visibility inside the large wrecks is good if the sediment is not disturbed and the wrecks are ideal for penetration and technical penetration diving. The better wrecks for diving have been buoyed underwater to make it harder for the local fishermen to find them. The bay is policed to stop people stealing from the wrecks and dive operators

and divers require permits. The coral life is poor, but the fish and invertebrate life can be good. Turtles still nest on the beaches.

Among the wrecks, the **Hell Ship** *Oryoko Maru*, ☐6 400m (1312ft) west of Alava Pier, has been flattened by explosives for navigational reasons. Now a tangled mass forming an artificial reef, it has good marine life. The *Seian Maru*, ☐7 between Alava Pier and the northern end of the runway, lies on her port side in 27m (89ft). The cavernous holds are easy to penetrate and marine life is good.

The massive World War I protected cruiser, the ex-*USS New York* ☐8, was scuttled in 1941 and now lies on her port side west-southwest of the *Seian Maru* ☐7 at 27m (89ft). Most impressive are the large 20cm (8in) guns that

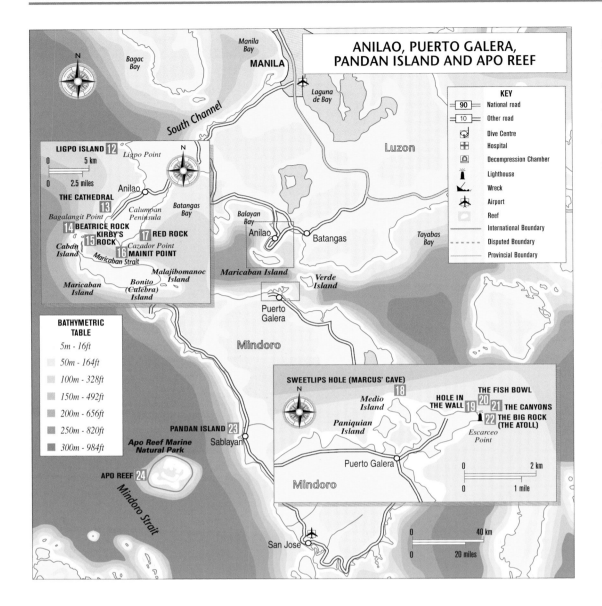

including huge frogfish (Antennariidae). **Mainit Point** [16], Cazador Point on the charts, is exposed to currents and the wind. Rocks break the surface and form mini drop-offs from 5m (16ft) to more than 30m (100ft). The marine life is plentiful and varied, including Whitetip Reef Sharks resting in a cave. At **Red Rock** [17], on the east side of the Calumpan Peninsula, there is an underwater coral mound. **Beatrice Rock** [14], at the northern end of Maricaban Strait, is an exposed series of short drop-offs with channels in between from 5 to 27m (16 to 89ft). There are large barrel sponges, black, soft and stony corals, anemones with clownfish, turtles, Blue-ringed Octopuses, nudibranchs, sea stars and dense populations of reef fish.

Kirby's Rock [15], on the northeast face of Caban Island, protrudes above the water. On its shoreward side it drops to 5m (16ft) and then the reef slopes upwards to the shore with good coral cover, fish and macro life. On the seaward side the rock drops as a wall to 20m (65ft) before shelving off on sand with coral patches. This wall is rich in marine life, including Gorgonian Sea Fans, Feather Duster and Christmas Tree Worms, nudibranchs, flat worms and sea cucumbers.

Bonito (Culebra) Island and Malajibomanoc Island are marine sanctuaries with coral heads on sandy slopes, which descend from 6m (20ft) to 24m (79ft).

PUERTO GALERA

Just south of Anilao on the island of Mindoro, Puerto Galera is the Philippines' busiest diving destination and with good reason. Famous for its diversity, it has everything divers could wish for except the largest sharks. There is diving of all standards, from easy dives for training and novices to high-voltage dives in strong currents and some deep dives where large animals are encountered. In recent years several wrecks have been sunk for divers, technical diving has become common and world record depths have been attained. The region was already known for its macrophotography, but some operators have been looking harder

---

are still in position and intact. There is an abundance of soft corals, sponges and hydroids, lionfish, triggerfish, Spotted sweetlips, Bluespotted Ribbontail Rays, fusiliers, batfish and big groupers. A **landing craft** [9] sits upright at 35m (115ft) between the southern end of the runway and Grande Island. The freighter *El Capitan* [10] lies on its port side by the inner channel marker buoy of Ilanin Bay. The gunboat *San Quintin* [11], which was scuttled by the Spanish to protect them from American attacks in 1898, lies between Grande Island and Chiquita Island.

ANILAO

The close proximity of Anilao to Manila, 124km (77 miles), makes it a popular centre for day and weekend trips. Most of the diving consists of coral slopes or steps of small drop-offs and shallow coral gardens among sandy

patches. The smaller fish and invertebrate life is profuse. Some marine sanctuaries have been set up and nearly all the dives are good, though many can have fierce currents.

Easily circumnavigated in one dive, **Ligpo Island** [12], west of Ligpo Point, is not for novices when the currents are running. There is a small drop-off and a cave on the east side and an underwater seamount on the west side, which slopes off deep. Pelagic species are common. **The Cathedral** [13], off Bagalangit Point, is a marine sanctuary and is probably the best-known Philippine dive site. It has been seeded with coral from elsewhere and is now teeming with fish, due to fish feeding. The site resembles a roofless cavern between two seamounts and has a small cross, planted at 15m (50ft) by the ex-Philippine President Fidel Ramos, in 1983 and blessed by Pope John Paul II. There is everything here, and finding most of the creatures that muck divers enthuse about, including frogfish, ghost pipefish and Harlequin Shrimps. Scientists have studied the area since the University of the Philippines Marine Biological station was set up in 1934. The UNESCO Man and Biosphere Programme declared it a marine reserve in 1974.

VERDE ISLAND PASSAGE

There is a myriad of good dives over a wide area, of which only a few can be highlighted here. Straight out from Batangas Channel, **Sweetlips Hole (Marcus' Cave)** [18], is best suited to technical divers with recent deep experience. Sweetlips Hole is at 45m (150ft), where it is good to watch the action of resident shoals of batfish and sweetlips. At Marcus' Cave, Whitetip Reef Sharks rest on sand at 50m (165ft), while many other species of fish shoal around. The cave contains a memorial stone to Marcus, although he did not die diving.

At **Hole in the Wall** [19], just west of Escarceo Point, divers allow for the currents and descend several stepped drop-offs to the hole in the wall at 12m (40ft). The hole is coated with multicoloured sponges and crinoids and teems with reef fish. Northeast of Escarceo Point, **The Fish Bowl** [20] is an advanced dive within a bowl-shaped depression at 40m (130ft), where divers observe Whitetip Reef and Grey Reef Sharks, large tuna and shoals of many species including Rainbow Runners (*Elagatis bipinnulata*) and Oriental Sweetlips (*Plectorhinchus vittatus*). Nearby, **The Canyons** [21] is for advanced divers. Divers drift past Hole in the Wall, race over several small drop-offs covered with soft corals and sponges, pass two smaller canyons en route to the main one, which is teeming with fish, including Six-banded Angelfish (*Pomacanthus sexstriatus*), Royal Angelfish (*Pygoplites diacanthus*) and Emperor Angelfish (*Pomacanthus imperator*). Divers are eventually swept onto a 1.5m (5ft) anchor, where they can muster before letting go to be swept away in the current and decompress in open water

after this high-voltage drift dive. Southeast of Escarceo Point, **The Big Rock** (The Atoll) [22] is an atoll-shaped rock 15m (50ft) wide, rising from 33m (108ft) to 21m (69ft), with many species of fish including lionfish and Bluespotted Ribbontail Rays.

PANDAN ISLAND [23] AND APO REEF [24]

Further south, off the west coast of Mindoro, Pandan Island has been declared a marine park by the local government and is proving to be another top diving region with 80 per cent coral cover.

Pandan Island is only 32km (21 miles) from Apo Reef, a large, offshore marine sanctuary with everything from good corals to large sharks. The whole northeast side of the reef consists of drop-offs and overhangs where sharks and shoals of large fish gather while the northern, eastern and southern sides have steep walls with turtles and pelagic species including Manta Rays.

VISAYAS

A large spread of islands in the central Philippines, the Visayas is known for calm waters, sun-drenched, palm-lined, white sand beaches and diving all-year round.

BORACAY, CARABAO AND MANIGUIN ISLANDS

Lying just north of Panay Island, Boracay's White Sand Beach was cited the best in the world in *The BMW Tropical Beach Handbook*. The diving is as good as the beach with many varieties of soft, leathery, whip, *Tubastrea* Cup, black and stony corals, large barrel sponges and abundant fish life including sharks, Manta Rays, turtles and sea snakes. Nearby, Carabao Island to the north and Maniguin Island to the southwest are equally good.

Northwest of Guiniuit Point, the northwest point of Boracay, **Yapak 1** [26] **and 2** [25] are the divemasters' favourite sites. A wall, covered in healthy marine life, rises to 30m (100ft). Out in the blue, Humphead

ABOVE *The bridge of the armoured cruiser* USS New York. *Launched in 1897, renamed* USS Saratoga *in 1911 and* USS Rochester *in 1917, she was finally scuttled in Subic Bay in December 1941.*

(Napoleon) Wrasse and Grey and Whitetip Reef Sharks are common; Scalloped Hammerhead Sharks, Manta Rays and Eagle Rays are sometimes seen. The south side of **Crocodile Island** [27] has a drop-off 60m (200ft) long, dropping from 7m (23ft) to 25m (80ft), with prolific soft corals and gorgonias. **Laurel 1** [28], on the northeast side of Laurel Island, has soft corals, *Tubastrea* Cup Corals and prolific fish and invertebrate life. **Buruanga** [30] and **Black Rock** [31], off the west face of Panay Island, are very good. **West Wall** [29], on the southwest face of Carabao Island, has a wall 200m (656ft) long. **Maniguin Island** [32], 48km (26 nautical miles) southwest of Boracay, has massive reefs and abundant marine life, including Bumphead Parrotfish, Eagle Rays, Spiny Lobsters and caves containing sleeping Whitetip Reef and Nurse Sharks.

CEBU – MALAPASCUA ISLAND

Malapascua Island, off the northern tip of Cebu Island, is a new destination making a name for itself as a base for muck and macro diving and a Thresher Shark cleaning station. The nearby marine sanctuary of **Gato Island** [33] has everything from sea horses and frogfish to sea snakes, bamboo and larger sharks and spectacular caves and rock formations. The seamount of **Monad Shoal** [34] rises from deep water to 15m (50ft), with many large fish and sharks, but is particularly noted for sightings of Thresher Sharks, which peak from May to January. With spectacular overhangs and walls, shoals of tuna, jacks and barracuda can be seen here.

CEBU – MACTAN ISLAND AND THE NEARBY ISLANDS AND TALONG AND CAPITANCILLO ISLANDS

Mactan International Airport has made **Mactan Island** [37] the most developed resort area in the Philippines. The better ones encourage marine conservation and professionalism. The better dives are on steep drop-offs with some walls and caves. Strong currents are the norm. Spear-fishing is still common near Mactan Island, but **Capitancillo** [35], **Talong** [36] and **Cabilao Island** [52] have good fish life.

CEBU – MOALBOAL AND PANAGSAMA BEACH

On the southwest coast of Cebu, 3km (2 miles) from Moalboal town, is **Panagsama Beach** [38]. Apart from Badian and Green islands, most of the accommodation is relatively cheap. The diving is good along Panagsama Beach, Badian and **Sunken** [40]

islands, but the main attraction is further offshore at **Pescador Island** [39]. Barely 100m (330ft) square and 6m (20ft) high, this coralline limestone island is a microcosm of all that is good in the region. Surrounded by deep water, the narrow coral reef slopes gently to between 3m (10ft) and 9m (30ft) before dropping vertically as a wall to 40m (130ft). There is almost everything here: caves, crevices and overhangs are covered in *Tubastrea* Cup Corals, colourful soft corals and Gorgonian Sea Fans. The sponges are covered in alabaster sea cucumbers. Shoals of sweetlips, surgeonfish, snappers, fusiliers, anthias, catfish, chromis, jacks, damsels and Moorish Idols abound. Humphead (Napoleon) Wrasse (*Cheilinus undulatus*) and Whitetip Reef Sharks are in deeper water. Whale Sharks are often seen both here and along the beach.

Near Santander at the southern tip of Cebu, **Liloan Point** [41] has strong currents. The best diving is west of Liloan Point. There are sandy slopes with large rocks and coral heads that are drift-dived down to 25m (80ft). There is a good variety of reef fish, Bluespotted Ribbontail Rays and Garden Eels are common and Manta Rays appear from March to June. Further out from Liloan Point the currents rage across a wall that goes down to 60m (200ft). Known as **The Wall of Death** [42], this site is only for experienced divers.

[43] SUMILON ISLAND

The first marine sanctuary in the Philippines covers the entire west side of Sumilon Island where the reef flat goes over a drop-off at 18m (60ft) down to sand at 35m (115ft), with good stony corals, black corals, Gorgonian Sea Fans and some small caves. There are lots of juvenile fish. The east and south sides are sandy slopes with coral heads and the marine life includes Garden Eels, sea snakes, turtles and Manta Rays. The currents can be strong.

LEFT *Typical of the mixed stony corals at Pescador Island off Moalboal, these are mainly Lettuce Corals (*Montipora*).*

44 DANJUGAN ISLAND – NEGROS

The Philippines Reef and Rainforest project was launched to conserve Danjugan Island in 1994. A small island off the west coast of Negros Island, it was purchased by the project and volunteers set about studying it, removing alien species on land and allowing underwater species to regenerate. There is a profusion of *Dendronephthya* Soft Tree Corals, gorgonias and sponges and sizable areas of stony corals. There are rare Peppermint Sea Cucumbers (*Thelenota rubrolineata*). Shoals of angelfish, butterflyfish, bannerfish, damselfish, Moorish Idols, jacks, fusiliers, unicornfish and triggerfish are common. Anemones with clownfish are plentiful; on the sand are sea stars and sea cucumbers. Green and Hawksbill turtles can be seen.

DUMAGUETE/SIBULAN – NEGROS

Off Sibulan, **Tacot** 45 is a seamount rising from a depth of 23m (75ft) to 13m (43ft). The site attracts large pelagic species as well as reef fish. There are some big Gorgonian Sea Fans, boulder corals, *Acropora* table corals and plenty of crinoids. Southeast of Sibulan, at **Calong-Calong Point** 46 the reef slopes for 2.5km (1.5 miles) with coral heads from 4m (13ft) to 24m (79ft), where it becomes a sandy bottom. There are many varieties of soft and stony corals, some large Gorgonian Sea Fans and barrel sponges. Most local reef fish are represented here, including lots of pufferfish and Bluespotted Ribbontail Rays. Both sites have strong currents.

APO ISLAND – NEGROS

Not to be confused with Apo Reef off Mindoro, Apo Island off Negros is one of the many success stories of Philippines diving. Destructive fishing ceased completely here in 1997. Silliman University staff helped organize the local people into marine management

RIGHT *The rare Red Lined or Peppermint Sea Cucumber (*Thelenota rubrolineata*) can grow to nearly 1m (3ft) long.*

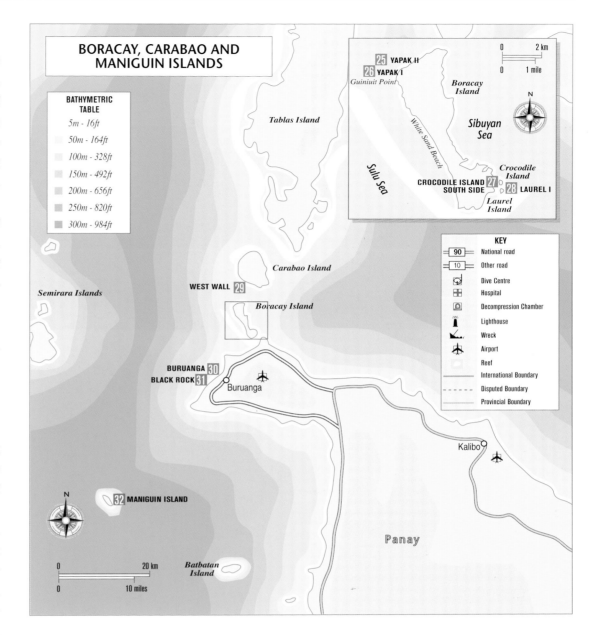

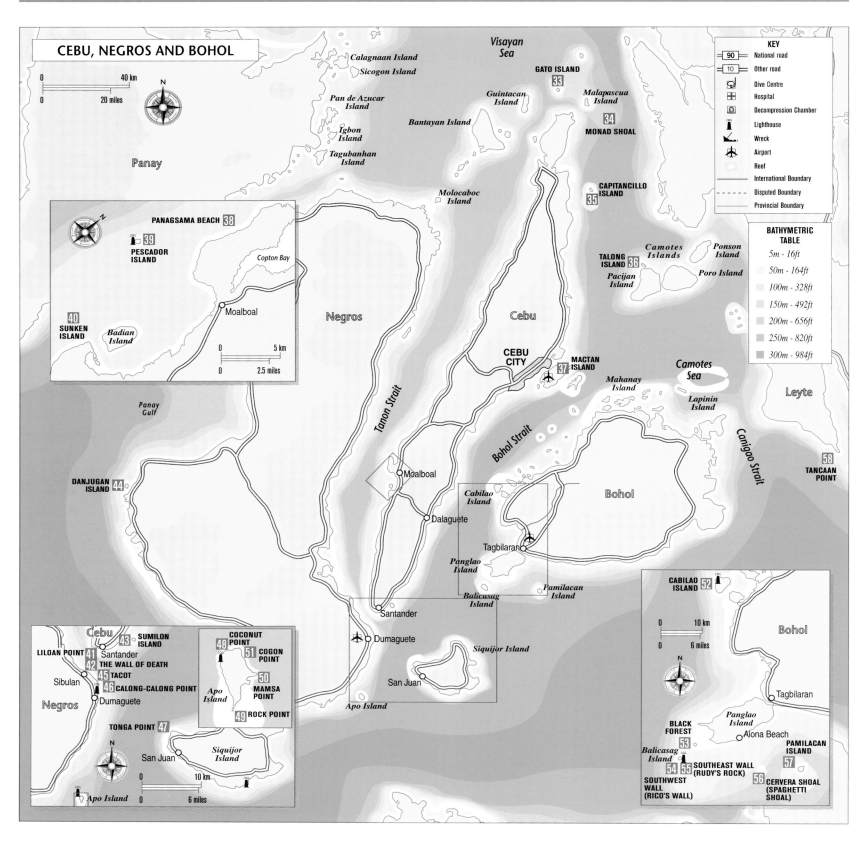

CEBU, NEGROS AND BOHOL

committees who set up marine reserves, including a no-fishing sanctuary. Aided by municipal governments, residents have continued to prevent reef damage by fishermen and divers, both within and outside the sanctuary. Divers and snorkellers must register and pay a small fee, may not wear gloves and there is a limit of 15 divers, including three dive

guides. *Bancas* (boats) must use the fixed moorings where provided and may only use anchors in designated areas. Larger boats must use the moorings.

At **Rock Point** 49 the prolific fish life includes many clownfish in anemones. East of Rock Point, the marine sanctuary is a mixture of walls, slopes with coral heads and sandy

patches with black corals. Clams have been seeded on the western side and turtles and Manta Rays are common. **Mamsa Point** 50 slopes to 25m (80ft) with a mixture of stony corals, black corals, whip corals and prolific fish life. South of Olo Point, **Cogon Point** 51 slopes to 20m (65ft), followed by an overhanging wall to 30m (100ft) with good stony corals, *Tubastrea* Cup Corals and abundant fish life. The slope at Olo Point also has Whitetip Reef Sharks and shoals of jacks. **Coconut Point** [48] usually has a strong current on its slope to 40m (130ft). The currents attract fish, barracuda, sweetlips, jacks and tuna, groupers, surgeonfish, fusiliers, triggerfish, angelfish, butterflyfish, moray eels, lionfish, scorpionfish, Vlaming's Unicornfish and Whitetip Reef Sharks.

SIQUIJOR ISLAND

Siquijor Island has great diving, but it can be tricky to land in parts because the water is very shallow near the beach. There are many large basket sponges, healthy stony corals and it is teeming with fish.

At the northern end of the southwest arm of Siquijor Island, **Tonga Point** [47] has a slope down to 12m (40ft), then a drop-off down to more than 40m (130ft), with spur and groove coral formations, *Acropora* table corals, lettuce corals and Gorgonian Sea Fans. Offshore from San Juan town it is much the same, with the addition of Ribbon Eels.

PANGLAO ISLAND, ALONA BEACH, BALICASAG, PAMILACAN AND CABILAO ISLANDS – BOHOL

Located off the southwestern tip of Bohol, the coralline limestone island of Panglao is joined to the mainland near Tagbilaran by a causeway. It is known for its quiet beach resorts, especially along Alona Beach. Offshore, Balicasag, **Pamilacan** [57] and **Cabilao Islands** [52], have some of the best diving in the Philippines. The diving is varied with coral gardens near the surface, but the main attraction is the steep walls with caves and crevices that harbour rich fish and invertebrate life. Out in strong currents, they also have large pelagic species, Manta Rays, Scalloped Hammerhead

RIGHT *A large shoal of Bigeye Trevally* (Caranx sexfasciatus) *circling where Rudy's Rock meets the eastern end of Rico's Wall.*

Sharks and Whale Sharks. The diving *bancas* (boats) here tend to be larger than elsewhere because they are used for diving safaris as far afield as Camiguin Island and Southern Leyte.

Balicasag Island, 6km (4 miles) southwest of Panglao Island, is a microcosm of the best diving in the region. On the south, from the buoy, outside Balicasag Dive Resort, is 400m (440yd) of marine sanctuary. Vertical walls over deep water in strong currents mean healthy reefs with pelagics including Scalloped Hammerhead and Whale Sharks. The **Southwest Wall (Rico's Wall)** [54] has a coral garden on a shelf from 7m (23ft) to 11m (36ft), then a wall to 35m (115ft). At the eastern end there is a huge shoal of Bigeye Trevally (*Caranx sexfasciatus*) where this dive joins **Rudy's Rock** [55]. The Southeast Wall (Rudy's Rock) is much the same, except that Green Turtles are found here. The northeast slope, **Black Forest** [53], is a fast drift dive where, below 30m (100ft), there are forests of black corals.

The seamount **Cervera Shoal** (Spaghetti Shoal) [56] rises to 12m (40ft), 15km (9 miles) east of Balicasag Island. Its name derives from the black-and-white sea snakes (*Laticauda columbrina*) and is often called Snake Island.

The northwest side of **Pamilacan Island** [57], 23km (14 miles) east of Balicasag Island, is a drift dive with prolific marine life, including Manta Rays.

West of Bohol, **Cabilao Island** [52] is known for an advanced deep dive off the northwest point, where Scalloped Hammerhead Sharks can be seen in December and January. Drifting either side of the southwest point there is abundant marine life, including Gorgonian Sea Fans, all varieties of sponges, Ribbon Eels (*Rhinomuraena quaesita*) and Garden Eels (*Heteroconger hassi*).

SOUTHERN LEYTE

A new location for Philippines diving, Southern Leyte has beautiful coral gardens and drop-offs. The coral gardens are mostly in pristine condition and where they are not, the quality of the corals improve with depth. As diving here is new, the fish are curious of divers. The 3km (2-mile) coral garden on the west side of **Tancaan Point** [58] can produce five separate dives. The current can get too strong for photography, but it is still a great drift dive. Fish and invertebrate life is profuse, including huge sea snakes and Whale Sharks (*Rhincodon typus*) from November till June.

REGION PALAWAN
BUSUANGA, CORON AND THE CORON WRECKS – CALAMIAN ISLANDS AND MAINLAND PALAWAN

For many years the wrecks around Busuanga Island, particularly in Coron Bay, were one of Philippine diving's best-kept secrets, because Coron was difficult to reach. However, the transport problem has been solved and it is now more accessible. A miniature version of Truk Lagoon, the area is littered with World War II Japanese shipwrecks that were sunk by Task Force 45 carrier-based aircraft on 24 September 1944, in preparation for the American landing on Leyte. Most of them are auxiliary fleet rather than warships. Many of these wrecks have now been found in recreational diving depths. Strong currents are rare.

Coron Island has spectacular scenery, with imposing limestone cliffs, tiny isolated beach coves and freshwater lakes. Apart from live-aboard boats, the diving in the south is from relatively cheap accommodation, while Club Paradise has luxury resorts in the north.

The diving is not all on wrecks, though these are the reason why most divers would come here. **Dimakya Island** [59] has a particularly good house reef. **Cayangan Lake** [70] contains creatures of both salt and freshwater and is fed by a hot spring. As divers go deeper it gets very hot. **Gunter's Cathedral** [73] is a delightful hidden cavern with an underwater entrance for experienced divers to explore.

As at **Fondeado Island** [90] off mainland Palawan, it is sometimes possible to find Horseshoe Crabs – living fossils of our world millions of years ago.

CORON'S WRECKS AND SITES

Just off the beach on the east side of Malajon Island, the **Black Island Wreck** [61] sits upright, but down the sandy slope from the shore. The bow rests on the bottom at 32m (104ft) and the stern at 20m (65ft). The origins of this 45m (150ft) coastal vessel are not known. It is teeming with small bait-fish and larger reef fish.

On the outer edge of the Lusteveco Company's pearl farm, south of Concepción village on Busuanga Island, lies the Concepción Wreck. For some time it was believed that it was the *Taiei Maru*, but recent researchers think that it is the *Okikawa Maru* [62]. Lying almost level with a slight list to port, this oil tanker is a good wreck for penetration with the main deck at 16m (52ft) and a maximum depth of 26m (85ft). There are good corals, sponges and fish including the ubiquitous lionfish and scorpionfish.

The *Akitsushima* [63] is one of the few true warships among the Coron wrecks. Lying between Lajo Island and Manglet Island, this 148m (487ft) flying boat tender lies on its port side in 38m (125ft) of water with the starboard side at 20m (65ft). The ship can be penetrated with care, but this is an advanced dive due to the depth. Large groupers lurk in the hull and shoals of barracuda, tuna and snapper are found along it.

At the southern end of Lusong Island there is the shallow wreck of a **Gunboat** [64]. The stern breaks the surface at low tide. The name of the wreck between the northern ends of Lusong Island and Tangat Island is not known. A 137m (450ft) Japanese Freighter, the wreck [65] lies on its starboard side in 25m (80ft) of water with the port side at 12m (40ft). A pretty dive, the port side hull has

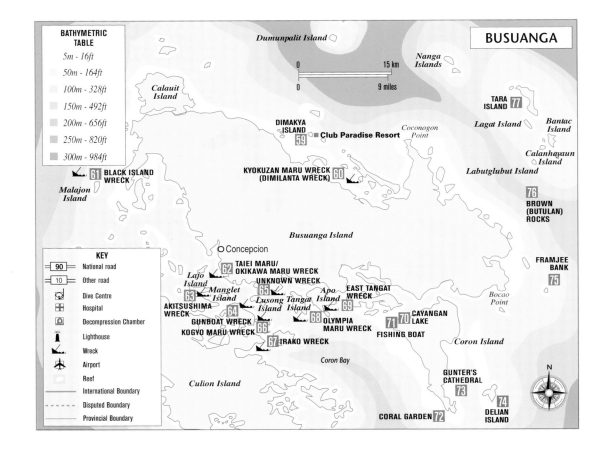

ABOVE *The wreck of a wooden fishing boat in relatively shallow water just south of the entrance to Coron's Cayangan Lake. It is festooned with corals and sponges that grow quickly in these warm waters.*

ABOVE *A lionfish (Pterois volitans) positions itself with the sun above it, like an aircraft in a dogfight, as it hunts among the superstructure of the Black Island Wreck, which teems with bait-sized fry.*

many large lettuce corals, black corals and sea anemones with clownfish. The abundant fish life includes Golden Rabbitfish (*Siganus guttatus*). South of this unknown wreck, the 158m (520ft) Japanese Freighter, **Kogyo Maru** 66 lies on its starboard side at 34m (110ft) with the port side at 22m (72ft). South of the *Kogyo Maru*, the 147m (482ft) Japanese refrigerated provision ship, **Irako** 67 is almost upright in 42m (138ft) of water with the main deck at 34m (112ft). Because of the depth, penetration is an advanced dive, but the superstructure has soft corals, sponges and profuse fish life.

West of the southwest end of Tangat Island, the wreck that used to be called the Tangat wreck has now been identified. Known as the **Olympia Maru** 68, she is a 137m (450ft) Japanese freighter lying on her starboard side at 25m (80ft), with the port side at 12m (40ft).

This site is a good introduction to wreck diving for novices and has good marine life. It is still not known what the 40m (130ft) **East Tangat Wreck** 69 actually is. Lying at the southeast side of Tangat Island, partly salvaged and listing to starboard down a sandy slope, the stern is at 22m (72ft) and the top of the bow at 3m (10ft).

The rotting remains of a **wooden fishing boat** 71 lie in 12m (40ft) of water a few hundred metres southwest of the entrance cove to Cayangan Lake on Coron Island. The 35m (115ft) vessel has lots of marine life and is perfect for novices' early dives.

Cayangan (barracuda) Lake 70 is a freshwater lake fed by a hot spring 30m (100ft) inland from the centre of the northwest face of Coron Island. It can be reached by a short but easy rock climb, though a second trip may be necessary for equipment. Diving is in

freshwater that becomes hotter and hotter with the descent. Around the perimeter, salt and freshwater mix and barracuda, Golden Rabbitfish, snappers, catfish and several species of shrimp and shellfish are seen.

There is a good **Coral Garden** 72 a few hundred metres northwest of Calis Point, the south point of Coron Island. **Gunter's Cathedral** 73 is north-northeast of Calis Point. Underwater, in a wide, open cavern in the limestone cliffs, a narrow, dark channel in the floor leads to the Cathedral cavern. En route are Spiny Lobsters and cowrie shells as divers swim towards a gleam of light and come out at the bottom of a chamber 20m (65ft) high, with shafts of sunlight descending from a large hole in the roof. Novices should fix a safety guideline from outside because it is easy to stir up sediment, making it difficult to see the way out again.

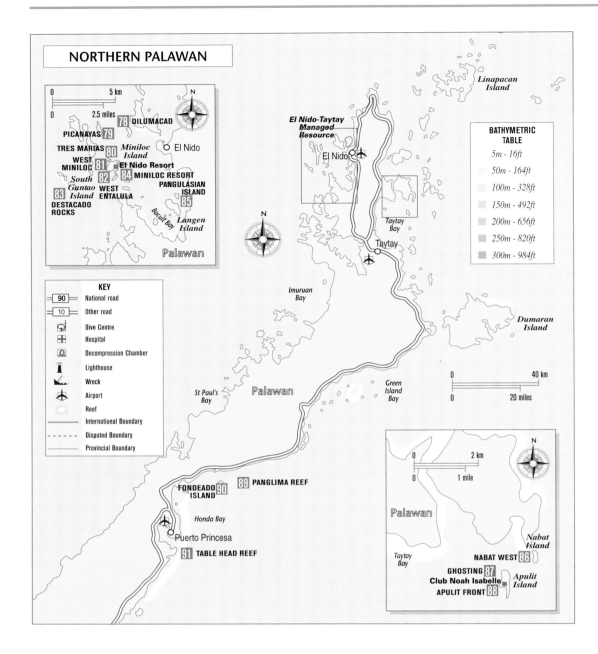

NORTHERN PALAWAN

0   5 km
0   2.5 miles

78 DILUMACAD
PICANAYAS 79
TRES MARIAS 80 Miniloc Island ○ El Nido
WEST MINILOC 81 El Nido Resort
South 82 84 MINILOC RESORT
Guntao Island PANGULASIAN ISLAND
83 WEST ENTALULA 85
DESTACADO ROCKS
Bacuit Bay
Langen Island
Palawan

Linapacan Island

El Nido-Taytay Managed Resource

El Nido ✈

Taytay Bay

✈ Taytay

BATHYMETRIC TABLE
5m - 16ft
50m - 164ft
100m - 328ft
150m - 492ft
200m - 656ft
250m - 820ft
300m - 984ft

Imuruan Bay

Dumaran Island

KEY
90	National road
10	Other road
⌂	Dive Centre
✚	Hospital
⬒	Decompression Chamber
⌇	Lighthouse
⚓	Wreck
✈	Airport
▢	Reef
——	International Boundary
---	Disputed Boundary
——	Provincial Boundary

St Paul's Bay

Palawan

Green Island Bay

0   40 km
0   20 miles

FONDEADO ISLAND 90
89 PANGLIMA REEF
Honda Bay
✈ Puerto Princesa
91 TABLE HEAD REEF

0   2 km
0   1 mile

Palawan

Nabat Island
Taytay Bay
NABAT WEST 86
GHOSTING 87
Club Noah Isabelle Apulit Island
APULIT FRONT 88

The north and south ends of **Delian Island** [74], 5km (3 miles) east-northeast of Calis Point have good shallow diving and snorkelling over coral gardens with many small reef fish and shoals of immature fish. **Framjee Bank** [75], 19km (12 miles) east of Bocao Point, the southeast extremity of Busuanga Island, is a sunken bank in 5m (16ft) of water; so it can be difficult to find without either a local boatman or GPS. The corals are poor, but when the currents are running large pelagic species come in to feed. Sharks, tuna, Rainbow Runners and trevallies are common. About 37km (23 miles) southeast of Coconogon Point (the northeast point of Busuanga Island) there is good diving on the west, south and east sides of the southern of two rocks 50m (163ft) high, called **Brown (Butulan) rocks** [76]. They are 2km (1 mile) south of Bantac, Calanhayaun and Lubutglubut islands. The rocks are a breeding ground for Cuttlefish (*Sepia pharonis*) and occasionally have Scalloped Hammerhead Sharks. Reef sharks and Guitar Sharks are found on the west side of **Tara Island** [77], 29km (18 miles) northeast of Coconogon Point.

Another top dive is the *Kyokuzan Maru*, also known as the **Dimilanta Wreck** [60] because it is close to the shore of Dimilanta Island. This 152m (500ft) Japanese freighter lies almost upright in 43m (131ft) of water with the main deck sloping from 22 to 28m (72 to 92ft). Almost intact and easily penetrated, there is a milky-white, mist-like haze being released by the cargo in some holds. WWF-Philippines are conducting research on Dugongs (sea cows) at **Club Paradise's Dimakya Island** [59].

NORTHERN PALAWAN

The Government of the Philippines proclaimed Bacuit Bay a marine reserve in 1991 and the protected area was expanded to

LEFT *One of the many large Marbled Groupers (Epinephelus polyphekadion) in Taytay Bay. They feed mainly on crustaceans and occasionally on small fish.*

ABOVE *This coral scene is made up of* Dendronephthya *Soft Tree Corals, a Gorgonian Sea Fan (*Melithaea squamata*) and a feather star.*

include parts of the municipality of Taytay, on the other side of Palawan, in 1998. It is now known as El Nido-Taytay Managed Resource, a special zone for conservation. This is an attempt to protect what is considered by many conservationists to be one of the last ecological frontiers in the Philippines.

BACUIT BAY, NORTHWEST PALAWAN – EL NIDO

El Nido, at the northwestern tip of Palawan, is named after the nests of swiftlets (*Collocalia fuciphaga*) found in crevices on its limestone cliffs. These nests, *nido* in Spanish, are used to make bird's nest soup. Small entrepreneurs built the original resorts, but it was the Ten Knots Development Corporation, under the

name El Nido Resorts, that fully advertised the region's potential as a tourist paradise. It took over others and today has exclusive resorts on Miniloc, Pangulasian and Langen Islands. These up-market resorts offer more than 20 sites from gradual slopes to drop-offs and walls where turtles, dolphins, whales, Whale Sharks and Manta Rays have been seen.

Miniloc Island has a marked dive trail established by the University of Edinburgh at the southeastern side of the island. Depths range from 12m (40ft) to 25m (80ft). Fish-feeding occurs at 18m (60ft) in front of **Miniloc Resort** [84], with habituated fish such as groupers, trevallies and Humphead (Napoleon) Wrasse. There are drop-offs from 24m (79ft) to 33m (108ft) with rich fish life at

West Miniloc [81] and 24m (79ft) to 36m (118ft) at West Entalula [82]. Submerged reefs such as Picanayas [79] 15m (50ft) are common. Dilumacad [78] has a cave wide enough for two divers at 12m (40ft). At the west side of South Guntao Island, Destacado Rocks [83] is the deepest dive in Bacuit Bay. The depth can reach 45m (150ft). The southern tip of Pangulasian Island [85] has rich marine life and, northwest of Miniloc Island, Tres Marias [80] often has turtles and Manta Rays.

TAYTAY BAY, NORTHEAST PALAWAN – CLUB NOAH ISABELLE

An up-market resort offering diving among other facilities, Club Noah Isabelle on Taytay Bay's Dragon Island of Apulit, gives a percentage of its income to various island ecosystems and a programme to conserve the remaining Dugong (sea cow) population. As with El Nido, the main clientele are South Asians, so the resort's rental equipment caters for the South Asian body-size. If you require fins to fit a larger foot, take your own.

The ban on fishing within one mile of Apulit Island has had its effect on sites outside the no-fishing zone, as larger species and food species are common. **Apulit Front** [88], 140m (460ft) south of the resort's main boat jetty, is used for fish-feeding, which has resulted in an impressive gathering of large Humphead (Napoleon) Wrasse, Marble, Peacock and Coral Groupers, jacks and trevallies, as well as a myriad of smaller fish. West of the west beach, **Ghosting** [87] is a submerged reef between 6m (20ft) and 15m (50ft), recovering from blast-fishing and displaying a surprising variety of fish. Well away from Apulit Island, isolated rocks, such as on the west side of **Nabat Island** [86], have walls continuing steeply down to sand and harbouring everything from nudibranchs to Gorgonian Sea Fans and big fish. Despite being outside the no-fishing limit there are huge trevallies, Humphead (Napoleon) Wrasse, Bumphead Parrotfish, lionfish, pufferfish, angelfish, butterflyfish, batfish, snappers and soldierfish.

PUERTO PRINCESA – CENTRAL PALAWAN

The diving around Puerto Princesa itself is mainly used for training novices. To the north, **Fondeado Island** 90 and **Panglima Reef** 89, together with **Table Head Reef** 91 to the south, have slopes to small drop-offs and can have strong currents.

SULU SEA AND MINDANAO

The Sulu Sea has countless isolated reefs and islets with world class diving. Many sites are strictly live-aboard destinations and some of them can only be visited for four months of the year for weather reasons, but large animals are guaranteed. The best-known reefs for diving are the Tubbataha reefs, 182km

(98 nautical miles) southeast of Puerto Princesa on Palawan Island, which together with Jessie Beazley Reef, make up the Tubbataha Reef National Marine Park.

THE SULU SEA – JESSIE BEAZLEY REEF – TUBBATAHA REEFS – BASTERRA REEF – ARENA ISLAND – CAVILI ISLAND AND CALUSA ISLAND

The Tubbataha reefs consist of two large reefs, with inner lagoons, separated by a 7km (4-mile) channel. At low water there are several sand cays. South Islet has a solar-powered lighthouse at the southern end. The wreck of the *Delson* is high and dry on the reef, east of the lighthouse. Jessie Beazley Reef is 23km (14 miles) northwest of North Islet. Basterra Reef is 93km (58 miles)

southwest of South Islet, with the wreck of the *Oceanic* high and dry on the east side. Arena Island is 89km (55 miles) northeast of Tubbataha North Islet. **Cavili Island** 103 is 9km (6 miles) northeast of **Arena Island** 104. **Calusa Island** 102 is 19km (12 miles) west-northwest of Cagayan Island. All these reefs consist of vertical walls or steep drop-offs, rising from great depths and teeming with fish. Currents are strong and often reverse during a dive, so be sure to have several methods of attracting your chase boat's attention when on the surface.

Jessie Beazley Reef 92 has a rich coral slope from 5m (16ft) to 10m (33ft), then a wall to 40m (130ft). The reef top is covered in lettuce and leathery *Sarcophyton* corals and teems with small reef fish. The walls

ABOVE *Schooling (Pennant) Bannerfish (Heniochus diphreutus) over Basterra Reef. Adults school above the bottom to feed on zooplankton, but juveniles sometimes act as cleanerfish on larger fish.*

ABOVE *This violet or purple fire coral (Distichopora violacea) can inflict a mild sting. It is found in crevices or under overhangs or roofs where there is strong water movement.*

have everything from huge Gorgonian Sea Fans, barrel sponges and *Dendronephthya* Soft Tree Corals to Whitetip, Blacktip, and Grey Reef Sharks. There are many large shoals of fish.

On Tubbataha Reef's North Islet, the **North Face** 93 has a sandy slope with coral heads to 15m (50ft), before dropping as a wall to great depths, with Guitar Sharks, Variegated (Leopard) Sharks and Manta Rays. **The East Face** 96, **Southwest Corner** 94 and **Southeast Corner** 95 are similar with large Gorgonian Sea Fans and soft corals below 30m (100ft). True Giant Clams, Leopardfish Sea Cucumbers and Tawny Nurse Sharks are just some of the prolific marine life.

On Tubbataha Reef's South Islet, the **North and Northeast Ends** 97 slope to 10–20m (33–65ft), then become walls down into the depths. The **South, Southeast and Southwest Ends** 98 are similar, but with a larger area of shallow reef top.

Basterra Reef is very small with diving similar to that of Jessie Beazley Reef, but with even more fish action. At the **North End** 99, beginning at the wreck of the *Tristar B*, there is a gentle slope to 10m (33ft); then a wall into the depths. Around the wreck the coral is damaged by blast-fishing, but plenty of fish shelter against the wreck and 50m (165ft) away the reef is rich again. The **East Face** 101 has better stony corals, as does the **South Wall** 100, which also has countless large pelagic visitors.

Calusa, Cavili and Arena Islands are less remote and have drop-offs rather than walls.

The reef tops have been blast-fished, but because drop-offs are not good for blast-fishing, these are still healthy.

CAMIGUIN ISLAND

Camiguin Island is just off the northwest coast of Mindanao, but is usually reached from the Visayas and often dived as a safari by Visayan operators. It is one of the most beautiful destinations in the Philippines, with hot springs and seven volcanoes. Most of its beaches are dark volcanic sand. The pristine environment received an environmental travel award, but the island was hit badly by typhoon Lingling (also known as Nanang) in November 2001. Shallow reefs have been damaged, but the fish and invertebrate life and the deeper corals are unaffected.

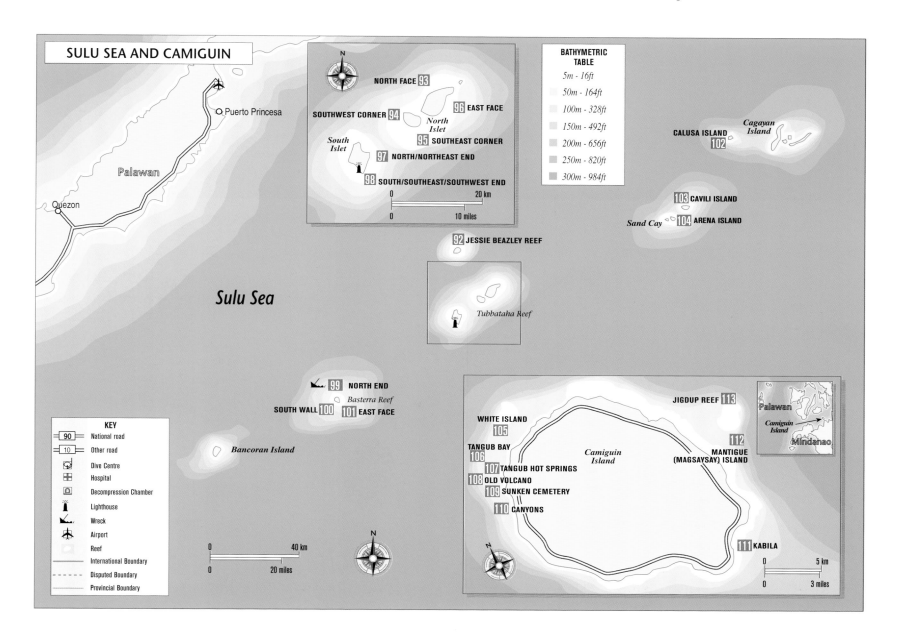

Northwest of the main island, **White Island** 105 is a large submerged reef near the visible sand cay of the same name. A gentle slope of stony and soft corals from 6m (20ft) to 26m (85ft), its countless fish include the rare Clown Grouper (*Pogonoperca punctata*). West of Camiguin Island, several dives are close together: **Tangub Bay** 106, **Tangub Hot**

Springs 107, **Old Volcano** 108, **Sunken Cemetery** 109 and **Canyons** 110. These dives cover lunar-like terrain, with volcanic rocks on dark sand. There is a slope from 3m (10ft) to 35m (115ft) with lots of fish, sea stars and turtles and Spanish Dancer nudibranchs out at night.

Southeast of Camiguin Island, **Kabila** 111 slopes from 3m to 35m (10ft to 115ft) with

rich marine life. To the northeast, **Mantigue (Magsaysay) Island** 112 has small walls with abundant corals and fish. North of Mantigue Island, **Jigdup Reef** 113 has a slope with ledges from 3m (10ft) to 35m (115ft) on the east side. On the west side is a wall from 3m (10ft) to 40m (130ft), with small caverns, prolific fish life and Manta Rays from December to March.

MINDANAO

Mindanao is the Philippines' second-largest island after Luzon. Mountainous, it is popular for trekking, its picturesque lakes and interesting tribes. There has been tension between central government and some Muslim groups, with terrorist activity at Pearl Farm Resort and General Santos City, but security has been increased considerably.

DAKAK

Off Dapitan Bay, Dakak has several dive sites along the coast and around **Liuay Rock** 121 that are fine for novices, but the better sites are at **Tagolo Point** 120 and the offshore islands and reefs.

At Silinog Island, the reef drops beyond 40m (130ft). The west side has gentle slopes and coral thickets, with many species of invertebrates, pufferfish, angelfish, butterflyfish, snappers and groupers. The east side has **Cesar's Reef** 117 to the north and **Octopus Wall** 118 to the south. For experienced and technical divers there is **Conrad's Wreck** 119, an old liner lying at 55m (180ft) with its highest point at 40m (130ft).

Aliguay Island slopes beyond 40m (130ft) as sand with coral heads. The shallows on the west are ideal for novices or muck diving. On the east side, **Eskuelahan** 114 and **Romy's Reef** 115 have strong currents.

The northeast of **Challenger Reef** 116, a submerged reef ascending from the depths to

DAKAK

114 ESKUELAHAN
Aliguay Island
115 ROMY'S REEF
116 CHALLENGER REEF

CESAR'S REEF
Silinog Island 117
CONRAD'S WRECK 119 118
OCTOPUS WALL

BATHYMETRIC TABLE
5m - 16ft
50m - 164ft
100m - 328ft
150m - 492ft
200m - 656ft
250m - 820ft
300m - 984ft

Sulu Sea

TAGOLO POINT 120
LIUAY ROCK 121
○ Dakak

Dapitan Bay

Mindanao

KEY
90	National road
10	Other road
	Dive Centre
	Hospital
	Decompression Chamber
	Lighthouse
	Wreck
	Airport
	Reef
	International Boundary
	Disputed Boundary
	Provincial Boundary

0   10 km
0   5 miles

LEFT *A family of False Clown Anemonefish* (Amphiprion ocellaris) *outside their host anemone* (Heteractis magnifica), *which closes as the light dims in the evening.*

38m (125ft), has prolific marine life, but is only for experienced divers. **Tagolo Point** 120 descends beyond 40m (130ft) and has strong currents attracting pelagics.

DAVAO PEARL FARM

Pearl Farm Beach Resort has two **World War II wrecks** 122 123 in front of its accommodation, which can only be dived if you are staying at the resort. There are several other dive sites around Malipano and Talicud Islands.

PEARL FARM

The furthest buoy from Pearl Farm jetty marks a 40m (130ft) Japanese Freighter lying on sand at 35m (115ft) with a mast from 20m (65ft) to 27m (89ft). It is an easy ship for experienced divers to penetrate. The nearest buoy to Pearl Farm jetty marks a 35m (115ft) Japanese Freighter lying on its side at 28m (92ft). Both wrecks have rich marine life.

At the southwest side of Talicud Island, **Mansud Wall** 125 is one of the best dives in the Gulf of Davao. Usually sheltered, it slopes gently to 10m (33ft), then drops to sand at 30m (100ft), with good corals and fish life including shrimpfish, sea snakes and snake eels. At the Southeast side of Talicud Island there is a 4km (2-mile) stretch of good **Coral Gardens** 124 sloping gently from 5m (16ft), which has been declared a marine sanctuary.

GENERAL SANTOS

Sarangani Bay has a wealth of good diving that has barely been touched. There has been some blast-fishing and, more recently, sediment from fish farming, but large areas are pristine. Many of the dive sites are accessed from private land so you require permission and a key to the gate.

On the west side of the bay north of Partridge (Tampuan) Point, **Lautengco** 129 has a gentle slope to 10m (33ft) before the reef drops off into the depths. Deeper down the stony and soft corals are good. There are large Gorgonian Sea Fans, feather stars, sea stars and a variety of fish species. **Partridge (Tampuan) Point** 130 and **Tampuan Wall** 131 are

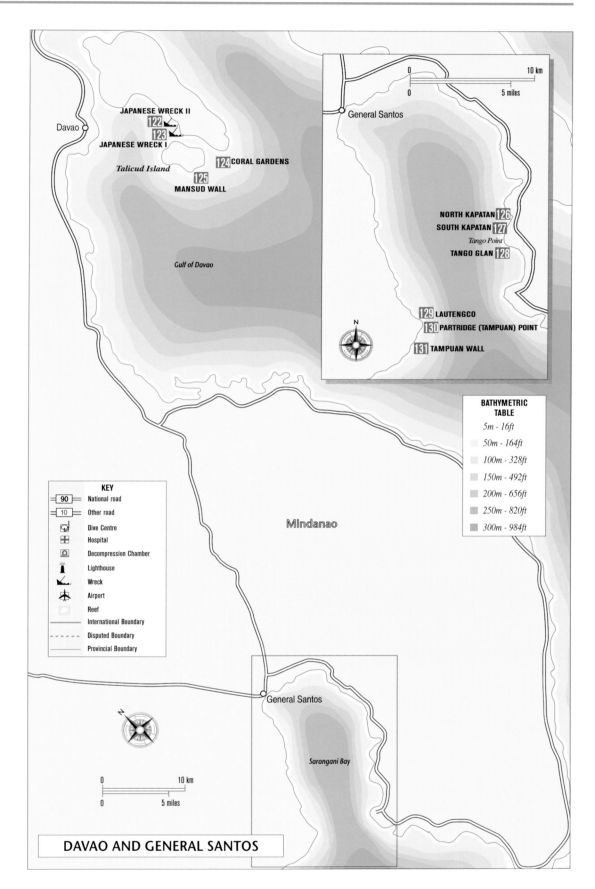

similar with prolific fish life, including clownfish in anemones and Humphead (Napoleon) Wrasse and good coral gardens.

On the east of the bay, north of Tango Point, **North Kapatan** 126 has a deeper slope of sandy gullies and coral heads to

beyond 40m (130ft) with abundant fish life and *Notodoris minor* nudibranchs. **South Kapatan** 127 is similar with many varieties of sea stars and nudibranchs. South of Tango Point, **Tango Glan** 128 has a steeper slope and more *Porites* coral.

MICRONESIA

by Michael Aw

ACROSS THE VAST EXPANSE OF THE WESTERN Pacific Ocean, 2148 islands lie scattered across 4,849,000 sq km (1,872,200 sq miles) of big blue sea. Together, they total just 1153 sq km (445 sq miles) of land. Lying east of the Philippines, Micronesia broadly comprises the islands of the Republic of Palau, Guam, the Federated States of Micronesia (Yap, Chuuk, Pohnpei and Kosrae), the Commonwealth of the Northern Marianna Islands and across to the Marshall Islands far southwest of Hawaii.

The islands of Micronesia are small, but tremendously varied. The largest is Guam at 541 sq km (209 sq miles), followed by Balbeldoap of Palau at 396 sq km (153 sq miles) and Pohnpei at 334 sq km (129 sq miles).

Geologically, Micronesia is as diverse and varied as its megafazzo cultures, traditions and history. Guam and Palau are both exposed peaks of an undersea ridge rising from the Mariana Trench, the deepest oceanic trench in the world. Kosrae, Pohnpei and

Weno (Chuuk) are volcanic islands and Yap is an uplifted section of the Asian continental shelf that just happened to float into the region. Because most of the islands are far from each other, they are like oases in the saltwater desert, refuges for planktonic larvae to settle and procreate. These are also 'motels' or pit stops for pelagic animals like oceanic sharks, orcas and whales on Pacific crossing.

The geological formation in the region also presents wide-ranging diving possibilities – from blue holes, cave systems above ground and underwater, uplifted marine lakes, rocks, islands and abyssal walls to the lost city of

TOP LEFT *Chuuk is worth exploring with a local guide. The lush tropical vegetation hides a treasure trove of World War II memorabilia.*

TOP RIGHT *The Rock Islands, 200-odd islets strewn across the 80km (50 mile) lagoon between Koror and Peleliu is a network of bays, channels and coves, perfect for exploring by kayak.*

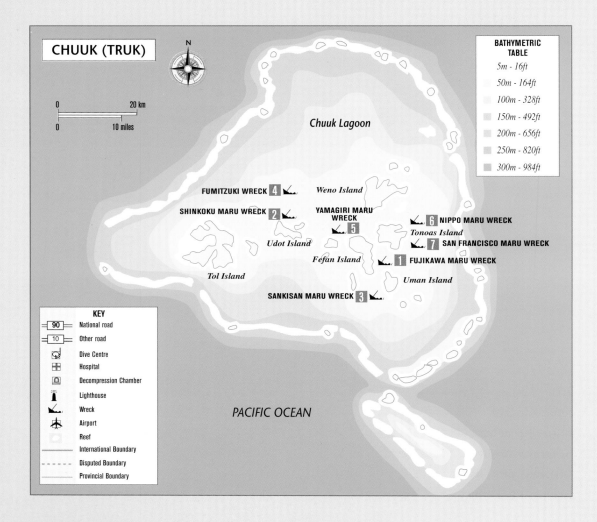

CHUUK (TRUK)

Chuuk Lagoon

0 ___ 20 km
0 ___ 10 miles

FUMITZUKI WRECK **4**

SHINKOKU MARU WRECK **2**

Weno Island

YAMAGIRI MARU WRECK **5**

6 NIPPO MARU WRECK

Tonoas Island

7 SAN FRANCISCO MARU WRECK

Udot Island

Fefan Island **1** FUJIKAWA MARU WRECK

Tol Island

Uman Island

SANKISAN MARU WRECK **3**

PACIFIC OCEAN

BATHYMETRIC TABLE	
	5m - 16ft
	50m - 164ft
	100m - 328ft
	150m - 492ft
	200m - 656ft
	250m - 820ft
	300m - 984ft

KEY

90	National road
10	Other road
	Dive Centre
	Hospital
	Decompression Chamber
	Lighthouse
	Wreck
	Airport
	Reef
	International Boundary
	Disputed Boundary
	Provincial Boundary

Nan Madol, which means Places in Between after the numerous islets cross-cut by waterways, lies on the southeast coast of Pohnpei Island, on a reef area referred to as Sounahleng, or Reef of Heaven. It consists of 92 man-made islets, covering an area of about 80ha (200 acres), with each believed to have served as a site for specialized activities. Buildings were constructed of long, log-like basalt stones from quarries on the island. High-walled rectangular enclosures were built and filled with coral rubble to form the islets' floors.

Nan Madol, an archeological site on a coral reef left by the mysterious culture of Pohnpei. World War II did not leave the region unscathed. Control of the Pacific theatre was essential to winning the war and the islands of Micronesia were the stages for the logistical bases of American and Japanese occupation. Most of the battles were naval, thus remnants of war, wrecks of ships and planes are found on and around nearly every island. Notably, an American offensive on 17 February 1944, called Operation Hailstorm, resulted in hundreds of Japanese wrecks in the vast lagoon of Truk (or Chuuk, to be politically correct). From a tourism perspective, the horrific time of war has at least left the island with a treasure trove for divers. Micronesia's underwater heritage, with its plethora of lush tropical islands, offers a lifetime of exploration.

CHUUK (TRUK)

Chuuk is legendary for the quality of its wreck diving – it has even been called 'the standard by which all wreck diving is measured.' This maritime graveyard is a legacy of Operation Hailstorm, a US aerial assault and one of the most devastating in maritime warfare. On 17–18 February 1944, day and night, aircraft from nine carriers unleashed wave after wave of bombs and torpedoes. The Japanese lost 260 planes, nearly 60 vessels and thousands of troops, compared to the US loss of a mere 26 aircraft. The 180,000 tonnes of Japanese ships that were sunk in just two days set a grim world record.

Over the next five-and-a-half decades, the warm tropical water and the richness of the Indo-Pacific and tidal currents combined to transform these hulks of war into an artificial

reef acclaimed as the best in the world. The Ghost Fleet of Truk has come alive, vibrant and active once more, but serving a different cause. The variety of wrecks within the sport-diving range is impressive: submarines, Japanese Zeros, Betty bombers, destroyers and submarine tenders to supply ships. Like good wine, they improve with age. Guns now wear garlands of sponges, tunicates and hydroids, exploding with kaleidoscopic soft corals. The war tanks on the deck of *San Francisco Maru* at 55m (180ft) blossom with white flower corals (*Clavulariidae*).

The Top Seven Wrecks

The ***Fujikawa Maru*** ☐1, a freighter, is the ambassador of the wrecks in Chuuk. She has lush coral growth on crossbeams, derricks, and a mast that looms toward the sky. In the

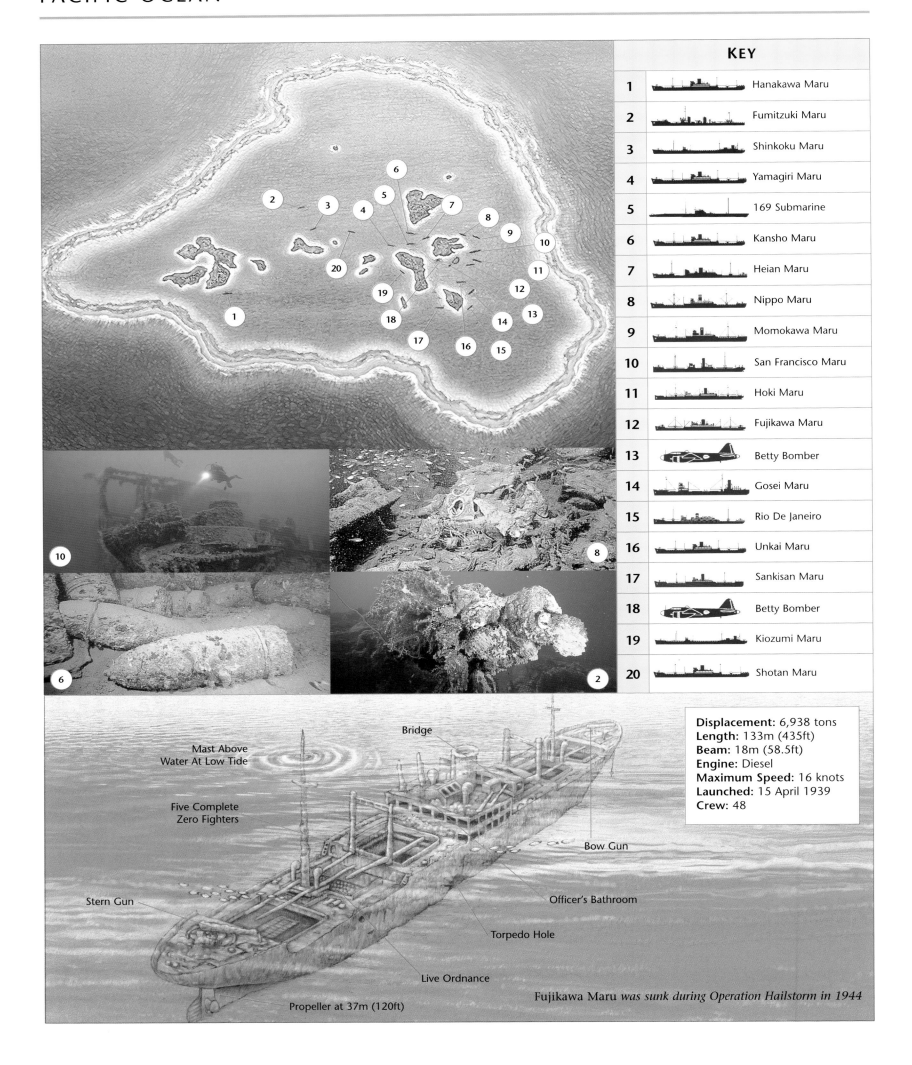

KEY

1		Hanakawa Maru
2		Fumitzuki Maru
3		Shinkoku Maru
4		Yamagiri Maru
5		169 Submarine
6		Kansho Maru
7		Heian Maru
8		Nippo Maru
9		Momokawa Maru
10		San Francisco Maru
11		Hoki Maru
12		Fujikawa Maru
13		Betty Bomber
14		Gosei Maru
15		Rio De Janeiro
16		Unkai Maru
17		Sankisan Maru
18		Betty Bomber
19		Kiozumi Maru
20		Shotan Maru

Displacement: 6,938 tons
Length: 133m (435ft)
Beam: 18m (58.5ft)
Engine: Diesel
Maximum Speed: 16 knots
Launched: 15 April 1939
Crew: 48

Mast Above
Water At Low Tide

Bridge

Five Complete
Zero Fighters

Bow Gun

Officer's Bathroom

Stern Gun

Torpedo Hole

Live Ordnance

Fujikawa Maru was sunk during Operation Hailstorm in 1944

Propeller at 37m (120ft)

cargo holds there are remnants of spare parts for fighter planes. The bow and stern guns are still in place.

Depth: 9m (30ft) to stack, 18m (60ft) to deck and 34m (1121ft) to bottom. Length: 133m (436ft).

The **Shinkoku Maru** 2 (Nation of God), a tanker, is undoubtedly the signature wreck of the lagoon, with a lush, sensuous and generous hull decorated with multicoloured soft corals from end to end. There is an operating table, a kitchen and human remains. The bow guns are the most impressive among her peers. End sections are overwhelmed with long whip corals, millions of glass and cardinal fish. Do not miss this wreck.

Depth: 12m (40ft) to bow gun and top of bridge, 38m (125ft) to propeller.

Sankisan Maru 3, a freighter, has the most beautiful foremast. It is completely encrusted with stony corals and droopy soft corals, sponges. It swarms with blennies, hawkfish and enigmatic blue wrasses. The front section is remarkably well preserved, but the section from bridge to stern was completely blown away on the first day of the raid. An ideal wreck for the second or third dive of the day.

Depth: 3m (10ft) to crosstree of foremast, 15m (50ft) to deck and 24m (79ft) to bottom of bow.

Fumitzuki 4, a destroyer, is a true warship and in her heyday she attained an impressive 37-knot cruising speed. Armaments of guns and torpedo launchers are still in place. It is an interesting wreck in fairly good condition. Marine growth on the davits is prolific. On one gun platform there is a display of gas masks, crockery and bullets.

Depth: 38m (125ft) to bottom, 30m (100ft) to superstructure. Length: 103m (338ft).

The stern of the **Yamagiri Maru** 5, a freighter, is decorated with purple *Dendronephthya* Soft Tree Corals and millions of glassfish swarm between the blades of her propeller. Lying on her port side, the view to the sky from beneath this wreck is almost surreal. The 220m (722ft) wreck was an ammunition

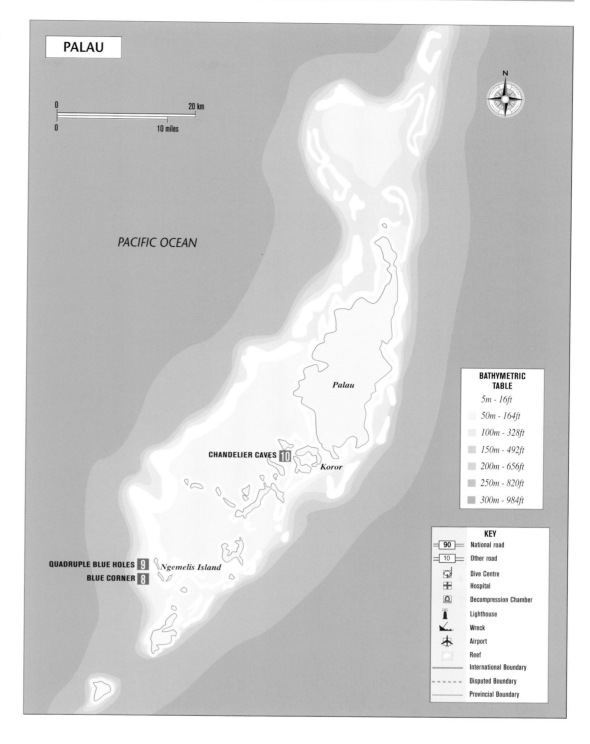

PALAU

PACIFIC OCEAN

Palau

CHANDELIER CAVES 10
Koror

QUADRUPLE BLUE HOLES 9 \ *Ngemelis Island*
BLUE CORNER 8

0   20 km
0   10 miles

BATHYMETRIC TABLE
5m - 16ft
50m - 164ft
100m - 328ft
150m - 492ft
200m - 656ft
250m - 820ft
300m - 984ft

KEY
90   National road
10   Other road
Dive Centre
Hospital
Decompression Chamber
Lighthouse
Wreck
Airport
Reef
International Boundary
Disputed Boundary
Provincial Boundary

ship for Japan's super battleship *Musahi* and the biggest shells used in the Pacific war, 46cm (18in), are found on this wreck. There are steamrollers in hold number 5.

Depth: 15m (50ft) to starboard beam, 34m (112ft) to bottom. Length: 133m (436ft).

Nippo Maru 6, a freighter, is one of the most fascinating wrecks in the lagoon for those interested to see an array of military artifacts and armaments. Three guns and tanks sit on the main deck, all pointing at the sky. There are also plenty of guns, trucks, radio equipment, hemispherical beach mines,

acid bottles and shells to amuse the inquisitive. The density of jellyfish around the wreck is fascinating. The vessel rests upright with a considerable list to port. Sunk within the first hour of the invasion, this wreck sits in deeper water and is for experienced divers only.

Depth: 24m (79ft) to bridge, 35m (115ft) to deck and 38m (125ft) to hold. Length: 107m (351ft).

San Francisco Maru 7, a freighter, is one of the most photographed wrecks in the lagoon for three reasons: it is deep, the water is clear, and the three tanks on the deck

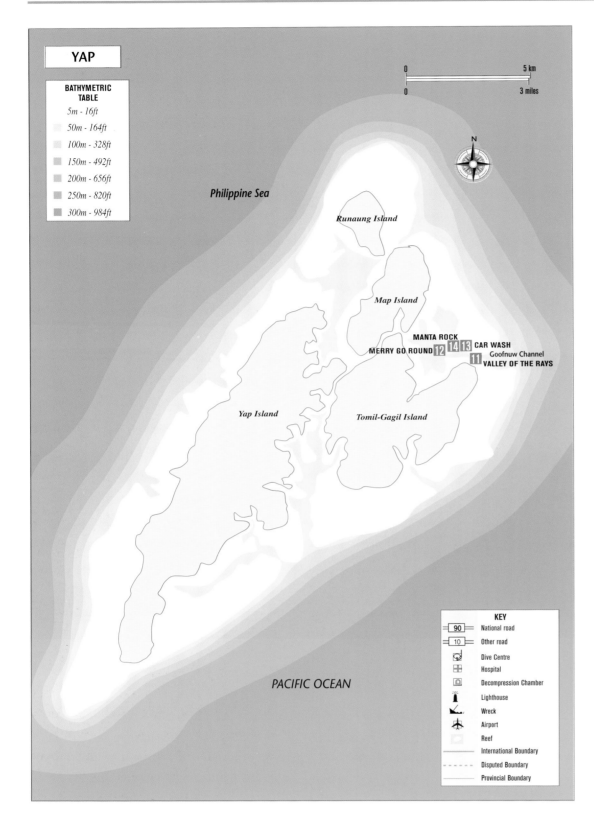

YAP

BATHYMETRIC TABLE

5m - 16ft
50m - 164ft
100m - 328ft
150m - 492ft
200m - 656ft
250m - 820ft
300m - 984ft

0   5 km
0   3 miles

N

Philippine Sea

Runaung Island

Map Island

MANTA ROCK
MERRY GO ROUND 12 14 13 CAR WASH
Goofnuw Channel
11 VALLEY OF THE RAYS

Yap Island

Tomil-Gagil Island

PACIFIC OCEAN

KEY

90	National road
10	Other road
	Dive Centre
	Hospital
	Decompression Chamber
	Lighthouse
	Wreck
	Airport
	Reef
	International Boundary
	Disputed Boundary
	Provincial Boundary

accessible in clear water with a visibility that averages 40m (130ft). Vast numbers of sharks, mantas, Eagle Rays, turtles, dolphins and migratory pelagics convene at the crossroads of the world's three major ocean currents.

Land-locked marine lakes, linked to the sea through narrow channels, are breeding grounds for sharks, jellyfish, crocodiles and rare critters. Uplifted marine lakes, home to millions of non-stinging jellyfish, are a short, easy uphill hike through a tropical rainforest. Submerged multichamber caves, hauntingly beautiful, are also easily accessible.

8 Blue Corner

Blue Corner is a triangular, flat-topped promontory, which projects some 45–70m (150–230ft) into deep water. Situated off the edge of Ngemelis Island, this world-famous site is the ultimate in adrenaline diving, or sensory overload in local terminology. Swift currents provide rich feeding for soft corals and fans on the outer, deeper point of the promontory and attract schools of pelagics. Abundant in shark action, the site teems, not just with large schools of Moorish Idols, but Napoleon Wrasse, groupers, barracuda, Whitetip Reef Sharks, turtles, moray eels, jacks, mantas and huge Blotched Fantail Rays. Especially when the current is running, the action seems endless and electrifying. The site is a reef flat that starts at about 12m (39ft) over a huge area, jutting out into the sea before dropping quickly to form a wall. Gorgonian Sea Fans and plate corals are prolific.

9 Quadruple Blue Holes

Just beyond Blue Corner, along the same wall, four vertical shafts lead down from a depth of 1.5m (4ft) straight into a series of immense caverns which are open to the sea. Descending down any one of these chimneys is a spiritual experience. As you descend into this cathedral-like chamber, the light diffuses through a spectrum of turquoise blue to sapphire and finally dissolves in darkness below. At high noon, the rays of sunlight pouring through these shafts evoke a religious setting.

against the bridge are hauntingly photogenic. The forward hold is full of mines and there are half-tracked vehicles in the cargo area. The forward mast has interesting coverage and can be used for ascent to maximize photographic productivity underwater.

Depth: 45m (145ft) to deck, 52m (171ft) to stern and 58m (190ft) to forward hold. Length: 118m (387ft).

PALAU

Situated closest to the core of biodiversity, the Indo-Australasian archipelago, the splendour of Palau is mostly beneath the waves. The coral reef has over 1,500 species of fish and an equally astounding coral diversity. Reef flats plummet quickly to depths beyond 2000m (6562ft). Blue holes, huge caverns and immense growths of sessile life are easily

ABOVE *Wreck diving in Micronesia offers military artefacts and armaments, including trucks, tanks and radio equipment.*

ABOVE *Cuttlefish are commonly found hovering over staghorn corals, which are ideal for hiding their eggs from predators.*

Though the first exit is at 28m (92ft) most divers are lured to the second at 38m (125ft). The bottom is sandy and Leopard sharks often lurk along the corridor. Ascend along the outer wall and, if the current is swift, it will be a quick drift down to Blue Corner.

10 Chandelier Caves

Accessible to most divers, Chandelier Caves were once air-filled caverns, possibly millions of years ago when the sea level was much lower. The cave system of four interconnecting chambers beneath a rock island are almost directly across from Sam's Dive Tours. The entrance is about 8m (25ft) below the surface and the short tunnel opens up to a huge chamber with a ceiling of stalactites and clear water, creating an illusion of endless visibility.

In the deeper recesses the chambers are filled with a sparkling field of helictites, delicate calcite crystal mirrored upon the lens of still, clear water. Even with dive lights, the senses are easily tricked, until you break surface to find air-filled chambers dripping with twinkling stone formations. If the spirit moves you, venture to the last chamber where the cave rises sharply to allow you to stand head and shoulders out of the water. If you remove your gear, a narrow passage leads to a completely dry chamber, an enchanting fantasy-land where few have ever been before.

YAP

Tourists are attracted to Yap partly for its culture, but mostly for its spectacular diving opportunities, including the experience of meeting eye to eye with giant Manta Rays. Elsewhere, sightings of mantas are less common, let alone the opportunity of swimming with them, but in Yap the first dive operator has discovered a few cleaning stations where mantas can be observed up close every day of the year. Up to four of them sometimes wait in the queue for a turn to have parasites removed from their undersides by small wrasse and butterflyfish. It is a captivating experience to see such majestic and gentle creatures hovering almost motionless while being attended to by their associates on the reef. It is not uncommon to find 12 magnifi-

cent animals, each with a wingspan of about 4m (13ft), swooping and turning like a squadron of stealth bombers in flight, silhouetted against the morning sun.

Goofnuw Channel: Valley of the Rays 11, Car Wash 13 & Manta Rock 14

Goofnuw channel is the premier location for mantas. There are three cleaning stations in the channel at depths of 15m (50ft) to 22m (72ft). **Merry Go Round** 12 is near the end of the channel dominated by a huge outcrop of lettuce corals. Generally the visibility is poor, but the mantas are often seen soaring in endless circles around this lettuce patch. Car wash and Manta Rock are both coral pinnacles that rise to about 10m (33ft) from the surface. Lots of mantas congregate at ebb tide. These rocks provide ideal shelter from tidal current, which may run to about 7km/h (4 knots). Though the mantas are the primary attraction, the staghorn corals on the reef slope are prolific and healthy. Whitetip Reef Sharks, octopuses and turtles are also local denizens. The best time to dive is in the morning.

MELANESIA

by Andy and Angie Belcher

MELANESIA ENCOMPASSES THE ISLANDS OF the western Pacific Ocean, beginning at Papua New Guinea and then flowing in a great crescent shape to include the Solomon Islands, Vanuatu, New Caledonia and Fiji. It is a region of widely scattered archipelagos – over two thousand splinters of land that, if placed together, would cover an area barely the size of the smallest European province.

The islands of Melanesia reflect the area's geological diversity, ranging from low-lying coral atolls with necklaces of reef to slabs of volcanic rock with mountains that spit flame.

Melanesia straddles the Pacific Rim, a volcanic chain created by the collision of the Pacific and Australian plates, and as a result is often at the receiving end of seismic activity. But volcanic action is not all that has rocked these islands. During World War II the region was the battle ground between Japanese and American forces, and wreckage from that time still lies in the now-peaceful waters, creating a submarine war museum for visiting divers.

TOP LEFT *Solomon Islands. Tropical clouds build up behind Kennedy Island, one-time refuge of John F Kennedy when his patrol boat, PT109, was sliced in two during World War II.*
TOP RIGHT *Hide Away Island nestles like a gem on a velvet background of magical sea in various shades of blue.*

The word Melanesia derives from the Greek word *melas* for black, (the inhabitants had darker skins than the Polynesians to the east) and *nesos* for islands. Early migratory waves across the Pacific and later colonization have resulted in a rich diversity of cultures.

Fiji has an established dive infrastructure, a range of accommodation and package deals. New Caledonia and Vanuatu, formerly known as the New Hebrides, blends French flair with Melanesian magic, while the Solomon Islands are the dream realm of the wreck diver.

FIJI

If there is one word that sums up Fiji it is friendliness. And the one word you will repeatedly hear when you visit these islands is *Bula*, a hearty and genuine greeting that will be offered by nearly everyone you encounter. Fiji consists of two major islands, Viti Levu and Vanua Levu, surrounded by more than three hundred smaller islands and atolls within a complex system of barrier reefs. Located on Melanesia's eastern boundary, Fiji is the meeting place of Melanesia and Polynesia. It also has a large Indian population originally brought in by the British to work on the sugar cane plantations. Fiji's central position in the Pacific has made it a focal point for travellers and trading.

Fiji's well-known dive sites are all grouped in clusters, usually because they share under-

sea plateaus or atoll formations. There are more than 1000 recorded species of fish, several hundred types of coral and sponges and an infinite array of crustaceans, molluscs, anemones, worms and other invertebrates. The diving is varied. Some sites, with their sheer deep walls and wild currents are best left to experienced divers, but there are endless shallow fringing reefs and protected lagoons suitable for beginners.

RESEARCH AND CONSERVATION

Many of Fiji's dive operators are involved with marine research and conservation programmes. Some assist by measuring water temperatures, salinity and current. Others collect reef specimens for analysis for medical uses. Beqa Divers is monitoring the proposed Namosi copper mine's plan to deposit tailings in the Beqa channel (this is only a plan and no effluent pipeline has yet been built). They monitor existing effluent pipelines in the Suva/Levuka area for leaks or damage. Dive operators participate in ongoing discussions with marine biologists of the University of the South Pacific, the Department of Fisheries and fishermen on sustainable fish farming and any changes to reef structure or animals.

On Kadavu, there are also projects under way to establish three marine parks. These are planned for the areas around Namalatta, Astrolabe and Cape Washington.

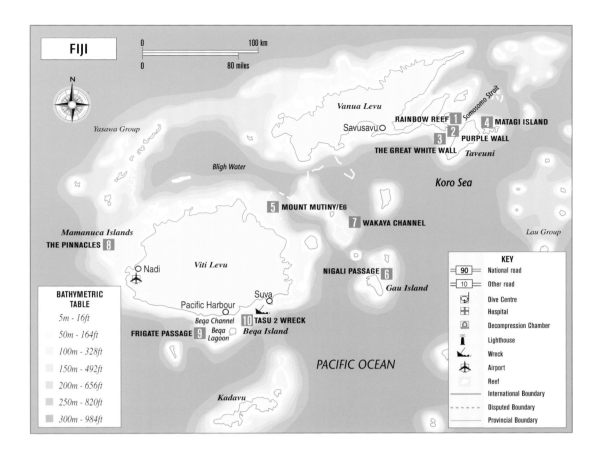

NORTHERN FIJI

The colour, size and profusion of soft corals are sensational – the result of fierce, nutrient-rich currents which sweep in and around the Somosomo Strait between Vanua Levu and Taveuni, giving Fiji the reputation of soft coral capital of the world. The Rainbow Reef, **Purple Wall** 2 and The Great White Wall are all accessible by boat from shore bases.

Divers, especially underwater photographers, are drawn to Taveuni by nature's colourful landscaping. The island, Fiji's third largest, is 40km (25 miles) long, and also known as The Garden Island. And lives up to its name as home to most of Fiji's bird species and the Tagimaucia flower. **Matagi Island** 4, a five-minute boat ride from Taveuni, is a favoured land-base for divers.

Rainbow Reef 1 is about 20 minutes by boat from Taveuni. It can have current, but good snorkelling is possible. The 30–km (20–mile) reef extends into the Somosomo Strait between Taveuni and Vanua Levu.

The Great White Wall 3 is a drift dive with strong currents and immediate descent is required. Visibility is about 20–30m (65–100ft) and the average depth 30m (100ft).

The wall drops to between 60m (200ft) and 80m (260ft), way beyond the maximum recommended sport diving depths.

The Somosomo Strait narrows abruptly and the water moving through this gap at speeds of up to 6km/h (3 knots) is further constricted by a number of reefs, one of which is Rainbow Reef. After descending about 10m (33ft) divers swim through a reef-top-tunnel decorated with luminous soft white corals, gorgonias, crinoids and clouds of tiny orange anthias (fish). As they emerge from the passageway at 24m (80ft) the reason for the dive's reputation is revealed. The current carries divers along a vertical wall smothered in white soft corals. The trick is to start the dive just as the current turns, so that divers can be carried gently along the wall and then fin back to the dive boat without undue exertion.

CENTRAL FIJI

The deep, rich, ocean channel between Fiji's two main islands is separated by two separate barrier reefs. Trade winds, currents and a rich nutrient flow make the diving wild and dynamic. Pinnacles, current-flushed reef passages and bommies submerged in small

TOP *Kadavu's garden grottos are for those who love beauty. Walls, drop-offs and reef passages provide limitless choices.*

ABOVE *The bommies of Beqa Lagoon (pronounced Benga) are riddled with tunnels and openings smothered in every conceivable colour and class of coral.*

lagoons, are just part of what is still largely an unexplored reef system. Mount Mutiny, Nigali Passage and the **Wakaya Channel** 7 are just some of the top sites.

Mount Mutiny 5, also known as E6, is situated in Bligh Water between Viti Levu and Vanua Levu. This is a seamount rising from 914m (3000ft), with the tip just breaking the surface at low tide. It is an open-water dive, accessible by live-aboard, with some current and excellent visibility. The average depth is 20m (65ft). It involves a swim-through of a crescent-shaped passage adorned with gorgonias and soft corals, leading to The Cathedral, or the Sistine Chapel as it is sometimes called. Depending on the time of day, shafts of light filter through holes in the coral formations bathing the passage in an almost spiritual glow. The area is favoured by photographers for its wide-angle, colourful images. Hammerheads, tuna and other pelagics scour the perimeter of the E6 seamount.

The Yasawa Group in the west and Lau Group in the east of this area are the great underwater playgrounds for live-aboard dive vessels. Divers enjoy vast unexplored territories and visits to traditional village communities, where they are given the opportunity to participate in local rituals, in particular the kava ceremony. To visit Fiji and not experience kava is unthinkable. This local drink, made from the crushed roots of the kava plant, has been described as 'looking like dirty water and tasting like dirty socks.' It has a narcotic effect and can leave the mouth slightly numb. The bizarre mushroom-shaped islets and crystal clear waters of Fulaga Lagoon in the Lau Group have been known to make visiting divers wonder if they are experiencing the hallucinating effects of a kava overdose.

Nigali Passage 6 is just off Gau Island, and access is by live-aboard boat. There is some current depending on the tide. It is a drift dive with an average depth of 24m (80ft). The passage carries water from deep ocean into a shallower lagoon. The stronger the current the more prolific the fish life. It is best as a drift dive with the current taking divers out into deeper, calmer waters. Here you will find the Cabbage Patch, a huge area of stony corals named after the leafy appearance and colour of the coral. Barracuda, Grey Reef, Whitetip and Blacktip Sharks are all resident.

SOUTHERN FIJI

Beqa Lagoon (pronounced Benga), off the south coast of Viti Levu, is one of the best-known dive areas in Southern Fiji. Strong currents rush through the passages, carrying with them schools of large pelagics. The

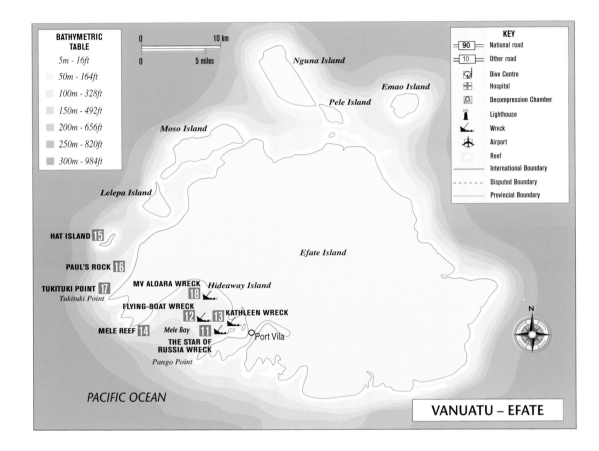

ABOVE *Gotham City, just a short boat ride from Plantation Island swarms with an assortment of reef fish following divers in the feverish expectation of being fed.*

lagoon itself has lots of big bommies (coral heads) riddled with tunnels that are festooned with a tremendous display of soft corals.

The *Tasu 2* [10], a scuttled trader, lies 48km (30 miles) west of Suva. Dive operators launch from Pacific Harbour. The site offers sheltered, shallow waters, good visibility and little current. The average depth is 15m (50ft). This wreck rests in about 20m (65ft). Although stripped of much of its original fittings, the rails and rungs make great photographic subjects, as do the prop and rudder which lie wedged in the white sands of the ocean floor.

The Pinnacles [8] is situated near the Mamanuca Islands. Access is by dive boat from one of several resorts on Plantation Island, Castaway, or Musket Cove. It is diveable in most conditions. There can be some current on the surface and visibility averages 15m (50ft). The average depth of the dive is 15–20m (50–65ft), with a maximum of 24m (80ft). It is a bommie rising up to within 6m (20ft) of the surface. The top is jam-packed with anemones and resident clownfish. A small swim-through near the base is a novelty for newer divers.

Frigate Passage [9] is at the southwest entrance to Beqa Lagoon. Access is by dive boat from shore bases at Beqa Island or Pacific Harbour. Visibility is often more than 20m (65ft). Two large coral heads in the entrance of the passage are riddled with small tunnels and caves which are fun to explore. Active and plentiful supplies of pelagic species pass through the passage.

VANUATU

Vanuatu, formerly known as the New Hebrides, consists of four main islands and a string of smaller ones. The total land mass of around 13,000 sq km (5000 sq miles) ranges from towering volcanic cones clad in dense rainforest to low-lying coral islands with deep natural harbours. It is recognised as one of the most culturally diverse countries in the world. While both French and English are spoken, the majority of Ni-Vanuatu speak Bislama, a quirky rendition of English. 'Mi laikem daiva long Vanuatu tumas!' translates as 'I like diving in Vanuatu very much!'

Diving is still confined to two of the largest islands, Espiritu Santo and Efate, where the sleepy capital of Port Vila is located. Despite the often-limited visibility in Port Vila's harbour, there are three regularly visited wrecks there. *The Star of Russia* [11] is an easily penetrated three-masted ship built in 1875. It now lies in 30m (100ft) of water. There is a **Sandringham flying-boat** [12] at 40m (130ft) and the scuttled trader *Kathleen* [13] lies at a depth of 35m (115ft).

Several buoyed sites at **Mele Reef** [14], less than half an hour from Port Vila, are well protected in most weather conditions. The plate and staghorn coral formations make it a popular site for novice divers and photographers alike. Better visibility and more spectacular terrain can be found closer to the entrance of the bay around Pango Point. For advanced divers the waters surrounding North Efate's offshore islands hide an intact corsair fighter, anti-submarine nets, buoys and boom gates. **Hat Island** [15] and Paul's Rock (one of Vanuatu's best marine reserves) are also popular dives.

Paul's Rock [16] is a seamount rising from 70m (230ft) to within 1m (3ft) of the surface, 800m (880yd) offshore from North Efate. Access is by boat and it is diveable in most conditions with a visibility of 10–20m (33–65ft). The average depth is 20m (65ft) and the maximum 70m (230ft). It offers gorgonia tunnels, swim-throughs and interactive fish life.

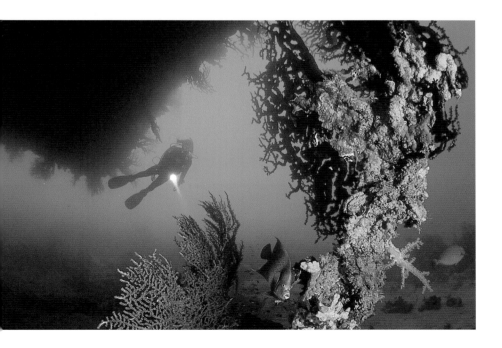

ABOVE *Corals hang seductively beneath the shaded bow of the* SS President Coolidge, *which rests off the island of Espiritu Santo.*

ABOVE *Million Dollar Point is the historian's paradise. Acres of discarded war machinery litters the coastline both above and below the water.*

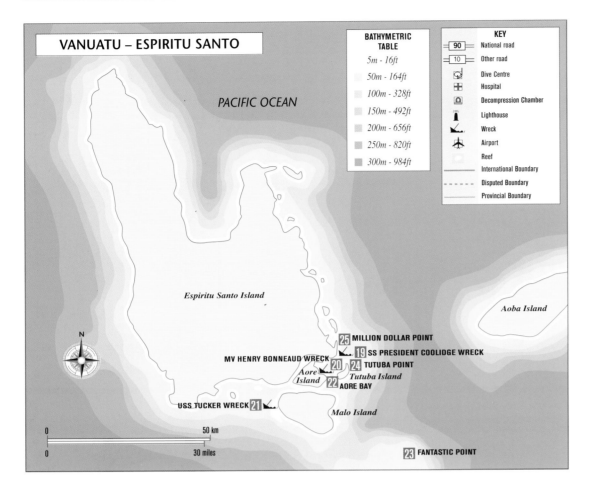

VANUATU – ESPIRITU SANTO

PACIFIC OCEAN

Espiritu Santo Island

Aoba Island

25 MILLION DOLLAR POINT
19 SS PRESIDENT COOLIDGE WRECK
MV HENRY BONNEAUD WRECK
20 24 TUTUBA POINT
Aore Island
22 Tutuba Island
AORE BAY
USS TUCKER WRECK 21
Malo Island
23 FANTASTIC POINT

0   50 km
0   30 miles

BATHYMETRIC TABLE

5m - 16ft
50m - 164ft
100m - 328ft
150m - 492ft
200m - 656ft
250m - 820ft
300m - 984ft

KEY

90 National road
10 Other road
Dive Centre
Hospital
Decompression Chamber
Lighthouse
Wreck
Airport
Reef
International Boundary
Disputed Boundary
Provincial Boundary

ABOVE *A diver swims over the top of Paul's Rock. This solitary seamount rising 800m (2600ft) offshore, is regarded as one of Vanuatu's best marine sanctuaries.*

The **MV Aloara** [18] is situated 550m (1805ft) offshore from Hideaway Island, Port Vila, Efate. This 30m (100ft) former island trader was sunk in November 2001 to create an artificial reef. The boat lies on its side near the edge of a reef. Access is possible by small boat in most conditions. Visibility is 20–30m (65–100ft) and there may be a slight current. The average depth is 20m (65ft) and the maximum 25m (80ft).

Tukituki Point [17] offers a labyrinth of canyons which are pierced at midday by the sun, creating shimmering curtains of light.

Dive operators in Port Vila go to great lengths in their effort to manage the reefs. They have, for instance, designated special areas as unofficial marine sanctuaries – a concept which is paying big dividends in terms of increased marine life.

Most diving visitors to Vanuatu are lured north to the archipelago's largest island, Espiritu Santo. It was here that author James A Michener was stationed during World War II and from which he drew inspiration for his book *Tales of the South Pacific*.

The main attraction of Espiritu Santo is the wreck of the **SS President Coolidge** [19], the largest, easily accessible shipwreck in the world. The 200m (654ft), 22,350–tonne luxury liner had a beam of 25m (80ft). She was converted to a troop ship during the war and run ashore after hitting two American mines while negotiating the channel in an attempt to reach the sheltered harbour. Moorings have been placed at regular intervals along the wreck to allow for quick and easy access. This wreck is huge.

It is recommended that divers prepare for deep and wreck dives before arriving in Santo. The wrecks of the **MV Henry Bonneaud** [20] and the **USS Tucker** [21] as well as many lovely stony coral reefs – **Aore Bay** [22], **Fantastic** [23] and **Tutuba Point** [24] – ensure variety.

The **President Coolidge** [19] in Santo Harbour was declared a Vanuatu Marine National Park in 1983. Access is possible from shore and by boat. It is diveable in most conditions, but silts easily. The average depth is 35–45m (115–150ft). The maximum depth is 60m (200ft) as per code of practice.

There is plenty to see outside the wreck, but most divers like to do at least one penetration dive. The most popular choices are to view The Lady at 45m (150ft), a beautiful porcelain wall plaque which once graced the smoking room, the engine room at 48m (158ft) or the swimming pool at 56m (184ft).

The ship lies on her port side. The bow rests in about 20m (65ft) of water while the stern drops away to 70m (230ft). Like any penetration dive, silt-outs are always a possibility. The wreck is a complex structure with a maze of passageways and compartments that can confuse even the most experienced diver. The majority of diving takes place between the bow and the bridge area at around 40m (130ft). The promenade deck is still littered with war debris. Rifles, bayonets, helmets and gas masks rest where they fell more than half a century ago. Trucks, jeeps, anti-aircraft guns and shells lie abandoned in the holds. *The President Coolidge* is advanced diving and diving with a guide is mandatory.

RIGHT At midday curtains of light fall through reef-top openings illuminating the interiors with magical light. This is a common sight throughout the Solomons and Vanuatu.

Million Dollar Point 25 is situated in Santo Harbour and is accessible from shore. It is diveable in most conditions and visibility averages 10–15m (33–50ft). The average depth is 10m (33ft) and the maximum 40m (130ft). There are trucks, bulldozers, boats, surplus army equipment and many small, exotic marine creatures have made their home in the wreckage.

At the conclusion of World War II millions of dollars worth of surplus army equipment was scuttled, driven or dropped off a jetty in Santo Harbour. The rusted remains can be seen on the beach and continue below the surface to 40m (130ft), spreading over a wide area. Great for fossicking and photography, especially macrophotography.

SOLOMON ISLANDS

The Solomon Islands comprise a volcanic and densely forested group of six main islands surrounded by more than 800 smaller islands, of which only about one third are populated. American and Japanese war veterans know the Solomon Islands well. During World War II, Guadalcanal, the main island, was a strategic point in the bitter struggle by American forces to repel the Japanese in the Pacific. The ensuing naval and air battles left hundreds of planes and ships wrecked on land and in the ocean. Some of the best wreck dives are conveniently close to shore and have attracted masses of fish and an incredible variety of coral life. Many wrecks start in depths shallow enough for snorkelling and then plummet down well past the limit for safe sport diving.

Tragically, parts of the Marovo lagoon are under threat from logging companies which are clear-felling to extract rosewood and ebony timbers. As well as depleting the resource, heavy run-off during the rainy sea-son creates tides of red silt into the lagoon smothering mangroves and corals. In another area, foreign tuna boats haul in huge catches of baitfish depleting the food source of the larger species. On a more positive note, eco-tourism is being encouraged, using local resources and knowledge.

The most accessible diving is in three main areas: Guadalcanal, Marovo Lagoon and Gizo.

GUADALCANAL

Due to land issues all diving around Guadalcanal has been put on hold. When they are accessible, the dives around Guadalcanal suit both novice and experienced divers. **Bonegi One** 26, **Bonegi Two** (***Kinugawa Maru***) 27 and the ***Ruiniu*** 28 are a trio of Japanese transporters bombed and then run ashore in an attempt to salvage supplies. Their bows are in shallow water – as little as 3m (10ft) – and their sterns lie at between 30m (100ft) and 40m (130ft). The fantastic fish life and prolific coral growth on these war relics provide a thought-provoking juxtaposition of life and, sometimes violent, death.

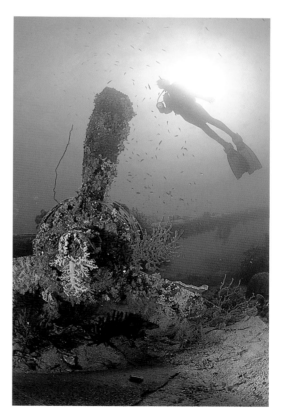

ABOVE A shroud of pastel-coloured corals covers this P-38 fighter which lies in 10m (33ft) of water off the end of the Seghe Airport runways at Marovo Lagoon.

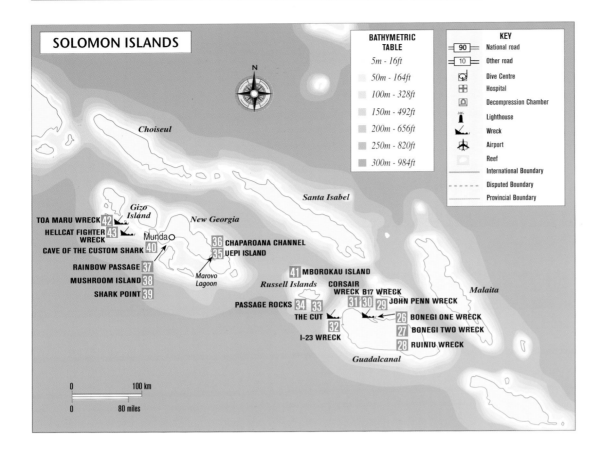

SOLOMON ISLANDS

BATHYMETRIC TABLE

5m - 16ft
50m - 164ft
100m - 328ft
150m - 492ft
200m - 656ft
250m - 820ft
300m - 984ft

KEY

90 National road
10 Other road
Dive Centre
Hospital
Decompression Chamber
Lighthouse
Wreck
Airport
Reef
International Boundary
Disputed Boundary
Provincial Boundary

Choiseul

Santa Isabel

Gizo Island

TOA MARU WRECK 42
HELLCAT FIGHTER WRECK 43
CAVE OF THE CUSTOM SHARK 40
Munda
New Georgia
36 CHAPAROANA CHANNEL
35 UEPI ISLAND
RAINBOW PASSAGE 37
MUSHROOM ISLAND 38
SHARK POINT 39
Marovo Lagoon
Russell Islands
41 MBOROKAU ISLAND
CORSAIR WRECK B17 WRECK
PASSAGE ROCKS 34 33
THE CUT
32
I-23 WRECK
31 30 29 JOHN PENN WRECK
26 BONEGI ONE WRECK
27 BONEGI TWO WRECK
28 RUINIU WRECK
Malaita
Guadalcanal

0 100 km
0 80 miles

ABOVE *Riddled with bullets, this B17 bomber was ditched in the shallow waters offshore of Honiara. Her heavily-armed 50-calibre machine guns still aim at a silent enemy.*

Serious technical divers can now access some of the deeper wrecks lying in Iron Bottom Sound, renamed as a result of the graveyard of wrecks sunk during the Guadalcanal Campaign. Many of these wrecks exceed sport diving depth limits, but others like the troopship *John Penn* 29, which is 36m (118ft) at its shallowest point, can be dived with guides supplied by local operators. A heavily armed B17 30, a **corsair** 31 and a **I-23 submarine** 32, which can be accessed from shore, as well as the potential to discover undiscovered wrecks make Guadalcanal a wreck diver's dream.

RUSSELL ISLANDS/MAROVO LAGOON

The Russell Islands are a compulsory stop for live-aboard boats heading for Marovo Lagoon, the second-largest lagoon in the world. These volcanic islands, accessible only by boat, are covered in thick, verdant tropical growth and rise straight out of the deep. At some sites the boat can tie up to vegetation and hang back, at others diving is done from tenders. Some islands have a 'lip' where the boat can anchor while the stern hangs over the deep.

The diving is exciting and diverse. There are cuts, canyons, custom caves and currents. Custom caves, above or below water, belong to a village and are controlled by customary laws. Currents encourage coral growth to delight wide-angle photographers, while the seemingly uninspiring coral rubble with silt-coated war wreckage (like that at White Beach) are home to the type of bizarre marine life that delights macrophotographers.

Visibility can be exceptional although there is some variation according to season, coral spawning or plankton blooms. Fish life is prolific with great schools of swirling barracudas and jacks. Highlighting the best dives around these islands is nearly impossible.

The Cut 33, a crevice 5m (16ft) wide, carved about 100m (330ft) into Leru Island, is accessible by live-aboard. It is best dived at midday when shafts of sunlight stream through the openings above, bathing divers in an almost spiritual light. At the end of the corridor you surface into a jungle to be serenaded by the calls of birds and insects. This is a sheltered site with visibility of 15–30m (50–100ft). The average depth is 10–12m (33–40ft), with a maximum of 16m (52ft).

Uepi Island [35] (pronounced Ooo-pee), a raised coral reef situated within Marovo Lagoon, has a diverse marine ecosystem and provides an idyllic land-based dive operation. There are plenty of coral gardens, drop-offs, ledges and gullies. The **Chaparoana Channel** [36], running between Uepi and a smaller island is a highway for sharks, rays, turtles and even the occasional whale. The Marovo area is also renowned for its exquisite ebony woodcarvings known as Spirit of Solomon.

Further to the west in the Roviana Lagoon is Munda. This was once the home of the headhunting Roviana people and there are still many remnants and artefacts. The names of the dive sites around this region describe what you can expect to see: **Rainbow Passage** [37], **Mushroom Island** [38] and **Shark Point** [39].

The Cave of the Custom Shark [40] is at Dnokendnoke Island, Roviana Lagoon, and can be reached in 30 minutes by small boat from Munda. Visibility at the sinkhole can deteriorate after heavy rain. The average depth is 15m (50ft) and the wall drops away to around 800m (2625ft) at the cave's ocean exit.

It is a penetration dive through a freshwater sinkhole out into the ocean on the other side of the island. Divers descend 15m (50ft) down a crystal clear freshwater pool on the island. The shaft widens and turns a bend just wide enough to negotiate the odd stalagmite which obstructs the path. Just as you lose all light and get that claustrophobic feeling, a layer of transparent blue light, the exit point, comes into view.

Mborokau Island [41], also known as Mary Island, is situated between the Russell Islands and Marovo Lagoon. Visibility can be exceptional and the sites are diveable in most conditions. The average depth depends on the actual site, but is usually between 5m (16ft) and 15m (50ft).

Fish life is prolific, with swirling jacks and schooling barracuda. There is an assortment of macro life, such as Harlequin Ghost Pipefish and camouflage crabs.

Passage Rocks [34], in the Russell Islands, is accessible by live-aboard boat. It can have strong currents and it is best to dive on the leeward side. The average depth is 20m (65ft).

These two tiny islets rest on a 10m (33ft) deep volcanic tabletop. At 25m (80ft) giant pink gorgonias and yellow soft corals cover the overhanging walls. Rays, sharks and massive schools of fish are always in residence. Thousands of tiny blue and yellow fusiliers hang around the bommies on the plateau.

GIZO

The excitement at Gizo starts when you land on a small narrow island consisting of nothing but its small, narrow runway, and doesn't finish until you've sat on a natural bench in 18m (60ft) of water at Grand Central Station. There divers can witness the hurried comings and goings of sharks, rays, and amberjacks in a frenetic underwater city. Situated in the Western Province, Gizo is surrounded by endless lagoons, volcanic islands and crystal bays and offers excellent and easy diving on wrecks, reefs and drop-offs. Nearly all the dive sites are 15–20 minutes from the wharf. The marine life is busy and unspoiled, but the wrecks of the ***Toa Maru*** [42] and the tiny Hellcat fighter are the most popular.

Toa Maru can be reached from Gizo by boat and lies in a sheltered bay diveable all year round. Visibility averages 15–20m (50–65ft). The average depth is 20–25m (65–80ft), with a maximum of 37m (121ft).

This 140m (460ft), 6990 tonne Japanese transporter lies on her starboard side with her bow in 12m (40ft) and stern in 37m (121ft). There are saki urns, gas masks, bayonets and even a tank lying upside down outside the main hold. We returned from one photographic trip to realize that the model had been elegantly perched on top of a pile of live mortars! Guided penetration dives take divers through the bridge, past the galley with its

TOP *This colourful nudibranch* (Nembrotha kubaryana) *has many colour variations.*
ABOVE *This crab,* (Hoplophrys oatesii), *mimics the colours and lines of the pink soft coral growing on war debris at White Beach, Marovo Lagoon.*

huge woks and ovens, into the massive engine room and its tangle of cables and valves and into the crockery room where sacks of plates and cups now hold easily disturbed layers of silt.

The Hellcat Fighter [43] lies in shallow water near a small island. It is accessible by boat, and is about one hour from Gizo. Visibility averages 10m (33ft). The average depth is 10m (33ft), with a maximum of 12m (40ft).

Still intact, this fighter was ditched after being shot down by a compatriot in 1943. It is an easy and fun dive and can be snorkelled. Divers enjoy being photographed sitting in the cockpit. It is surrounded by patches of cabbage and staghorn coral. The excitement of visiting Melanesia is not in what you know, but in what awaits discovery. Unexplored reefs, undiscovered wrecks and unrecorded marine life await the adventurous diver.

PAPUA NEW GUINEA

by Bob Halstead

IN THE ERA WHEN THE PACIFIC AND ASIA were being explored, invaded and colonized by Europeans, Papua New Guinea was largely ignored. Its formidable mountain ranges might have held the promise of fabled golden treasures, but the mountains soared above shores tangled with impenetrable jungle and were protected by fierce inhabitants and treacherous reefs, both capable of giving intruders lethal surprises.

What made Papua New Guinea so inaccessible for early foreign explorers is the very thing that attracts modern adventurers to this astonishing country. It is one of the world's last remaining wilderness areas. However, it is not the desolation of the landscape or a harsh climate that has kept Papua New Guinea pristine, but its opulence and abundance that made it inaccessible. Nature went crazy in this area and produced such a lush display of mountains, volcanoes and rivers, swampy plains, rainforests and coral reefs, that Europeans had a hard time taming them and

TOP LEFT *Milne Bay. Fringing reefs in this region often have deep water close by and mild currents parallel to shore.*

TOP RIGHT *Offshore reefs such as this one in Milne Bay, can have complex channels and drop-offs. These fascinating dives often involve encounters with sharks and pelagics.*

surviving. Even Papua New Guineans, whose ancestors are believed to have settled from Asia some 50,000 years ago, have mostly stayed isolated from each other, resulting in the evolution of over 800 languages and a kaleidoscope of colourful and distinct cultures.

For divers, a significant feature of the country's reefs is that deep water comes very close to shore. Offshore winds produce calm seas and upwellings, as a result of which these reefs support a multitude of marine creatures. Delicate coral formations that could never grow on barrier reefs subjected to storm waves thrive in the clear, but sheltered waters. Sea fans and soft corals often reach enormous size, and large pelagic fish patrol the edge of the reef.

Shallow sandy or sea grass areas near beaches, some of which slope quickly to deep water, make for fascinating muck diving and the chance to discover the bizarre marine critters that live there.

Offshore from the mainland and big islands are countless small islands and reefs, many of which are uninhabited and uncharted. Although more exposed to the weather they are usually blessed with year-round visibility in excess of 40m (130ft). Some get enough nutrients to support soft corals and giant sea fans and sea whips. These occur deeper than their inshore relatives and are usually found between 20m (66ft) and 50m (165ft) down.

In addition to the magnificent reefs there are hundreds of wrecks scattered throughout the waters. These include ships, submarines and aircraft, many in excellent condition, some of which are perfect, untouched time capsules now transformed into coral wonderlands. There is still much scope for exploration. There are many aircraft and ship-wrecks – and indeed reefs – in Papua New Guinea that have not yet been dived. Rarely does a year go by without some significant discovery being made.

CARL'S ULTIMATE, EASTERN FIELDS

Eastern Fields is a Coral Sea reef complex situated about 167km (104 miles) southwest of Port Moresby. The dive sites are only accessible by live-aboard boat. Like most true Coral Sea reefs it boasts excellent visibility, untouched coral growth and plenty of big fish and shark action.

Carl's Ultimate [1] sits in the northern entrance to the Eastern Fields lagoon and experiences tidal currents. The outer tip has been scoured into cave-like passages filled with pink soft corals and the whole reef is adorned with sea fans and Dendronephthya Soft Tree Corals. The fish life, including some impressive Giant Groupers (*Epinephelus lanceolatus*) and Potato Cod (*E. tukula*) is staggering.

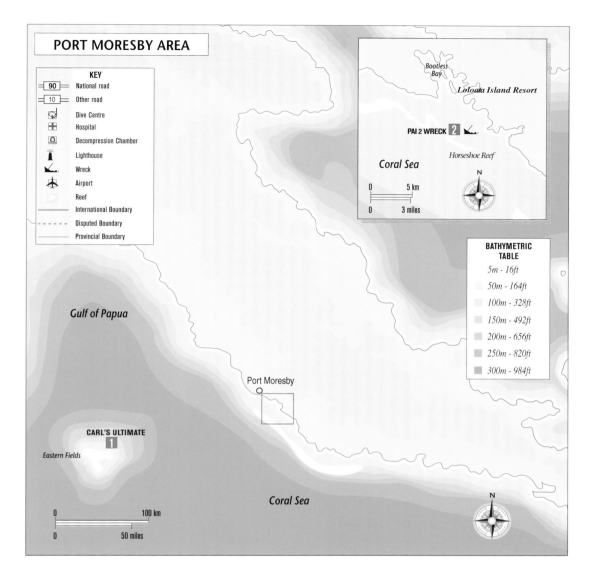

KEY

90	National road
10	Other road
	Dive Centre
	Hospital
	Decompression Chamber
	Lighthouse
	Wreck
	Airport
	Reef
	International Boundary
	Disputed Boundary
	Provincial Boundary

Bootless Bay

Loloata Island Resort

PAI 2 WRECK 2

Coral Sea

Horseshoe Reef

0 — 5 km
0 — 3 miles

Gulf of Papua

BATHYMETRIC TABLE

5m - 16ft
50m - 164ft
100m - 328ft
150m - 492ft
200m - 656ft
250m - 820ft
300m - 984ft

Port Moresby

CARL'S ULTIMATE 1

Eastern Fields

Coral Sea

0 — 100 km
0 — 50 miles

The tidal currents should be assessed carefully and the boat moored at the down-current end of the reef. Do not anchor. Divers can then be taken by tender to the up-current end and dropped at the edge of the reef. The top of the reef is only 7m (23ft) deep and the reef, which is sausage-shaped, has over 40m (130ft) of water around it. Most of the dive should be planned for the end of the reef receiving the current, to be followed by a shallower drift or swim-back to the moored boat.

Because of the shape and isolation of the reef, navigation is easy. A gentle incoming current is preferable and times of maximum current should be avoided. The reef also boasts a multitude of interesting smaller critters including the recently described Whitebarred Wrasse (*Pseudocheilinus ocellatus*) known only from the oceanic Coral Sea. Lacy scorpionfish (*Rhinopias aphanes*), can be seen on the reef edge.

THE WRECK OF THE PAI 2, PORT MORESBY

Diving at Port Moresby is particularly good for exotic marine life, and the outer barrier reef is only a few kilometres offshore. There are many wrecks, recent and historical, lush reefs with drop-offs, reef passes and fascinating muck dives.

The most popular area is out of Bootless Bay, a 15-minute drive from the Airport and home to Loloata Island Resort. Horseshoe Reef on the outer barrier provides some excellent sheltered dive sites, including the **wreck of the *PAI 2* 2**, a scuttled fishing trawler. The wreck sits in 30m (100 ft) of water close to Horseshoe Reef, which is awash at low tide. Upright and still with its masts and wheelhouse intact, this wreck has improved over the years and now is the home for many tame fish including Mangrove Snappers (*Lutjanus argentimaculatus*) and Saddleback Coral

TOP *Carl's Ultimate cave passages provide a popular swim-through for black trevally (*Caranx lugubris*) and divers alike.*

ABOVE *A diver frames herself with colourful soft corals on the ladder and mast structure of the wreck of the* PAI 2, *a scuttled fishing trawler on Horseshoe Reef.*

Grouper (*Plectropomus laevis*). The masts are decorated with a colourful display of Dendronephthya Soft Tree Corals. Red-stripe Anthias, also known as One-stripe Anthias (*Pseudanthias fasciatus*), usually found in much deeper water, swarm on the wreck.

Boats can tie up to a permanent mooring established on the wreck and descend to the superstructure and masts at 15m (50ft). Currents tend to be slight and easily manageable. Visibility is variable, but often 25m (80ft) after passing through a murkier surface layer.

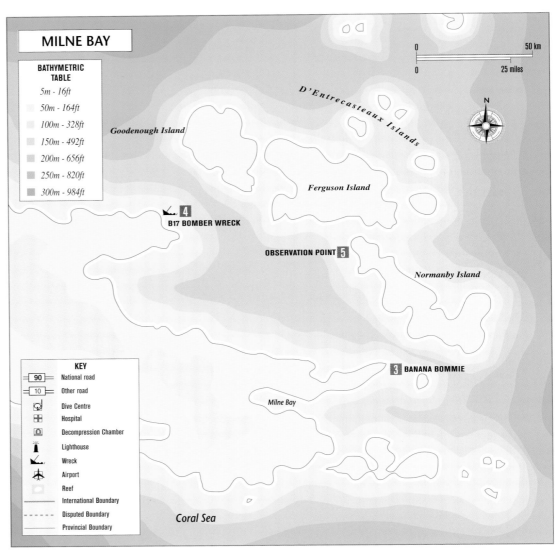

MILNE BAY

BATHYMETRIC TABLE

5m - 16ft
50m - 164ft
100m - 328ft
150m - 492ft
200m - 656ft
250m - 820ft
300m - 984ft

Goodenough Island

D'Entrecasteaux Islands

Ferguson Island

4 B17 BOMBER WRECK

OBSERVATION POINT **5**

Normanby Island

3 BANANA BOMMIE

Milne Bay

Coral Sea

KEY

90 — National road
10 — Other road
Dive Centre
Hospital
Decompression Chamber
Lighthouse
Wreck
Airport
Reef
International Boundary
Disputed Boundary
Provincial Boundary

TOP *Bathed in a steady current, Banana Bommie is smothered in corals and feather stars, and swarms with fish.*

ABOVE *The top turret gun of* Blackjack, *a World War II B17 bomber lying in deep water. It is still in near perfect condition. The cockpit can be viewed through open side windows.*

3 BANANA BOMMIE, MILNE BAY

This sensational reef now has a mooring on top in 5m (16ft) of water. Boats should not anchor. In ideal conditions there is a slight and easily manageable current from the west. However, sometimes the current can get as fast as 4km/hour (two knots) and the dive should be avoided at these times. Divers should remember that the current running over the top of this reef is much stronger than the current experienced once a short distance down the reef slope.

The west side slopes steeply to about 27m (90ft) to a sandy bottom with scattered small coral heads. A forest of large garden eels live in the sand and, as the sand slopes towards the reef, several Red Lined or Peppermint Sea Cucumbers (*Thelenota rubrolineata*) will be seen. These are popular with photographers because of their brilliant colours.

The sides of the reef are thick with black corals, sea fans and soft corals, crinoids, anemones and zillions of fish. Coral Groupers or Red Coral Trout (*Cephalopholis miniata*) are very common and are not shy of divers. Barramundi Cod or Humpback Groupers (*Cromileptes altivelis*) are a prize find.

The eastern side can be dived on the rare occasions that the current is from the east. However, it is not as rich as the western side.

At the edge of the reef huge schools of Fairy Basslets (*Pseudanthias* spp.) feed on plankton borne by the current. It is a fabulous sight.

4 B17 BOMBER WRECK, BLACKJACK, MILNE BAY

The area is exposed to strong southeast and northwest winds and often has a current over the site from the southeast. It should not be attempted except in calm conditions.

The best plan is for a direct ascent to the aircraft, a single slow pass over the wings, nose and cockpit areas finishing at the tail. The starboard tailplane is bent upwards and points to the exit for the dive, which is a reef slope at about 45° leading to a vertical wall ideal for making a slow, safe ascent. The wall rises to 3m (10ft) of water. This is a deep dive requiring decompression stops, often with current present, and should not be attempted by inexperienced divers. It may be dived at 40m (130ft), but the sandy bottom is at 48m (158ft). Visibility in good conditions can reach 40m (130ft). The wreck is exceptionally intact and has guns and other artefacts for the

MUCK DIVING

First coined by Bob Halstead in Papua New Guinea, muck diving is usually done over a silty or sandy bottom, but it can also be over coral rubble. Concentrated observation will locate small and often colourful or weird creatures camouflaged against their environment. Having realized the possibilities, divers soon found creatures they had previously missed in Indonesia's Lembeh Strait, Borneo's Mabul, Kapalai and Lankayan and in the Philippines' Anilao, Boracay, Puerto Galera and Malapascua. Often it was a case of the visibility being so good that no one had bothered to look for such small creatures.

Most divers will need local guides to help locate these creatures. Many are so small that it is worth carrying a magnifying glass: tiny commensal shrimps and crabs on larger animals and gobies and pygmy sea horses on gorgonias.

diver to see. Divers should resist the temptation to penetrate the fuselage, which has many loose wires hanging around. The cockpit can be viewed and photographed through the open side windows. A machine gun at the tail of the aircraft still swivels in its mount. A Giant Grouper is occasionally seen. A film describing the aircraft's war history and its eventual discovery, *Black Jack's Last Mission*, was produced in 1988. There are excellent reef dives near the wreck, particularly at the southeast entrance to the channel in which it lies; and the wall by the wreck can be dived by those not interested in deep wreck diving.

5 OBSERVATION POINT, MILNE BAY

This is one of the most famous of Milne Bay's muck dives. Boats can anchor on the sandy slope in the passage between the point at the northwestern tip of Normanby Island and the small island, with the stern tied to a tree on the sandy beach. Villagers are friendly and have built rest houses for visiting divers. The site is sheltered in all weather and particularly good when the southeaster blows. There is sometimes a slight current over the site. Visibility depends on the weather, but is usually between 8m (25ft) and 30m (100ft).

This is not a glamorous site, but it offers opportunities for finding unusual marine life. A coral reef has sea grass and mangroves in the shallows. This borders a steep, sandy slope littered with crinoids, dead leaves and other debris. Down the slope, in the middle of the passage at about 40m (130ft), are sea pens and small soft corals. The area supports an array of creatures not found on coral reefs, including ghost pipefish; sand darters (divers) and razorfish (*Iniistius sp.*); shrimpfish (*Aeoliscus strigatus*); Dwarf or Shortfin Lionfish (*Dendrochirus brachypterus*); octopuses; cuttlefish; *Inimicus* and

TOP *A muck dive, Observation Point, reveals its treasures only after careful scrutiny. This new species of sand darter (*Trichonotus halstead*) is named after the author and his wife.*

ABOVE *Stalactites have formed over the skulls in this Milne Bay cave. They were probably taken as war trophies in ancient wars.*

other scorpionfish; helmet shells; frogfish; fire urchins and juvenile batfish. A new species of sand darter, *Trichonotus halstead*, named after the author and his wife, was discovered here.

The creatures vary, but there are always superb macrophoto opportunities for unusual creatures. Care should be taken not to stir up the bottom. A Saltwater or Estuarine Crocodile, *Crocodilus porosus*, was seen here and photographed underwater. The BBC programme *Blue Planet* filmed a mating sequence of the Flamboyant Cuttlefish here.

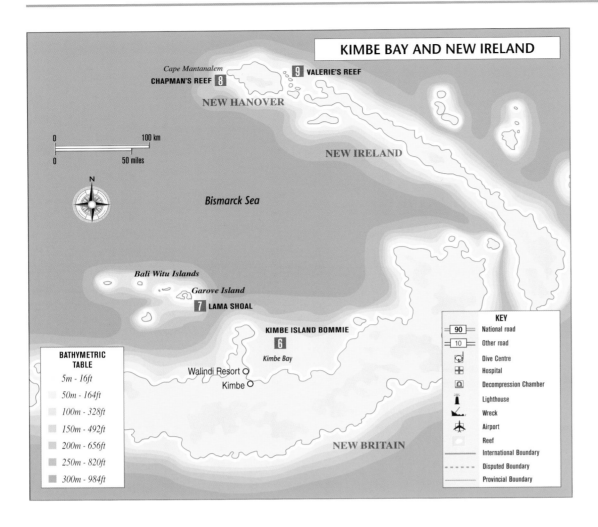

KIMBE BAY AND NEW IRELAND

Cape Mantanalem
CHAPMAN'S REEF 8
9 **VALERIE'S REEF**

NEW HANOVER

NEW IRELAND

Bismarck Sea

Bali Witu Islands

Garove Island

7 **LAMA SHOAL**

KIMBE ISLAND BOMMIE
6

Kimbe Bay

Walindi Resort
Kimbe

NEW BRITAIN

BATHYMETRIC TABLE	
5m - 16ft	
50m - 164ft	
100m - 328ft	
150m - 492ft	
200m - 656ft	
250m - 820ft	
300m - 984ft	

KEY	
90	National road
10	Other road
	Dive Centre
	Hospital
	Decompression Chamber
	Lighthouse
	Wreck
	Airport
	Reef
	International Boundary
	Disputed Boundary
	Provincial Boundary

ABOVE *Lama Shoal has extraordinary fish life. However, it is carpeted with large areas of stinging Corallimorpharians (Discosoma sp.), which should never be touched.*

6 KIMBE ISLAND BOMMIE KIMBE BAY

Kimbe Island is in the middle of Kimbe Bay about an hour's boat ride from Walindi Resort. The bommie is close to the island and marked with a mooring. Boats should not attempt to anchor, especially as the top of the bommie is 27m (90 ft) deep. The site is weather-dependent and difficult to dive in strong southeast trade winds or northwest swells.

Visibility is, however, usually excellent and often reaches 50m (165ft). The dive is best when there is a slight current (less than one knot) running, when all the fish come to feed. The reef abounds with life and is richly deco-rated with stony and soft corals and gorgonias. There are some ridges extending from the pinnacle into water too deep to dive. This is one of the best sites in the area to see schools of big fish, depending on the current. On a still day you will wonder what the fuss is about, although the scenery is always great.

Whales and dolphins are often seen in the area and divers have reported, and filmed, awesome experiences, particularly with Orcas.

7 LAMA SHOAL NEW BRITAIN

Lama Shoal, almost two kilometres (one nau-tical mile) east of Garove Island in the Bali Witu Islands, is exceptional for fish action. After descending to the top of the reef, where there is a mooring in about 8m (25ft), divers should make their way against the current to the side receiving the current to see schools of barracuda and Bigeye Trevallies. Dogtooth Tuna patrol the drop-off among schools of other reef fish. Sharks are occasionally seen. Princess Anthias, (*Pseudanthias smithvanizi*) swarm over the reef and lionfish are common.

Visibility is usually excellent – at least 40m (130ft). On the sloping, descending to well below 50m (165ft), are many large bushes of black coral, sea whips and barrel sponges. An unusual feature of this reef is that the top and upper slope is carpeted with a small brown anemone-like creature. This is a giant colony of Corallimorpharians, which are dangerous to divers. These animals capture prey not merely by stinging them, but by enclosing them in their mantle, which shapes itself into a sphere with a small opening at the top. If a shrimp or fish wanders into the opening it immediately closes and traps the animal. The Corallimorpharian is dangerous to divers because it has a potent defensive sting which can penetrate a Lycra suit. If you disturb the animal it produces a mass of white acontia, which contains stinging cells. The stings can produce secondary symptoms such as neuritis. Do not touch these creatures.

The site is exposed to strong southeast winds, but otherwise quite sheltered and a worthwhile dive, particularly in the evening when the fish life is magic.

8 CHAPMAN'S REEF, NEW HANOVER

Chapman's Reef is located just south of Ao Island near Cape Matanalem, New Hanover. It features an incredible drop-off with huge school of barracuda, and masses of pelagic fish. There is often a strong current, usually from the southeast, but this is manageable for experienced divers. However the reef does experience swells and is partly exposed, making mooring impossible in windy conditions. Visibility is usually excellent and can reach 50m (165ft). The reef top is at 10m (33ft), but the drop-off reaches well over 50m (165ft).

A ridge reef runs parallel to shore, sloping deeply at the sides and with a massive drop-off at its eastern end. The trick is to get over the drop-off when there is a current flowing over it. Once over the edge of the reef the diver is largely sheltered from the effects of the current and can just pick a depth and watch the world go by. Sharks and giant Queensland Groupers cruise through huge schools of fish. Pelagics, including big Dogtooth Tuna, hunt in the evenings. The reef is carpeted by soft corals and there are sea fans down the drop. If the boat is close to the edge the best technique is to swim quickly to the northern side of the ridge where a back eddy will help the diver to the drop-off. Getting over the edge of the drop is the hardest part.

Sometimes the dive is made from an inflatable that drops divers up-current of the edge. The strength of the current is largely unpredictable, but it appears to be stronger on the neap tides, rather than on the springs as one would expect. There is usually a period during the day when the current slackens and then it is possible to dive with the school of barracuda on top of the ridge, which will circle around a diver. A deep crack, filled with fish, runs across the ridge at the eastern end.

9 VALERIE'S REEF KAVIENG

Valerie's Reef has a resident population of Silvertip Sharks (*Carcharhinus albimarginatus*). The initial dives were made from the dive boat *Telita* with Valerie Taylor and the reef is named for her. Boats can moor on top of a sloping stony coral reef in 12m (40ft) of water. As soon as the boat is moored sharks can be seen swimming below. Indeed, the sharks will come to the boat if anchored anywhere within a radius of 9km (6 miles) of the reef.

Best conditions are when a slight current is running from the southeast and light winds. Ocean swells may be present. Visibility is excellent unless there has been recent heavy rain. The reef slopes away to over 40m (130ft).

Shark feeds have previously been held at this site, but regular feeding is no longer needed to attract sharks. No Grey Reef Sharks have ever been seen. However, a Great Hammerhead (*Sphyrna mokarran*) did come to the bait once, at which time the Silvertips immediately disappeared. The number of sharks has declined in recent years because of illegal fishing. However, a small population of large sharks remains at the site. These sharks do not act aggressively if there is no bait in the water. This is a rare and valuable dive site that enables divers to get within touching distance of large sharks in clear, shallow water. The sharks remain for a long time and it is possible to return to the boat directly above for more film and air and continue the dive. Snorkelling is not advised.

ABOVE *A diver is encircled by a school of Chevron (Blackfin) Barracuda (*Sphyraena qenie*) during a period of slack tide on top of the ridge at Chapman's Reef.*

EASTERN AUSTRALIA

by Michael Aw

TOUTED AS ONE OF THE SEVEN WONDERS OF the natural world, from the air the Australian Great Barrier Reef looks like a string of necklaces along the northern coast of Queensland. It is the only living biological community on our planet visible from space and is the earth's longest reef system. Labyrinths of green and blue in irregular patterns are broken up by sand cays and forested islands. They stretch out like the shadows of witches' hands over an expanse of 2000km (1250 miles), making this barrier the most complex and extensive coral reef system in the world.

However, the name is partly a misnomer. It is a barrier, but it is not one continuous reef. It comprises 2800 individual reefs, shoals and over 900 continental and coral islands, covering a total area of 34 million hectares (84 million acres). An amazingly diverse and incredible abundance of marine life supports this ecological wonderland. It is on a shallow plateau that, in the northern sector, lies between 30 and 50 miles offshore, dropping

TOP LEFT *Heron Island on the southern end of the Great Barrier Reef offers one of the best examples of barrier reef ecology. The resort is a great platform for divers, snorkellers and family vacations.*
TOP RIGHT *Lizard Island serves as base for OceanNEnvironment Australia, from which they conduct marine research.*

off into the chasm of the Coral Sea. The majority of this vast ecosystem remains inaccessible to the masses and unscathed by man's influence. Its diverse habitats support over 450 species of coral, over 1500 species of fish, hundreds and thousands of invertebrate species such as worms, crustaceans, echinoderms, molluscs, and sponges. 23 marine mammals, 16 species of sea snakes and six of the world's seven species of sea turtles are also found in the region. Migratory and resident sea birds breed on the reef's tropical cays and islands while Dugongs and whales use the area as refuge, mating and feeding ground. This great biological richness is thought to reflect the maturity of an ecosystem that has evolved over millions of years.

ENVIRONMENTAL PROTECTION

Due to increased awareness of the complexity and fragility of this barrier, and the impact of human activity, the Commonwealth Government passed the Great Barrier Reef Marine Park Act in 1975. The objective was to protect and regulate use of the reefs by creating designated zones in the entire complex. Divided into the Far Northern, Cairns, Central and Mackay/Capricorn sections, the Great Barrier Reef Marine Park Authority (GBRMPA), now administers the system with its headquarters in Townsville, Queensland. The zoning allows areas for tourism access, commercial fishing

and scientific research. General Use zoning allows for all commercial activities except mineral extraction; the Marine National Park zoning restricts the removal of marine organisms, although limited fishing is allowed in some areas; and the Preservation and Scientific Research zones are off limits to all but scientists studying the reef. In partnership with James Cook University and the Australian Institute of Marine Science, the park is the benchmark of coral reef management systems in the world.

The Great Barrier Reef's special resources and its significance to life on our planet were formally recognized with an inscription to the UNESCO World Heritage list in 1981. It is one of the few to have satisfied all criteria required to receive the honour defined by the World Heritage Convention. East of the Great Barrier Reef are the reef complexes, uninhabited islands and sand cays of the Coral Sea, many of which lie over 200 nautical miles off the coast of Australia. An expanse of nearly 2.5 million sq km (1 million sq miles) of ocean, the Coral Sea contains hundreds of separate reefs, atolls, cays and seamounts. Many of these rise thousands of feet from the ocean floor to just beneath the surface.

The Coral Sea reef system differs from that of the Great Barrier Reef. Exposed to the power of the immense Pacific Ocean, the reef flat does not boast large expanses of coral.

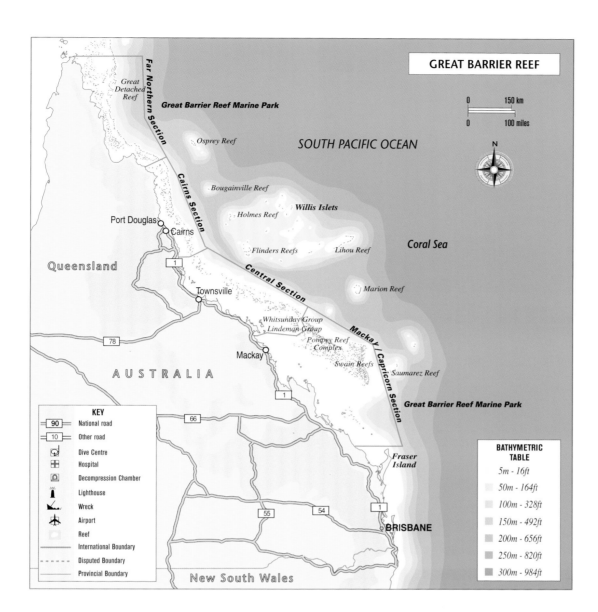

Like an oasis in a desert, the many submerged reefs attract a wide variety of fish either in schools of vast numbers or as solitary animals. The topography of the Coral Sea's formations includes spectacular walls, steep drop-offs and lone seamounts, as well as shallow gardens and gently sloping gradients. Renowned for crystal clear water with an average visibility in excess of 40m (130ft), a diver can appear suspended in air against a vertical wall laced with huge fans. The Coral Sea Reefs present an amazing display of massive Gorgonian Sea Fans and Sea Whips, and massive bright yellow soft corals. Sharks and pelagics are ever present while nudibranchs, anemones, unusual tropical fish, invertebrates, and huge schools of fish are predictably found. Surrounded by the shear beauty of these reefs in gin-clear water, divers need to pay attention to depths and bottom time.

The Great Barrier Reef, on the other hand, is an immense shallow area, averaging 15–30m (50–100ft) deep and 80–160km (50–100 miles) wide. Between the tides, an enormous volume of water roars in and out of the system daily. Fast currents of the turbid lagoon-type flow over sites within the reef, sometimes resulting in visibility of just 10m (33ft).

ACCESSIBILITY

However, quite a number of dive sites are not only very good, but can be reached from Cairns and the Whitsunday Islands by dayboat operators. Without a doubt live-aboards are the best option for serious divers who want to sample the Great Barrier Reef. Generally, live-aboard expeditions from Cairns and Townsville incorporate the Barrier Reef's Cod Hole, Pixie Pinnacles, Temple of Doom and the *Yongala* wreck into their itineraries.

TOP *A Coral Grouper hiding among the fronds of corals, from a photographer mistaken for a spearfisherman. Only five per cent of the Great Barrier Reef is protected marine reserve.*

ABOVE *Sergeant Major fish (*Abudefduf *spp.) shelter near stony coral. Many coral colonies are exposed at low tide in the Barrier Reef system.*

Queensland's scuba diving community, especially around Cairns, Port Douglas and Townsville, is a mature industry. It is well regulated by legislation, requiring high standards of safety control. Since most of the reef lies from 16km (10 miles) to 300km (187 miles) off the coast, most diving and snorkelling is done from boats or pontoons. There are facilities in most major towns along the Queensland coast, from where dive trips to the Great Barrier Reef can be arranged.

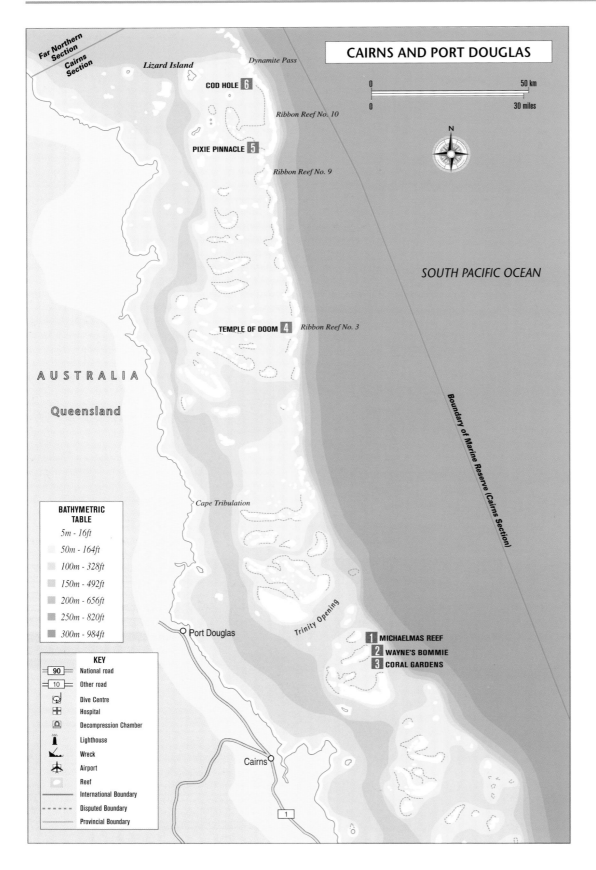

CAIRNS AND PORT DOUGLAS

there are over 50 vessels operating out of Cairns, Airlie Beach, Townsville, Port Douglas and Gladstone. With such an immense reef system, exploring the Great Barrier Reef and Coral Sea could take a lifetime and even then, one would only see a small part of it.

CAIRNS AND PORT DOUGLAS

Cairns is the gateway to the Great Barrier Reef with hundreds of operators offering resort-based diving and live-aboard trips, all departing from the doorstep of Cairns or Port Douglas. These vary in degree of comfort, exclusivity and budget, from single day trips to 10-day live-aboard expeditions to the clear waters of the Coral Sea. While some of the sites easily reached by day trip from Cairns are spectacular, the top sites are in the northern section of the Great Barrier Reef Marine Park. North of Cairns, the Ribbon Reefs comprise a string of 10 coral ramparts and cover a distance of about 160km (100 miles) from Lizard Island almost to Cape Tribulation.

There are many famous sites to choose from such as Pixie Pinnacle, The Temple of Doom, and Dynamite Pass, but there are also many spectacular sites not frequented by the 'regular-departure' live-aboards, and one can stop almost anywhere and expect a fabulous dive. Coral formations vary from beds of huge plate corals to isolated pinnacles sustaining an amazing display of fish life, to walls and channels for perfect drift dives as well as caves, canyons and shallow coral gardens. The best way to appreciate the Great Barrier Reef is a short live-aboard trip to the Ribbon Reefs. One boat offers four to five day trips leaving Cairns every Tuesday and Friday. The Friday trip includes Osprey Reef renowned for an abundance of sharks and a couple of dives at the world-famous Cod Hole. During winter you may even swim with the Dwarf Minke Whales around the Ribbon Reef area. As always, the sites on the edge of the very outer Great Barrier Reef have better visibility than fringing islands and patch reefs closer to the mainland.

On a number of the day trips that are offered on catamarans at Cairns, Port Douglas and Townsville, videos about the reef are shown on the outward and return trips. Guided snorkelling tours are presented at most centres, and general snorkelling, scuba diving and introductory dive packages are also available. Some dive operators present underwater naturalist courses, which are certificate courses presented as workshops over two days full-time, or part-time over a week. Marine biologists regularly present talks on various aspects of marine biology. For extended expeditions to the Coral Sea and the Ribbon Reefs,

TOP SITES

1 MICHAELMAS REEF

About 45km (28miles) northeast of Cairns, Michaelmas has extensive coral coverage and a number of pinnacles, which serve as food stops for pelagic fish. Tunas and jacks are often seen. Endowed with lush Gorgonian Sea Fans and soft corals, the reefs are popular. Thousands of sea birds nest at the sand cay at the southern end of the reef. Just off this cay are some lovely coral gardens and large numbers of pinnacles. **Wayne's Bommie** 2 consists of dozens of pinnacles that seem to be packed with fish life. You are likely to find giant clams nested on the bottom, shy cuttlefish, turtles, Whitetip Reef Sharks, Bluespotted Ribbontail (Fantail) Rays wedged under plate corals and even Manta Rays. There are more towering pinnacles at the **Coral Gardens** 3 which seem to attract a large selection of pelagic fish. Divers regularly encounter Dogtooth Tuna, Spanish Mackerel, Coral Grouper, Humphead (Napoleon or Maori) Wrasse, schools of fusiliers and barracuda, and reef sharks. The pinnacles are riddled with small caves and coated with lovely coral growths. Small reef fish are omnipresent and numerous invertebrates hide in the corals.

4 TEMPLE OF DOOM

One of the fishiest dive sites in the world, the Temple of Doom is a massive pinnacle on the western side of Ribbon Reef No. 3. It is over 30m (100ft) in diameter and justifiably known as the fish aquarium of the Barrier Reef. As soon as you hit the water you find yourself surrounded by large schools of yellow goatfish, Bluefin Trevallies, Bluelined Snappers, fusiliers, tuna, mackerel, barracuda and Coral Groupers. The site pulsates with life and luxuriates in a lush coverage of staghorn corals on the reef top. Because of its abundance and variety of fish and invertebrate life, Temple of Doom was the location selected for *Metamorphosea*, the world's first 24-hour dive that documented the cycle of life on a coral reef continuously from 12 noon to 12 noon in 1995. The pinnacle falls steeply to 30m (100ft) and the slope is generously covered with gorgonias, black coral trees, sea whips, sponges and some lovely soft corals. A number of small ledges cut into the pinnacle, making a suitable habitat for moray eels and crayfish. Whitetip Reef Sharks are also commonly seen, as are sweetlips, groupers (known locally as gropers), stingrays and Eagle Rays.

5 PIXIE PINNACLE

Located 165km (103 miles) north of Port Douglas, on the western end pass of Ribbon Reef No. 9 and No. 10, Pixie Pinnacle is like a large coral bommie protruding from the bottom, overflowing with colourful sea fans, and home to a profusion of reef life. It is one of the most illustrious dive sites in the world, home to every group of organism found on the Great Barrier Reef. Divers should take time to explore the many overhangs and small caves that riddle the pinnacle – each packed with beautiful, spiky soft corals, hydroid corals, *Tubastrea* corals and small gorgonias. The pinnacle rises from 40m (130ft) to near surface where it is just 15m (50ft) in diameter.

The walls are steep and coated with corals, anemones, sea whips, soft corals and gorgonias. Among the feather stars, sea whips and fans are swarms of pink Anthias (Fairy Basslets) feeding in passing currents. The fish life includes lionfish, groupers, hawkfish, wrasse, butterflyfish, cardinalfish, squirrelfish, filefish and angelfish. Reef sharks, Eagle Rays, barracuda, jobfish, fusiliers, mackerel and batfish swim off the pinnacle. Photographers will find that they quickly run out of film here. After dark, Pixie Pinnacle is even more

ABOVE *Goatfish swarm over the reef in large shoals, feeding as they go, at the Temple of Doom.*

ABOVE *Colonial or Seafan Anemones (*Amphianthus *spp.) are colonial and found mostly on dead whip corals and wrecks in deeper water.*

WHALES ON THE GBR
DWARF MINKE WHALES

The Ribbon Reefs are a string of twisting coral fortifications stretching along the outer edge of the Northern Great Barrier Reef. Designated Reef No. 1–10, the Ribbons can be up to 25km (15 miles) long, but rarely over 500m (1640ft) wide. On the ocean side, the reef plummets to several hundred metres, while the other side of the reef falls gently to shallow gullies conducive to lush coral gardens and outcrops.

Between June and July, the Dwarf Minke Whales visit the Ribbon Reefs and interactions with snorkellers are frequent. Though they are smaller than those of the North Atlantic, any encounter with whales underwater is an unforgettable experience. Cetacean biologists have yet to determine this Minke's taxonomic status, but it does appear to be a distinct subspecies of the typical Minke, *Balaenopera acutorostrata*.

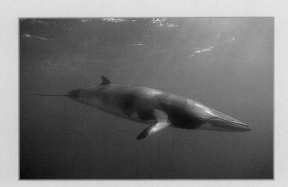

The maximum length reported of Great Barrier Reef Minke Whales is 9m (30ft), but those regularly sighted average about 5m (16ft). Females are usually about 1m (3ft) longer with an estimated weight of 6–7 tonnes. They belong to the suborder of *Mysticetes* in the 78 known species of cetacean (the biological classification/order of whales and dolphins). Minkes are rorquals. Their distinctive prominent head ridge and acutely pointed triangular snout with an all-round broad lower jaw, seemingly in perpetual smile, give them character. Their robust physique, insulated by several centimetres (inches) of blubber, makes them the roly-poly of the family. Like dolphins, minkes also use sound to 'see' their environment and look for food, friends and predators. Since enlarged outer ears would be useless underwater, their skulls sense sound vibrations directly, as do other cetaceans.

Though our Dwarf Minkes are similar in shape and form to their bigger cousins, they have some distinctive characteristics. The outer half of their flippers is dark grey to black, whereas the inner section is almost pure white. There is also a pure white patch on the shoulder area where the flipper meets the body. The area between the mouth and the flipper is dark grey to black. The top of the head is distinctly lighter than other parts of the body; this combination is said to be unique to the 'junior' minke whales.

Whales lead one of the most inconvenient lives on earth. They live in the ocean, but they must come all the way to the surface to breathe. They live with all the glorious chewy seafood around them, but they have no teeth. Minkes are baleen whales; rather than teeth, they have 200–300 pairs of baleen plates hanging from the roof of the mouth. The throat of the minke is designed to expand enormously and between their 300 pairs of baleen plates, they engulf tons of water in one gulp; usually full of krill and small schooling fish. There are no recorded sightings of feeding by the 'junior' minke in Australian waters. In fact, no one knows of their diving capabilities.

We do know, however, that our 'junior' minkes prefer to live in the southern hemisphere; they are sighted in warm, temperate and tropical waters of Australia, New Zealand, Southern Atlantic coast of South America and New Caledonia. Sightings have also been reported in Sub-Antarctic and Antarctic waters as far south as 65°S latitude in the summer months from December to March. Like other baleen whales they probably follow the same migration pattern between feeding grounds in the southern ocean and the tropical sea, but this is far from conclusive.

According to an Australian authority on minke whales, Dr Peter Arnold of the Museum of Tropical Queensland, they are sighted during the austral winter from as far south as the Swain Reef to as far north as Lizard Island. Sightings are seasonal and research indicates that 80% of encounters are in the months of June and July and they are frequently found near the southwest corner of Ribbon Reef No. 3, commonly referred to as Steve's Bommie and Temple of Doom. Swimming with whales is an incomparable experience – the awe of an eye-to-eye meeting with a massive cetacean several times your own size.

---

colourful under torchlight. Many small reef creatures appear, including Mantis Shrimps, flatworms, coral crabs, molluscs, decorator crabs, coral shrimps and nudibranchs. Nestled within colourful coral and caves are parrotfish, sea turtles, fusiliers and butterflyfish, somehow creating a surrealistic landscape worthy of a lifetime of exploration.

6 COD HOLE

In the northern end of Ribbon Reef No. 10, a patch reef of 10–25m (33–80ft) wide, is Cod Hole, world famous for its boisterous Potato Cod. As soon as divers enter the water, from six to twelve 100kg (220 lb) fish will show up for a free hand-out. Waltzing among the divers, the cod are accustomed to look out for the divemaster who will put on a show, hand-feeding them with offerings of fish and sometimes even a kiss on a fleshy cheek! A débâcle sometimes ensues while the big fish jostle each other, and sometimes the divers, to get the food. They have to be quick because several Leopard Morays, other groupers and large Humphead (Napoleon) Wrasse also home in for a free meal. Beware, the cod can be overzealous during feeding time and are known to swallow gloves, which will inevitably cause their demise. Strictly speaking, gloves should not be worn on this dive. Even without food offering, the cod are easily approached and will indeed pose for photographers. Though the Potato Cod is the main attraction, the reef is also populated by a variety of ornamental reef fish, rays, reef sharks and invertebrates. Pelagics often sweep past the reef; mackerels, tuna and Giant Trevallies are frequent visitors. Indeed, the Cod Hole is the signature dive of the Great Barrier Reef.

NORTHERN CORAL SEA

Blue, gin-clear water is the signature of Coral Sea diving. It is one of those magical places that give the illusion of being able to see forever underwater. Harbouring some of the most photogenic seascapes in the world, the marine life is astounding and spectacular. Some say the best diving in the world can be done here – with drop-offs one kilometre (half a mile) deep, pinnacles the size of office blocks, countless numbers of caves, huge gorgonias and soft corals, sharks, Manta Rays and schooling pelagic fish. The Northern Coral Sea reefs are completely different to most of those found in the south. Significantly, there are more sharks but fewer sea snakes. All these reefs are the tips of ancient mountains, long covered by rising seas. Some form large lagoon basins, others are just towering columns of coral, but all fall quickly into the abyss.

7 8 HOLMES REEF

Split into two halves, the reef structures of Holmes Reef lie just 220km (120 nautical miles) to the east of Cairns. It is a good example of the Coral Sea, which can be visited by day trip. It consists of East and West Holmes and two small sand banks that break surface at low tide. Below, steep slopes and vertical walls rise from 1500m (5000ft); and caves, tunnels and caverns are dotted around shallow, sheltered lagoons. When the current is running, the diving at the

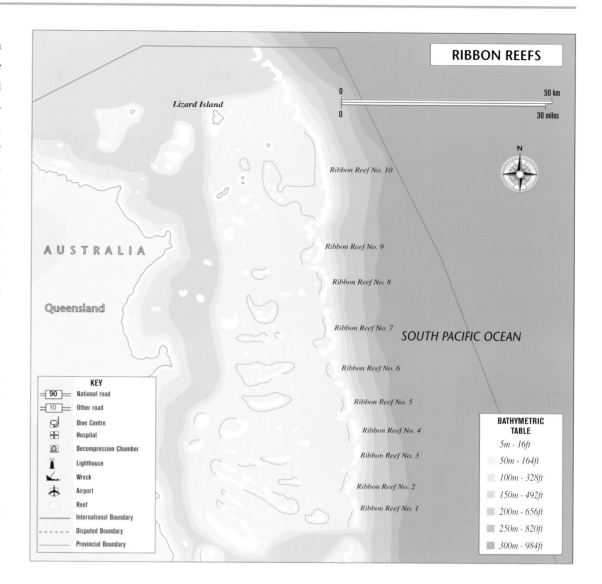

RIBBON REEFS

Lizard Island

AUSTRALIA

Queensland

Ribbon Reef No. 10

Ribbon Reef No. 9

Ribbon Reef No. 8

Ribbon Reef No. 7   SOUTH PACIFIC OCEAN

Ribbon Reef No. 6

Ribbon Reef No. 5

Ribbon Reef No. 4

Ribbon Reef No. 3

Ribbon Reef No. 2

Ribbon Reef No. 1

KEY

90	National road
10	Other road
	Dive Centre
	Hospital
	Decompression Chamber
	Lighthouse
	Wreck
	Airport
	Reef
	International Boundary
	Disputed Boundary
	Provincial Boundary

BATHYMETRIC TABLE

5m - 16ft
50m - 164ft
100m - 328ft
150m - 492ft
200m - 656ft
250m - 820ft
300m - 984ft

ABOVE *Several Potato Cod (Grouper)* (Epinephelus tukula) *of up to 100kg (220 lb) will show up for a free hand-out as soon as divers enter the water at Cod Hole.*

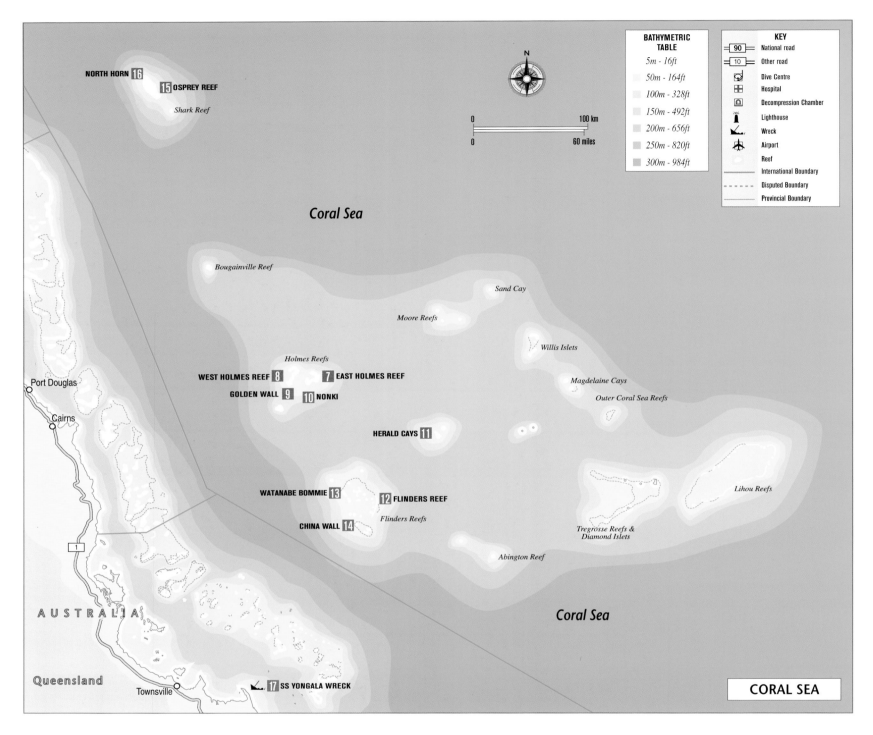

Golden Wall 9 – a sheer coral wall covered with lush yellow sponges and soft corals – is an adrenaline fix, as one flies along the wall that dissolves into the blue yonder with its incredible visibility. Enormous gorgonias lace the walls. Turtles, Manta Rays, schools of pelagics, sharks and even the occasional Whale Shark can be seen here. **Nonki** 10, a dive site named by a Japanese diver, is a comparatively easy-going site comprising three huge pinnacles rising from 30m (100ft) to 5m (16ft). There are overhangs and caverns cut into the pinnacles, all cov-

ered with sessile animals and soft corals. Various colours of sea fans jostle for space against a profusion of stony corals, which cover the entire pinnacle slope.

11 HERALD CAYS

Lying 100km (62 miles) to the southeast of Holmes Reef, the Herald Cays are two sandy islets that are home to a unique selection of rare sea birds, including terns and frigates. This twin reef complex is surrounded by steep drop-offs, with a sheltered lagoon between them. The drop-offs are packed with

a variety of stony and soft corals, delicate hydroid corals, *Tubastrea* corals, black coral trees, verdant soft corals, orange Gorgonian Sea Fans, Gorgonian Sea Whips, sponges and expanses of stony coral. Reef fish are abundant and large schools of pelagic fish, groupers (locally known as gropers), Humphead (Napoleon or Maori) Wrasse or Eagle Rays visit. Reef sharks become constant companions, and the occasional Whitetip Reef Shark sleeps in a cave. Herald Cays is also nesting ground for Green Sea Turtles which visit the region to lay their eggs in the last few months of the year. Hundreds of turtles come into the cay for a night to nest. Hatchlings emerge in January. Herald Cays is seldom visited and a treat for divers who also enjoy the natural wonders of the Great Barrier Reef and Coral Sea above the tide.

12 FLINDERS REEF

One of the larger of the Coral Sea reef systems, Flinders Reef includes a cluster of reefs in an area of 66 by 26km (41 by 16 miles). Because it is only 220km (137 miles) from Townsville, it is the most popular and regularly visited of all the Coral Sea Reefs. The Flinders Reef is multifaceted with coral formations, cays and two islets just above the surface, which are home to sea birds, turtles, and hermit crabs. Sites vary from 1000m (3281ft) walls and arrays of pinnacles, to coral gardens and seamounts emerging from the ocean depths. Grey Reef, Blacktip Reef and Silvertip Sharks, barracuda, Bigeye Trevallies and rays as well as the exotic cuttlefish, sea hares and Whitemouth Morays are seen. In sandy lagoons, small coral heads are home to parrotfish, triggerfish, pufferfish, Humphead (Napoleon or Maori) Wrasse, coral trout, gobies, blennies and various molluscs and sea stars.

On the western side of Flinders is **Watanabe Bommie** 13, a giant pinnacle regarded as one of the most action-packed dive sites in the Coral Sea. Though the towering pinnacle is encrusted with wonderful corals, it is the swarms of barracuda, Bigeye Trevallies, Rainbow Runners, Leopard Coralgrouper, Dog-tooth Tuna, surgeonfish, and clouds of fusiliers that make this site appealing to divers. Often one can find oneself engulfed in an electrifying commotion as the sharks and jacks chase the fusiliers through a whirlpool of silvery barracuda – an experience one will want to relive frequently. **China Wall** 14 is another exciting dive in the Flinders vicinity. The wall face is covered with soft corals, sponges, gorgonias, feather stars and small stony coral colonies. Large fish such as tuna, mackerel, Rainbow Runners and Giant Trevallies are predictably sighted.

NORTH HORN AND OSPREY REEF

Osprey Reef 15 lies in the Coral Sea nearly 160km (100 miles) to the east-northeast of Lizard Island. This Coral Sea reef is 21km (134 miles) long and boasts more than 30m (100ft) visibility and 1000m (3300ft) vertical walls. Many divers consider this reef to be the ultimate reef diving adventure. Not only can the largest and most spectacularly coloured soft corals in the world be found here, but the large reef system also has a healthy shark population and **North Horn** 16, a reef shelf at a depth of between 12m (40ft) and 45m (150ft), is world famous for its shark action. Often divers will descend into a group of five or six resident Whitetip Reef Sharks and several Grey Reef Sharks. In deeper water Silvertip Sharks are often found among coral outcrops and, if one is moderately lucky, oceanic Whitetip sharks, Great Hammerheads, Thresher and the odd lone Tiger Shark. North Horn is also the site where most live-aboards conduct their shark feeds. However, even without the hand-out, the shark interaction is exceptionally good. One of the most significant features of this reef is the population of hammerhead sharks. In winter and spring large schools of hammerheads are predictably seen off the wall. Besides the sharks, the shelf is also home to large friendly Potato cod, schools of trevallies and barracudas. Eagle Rays and Manta Rays are also often seen. Of course, when you get bored with the big-fish action, there's always the giant soft corals found in deeper water.

17 WRECK OF THE *YONGALA*

Undoubtedly Queensland's best wreck dive is the SS *Yongala*, a passenger and general cargo steamer lost in a cyclone in 1911. The wreck owes its popularity not to its history or superstructure, but to the amazing concentration of fish life that now resides on the wreck. It is now protected under both the GBR Marine Park regulations and the Commonwealth's Historic Shipwreck Act (1976). Resting on a 30m (100ft) bottom, just 24km (15 miles)

offshore, the wreck is easily accessible from Townsville and easily located by permanent mooring. The vessel lies on its starboard site, with the deepest point at 33m (108ft) under the bow. Descending to the wreck is an overwhelming experience, requiring a swim through myriad layers of batfish and Sweetlips. The deck at 15m (50ft) is completely encrusted with sessile life, anemones with clownfish and one will be surrounded by groupers, sea snakes and Blotched Fantail Ray. One particularly overgrown grouper is nicknamed VW – because of its size. Large oysters line the wreck's interior and underside, and piles of dead shells lie on the sand. The entire surface of the hull is covered with chunky sponges and coral growth. Seemingly this 110m (360ft) wreck has become the oasis in the desert sea. Many consider the *Yongala* to be one of the world's top dive sites. However, due to its proximity to shore, dives are often cancelled due to bad surface conditions and, of course, the *Yongala* is addictive – once is never enough.

ABOVE *Wrecks are protected under the GBR Marine Park regulations and also the Commonwealth's Historic Shipwreck Act of 1976.*

NEW ZEALAND

by Wade Doak

DIVING IS ONE OF NEW ZEALAND'S MANY adrenaline-charged outdoor activities. The country's intricate coastline is almost as long as that of the continental United States of America, but the total population is only four million. Diving experiences range from the Poor Knights Islands in the north to the spectacular fiords of the southwest region. There are even good diving locations within an hour's drive of the main city, Auckland. Water temperatures range from thin sheet ice in the southern fiords in winter to 24°C (75°F) in the northern bays in peak summer. Make no mistake, however, protective suits are needed.

Most visitors would prefer the warm period despite the possibility of cyclones, but winter offers the opportunity of a side trip to world-class ski fields.

A process is under way to protect ten per cent of coastal waters with total no-take marine reserves. Severe penalties are in place for violating such areas with huge fines even for feeding the fish.

TOP LEFT *A yacht sails by a sea arch carved from volcanic rock as it enters South Harbour off Aorangi Island.*

TOP RIGHT *The rugged islands are protected as a marine reserve and landing is strictly forbidden without prior permission. The intention is to protect ten per cent of coastal waters.*

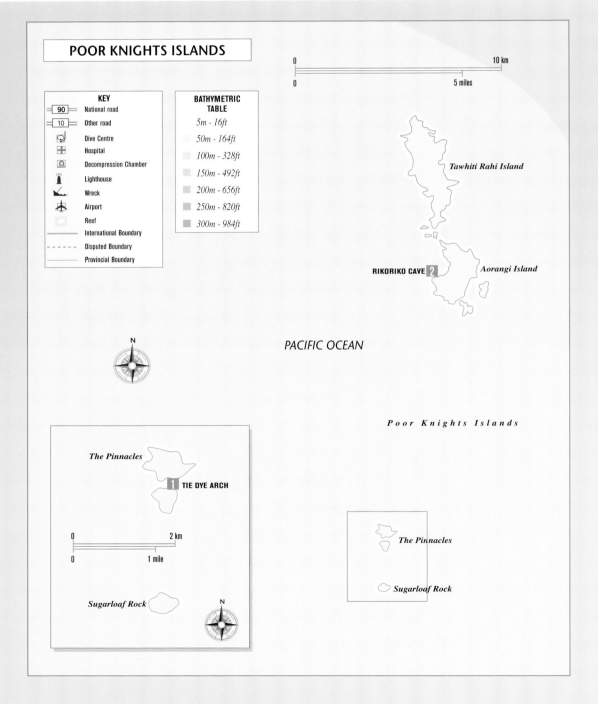

POOR KNIGHTS ISLANDS

Situated just 23km (14 miles) off the North Island, the uninhabited Poor Knights offer world-class diving in a marine reserve. The main island group is some 5km (3 miles) long and 800m (a half mile) wide. It consists of flat-topped, high-cliffed and densely forested volcanic rocks, and is home to a prolific number of birds. Landing is forbidden except with prior permission. The islands offer sanctuary to some fascinating creatures, including the Tuatara – a lizard-like living fossil that occurs only on New Zealand's offshore islands – and some giant insects. The islands are the only nesting grounds on earth for a species of petrel that feeds in the arctic. Between descents, resting divers can delight in the songs of forest birds, while being on the alert for occasional free-falling giant wetas (huge, ugly grasshoppers).

The Poor Knights Islands were created 10 million years ago when a volcano off North Island's east coast burst through the earth's crust in a display of boiling molten rock. As the lava cooled, gas pockets, hot water and high-pressure steam sculpted the landscape into a maze of corridors, grottoes and curved domes. Over time, with rising sea levels, the ocean eroded and carved the volcanic rock into a vast labyrinth. Diving here is like flying through the galleries of a giant's castle. Strange experiences might include an encounter with a giant salp, a transparent, open-ended floating barrel big enough for a diver to enter and swim around inside.

The waters of the Poor Knights boast a wider range of fish species than the rest of New Zealand, and their size and approachability are

a delight. It is a fusion of subtropical and temperate species, which includes coral fish, kelpfish (*Chironemus marmoratus*), demoiselles, wrasse, scorpionfish, and five species of moray.

Divers usually commute daily from Tutukaka, although it is possible to arrange overnight trips for parties of eight. A 30-minute drive from the city of Whangarei, Tutukaka is also the gateway to a popular surfing spot, an array of tiny sheltered coves and isolated beaches, mangroves, and the idyllic Matapouri Bay.

☐ TIE DYE ARCH

At the Pinnacles is a submerged throughway which can be entered at twin gothic archways. The ocean courses steadily through a submerged hallway that is the equivalent of six storeys high, to give the diver the surrealistic feel of swimming through Westminster Abbey. Spread over every inch of the vaulted ceilings, broad walls and the massive boulders on the floor is a crazy quilt of tiny mouths – a celebration of ocean life at its best. Fish often cram the hallway wall to wall and in summer squadrons of stingrays cruise the portals.

ABOVE RIGHT *In deeper water there are sponges and night-stalking Mosaic Morays find daytime refuge in cracks surrounded by feather stars, mossy bryozoans and coralline structures.*

RIGHT *In clear water and good light penetration kelp flourishes among Erect Sponges, and other filter feeders.*

2 RIKORIKO CAVE

One of the largest sea caves in the world, Riko-riko Cave, which is a 60m (200ft) sphere half filled with ocean. A surface cul de sac, its tubular entrance is large enough to admit yachts. As you swim towards the back of the cave, choosing a depth of only 10m (33ft), the light level drops dramatically until it is equivalent to the light at an ocean depth of 100m (330ft). As your eyes adjust to the twilight, you will see conditions similar to that on the continental shelf: reef fish galore, walls of gorgonias, yellow sea daisies (zoanthids), cleaner shrimps. In the furthest recesses lives a tiny, salad green solitary polyp. Previous records of its habitat were from sunless regions 2000m (6562ft) down.

The Poor Knights have much to offer in addition to its wealth of sea caves and steep walls. Between the islands, sand-floored avenues and steep pinnacles provide optimal conditions for reef fish: constant, gentle currents from the tropics, shelter from wave violence, and sunlit seaweed jungles. Many divers prefer seaweed forests to coral reefs because, without the fluctuant grace and colour of seaweed and other sea plants, the reef can become a 'treeless' monotony.

3 FIORDLAND – SW NEW ZEALAND

A descent in Fiordland is among the weirdest of dives. A world of drowned U-shaped valleys; 200 kilometres of the most deeply indented coastline on earth and one of the world's wettest places, with up to 9m (30ft) of annual rainfall. Along each fiord a river of fresh water up to 10m (33ft) deep flows. A tanin-stained, chill surface layer conceals a warm, crystal clear, twilit world where black corals grow along a contour from 10m (33ft) to around 50m (165ft). You leap from the charterboat into stinging cold beer – there's a shimmering, oily effect where fresh water meets salt. You blink – visibility opens up to 30m (100ft) and a warm flow wafts in from the sea. It's a world tipped on edge, seething with fish and so bizarre it could be a reef on some alien planet.

Red corals, sea pens and black coral galore like huge white apple trees, thick trunks, multibranched, with boldly patterned snake stars entwined on every stem. Penguins, seals, curious Bottlenose Dolphins – in Fiordland you dive one of Earth's last pristine places, its life patterns scarcely changed since the last ice age ten thousand years ago.

Marine life is extremely diverse, with many invertebrates, especially black coral trees. Calm conditions on the vertical walls make encrusting life very accessible. There are Bottlenose Dolphins all year, mainly in Doubtful and Dusky Sounds, sometimes Milford.

Of the penguins, Little Blues can be seen all year and the Fiordland Crested from July to December. There are seals in most fiords, but it is not advisable to dive with seals from December to January.

Sea pens and deep water species can be seen at divable depths.

GOAT ISLAND MARINE RESERVE AT LEIGH

Since becoming New Zealand's first marine reserve in 1977 Goat Island just keeps on getting better. Ninety minutes' drive north of Auckland city, it compresses the best of NZ inshore diving into one area – a gateway to the ocean seething with marine life, with unbelievably friendly fish, huge rock lobsters (called crayfish in New Zealand) and waving kelp forests.

LEFT *Fifty miles north of the Poor Knights, in a sheltered cove at the Cavalli Islands, the famous* Rainbow Warrior *lies in her grave, a shrine for visiting divers and a Taj Mahal of jewel anemones.*

ABOVE *Jewel Anemones* (Corynactis haddoni) *form colonies of same-hue individuals because they reproduce asexually by budding (as well as sexually). The subtle arrays of colours and diadem patterns are photogenic.*

ABOVE *Tiny triplefins of many species abound at all New Zealand dive sites and delight photographers with their vivid patterns, inquisitive attitude and feisty mien. Nest-guarding males will even drive off divers.*

Big snappers are the dominators, at the top of the local food chain, sweeping to and fro with curious eyes, powerful jaws, argent gill plates and spikey dorsal fins that rise like hackles during skirmishes. Just as shot silk catches the light, their iridescent freckles glow or fade to copper with each turn. Amid them weave Pin Striped Parore (*Girella tricuspidata*) known elsewhere as Luderick or Blackfish, silvery slim Kahawai (*Arripus trutta*) or Australian Salmon, triggerfish, Blue Maomao (*Scorpis violaceus*) and wrasses with rat-like teeth. A kelpfish clings to the rock with its hand-like pectorals. A big Blue Cod (*Parapercis colias*), frowning mouth agape, arches its back ready to strike.

You can dive on the deeper water **Sponge Garden** 4 , explore seaweed jungles near the **Waterfall** 5 or the **caves** 6 at the north tip of Goat Island where transient dolphins ambush prey, but wherever you descend here, fish surround you like a pop star. For the fish watcher Goat Island is a one-stop shop.

Marine life is diverse with a variety of invertebrates. Reef fish are abundant, large and tame. Dolphins and orca are transients.

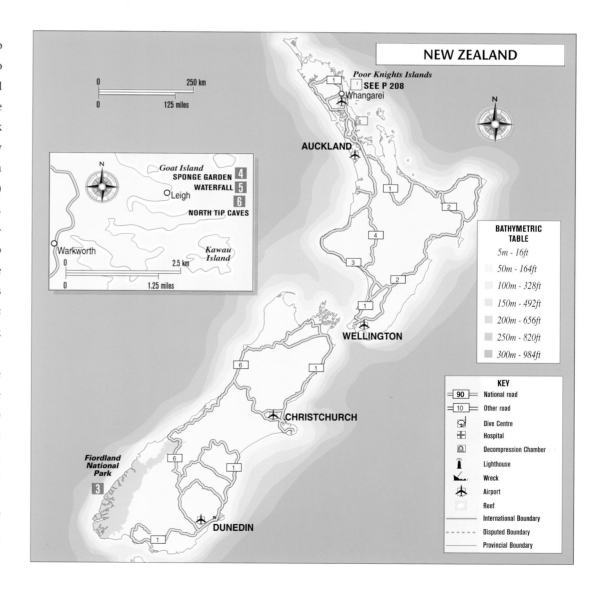

CANADA

by Lawson Wood

VANCOUVER ISLAND LIES IN A NORTHWESTERLY orientation just off the coast of British Columbia in western Canada. The island is the same length as England and has a total land area equivalent to all of Ireland. It takes around three hours to travel from the east to the west coast and over seven hours to travel from Victoria, the island and state capital in the south, all the way up the east coast to Port Hardy.

The trip across to Departure Bay on Vancouver Island takes around one and a half hours by *BC* ferry from Horseshoe Bay, just north of Vancouver. Nanaimo is a gateway town for the island and most visitors arrive at this well-laid-out city. Hotels and guesthouses offer good quality accommodation at little expense. Nearby dive shops are able to fill Nitrox and Trimix for the aficionados of the technical side of the sport.

One of the most outstanding aspects of diving around Vancouver Island is the chance encounter with large animals such as whales, sea lions, Giant Octopuses and the millions

TOP LEFT *Also called The Thousand Islands, the Pacific Rim National Park covers huge tracts of Vancouver Island's west coast.*

TOP RIGHT *Humpback Whales follow the salmon up Vancouver Island's west coast and can be seen breaching in Barklay Sound. Individuals are recognized by markings on the tail.*

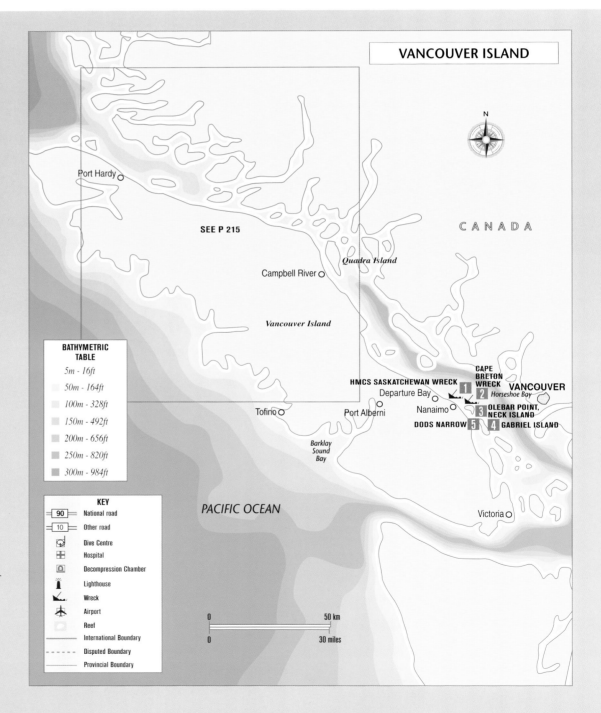

VANCOUVER ISLAND

CANADA

SEE P 215

Port Hardy

Quadra Island

Campbell River

Vancouver Island

HMCS SASKATCHEWAN WRECK
CAPE BRETON WRECK
Departure Bay
Tofino
Port Alberni
Nanaimo
VANCOUVER
Horseshoe Bay
OLEBAR POINT, NECK ISLAND
DODS NARROW
GABRIEL ISLAND

Barklay Sound Bay

PACIFIC OCEAN

Victoria

BATHYMETRIC TABLE

5m - 16ft
50m - 164ft
100m - 328ft
150m - 492ft
200m - 656ft
250m - 820ft
300m - 984ft

KEY

90	National road
10	Other road
	Dive Centre
	Hospital
	Decompression Chamber
	Lighthouse
	Wreck
	Airport
	Reef
	International Boundary
	Disputed Boundary
	Provincial Boundary

0 ____ 50 km
0 ____ 30 miles

of salmon which pass through the rivers each spawning season. Giant Octopuses (*Enteroctopus dofleini*) can be found all over, often making their home in the jumbled concrete blocks used in the construction of ports and marinas. Growing to a span of 9m (30ft), a full-grown adult can be quite formidable, but they are actually quite shy. They only venture out at dusk to feed at night on large Puget Sound Crabs. Their lairs are easy to spot because of the debris field of broken crab and clam shells littering its entrance.

NANAIMO

Nanaimo has some superb diving and should not be overlooked in the rush to dive the exposed western or northern coastline. The *HMCS Saskatchewan* and the **Cape Breton** [2] are located just offshore. Nearby Neck Island, Gabriel Island and **Dods Narrows** [5] are exceptional for photography and marine life encounters. Nanaimo and the state capital, Victoria, were the only places where we stayed at independent hotels. The rest of the diving is done from dive lodges on the island.

[1] *HMCS SASKATCHEWAN,*

Twenty minutes east of Nanaimo is the final resting place of the *HMCS Saskatchewan*, a former Canadian Navy frigate, which was sunk as an artificial reef in 1997. The Fraser River run-off tints the surface layers of the water a peaty brown (no problem for us Scottish divers), but below this halocline the vista opens up to reveal the massive ship. Its shallowest end is at 20m (65ft), dropping to 34m (112ft). Nearby Snake Island has a population of around 150 harbour seals which often 'buzz' you on the wreck, which is great fun.

TOP RIGHT *The Canadian frigate* HMCS Saskatchewan *was sunk as an artificial reef in 1997. The main deck is at 20m (65ft).*

RIGHT *Due to the nutrient-rich water along the east coast of Vancouver Island, wreckage is quickly covered in a patina of Plumose Anemones, feather stars and sea urchins.*

③ OLEBAR POINT,
④ GABRIEL ISLAND

The wall at Gabriel Island just drops away from the rolling edge at 12m (40ft) in vertical slabs way beyond sport diving depths on air. My dive buddy for the day was an ex-Canadian Navy diver using a military-issue rebreather and he dropped to over 80m (260ft) for his 45-minute dive. Back in reality at 25m (80ft) there are horizontal ledges which have shrimps, sea cucumbers, sea stars and groupers. The wall has thousands of large red anemones, very similar to Dahlia Anemones.

BARKLAY SOUND BAY

Three hours' drive to the west brings you to Port Alberni where you catch the *Lady Rose* ferry down the Alberni fiord. The remote site is isolated in massive Barklay Sound Bay where Humpback Whales breech the surface chasing the migrating herring schools, and Steller Sea Lions bask on the rocky offshore islands, barking at the passing divers.

Barklay Sound is also one of the few locations where one can see the Six-gill Shark (*Hexanchus griseus*). Thought to be extremely rare and to have preferred deeper, dark waters, Six-gilled Sharks are now seen regularly during the summer months where they have around 40 pups in the shallow waters of the sound.

Further up the coast is Tofino, situated in the heart of the Pacific Rim National Park, excellent for someone looking for whale action. A 45-minute flight, the cost of which

TOP LEFT *Copper Cliffs off Quadra Island drop vertically to over 30m (100ft) and are smothered in jewel anemones, Plumose Anemones, fan worms, and sea stars.*

CENTRE LEFT *The Wolf Fish (Eel)* (Anarrhichthys ocellatus) *is quite approachable. Its ugly visage is a symbol of Vancouver Island diving.*

BOTTOM LEFT *Sculpins dot the crevices and walls on all the dive sites. Several species of sculpin are found in these waters and most have the ability to change their coloration.*

DEEP-WATER NUTRIENTS

Most marine organisms live near the surface, but those that die without being predated, sink, and as they sink, they slowly decompose and release nutrients back into the water. Thus ocean deep water is rich in nutrients. When upwelling occurs, these nutrients are forced to the surface where they stimulate the growth of algae and phytoplankton living near the surface. These, in turn, form the base of the ocean's food chain, so that when they prosper, all the larger organisms also feed well.

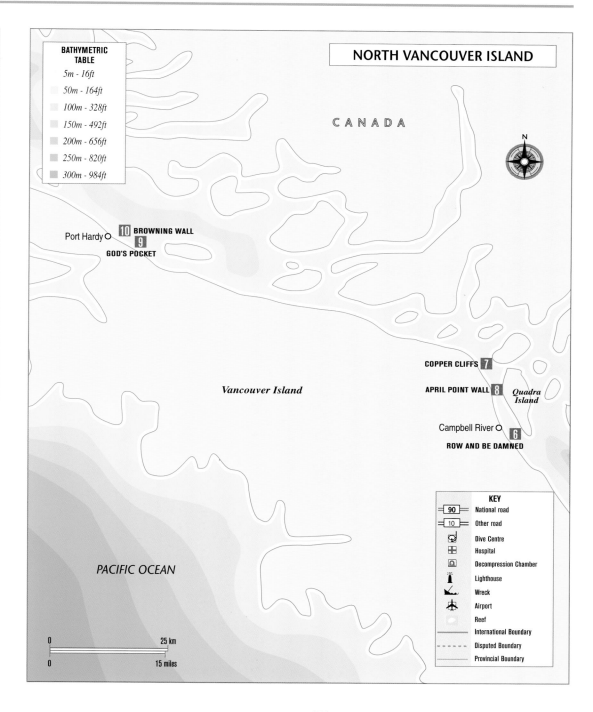

NORTH VANCOUVER ISLAND

BATHYMETRIC TABLE
5m - 16ft
50m - 164ft
100m - 328ft
150m - 492ft
200m - 656ft
250m - 820ft
300m - 984ft

CANADA

Port Hardy ○ · [10] **BROWNING WALL**
[9]
GOD'S POCKET

Vancouver Island

COPPER CLIFFS [7]

APRIL POINT WALL [8] *Quadra Island*

Campbell River ○ [6]
ROW AND BE DAMNED

PACIFIC OCEAN

KEY
90 National road
10 Other road
Dive Centre
Hospital
Decompression Chamber
Lighthouse
Wreck
Airport
Reef
International Boundary
Disputed Boundary
Provincial Boundary

0 — 25 km
0 — 15 miles

can be shared by three people, will get you to the natural hot springs, which flow into the sea at over 40°C (105°F). The Thousand Islands, as they are known, look superb from the air as well as underwater with some fabulous walls, exciting drift dives, tons of marine life, with fish eagles and whales seen on virtually every trip out in the boat.

QUADRA ISLAND, CAMPBELL RIVER

Moving back to the east coast and up-island, the next centre for diving is Campbell River, a short ferry ride across to Quadra Island. Campbell River is famous for its strong currents, vertical walls and abundance of marine life at sites such as Row and Be Damned, **Copper Cliffs** [7] and **April Point Wall** [8].

Row and Be Damned [6] is another wall dive where converging currents pull the kelp flat and sweep the outer rocks bare of anything other than encrusting coralline algae and huge Puget Sound Crabs that appear oblivious to the water movement. At the bottom of the wall, at 20m (65ft), there are some huge boulders that offer shelter to more delicate marine organisms such as the small Strawberry Anemone and the brilliantly

coloured Snubnose Sculpin (*Orthonopias triacis*). Other colourful fish here are the Painted Greenling (*Oxylebius pictus*) with its brilliant red vertical bands and the similarly coloured Tiger Rockfish (*Sebastes nigrocintus*), which is quite shy, but also brilliantly marked.

It is possible to snorkel the Campbell River to view thousands of salmon in spawning season.

God's Pocket [9] is a 30-minute ferry ride east of Port Hardy, which has fish eagles instead of seagulls. (And casual sightings of bears wandering across the main road.) Everything here is bigger, brighter, more colourful and with more of it, than at any other temperate water destination in the world.

[10] BROWNING WALL, PORT HARDY

If you were to combine all the previous dives, add a few whales, Wolf Fish and Puget Sound Crabs, then you will have Browning Wall. It has kelp and sea urchins, northern basket stars and even the rarer Grunt Sculpin (*Rhamphocottus richardsoni*). At only about 10cm (4in) long, it has a pig-like snout and large pectoral fins with extended fin rays which it uses as feet on which to hop around along the sea bed. It is drab in colour with a marbled appearance, except for its tail, which is bright orange. It also poses well for the camera.

WEST COAST: USA

by Lawson Wood

CATALINA ISLAND, CALIFORNIA

CATALINA ISLAND, A SHORT, HIGH-SPEED FERRY ride from Long Beach in southern California, was once owned by the Wrigley family (of chewing gum fame). Rugged and remote, the island is an outpost for a herd of wild buffalo and the small rocky islets around the island are home to Californian Sea Lions. Almost split in two, but connected by an isthmus, the northern village is called Two Harbors and has no paved roads. Principle access is by boat. The main settlement is Avalon at the southeastern end of the island. Very laid-back, the island certainly works at a more leisurely pace. Situated around a sheltered bay, the small, rather quaint village is dominated by the old casino which, built in the 1930s, was never actually used as a casino. The underwater scenes in the tile work at the entrance are exquisite, undoubtedly inspired by the wealth of marine life to be found in the surrounding seas.

TOP LEFT AND RIGHT *Avalon Bay on Catalina Island is dominated by the old casino at the northern end of the bay. Quiet during the winter months, the bay is filled with pleasure craft in summer. The Casino Point Marine Park is one of the high-yield photographic sites, giving maximum footage for minimum effort.*

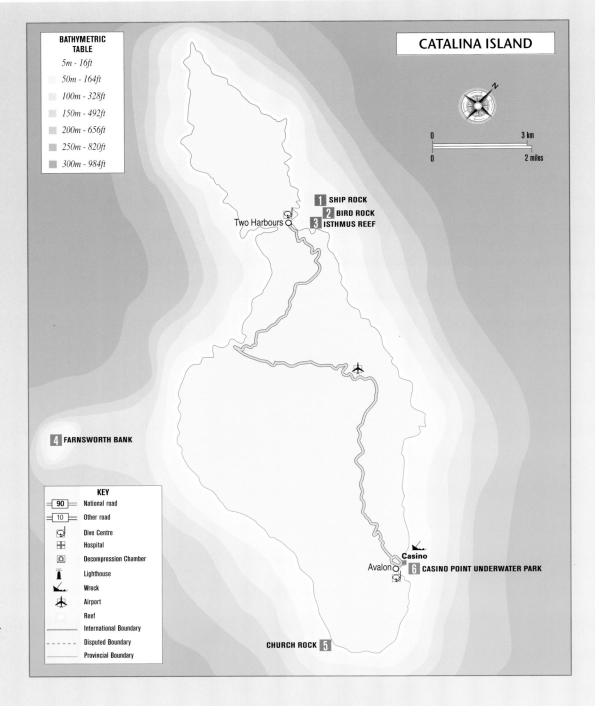

CATALINA ISLAND

BATHYMETRIC TABLE
- 5m - 16ft
- 50m - 164ft
- 100m - 328ft
- 150m - 492ft
- 200m - 656ft
- 250m - 820ft
- 300m - 984ft

0 — 3 km
0 — 2 miles

Two Harbours

1 SHIP ROCK
2 BIRD ROCK
3 ISTHMUS REEF

4 FARNSWORTH BANK

KEY
- 90 National road
- 10 Other road
- Dive Centre
- Hospital
- Decompression Chamber
- Lighthouse
- Wreck
- Airport
- Reef
- International Boundary
- Disputed Boundary
- Provincial Boundary

Casino
Avalon 6 CASINO POINT UNDERWATER PARK

CHURCH ROCK 5

The dive sites are varied and, while the predominant feature is kelp, the underwater topography includes archways, gullies, canyons, wrecks and vertical walls. North of Two Harbors there are several sites around offshore rocks. **Ship Rock** 1 is popular, particularly the northern face as it drops 36m (118ft) to a sandy sea floor where angel sharks are common. On the inward side, there is a confusing mass of rocks, gullies and canyons – superb for photography, but making it easy to lose your sense of direction. The walls have gorgonias, and octopuses as well as large sea bass can be found here. Time on the surface requires vigilance, since there is a lot of boat traffic in the area during the summer months.

Rather smelly, guano-covered **Bird Rock** 2 has an excellent wall and a spur of rock that juts out to the south. Topped with kelp, the cliff rapidly gives way to large colourful Gorgonian Sea Fans, nudibranchs and the amazing Bluebanded (Catalina) Goby, which has a brilliant blue coloration to the head and a red body.

Nearby **Isthmus Reef** 3 barely reaches the surface and is best dived in calm water when the kelp-covered top is more visible. This open-water site has sea lions, sheephead, lobsters, rockfish and, on the lower slopes, cat sharks and large rays. While divers wait in the water for the dive boat to pick them up, they will be able to see some superb jellyfish and pelagic tunicates near the surface.

The **Farnsworth Bank** 4 to the west of the island is well known among Californian divers for the diversity of life amid these offshore pinnacles. Current should be expected and the site gets deep very quickly in every direction, making it difficult to plot during rough weather.

At the southernmost point is **Church Rock** 5. Exposed to surge, the rock is at the confluence of the strong currents which flow between the San Pedro Channel and the Santa Barbara Passage. Large boulders offer protection against the worst of the swell and it is here that you can find lobsters, sheephead and the ubiquitous Garibaldi.

The **Casino Point Underwater Park** 6 to the north of Avalon has a lush kelp forest, encounters with big rays and small sharks, (the perfect order) occasional sea lions, tons of brilliantly coloured fish (Garibaldi) and nudibranchs by the dozen. There is easy shore access and even lockers where personal items can be stored. The local dive shop supplies small carts in which you can convey your air tanks around the promenade to the marine park or arranges transport for you in the back of the shop's pickup truck. The local hotels also arrange transportation of equipment.

Looking down at the marine park from the shore, the kelp forms a thick blanket that covers the water surface and in calm weather it appears thick enough to walk across. Around February and March the forest is still quite open and new, with curved shoots and air bladders forming at the ends of the stalks. Small schools of fish move lazily through the leafy glades and the occasional large stingray or electric ray may cross this protected area. The marine park has a few small wrecks and assorted engine bits, overgrown with purple encrusting algae, but the kelp forest is the main attraction. This type of kelp (*Macrocystis pyrifera*) has large multilimbed holdfasts, thin stalks topped with large leafy blades and air bladders that keep the algae buoyant. In the right conditions, this can extend over 60m (200ft), with a growth rate of over 60cm (24in) per day at the height of the growing season. Swimming through it gives the diver the same sensation as being in a terrestrial forest.

Looking closely at the kelp you can find snails, nudibranchs, sea urchins, cucumbers, kelp fish and the ubiquitous bright orange member of the damselfish family, the Garibaldi. These highly inquisitive fish are always in your face and, whenever you stop to take a closer look at the marine life, the garibaldi show up in their dozens.

Catalina Island and the Casino Point Marine Park are considered high-yield underwater photographic sites, with maximum footage for minimum effort.

TOP *In the spring, jellyfish are commonly found in the kelp forest as the bi-annual plankton bloom brings new life to the underwater domain.*
ABOVE *The kelp forest at Church Rock in the south forms glades, not unlike a terrestrial forest, which are home to the inquisitive Garibaldi.*

BAJA CALIFORNIA SUR

by Lawson Wood

DIVERS TEND TO THINK OF MEXICO AS A Caribbean diving destination, but the quality of diving and diversity of marine life on the Pacific coast exceed that of the Caribbean. There are fewer people, using fewer dive centres and therefore there is less pressure on dive sites and better control over conservation measures. While much of the Pacific coastline is exposed to the oceanic swell, the sheltered Sea of Cortés is superb for diving, with regular sightings of whales, Manta Rays, large schools of hammerhead sharks, turtles and some of the most northerly coral reefs to be found in the Pacific.

The long finger of land which juts down from California off the west coast of Mexico is known as Baja and almost land-locks a massive stretch of Pacific waters known as the Sea of Cortés. Named after the Spanish explorer, the sea has marine links with not only the Pacific Ocean, but also an ancient link with the Caribbean before the Central American isthmus was formed. Many species of marine life are endemic and others are indigenous to both oceans, such as the small Orange Cup Corals (*Tubastrea coccinea*), which cover the lower shaded reefs and under overhangs. Out on the isolated seamounts such as El Bajo, divers are often treated to (though not guaranteed) schools of 200 or more hammerhead sharks and thousand of jacks that swirl around the

divers constantly. Marine life is profuse and, although constantly reminiscent of Caribbean waters, the diving is a mix between that of the Mediterranean, Caribbean and Atlantic, with British diving represented by the only rigid inflatable diving boat in western Mexico at a club in La Paz.

The route north takes divers past Isla Espiritu Santa, through schools of Spinner Dolphins, past giant Manta Rays splashing near the surface beyond a set of lonely pinnacles called Los Islotes (the Islets). This can be planned as the second dive of the day. Situated well offshore, these lonely pinnacles host the largest rookery for the brown California Sea Lion in Mexico. There are smaller rookeries located on nearby Isla Espiritu Santo and Cabo San Lucas, which is at the 'Lands End' of Baja.

1 EL BAJO

El Bajo is one of a series of three submarine seamounts about 25m (80ft) below the surface. The pinnacle is covered on all sides by large Gorgonian Sea Fans and sponges, all of which appear to have been pulled into curious flattened shapes as a result of the almost constant tidal race that cut through the pinnacles. On the bottom, the tidal race runs in the opposite direction, resulting in a distinct halocline with the change in water temperature and salinity. Exhilarating diving

is possible amid schools of King Angelfish, barracuda, pufferfish, rabbit fish. There and Longnose Hawkfish.

2 LOS ISLOTES

The best place in Mexico for interaction with sea lions, is Los Islotes. This delightful experience is possible all year round and the site often gets busy with dive boats and locals who venture out to the islands to snorkel in safe, calm waters. During a recent dive we watched the larger bull sea lions hold court over their harem, sometimes lunging threateningly at us, baring their teeth. However, as long we kept clear of the females' resting sites, the bulls left us alone and even allowed us to interact with the juveniles. These boisterous youngsters flopped their way over the polished boulders to their diving platforms and dive-bombed us, pulling playfully at our fins, frightening the life out of us as they twisted and cavorted around us. They would rush

TOP LEFT *Cabo San Lucas is where the Pacific meets the Gulf of California. The waters are particularly rich in marine life.*

TOP RIGHT *Los Islotes to the north of La Paz is home to the largest population of sea lions in Mexico. Once joined to the mainland, it is now a designated conservation area.*

BAJA CALIFORNIA SUR

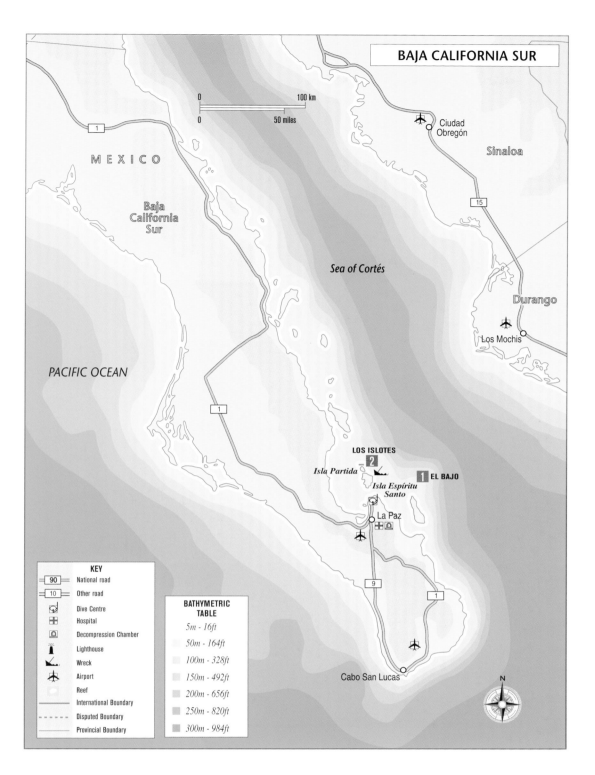

KEY

90	National road
10	Other road
	Dive Centre
	Hospital
	Decompression Chamber
	Lighthouse
	Wreck
	Airport
	Reef
	International Boundary
- - -	Disputed Boundary
	Provincial Boundary

BATHYMETRIC TABLE

5m - 16ft
50m - 164ft
100m - 328ft
150m - 492ft
200m - 656ft
250m - 820ft
300m - 984ft

straight at a diver's face, bare their teeth and whip away in a cloud of expelled air bubbles. While rather awkward on the rocks, the sea lions seem able to fold themselves in half and perform a mind-boggling series of movements at breakneck speed, a display which left us bemused at our ungainly and clumsy performance in the water.

Los Islotes is one huge rocky spur that has been eroded away in the centre, creating a flat rocky platform virtually at sea level with boulders located at either end. The rocky stacks are covered in guano, which glistens in the afternoon sun, from nesting seagulls, frigate birds and the occasional pelican. Topped by straggly cactus, the easterly stack is more sheer and is cut by a massive tunnel. Although not negotiable by boat, it is perfect for divers as the depth here is around 15m (50ft). The depth beside the platform, and the best chance for playing with the sea lions, is at only 6m (20ft). The surrounding area has huge boulders, all covered in small coral growths, sea fans, nudibranchs, colourful blennies and starfish (sea stars). There are few large fish close to the rocky shoreline.

TOP *Schools of colourful fish are commonplace on the outer seamounts where strong currents bring nutrient-rich waters into the Sea of Cortés.*
LEFT *Friendly and inquisitive, the sea lions readily approach divers and snorkellers to play. Juveniles love the interaction, often tugging on fins or dive-bombing divers close to the rookeries.*

THE GOLDEN TRIANGLE

by Jack Jackson

THE DIVER'S GOLDEN TRIANGLE IS MADE UP of Ecuador's Galápagos Islands and the live-aboard-only destinations of Costa Rica's Cocos Island and Colombia's Malpelo Island off the west coast of Central America. Although close to the equator, deep, cold currents hit these volcanic seamounts, the surface waters are relatively warm, but the currents below various thermoclines are remarkably cold. When they hit the seamount they well up, carrying rich nutrients from deep water. These nutrients attract smaller species, which in turn attract the larger species that prey on them and these attract a vast array of pelagic life. Cocos and Malpelo have small amounts of coral that must be avoided, but hanging on to volcanic boulders to avoid being swept away is allowed.

The Galápagos consists of 13 major islands, six smaller islands and 70 islets and rocks spread over a wide area in the Humboldt (Peru) Current, where water temperatures can be as low as 10°C (50°F). This current mixes

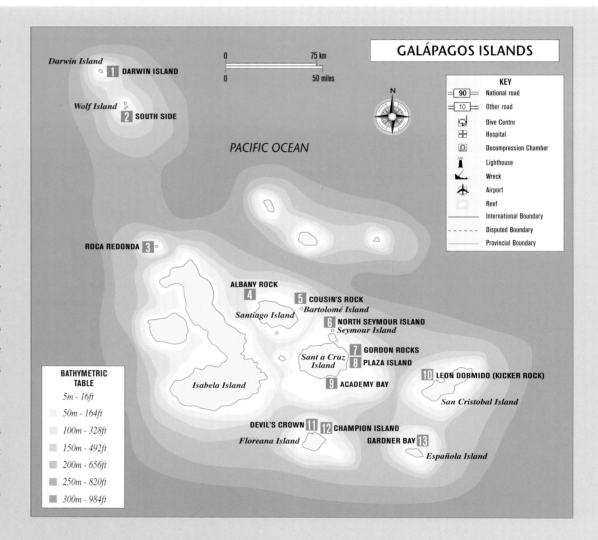

GALÁPAGOS ISLANDS

PACIFIC OCEAN

Darwin Island ── 1 DARWIN ISLAND

Wolf Island ── 2 SOUTH SIDE

ROCA REDONDA 3

ALBANY ROCK 4
5 COUSIN'S ROCK
Santiago Island ○ *Bartolomé Island*
6 NORTH SEYMOUR ISLAND
Seymour Island
7 GORDON ROCKS
Sant a Cruz Island 8 PLAZA ISLAND
Isabela Island 9 ACADEMY BAY
10 LEÓN DORMIDO (KICKER ROCK)
San Cristobal Island

DEVIL'S CROWN 11 12 CHAMPION ISLAND
Floreana Island GARDNER BAY 13
Española Island

KEY

90	National road
10	Other road
	Dive Centre
	Hospital
	Decompression Chamber
	Lighthouse
	Wreck
	Airport
	Reef
	International Boundary
	Disputed Boundary
	Provincial Boundary

BATHYMETRIC TABLE

5m - 16ft
50m - 164ft
100m - 328ft
150m - 492ft
200m - 656ft
250m - 820ft
300m - 984ft

0 ─── 75 km
0 ─── 50 miles

TOP LEFT *The only lizard in the world that can feed in the sea, Marine Iguanas are found throughout the Galápagos. Glands connected to the nostril allow salt to be expelled.*

TOP RIGHT *Teeming with birdlife, the arch at Darwin Island is an imposing sight on the surface, but even more spectacular underwater.*

with several warmer currents here to produce a mixture of temperate and warm water species. The islands are famous for having many endemic species of fauna and flora. The government of Ecuador designated some of the Galápagos Islands a wildlife sanctuary in 1935. The Galápagos Marine Resources

Reserve was created in 1986 to protect the surrounding waters and designated a United Nations world heritage site in 1998.

Cocos and Malpelo islands are in the Equatorial Countercurrent. Cocos Island is 8km (5 miles) long, has two natural harbours on its north coast and is surrounded by outlying pinnacles. In 1982 the island was designated Cocos Island National Park and is another important repository of indigenous species. Malpelo is not much more than a huge rock pinnacle, where the difficult landing requires gymnastic abilities. It is surrounded by smaller outlying pinnacles. Large swells are common at both destinations.

At all three destinations the diving is for relatively experienced divers who are used to rough surface conditions and strong currents, which can change at any time. When planning a trip it is also important to note that different boats often have different names or translations for dive sites.

GALÁPAGOS

The Galápagos Islands are located 1000km (600 miles) west of the mainland of Ecuador. An all-round diving destination, they also have shoaling hammerheads, which are most prolific around the islands of Wolf and Darwin. A mixture of cold and warm currents gives the waters of the Galápagos islands species that are endemic to cold and warm water, with exciting sightings of hammerhead sharks, Galápagos Sharks, Manta Rays, Whale Sharks and interactions with

sea lions. Some of the diving is on isolated rocks rising straight out of the sea. Some journeys between sites are quite long and most islands have several names.

For the Golden Triangle, the most important sites are the remote islands of Darwin and Wolf as they have warmer water and the most hammerhead sharks. These islands are the least affected by the cold Humboldt Current and there is even some plate coral off Darwin, an unusual sight in the region. Galápagos Sea Lions, Galápagos sharks, Sperm Whales and Ocean Sunfish are also encountered. Currents are sometimes unpredictable and strong downwellings are common. Roca Redonda is known for strong currents and downwellings. Targus Cove on Isabela Island has a 1.2m (4ft) sea star (*Luidia superba*), Bartolomé has Galápagos Penguins. Cousin's Rock has, among others, Black Coral.

The most northerly island, **Darwin** 1, is north-northwest of Wolf Island. Teeming with bird life, the Arch is a splendid sight from the surface, but even better underwater. Sitting on a plateau below the surface, the wall drops off into the depths – a focal point for the fish. Dolphins and the occasional Whale Shark

swim at the surface. Countless Scalloped Hammerhead Sharks shoal underwater. There is a natural viewing platform at 18m (60ft) on the ocean side of the Arch. More of the warmer water fish, such as Moorish Idols, are found here than off the islands further south, where the water is colder. Other animals found here are Galápagos Sharks, Eagle Rays and Green and Hawksbill Turtles. The area around Darwin Island has no protection, anchorage is poor, the surface can be rough and the strong currents change quickly.

Wolf Island consists of one main island with two smaller ones at each end. The main dive site is on the island's **South Side** 2 where fallen boulders create a slope of rocks leading to sand at 45m (150ft) with an abundance of marine life. Shoaling Scalloped Hammerhead Sharks pass across the reef from the shallower area over the rocks towards deeper water. There are also many surgeonfish, butterflyfish and pufferfish, Galápagos Sharks, Manta Rays, Eagle Rays, turtles and sea lions. The currents are unpredictable and change quickly. Visibility can change from 9m (30ft) to 30m (100ft) between dives.

Off the northwest of Isabela Island, **Roca Redonda** 3 thrusts through the surface,

ABOVE *The strange-looking Red-lipped Batfish, with leg-like appendages and unicorn-like nose, crawls and hops like a frog.*

ABOVE *Like other gobies, the Galápagos Bluebanded Goby spends most of its time resting on the bottom near a crack in the reef where it can retreat.*

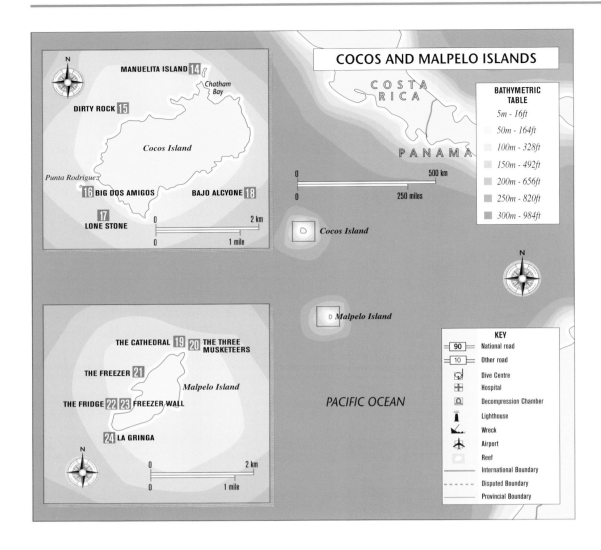

COCOS AND MALPELO ISLANDS

MANUELITA ISLAND [14]

Chatham Bay

DIRTY ROCK [15]

Cocos Island

Punta Rodríguez

[16] BIG DOS AMIGOS   BAJO ALCYONE [18]

[17] LONE STONE

COSTA RICA

PANAMA

BATHYMETRIC TABLE

5m - 16ft
50m - 164ft
100m - 328ft
150m - 492ft
200m - 656ft
250m - 820ft
300m - 984ft

500 km

250 miles

0   2 km

0   1 mile

Cocos Island

Malpelo Island

THE CATHEDRAL [19] [20] THE THREE MUSKETEERS

THE FREEZER [21]

Malpelo Island

THE FRIDGE [22] [23] FREEZER WALL

[24] LA GRINGA

PACIFIC OCEAN

0   2 km

0   1 mile

KEY

[90]	National road
[10]	Other road
	Dive Centre
	Hospital
	Decompression Chamber
	Lighthouse
	Wreck
	Airport
	Reef
	International Boundary
	Disputed Boundary
	Provincial Boundary

ABOVE *The Guineafowl Pufferfish* (Arothron meleagris) *are poor swimmers with movement produced by the sculling action of the fins and, to a lesser extent, the tail.*

while underwater shoals of barracuda, sea lions and reef fish swirl around the divers. With strong currents and downdrafts, hammerheads and Galápagos Sharks are found from 6m (20ft) to 15m (50ft). Fumaroles vent from the sand on the island's south side. Northwest of Santiago Island, **Albany Rock's** [4] west and east sides gradually slope down to sand at 45m (150ft) with similar fish life. East of Santiago Island, the uninhabited island of Bartolomé is popular as it is the northern limit of endemic Galápagos Penguins that dive to 12m (40ft). North of Bartolomé is **Cousin's Rock** [5], a small rock 9m (30ft) high and a few hundred feet long. It is an exciting dive with sea lions, reef sharks, hammerheads, Eagle and Manta Rays.

North of Santa Cruz Island is **North Seymour Island** [6], which has garden eels and, when the currents are strong, it teems with fish. Northeast of Santa Cruz Island, **Gordon Rocks** [7] has a 90m (300ft) volcanic crater. Currents vary and are often only for experienced divers, but the prolific marine life includes sleeping turtles, Black Coral and stingrays. South of Gordon Rocks, **Plaza Island** [8] has an easy, shallow dive with sea lions. Operators on Santa Cruz Island have several dive sites around **Academy Bay** [9].

Leon Dormido (Kicker Rock) [10], west of San Cristóbal Island, has many moray eels among the rocks. Floreana Island has several dive sites with **Devil's Crown** [11] and **Champion Island** [12] to the east having spectacular marine life. Off Española Island, **Gardner Bay** [13] has sea lions and prolific fish life.

COCOS ISLAND

The diving at Cocos and Malpelo islands provides fish action off sheer granite cliffs that plunge into deep water. These regions teem with big fish, but the main interest is the shoals of hundreds of female hammerheads that line up in the strong currents by day and leave to feed at night. Even without the hammerheads, there will be big-animal action, with Whale Sharks, Manta and Mobula Rays and also packs of Eagle and Marbled Rays.

Juvenile Whitetip Reef Sharks are everywhere. Divers descend rapidly to around 15–25m (50–80ft), find a crevice in the rocks, wedge in and wait for the fish to approach.

Cocos Island is 600km (375 miles) off the mainland. Strong currents are present at many sites, particularly those with exciting action such as Alcyone, Dirty Rock or Manuelita Island. All species here grow large. Whitetip Reef Sharks are everywhere, but most divers come to see the large shoals of Scalloped Hammerhead Sharks. Sometimes these sharks are encountered near the surface, but mostly they are found below the thermoclines. The majority of the diving is between 18 and 30m (60 and 100ft), occasionally 40m (130ft). Squadrons of Scalloped Hammerhead Sharks appear out of the blue, swim by majestically and recede into the distance to be replaced by further shoals of ten, twenty, fifty, even hundreds at a time. Hammerheads tend to be spooked by the noise of exhaust bubbles. For that reason live-aboard boats offer training in rebreathers so that divers can get closer to them. Exhaust bubbles do not worry the other inhabitants here, such as Yellowfin Tuna, snappers, groupers, moray eels, trumpetfish, frogfish, Red-lip Batfish, Whale Sharks, Humpback Whales, Sailfish, Manta Rays, shoaling Mobula Rays and Eagle Rays, Silky Sharks, Galápagos Sharks, and dolphins. Mobula Rays often approach divers, wanting to have their bodies rubbed as if by cleaner fish. All crevices in the reef are packed with fish hiding from the current and predators.

Bait-balls, dense shoals of jacks and other species that are attacked by sharks, dolphins and tuna are often found. Divers should be very careful, as sharks will snatch at anything when involved in feeding frenzies.

Northeast of Cocos, north-northwest of Chatham Bay, **Manuelita Island** 14 has a sheer wall and deep boulders on the west side and shallow plate corals on the east. Whitetip Reef sharks and Marbled Rays are stacked atop each other on the rocks and Scalloped Hammerhead Sharks come in close for cleaning at

depths of 14–45m (45–150ft). Off Cocos's northwest corner, **Dirty Rock** 15 has massive boulders sloping down the south side. A channel 100m (330ft) wide separates the main rock from a collection of pinnacles with prolific fish life including Eagle, Manta and Marbled Rays and large shoals of jacks.

Southwest of Cocos, off Punta Rodriguez, **Big Dos Amigos** 16 has an arch 14m (45ft) high and an 18m (60ft) pinnacle off the southeast side. Rainbow Runners, snappers and jacks shoal through the arch and hundreds of hammerheads swim between the islet and the pinnacle at depths of 20–35m (65–115ft). Southeast of Big Dos Amigos, **Lone Stone** 17 also has abundant fish life, including shoals of Mobula Rays and lone Marbled Rays down to 30m (100ft).

Southeast of Cocos, **Bajo Alcyone** 18, a seamount with its top 25m (80ft) from the surface, is one of the best sites for shoaling hammerheads and most other large fish.

MALPELO ISLAND

Declared a national park in 1980, Malpelo Island, 500km (310 miles) off the western coast of Colombia, is a collection of jagged pinnacles protruding from the ocean. One pinnacle, 3km (2 miles) by 0.4km (0.25 miles), is much larger than the others, but doesn't have a good sheltered anchorage. There are Scalloped Hammerhead Sharks shoaling at the surface as well as deeper down. Shoals of Silky Sharks are also seen. A previously unidentified shark is found here. It is similar in appearance to a Sand Tiger/Grey Nurse/Raggedtooth Shark, but is larger and has bigger eyes. Females of up to 6m (20ft) have been found. It is thought to be a version of the Smalltooth Sandtiger Shark (*Odontaspis ferox*).

Currents are variable, so that one charter can have a quiet time and on the next outing divers are rammed against the rocks in 'washing machine' turbulence.

Dive sites at Malpelo are similar to those at Cocos but the seas can be wilder. Hundreds of moray eels swim around with large snappers, groupers and Manta Rays. **The**

TOP *Hermit crabs often encourage* Calliactis *anemones to settle on their shell. When it changes shells, the crab coaxes the anemones to change shells with it.*

ABOVE Tubastrea *and* Dendrophyllia *corals are not light-dependent.*

Three Musketeers 20, a group of pinnacles off the northern end of Malpelo, have a series of tunnels and caverns. The largest of these, **The Cathedral** 19, is full of fish including baitfish and Whitetip Reef Sharks. The water temperature below the thermoclines is reflected in the names of sites on the island's north side, such as **The Freezer** 21, **The Fridge** 22 and **Freezer Wall** 23. **La Gringa** 24 is another site where female Scalloped Hammerheads line up in strong currents off the wall during the day.

THE CARIBBEAN SEA

by Jack Jackson

COMPARED WITH THE OCEANS, THE CARIBBEAN SEA, a suboceanic basin of the western Atlantic, is minute. It has a surface area of only 2,754,000 sq km (1,063,000 sq miles) and lies between 9°N and 22° N and between 89°W and 60° W. To the north it is bounded by the Greater Antilles islands of Cuba, Hispaniola (Haiti and the Dominican Republic), Jamaica, and Puerto Rico and to the south by the coasts of Panama, Colombia and Venezuela. To the west it is bounded by the Yucatán Peninsula of Mexico, Guatemala, Belize, Honduras, Nicaragua and Costa Rica and to the east by the Lesser Antilles chain, consisting of the island arc that extends from the Virgin Islands in the northeast to Trinidad and Tobago off the Venezuelan coast in the southeast.

The preferred oceanographic term for the Caribbean is the Antillean-Caribbean Sea which, together with the Gulf of Mexico, forms the Central American Sea. It is presumed to have been connected with the Mediterranean during Palaeozoic times and to have separated from it as the Atlantic Ocean was formed. Connections with the Pacific Ocean were lost when South America welded to Central America, closing the isthmus of Panama. This greatly altered the currents of the Caribbean Sea and the North Atlantic and limited the number of species found in the Caribbean.

Most of the islands are fringed by coral reefs and have gentle currents. The islands and connecting ridges of the eastern Caribbean prevent the interchange of deep water from the Atlantic, so the tides are smaller and visibility good. The region also has sophisticated infrastructures, a mild tropical climate, ideal conditions for novices and leisurely diving, a potpourri of diverse cultures and a laid-back attitude to life.

The islands vary from mountainous and lush to almost flat and arid, but the diving does not vary much. The islands bordering the Atlantic have more of the larger pelagic species on their Atlantic coasts. Stronger currents give exciting drift-dives off such places as Cozumel and Tobago; and trade winds produce rough seas on the windward sides of Aruba, Bonaire and Curaçao.

ABOVE *A Trumpetfish* (Aulostomus maculatus) *and a shoal of Blue Tangs* (Acanthurus coeruleus) *over the coral reef. Trumpetfish can change colour to match the background.*

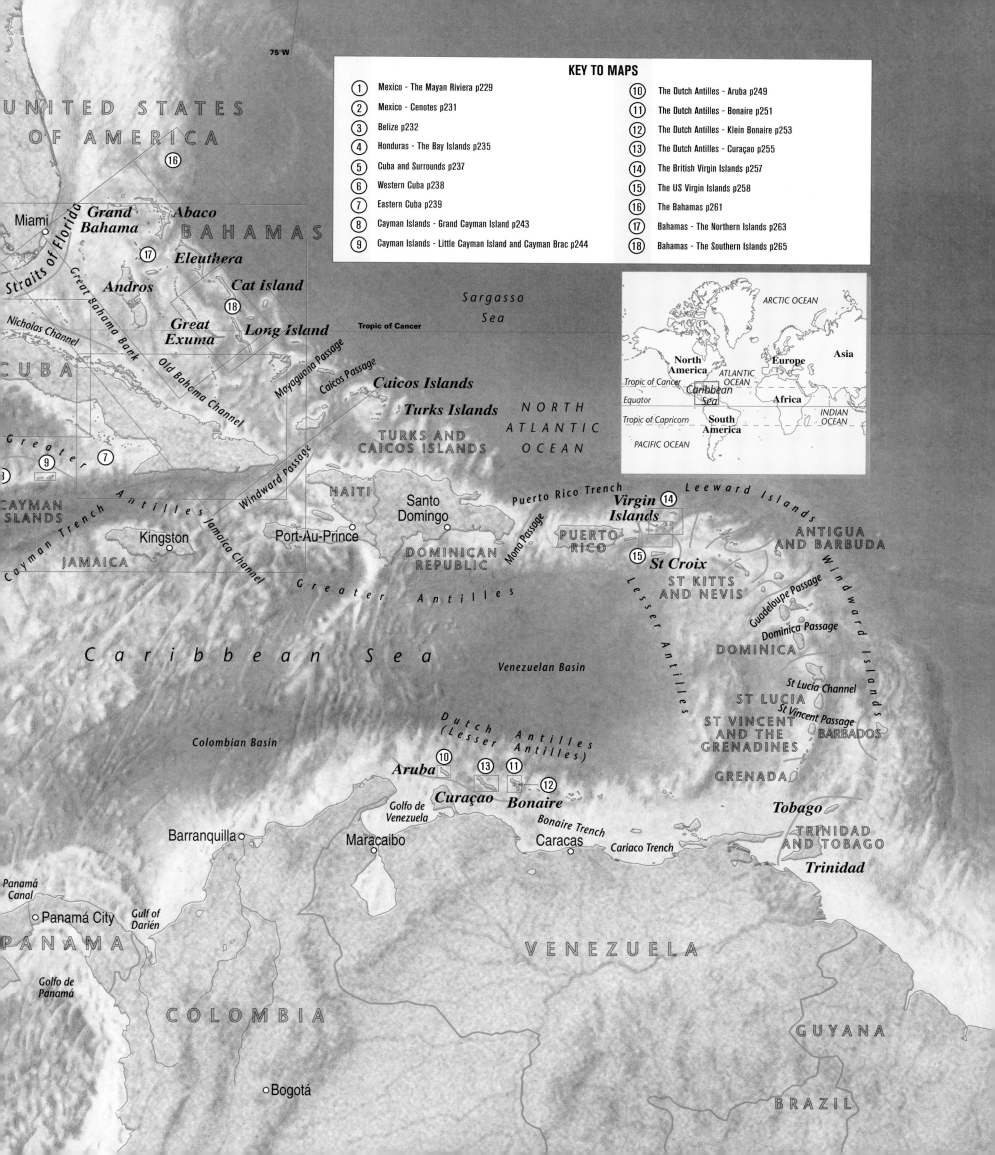

KEY TO MAPS

1. Mexico - The Mayan Riviera p229
2. Mexico - Cenotes p231
3. Belize p232
4. Honduras - The Bay Islands p235
5. Cuba and Surrounds p237
6. Western Cuba p238
7. Eastern Cuba p239
8. Cayman Islands - Grand Cayman Island p243
9. Cayman Islands - Little Cayman Island and Cayman Brac p244
10. The Dutch Antilles - Aruba p249
11. The Dutch Antilles - Bonaire p251
12. The Dutch Antilles - Klein Bonaire p253
13. The Dutch Antilles - Curaçao p255
14. The British Virgin Islands p257
15. The US Virgin Islands p258
16. The Bahamas p261
17. Bahamas - The Northern Islands p263
18. Bahamas - The Southern Islands p265

75°W

UNITED STATES OF AMERICA

Miami

Grand Bahama
Abaco
BAHAMAS
Straits of Florida
Great Bahama Bank
Eleuthera
Andros
Cat Island
Great Exuma
Long Island
Nicholas Channel
Old Bahama Channel
Mayaguana Passage
Caicos Passage

CUBA

Tropic of Cancer

Sargasso Sea

ARCTIC OCEAN
North America
ATLANTIC OCEAN
Europe
Asia
Tropic of Cancer
Caribbean Sea
Equator
Africa
INDIAN OCEAN
Tropic of Capricorn
South America
PACIFIC OCEAN

Caicos Islands
Turks Islands
TURKS AND CAICOS ISLANDS
NORTH ATLANTIC OCEAN

Windward Passage

Greater Antilles
Jamaica Channel
Cayman Trench

CAYMAN ISLANDS

Kingston
JAMAICA

HAITI
Port-Au-Prince

Santo Domingo

DOMINICAN REPUBLIC

Puerto Rico Trench
Mona Passage
Virgin Islands
PUERTO RICO
St Croix

Leeward Islands

ANTIGUA AND BARBUDA

ST KITTS AND NEVIS

Guadeloupe Passage
Dominica Passage
DOMINICA

Windward Islands

St Lucia Channel
ST LUCIA
St Vincent Passage
ST VINCENT AND THE GRENADINES
BARBADOS

GRENADA

Caribbean Sea

Venezuelan Basin

Colombian Basin

Dutch Antilles (Lesser Antilles)

Aruba
Curaçao
Bonaire

Golfo de Venezuela
Bonaire Trench
Cariaco Trench

Tobago
TRINIDAD AND TOBAGO
Trinidad

Barranquilla
Maracaibo
Caracas

Panamá Canal
Panamá City
Gulf of Darién
PANAMA
Golfo de Panamá

VENEZUELA

COLOMBIA

GUYANA

Bogotá

BRAZIL

THE CARIBBEAN SEA

While themed dives (diving with stingrays, sharks or dolphins) are popular, reefs are the main attraction and many of the islands have initiated artificial reef programmes by sinking ships and aeroplanes that had been cleaned to be environmentally sound. Some 'treasure ships' have been located, dating from the Spanish colonial period, when the world's richest maritime trade was prey to pirates, naval engagements and storms. Several more modern wrecks are regularly dived.

The Caribbean climate is tropical, but there are many local variations depending on the altitude of mountains, local currents and the trade winds. Rainfall varies from about 254mm (10 in) per year on the island of Bonaire to 8,890mm (350 in) per year in regions of Dominica. The Northeast Trade Winds dominate the area with an average velocity of 15–30km (9½–20 miles) per hour.

Storms of hurricane strength occur seasonally in the northern Caribbean and in the Gulf of Mexico, but are rare in the far south. Although the exact path of a hurricane is unpredictable, most form near the Cape Verde Islands in the eastern Atlantic and follow the path of the trade winds into the Caribbean and the Gulf of Mexico. The hurricane season is June to November, but they are most frequent in September. The Caribbean has fewer hurricanes than the Gulf of Mexico or the western Pacific, where they are called typhoons.

Mixed tides (both diurnal and semidiurnal) occur in the Caribbean and the Gulf of Mexico and are much smaller than those in the main Atlantic Ocean, usually less than 1m (40 in). Storm surges caused by hurricanes can cause local sea levels to rise by 1m (40 in).

TOPOGRAPHY

The Caribbean's greatest known depth is the Cayman Trench, also known as the Bartlett Deep or Bartlett Trough. It runs east-northeast to west-southwest between Cuba and Jamaica reaching 7,686m (25,216ft) below sea level.

Although the interior of the Caribbean is tectonically inactive, its margins are not. Volcanic activity and earthquakes produced by the interactions between crustal plates are common as the elongated plate of the Caribbean Sea is bordered to the west and east by subduction zones where other plates slide beneath the Caribbean Plate. The northeast edge of the Cocos Plate runs parallel to the Pacific coast 95–200km (60–125 miles) offshore. This plate abuts on the southwest edge of the Caribbean Plate, whose northern edge is marked by fault zones extending across southern Guatemala to include the active Cayman trough. To the north and northwest, the American Plate is relatively stable and has allowed the accumulation of limestones on the Yucatán Peninsula. The eastern edge of the Cocos Plate is in contact with the Panama

block of the Nazca Plate. The Cocos Plate is moving northeast relative to the Caribbean Plate at a rate of 10m (33ft) per century which, by geologic standards, is very fast.

At the eastern end of the Caribbean Sea, the volcanic islands forming the island arc of the Lesser Antilles mark the edge where the North Atlantic Ocean floor is sliding under the Caribbean Plate.

The Caribbean Sea is divided into five submarine basins separated from one another by submerged ridges and rises – the Yucatán, Cayman, Colombian, Venezuelan, and Grenada basins. The Yucatán Basin is separated from the Gulf of Mexico by the Yucatán Channel between Cuba and the Yucatán Peninsula. It has a sill depth (the depth of the submarine ridge between basins) of about 1,600m (5,250ft). To the south the Cayman Basin is partially separated from the Yucatán Basin by the Cayman Ridge, a narrow ridge that extends from Guatemala towards the southern part of Cuba. This ridge rises above sea level as the Cayman Islands. Further south, the Nicaraguan Rise is a wide triangular ridge with a sill depth of about 1,220m (4,000ft), which runs from Honduras and Nicaragua to Hispaniola. It separates the Cayman Basin from the Colombian Basin and rises above the surface as the island of Jamaica. The Colombian Basin is partly separated from the Venezuelan Basin in its northern half by the Beata Ridge, but these two basins are connected by the submerged Aruba Gap at depths greater than 3960m (13,000ft). To the east, the Aves Ridge, which is broken at its southern end, separates the Venezuelan Basin from the small Grenada Trough, whose eastern limit is the islands of the Antillean arc.

CURRENTS

High in oxygen content, North Atlantic Deep Water enters the Caribbean beneath the Windward Passage, which runs between east Cuba and northwest Haiti on Hispaniola. It then divides to fill the Yucatán, Cayman, and Colombian basins at depths of around

---

THE WEST INDIES

The West Indies stretch more than 3200km (2000 miles) from Cuba almost to the north coast of South America. Principally divided into the Greater and Lesser Antilles, this island chain separates the Caribbean Sea from the Atlantic Ocean. Other islands of the region are isolated groups on the continental perimeter of the Antilles, including the Bahamas, Trinidad and Tobago, and the Netherlands (Dutch) Antilles.

The shape and alignment of the Greater Antilles, Cuba, Jamaica, Hispaniola (Haiti and the Dominican Republic), and Puerto Rico, are determined by an ancient chain of mountains that extended from Central America through the Caribbean. Remnants of this chain are found in the Blue Mountains of Jamaica, the Sierra de los Órganos and the Sierra Maestra in Cuba and Duarte Peak, 3170m (10,400ft), in the Dominican Republic, the highest point in the Caribbean.

1,980m (6,500ft). This Caribbean Bottom Water also enters the Venezuelan Basin, introducing oxygen-rich water at depths of 1,800–2990m (5,900–9,800ft). Subantarctic Intermediate Water enters the Caribbean below the Anegada Passage at depths of 490–1,000m (1,600–3,300ft). At the Antillean arc, the shallow sill depths block the Antarctic Bottom Water, with the result that the bottom temperature of the Caribbean Sea is around 4°C (39°F), as opposed to the Atlantic bottom temperature of less than 2°C (36°F).

Surface currents enter the Caribbean mainly through the channels and passages of the southern Antilles. The Guiana Current and part of the North Equatorial Current flow past Saint Lucia almost unimpeded. The trade winds push these waters through the Yucatán Channel into the Gulf of Mexico. In the western Caribbean and the Gulf of Mexico, the trade winds force the surface waters northwards, away from the mainland, causing nutrient-rich upwellings.

The wind-driven surface water builds up in the Yucatán Basin and the Gulf of Mexico, resulting in a higher average sea level than in the Atlantic Ocean. This forms a hydrostatic head, thought to be the main driving force behind the Gulf Stream.

The Gulf Stream is fed by the westward-flowing North Equatorial Current moving from North Africa to the West Indies. This current splits into two off the northeast coast of South America, forming the Caribbean Current, which passes into the Caribbean Sea and through the Yucatán Channel into the Gulf of Mexico, and the Antilles Current, which flows to the north and east of the West Indies. The Caribbean Current flows back into the Atlantic through the Straits of Florida between the Florida Keys and Cuba as the Florida Current. Diverted northeast by the submerged Great Bahama Bank southeast of the Florida Peninsula, this swift current combines with the Antilles Current and then flows roughly parallel to the eastern coast of North America to Cape Hatteras. There part of the Gulf Stream forms a countercurrent that flows

TOP Fire corals (Millepora *spp.*) have many stinging nematocysts that produce a painful sting if they touch sensitive bare skin. Washing the stung area with vinegar immobilizes any unspent nematocysts.
ABOVE An adult Spotted Drum (Equetus punctatus). These fish inhabit secluded areas of the reef, under ledges and large debris or near small caves and only come out in the open to feed at night.

south and then west to rejoin the Gulf Stream on its seaward side along the coast of Florida and the Carolinas.

With its climate and recreational resources, the Caribbean has become one of the world's main winter vacation resorts and cruise ship destinations. Lack of capital and limited natural resources have discouraged most islands from large industrial development, though oil storage or production occurs on some.

Atlantic-Pacific shipping via the Panama Canal passes through the Caribbean, which means that oil spills from normal tanker operations and occasional large-scale tanker or other shipping catastrophes are a problem.

The Caribbean Sea suffers from the same problems of pollution, sedimentation and over-fishing as any of the oceans, but on a smaller scale. Many islands make an effort to conserve their marine habitat.

MEXICO

by Lawson Wood

THE YUCATÁN PENINSULA DIVIDES THE Caribbean Sea from the Gulf of Mexico. The island of **Cozumel** ☐1 lies just 30km (19 miles) southeast of Cancún on the peninsula. This small island has the largest concentration of dive centres, which puts an inevitable strain on the environment. Conservation measures are often defeated by the sheer number of divers at these sites all year round. All the sites off this island offer drift diving – not suitable for beginner divers.

Cancún is often overlooked, even though this holiday town is certainly perfect for learning to dive. Cancún is also a perfect base from which to explore the Yucatán. Reef diving is still very popular along the coast, but this exposed shoreline is often too rough to dive (unlike sheltered Cancún and western Cozumel). However, an alternative diving destination has been discovered.

TOP LEFT *Xcaret Lagoon in the Yucatán is at the terminus of an underground river which flows through this ancient limestone region to the sea, where a resort has now been established.*

TOP RIGHT *Isla Mujeres has superb sandy beaches and is only a short boat ride north of Cancún. The shallow reefs have some of the largest fish populations in the Caribbean.*

RIGHT *Splendid Toadfish (Sanopus splendidus) is an endemic species to this region.*

☐2 CANCÚN

The shores of Cancún have the most northerly coral reefs in the western Caribbean, protected to some extent by the islands of Isla Mujeres and Isla Contoy to the north in the Gulf of Mexico and, a few kilometres to the southeast, Cozumel, regarded as Mexico's only Caribbean island.

Most divers tend to stay on Cozumel, while Cancún has been largely overlooked due to its shallow, sheltered bay between Cancún and Isla Mujeres. The maximum depth of the

seabed in the bay is 9m (30ft) and the outside reefs bottom out at 17m (55ft). Virtually all the diving involves drift diving in a slight current and the dive boat captain will keep station over the divers as they progress along the reef. The reef is in fact old coralline limestone bedrock, testifying to the fact that this area was once dry land. At the northern limit of coral polyp distribution in the western Caribbean and Gulf of Mexico, there is little stony coral growth, except for Elkhorn, Staghorn, Star and Brain coral. Gorgonian

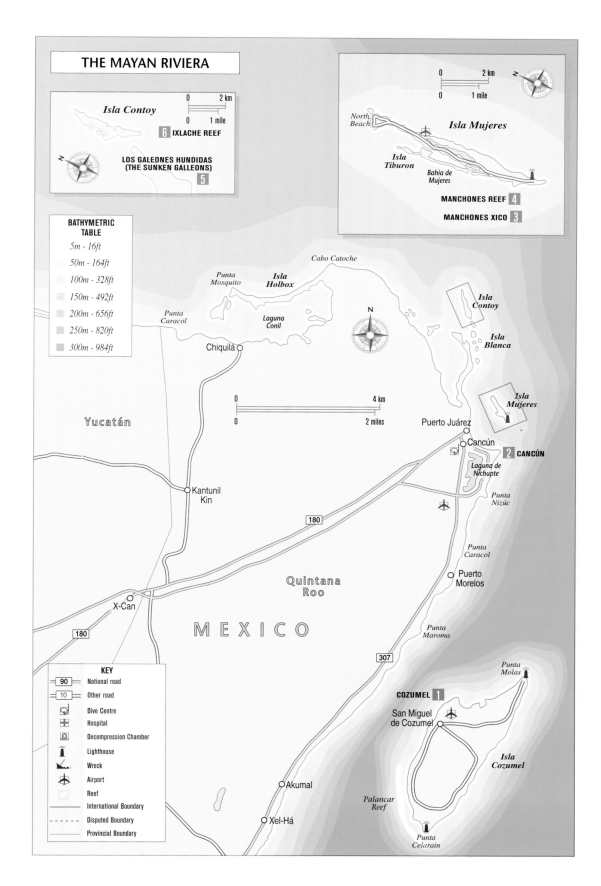

THE MAYAN RIVIERA

Isla Contoy

0 — 2 km
0 — 1 mile

6 IXLACHE REEF

**LOS GALEONES HUNDIDAS
(THE SUNKEN GALLEONS)
5**

0 — 2 km
0 — 1 mile

Isla Mujeres

North
Beach

Isla
Tiburon

Bahia de
Mujeres

MANCHONES REEF 4

MANCHONES XICO 3

**BATHYMETRIC
TABLE**

5m - 16ft
50m - 164ft
100m - 328ft
150m - 492ft
200m - 656ft
250m - 820ft
300m - 984ft

Cabo Catoche

Punta
Mosquito

**Isla
Holbox**

Punta
Caracol

Laguna
Conil

Chiquilá

N

**Isla
Contoy**

**Isla
Blanca**

0 — 4 km
0 — 2 miles

Puerto Juárez

**Isla
Mujeres**

Cancún

2 CANCÚN

Laguna de
Nichupte

Punta
Nizúc

Yucatán

Kantunil
Kin

180

Punta
Caracol

Puerto
Morelos

**Quintana
Roo**

X-Can

180

M E X I C O

Punta
Maroma

307

Punta
Molas

COZUMEL 1

San Miguel
de Cozumel

KEY

90	National road
10	Other road
	Dive Centre
	Hospital
	Decompression Chamber
	Lighthouse
	Wreck
	Airport
	Reef
	International Boundary
	Disputed Boundary
	Provincial Boundary

**Isla
Cozumel**

Akumal

Palancar
Reef

Xel-Há

Punta
Celarain

TOP RIGHT *A typical cavern entrance in Quintana Roo to part of the massive labyrinth of cenotes which honeycomb the region. This fresh water diving is becoming increasingly popular.*

CENTRE RIGHT *This juvenile Caribbean Reef Squid (Sepioteuthis sepioidea) is commonly found around shallow reefs at night where it hunts for shrimps and small pelagic fish. They can be approached easily if you do not shine your dive lights directly at them.*

RIGHT *This Green Moray Eel and Banded Coral Shrimp have a symbiotic relationship on the reef, where the shrimp cleans the moray eel of parasites and in return gains protection and can feed on scraps.*

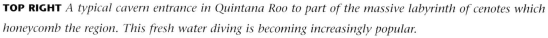

TOP *Inside the Gran Cenote, the huge cavern's passageways run for kilometres and are lavishly decorated with different types of formation, which have been sealed in time by the crystal clear fresh water.*

ABOVE *At the entrance to Car Wash Cenote there is a pile of debris from fallen trees and leaves which should be avoided, because disturbing the sediment will spoil the otherwise superb visibility.*

corals and sea fans predominate. Colourful sponges are evident as are a significant number of species of algae, all of which make an ideal home for parrot fish, wrasse, blennies, gobies, angel and butterfly fish. Some of the most colourful fish in the entire Caribbean can be found around these shallow reefs.

Much of the diving is done by trainees and first-time visitors to Cancún, who are intent on catching another flavour of the Caribbean. All the diving centres offer beginner's courses to a very high standard. The largest diving operators and the ones who do the most advertising are not necessarily the best, although these are run very efficiently and will try to give tourists what they are looking for.

ISLA MUJERES

Many visitors who first come to Isla Mujeres on a day trip return for a lengthier stay on their next vacation. The island's people are laid-back and even topless sunbathing is allowed on North Beach. The shallow reefs around Isla Mujeres teem with life and, although much of the reefs are shallow and low lying, this does not seem to deter large numbers of fish. At **Manchones** ③ ④, the snorkelling is particularly popular and there is just sufficient depth to keep hands off the coral. The reefs are quite convoluted with many little gullies and canyons for divers to swim through and fish-watch. It is a popular dive site with operators from both Isla Mujeres and Cancún.

ISLA CONTOY

Isla Contoy is on the limit of the northern coral distribution into the Gulf of Mexico. The long shallow reef that stretches north from Isla Mujeres to Isla Contoy is called **Ixlache Reef** ⑥ and offers an opportunity to see some massive brain corals. Also on the way is a shallow reef called **Los Galeones Hundidas** ⑤ (The Sunken Galleons) in water no deeper than 4½m (15ft) where there is reputed to be the scattered remains of a number of ancient shipwrecks.

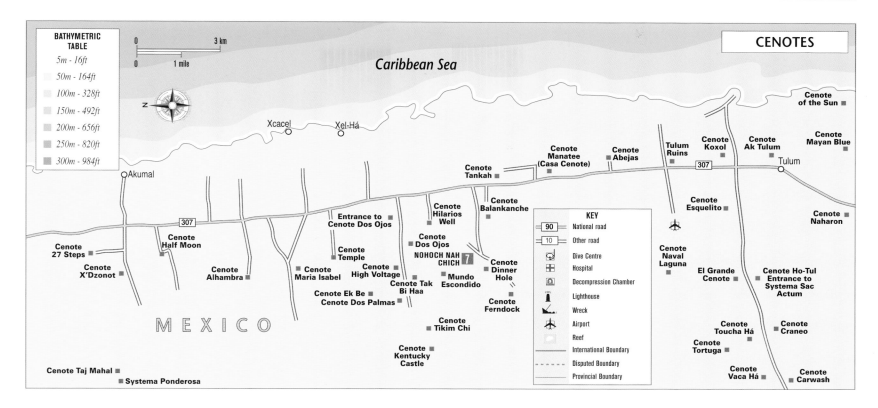

BATHYMETRIC TABLE

5m - 16ft
50m - 164ft
100m - 328ft
150m - 492ft
200m - 656ft
250m - 820ft
300m - 984ft

CENOTES

Caribbean Sea

Xcacel   Xel-Há

Akumal

MEXICO

Cenote 27 Steps
Cenote X'Dzonot
Cenote Half Moon
Cenote Alhambra
Entrance to Cenote Dos Ojos
Cenote Temple
Cenote Maria Isabel
Cenote High Voltage
Cenote Tak Bi Haa
Cenote Ek Be
Cenote Dos Palmas
Cenote Hilarios Well
Cenote Dos Ojos
NOHOCH NAH CHICH 7
Mundo Escondido
Cenote Balankanche
Cenote Dinner Hole
Cenote Ferndock
Cenote Tikim Chi
Cenote Kentucky Castle
Cenote Taj Mahal
Systema Ponderosa
Cenote Tankah
Cenote Manatee (Casa Cenote)
Cenote Abejas
Tulum Ruins
Cenote Koxol
Cenote Ak Tulum
Tulum
Cenote of the Sun
Cenote Mayan Blue
Cenote Naharon
Cenote Esquelito
Cenote Naval Laguna
El Grande Cenote
Cenote Ho-Tul Entrance to Systema Sac Actum
Cenote Toucha Há
Cenote Tortuga
Cenote Vaca Há
Cenote Craneo
Cenote Carwash

KEY

90	National road
10	Other road
	Dive Centre
	Hospital
	Decompression Chamber
	Lighthouse
	Wreck
	Airport
	Reef
	International Boundary
	Disputed Boundary
	Provincial Boundary

All dive centres are PADI certified and they will take care of your every diving need. Although Cancún is generally considered an all-round vacation resort rather than a diving destination, I have never seen so many fish in one place as among the shallow reefs and mini-walls of the sheltered bay between Isla Mujeres and Cancún.

CENOTES

Beneath the apparent solid limestone rock of the Yucatán Peninsula lies a huge network of caves that have been, for the most part, submerged for millennia. With new techniques and diving equipment, penetration of these vast underwater cave systems has opened a new frontier for exploration.

The entire Yucatán Peninsula was underwater more than 65 million years ago. During the last ice age the sea level dropped and left a huge raised plateau of soft porous limestone. The bedrock composition of this plateau is volcanic in origin, but it is only the top layers of ancient coralline limestone that we are able to explore. This huge porous shelf is made up of sedimentary rocks, dead corals, shells and the breakdown of lime left behind by their decomposition. The limestone which makes up the peninsula dates from the Pleistocene and Holocene eras. This limestone bedrock is susceptible to erosion and tropical rainstorms, coupled with acid rain from neighbouring volcanoes over the centuries, have created huge underground caverns and wells.

A cenote is the collapsed ceiling of an underground cave system and can be regarded as a window in the dense jungle floor to the crystal clear underground rivers that honeycomb the entire Yucatán Peninsula. Around 80–90 cenotes have been located in the Yucatán and most have been explored to some degree over the years. The most famous is **Nohoch Nah Chich** 7, which has been recorded in the *Guinness Book of Records* since 1992 as the world's largest underground cave system. Around 50 of the cenotes are found along the Akumal/Tulum Corridor and are now well mapped, but still not completely explored. The name cenote comes from the Mayan word *tzonot*, which means 'well' or 'sinkhole.' Cenotes were not only the primary source of fresh water, but were also sacred places where sacrifices and other rituals were performed. At a number of the major sites such as Chichen Itza, the Maya prayed to the Rain God, Chac. Since the early 1980s over 160km (100 miles) of underground passageways have been surveyed.

ABOVE *At Gran Cenote, as in many of the accessible sites, signs warn divers not to proceed without proper training and equipment.*

WESTERN CARIBBEAN

by Lawson Wood

THE DIVING OFF THE WESTERN CARIBBEAN Barrier Reef is interesting as it covers many atolls, islands and nations. Each group is different. Most have tourism, but there are also undived areas of reef only accessible by live-aboard boat, of which there are several.

Belize changed its name from British Honduras when it gained independence from Great Britain in 1981. Still mainly English speaking, the population is made up of the descendants of slaves first brought to the colony of Jamaica. The principle industry on land is still forestry, sugar cane and oranges and their associated processing plants, while the offshore islands are geared up for fishing and tourism. Located between Mexico to the north and Guatemala and Honduras to the south, the country appears to have been made for diving, with the second-largest barrier reef in the world just a few kilometres (miles) from the mainland and three coral atolls (Turneffe Island Atoll, Lighthouse Reef and Glover's Reef).

TOP LEFT *Cochine Grande off the Bay Islands of Honduras, where Manta Rays and other large pelagic fish are seen regularly.*

TOP RIGHT *The Bay Islands of Honduras are renowned for its concentration of invertebrate life. Many of the coastal villages are only accessible by boat and are not linked by roads.*

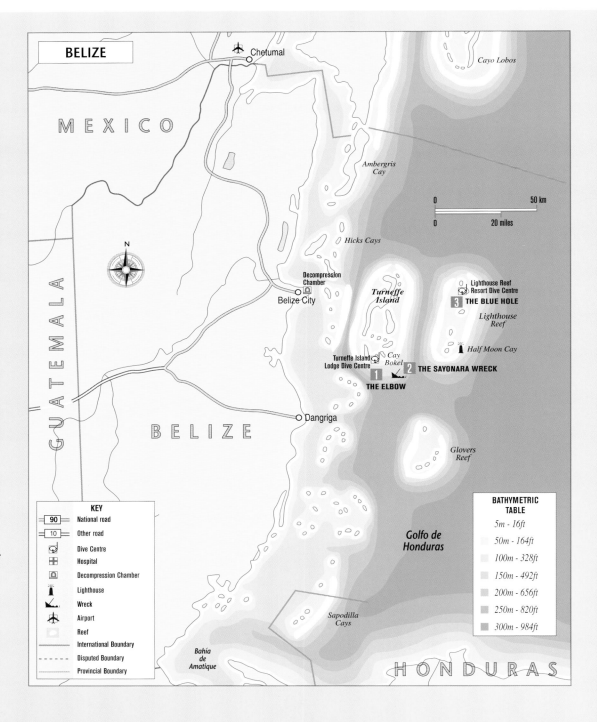

BELIZE

Chetumal

MEXICO

Cayo Lobos

Ambergris Cay

0 — 50 km
0 — 20 miles

Hicks Cays

GUATEMALA

N

Decompression Chamber

Belize City

Turneffe Island

Lighthouse Reef Resort Dive Centre

3 THE BLUE HOLE

Lighthouse Reef

Half Moon Cay

Turneffe Island Lodge Dive Centre

Cay Bokel

1 **2** THE SAVONARA WRECK

THE ELBOW

Dangriga

BELIZE

Glovers Reef

Golfo de Honduras

KEY

90	National road
10	Other road
	Dive Centre
	Hospital
	Decompression Chamber
	Lighthouse
	Wreck
	Airport
	Reef
	International Boundary
-----	Disputed Boundary
	Provincial Boundary

BATHYMETRIC TABLE

5m - 16ft
50m - 164ft
100m - 328ft
150m - 492ft
200m - 656ft
250m - 820ft
300m - 984ft

Sapodilla Cays

Bahía de Amatique

HONDURAS

BELIZE
TURNEFFE ATOLL

Turneffe Island Atoll is one of the most important biological systems in the Caribbean with lush mangroves, littoral palm forests and pristine coral reefs where the elusive manatee and playful dolphins can be found. Volunteers from Coral Cay Conservation collect scientific data and are working to survey the forests, lagoons and reefs throughout the 350 sq km (135 sq miles) of Turneffe Atoll. This is part of a national drive to establish a management plan for the protection and sustainable use of the atoll's outstanding biodiversity. Turneffe Atoll is the largest of the three coral atolls in Belize and the only one with an extensive cover of mangrove. There is diving at the southernmost point, **The Elbow** 1. Shallower dives, more suitable for novices, can be found on the western, more sheltered, shoreline. More challenging dives in tidal surge and currents are found on the southeast corner.

There is an artificial reef to the south of the shallower sites called the *Sayonara* 2. This former passenger and cargo boat was sunk in 1985 and sits in a maximum depth of 15m (50ft) with a list to starboard. Since it is of wooden construction, it is deteriorating rapidly and exploration inside is discouraged. It is great for invertebrate spotting and there are good gorgonian corals and sponges.

LIGHTHOUSE REEF AND THE BLUE HOLE 3

Situated 65km (40 miles) east of Belize City and originally known as the Eastern Reefs, Lighthouse Reef was named after the lighthouse on Half Moon Cay. This reef is the farthest from the mainland and known for its better-than-average underwater visibility. However, what makes this atoll special is the massive natural blue hole in the centre of the lagoon. Forming a near perfect circle, it is 300m (1000ft) in diameter and drops 124m (412ft). It was made famous by a Jacques Cousteau *Calypso* expedition in 1970. There are two narrow passageways through the very shallow surrounding reef. The shallowest of

the internal caverns with stalactites starts at 43m (140ft), dating to when the sea level was 105m (350ft) shallower during the last ice age some 15,000 years ago. Lighthouse reef has excellent stony and gorgonian coral growth, but they are in competition with the much more vigorously growing algae and sponges.

TOP *In the Blue Hole at Lighthouse Reef, divers can encounter enormous stalactites at around 50m (165ft), some over 12m (40ft) long.*

ABOVE *Scrawled filefish (Aluterus scriptus) are generally fairly wary of divers during the day, but easily approached at night, drifting amid moving sea fans and plumes.*

TOP *The Caribbean clingfish (*Arcos rubigi-nosus)*, although rare in other areas of the Caribbean, is found regularly on most night dives at Cayos Cochinos.*

ABOVE *White-speckled nudibranch (*Pauleo juba-tus) *can be found from May to September on various species of sea plume.*

HONDURAS
THE BAY ISLANDS

The Bay Islands off Honduras to the south comprise eight islands and 65 associated cays. There is also superb diving off its three north-ern islands that form part of the same barrier reef running parallel to the Central American coast. Located 64km (40 miles) north of Hon-duras, the three main islands are **Utila** 4 **Roatan** 5 and **Guanaja** 6. **Cayos Cochinos** 8 is closer to the mainland. It has a vertical wall, with the reef crest at 6m (20ft) protecting a shallow coral garden. There are also seamounts (coral islands below the sur-face), which are always filled with pelagic species such as Ocean Triggerfish.

The Payan Indians, closely related to the Maya, introduced agriculture and traded extensively with neighbouring areas. All this changed when Columbus sailed into Guanaja in 1502 on his fourth voyage of discovery and named the island the Isle of Pines. Much of the local population were enslaved in the ensuing years. The name Honduras translates to something like Deep Sea. The town of Savannah Bight on Guanaja was a notorious pirate lair and Port Royal on Roatan was the scene of a particularly brutal raid in 1792. English settlers reintroduced agriculture, while Scottish shipbuilders and fishermen rebuilt the trade economy. The islands were ceded by the British to Honduras in the late 1800s. The language and customs are gradu-ally changing to Spanish as mainland Hondurans migrate to the islands seeking work and an island way of life.

The abundance of marine life – mainly large groupers, moray eels, jacks, Manta Rays and Whale Sharks, which are becoming rare in other areas of the Caribbean – and under-water visibility of over 30m (100 ft) make it attractive to divers.

7 JADO TRADER

A freighter that worked between the inner islands of the western Caribbean, the *Jado Trader*, was deliberately sunk as an artificial reef in 1987. Now resting on her starboard side near a healthy reef, the wreck lies 2km (1¾ mile) offshore of southern Guanaja. Rest-ing in 33m (110ft) of water, there are obvious depth and time limitations to diving on her. Largely intact, the ship's spars, mast and rig-ging stretch out at right angles to the ship, creating an excellent holdfast for gorgonian corals and long colourful sponges. The masts attract schools of small fish, with small hunting packs of angelfish, parrotfish and wrasse. More sedentary fish such as moray eels are also common. Two huge Green Moray Eels are always seen on the wreck and there are several other smaller species. The entire superstructure, decks and winching equipment are now covered in encrusting algae and sponges; their brilliant colours picked out by the divers' torches. The underside of the hull is home to lobsters and large, inquisitive grouper.

The wreck is located far offshore and in an area of tidal current, so that there is a higher-than-average presence of marine life. There are always large packs of jacks and barracuda preying on the smaller species of fish.

8 CAYOS COCHINOS

The 11 small cays of Cayos Cochinos (Hog Islands) are surrounded by a fringing reef and a further barrier reef, offering additional protection to the lush islands. Perfect for wall diving, the inner lagoon has a wide sandy area with sand chutes and coral canyons, all of which converge on the reef crest only 3m (10ft) from the surface. The wall drops near vertically to 36m (120ft) before it starts to slope steeply into the depths where Manta Rays and hammerhead sharks have been seen. As you travel along the wall to the southwest there is a narrow pinnacle that rises from the depths. The channel between the pinnacle and the reef is a mass of deep-water gorgonias, Creole Wrasse and feeding parrotfish.

Off the wall, a Manta Ray may be interested enough to hang around for over 30 minutes, spiralling round the divers, feeding on the rising plankton. The Gorgonian Sea Fans are all of good quality and some of the rope sponges and barrel sponges reach enormous proportions. Flamingo Tongue shells, clingfish and various nudibranchs all make their home on these sea fans and are always a delight to find.

The shallower sandy patch and associated reef is perfect for night dives, because the shallowness allows for extended periods of exploration without time penalties. There are

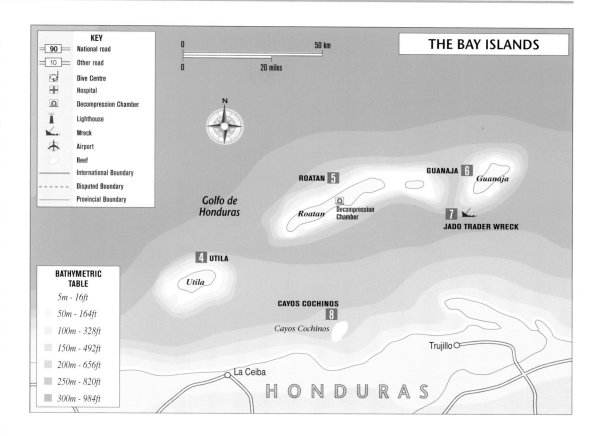

THE BAY ISLANDS

KEY
- 90 National road
- 10 Other road
- Dive Centre
- Hospital
- Decompression Chamber
- Lighthouse
- Wreck
- Airport
- Reef
- International Boundary
- Disputed Boundary
- Provincial Boundary

BATHYMETRIC TABLE
- 5m - 16ft
- 50m - 164ft
- 100m - 328ft
- 150m - 492ft
- 200m - 656ft
- 250m - 820ft
- 300m - 984ft

Golfo de Honduras

ROATAN 5

GUANAJA 6 Guanaja

Roatan Decompression Chamber

7 JADO TRADER WRECK

4 UTILA

Utila

CAYOS COCHINOS 8

Cayos Cochinos

Trujillo

La Ceiba

H O N D U R A S

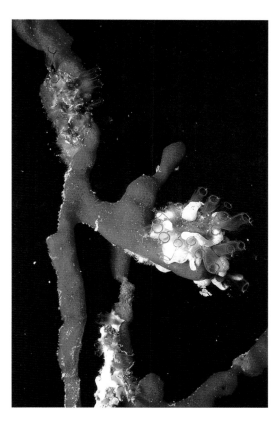

giant Channel Clinging Crabs (*Mithrax spinosissimus*), scorpionfish, spiny lobsters and shrimps of numerous varieties. The edge of the sand patch is also home to toadfish. They use the undersides of coral boulders as sounding boards and their distinctive croaking can be heard over long distances underwater.

ABOVE LEFT *Golden Crinoids* (Davidaster rubiginosa) *are fairly abundant. Hiding from direct sunlight, they only come out to feed at night.*

ABOVE *Colourful sponges are synonymous with the reefs of the western Caribbean and most are host to many different types of marine life, such as these delicate Bulb Tunicates.*

CUBA

by Jack Jackson

SHAPED LIKE A SLEEPING CROCODILE, CUBA lies 145km (90 miles) south of Florida between Jamaica and the Bahamas. Washed by the Atlantic Ocean in the north, the Caribbean Sea to the south and the Gulf of Mexico to the west, its 5746km (3563mile) coastline teems with fish, making it probably the most prolific diving destination in the Caribbean for animal life.

Although the Isla de la Juventud is Cuba's best-known diving region, foreign investment has constructed top-class hotels in other areas where good diving exists. These hotels – as well as the introduction of a barge, which was converted into a floating hotel; and live-aboard boats, which are opening up the marine park of Los Jardines de la Reina – have placed Cuban diving firmly on the international diving map.

There are many more dive sites than those described here and different operators also have different names, or translations of names, for many of them.

TOP LEFT *The Caribbean coast of Cuba. The beach and deep water jetty at Playa Ancon has facilities for all water sports.*

TOP RIGHT *The Atlantic coast of Cuba. One of the earliest areas developed for beach tourism, Varadero's 20km (12½ miles) of fine white sand is one of the cleanest beaches in the world.*

1 HAVANA

Along Cuba's Atlantic coast, Havana has good diving at Playas del Este in the east and to the north of Marina Hemingway, which lies to the west of Havana. Although foreign visitors rarely try it, diving near the capital is good and consists of shelves descending in steps into very deep water. There are also several wrecks.

VARADERO

Varadero, 140km (90 miles) to the east of Havana, has many dive sites and excursions to Playa Girón on the opposite, Caribbean, coast. It is one of the longest established resort areas and well organized for diving, with over 30 dive sites. About 20km (12½ miles) west of it there are several sites off Matanzas, but **Playa Coral** 2 is among the most popular. The site has many gullies descending to a wall at 2–8m (6½–25ft) with Elkhorn and Staghorn coral, sponges and gorgonias, including sea fans and Black Coral in the deeper water. The fish life includes cornetfish and trumpetfish. There are over 30 species of coral down to 20m (65ft) and a series of three caves at 8–10m (25–33ft).

Inland, 18km (11 miles) southwest of Varadero, **Cueva de Saturno** 3 (Saturno Caves) are a series of caves flooded with both fresh and seawater and containing stalactites, stalagmites and blind shrimps.

Penetration to the further chambers is only for trained cave divers. The water is cold, so a good wetsuit is required.

North of Punta Hicacos, there are several wrecks which were cleaned and sunk for divers. The 102m (335ft) **Russian patrol ship** 4 (*barco patrullero* in Spanish), lies in 28m (92ft) of water. The 40m (130ft) wreck, referred to in Spanish as **Coral Negro** 5, and the 36m (118ft) tugboat **Remocador** 6 lie at a depth of 20m (65ft). A **Russian AN-24 aircraft** 7 lies at a depth of 15m (50ft) and **La Cohetera** 8 is at 18m (60ft).

Northeast of Cabezo del Cayo and Cayos Blancos, the 40m (130ft) **Barco Hundido** 9 (Sunken Ship), also called *Neptuno*, is a popular site because it is not deep. It lies at a depth of only 10m (33ft), with good visibility and good marine life.

CAYO COCO

Cayo Coco, 100km (62 miles) northeast of Ciego de Ávila, is accessible by vehicle via a 27km (17 miles) causeway. It has relatively new hotel developments along brilliant white sand beaches and spectacular diving. The sites have not seen many divers so reef and nurse sharks are often encountered. North of Cayo Coco, **La Jaula** 10 has four slightly different sites, the seabed being covered in Gorgonian Sea Fans, Sea Rods and Sea Whips interspersed with clumps of stony corals and rich fish life.

SANTA LUCÍA

Santa Lucía, 180 km (112 miles) northeast of Camagüey, has attractive reefs and wrecks with many pelagic species, including Eagle Rays, stingrays and Manta Rays.

The main dive site at Santa Lucía is the **Mortera** wreck [11]. This Spanish merchant ship sank north of the Bahia de Nuevitas in 27m (89ft) of water after a collision in 1896. It is now well colonized by marine creatures and the fish life includes Bull Sharks.

Northeast of the Bahia de Nuevitas, **Escalón** [12] is a sandy ledge with diverse marine life along the top of a drop-off at 20m (65ft). North of Santa Lucía is **Poseidon 2** [13], a dense coral garden on a ledge at 18m (60ft), before the seabed slopes down to 30m (100ft).

GUARDALAVACA

Guardalavaca has wrecks, walls, caves and terraces. The area also has other attractions besides diving. Northwest of the Bahia de Vita is **Cadena** [14] (Chain), a dive which follows the marine life that developed around a dropped chain at 20m (65ft). Northwest of Guardalavaca, **Corona** [15] has a colourful wall with rope and encrusting sponges from 20m (65ft) to 40m (130ft). The abundant fish life includes Blacktip Reef Sharks. Northeast of Guardalavaca there is another of many sites called **Aquarium** [16] after its abundant fish life at 10–15m (33–50ft).

SANTIAGO DE CUBA

At the eastern end of Cuba's Caribbean coast, 863km (535 miles) east of Havana, the Santiago de Cuba region has more than 70 dive sites and excellent marine life among channels, caves and wrecks. Apart from the wreck

TOP RIGHT *The Indigo Hamlet (Hypoplectrus indigo) is a shy and relatively rare Seabass that swims about near the bottom, feeding on small fish and crustaceans.*

RIGHT *The Blue Tang (Acanthurus coeruleus) is one of many fish that change colour patterns as they develop from juvenile to adult.*

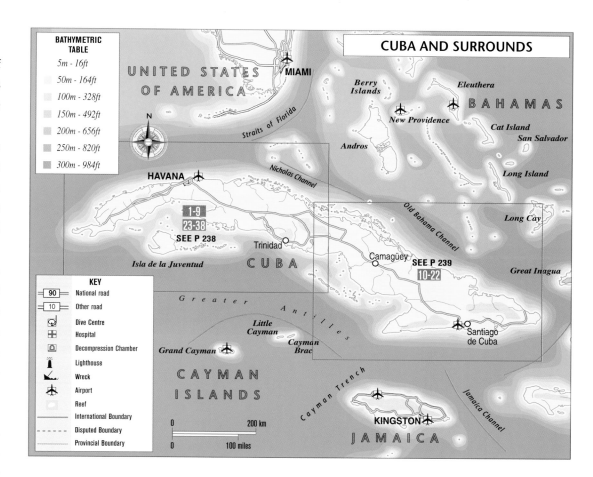

CUBA AND SURROUNDS

BATHYMETRIC TABLE
5m - 16ft
50m - 164ft
100m - 328ft
150m - 492ft
200m - 656ft
250m - 820ft
300m - 984ft

KEY
90 National road
10 Other road
Dive Centre
Hospital
Decompression Chamber
Lighthouse
Wreck
Airport
Reef
International Boundary
Disputed Boundary
Provincial Boundary

UNITED STATES OF AMERICA
MIAMI
Straits of Florida
HAVANA
1-9
23-38
SEE P 238
Trinidad
Isla de la Juventud
CUBA
Camagüey
SEE P 239
10-22
Nicholas Channel
Old Bahama Channel
Berry Islands
Eleuthera
BAHAMAS
New Providence
Cat Island
San Salvador
Andros
Long Island
Long Cay
Great Inagua
Santiago de Cuba
Greater Antilles
Little Cayman
Cayman Brac
Grand Cayman
CAYMAN ISLANDS
Cayman Trench
KINGSTON
JAMAICA
Jamaica Channel

0   200 km
0   100 miles

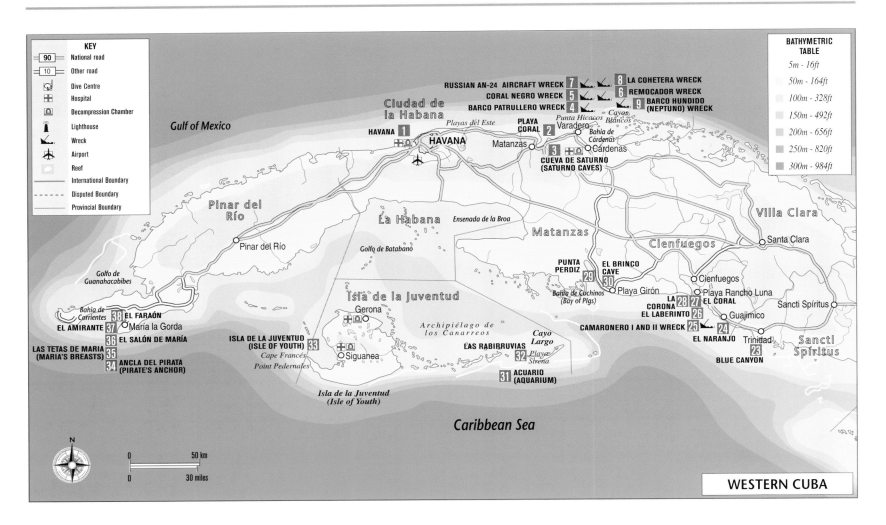

ABOVE *A distinctive adult female Stoplight Parrotfish* (Sparisoma viride)*. The teeth of all parrotfish are fused into beak-like plates, which most use to scrape the algal film from stony coral or rock, while a few eat leafy algae or living stony coral.*

of the *Cristóbal Colón*, the reef platform slopes to 35m (115ft) and then drops off into depths greater than 1000m (3300ft) – so there are plenty of pelagic species in addition to the excellent marine life both on and off the narrow reef flat. Where it descends into the abyss, divers can observe large fish, but the main attraction in this area is the sunken Spanish warship *Cristóbal Colón* 17 close to the shore near La Plata. The wreck lies down the slope to 30m (100ft).

LOS JARDINES DE LA REINA

South of Ciego de Avila, Los Jardines de la Reina (The Queen's Gardens), is a chain of 250 uninhabited coral reefs stretching for over 160km (100 miles) some 80km (50 miles) offshore. It is a marine park, and therefore access is restricted and commercial fishing banned. As well as small fish there are massive Goliath Groupers, shoals of Tarpon and jacks and Silky, Blacktip Reef and Bull Sharks. Known to Americans as Lost Paradise Keys, Los Jardines de la Reina National Park

has 50 pristine dive sites, most of them protected from winds and currents, with many more still to be explored. There are hundreds of small cays surrounded by mangroves. The area teems with reef fish, including huge barracuda, groupers and sharks.

Cabezo de Coral Negro 18 is known for Blacktip, Bull and sometimes Silky Sharks at 35–40m (115–130ft). Southeast of Cayo Anclitas is **La Cueva del Pulpo** 19, which is

RIGHT *Bipinnate Sea Plume Gorgonian (Pseudopterogorgia bipinnata) colonies grow in a single plane with primary and secondary branches.*
FAR RIGHT *In deep water Yellow Tube Sponges (Aplysina fistularis) are longer, without the staghorn-like growths found in shallow water.*

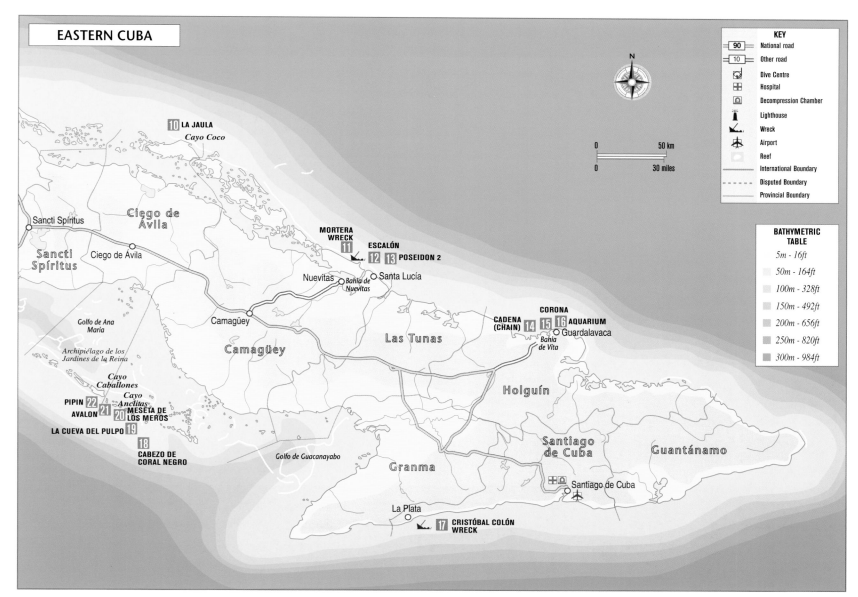

AMERICAN DIVERS GOING TO CUBA

Due to the US embargo on Cuba, Americans who visit Cuba at their own expense, without US Government permission, cannot legally spend money in Cuba. There is no law specifically forbidding American citizens to travel to Cuba, provided they do it under fully escorted and fully sponsored programmes. American divers have got around this problem for many years by booking an all-inclusive, pre-paid trip through a non-US or non-Cuban tour operator, usually in Canada or Mexico. The most common gateways are Cancún, Toronto, Panama, Nassau and Montreal, but you can also use the Cayman Islands, Jamaica and Costa Rica.

Although popular, travel to Cuba is a 'grey' area and after years of the government turning a blind eye the Bush administration is clamping down on it. If American citizens do travel to Cuba in this way, they should make sure that immigration officials within Cuba stamp their tourist card or visa and not their passport. On return to the US, if customs officials ask them to fill out a form listing the countries visited since departure, they should not list Cuba. If they receive any other related forms, they should ask their tour operator for advice before filling them in.

ABOVE *A stand of Pillar Coral (Dendrogyra cylindrus). Spires grow from a common base and are found on flat or slightly sloping bottoms.*

best known for large pillar corals, a cave, and Goliath Groupers. **Meseta de los Meros** [20] is particularly known for its groupers down to 32m (105ft). West of Cayo Anclitas is **Avalon** [21], which has abundant fish life at 37m (121ft), which in turn attracts Blacktip, Bull and many Silky Sharks. South of Cayo Caballones is **Pipin** [22], which has sandy gullies among Brain and Star Corals on a gentle slope from 15m (50ft) to 22m (72ft).

CIENFUEGOS, GUAJIMICO AND TRINIDAD

The Cienfuegos, Guajimico and Trinidad areas have a maze of small walls and sandy gullies lined with sponges and gorgonias, including sea fans and sea rods. The growth on the seabed harbours reef fish, lobsters, shrimps, nudibranchs and crabs. Fish species include moray eels, Nassau Groupers, Blue Tangs, Queen Triggerfish and snappers, while Batwing Coral Crabs are common in this area.

The coast of Trinidad has 21 dive sites and one of the longest coral reefs in Cuba, known for its Black Coral and Whale Sharks. West of Trinidad, **Blue Canyon** [23] is the largest of several channels descending to a drop-off at 20–30m (65–100ft), with abundant marine life.

Guajimico has 16 dive sites, one of which, **El Naranjo** [24], is a colourful dive with Lettuce and Fire Corals, gorgonians and many species of snappers at 7m (23ft).

Camaronero I and II [25] are two deliberately sunk fishing boats lying at 10–25m (33–80ft). Northwest of the wrecks is **El Laberinto** [26], a labyrinth of sandy gullies, coral heads and gorgonias from 10m (33ft) to 27m (89ft). North of El Laberinto is **El Coral** [27], which has a pillar coral 7m (23ft) high – one of the largest in the world.

Cienfuegos, described as the Pearl of the South, has 30 dive sites characterized by calm waters and large reefs with deep, wide channels dropping down from 10m (33ft) to 40m (130ft). South of Playa Rancho Luna, **La Corona** [28] has narrow coral channels more than 10m (33ft) deep, descending sharply to a sandy plateau carpeted with gorgonias and many large fish.

PLAYA GIRÓN

Northeast of Cayo Largo, Playa Girón (Bahia de Cochinos – the Bay of Pigs) has drop-offs, gorgonias, sponges, barracuda, Tarpon, groupers and wrecks. There are 14 dive sites, some with steep drop-offs, a good collection of pelagic species and an inland cave. On the east side of the Bahia de Cochinos, **Punta**

Perdiz [29] has a good drop-off around 18m (60ft) and good marine life from 10m (33ft) to more than 40m (130ft). Inland, 2km (1½ mile) northwest of Playa Girón, **El Brinco Cave** [30] should only be dived in the company of a local guide. It has blind fish, but no stalactites or stalagmites.

CAYO LARGO

Cayo Largo, the largest island in the archipiélago de los Canarreos, has many shallow coral gardens, but the best walls often start below 30m (100ft). Canyons harbour countless reef fish and reef sharks are found along the walls. Some drop-offs begin at 6m (20ft) and descend into the depths. Tunnels full of jacks, Tarpons, large groupers and Green and Hawksbill Turtles are common. Cayo Largo has more than 30 dive sites. Southeast of Faro los Ballenatos, **Acuario** [31] (another Aquarium) is another area of patch reefs and holes with prolific fish life at 12–15m (40–50ft). Southwest of Playa Sirena, **Las Rabirruvias** [32] has coral heads and gorgonias on sand at 5–8m (16–25ft).

ABOVE *Flamingo Tongue Snail (Cyphoma gibbosum) on a gorgonian. These snails feed on gorgonias in all types of habitats.*

ABOVE *The Azure Vase Sponge (Callyspongia plicifera), with its elaborately convoluted exterior, grows alone or in twos and threes.*

ABOVE *Batwing Coral Crabs (Carpilius corallinus), often only seen at night, can be seen during the day off Playa Ancon.*

☒ ISLA DE LA JUVENTUD (THE ISLE OF YOUTH)

The Isla de la Juventud (Isle of Youth), previously known as the Isle of Pines, attracts the most divers. A shallow reef crest with caves, crevices, canyons and drop-offs into the Gulf of Mexico, this area has one of the oldest marine reserves in the world. Many of Cuba's premier dive sites lie along its southwest shore. The diving is based on Hotel El Colony on the coast west of Siguanea, but the dive sites stretch from Cape Francés to Point Pedernales and include a 6km (4mile) strip known as the Pirate Coast. Highly organized with a fixed restaurant complex for lunch, there are nearly 60 marked dive sites and most have fixed moorings to minimize anchor damage. Sheltered from the prevailing east-southeast winds, and with minimal currents, the fish life is profuse, tame and approachable. Some sites are at 30m (100ft) with valleys descending to between 50m (165ft) and 80m (260ft). The reefs are forested with Gorgonian Sea Fans, Sea Plumes and Sea Rods as well as Bowl, Tube, Vase and Octopus Sponges.

Large shoals of Tarpon barely condescend to move aside as you swim through them. Barracuda, Rainbow Runners, Trumpetfish, Red Snappers, Schoolmaster Snappers and Yellowtail Snappers follow you around. Spiny lobsters, Batwing Coral Crabs and Green Moray Eels abound and stingrays are found on the sand. The myriad of friendly fish include Queen Angelfish, French Angelfish, Queen Triggerfish, Sargassum Triggerfish, Black Durgon, Ocean Surgeonfish, Blue Tangs, butterflyfish, grunts, groupers, Spanish Hogfish, parrotfish and Scrawled Filefish.

North-northeast of Cape Francés there are three shipwrecks which are well colonized by marine life.

MARÍA LA GORDA

An UNESCO biosphere reserve situated along the Caribbean coast, 300km (190 miles) west of Havana, María la Gorda has one of the most protected reef areas in Cuba. Most of the dive sites are close to shore. They are noted for corals, gorgonias, fans, sponges, snappers, barracuda, Eagle Rays and stingrays, while Whale

Sharks are seen from September to November. The area has 39 of Cuba's best dive sites, though some of them are beyond recreational diving depths on air.

Ancla del Pirata ☒ (Pirate's Anchor) is named after a large 18th century anchor resting against coral at 15m (50ft). **Las Tetas de Maria** ☒ (Maria's breasts) is named after the rock formations that jut out to sea from the land. Sandy channels and large coral heads are the most prominent features of this site.

Northwest of Las Tetas de Maria is **El Salón de María** ☒. This is a cave characterized by its sponges at 20m (65ft). There are three entrances. Northwest of El Salón de María is **El Amirante** ☒, a drop-off starting at 27m (90ft) and covered with large sponges, gorgonias and Black Coral at 30m (100ft). The prolific fish life includes Tarpon, angelfish, grunts and groupers and the occasional Whale Shark. On the east side of the Bahia de Corrientes, **El Faraón** ☒ is known for a 2m (6½ft) Barrel Sponge on the top of a drop-off at 20m (65ft). The marine life is prolific with Black Corals at 35–40m (115–130ft).

CAYMAN ISLANDS

by Lawson Wood

ORIGINALLY CONNECTED TO CUBA TO THE northeast by a now submerged mountain range, the Cayman Islands were discovered in 1503 by Christopher Columbus during his second Caribbean voyage of discovery. Located in the central Caribbean, the three coral-topped former mountains are Grand Cayman, Cayman Brac and Little Cayman. Still a British crown colony, the islands are subject to British laws and customs, although they have their own national currency, the Cayman dollar, used alongside the American dollar.

Each island has its own atmosphere and, of course, great diving and snorkelling. Grand Cayman is 35km (22 miles) long and the largest of the three islands. It is also known for 'the best 3½m (12ft) dive worldwide' at Stingray City where, for many years now, thousands of tourists have experienced the thrill of hand-feeding stingrays. One section of the area is known as The Sandbar and, with the water as shallow as 1m (3ft), this makes a perfect

TOP LEFT Little Cayman Island has excellent walls along the Bloody Bay Wall and Jackson Bight, where there are massive caverns and sand chutes which disect the fringing coral heads.
TOP RIGHT At The Sandbar you can interact with Southern Stingrays in the safety of only a few feet of water.

location for interaction with these amazing creatures which have 'trained humans' to feed them tasty morsels. The famous Cayman Trench can be explored here to a depth of 300m (1000ft) by a deep submersible.

Cayman Brac, 120km (75 miles) to the northwest, is home to a Russian frigate which was sunk deliberately in September 1996 to serve as an artificial reef. Just 11km (7 miles) away is Little Cayman Island, reputed to have the best wall diving in the Caribbean.

The Caribbean's deepest oceanic valley, the Cayman Trench, comes close to the southern shores of these islands. The Cayman Trench is responsible for the better-than-average clarity of water, because all suspended particulate matter quickly drops into the deep, leaving the shallow waters perfect for snorkelling and diving. Grand Cayman is on all Caribbean cruise ships' routes and hundreds of thousands of visitors from all over the world are discovering these magical islands for scuba diving, snorkelling, swimming, banking, shopping and just plain relaxing in a safe country where the locals are welcoming.

Over 100 dive operators, hotel and condominiums are members of the Cayman Tourism Alliance (CTA), formerly known as the CIWOA (Cayman Islands Watersports Operators Association). These islands are also regarded as one of the safest dive locations in

the world, with a special programme of conservation and safety education adopted by all the dive centres in the alliance.

The Department of the Environment maintains the Marine Parks and has introduced over 280 permanent mooring buoys around the islands. The moorings for dive boats and yachts are changed every year to allow coral regeneration and to spread the load of diver pollution. The department was also responsible for the survey and cleanup work on the former Russian frigate, which was sunk off Greenhouse Reef to the north of Cayman Brac, and is involved in continuous monitoring of marine habitats around the islands. The majority of the diving and snorkelling on all three islands is from day boats, which usually entail a 10–20 minute ride to the site. Moorings are only equipped for one dive boat at a time and the principle of first come, first served applies. However, qualified divers can hire equipment and shore-dive in a number of specific locations without the time limits imposed by dive centres.

GRAND CAYMAN ISLAND

Located inside the sheltered lagoon and protected by Grand Cayman Island's famous North Wall, are two of the world's legendary dive locations. **Stingray City** ☐1 and its counterpart, The Sandbar ☐2, have been featured in *National Geographic* and promoted

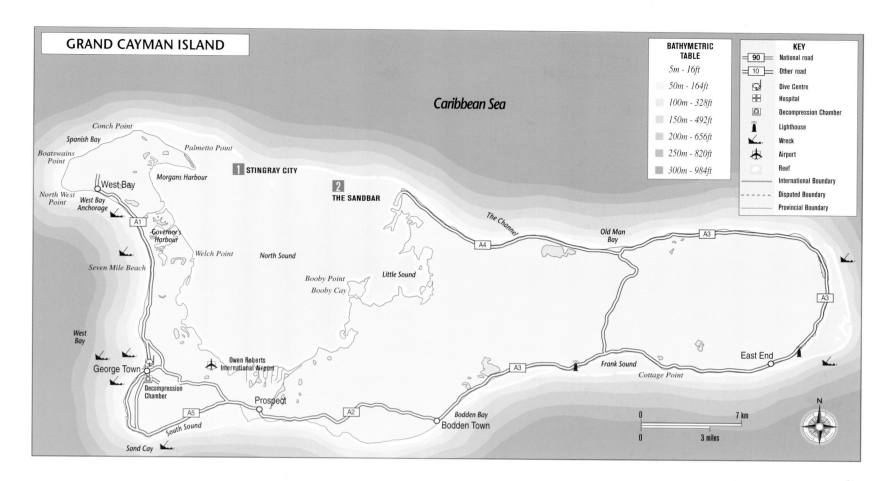

GRAND CAYMAN ISLAND

Caribbean Sea

BATHYMETRIC TABLE

5m - 16ft
50m - 164ft
100m - 328ft
150m - 492ft
200m - 656ft
250m - 820ft
300m - 984ft

KEY

90 National road
10 Other road
Dive Centre
Hospital
Decompression Chamber
Lighthouse
Wreck
Airport
Reef
International Boundary
Disputed Boundary
Provincial Boundary

Conch Point
Spanish Bay
Palmetto Point
Boatswains Point
Morgans Harbour
1 STINGRAY CITY
2 THE SANDBAR
West Bay
North West Point
West Bay Anchorage
A1
Governor's Harbour
Welch Point
North Sound
The Channel
Old Man Bay
A4
A3
A3
Seven Mile Beach
Booby Point
Booby Cay
Little Sound
West Bay
Owen Roberts International Airport
George Town
Decompression Chamber
Prospect
A5
South Sound
Sand Cay
A2
Bodden Bay
Bodden Town
Frank Sound
Cottage Point
East End

0   7 km
0   3 miles

N

throughout the world in film, video and magazine articles. The Sandbar is the most popular with tourists, because it makes it possible for those unable or unwilling to dive to enjoy the spectacular stingray feeding in waters only 1m (3ft) deep.

The stingrays here are the Southern Stingray (*Dasyatis americana*). There are several large groups of these rays, totalling about 250, that have become habituated over many years to hand-feeding. They are able to detect the scent of food in the water and also associate the sound of boat engines with food. Stingrays do not have teeth; instead they have a pair of bony rasping plates. You feed them like a horse, with fish bait held in the open palm. When feeding, it is not uncommon for a ray to envelop you in its 'wings.' Free meal over, the stingrays quickly revert to their normal feeding behaviour of foraging on the sand flats for small crustaceans and molluscs. This curious mix of nature and enterprise has been enjoyed by several hundred thousand tourists attracted by the interaction with one of nature's amazing phenomena.

ABOVE *Orange Ball Corallimorph* (Pseudocorynactis caribbeorum) *have bright orange ball tips to each tentacle. They are often misnamed the Orange Ball Anemone due to the resemblance.*

ABOVE *Bigeye Scad* (Selar crumenophthalmus) *often come in huge schools in April and May when they are rounded up by Dolphin Fish and tuna and ferociously attacked.*

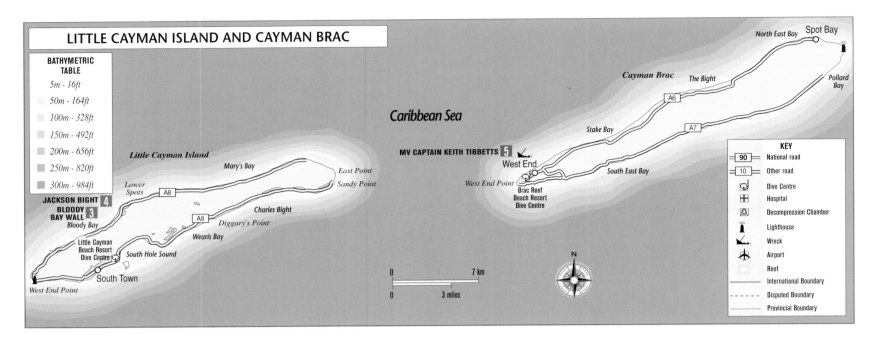

LITTLE CAYMAN ISLAND

Bloody Bay Wall ③ and **Jackson Bight** ④ to the north of Little Cayman are both highly regarded. In the southwest, the reef crest is only 6m (20ft) deep and the wall drops vertically for several hundred metres, well beyond the safe diving limit. The top of the reef is made up of hard pan – the ancient coralline shoreline topped by sparse gorgonian and stony corals, but is home to huge quantities and varieties of reef fish.

As you travel to the northeast along the reef crest, the wall becomes more convoluted and is deeply undercut in some sections, making it the perfect habitat for shade-loving creatures such as squirrelfish, Channel Clinging Crabs and lobsters. Towards the Jackson Bight section, the hard pan gives way to a wide, gently sloping sandy-bottomed lagoon protected by the outer reef. Here the reef is cut through by numerous caves, caverns, sand chutes and canyons connecting the sandy lagoon to the outer vertical cliff wall.

TOP LEFT *Bluestriped Lizardfish* (Synodus saurus) *are common around the shallow reefs, but hide under the sand to ambush prey.*
LEFT *During early summer, Balloonfish* (Diodon holocanthus) *can often be found in pairs or groups of three or four as they pursue the age old mating ritual.*

One of the greatest thrills in this area is the regular appearance of Eagle Rays that forage for crustaceans under the sand, their pointed snouts equipped for the purpose. Graceful in motion, their spotted backs and long whip-like tails distinguish them from the much smaller, bottom-hugging Southern Stingrays which are also common in these sand flats.

The shallower rubble-filled areas at the bottom of the inner mini-wall are home to Sailfin Blennies, which ferociously protect their old worm-cast burrows. Many of the smaller stones have attached corkscrew anemones and their attendant pistol shrimps. The name pistol shrimp comes from the sound that the larger of their two claws makes when striking out in defence or attack. The shallower coral canyons are also home to huge schools of silversides which congregate during July to September in large moving shoals for protection from the main hunters of the reef – the jacks, Tarpon and barracuda.

CAYMAN BRAC

Renamed the **MV Captain Keith Tibbetts** 5, after a resident of Cayman Brac, the Russian frigate was built in 1984 at Nadhodka in the USSR at a cost of US$30 million. The 100m (330ft) ship had a beam of 13m (43ft), and weighed 1590 metric tons and had a ship's complement of 11 officers and 99 enlisted personnel. Stationed in Cuba during the Cold War, she was never involved in any conflict. When the USSR dissolved in 1992, the newly created Russian Republic took over the operational control of the old Soviet base on Cuba. However, due to the economic upheaval in Russia, the base could not be supported financially and in 1993 the base and all the ships stationed in the Caribbean were removed from active duty.

When the ship was finally sunk in September 1996, Jean-Michel Cousteau, in full scuba gear, stayed on board as she went down. Later that night, after we had completed filming for the day, he said '...fear did not come into it, this is something that I have always wanted to do and the preparations, to ensure that there

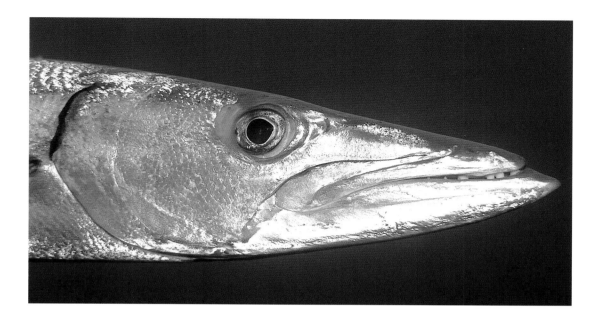

TOP *Great Barracuda (*Sphyraena barracuda*) are seen on most dives. They are attracted to the shade offered by dive boats and are often the first fish divers encounter.*
ABOVE *The classic view of the Channel Clinging Crab (*Mithrax spinosissimus*) at night when it climbs up onto the swaying sea fans. It grows to span over 1m (40 in) to the ends of its claws.*

would be no accidents, were meticulous. What did cause a moment of anxiety was when the aluminium superstructure cracked open in two places, splitting the living quarters with a resounding crack...'

The main part of the hull lists only slightly to starboard and is perfectly placed in a sand-chute that plunges over the wall off the north shore of Cayman Brac. On either side are healthy sections of coral reef carpeted with

huge barrel sponges. The bow has now almost sheered off and lies at a much more acute angle, but now the ship looks much more like the wreck she has become, rather than an old ship sunk as a tourist attraction. Completely covered in marine growth, with some fine examples of gorgonian and stony corals and sponges, this former engine of war is now an extension of the healthy reef and home to a myriad of fish and invertebrates.

CAYMAN TRENCH

EXPLORING THE DEEP

Until recently it was only members of the scientific community who had the opportunity to visit the depths of the ocean in the quest for knowledge. It was unthinkable that some day tourists would be able to enjoy the same freedom. The 6.6m (22ft) *Atlantis Research Submersible*, based in George Town on Grand Cayman can take two passengers down the Cayman Trench to a depth of 300m (1000ft). The adventure begins some 30 minutes before leaving shore, with a slide show of the dive you are about to undertake. The most disconcerting part of the experience is when the captain states: 'If I die, hit this emergency button and breathe from this.' The two passengers and captain sit in the forward compartment looking out of a window 6cm (2 in) thick and 1m (40 in) in diameter.

This twilight world hosts species of marine life only rarely seen. Due to its filtration by the water, the colour red is the first to disappear, gradually followed by the other colours in the ascending order of electromagnetic energy, until everything takes on shades of blue-grey. At the 100m (330ft) level the captain switches on his powerful 600 watt halogen lamps and the sponge belt's colour is revealed in all its splendour, with brilliant reds and yellows. Many of the deeper sponges and some corals feed on the marine 'snow' which falls from shallow waters into the depths of the Cayman Trench. At 240m (800ft) the lights penetrate 100m (330ft). Huge boulders of ancient limestone are topped with curiously shaped crinoids, a distant cousin of prehistoric sea lilies and huge arrow crabs. Surprisingly there are quite a few fish hunting in these depths, taking advantage of our powerful lights. The debris on the slope is made up of sand and the skeletal remains of sea creatures over the millennia. This breathtaking experience should not be missed by anyone with a sense of adventure.

Not to scale – some of the smaller species have been enlarged for clarity.

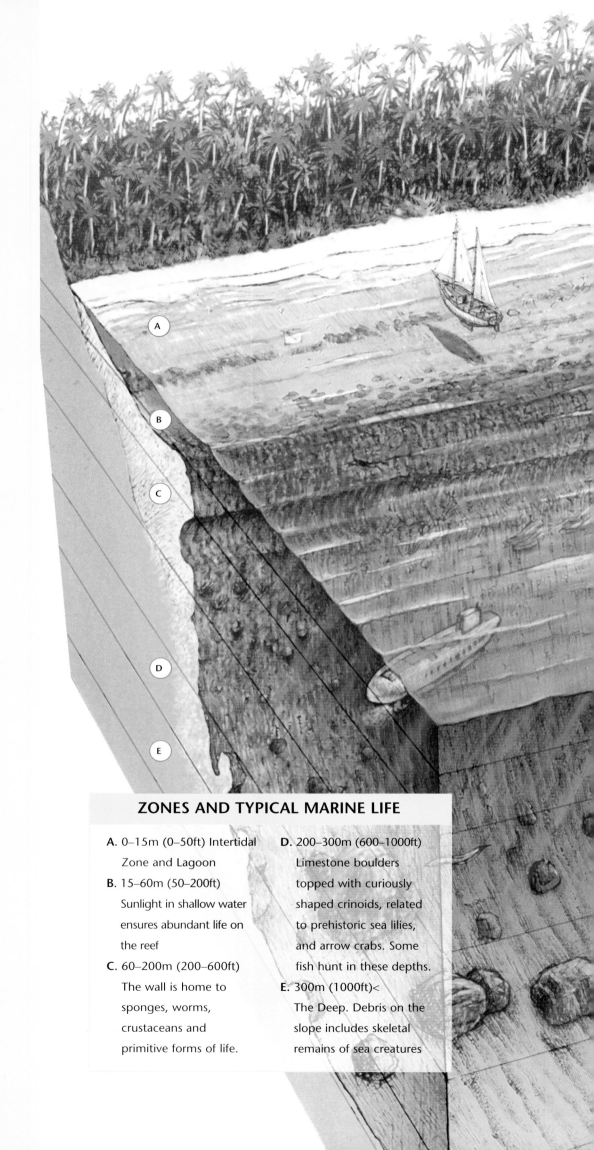

ZONES AND TYPICAL MARINE LIFE

A. 0–15m (0–50ft) Intertidal Zone and Lagoon

B. 15–60m (50–200ft) Sunlight in shallow water ensures abundant life on the reef

C. 60–200m (200–600ft) The wall is home to sponges, worms, crustaceans and primitive forms of life.

D. 200–300m (600–1000ft) Limestone boulders topped with curiously shaped crinoids, related to prehistoric sea lilies, and arrow crabs. Some fish hunt in these depths.

E. 300m (1000ft)< The Deep. Debris on the slope includes skeletal remains of sea creatures

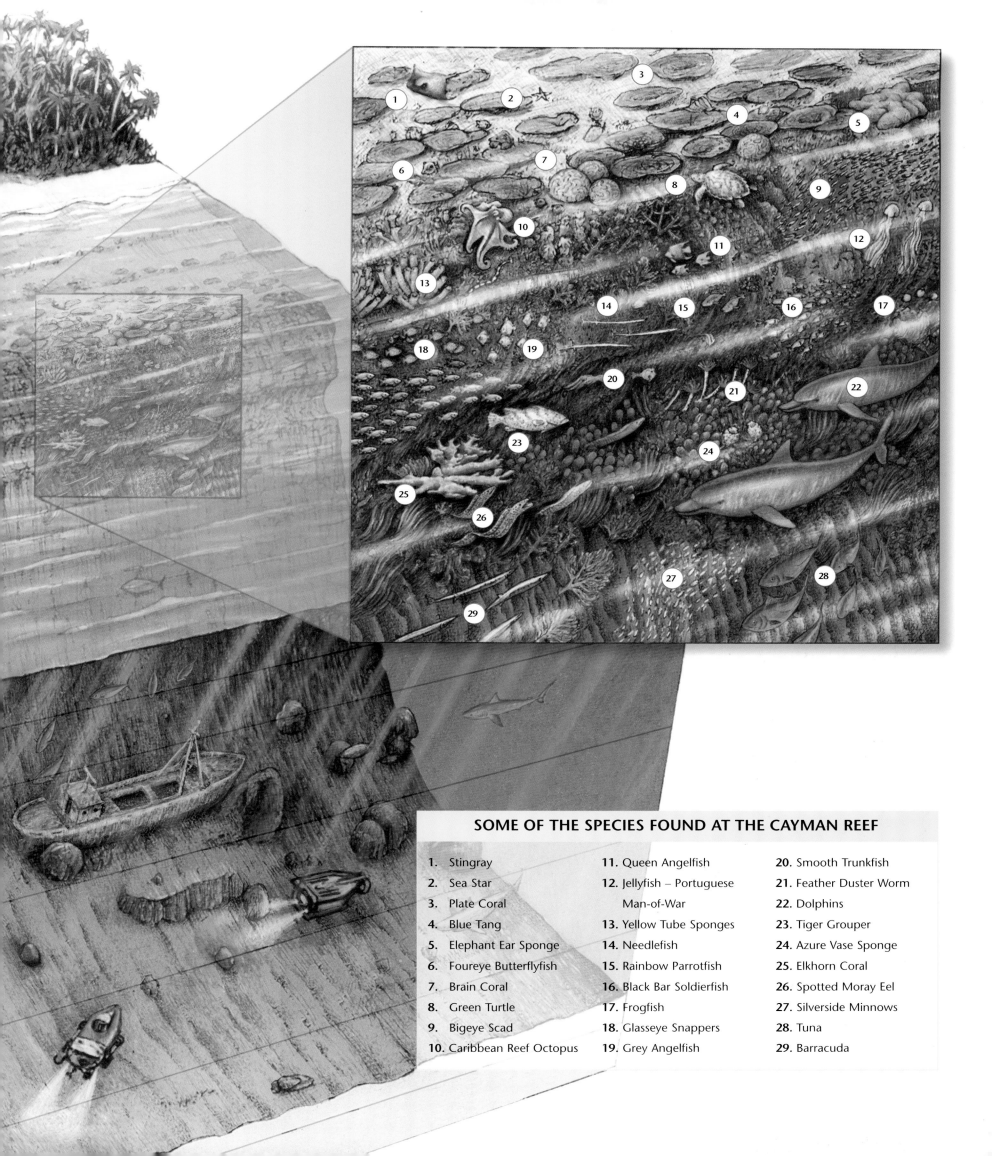

SOME OF THE SPECIES FOUND AT THE CAYMAN REEF

1. Stingray
2. Sea Star
3. Plate Coral
4. Blue Tang
5. Elephant Ear Sponge
6. Foureye Butterflyfish
7. Brain Coral
8. Green Turtle
9. Bigeye Scad
10. Caribbean Reef Octopus

11. Queen Angelfish
12. Jellyfish – Portuguese Man-of-War
13. Yellow Tube Sponges
14. Needlefish
15. Rainbow Parrotfish
16. Black Bar Soldierfish
17. Frogfish
18. Glasseye Snappers
19. Grey Angelfish

20. Smooth Trunkfish
21. Feather Duster Worm
22. Dolphins
23. Tiger Grouper
24. Azure Vase Sponge
25. Elkhorn Coral
26. Spotted Moray Eel
27. Silverside Minnows
28. Tuna
29. Barracuda

DUTCH ANTILLES

by Jack Jackson

TOP LEFT *Pounding surf on the windward side of Aruba has cut eight natural bridges in the limestone. Andicuri Bridge, 8m (25ft) high and 30m (100ft) long, is the largest.*

TOP RIGHT *Curaçao is the largest of the ABC islands, with the most varied diving. Santa Martha Bay has sheltered anchorage.*

ARUBA

Aruba has the best beaches and is the most Americanized of the Dutch Antilles. The island has plenty of other activities and is ideal for non-diving partners or family. The reefs on the leeward (southern) coast mainly slope gently from 5m (15ft) to 18m (60ft) and then drop off at an angle of 40–60° to a sandy seabed with coral heads at 30–40m (100–130ft). The west coast is flatter and, except for Malmok Reef, ranges from 11m (35ft) to 18m (60ft). Diving operators often have their own names for sites.

Aruba has a number of conservation and cleanup programmes, mooring buoys and a marine park. Some divers avoid the peak cruise ship months of December and January when the most popular sites become crowded.

Southeast of the lighthouse, the **California wreck** 1 rises to 9m (30ft) and is surrounded by large coral formations and an abundance of reef fish including Goliath Groupers (*Epinephelus itajara)*, barracuda and the occasional shark. However, it is located in the choppy seas and strong currents of the island's windward side, so it is not suitable for novices.

Off Arashi Beach, **Arashi Airplane** 2 has a twin-engined Beechcraft sitting in 10m (33ft) of water. Its propellers have fallen off, but the passenger cabin is full of shoaling fish. Sergeant Majors, jacks, goatfish, grunts, angelfish, butterflyfish, parrotfish and pufferfish swim around the outside.

The 120m (400ft) German freighter ***Antilla*** 3 requires several dives. She was scuttled off Malmok Beach in 1940 and lies in 18m (60ft) of water, listing to port, with part of her starboard side above water. The hull is festooned with invertebrates and the fish life includes Sergeant Majors, parrotfish, moray eels, Trumpetfish, snappers, Queen Angelfish, groupers and many species of shoaling fish. The oil tanker ***Pedernales*** 4 was torpedoed off Hadicurari Beach in 1942 and what remains of her lies in several large pieces at 8m (25ft).

Off **Oranjestad harbour** 5, the slope gradually drops from 12m (40ft) to 30m (100ft) past heads of Brain Corals, sponges and gorgonias with Green Moray Eels, French Angelfish, Spotted Eagle Rays, stingrays, sea horses and an old pilot boat. **Sonesta Airplane** 6, a Convair–400, sits upright in 15m (50ft) of water off Sonesta Island. The doors and most of the interior were removed so the aircraft is easy to penetrate and the propellers are still attached to the engines. The site begins around 5m (16ft) and the reef continues down to 30m (100ft).

East of **Skalahein** 7 is the spectacular wreck of the 75m (250ft) freighter ***Jane Sea*** 8, which was deliberately sunk as an artificial reef. Sitting upright with the propeller at 29m (95ft), there is plenty of colour, Orange *Tubastrea* Cup Corals, Fire Coral and

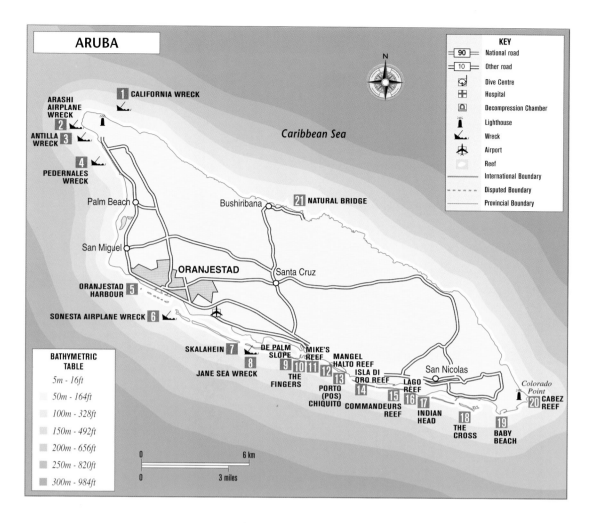

ARUBA

KEY

90	National road
10	Other road
	Dive Centre
	Hospital
	Decompression Chamber
	Lighthouse
	Wreck
	Airport
	Reef
	International Boundary
	Disputed Boundary
	Provincial Boundary

Caribbean Sea

1 CALIFORNIA WRECK

ARASHI AIRPLANE WRECK 2

ANTILLA WRECK 3

4

PEDERNALES WRECK

Palm Beach

San Miguel

ORANJESTAD

ORANJESTAD HARBOUR 5

SONESTA AIRPLANE WRECK 6

SKALAHEIN 7

8

JANE SEA WRECK

DE PALM SLOPE 9

MIKE'S REEF

THE FINGERS 10 11

PORTO (POS) CHIQUITO 13

Bushiribana

21 NATURAL BRIDGE

Santa Cruz

MANGEL HALTO REEF 12

ISLA DI ORO REEF 13

14

COMMANDEURS REEF 15

16 LAGO REEF

17 INDIAN HEAD

San Nicolas

18 THE CROSS

19 BABY BEACH

Colorado Point

20 CABEZ REEF

BATHYMETRIC TABLE

5m - 16ft
50m - 164ft
100m - 328ft
150m - 492ft
200m - 656ft
250m - 820ft
300m - 984ft

0   6 km

0   3 miles

---

red and pink encrusting sponges are found on the hull and Black Corals on her port side. The wreck attracts shoaling fish, while Brain Corals and Gorgonian Sea Fans can be found around her. **De Palm Slope** 9, off De Palm Island is a good shore dive from 5m (16ft) to deep water. **Mike's Reef** 11, southeast of **The Fingers** 10 is one of the best reef dives in Aruba. A rock garden beginning at 8m (25ft) and descending to 27m (90ft), it is dominated by Brain Corals, Star Corals and Gorgonian Sea Fans and colourful sponges. Its varied fish life includes Rainbow Runners. **Mangel Halto Reef** 12 slopes steeply from 5m (15ft) down to 34m (110ft) and has sea horses. **Porto (Pos) Chiquito** 13 is a pretty shore dive of great diversity down to 25m (80ft). Once called Snapper City, there are countless fish. Easily accessible from shore, it is regularly used for night diving and is popular for observing coral spawning in September and October.

Isla Di Oro Reef 14, off Saveneta, is similar to Mangel Halto. **Commandeurs Reef** 15 slopes from 12m (40ft) into the depths with

Leaf and Sheet coral and rich fish life. **Lago Reef** 16 is one of Aruba's deepest dive sites with beautiful coral formations, Gorgonian Sea Fans, sponges, sea anemones and abundant crustacean and fish life down to 37m (120ft). **Indian Head** 17 is named after a large coral formation resembling a head.

The Cross 18 has good coral heads and an assortment of Gorgonian Sea Rods, Sea Whips and Sea Fans and bountiful fish life down to 18m (60ft). The site has a 3m (10ft) memorial embedded in the seabed. **Baby Beach** 19 slopes from 6m (20ft) to 18m (60ft) with large formations of Elkhorn Coral and Sheet Coral making good hiding places for crabs, lobsters and octopuses. South of Colorado Point, **Cabez Reef** 20 has rough seas with strong currents. For experienced divers there are amberjack, barracuda and Rainbow Runners as well as many species of reef fish.

Natural Bridge 21, off the largest of the natural bridges near Bushiribana, can be dived during calm weather on the windward side of the island by advanced divers. Descending to

33m (110ft), there are huge boulders and large formations of Fire, Brain and Star Coral, Black Coral, Gorgonian Sea Fans, Sea Rods and Sea Whips and large Barrel Sponges.

BONAIRE

Bonaire vies with Grand Cayman and Cozumel as the top Caribbean destination for American divers and is a world leader in the preservation of underwater resources. The whole island is a protected marine park. Two areas have been designated marine reserves where no diving is allowed: north from Boca Kayon to Boca Slagbaai, and west of Karpata. Lac Bay is protected because of its mangroves and sea-grass beds. Heavily dived sites are closed off sporadically to allow recovery. Divers must attend an orientation session and

THE CARIBBEAN SEA

TOP *The cabin of the Arashi Airplane wreck (a Beechcraft) on Aruba is a haven for mixed shoals of fish, mainly Schoolmaster Snappers and French Grunts.*

CENTRE *A winch on Aruba's Jane Sea wreck. It is colourful with Orange Cup Corals Fire Corals, sponges and shoals of Sergeant Majors.*

ABOVE *Brown or Yellow-edge Chromis (Chromis multilineata) on Aruba's Antilla wreck. The dorsal fin and the tail are edged in yellow.*

purchase a Marine Park Tag before diving on Bonaire. This tag is valid for one year and is not transferable. Mainland Bonaire has a system of well-marked roads with yellow-painted rocks marking the access points for shore-dive sites. Boat dives are also organized several times a day to all the popular sites and this is the only way to dive the sites of Klein Bonaire.

Most Bonaire diving takes place on the leeward southern and western coasts. The coastline consists of coral rubble or sand beaches down to a drop-off from 5–12m (16–40ft) to more than 40m (130ft). In the centre of the southern section, between Punt Vierkant and Salt Pier, there is a double-reef system referred to as the **Alice in Wonderland** 42 double-reef complex. The reef slope is at a shallow angle and descends to a sandy channel at 20–30m (65–100ft), then there is a second reef on the other side. On Klein Bonaire, buttresses and steep reef slopes are dominant. On the windward, east side of the island there is a shelf and then a drop-off 12m (40ft) from the shore, this descends to a coral shelf at 30m (100ft) and then drops down to the ocean floor. The sea here is rough for most of the year, but often calms down in October or November.

One of the most popular dives on Bonaire is under the town pier in the capital, Kralendijk. For safety reasons due to shipping movements, permission is required.

MAINLAND BONAIRE

Most of Bonaire's sites are on the sheltered south and west coasts. The shallow reef flat is thick with Elkhorn, Star, Fire and Staghorn Coral, Gorgonian Sea Fans, Sea Rods and Sea Whips with nudibranchs, sea horses, Peacock Flounders, angelfish, butterflyfish, goatfish, Trumpetfish, pufferfish, Black Durgon and Spanish Hogfish. The drop-offs have Brain and Star Coral, Elephant Ear, Barrel and Tube Sponges, groupers, grunts, trunkfish, wrasse, snappers and parrotfish with pelagics deeper down. *Tubastrea* Coral grows in the shade.

Located along the northwest coast of Washington Slagbaai Park, **Playa Bengé** 22 has strong currents. A classic example of spur and

groove formations, the shallows have Star and Staghorn Corals, Blade Fire Coral and large Gorgonian Sea Fans. The drop-off is a long swim out to 40m (130ft) and has Tiger Groupers and stingrays. Just north of the no diving reserve, **Boca Slagbaai** 23 has six concrete replicas of cannons buried for the film *Shark Treasure*. There are barracuda, Tarpon, Whitespotted Filefish and shoals of Palometa. At the southern end of the cove, there are two real cannons in 3m (10ft) of water. The drop-off begins at 12m (40ft) and drops to 40m (130ft) with Horse-eye Jacks, Tiger Groupers and Schoolmaster Snappers.

Just north of Kralendijk and off the national parks foundation, STINAPA Bonaire (Stichting Nationale Parken), **Karpata** 24 has spur and groove formations from 10m (33ft) down to sand at 30m (100ft). Heading east, exploring the drop-off, divers will find several large anchors and great marine life. **La Dania's Leap** 25 is one of Bonaire's few vertical walls, with numerous canyons and sand shoots. Off Devil's Mouth, **Rappel** 26 is one of the best dives on Bonaire with large gorgonias and Star Corals and an abundance of nudibranchs in the shallows. There is a cave sheltering large groupers 73m (240ft) south of the mooring. **Ol' Blue** 27 lies just off a long coral beach, west of **1000 Steps** 28. A shelf at 6m (20ft) extends seaward for 90m (300ft), covered with rich marine life. The drop-off descends from 10m (33ft) to sand at 45m (150ft). In front of the southernmost of the Radio Netherlands transmitter pylons, 1000 Steps has a gentle slope to 10m (33ft) with stony corals and gorgonias. A steeper drop-off then descends to 40m (130ft) with shoals of Schoolmaster Snappers. Hawksbill Turtles, Manta Rays, dolphins and a Whale Shark have been seen. Originally called Witches Hut, **Weber's Joy** 29 is a favourite with underwater photographers. The shallow reef shelf drops off from 13m (40ft) to 40m (130ft) with healthy corals and fish life.

Barcadera 30, opposite the Bonaire Marine Park Headquarters, **Andrea II** 31, just north past the desalination plant, **Andrea I** 32 and

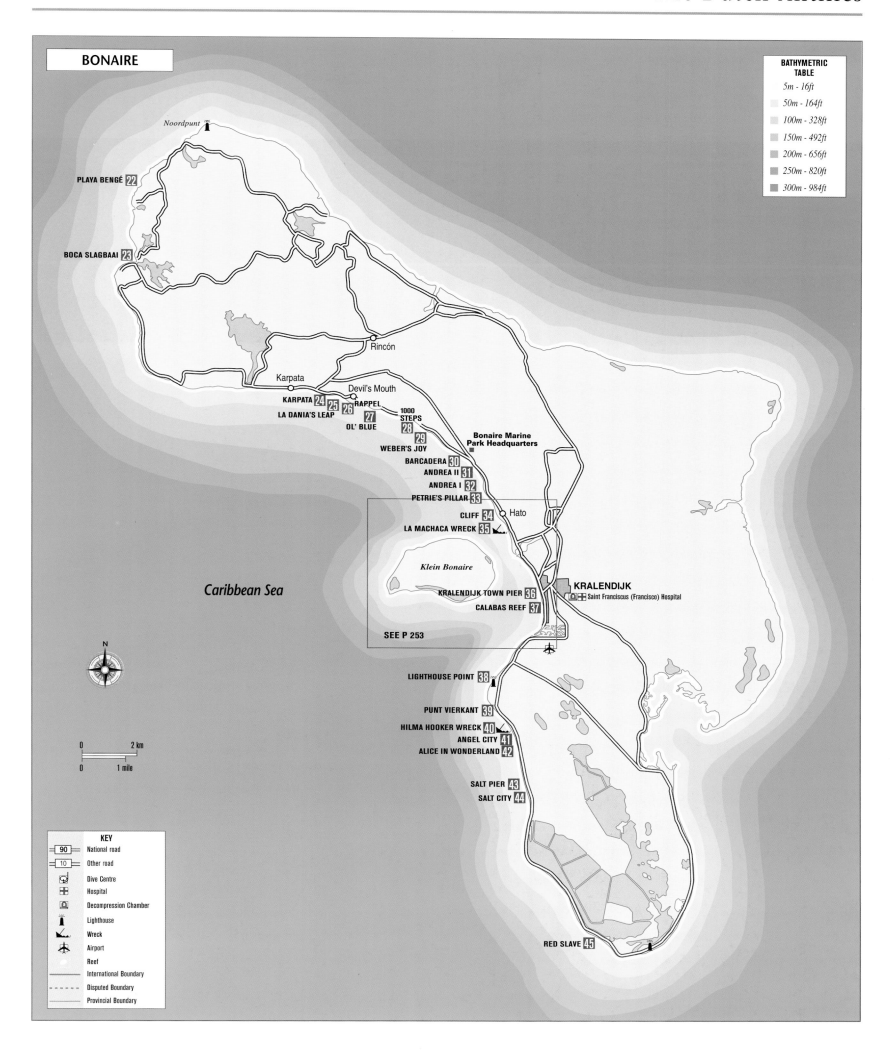

BONAIRE

BATHYMETRIC TABLE

5m - 16ft
50m - 164ft
100m - 328ft
150m - 492ft
200m - 656ft
250m - 820ft
300m - 984ft

Noordpunt

PLAYA BENGÉ 22

BOCA SLAGBAAI 23

Rincón

Karpata

Devil's Mouth

KARPATA 24 25
LA DANIA'S LEAP 26 RAPPEL
27
OL' BLUE 28 1000 STEPS
29
WEBER'S JOY
BARCADERA 30 Bonaire Marine Park Headquarters
ANDREA II 31
ANDREA I 32
PETRIE'S PILLAR 33
CLIFF 34 Hato
LA MACHACA WRECK 35

Klein Bonaire

Caribbean Sea

KRALENDIJK TOWN PIER 36
CALABAS REEF 37

KRALENDIJK
Saint Franciscus (Francisco) Hospital

SEE P 253

N

LIGHTHOUSE POINT 38

PUNT VIERKANT 39
HILMA HOOKER WRECK 40
ANGEL CITY 41
ALICE IN WONDERLAND 42

SALT PIER 43
SALT CITY 44

0   2 km

0   1 mile

RED SLAVE 45

KEY

90	National road
10	Other road
	Dive Centre
	Hospital
	Decompression Chamber
	Lighthouse
	Wreck
	Airport
	Reef
	International Boundary
	Disputed Boundary
	Provincial Boundary

The Dutch Antilles

Petrie's Pillar [33], are good dives for novices. At **Cliff** [34], in front of the Hamlet Villas, north of Captain Don's Habitat, a channel runs through Elkhorn Coral onto a shelf with gorgonias and stony corals. The drop-off descends as a short wall from 9m (30ft) to 22m (70ft) then slopes to sand at 40m (130ft) with abundant fish life. The house reef at Captain Don's Habitat is called *La Machaca* [35] after the wreck of a fishing boat. Most of the reef fish encountered on Bonaire can be found here, including Bigeyes and Tarpon.

Kralendijk Town (North) Pier [36] is only 9m (30ft) deep and the pier's stanchions are home to a rich world of small invertebrate life and other creatures seeking shelter or a meal. The fish life includes juvenile French Angelfish, Frogfish, drums and soapfish.

Calabas Reef [37] is another good site with prolific marine life including Creole Wrasse. The drop-off starts at 9m (30ft) and slopes down to 27m (90ft). **Lighthouse Point** [38], off Punt Vierkant Lighthouse, has a sandy sloping bottom rather than a drop-off. There are lots of Gorgonian Sea Rods, Sea Whips and Sea Plumes together with Staghorn and Star Corals and great fish life down to 30m (100ft). **Punt Vierkant** [39], north of the Trans World Radio transmitting pylons, marks the start of the double-reef system, part of the Alice in Wonderland complex. Almost everything is found on the many dive sites here.

The 72m (235ft) freighter *Hilma Hooker* [40] was caught carrying marijuana and deliberately sunk north of **Angel City** [41] in 1984. She now rests at the bottom of the reef slope on her starboard side at 30m (100ft), the highest point of the vessel is at 18m (60ft). **Salt Pier** [43], the salt loading pier, is like Town Pier with the stanchions covered in coral and sponge growth and acting as shelter for many juveniles. South of it, **Salt City** [44] is still part of the double-reef system with stony corals, Palometa, Sand Tilefish, Garden Eels and, occasionally, Eagle Rays and turtles.

Turtles are seen regularly south of Salt Pier. The water gets rougher and the currents stronger on approaching the southern tip of

the island and losing the shelter from the wind. Off the more southerly group of slave huts, **Red Slave** [45] is only recommended for advanced divers, the fish life is abundant and includes Nassau groupers and large pelagics.

KLEIN BONAIRE

Klein Bonaire's sites are treated as boat dives, although many are close to shore if you are already on the island. Most sites are good for snorkelling. Many of them are similar with small differences in topography and fish life according to the substrates and currents.

Sampler [46] is the most northerly dive of Klein Bonaire. The shallows are mostly sand with patches of finger, Brain and Mustard Hill Corals, together with parrotfish, French

TOP *Massive Orange Elephant Ear Sponges (Age-las clathrodes) can grow to 2m (6½ft). The fish is a Dusky Damselfish (Stegastes fuscus).*

ABOVE *A shoal of Smallmouth Grunts (Haemulon chrysargyreum) find shelter among the stanchions of Kralendijk's Town Pier in Bonaire.*

Angelfish and snappers. The drop-off begins at 12m (40ft) with gorgonias, sponges, stony corals, Spotted Moray Eels, Trumpetfish, cowfish, Whitespotted Filefish, soldierfish, squirrelfish and jacks down to 40m (130ft). Heading west, **Knife** [47] and **Leonora's Reef** [48] have Elkhorn Coral in the shallows, Yellowfin Mojarras, Bermuda Chubs and Yellowhead Jawfish.

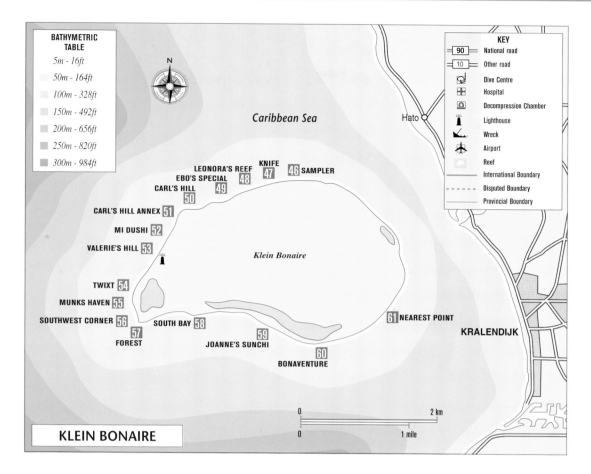

BATHYMETRIC TABLE

5m - 16ft
50m - 164ft
100m - 328ft
150m - 492ft
200m - 656ft
250m - 820ft
300m - 984ft

KEY

90 National road
10 Other road
Dive Centre
Hospital
Decompression Chamber
Lighthouse
Wreck
Airport
Reef
International Boundary
Disputed Boundary
Provincial Boundary

Caribbean Sea

Hato

LEONORA'S REEF
EBO'S SPECIAL 48
CARL'S HILL 50
KNIFE 47 46 SAMPLER
49
CARL'S HILL ANNEX 51
MI DUSHI 52
VALERIE'S HILL 53
Klein Bonaire
TWIXT 54
MUNKS HAVEN 55
SOUTHWEST CORNER 56
57
FOREST
SOUTH BAY 58
JOANNE'S SUNCHI 59
BONAVENTURE 60
61 NEAREST POINT
KRALENDIJK

0   2 km
0   1 mile

KLEIN BONAIRE

The dive sites around the southwest corner of Klein Bonaire are as good as any in the Caribbean. **Ebo's Special** 49 is a microcosm of all that is good in Bonaire's diving. The drop-off begins at 8m (25ft) and slopes into the depths. The slope is overgrown with gorgonias, sponges and Black Corals and it harbours countless fish. **Carl's Hill** 50, at the northwest tip, has a wall down to a sandy bottom at 22m (70ft) before sloping off to 45m (150ft). The shallows have Elkhorn and Pillar Coral and prolific fish life, including shoals of Blue Tangs. **Carl's Hill Annex** 51 also has sea horses. **Mi Dushi** 52 has abundant fish life. **Valerie's Hill** 53 has numerous sponges and Black Corals. Near the lighthouse, divers can experience problems with currents, but they are not as strong as those at Munks Haven or Southwest Corner. Rich stony and gorgonian coral growth mark the shallow shelf. The drop-off has undercut Star Corals forming mushroom-like shapes and it harbours many species of fish, including Goliath Groupers. **Twixt** 54, **Munk's Haven** 55 and **Southwest Corner** 56 have similar Staghorn and Star Coral interspersed with gorgonias and sponges in strong currents. The drop-off slopes steeply from 12m (40ft) down to sand at 37m (120ft), with countless fish. **Forest** 57 and **South Bay** 58 are similar dives. **Joanne's Sunchi** 59 has sand chutes, large tube sponges and good fish life. **Bonaventure** 60 has both Lined and Longsnout Sea Horses. **Nearest Point** 61 has lush gorgonian growth on the sand. The drop-off begins at 13m (40ft) with Black Corals and abundant fish life in deeper water. The dive sites nearest the mainland shore are the most sheltered and have large stony corals.

ABOVE *A day boat on a fixed mooring above Giant Slit-Pore Sea Rods (*Plexaurella nutans*). They grow tall with thick stalks and very little branching.*

CURAÇAO

The most European of the three islands, Curaçao has more variety above and below water. Willemstad, with its colonial architecture, Christoffel National Park, restaurants, casinos and variety of water sports will occupy non-diving companions.

Curaçao is much larger than Aruba and Bonaire, so the diving operators outside

SHORE DIVING AND THEFT

Dive operators can organize suitable vehicles for shore diving. Some operators have their own or are in a position to arrange a 10 per cent discount. Double-cab pick-up trucks are the preferred vehicles. Divers should remember to take with them only what they need in the water. It is not advisable to leave valuables in an unattended vehicle while diving. Some shore dives on Curaçao are accessed from private property and in these instances there is a small charge for entry.

Willemstad tend to be spread along the leeward coast and only dive on the sites that are within a 15-minute boat ride of their jetties. Divers who wish to dive further afield can hire a vehicle for a shore dive.

The typical fringing reef is a shallow reef shelf in 5–12m (16–40ft) of water, a drop-off with a 45° slope or less, and then sand shelving into the deep. The reef is steeper at sites in the middle and east of the island. Shore diving is better in the north, while in the south the drop-offs are steeper with depths of 40m (130ft) and usually less than 150m (500ft) from the shore. Coral diversity is high with some 50 hermatypic species recorded.

The entire western side of the island, from Noordpunt (North Point) to Oostpunt (East Point), is one large dive site. The stretch from West Point to the Light Tower on Cape Saint Marie is called Bando Abao Underwater Park and that from Bullen Bay to the Princess Beach Hotel is called Central Curaçao Underwater Park. These are unofficial parks, but the stretch from Princess Beach to East Point has been declared the Curaçao Underwater Park.

Conditions at the northwestern sites are calm. The southeast has less shelter from rough seas and currents, but sites may be calmer in the early morning. The major shore sites are marked with numbered white stones, similar to the yellow ones on Bonaire.

The reefs on Curaçao see fewer divers and have slightly more variation in topography than those on Bonaire, but the organisms encountered are much the same. Bluespotted Cornetfish are more common in the shallows. The drop-offs begin at 5–12m (16–40ft) and descend below 40m (130ft). Deeper down, the stony corals, sponges and gorgonias become denser and shelter a multitude of invertebrates including lobsters, Banded Coral Shrimps and Christmas Tree Worms.

When conditions are good, **Watamula** 62 is Curaçao's finest reef dive. It is similar to Mushroom Forest, but even more lush and overgrown. The seabed is a gentle slope covered in Star and Brain Corals, gorgonias, anemones and vase, basket and tube sponges that shelter a multitude of fish and invertebrates. Depths are below 40m (130ft).

At Westpunt **Playa Kalki** 63 is also called Alice in Wonderland. The bottom slopes gradually, and from 9m (30ft) it resembles rolling hills covered in coral. There are gorgonias and Star Coral at about 18m (60ft) and Plate Coral below 30m (100ft). Near Landhuis Jeremi, **Playa Jeremi** 64 offers easy shore diving, protected from most of the weather and ideal for night diving. Flying Gurnards are found on the seabed at 5m (16ft).

Playa Lagun 65 is one of the island's top dives. There are several small caves and a 45° drop-off at 10m (30ft), which descends to a second drop-off at 45m (150ft) with profuse marine life. Off the point south of **Santu Pretu** 66, **Mushroom Forest** and **The Cave** 67 vie with Watamula as the island's top dive site. It is named after the many large heads of Star Coral that have been eroded at their base to turn into mushroom shapes. There is a drop-off, but the main interest is on the inshore shelf at 12–15m (40–50ft), where the coral heads are a riot of colour from encrusting marine life. The animals include turtles and Nurse Sharks. Directly inshore,

ABOVE *A diver surveys the massive Boulder Star Corals (*Monastrea annularis*) at Curaçao's Watamula dive site. It vies with Mushroom Forest as the finest site off Curaçao.*

RIGHT *A diver looks into the wheelhouse of the wreck of the* Superior Producer. *The inside of the wheelhouse, shaded like a cavern, is covered in bright Orange Cup Corals (*Tubastrea coccinea*).*

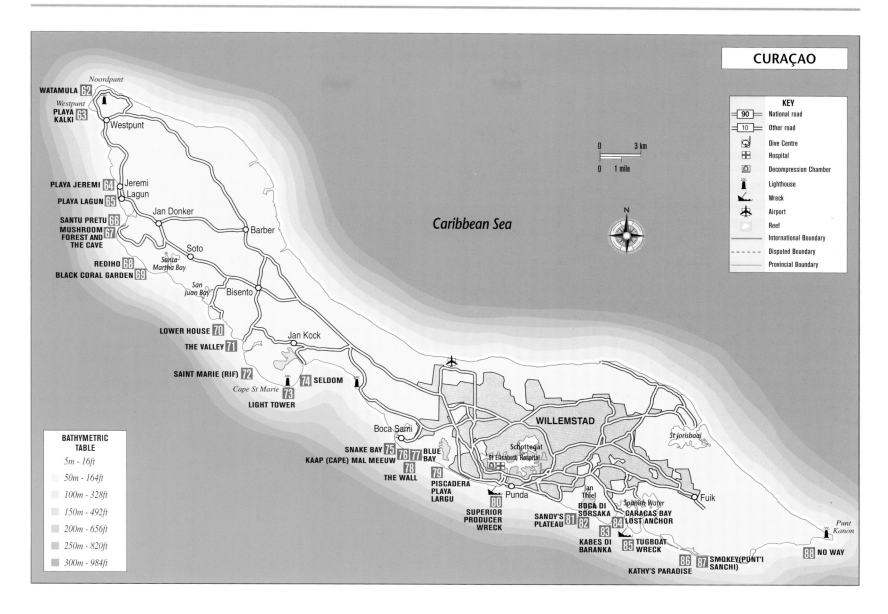

The Cave is 6m (20ft) deep with a huge entrance. Shoals of sweepers dash around, *Tubastrea* Cup Corals encrust the roof and slipper lobsters crawl around.

Off San Nicolas, **Rediho** 68 and **Black Coral Garden** 69 have no shelter, so conditions can be rough. The steep drop-off begins at 12m (40ft) and descends below sport diving depths. There is a colossal Black Coral forest and profuse fish life. Turtles are common while Manta Rays and Whale Sharks have been seen. **Lower House** 70 has a rich slope from 9m (30ft) to sand at 40m (130ft). Lobsters and Spotted Drums are common. At Port Marie Beach, **The Valley** 71 is another of the island's top sites – two healthy parallel reefs, with a valley in between, which are home to a variety of reef life, including Nurse Sharks. Off Habitat Curaçao, **Saint Marie (Rif)** 72 is another top dive with abundant marine life.

Either side of Cape Saint Marie, **Light Tower** 73 and **Seldom** 74 are for advanced divers. The drop-off is a steep slope from 7m (23ft), with strong currents giving healthy marine life, including a shoal of barracuda.

South of **Snake Bay** 75, **Kaap** (Cape) **Mal Meeuw** 76 can be rough, but the currents along the wall produce healthy marine life. Off **Blue Bay** 77, **The Wall** 78 falls off steeply from 9m (30ft) into the depths with Sheet Coral, Black Coral, gorgonias, turtles and Eagle Rays. **Piscadera Playa Largu** 79 is a popular spot to see sponges spawning in September and October.

Just west of the harbour entrance, the wreck of the *Superior Producer* 80 sits upright on sand at 34m (110ft). Parts of the hull and the interior of the wheelhouse are carpeted with Orange *Tubastrea* Cup Corals and colourful encrusting sponges.

There are several top dives off Jan Thiel. **Sandy's Plateau** 81 and **Boca di Sorsaka** 82 have dense coral growth and prolific fish life. At Caracas Bay, **Kabes Di Baranka** 83 and **Caracas Bay Lost Anchor** 84 have a wall descending to a ledge at 33m (110ft) before shelving into deeper water with lots of pelagic species. **Tugboat** 85 is a wreck small enough to be photographed as a whole. There is a 45° sloping drop-off from 9m (30ft). Offshore Fuik Bay, **Kathy's Paradise** 86 and **Smokey (Punt'i Sanchi)** 87 have strong currents.

There are a number of spectacular sites approaching the East Point (Punt Kanon) that are exposed, with strong currents, but worth the effort by experienced divers. **No Way** 88 has an old Spanish cannon at 3m (10ft). The tiny uninhabited island of Klein Curaçao, almost two hours southeast of Curaçao has more top sites.

VIRGIN ISLANDS

by Lawson Wood

THE VIRGIN ISLANDS, NAMED AFTER ST URSULA and her 11,000 virgin followers, were discovered by Christopher Columbus during his second voyage of discovery of the West Indies in 1493. The Islands are located 95km (60 miles) east of Puerto Rico and 1800km (1100 miles) southeast of Miami. Originally settled by Ciboney, Arawak and Carib Indians, the indigenous population was wiped out by the Spanish in their thirst for gold. Over the following years, the islands were fought over and settled by the Dutch, Danish, British, French and Spanish explorers, marauding pirates, plantation owners and Quakers.

Primarily known for their excellent cruising and safe anchorages in a multitude of secluded bays and inlets, with generally shallow water, perfect for sport diving, the Virgin Islands are rapidly becoming one of the most popular diving destinations in the Caribbean. Their geographical position probably contributes

TOP LEFT *The islands of St John in the US Virgin Islands and Tortola in the BVI in the background are separated by a narrow channel.*

TOP RIGHT *The group of rocks known as the Indians in Sir Francis Drake Channel has shallow diving, but can only be reached by boat.*

RIGHT *The wreck of RMS* Rhone *near Salt Island is split into two sections, one deep and the other shallow.*

most to the diversity of marine life found around these islands, as the Gulf Stream flows through the islands on its way up, past the Bahamas and on to Bermuda in the eastern Atlantic. The island group is split into two distinct and entirely separate areas. To the north is the British Crown Colony of the British Virgin Islands, comprising some 60 islands and cays, of which 16 are inhabited. To the south lie the United States Virgin Islands, an unincorporated territory of the USA with three main islands and a further associated 65 islets and cays.

THE BRITISH VIRGIN ISLANDS

The British Virgin Islands are clustered around the Sir Francis Drake Channel and are of granite origin – only Anegada in the north is a true coral island. Once a huge subterranean mountain plateau, the islands are clustered around a wide, shallow bay, perfect for yachting and sport diving. Once the home base of pirates including Henry Morgan, Sir John Hawkins and Blackbeard, tales of hidden treasure brought speculators from all over the world in the early days of colonization.

While Tortola is the main island, much of the diving is actually carried out on her satellites of Ginger Island, Cooper Island, Salt Island (where the wreck of the *Rhone* can be found), Dead Chest, Peter Island and Norman

Island. To the north of Tortola lie Jost Van Dyke, Guana Island, Great Camanoe, the Dogs (named after the barking sound from the now-extinct population of Caribbean seals), Mosquito Island, Eustatia, Necker Island and Beef Island where the international airport is situated. To the northeast is the true coral island of Anegada, formed on the northern ridge of the now-submerged ancient volcano. More sparsely populated than any of the other islands, its barrier reef is credited

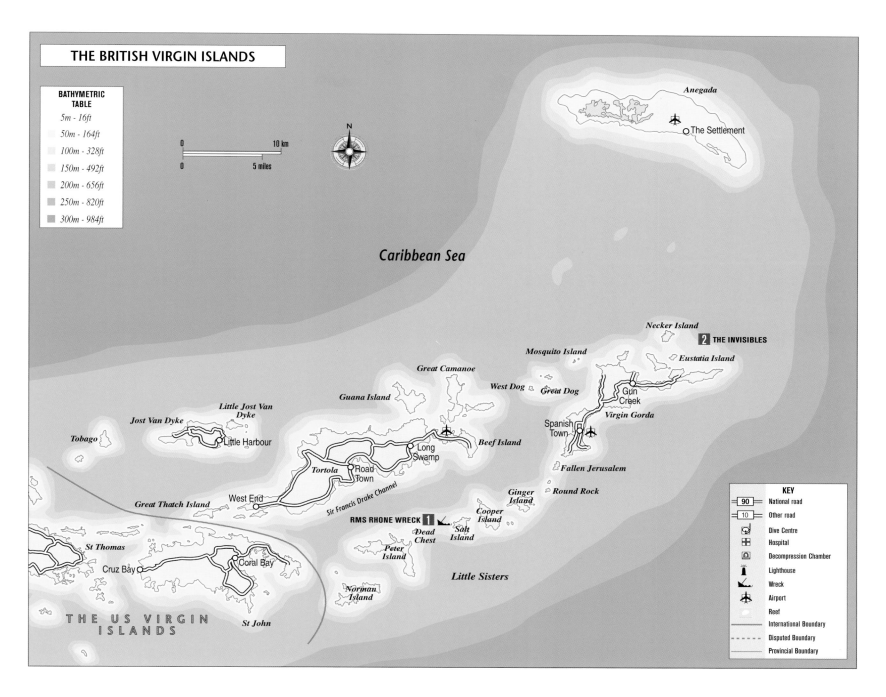

THE BRITISH VIRGIN ISLANDS

BATHYMETRIC TABLE
- 5m - 16ft
- 50m - 164ft
- 100m - 328ft
- 150m - 492ft
- 200m - 656ft
- 250m - 820ft
- 300m - 984ft

KEY
- 90 — National road
- 10 — Other road
- Dive Centre
- Hospital
- Decompression Chamber
- Lighthouse
- Wreck
- Airport
- Reef
- International Boundary
- Disputed Boundary
- Provincial Boundary

Caribbean Sea

Anegada — The Settlement

Necker Island — **2** THE INVISIBLES

Mosquito Island · *Eustatia Island*

Great Camanoe · *West Dog* · *Great Dog* · Gun Creek

Guana Island · *Virgin Gorda* · Spanish Town

Little Jost Van Dyke · *Jost Van Dyke* · Little Harbour · Long Swamp · *Beef Island*

Tobago · *Fallen Jerusalem*

Tortola · Road Town · *Ginger Island* · *Round Rock*

Great Thatch Island · West End · *Sir Francis Drake Channel* · *Cooper Island*

RMS RHONE WRECK **1** · *Dead Chest* · *Salt Island*

St Thomas · *Peter Island*

Cruz Bay · *Little Sisters*

Coral Bay

Norman Island

THE US VIRGIN ISLANDS · *St John*

---

with over 300 shipwrecks, many of which have been researched by Bert Kilbride, the former Receiver of Wreck for the islands.

The National Parks Board have installed over 200 mooring buoys since 1989, which have eliminated anchor damage at sites. Now a system of first come first served applies to all dive boats and private yachts, with the size of the boat determining which mooring to take.

1 WRECK OF *RMS RHONE*

The 95m (310ft) Royal Mail Steamer *Rhone* was launched on 11 February, 1865 and considered one of the finest steel-hulled transatlantic ships of her generation. During a particularly violent hurricane, which

struck the islands in October 1867, she lost her main anchor and chains and was swept onto the rocks at Salt Island, broke her back and split in two, with great loss of life and few survivors.

The forward part of the hull and bowsprit lie on their starboard side parallel to the shore in 27m (90ft). The decking has rotted away, leaving her ribs exposed and easily negotiated by divers. There are always large schools of snapper and grunt around the ship and while bottom time is limited due to the depth, the wreck is a superb dive. The stern of the ship lies at right angles to the shore, with her four-blade propeller and the remains of her sternpost in less than 6m (20ft) of water. Part

of the hull forms a small cavern where light-sensitive fish, such as squirrelfish and large grouper, can hide. Divers can swim along the entire length of her propeller shaft and gearbox. Separate from both sections, but in line with the stern, is the large square section of the boilers and part of her mid-decking, now covered in brightly coloured Gorgonian Sea Rods and Whips. The shallow section of the wreck is particularly popular at night because it is home to thousands of invertebrates including squid, octopuses, nudibranchs, snails, crabs and shrimps.

The *Rhone* is now regarded as one of the top ten wrecks in the world and the area surrounding and including the wreck has been

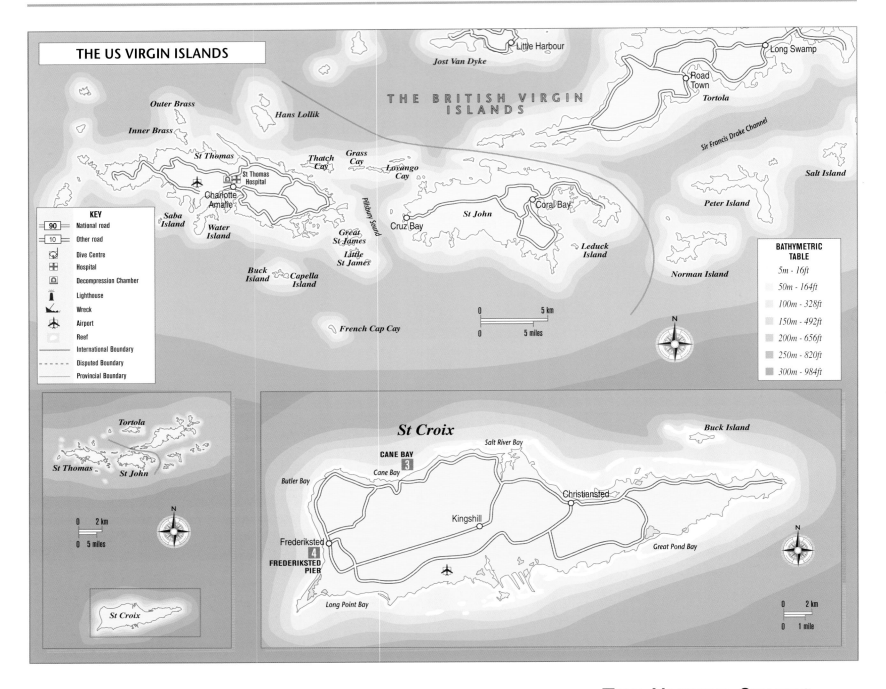

THE BRITISH VIRGIN ISLANDS

KEY

90	National road
10	Other road
	Dive Centre
	Hospital
	Decompression Chamber
	Lighthouse
	Wreck
	Airport
	Reef
	International Boundary
	Disputed Boundary
	Provincial Boundary

BATHYMETRIC TABLE

	5m - 16ft
	50m - 164ft
	100m - 328ft
	150m - 492ft
	200m - 656ft
	250m - 820ft
	300m - 984ft

St Croix

CANE BAY **3**

FREDERIKSTED PIER **4**

declared a national marine park – the first of its kind in the British Virgin Islands. Numerous moorings have been installed around the site and the wreck is the favoured dive site of all the dive shops.

VIRGIN GORDA

The Invisibles [2] are due east of Necker Island and form part of Eustatia reef, which in its wider reef formation eventually becomes part of the southern side of Horseshoe Reef. The latter is the third-largest barrier reef in the Caribbean and the final resting place of hundreds of shipwrecks. Little more than a couple of granite peaks surrounded by a jumble of huge, wave-sculpted granite blocks, most dive

centres only find the location by looking for the breaking waves over the rocks. Numerous caverns, gullies and under-hanging walls have are formed by the position of the boulders. Although poor in large coral growth, every surface is smothered in large Atlantic Thorny Oysters and brilliantly coloured encrusting sponges. The undersides are aflame with golden cup-corals, their brilliant orange and yellow polyps extended to feed on the passing plankton on this exposed site. To the north of the granite boulders there is usually a large school of Atlantic Spadefish. However these are always in open water – and about 100m (330ft) offshore – and therefore unlikely to be seen by most sport divers.

THE UNITED STATES VIRGIN ISLANDS

Formerly known as the Danish West Indies, these islands were bought by the USA in 1917 for $25m. The northern islands of St John and St Thomas are situated a few kilometers (miles) southeast of Tortola and are part of the same island group as the British Virgin Islands.

St Thomas is the USVI capital and main tourist island, with thousands of cruise shippers arriving annually into Charlotte Amalie harbour. Thatch Cay to the north is the largest of the satellites, while Outer and Inner Brass, Saba Island, Water Island, Birsk Island, Capella Island and Great St James Island, are all popular for diving. St John is the smallest

ABOVE LEFT *Many of the inshore shallow reefs are of granite carved by eons of wave action and covered in small corals and sponges.*

ABOVE RIGHT *Shade-loving fish like French Grunts* (Haemulon flavolineatum) *can be found under the granite boulders.*

and least developed, with two thirds of the island given over to a national park. The largest of her offshore islets or cays are Leduck Island, Congo Cay and Grass Cay.

Most of the local cruzans of St Croix (pronounced Saint Croy) are either involved in the tourism or oil industries, which have taken over from the large sugar cane plantations of the early Danish settlers. The capital, Christiansted, is in the northeast, set on a bay now filled with yachts, protected by an offshore reef, called Long Reef. Nearby, the National Park of Buck Island has excellent beaches. The other main town, Frederiksted, on the west coast, has some delightful diving off the old pier.

ST CROIX

A 25-minute drive west of Christiansted is **Cane Bay** ③, primarily used by the locals. Beaches are not all that evident along the north shore of St Croix and most are just a narrow strip before you reach the raised platform of the old ironshore. The top of the reef shallows is a classic spur and groove reef with long fingers of coral interspersed by sand and coral rubble gullies, the perfect habitat for Yellowhead Jawfish, Flying Gurnards and Peacock Flounders. The corals in this area are not that great, but as you reach the outer reef crest beyond 100m (330ft) from the shore, the corals grow larger, the sponges are more prolific and there is less algae intrusion. The Cane Bay area is renowned for its well-developed field of many different varieties of sea fans. On closer inspection, these fans harbour one of the most common molluscs in the Caribbean, the Flamingo Tongue (*Cyphoma gibbosum*) and its much rarer cousin the Fingerprint Cyphoma (*Cyphoma signatum*).

The main town on the sheltered west coast of St Croix is Frederiksted. It has some superb diving off the **new town pier** ④. Local divers have collected all the debris from the construction and placed it in small heaps beneath the shaded area between the pillars and this is where you will find the resident sea horses, frogfish, juvenile French Angelfish and Spotted Drum. Rather boring on first inspection, the new pier's pilings are now covered in a thin layer of sponges, tunicates and small corals.

This new facility has replaced the fabled old Frederiksted Pier, reputed to have been the best pier dive in the Caribbean. However, much of the old pier was destroyed during the new construction, leaving only three 'dolphins', (separate mooring facilities) unattached to the main facility. It is around these leg supports that most of the marine life is found. Access is directly from the shore or from the pier itself before 19:00 when the gates are locked to vehicular traffic. Average depth is only 6m (20ft) and it is one of the best night dives. These old piers had Orange Ball Corallimorph, Redeye Sponge Crabs, hundreds of juvenile spiny lobsters and Spotted Spiny Lobsters and the most octopuses found in one small area, often three or four per square metre (square yard). Boxfish, trunkfish, Blue Tangs, soapfish and Red Night Shrimps were everywhere. Often neglected in the rush to dive the excellent reefs and wrecks on these Caribbean islands, the functional, often ugly structures which we see above the water belie the fact that below them there are secret gardens waiting to be discovered.

THE BAHAMAS

by Lawson Wood

DISCOVERED IN 1492 BY CHRISTOPHER Columbus, the Islands of the Bahamas are set astride the Tropic of Cancer and situated only 30 minutes' flying time southeast of Florida. Originally called Bajamar (shallow seas) by Columbus, the name eventually changed to Bahama. It was made famous by the series of films based on Ian Flemming's fictional hero James Bond, as most of the underwater action was filmed around the islands. The wrecks used as props lie around Nassau and some of the cavern locations are in the Exuma chain.

During the last Ice Age, the Bahamas were the top of a plateau more than 90m (300ft) above sea level. As the ice melted, the waters rose, submerging the plateau. Mostly just a few meters deep, the plateau is cut by a deep trench, called the Tongue of the Ocean, created by the upwards thrust of tectonic plates. Many of the shallow islands are riddled with caves filled with stalagmites and stalactites.

The Bahamas, although not located in the Caribbean Sea, are nevertheless associated

TOP LEFT *The Bimini Islands, to the northeast of the Bahamas and the closest point to Florida, are home to wild spotted dolphins and the underwater rock formations that have become known as the Atlantis Road.*
TOP RIGHT *The remains of the* Sapona, *the former concrete ship wrecked in 1926.*

with the Caribbean and are regarded as one of the top diving locations in the world and certainly the number one location where divers can be guaranteed action with sharks. Most people know the Bahamas by their respective tourist locations, yet they comprise more than 700 islands, 2500 small cays and are scattered over approximately 259,000 sq km (100,000 sq miles) of ocean. The larger islands of New Providence, Andros and Grand Bahama offer some of the most varied scuba diving in the Caribbean. However, it is the smaller islands to the south that are considered by many to have the best diving that the islands have to offer. This is for divers who enjoy vertical walls, challenging drift dives and even encounters with larger mammals – such as happens during the migration of the Humpback Whales from December through February. Because of the parallel formation of the reefs and the close proximity of each of the dive sites, the dive types are split into three different depth ranges to suit different standards of diver. Most diving is done as a twin-tank dive in the morning and a single-tank dive in the afternoon. This means that you will venture out on a boat for two dives leaving around 8:30 and returning around lunch time, with the deepest dive being the first dive of the day, followed quickly by a medium site and a shallow (or training) site in the afternoon.

THE NORTHERN ISLAND GROUPS
WALKERS CAY

Walkers Cay is famous for two pastimes: ocean fishing and the Shark Rodeo. The island has a fishing resort, with its own marina, which hosts regular international fishing competitions. The fish scraps from the competitions are frozen into big drums, called chumsickles, which are used on an infrequent basis to attract sharks into a feeding arena. Over 150 sharks of several species attend these feeds in what can only be described as high-voltage action. The dive sites are for the most part protected by an outer barrier reef and close together – as little as 10 minutes travel time. Known for the interlocking caverns, caves and swim-throughs, much of the diving is similar to the offshore reefs of Bermuda.

Spiral Cavern 1 is 15 minutes northwest of Walker's Cay Marina and can be reached by boat only. The water can be choppy. The average visibility of 15m (50ft) is reduced considerably during the shark feed.

GRAND BAHAMA ISLAND

Grand Bahama has a mixed terrain with an ancient limestone rocky base and small rolling hills covered in scrubby vegetation. As you fly over the island, you are struck by the colour of the water, ranging from light turquoise to the near-black of the circular

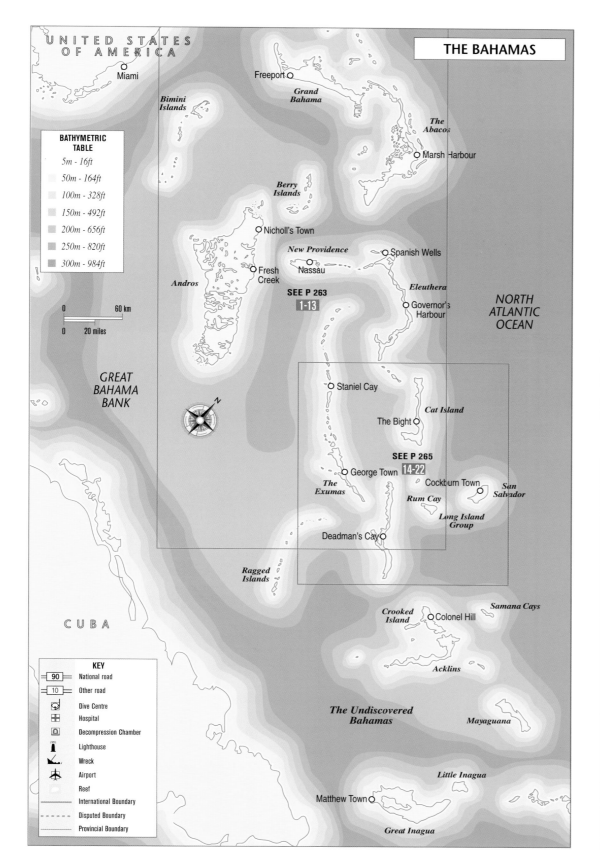

BATHYMETRIC TABLE

5m - 16ft
50m - 164ft
100m - 328ft
150m - 492ft
200m - 656ft
250m - 820ft
300m - 984ft

UNITED STATES OF AMERICA

Miami

Freeport

Grand Bahama

Bimini Islands

The Abacos

Marsh Harbour

Berry Islands

Nicholl's Town

New Providence

Spanish Wells

Andros

Fresh Creek

Nassau

SEE P 263
1-13

Eleuthera

Governor's Harbour

NORTH ATLANTIC OCEAN

0   60 km
0   20 miles

GREAT BAHAMA BANK

Staniel Cay

Cat Island

The Bight

SEE P 265
14-22

George Town

Cockburn Town

San Salvador

The Exumas

Rum Cay

Deadman's Cay

Long Island Group

Ragged Islands

CUBA

Crooked Island

Colonel Hill

Samana Cays

Acklins

The Undiscovered Bahamas

Mayaguana

KEY

90   National road
10   Other road
     Dive Centre
     Hospital
     Decompression Chamber
     Lighthouse
     Wreck
     Airport
     Reef
     International Boundary
     Disputed Boundary
     Provincial Boundary

Little Inagua

Matthew Town

Great Inagua

sinkholes inland to the green of the shallow grass beds dropping off to indigo off the wall, where most of the diving is done. The dive centres on Grand Bahama all operate along the same stretch of southern coastline and all the dive sites are protected by mooring buoys to prevent anchor damage.

Under these scrub-covered hills is one of the island's greatest assets – huge subterranean sink wells, similar to the cenotes of the Yucatán in Mexico. These underground passage-ways are currently being explored and mapped by Rob Palmer's Blue Holes Founda-tion, headed by his wife Stephanie Schwabe.

TOP *Social Feather Duster Worms* (Bispira brun-nea) *are tiny fans which grow in clumps at the base of sea fans. They prefer shallow water for its bright sunlight and moving water.*

ABOVE *Boulder Brain Corals* (Colpophyllia natans), *one of the main reef builders in the Bahamas, prefer cooler, nutrient-rich water.*

THE CARIBBEAN SEA

The reefs along the south shore of Grand Bahama Island are of a classic spur-and-groove formation – the result of wind and wave action over millennia. There is a secondary inner barrier reef, similar to the reef formations around Bermuda that protects the islands from the worst of the storms.

The majority of the dives are just a short boat trip from the marina in Freeport. It is also from here that visitors can have real hands-on experience with a group of Bottlenose Dolphins. The **Dolphin Dive** 2 enables you to dive with these masters of the sea in their open ocean environment.

There are several locations which offer interaction with a number of species of sharks. This type of 'pay and display' diving

ABOVE *A shark feed on Grand Bahama Island is often the first opportunity for many divers to witness these wild animals as they come in and take bait from experienced shark wranglers*

makes it possible for divers, for a little extra money, to sit back on the seabed and watch these maligned creatures being stroked and hand-fed. Essentially, these are spectator sports, with divers positioned in a semicircle and staying still while large groups of Caribbean Reef Sharks come in and take bait from the experienced shark wranglers dressed in chain mail suits.

There is a daily shark-feeding programme at the **Hydro Lab (Shark Junction)** 3 just 10 minutes' boat ride from the dock. A detailed lecture is given before each trip and divers are made aware of the risks involved in hand-feeding large wild animals.

BIMINI

Bimini, referred to as the Gateway to the Bahamas, is just 79km (49 miles) east of Miami. Made up of two main islands, North and South Bimini, a few rocky cays and a large area of sand flats used by sports fishermen hunting bonefish. Little is known of Bimini's early history and the Lucayan, Taino and Arawak Indians. There is an enduring myth about the discovery of an ancient underwater road, reputed to be from Atlantis, based on the column-like formations in 6m (20ft) of water, clearly discernible from the air. Spanish explorer Juan Ponce de Leon also sought the fountain of youth on South Bimini. The more worldly can visit Hemingway's old haunt, The Complete Angler, in the capital, Alice Town, on North Bimini.

Much of the diving is done around the shallow inshore reefs and cays that are home to some of the largest schools of fish in the Bahamas, with sightings on every dive of reef sharks, Nurse Sharks and barracuda. Operators offer two exhilarating underwater experiences. Northwest of South Cat Cay, at the south end of the Bimini chain of islands, is **Tuna Alley** 4, which can be reached by boat only. It is exposed and tidal, with current. **The Victories** 5 is 3km (2 miles) south of Tuna Alley and you can expect surface surge and tidal current.

ANDROS

Of special interest to divers is the eastern seaboard of Andros, which has the third-longest barrier reef in the world, running parallel to the coast for 225km (140 miles). There is a massive, almost impenetrable inner barrier of Elkhorn Coral that takes the brunt of the bad weather and stormy seas. However, it is the outer edge of the wall that divers come to see. It drops 1800m (6000ft) into the Tongue of the Ocean with canyons, sand chutes, caves, caverns and blue holes.

Andros Island has the highest concentration of blue holes in the Bahamas. For the most part, these are gigantic circular depressions in the limestone matrix that lead to undersea caverns filled with stalactites and stalagmites. The **Ocean Blue Hole** 6 in North Andros is particularly well known. On entering the gloomy world of sulphurous water, tinged green, it is even possible for divers to smell this sulphur underwater, through their face masks. There are shallow blue holes within the inner barrier reef and deep sinkholes on the island, the majority of which are unexplored, with virtually all of them connecting. Due to the extreme conditions surrounding the exploration of these caverns, a number of divers have lost their lives over the years. It is imperative to receive instruction with qualified guides. Rob Palmer's Blue Holes Foundation on Grand Bahama will be able to advise on any aspect of blue holes diving.

Small Hope Bay Lodge and Dive Resort just north of Fresh Creek has been at the forefront of blue hole exploration since 1960.

One of the more exciting and perhaps most serious dives is under the **United States Naval Buoy** 7, or DNM (Deployed Noise and Measurement Buoy), which is used for submarine tracking and exercises by NATO. The buoy is anchored to the seabed in 1800m (6000ft) of water and when you jump over the side of the dive boat, you know that it is a long way down. The attraction of the dive is not only the deep-water, open-ocean experience, but also the high probability of encounters with

Silky Sharks (*Carcharhinus falciformis*). The naval buoy is 6m (20ft) in diameter and the flat underside has become overgrown with algae. This attracts pelagic fish which eat the algae, small organisms land there during the planktonic stages of their lives and are preyed upon by larger creatures and so on up the food chain until the sharks show up. The sharks are also attracted by the vibrations of the attaching cable as the current passes through this natural deep-water trench. This is a superb open-ocean encounter, but only for experienced divers.

NEW PROVIDENCE (NASSAU)

The diving along the south shore of New Providence Island is diverse. Apart from the huge number of wrecks, many of which have been used as Hollywood film props, the island offers the opportunity to dive with sharks under relatively controlled conditions – it is important to remember that these are wild animals, competitive, and at the top of the marine food chain.

The Bahamas became the diving world's most important shark destination after lengthy habituation of large numbers of, primarily, Caribbean Reef Sharks (*Carcharhinus perezi*). While these sharks are the mainstay of the island's diving industry, the wall dives are splendid because the edge of the continental shelf starts in quite shallow water, at around 12m (40ft). Therefore, unlike other areas of the Bahamas, it is not necessary to undertake a deep dive with limited time just to get to the edge of the wall for regular encounters with large schools of pelagic fish. Divers visit this 1800m (6000ft) drop-off every day of the year. The south shore was used as a film prop in the *Flipper* movie. There are drop-offs, an abundance of fish, and coral reefs littered with wrecks, many of which have been used as props in a number of James Bond movies.

The **James Bond wrecks** 8 south of Clifton Point, are close to shore, but can only reached by boat. The conditions are generally quite sheltered.

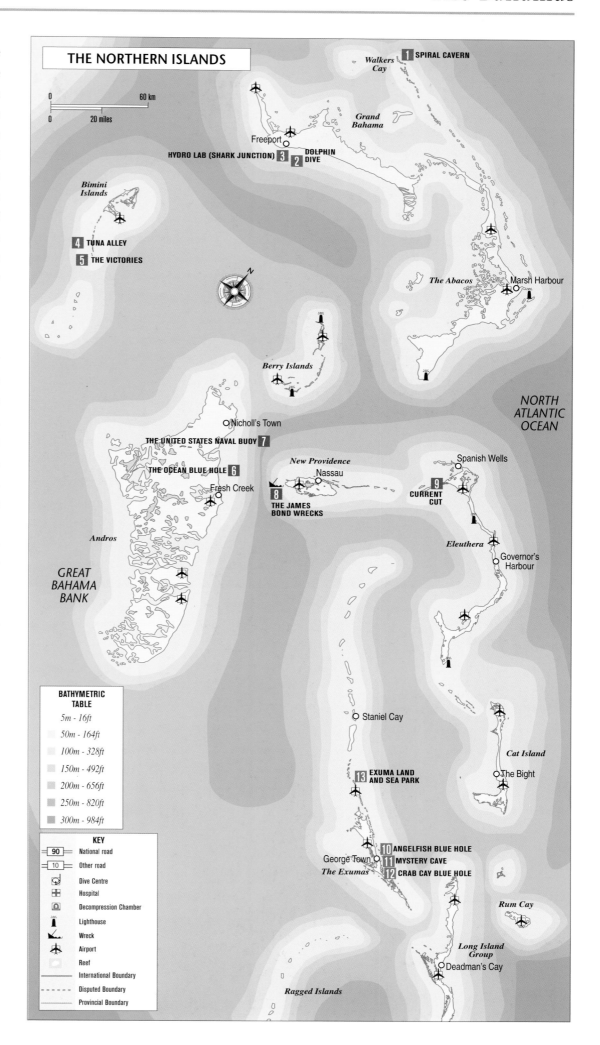

TOP *Longlure frogfish* (Antennarius multiocellatus) *are rendered almost invisible by their shape and coloration.*

ABOVE *The Bahamas are renowned for the small schools of Grey Angelfish* (Pomacanthus arcuatus), *which inhabit the inner reefs.*

ELEUTHERA

Eleuthera, called Cigatoo by the locals, is now known as the birthplace of the Bahamas. Harbour Island, Brisland to the locals, is the oldest settlement and original capital of the Bahamas. Harbour Island was founded before the United States became a nation. Much of the diving and snorkelling takes place on the more exposed ocean side of the island and inside the protective barrier reef off the north of the island. This reef is 11km (7 miles) long

and known as The Devil's Backbone due to the jagged coral ridges that come close to the surface in many areas, and have been responsible for the destruction of many ships.

Travelling south down the island, the main settlement is Governor's Harbour which has its own airstrip, a sheltered cove and a resort suitable for couples with children. In the extreme south of the island, off the vertical drop-offs south of Bannerman Town, is a reef that stretches southeast past Little San Salvador and then on to Cat Island. Little San Salvador has been sold to the Princess Cruise Line and casual visitors are discouraged. So live-aboard dive boats are the best way to dive these pristine reefs and walls.

Probably the best-known dive in the area is not really a dive as we know it, and there is little coral growth. **Current Cut** 9 is essentially a race along the seabed with a strong localized tidal current, with speeds reaching up to 19km/h (10 knots). Divers are dropped into the water at the peak of the tidal race about two and a half hours either side of high or low water. There are no corals between the two islands, but there are large numbers of fish, particularly those which like fast tidal streams such as Eagle Rays and Blacktip Reef Sharks. The current moves so fast, and the dive is so short, that divers take two or three exhilarating shots at the current.

EXUMAS

Directly opposite George Town, the capital of the Exumas, is Stocking Island with an adjacent barrier reef which stretches over 7km (4 miles). The reefs are pristine, but relatively shallow and subject to autumn storms. However, the islands are better known for the sheltered diving in blue holes. **Angelfish Blue Hole** 10, in the shelter of Stocking Island, is a vertical shaft that drops to 29m (97ft) before branching off at right angles. Nearby is **Mystery Cave** 11 with thousands of metres already explored underground. **Crab Cay Blue Hole** 12 starts in only 4m (13ft) of water. To the north of the island chain is the **Exuma Land and Sea Park** 13, set up by the Bahamas

Government. Covering 285 sq km (110 sq miles), there are hectares (acres) of Staghorn and Elkhorn Coral, mangrove forests, which are essential fish nurseries, and numerous blue holes, caverns and caves. The northern islands of the sea park are bordered to the west by a shallow sandy bay where much bonefish-fishing and conch collecting is done. On the eastern shores, the edge of the continental shelf comes close to shore, offering spectacular, unspoiled diving only rarely visited by live-aboard dive boats.

THE SOUTHERN ISLANDS
CAT ISLAND

Cat Island is midway down the Bahamas archipelago, northwest of San Salvador. It is 79km long (48 miles) and has been described as one of the most beautiful of the Bahamas, with the highest point in the chain at the Hermitage on Mount Alverina at 62m (206ft). This famous monastery was built by Father Jerome (John Hawes), an Anglican who converted to Roman Catholicism. The island probably received its present name from a contemporary of the infamous pirate Edward 'Blackbeard' Teach – Arthur Catt – who used the island as a staging post for his raids. It also has a large number of feral cats that were left when the Spaniards abandoned their settlements. One of the least dived areas in the Bahamas, the majority of the diving here is done along the south coast in Cutlass Bay, between Columbus Point in the east and **Devil's Point** 14 in the west. The reef wall starts at only 15m (50ft) and plummets down with gullies, canyons, chimneys and swimthroughs. This is virgin territory at its best.

SAN SALVADOR

Located 320km (200 miles) east-southeast of Nassau and southeast of Cat Island, San Salvador is known as the original landfall of Christopher Columbus on 12 October 1492. Known as Guanahani by the Arawak Indians, the it is quite small at 20km (12 miles) long by 8km (5 miles) wide. Famous for its crystal clear and flat, calm waters, the walls are for the most part pristine and vertical. All dive sites have mooring buoys to prevent anchor damage. However, it is the outer vertical wall dives that are of greatest interest, with dives such as **The Telephone Pole** 15 , **Devil's Claw** 16 and **Double Caves** 17 offering outstanding scenic diving.

Most of the dives are 5–15 minutes south from Riding Rock Marina. On a couple of the sites you are greeted by gregarious Nassau Groupers (*Epinephelus striatus*). If you want a grouper in your face, this is the island. Well used to being handled, these fish are willing to pose for queuing photographers. The dives on the outer and west-facing walls have huge sculpted sand chutes, caves and deep slashes in the reef, topped by elegant sea fans, all surrounded by masses of fish. The outer walls have hundreds of wire corals spiralling into the depths. Groups of Black Jacks (*Caranx lugubris*) mingle with Bermuda Chub (*Kyphosus sectatrix*). Keeping just out of arm's length, they will accompany divers for most of the dive. This area is also home to whip coral shrimps. At Double Caves there are regular sightings of hammerhead sharks (honest!).

CONCEPTION ISLAND

Located in the centre of the triangle created by Long Island to the west, Cat Island to the north and Rum Cay to the south, **Conception Island** 18 is uninhabited and has been declared a terrestrial and marine wildlife sanctuary by the Bahamas National Trust. The vertical walls plummet into the depths around the island and a number of turtles breed on the island.

Divers are now able to visit this remote island from Long Island. The trip takes between two and four hours, depending on the boat and weather conditions, rendering this an all-day expedition. Although the wall dives are deep, the reef edge is riddled with caverns and tunnels where silversides shoal in the summer months, buzzed by barracuda, jacks and tuna. Every sea fan appears to have Flamingo Tongue Snails (*Cyphoma gibbosum*) and tiny filefish hiding amid the sea plumes.

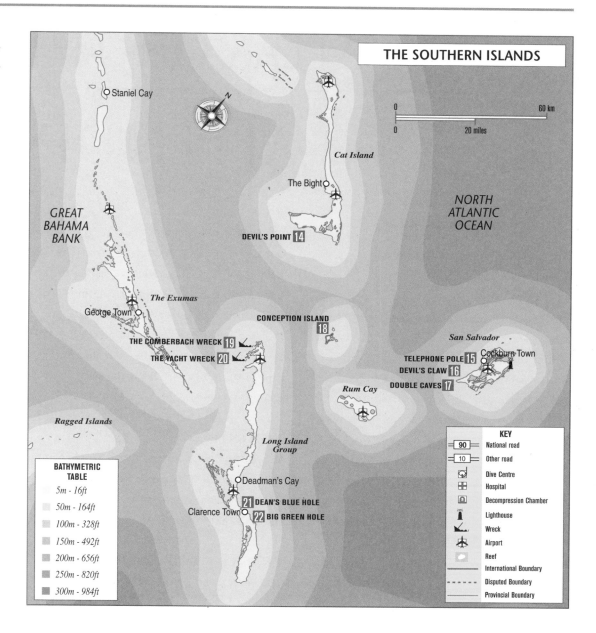

LONG ISLAND

Located to the southeast of the Exuma Chain, Long Island is 106km (66 miles) long. The island's 35 small communities are linked by the newly paved Queen's Highway.

As far as diving on Long Island goes, the corals are not that good inshore. However, there is a splendid wreck, the **Comberbach** 19 , which was a 30m (100ft) steel-hulled coastal freighter that plied its trade around the Exumas and Long Island. Intact and sitting upright, she was deliberately sunk as an artificial reef in the 1980s. Since then the ship has become home to large numbers of snappers, grunts and parrotfish which graze on the algae, corals and sponges that now completely cover the wreck. The engine room is accessible, as are the holds, the forward part of which has a wrecked Volkswagen van. Near

the *Comberbach* are the remains of **a yacht** 20 that was destroyed during a recent hurricane. It too is slowly being claimed by the sea, with several species of algae, corals and hydroids attaching themselves to the hull.

The island has rolling hills, which drop into the exposed eastern side's surf and on the west slopes down slowly to a massive shallow sandy bank that stretches over to the Exumas. **Dean's Blue Hole** 21 on the Atlantic side of the island is on private ground, so access is limited, but it is spectacular if you do get the chance. The **Big Green Hole** 22 at Lochaber, south of Clarence Town, is worth a visit, if only for the beaches. In the south, there are several old churches that are worth exploring.

Long Island is more of a stopping-off point for diving Conception Island and the shark diving that originated here over 20 years ago.

DIVE ATLAS OF THE WORLD

APPENDIX

ATLANTIC

EAST COAST USA

CLIMATE

This vast area has climates varying from the temperate north to almost Caribbean-like within the Gulf Stream and to the south. The northeastern USA can have temperatures below freezing from November to April. The Florida Keys and Bermuda are sub-tropical with temperatures from 18°–23°C (65°–73°F) in winter to 30°C (86°F) in summer. The hurricane season on the North Carolina coast and Florida Keys is from August to December, while for Bermuda it is June to November.

BEST TIME TO GO

All areas are best dived in the northern summer, but the hurricane season is a problem. However, those sites from North Carolina and further south, including Bermuda, can be dived all year round. The North Atlantic can get really rough, but Bermuda has wrecks all around the islands, making it possible to find leeward diving somewhere in most weathers.

GETTING THERE

The northern wrecks are reached from various cities including Atlantic City, New Jersey, New York and Massachusetts. North Carolina wrecks are similarly reached from various cities including Morehead City, Beaufort, Wilmington and Hatteras. The Florida Keys are reached via Miami. Bermuda can be reached directly from Europe or via the USA.

WATER TEMPERATURE

In the north, bottom temperature on wrecks such as the *Andrea Doria* can be as low as 7°C (45°F) and rarely rises above 15°C (60°F) in late summer. Off North Carolina it ranges from 13°C (55°F) in winter and spring, to 26°C (79°F) in late summer. In the Florida Keys, it can be as low as 22°C (72°F) from December to March and up to 29°C (84°F) from April to November. In Bermuda it ranges from 18°C (65°F) in January to 30°C (86°F) in August.

VISIBILITY

Visibility is poor in the north, but generally clear in the Gulf Stream – more than 15–30m (50–100ft). Ebb tides and stirred-up sand can limit visibility on some sites.

QUALITY OF MARINE LIFE

The wrecks in the north have cold-water species including lobsters. North Carolina has a mixture of cold-water species and tropical species that have travelled north in the Gulf Stream. The Florida Keys and Bermuda have a rich collection of tropical species.

DEPTH OF DIVES

The northern wrecks range from relatively shallow to quite deep and some exceed 60m (200ft). Most of the popular North Carolina wrecks are in the 24–46m (80–150ft) range. The *Bibb* is at 30m (100ft) and the *Duane* is at 28m (90ft). In Bermuda most wrecks are shallow, generally less than 30m (100ft).

RECOMPRESSION (HYPERBARIC) CHAMBERS

There are several facilities on the mainland of the USA. In Bermuda there is one at King Edward VII Memorial Hospital, Paget, Bermuda. Telephone 236 2345.

SNORKELLING

None on the wrecks, popular off the Florida Keys and Bermuda.

DIVE PRACTICALITIES

The northern wrecks are for very experienced divers only. The other wrecks can be enjoyed by most divers, though the deeper ones require more training.

All operators offer extensive facilities, diving courses and have equipment for hire, the larger ones offer Nitrox and technical diving.

UNITED KINGDOM

CLIMATE

The weather is very changeable, air temperatures are affected by the wind-chill factor. Summer is May to September and winter is October to April. Most divers use dry suits year round, though some use thick semidry suits in summer.

BEST TIME TO GO

Year-round if sheltered, but in summer only for offshore sites. Summer has the advantage of a high sun giving greater penetration of light into the water.

GETTING THERE

A good system of international and domestic flights, roads and ferries mean that all sites are easily reached.

WATER TEMPERATURE

Water temperature ranges from 2°–8°C (36°–46°F) in winter, to 9°–18°C (48°–65°F) in summer, depending on the depth. The west coast tends to be warmest and temperatures are highest in late summer.

VISIBILITY

Generally poor at 2–20m (6½–65ft), depending on the site and weather.

QUALITY OF MARINE LIFE

Many sites are very good, with a high density of seaweed and bottom-dwelling creatures, including anemones, crustaceans and nudibranchs, small shoals of fish sheltering from the current in the lee of the rocks, or in crevices, and many species of pelagic fish. There are some exotic visitors in the Gulf Stream and some introduced, alien species.

DEPTH OF DIVES

From the surface to depths well beyond the accepted limits of sport or recreational technical diving. Diving too deep is a common problem, so act sensibly.

RECOMPRESSION (HYPERBARIC) CHAMBERS

There are many hyperbaric chambers in the UK. Most are near the coast, but there are others inland for divers diagnosed with a problem associated with decompression later. Hyperbaric treatment is also used in treating diseases not connected with diving.

SNORKELLING

Not recommended in most places due to tidal currents and poor visibility.

DIVE PRACTICALITIES

All diving should be treated with respect even on calm summer days. At sea the tides can be vicious and the weather can change quickly. Most dives require slack water. Dives should be planned with knowledge of the local tides and weather forecasts. When diving with a day boat or live-aboard boat operating in the area, respect the planning of the skipper who would know the waters.

Dive operators would have most facilities and popular equipment; day and live-aboard boats would carry all necessary safety equipment. Divers should not dive in a dry suit without proper training in its safe use.

Divers should fully understand the problems and equipment requirements of diving in cold water before diving in lakes or quarries in winter.

SCOTLAND
SCAPA FLOW
CLIMATE

The weather is variable due to its exposed northern location. Scapa Flow is susceptible to fog in the early summer months as the land warms up, while the sea is still cold at around 7°C (45°F).

BEST TIME TO GO

The water is warmer from August to October, but this also coincides with an algae bloom. However, while visibility underwater may be poor at that time, there is also more light and the water is warmer.

GETTING THERE

There is a daily car ferry service from Scrabster on the Scottish mainland to Stromness, the centre for diving Scapa Flow. Daily flights into Kirkwall are also available through British Airways from Edinburgh and Aberdeen.

VISIBILITY

Best time is during the winter months (December to March) after the plankton blooms. The entrance to Burra Sound on the blockships is the clearest at any time of year because this is where the tidal movement sweeps the bad visibility away before it. However, the only drawback to this is the limited dive time at slack water – usually only around 20 minutes.

DEPTH OF DIVES

Average blockship is around 15m (50ft), the German war ships start in about 36m (120ft).

RECOMPRESSION CHAMBERS

Dial 999 and ask for the coastguard. They will automatically patch you through to the nearest decompression chamber if required.

CATHEDRAL ROCK
BEST TIME TO GO

After the spring plankton bloom, June to July are usually excellent and a perfect time for viewing seabirds diving underwater, beneath the towering cliffs of St Abbs Head.

HOW TO GET THERE

Travel up the A1 trunk road until you reach Scotland. Turn second right along the Eyemouth to Coldingham road, the A1107. In Coldingham village square, take a tight turning to your right, which is well sign-posted, to St Abbs. As you approach the village, the road splits into two. To get to St Abbs harbour take the main branch to the right. St Abbs is only about 7km (4 miles) off the A1.

VISIBILITY

Usually 6–15m (20–50ft). The winter months, between November and March, are generally best, but periodic winter storms can spoil this.

DEPTH OF DIVES

Shore dives average 8–14m (25–45ft).

SOUTH AFRICA/GREAT WHITES
CLIMATE

The western coast has cold currents washing up from Antarctica. Summer is from November to February and winter from May to July. The areas where shark diving is done have a Mediterranean climate with winter rainfall.

BEST TIME TO GO

April to September for diving with Great Whites at Seal Island. October to May for the Makos.

GETTING THERE

South African Airways has frequent scheduled flights. Most major airlines have scheduled flights either direct to Cape Town or to Johannesburg, with a connecting flight by domestic airline to Cape Town.

WATER TEMPERATURES

Great Whites: 13–19°C (55–66°F). Makos and Blues: 18–23°C (65–73°F).

VISIBILITY

Great Whites: 2–15m (6½–50ft). Mako and Blues 10–30m (33–100ft) and more.

QUALITY OF MARINE LIFE

Great White Sharks, seals and many small species of fish. On Mako and Blue dive trips, one can also see huge tuna and other large pelagic species.

DEPTH OF DIVES

Great Whites: just below the surface for cage dives. Mako and Blue Sharks: down to 15m (50ft).

RECOMPRESSION (HYPERBARIC) CHAMBERS

Closest chamber is in Simon's Town, 20 minutes from dive site.

SNORKELLING

Only on Mako and Blue Shark trips. All Great White dives are done with scuba.

MEDITERRANEAN

SPAIN (MEDAS ISLANDS) AND FRANCE

CLIMATE

Windy and cool in the spring with high rainfall. Average temperatures of 25°C (78°F) from June to October.

BEST TIME TO GO

June to September when light, warm offshore winds predominate. However, this is a year-round diving destination and when there is little rain, the weather is generally perfect for diving.

GETTING THERE

There are no direct flights to Estartit, so most visitors will fly to Barcelona or Gerona in Spain or Perpignan in France, all of which are about an hour's drive from Estartit.

WATER TEMPERATURES

Approximately 20°C (68°F) is average, so thick wet suits or dry suits are recommended. The temperature in the Mediterranean never drops below 10°C (50°F).

VISIBILITY

The River Tor governs the visibility around the islands. The clearest months with least rainfall are June to September.

QUALITY OF MARINE LIFE

Excellent for precious red corals and large grouper encounters.

DEPTH OF DIVES

All depths available, but the average is around 25m (80ft) and less.

RECOMPRESSION CHAMBERS

In La Estartit.

SNORKELLING

Very good off the Medas Islands as there are large schools of fish and grouper close to the shorelines.

DIVE PRACTICALITIES

Dive centres cater for large groups, so hire equipment is excellent quality, although most people bring own equipment. Dive schools teach in several languages and are affiliated to most major training organizations.

MALTA, GOZO, COMINO

CLIMATE

Very hot, with an average of 30°C (86°F) in the summer. It can be windy from the north, with very little rainfall, but expect small but very heavy showers in September.

BEST TIME TO GO

From May to the end of September, maximum temperatures will range from 30°C (86°F) to 34°C (93°F), with almost 13 hours of sunshine, so protect yourself accordingly. The power of the sun is often disguised by a northwesterly breeze, especially later in the year when the majjistral, as it is known locally, is at its strongest. The northeasterly wind is known as the grigal, and the northerly tramuntana causes the occasional winter storm. The warm sirocco that blows off the Sahara often makes the sea rough along southern shores, and all diving is then done on the north shore.

GETTING THERE

Air Malta has international flights to virtually all the major European cities. A number of other airlines and charter operators also fly into Malta. Transfer to Gozo can be done by helicopter or by regular ferry service.

WATER TEMPERATURE

From October to April temperatures are between 17° (63°F) and 28°C (82°F). Temperatures start to fall in November and are down to 14°C (57°F) in January and February, when thicker wet suits, even dry suits, are needed.

VISIBILITY

Over 45m (150ft) average off the shore at the deeper sites. In the shallow bays the average is 12m (40ft).

QUALITY OF MARINE LIFE

Very good for invertebrates and sea horses. Few large schools of fish, but what is there, is friendly.

DEPTH OF DIVES

Over 30m (100ft) average, but since most dives are shore dives, depths are available to suit all experiences.

RECOMPRESSION (HYPERBARIC) CHAMBERS

In Valletta on Malta.

SNORKELLING

Snorkelling is very good from the shore and most locals participate, so it can get busy at popular locations.

DIVING PRACTICALITIES

Teaching is done in many languages and islands are perfect for learning to dive. Best feature is the underwater topography with many caves and caverns.

Visitors need a Maltese diving permit. If your qualification is less than the equivalent of CMAS two-star diver, you need to dive with a Maltese-registered instructor at all times, and may need to sit another medical.

There are 28 diving operations registered with the Ministry of Tourism. Others (mainly German) operate seasonally in various hotels.

RED SEA

ISRAEL AND JORDAN

CLIMATE

Warm and dry in winter, but there can be cold spells. Average temperature 20°C (70°F). Hot and dry in summer averaging 35°C (95°F).

BEST TIME TO GO

This region is dived all year round, but is best in summer, June to August. High season for bookings is October to April.

GETTING THERE

In Israel, Eilat Airport can only accommodate small aircraft. A few divers fly to Tel Aviv and then travel on to Eilat by road, but charter flights go to the military airport at Ovda, 40 minutes from Eilat by road. Some divers cross the border to and from Aqaba in Jordan. In Jordan, most divers for Aqaba will change flights in the capital Amman, though now that the Eilat/Aqaba border is open it can be cheaper to travel via Israel. The Egyptians have recently enlarged Râs el Naqb airport to serve Taba and Nuweiba in the Sinai, so divers can cross into Israel at Taba from here, but the Egyptian customs at Taba can give problems.

WATER TEMPERATURE

Averages 25°C (77°F) in summer, 19°C (66°F) in winter.

VISIBILITY

Lower on average than at other Red Sea sites due to industrial and port activity along this part of the coast.

QUALITY OF MARINE LIFE

Surprisingly good. The fish are used to divers not being a threat so they allow them to approach closely. Swimming with dolphins at Dolphin Reef in Israel is a highlight.

DEPTH OF DIVES

Mostly shallow.

RECOMPRESSION CHAMBERS

Israel – Yoseftal Hospital, Eilat. Telephone (chamber) +972(0)8 6358023.

Jordan – The Princess Haya (Bint El-Hussein) hospital in the centre of Aqaba. Telephone +962(0)3 2014111.

SNORKELLING

Excellent over the shallows and with the dolphins at Dolphin Reef.

DIVE PRACTICALITIES

Good buoyancy control to avoid damaging the coral and some form of protective clothing against fire coral and stinging hydroids. The Israeli authorities now ban close approach to coral and newly-qualified dive masters can interpret this too literally. Ear infections, often caused by fungus, are common with divers and snorkellers. Use an ear-drying agent after each dive.

NORTH EGYPT

CLIMATE

Warm and mostly dry in winter, with an average temperature of 20°C (70°F), but cold and windy out to sea, a dry suit, semidry suit or thick wet suit is preferable. Hot and dry in summer, with an average temperature of 35°C (95°F), but the winds at sea can be strong, when wet suits are fine provided you have warm clothes available when on a boat. If you have booked a live-aboard, you are only exposed to the heat ashore when travelling.

BEST TIME TO GO

This region is dived all year round, but is best in summer, May to September. High season for bookings is October till April.

GETTING THERE

There are international airports at Râs Nusrâni (Sharm el Sheikh) for the Sinai and south of Hurghada for Hurghada and El Gouna. There is also a smaller airport at El Gouna. Both Sharm el Sheikh and Hurghada airports receive direct charter flights or connecting flights via Cairo. The Egyptians have recently enlarged Râs el Naqb airport to serve north Sinai with charter flights.

WATER TEMPERATURE

Averages 25°C (77°F) in summer, 19°C (66°F) in winter.

VISIBILITY

Visibility is least 20m (65ft) on fringing or nearshore reefs, except where divers or currents stir up the silt. However, 30–40m (100–130ft) is common over deep water.

QUALITY OF MARINE LIFE

Very good, a high density of stony and soft corals, gorgonias, other invertebrates and both reef and pelagic fish.

DEPTH OF DIVES

Depth of dive can range from the surface to well beyond the accepted limits of sport or recreational technical diving. Depths of 30–40m (100–130ft) are common for experienced divers, but 25m (80ft) is deep enough to see most things of interest.

RECOMPRESSION CHAMBERS

There are recompression chambers at Sharm el Sheikh opposite the naval harbour and the El Gouna Hospital north of Hurghada.

SNORKELLING

Almost everywhere, except where sharks are common, when a snorkeller on the surface can be mistaken for a fish in trouble.

DIVE PRACTICALITIES

Everywhere – good buoyancy control to avoid damaging the coral and some form of protective clothing against fire coral and stinging hydroids. At night there is an extra problem with lionfish. Ear infections, in the Red Sea often caused by a fungus, are common with both divers and snorkellers. Use an ear-drying agent after each dive.

SOUTH EGYPT

CLIMATE

Hot and humid on land in summer, but the winds at sea can be strong. Thin wet suits are fine, but it is wise to have warm clothes on the boat. If you have booked a live-aboard, you are only exposed to the heat ashore when travelling. Pleasantly warm on land in winter, but cold out to sea, a dry suit or thick wet or semi-dry suit will aid comfort between Port Safâga and El Quseir at that time. The Brothers Islands, Elphinstone Reef, Dædalus Reef, Gezîret Zabargad, Rocky Islet and St Johns are kept at a pleasant temperature in summer by the winds, but in the water it is warm enough for a thin wet suit.

BEST TIME TO GO

Fringing and nearshore reefs can be dived all year round, but are best May to September. High season for bookings is October till April.

The Brothers Islands, Dædalus Reef, Gezîret Zabargad, Rocky Islet and St Johns are best dived from May to July. Charters run in August and September, but the sea can be rough. Elphinstone is best dived from April to September.

GETTING THERE

There are two routes, depending on your destination. Live-aboards for the offshore islands and reefs must depart from Hurghada or the new Port Ghalib International Marina at Marsa 'Alam. For Hurghada there are charter flights or connecting flights via Cairo to Hurghada airport, which is midway between Hurghada and Port Safaga. Then there is an asphalt road if you are heading further south. Charter flights or connecting flights via Cairo now go to Marsa 'Alam airport for the operators based well to the south.

WATER TEMPERATURE

At Port Safâga to El Quseir – the average is 25°C (77°F) in summer, 19°C (66°F) in winter.

Further south to the Sudanese border – the average is 28°C (82°F) offshore in summer, 30°C (86°F) on fringing reefs, but can drop to 23°C (73°F) in winter.

At the Brothers Islands, Elphinstone Reef, Dædalus Reef, Gezîret Zabargad, Rocky Islet and St Johns the average is about 27°C (81°F) in summer.

VISIBILITY

At least 20m (65ft) on fringing or nearshore reefs, except where divers or currents stir up the silt on wrecks, 30–40m (100–130ft) is common over deep water.

QUALITY OF MARINE LIFE

Very good, a high density of stony and soft corals, gorgonias, other invertebrates and both reef and pelagic fish. Sharks of many types are found on the offshore reefs.

DEPTH OF DIVES

From the surface to depths well beyond the accepted limits of sport or recreational technical diving. Depths of 30–40m (100–130ft) are common for experienced divers but 25m (80ft) is deep enough to see most things of interest.

RECOMPRESSION CHAMBERS

The nearest chamber is at the El Gouna Hospital north of Hurghada and there is another in Sharm el Sheikh opposite the naval harbour.

SNORKELLING

Almost everywhere, except where sharks are common and a snorkeller on the surface runs the risk of being mistaken for a fish in trouble.

DIVE PRACTICALITIES

Everywhere – good buoyancy control is necessary to avoid damaging the coral. some form of protective clothing against fire coral and stinging hydroids is necessary. At night there is an extra problem with lionfish. Ear infections, in the Red Sea often caused by a fungus, are common in divers as well as snorkellers. Use an ear-drying agent after each dive.

Operators stock the minimum of equipment, divers are generally better off if they are self-sufficient: carrying all equipment and spares – any prescription medicines, decongestants, batteries and film.

SUDAN

CLIMATE

Pleasantly warm and dry in winter, but at that time the offshore winds can be very strong and it is wise to have warm clothes on the boat. In summer it can be unpleasantly hot on land with temperatures of 47°C (117°F), but you are only ashore when travelling, whereas at sea the temperature is comfortable, but humid. Thin wet suits are best in winter, but Lycra Skins are fine in summer.

BEST TIME TO GO

Sudan is dived all year. Most live-aboard boats operating out of Port Sudan only do so in winter, but it can get very windy and rough at that time. The best time to go is May till July and again in September. Avoid August when rain in nearby Ethiopia causes bad weather.

GETTING THERE

It is best to take a live-aboard boat from Egypt. Air connections are notoriously unreliable. Try to get an international flight via Cairo to Port Sudan rather than arriving at Khartoum. Most reliable are the flights from Jeddah, Saudi Arabia, but these are only available to Saudi Arabian nationals or expatriates working there.

WATER TEMPERATURE

Averages 28°C (82°F) in summer, 27°C (81°F) in winter. There can be highs of 30°C (86°F) in places, and these patches feel like a hot bath.

VISIBILITY

You can expect at least 20m (65ft), except where divers or currents stir up the silt on wrecks, while 30–40m (100–130ft) is common over deep water.

QUALITY OF MARINE LIFE

The greatest density and diversity of species in the Red Sea can be found in the Sudan, with excellent reef fish, stony, gorgonian and soft corals. The absence of large-scale commercial fishing means that there are plenty of pelagic species, especially sharks.

DEPTH OF DIVES

Diving is possible from the surface to depths well beyond the accepted limits of sport or recreational technical diving.

Depths of more than 30–50m (100–165ft) are common for experienced divers, but 25m (80ft) is deep enough for recreational divers to see most things of interest.

RECOMPRESSION (HYPERBARIC) CHAMBERS

There are working Hyperbaric Chambers in Jeddah (Saudi Arabia), but these are not available to most recreational divers. The nearest chamber available without bureaucratic problems is at El Gouna (Egypt), so dive conservatively.

SNORKELLING

Snorkelling is possible almost everywhere except where sharks are common – they can mistake a snorkeller on the surface for a fish in trouble.

DIVE PRACTICALITIES

Everywhere – good buoyancy control is essential to avoid damaging the coral and some form of protective clothing is necessary against fire coral and stinging hydroids. At night there is an additional problem with lionfish. Ear infections, in the Red Sea often caused by a fungus, are common in divers as well as snorkellers. Use an ear-drying agent after each dive.

It is important to take everything you are likely to need with you, including any prescription medicines. Operators do not stock any equipment and there are no dive shops. Batteries and even toilet paper can be unobtainable for months.

INDIAN OCEAN

EAST AFRICA

CLIMATE

Tanzania has two seasons: dry and rainy. Most of the year the country is dry, sunny and hot. In March and April heavy rainstorms often make roads impassable.

GETTING THERE

A few airlines fly to Tanzania, including South African Airways, Tanzania Air, British Airways and Gulf Air. The main airport is near the capital, Dar es Salaam. A new airport has been built near Mount Kilimanjaro, where KLM is the main operator.

RECOMPRESSION (HYPERBARIC) CHAMBERS

There is a fully functional recompression chamber in Mombassa, annually checked by the US Navy.

SEYCHELLES

CLIMATE

The southeast monsoon blows from mid-May to October, although the wind rarely exceeds 24km/h (15mph). The highest rainfall occurs around December and January, with the hottest months being March and April. Temperatures average about 27°C (80°F).

BEST TIME TO GO

May to December are best as far as the weather is concerned, but this also coincides with plankton blooms. However, the reduced underwater visibility is offset by the improved opportunity to see Whale Sharks and mantas.

GETTING THERE

British Airways and Air Seychelles run regular direct flights from London to Mahé.

WATER TEMPERATURE

Average 29°C (84°F), but does fluctuate with the spring and autumn plankton blooms, when temperatures may soar into the high 30s°C (90s°F) and lead to coral bleaching.

VISIBILITY

Average is 25m (80ft) inshore, but on the offshore seamounts and outer islands, visibility may exceed 45m (150ft).

QUALITY OF MARINE LIFE

The Seychelles suffered badly from the El Niño/Southern Oscillation Phenomenon and much of the inshore soft and leathery corals were lost. Not primarily known for their coral reefs, the stony and soft corals on the offshore granite boulders have recovered well and populations of fish life are at their highest level now. Most of the dive sites are just a 10 to 20-minute boat ride from shore.

WHALE SHARKS

Best time for Whale Sharks is in November, when large numbers of them congregate around the coastal shallows feeding on the rich plankton.

DEPTH OF DIVES

Inshore is 12–15m (40–50ft) offshore depths over 30m (100ft).

RECOMPRESSION (HYPERBARIC) CHAMBERS

At Victoria on Mahe.

SNORKELLING

Superb around all the islands. The Seychelles are a 'high yield' destination with lots of marine life for very little effort.

DIVE PRACTICALITIES

All levels catered for and dive instruction to the highest standard given in several languages.

CHAGOS

CLIMATE

The Chagos Archipelago lies just south of the equator, so the climate is tropical. Winds are mostly light northwesterly during October to April, and stronger southeasterly during May to September. Severe tropical cyclones are rare.

BEST TIME TO GO

Calmest conditions are from January to April. July is also reported to be relatively calm. Private yachts visit at any time, although most pass through during the period of the northeast monsoon in the northern Indian Ocean (November to April).

GETTING THERE

Getting to the Chagos is half the challenge. At present, under the terms of the Anglo-American defence agreement, no commercial activities are allowed in the Chagos. This includes dive charters. While things might change in the future, at present there are only two ways for divers to get there: you can either join or organize your own scientific expedition, or sail there by private yacht.

WATER TEMPERATURES

Water temperatures are consistently warm, varying from about 27°C to 31°C (80°F) to (88°F). A wet suit is not a necessity, but a thin neoprene or lycra suit will offer comfort on longer or repeat dives, as well as protection against scratches and stings.

VISIBILITY

Visibility is normally very good around these oceanic reèfs. Inside the atolls it can drop to 10m (33ft) on occasions, but visibility of 30m (100ft) or more is the norm outside the atolls.

QUALITY OF MARINE LIFE

Reef fish and invertebrate abundance and diversity are excellent. Nearly 800 species of reef fish have been recorded. Coral diversity is the highest in the central Indian Ocean. Although corals were badly affected by coral bleaching in 1998, recovery is now well under way.

DEPTH OF DIVES

Dives are on coral reefs, most of which reach the surface. On the outside of the atolls the reefs drop away to the ocean depths. So dive depths are very much a matter of personal choice. However, there are no recompression facilities available (military divers at Diego Garcia have their own facilities, but for non-military divers the nearest recompression chamber is in the Maldives). Consequently, dive profiles should be suitably conservative.

HOSPITAL AND RECOMPRESSION CHAMBERS

None for civilian use. There are excellent facilities at the US military base on Diego Garcia, but the island is definitely out of bounds to unauthorized persons. The nearest (small) hospital is on the island of Hithadhoo in Addu Atoll in the Maldives, over 480km (300 miles) to the north. The nearest reasonably sized and equipped hospital is on Malé in central Maldives, and the nearest recompression chamber on Bandos Island Resort nearby. Both are over 950km (600 miles) north of the Chagos.

SNORKELLING

Snorkelling on the coral reefs is superb. Reef fish are a particular attraction.

DIVE PRACTICALITIES

There are no facilities. You need to bring everything you need for diving; tools and spares for small repairs to equipment; first aid and prescription medicines; personal items and food.

MAURITIUS

CLIMATE

Mauritius has a maritime tropical climate with only two seasons – summer and winter – the difference between them being so marginal that spring and autumn are smudged out. During the summer months (November to April) temperatures can climb up to 35°C (95°F) at times and, combined with high humidity, can become very uncomfortable. During winter (May to October), the average temperature is a comfortable 25°C (77°F), humidity levels are reduced and the nights are cooler.

BEST TIME TO GO

Mauritius is dived all year round. Best months are October and November – usually the driest months and outside the normal cyclone season when the prevailing winds can be a problem.

GETTING THERE

Mauritius is a tropical island and therefore can only be reach by aircraft or by boat. Air Mauritius, SAA, Air France, British Airways, Condor, Emirates and Singapore Airlines have scheduled flights to Mauritius.

WATER TEMPERATURES

Water temperatures vary between 20°C (68°F) and 28°C (82°F) and thin wet suits are recommended. When diving on the drop-off, temperatures can descend below 20°C (68°F), depending on depth.

VISIBILITY

Inside the lagoon visibility can be as much as 20m (65ft), but on the drop-off it decreases to anything between 5m (15ft) and 15m (48ft), depending on depth.

QUALITY OF MARINE LIFE

Although Mauritius is a tropical island, it lies at the southern extreme of the tropics and therefore its marine life is not as rich and colourful as that of islands lying closer to the equator. Nevertheless, Mauritius has its fair share of marine beauty and things of interest for divers.

DEPTH OF DIVES

Most diving in Mauritius is done between 18m (60ft) and 25m (80ft), but some dives go down to 40m (130ft) and even beyond. However, this is only for very experienced divers.

RECOMPRESSION CHAMBERS

There is only one facility on the island, situated at the paramilitary Special Mobile Force unit at Vacoas, near Port Louis.

SNORKELLING

This can be done anywhere inside the lagoon that surrounds the island. The closer to the barrier reef and the drop-off beyond, the richer the marine life. However, this can mean a fairly long swim.

DIVE PRACTICALITIES

There are 23 dive centres in Mauritius that are registered with the Mauritius Scuba Diving Association. Each is run by professional staff and all are run from premises that are incorporated within a hotel or resort complex. Each offers equipment for hire and operates dive boats which take you to the drop-off. All necessary facilities are available on the island.

MOZAMBIQUE

PONTA DA BARRA

CLIMATE

Tropical, with a summer rainy season from November to April. Temperatures drop slightly during winter, May to October. Temperatures range from 15°C to over 32°C (60°F to 90°F).

BEST TIME TO GO

This is a year-round destination, although mantas and Whale Sharks are summer visitors.

GETTING THERE

There are two scheduled flights from Johannesburg (South Africa) to Inhambane every week. Guests are met and taken by car to the various hotels that line the beach of Barra and Tofo. For those who want to drive there, Barra is almost 1000km (over 600 miles) from Johannesburg and 400km (250 miles) from Maputo on reasonable roads.

WATER TEMPERATURES

The temperature ranges from a cool 21°C (70°F) in winter to a warm 29°C (84°F) in summer.

VISIBILITY

The visibility over the reefs is entirely dependent on the ocean currents. These move with the winds generated by the weather fronts along the coast of southern Africa. The northern winds bring the plankton blooms, while the southeasters bring the blue water.

QUALITY OF MARINE LIFE

Marine life is typical of the tropical reefs of the Indian Ocean, with a great variety to cater for all preferences, from the larger sharks and mantas to the tiny gobies, shells and small fry. The coast is frequented by Whale Sharks and mantas; there is even a manta cleaning station on one of the reefs. The mangroves offer a unique variety of marine inhabitants and the lucky few may even spot a Dugong or two.

DEPTH OF DIVES

The reefs closest to the shore are a shallow 6m (20ft) while the deepest reef – Giant Castle – reaches a depth of more than 35m (115ft).

RECOMPRESSION CHAMBERS

For minor injuries there is a hospital at Inhambane, but both diving lodges have evacuation policies to the nearest South African hospital (in Nelspruit) or recompression facility at Richards Bay in South Africa. However, it is a one person chamber so any more would need to go to Durban.

SNORKELLING

The sheltered bay offers great snorkelling at only 3-5m (10–16ft), but the best snorkelling experience, with the most to see, is to be had when drifting with the tide through the mangroves.

DIVE PRACTICALITIES

There are several hotels, self-catering facilities, camp sites and backpacker camps, but only two diving lodges – one at Ponta da Barra and the other at Praia do Tofo. Both facilities are fully equipped and include a dive school.

There are dive sites to suit all dive qualifications. Operators offer dive courses, equipment hire and refills. It is advisable to take malaria precautions.

BAZARUTO ARCHIPELAGO

CLIMATE

Typical tropical summer rains fall between December and March. Temperatures drop to 15°C (60°F) in winter and reach a summer high of 32°C (90°F).

BEST TIME TO GO

The archipelago is an all-year-round destination, although the winter months between March and September offer cooler nights and clear skies.

GETTING THERE

The best way to get to the archipelago is to fly to Vilankulo. At the moment there are two scheduled flights per week from Maputo and four from Johannesburg. Transfers to the islands can be done by small plane or by boat.

WATER TEMPERATURES

Range from a cool 22°C (72°F) to a warm 28°C (82°F) in summer.

VISIBILITY

Varies according to the surge and the currents.

QUALITY OF MARINE LIFE

Many tropical species of the Indian Ocean are found on these reefs. Pelagic fish frequent the open water and elusive Dugongs have been seen in the shallow channels between islands. These reefs are home to six species of marine turtles.

DEPTHS OF DIVES

The reefs closest to the islands are no deeper than 10m (33t), Cabo San Sebastian reaches 30m and more (100ft).

RECOMPRESSION CHAMBERS

In the event of an accident guests would be evacuated to a hospital in Nelspruit or Johannesburg in South Africa. The closest recompression chamber is at Richards Bay, also in South Africa. However, it is a one person chamber so any more would need to go to Durban.

SNORKELLING

Great snorkelling may be found around the islands and in the protected bays.

DIVE PRACTICALITIES

There are dive sites to suit all qualifications. It is advisable to take malaria precautions. All hotels on Benguerra and Bazaruto Islands have fully equipped dive facilities and schools.

PONTA DO OURO
CLIMATE

Tropical, with a summer rainy season between November and April. Temperatures drop slightly during winter, May to October. Temperatures range from 15°C (60°F) in winter to over 32°C (90°F) in summer.

BEST TIME TO GO

Ponta do Ouro is a year-round destination. The resident pods of dolphins are often seen along the coast, Whale Sharks are sighted for most of the summer – September to March, and sharks, such as the Zambezis and Silvertips, are summer visitors as well.

GETTING THERE

Ponta do Ouro is situated only a few kilometres (miles) north of the South African border where there is a car park for vehicles. All operators offer a meet-and-greet system. Alternatively, people with four-wheel-drive vehicles can negotiate the network of sandy roads. Although Maputo is only 120km (75 miles) further north by ferry (if it is working) or 175km (110 miles) by land, the road is so bad that it would take a four-wheel-drive vehicle up to six hours to make the distance. The alternative way to reach Ponta is by small aircraft. There are two small airstrips on either side of the border.

WATER TEMPERATURES

This can range from a cool 22°C (72°F) in winter to a warm 28°C (82°F) in summer.

VISIBILITY

The visibility over the reefs is entirely dependent on the ocean currents. These move with the winds generated by the weather fronts along the coast of southern Africa. A southwester brings gin-clear water from the open ocean and an easterly churns the sandy floor, resulting in murky conditions and then visibility drops to 10m (33ft).

QUALITY OF MARINE LIFE

Typical of the tropical reefs of the Indian Ocean, with a great variety to cater for all preferences, from the larger sharks and mantas to tiny gobies, shells and small fry. The coast is frequented by Whale Sharks and dolphins.

DEPTH OF DIVES

The reefs closest to the shore are a shallow 10m (33 ft), while the deepest reef – Pinnacles – reaches a depth of more than 40m (130ft).

RECOMPRESSION (HYPERBARIC) CHAMBERS

The closest and most accessible hospital and recompression facility is at Richards Bay in South Africa, 250 kilometres (155 miles) south of Ponta do Ouro. However, it is a one person chamber so any more would need to go to Durban.

SNORKELLING

The bay at Ponta is well protected and offers good snorkelling sites, in fact some 'pool sessions' for diver training are done in the bay.

DIVE PRACTICALITIES

There are at least eight dive operators that launch from the beaches at Ponta do Ouro and Malongane, all well equipped to cater for the international client.

There are dive sites to suit all dive qualifications. Operators offer dive courses, equipment hire and refills including trimix. It is advisable to take malaria precautions.

SODWANA/ ALIWAL SHOALS/ PROTEA BANKS
CLIMATE

Subtropical with hot and humid summers. Winters are pleasantly cool.

BEST TIME TO GO

Diving is generally good throughout the year and often very good between April and June.

GETTING THERE

International flights to Johannesburg, South Africa and then local flights to Durban. It is possible to hire a car in Johannesburg and drive to Sodwana Bay.

WATER TEMPERATURES

Averages 23°C (73°F) to 25°C (77°F).

VISIBILITY

Generally good, but during summer heavy rains can decrease visibility at Aliwal Shoal.

QUALITY OF MARINE LIFE

Excellent in most areas. Sharks, whales, dolphins, turtles, as well as spectacular fish and invertebrates abound.

DEPTH OF DIVES

Both shallow and deeper dives are available in Sodwana Bay and on Aliwal Shoal.

RECOMPRESSION CHAMBERS

The closest chamber is in Richards Bay. However, it is a one person chamber so any more would need to go to Durban. There is emergency evacuation from Sodwana. From Aliwal/Protea the closest chamber is Durban.

SNORKELLING

Good snorkelling is available near Sodwana Bay at Mabibi and Adlams. However, transport to these areas is currently restricted to tour operators.

PRACTICALITIES

Malaria precautions are recommended for Sodwana Bay.

MALDIVES
CLIMATE

The Maldives is in the monsoon belt of the northern Indian Ocean, and experiences fairly complex weather patterns. There are two seasons; a northeast monsoon (called *iruvai*) and a wetter southwest monsoon (*hulhagu*). From May to November the prevailing winds are from the southwest and bring an average of 215mm (8½ in) of rainfall and 208 hours of sunshine per month. Around mid-December the winds veer to the northeast and during this season rainfall averages at 75mm (3 in), with 256 hours of sunshine per month. Days are hot and humid with temperatures of about 25–30°C (77–86°F) and humidities of 60–70%.

BEST TIME TO GO

The Maldives is dived all year round, but you do need to be aware of the seasonal differences as the weather patterns have a strong influence on the currents, and the currents have a strong influence on visibility. There is no river run-off in the Maldives, so the seasonal rainfall has little effect on visibility. The most settled time of year is the northeast monsoon season. May is the wettest month.

GETTING THERE

Most passengers arrive to the Maldives by air. Hulule International Airport on Malé Island is served by a small number of international scheduled and charter airlines.

WATER TEMPERATURE

Averages 28°C (82°F) in the northeast season and may sometimes fall one or two degrees in the southwest season. Thermoclines are rare, but do sometimes occur in the northeast season doldrums (April).

VISIBILITY

Is strongly affected by prevailing currents. In the northeast season, with winds and currents from the northeast, there will be good visibility of 30–40m (100–130ft) on the east side of the atolls and poorer visibility of 20m (65ft) on the west side. In the southwest season, with winds and currents from the southwest, there will be good visibility 30–40m (100–130ft) on the west side of the atolls and poorer visibility 20m (65ft) on the east. If surface conditions are choppy, visibility may be reduced.

QUALITY OF MARINE LIFE

Prolific marine life with over 700 common fish species and many more still to be discovered and classified. Invertebrate species are thought to be in their tens of thousands. There is no large scale commercial fishing in the Maldives, with most of the local fishing fleets using just rod and line techniques.

DEPTH OF DIVES

The best reef life is between 5m (16ft) and 25m (80ft). The Maldivian government has set a 30m (100ft) depth limit on all diving.

RECOMPRESSION (HYPERBARIC) CHAMBERS

A private clinic operates a chamber on Bandos Island Resort in North Malé Atoll. There is also a chamber on Kuramathi Island Resort in Northern Ari Atoll. Facilities and levels of medical care are good but expensive – so it is essential to consider your insurance cover.

SNORKELLING

The snorkelling in the Maldives is fantastic and many of the resort islands have house reefs easily accessed from the shore. Snorkellers should be aware of the currents and discuss the local conditions with the staff at the dive centre before setting off.

DIVE PRACTICALITIES

The Maldives is a great place to learn to dive; the shallow turquoise lagoons offer the ideal environment. Ear infections are common in divers and snorkellers, but it can be prevented by washing out your ears with fresh water after each dive and then using a drying agent.

Currents in the Maldives can sometimes be strong and it is a good idea to have some type of surface marker device such as a flag or delayed SMB with you when diving. Standard scuba equipment can be hired from all dive centres, although some do not have wet suits. Some of the resorts and the better live-aboards now offer Nitrox.

PHUKET/MERGUI/ANDAMANS

CLIMATE

South west monsoon blows between May and October. This season experiences strong winds and rain coming from the southwest rendering the majority of sites in the Andaman sea inaccessible; even if the sites could be reached divers would almost certainly be welcomed by strong currents and limited visibility. The opposite applies during the northeast monsoon which blows between November and April. Which is the really the diving season.

WATER TEMPERATURES

The waters range between 27°C and 31°C (80°F and 88°F). Generally, exposure protection is not required while diving the offshore sites; however a number of divers do wear thin lycra suits as a barrier against stinging cells. Many divers don 3mm wet suits when diving sites far from land on live-aboard excursions, because these sites can be susceptible to sudden cold currents or thermoclines, some dramatically chilling the water by a breathtaking 10°C (50°F).

VISIBILITY

During the preferred season visibility in the Andaman sea can range from 5m (16ft) to above 30m (100ft).

QUALITY OF MARINE LIFE

The region boasts an enormous diversity of marine life. The corals are spectacular with an abundance of both stony and soft corals complementing the blue waters with radiant colours and breathtaking formations inviting prolific schools of fish to seek nutrition and shelter among their branches. Graceful majestic giants such as the Manta Ray and Whale Sharks are often sighted alongside other open ocean fish; barracuda, tuna, trevally and mackerel are all frequent visitors. There's also plenty of stony coral reefs with reef inhabitants of all sizes ranging from minute invertebrates to Giant Moray Eels.

DEPTH OF DIVES

The depths of dives range from 5m (16ft) down to 1000m (3000ft) drop offs in places such as Barren Island in the Andaman Islands. The average, however, is 20-40m (65–130ft).

SNORKELLING

There's a widespread selection of snorkelling sites, mostly over stony coral gardens, only a few of which are accessed from the beaches. So boat trips are in order.

PHUKET
BEST TIME TO GO

Best time is during the dry season, which falls between October and May, when the area experiences hot, sunny conditions and the seas are generally calm and water temperature ranges between 27° and 31°C (80° and 88°F).

GETTING THERE

Phuket International Airport can be reached directly from a number of destinations in the region. For those travelling from further afield, 14 domestic flights depart from Bangkok airport bound for Phuket daily. The flight time is 75 minutes. On arrival on Phuket it will be necessary to transfer by taxi or local air-conditioned minibus directly to the particular live-aboard operator.

WATER TEMPERATURES

Between October and May water temperature ranges between 27° and 31°C (80° and 88°F).

RECOMPRESSION (HYPERBARIC) CHAMBERS

The nearest recompression chamber is on the island of Koh Phuket.

PRACTICALITIES

International and domestic transport networks are good, with regular schedules of road, rail and air services. Dive operators centre around the PADI training agency, ranging from one-man concerns up to five-star facilities. Dive trips and education are obtainable

on arrival, but pre-booking is recommended. Retail of new equipment and spare parts covers many of the top brands.

MERGUI
BEST TIME TO GO

The dry season between October and May is hot and sunny, the seas are generally calm, with an average temperature of 28°C (82°F).

GETTING THERE

All trips depart from the port of Kaw Thaung on Victoria Point, which can be reached from the town of Ranong on the western coast of Thailand. Ranong can be reached by air directly from Bangkok or by road from Phuket Island. Phuket International Airport can be reached directly from a number of destinations in the region. For those already in Thailand, 14 domestic flights depart Bangkok domestic airport daily. The flight time is 75 minutes. At Phuket it will be necessary to transfer by taxi or local air-conditioned minibus to one of the operators. The easiest way is to make prior arrangements to be collected at the airport by your dive operator.

WATER TEMPERATURES

Between October and May the seas are generally calm, with an average temperature of 28°C (82°F).

RECOMPRESSION (HYPERBARIC) CHAMBERS

Nearest recompression chamber is in Phuket.

PRACTICALITIES

Entry considerations vary from season to season, the best is to contact your dive operator before departure.

ANDAMANS
BEST TIME TO GO

Between early January and May the surrounding seas are usually calm, with an average temperature of 28°C (82°F). The skies are clear with plenty of sunshine.

GETTING THERE

There are two ways of accessing these islands, which are owned by India. Live-aboard excursions depart directly from and return to Phuket Island in southern Thailand. Crossings average out at around the 40-hour mark. Alternatively, the islands can be reached indirectly by air via Calcutta or Madras; with a flight time of around two hours from either city.

RECOMPRESSION (HYPERBARIC) CHAMBERS

The nearest recompression chambers are on Phuket Island, Thailand.

PRACTICALITIES

A visa is required in order to enter India – these are issued by Indian Embassies. A separate visa is required to enter the Andaman Islands – these are automatically issued on arrival at Port Blair. For additional information consult your local Indian Embassy.

WESTERN AUSTRALIA
CLIMATE

The northern regions down to Ningaloo Reef are tropical with average land temperatures varying from about 26°C (80°F) to 32°C (90°F).

During summer, some land temperatures can reach over 38°C (100°F). The far south is temperate and averages around 20°C (68°F).

BEST TIME TO GO

Cocos and Christmas Islands: all year. Scott Reef, Seringapatam, Rowley Shoals: from August to November. Ningaloo Reef: from April to November. Rottnest Island: from October to June. Geographe Bay and *HMAS Swan*: from November to June. Albany and Esperance: from November to June.

GETTING THERE

Cocos and Christmas Islands: International flights from Jakarta and domestic flights from Perth. Scott Reef, Seringapatam and Rowley Shoals: domestic flights from Perth to Broome and then live-aboad from

Broome. All other sites: by road or flights from Perth.

WATER TEMPERATURE

Cocos, Christmas Islands, Seringapatam and Scott Reef: average 28°C (82°F). Rowley Shoals, Ningaloo: 26°C (80°F). Rottnest Island and Geographe Bay: 20°C (68°F). Albany and Esperance: 18°C (65°F).

VISIBILITY

Average around 20m (65ft).

QUALITY OF MARINE LIFE

Good, with many pristine coral reefs and temperate water invertebrates.

DEPTH OF DIVES

From the surface to depths beyond the accepted limits of sport or recreational technical diving. From the surface to 25m (80ft) is enough to see most things of interest.

RECOMPRESSION CHAMBERS

Fremantle, Perth.

SNORKELLING

Everywhere.

DIVE PRACTICALITIES

There are dive facilities everywhere. Western Australian Tourism Commission telephone: (+61-1300)361 351.

PACIFIC OCEAN

MALAYSIA
CLIMATE

Tropical, warm and humid year round. Temperatures rarely drop below 20°C (68°F), except on high ground, and are usually around 26°C–30°C (80°F–86°F) during the day.

Although monsoon winds affect the climate, strong winds are rare. Typhoons miss the country by several hundred kilometres, so that Borneo is referred to as The Land Below the Wind. Only the north of Peninsular Malaysia's east coast and Layang Layang close down tourism during their monsoon periods.

BEST TIME TO GO

Each area has two main seasons, the drier season and the so-called monsoon season, which in Malaysia is more accurately called the wetter season.

In Peninsular Malaysia, the west coast's drier season is November to March, and wetter season is April to October. The east coast's wetter season is November to March and drier season from April to October. Sabah's west coast is wettest from June to December, and driest from January to May. Layang-Layang can have bad weather at any time, but has its best weather from April to September. The islands around Pulau Sipadan can be dived all year, but the weather is calmest and driest from May to October. August is the high season for local holidays and turtle nesting.

GETTING THERE

To reach Peninsular Malaysia, fly to Kuala Lumpur International Airport, from where domestic flights connect with Pulau Tioman (direct) or the nearest town for onward land and ferry travel to other islands.

To reach East Malaysia – fly to Kota Kinabalu International Airport, from where special flights are available to Layang-Layang. Domestic flights connect to Tawau for Pulau Sipadan and other islands off Semporna. From Tawau you can either take a helicopter to Pulau Sipadan or continue by road to Semporna, followed by a speedboat ride to the islands. For Lankayan take a domestic flight to Sandakan then carry on by speedboat. Labuan can be reached by ferry from Kota Kinabalu as well as by air.

WATER TEMPERATURES

25°C (77°F) over deep water in the cooler season, to 31°C (88°F) in the warmer season, and 30°C (86°F) is common in shallow water.

VISIBILITY

In good conditions the visibility at Layang-Layang and Sipadan approaches the mythical 60m (200ft) and rarely drops below 30m (100ft). At Labuan, Pulau Perhentian, Pulau Lang Tengah and Pulau Tioman visibility varies from 3m (10ft) to 30m (100ft). At Pulau Aur, Pulau Redang and Pulau Tenggol visibility of more than 30m (100ft) is common.

QUALITY OF MARINE LIFE

Diverse and prolific, marine life is often tame and inquisitive. Large pelagics can be encountered even inshore.

DEPTH OF DIVES

The reefs at Layang-Layang and Pulau Sipadan descend to depths greater than sport divers should go, so act responsibly.

RECOMPRESSION (HYPERBARIC) CHAMBERS

The Malaysian Navy has hyperbaric facilities in Peninsular Malaysia at Lumut and in East Malaysia at Labuan. The Singapore navy has them in Singapore, while Borneo Divers has a two-man chamber in Sipadan.

SNORKELLING

Good snorkelling from the shore or in shallow water over coral reefs for all abilities.

DIVE PRACTICALITIES

Apart from Layang-Layang and Sipadan's Turtle Cavern, Malaysian diving is relaxed and suitable for all standards of divers. Layang-Layang can have strong currents. Carry a high-visibility late-deployment surface marker buoy, rescue tube or flag for attracting the attention of your boat cover.

All operators offer diving courses and have equipment for hire.

INDONESIA
CLIMATE

Two distinct seasons – the wet from November to March and dry from April to October. The month of July and August can be pretty windy. Average year-round temperature is between 27°C (80°F) and 31°C (90°F).

BEST TIME TO GO

April to June and October.

WATER TEMPERATURE & VISIBILITY

The waters of the Bunaken/Manado Tua Marine Park are mostly calm, providing ideal conditions for holiday divers and beginners, enabling even snorkellers to enjoy visibility of 12–30m (40–100ft). Diving conditions are exceptional, with visibility in the 15–30m (50–100ft) range, and water temperatures generally around 26–27°C (78–80°F).

DIVE PRACTICALITIES

The average diver might be quite comfortable in a bathing suit, but a lycra or thin neoprene suit is advisable, not least for protection from the many stinging hydroids. Night dives and multiple dives per day can leave you chilled even in warm water, so a 3mm wet suit is worth bringing.

PHILIPPINES

CLIMATE

Tropical, 23–36°C (73–97°F) with pronounced seasons. The dry season is from November to February and the wet season from June to October, when typhoons can occur in the northern half of the country.

BEST TIME TO GO

Year-round for most areas, except in the far north. April and May are reliably calm throughout the archipelago, December to June is the peak season. The Tubbataha reefs are only comfortably dived from March to the end of June.

GETTING THERE

Fly to either Ninoy Aquino International Airport (Manila), or Mactan International Airport (Cebu), then onward domestic flights to all major destinations, including Puerto Princesa, where you board live-aboard boats for the Tubbataha Reefs. Many destinations now have good ferry services.

WATER TEMPERATURES

25°C (77°F) in the cooler season to 31°C (88°F).

VISIBILITY

Generally excellent, more than 40m (130ft) on a flood tide.

QUALITY OF MARINE LIFE

Diverse and prolific. Large pelagics are regularly encountered on offshore reefs.

DEPTH OF DIVES

Many open-water reefs descend to depths greater than sport or recreational technical divers should dive, so act responsibly.

RECOMPRESSION (HYPERBARIC) CHAMBERS

Recompression Chambers are available in the Freeport Zone at Subic Bay, the AFP Medical Center in Manila and the VISCOM Station Hospital in Cebu. Evacuation Assistance can be obtained from AFP Search & Rescue Facilities in Metro Manila.

SNORKELLING

Good snorkelling from the shore or in shallow water over coral reefs from Bancas or live-aboard tenders.

DIVE PRACTICALITIES

In any open water area, Philippines diving can experience strong currents, especially at times of spring tides. For the Tubbataha Reefs, novices should be accompanied by experienced divers. Carry a high-visibility delayed deployment surface marker buoy or flag, a power whistle and an old CD for use as a heliograph, to attract the attention of your boat cover.

All land-based operators offer diving courses in several languages, and also have equipment for hire. Live-aboard boats, however, do not normally offer courses and only have a small selection of rental equipment, so come prepared.

MICRONESIA

CLIMATE

Tropical, with little seasonal variation. Temperatures range from 25°C to 30°C (77°F to 86°F). Dry season is from January to May.

Typhoon season is from August to December.

BEST TIME TO GO

August to November is the time to avoid Micronesia; most of the islands lie within the Pacific's typhoon belt, often bringing storms, cyclones and majestic swells.

GETTING THERE

By air from Guam, Palau or Manila.

WATER TEMPERATURES

28°C–30°C (82°F–86°F).

VISIBILITY

At Truk Lagoon it is from 12m (40ft) at low tide to over 30m (100ft) at high, depending on tides and location within the lagoon. Can be more than 30m (100ft) at Yap and Palau.

QUALITY OF MARINE LIFE

Schooling fish and invertebrate life. Soft and stony corals drape the wrecks.

DEPTH OF DIVES

Truk lagoon: most diving is at 12–24m (40–80ft). Some deeper wrecks are at 30–46m (100–150ft). Yap depths are around 15m (50ft) and Palau from 30m (100ft).

RECOMPRESSION (HYPERBARIC) CHAMBERS

The nearest fully operational chamber is in Guam. There is a chamber in Truk, but it is usually not operational. There are plans to get it working again.

SNORKELLING

Snorkelling is possible on a number of Truk's wrecks, although most require scuba. Good snorkelling on the reefs at Palau.

DIVE PRACTICALITIES

Conditions are normally calm at Truk Lagoon, with diving at all levels. Deep wrecks and penetration of wrecks should only be attempted by experienced divers accompanied by a local guide. Visibility in the Yap channels is best toward the end of a flood tide. At Palau, conditions depend on the strength of the current, and whether divers use reef hooks.

MELANESIA

CLIMATE

Melanesia covers a large area so there is some variation of climate among the different island groups. Overall the climate is tropical with daytime temperatures ranging between 25°C (77°F) and 32°C (90°F) falling 2–3 degrees at night. Daytime temperatures are rarely extreme due to the cooling winds blowing off the sea.

BEST TIME TO GO

April to October are generally the best months to visit the islands of Melanesia. January to March are the most humid months, with November to March being the monsoon, or wet, season with cyclones forming in the coral sea and steering towards Vanuatu and New Caledonia.

GETTING THERE

International airports at Suva-Fiji, Honiara-Solomon Islands and Port Vila-Vanuatu, receive flights from most major airlines via Australia and New Zealand. Domestic flights to outer islands are available in each country. Live-aboard dive vessels are a great way to visit otherwise inaccessible areas.

WATER TEMPERATURES

The warm tropical waters have an average temperature of 27°C (80°F), although there are variations according to currents and time of year.

VISIBILITY

Can be as good as 50m (165ft) or in rare instances as little as a few metres. Generally expect 25–30m (80–100ft). Best visibility is generally found around offshore dive sites.

QUALITY OF MARINE LIFE.

Overall the marine life around Melanesia is exciting, colourful, exotic and holds the real possibility of discovering new and unnamed species.

DEPTH OF DIVES

Shallow diving on reef tops to depths far beyond recommended sport diving depths. Best coral colours are in the shallows. Many wrecks lie in deeper waters.

RECOMPRESSION (HYPERBARIC) CHAMBERS

Best to avoid needing this facility, but there are small chambers in Suva-Fiji and Port Vila-Vanuatu.

SNORKELLING

Snorkelling is available nearly everywhere with good coral and fish life on most shallow reefs. Lycra suits are recommended to guard against coral cuts and stings as well as protection against sunburn.

DIVE PRACTICALITIES

Lycra suit or thin wet suits are recommended. Ear infections from the tropical warm waters are common. Use of an ear-drying agent is advisable. Malaria medication is strongly recommended for travellers to the Solomon Islands and Vanuatu. Gastro-intestinal problems can be a problem. Bottled water is recommended. Take a comprehensive first-aid kit and any personal prescriptions.

Visitor permits for stays of up to 30 days are issued on arrival, provided visitors have valid passports and onward or return tickets.

Most operators will want to see valid scuba certification or log books as proof of experience.

PAPUA NEW GUINEA

CLIMATE

Coastal climate varies considerably around PNG, but the wet season is typically January to March, and the southeast trade winds blow from May until November. Diving is possible year round as most of the best dive sites are sheltered and close to shore. Cyclones are very rare since PNG is too close to the equator.

BEST TIME TO GO

Diving is year-round with the calmest and warmest months being November to May and the clearest water from June to November. The wet season is from January through March, when it can be squally, except in Milne Bay, which is wettest in August and September. However, weather patterns are very variable from year to year and difficult to predict. Excellent diving can be had throughout the year in most areas.

Cyclones rarely affect the diving areas in Papua New Guinea, which is mostly outside the cyclone belt. However, sites bordering the Coral Sea may be rough if a cyclone is active further south.

GETTING THERE

Air Niugini flies direct to Port Moresby from Singapore, Manila and Australia. There are daily flights from Port Moresby to main centres round the country.

Note that Air Niugini has a special 20kg (44 lb) extra baggage allowance – total 40kg (88 lb) for international passengers – that may be claimed for dive gear. This should be checked when purchasing tickets, and claimed at check in.

WATER TEMPERATURES

Range from average highs of 29°C (84°F) around December and January to average lows of 25°C (77°F) during July and August in the south of Papua New Guinea and rising to 30°C (86°F) and 27°C (80°F) respectively in northern waters.

VISIBILITY

Visibility is usually better than 30m (100ft) on most of the popular dive sites. It can be affected by local rainfall, but this is very temporary. Some of the famous beach muck diving sites may have less visibility, but other sites regularly have visibility in excess of 50m (165ft).

QUALITY OF MARINE LIFE

PNG marine life is extraordinary both for biodiversity and abundance. The quality of the reefs is superb and the author's survey in 2002/3 showed them to be as good or better than they have ever been.

DEPTH OF DIVES

Deep dives are possible in PNG since deep water comes very close to shore. However, most dives are conducted in water less than 30m (100ft) deep on reefs which slope to shallow water less than 10m (33ft) deep.

RECOMPRESSION (HYPERBARIC) CHAMBERS

In Port Moresby.

SNORKELLING

There is excellent snorkelling on the sheltered fringing reefs along shore or around the many small islands throughout the country.

PRACTICALITIES

60-day tourist visas are available for K25 on arrival for passengers with valid passports and return or onward tickets. Visas for longer stays should be obtained before departure. Departure tax is included in ticket price, but there is now an Airport Services Tax at Port Moresby of K30 to be paid before departure.

Malaria prophylaxis is recommended for short-term visitors. Check with your doctor, generally Doxycycline is recommended, Larium is NOT. Try to avoid getting bitten by mosquitoes at night by wearing appropriate clothing and using insect repellent. Use alcohol-based ear drops every diving day to avoid ear infections, and scrub out coral cuts and apply an antibiotic ointment. DAN or other dive insurance is vital.

Fantastic people, art, culture and landscapes, superb diving. Avoid wandering around cities alone or at night, inappropriate clothing or ostentatious behaviour.

GREAT BARRIER REEF
BEST TIME TO GO

For the clearest water and to swim with Minke Whales you should go in July to September.

Otherwise from March to early December.

GETTING THERE

Cairns is the international gateway serviced by 10 international airlines, including Qantas, Malaysian Airlines, Singapore Airlines and Continental.

TRAVEL PRACTICALITIES

What to take with you on a day trip to the Great Barrier Reef: towel, swim suit, hat and sunscreen, sunglasses, casual shoes for walking on islands or hot decks, credit card and cash for purchasing souvenirs and snacks, camera and plenty of film, a change of clothes.

When booking your trip remember to check what is included. Dress lightly and comfortably. It is a good idea to leave passports and other valuables in the hotel safe. All visitors to the reef are charged a small fee for reef tax. This charge goes towards managing and preserving the Great Barrier Reef. If you are prone to seasickness take some medication prior to boarding the vessel. If you are not sure if you get seasick take some medication anyway. If you do get seasick don't worry, once you arrive at the reef it is calm and your motion sickness will generally go away. The best way to avoid seasickness is to have a good breakfast, stay in the fresh air, look at the horizon and keep your mind busy. Swimming also helps seasickness to disappear quickly.

NEW ZEALAND
POOR KNIGHTS
CLIMATE

Cool, wet and windy in winter (June to October). Often very dry from January to March.

BEST TIME TO GO

Year-round, but the water is warmer from December to May. In spring (August to November) the water is cool, but the ocean life is rewarding – for example you will see paper nautilus and giant salp.

GETTING THERE

There are flights from Europe to Auckland.

Take a rental car to Tutukaka, or fly to Whangarei. Most charters arrange transport from the local airport. Dive boats make the 28km (17-mile) crossing in approximately one hour.

WATER TEMPERATURES

Between 14°C (57°F) and 23°C (73°F). It is warmest from January to May.

VISIBILITY

20–50m (60–165ft). Varies depending on plankton blooms (more intense and frequent in spring). Best from January to July.

QUALITY OF MARINE LIFE

Extremely diverse – many invertebrates, especially nudibranchs. Calm conditions on vertical walls make encrusting life very accessible. Reef fish are abundant, large and friendly. Divers can see Eagle Rays and stingrays, moray eels and dolphins.

DEPTH OF DIVES

10–50m (33–165ft).

RECOMPRESSION CHAMBERS

The nearest recompression chamber is at Devonport, Auckland, for Poor Knights and Goat Island, at Christchurch for Fiordland.

SNORKELLING

Superb. Snorkellers can work in pairs. Ride-on kayaks supplied by some charter boats.

DIVE PRACTICALITIES

Dive certification required. Equipment hire in Tutukaka. Dive guides on most charter boats.

FIORDLAND
CLIMATE

Four seasons in one day throughout the year.

Winter is June to September, when there is not as much wind, the days are short and there is less rain. Wonderful diving with ice diving possible in smaller fiords during severe winter conditions.

Summer is from November through February, when there is more rain and wind, and long daylight hours.

BEST TIME TO GO
Year round is good, but the water is warmer in summer by 2 to 4 degrees. For night dives winter is better.

GETTING THERE
There are flights from Europe to Auckland and connecting flights to either Queenstown or Invercargill. There is daily bus transport from both airports to Manapouri or Te Anau. Rental vehicles are also available. Bigger groups can charter minibuses. From Te Anau or Manapouri a charter operator will organise transport to either Milford or Doubtful Sound where vessels are moored. The sailing time is about two to three hours.

WATER TEMPERATURES
Between 10°C (50°F) and 15°C (60°F) and is warmest from January to March. The water temperatures also vary due to rain: a freshwater layer is colder than salt.

QUALITY OF MARINE LIFE
Marine life is extremely diverse, with many invertebrates, especially Black Coral trees. Calm conditions on vertical walls make encrusting life very accessible.

Bottlenose Dolphins can be seen all year, mainly in Doubtful and Dusky Sounds, sometimes Milford.

Penguins: Little Blues can be seen all year; Fiordland Crested can be seen from July to December.

There are seals in most fiords. Not advisable to dive with seals from December to January.

Special: sea pens, deepwater species can be seen at divable depths.

DEPTH OF DIVES
10–50m (33–165ft).

SNORKELLING
Superb.

DIVE PRACTICALITIES
Dive certification is required. Equipment can be hired at Te Anau, Dunedin or Invercargill. There is only one dive boat that has all hire gear aboard. Dive guides on only two charter boats. Passenger submarine rides are possible in Milford to 182m (600ft).

GOAT ISLAND MARINE RESERVE, LEIGH
CLIMATE
Cool, wet and windy in winter (from June to October). Often dry from January to March.

BEST TIME TO GO
Year-round, but water is warmer from December to May.

GETTING THERE
There are flights from Europe to Auckland. Rental car north to Leigh in 90 minutes.

WATER TEMPERATURES
Between 14°C (57°F) and 22°C (72°F). Warmest from January to May.

VISIBILITY
5–15m (16–50ft). Varies depending on plankton blooms (more intense and frequent in spring). Best from February to June.

QUALITY OF MARINE LIFE
Extremely diverse; many invertebrates, especially nudibranchs. Reef fish are abundant, large and tame. Dolphins and Orcas are transients.

DEPTH OF DIVES
3–10m (10–33ft).

SNORKELLING
Superb. Dive from beach. Glass-bottom boat trips are available.

DIVE PRACTICALITIES
Equipment hire in Auckland or Leigh.

CANADA
VANCOUVER ISLAND
CLIMATE
The summer months from July to September are hot. You can expect lots of rain on Vancouver Island over November to April. Snow is to be expected on high ground from November through to May – several metres of it.

BEST TIME TO GO
Whale watching is done from March to November. The summer months are undoubtedly easiest for weather, but not necessarily for the best visibility because this is best from October to February.

GETTING THERE
There are direct flights into Vancouver from all of the major hub airports. You can then catch either a connecting flight to one of the smaller towns on Vancouver Island or catch the ferry from Vancouver to Nanaimo.

WATER TEMPERATURE
Water temperatures average only 8–10°C (46–50°F). Dry suits are recommended.

VISIBILITY
Average 15m (50ft) but this increases the further offshore you travel.

QUALITY OF MARINE LIFE
Super abundance of marine life, very rich in species and of course great chances to see whales.

DEPTH OF DIVES
All depths available.

RECOMPRESSION (HYPERBARIC) CHAMBERS
In Vancouver and Victoria.

SNORKELLING
Fun through some of the areas of fast-moving water and also good among the sea lions and whales.

DIVE PRACTICALITIES

For more experienced divers, because the water is cold and dry suits are recommended.

CATALINA ISLAND

CLIMATE

Hot in the summer months, but can be windy from the west.

BEST TIME TO GO

February to October is best – when the kelp is on its growing cycle. Diving is usually sheltered on Catalina against any offshore storms in the Pacific.

GETTING THERE

Flights to Los Angeles are available through all major air carriers. It only takes about one hour to transfer to the Catalina Express ferry terminal on Long Beach. Taxis are best.

WATER TEMPERATURE

Around 20°C (68°F) is average, thick wet suits or dry suits are recommended.

VISIBILITY

Usually 15–30m (50–100ft).

QUALITY OF MARINE LIFE

Superb kelp forest and sea lion activity.

DEPTH OF DIVES

Average 15m (50ft).

RECOMPRESSION CHAMBERS

In Long Beach and San Diego.

SNORKELLING

Very good in kelp forest shallows.

DIVE PRACTICALITIES

Cold water, so full 7mm wet suits required or dry suits.

MEXICO BAJA CALIFORNIA

CLIMATE

Can be windy from the north, but average is around 25°C (77°F).

BEST TIME TO GO

During November to February the young seal pups are at their most playful and inquisitive and, while the water is colder, it is certainly clearer. With the calmer seas of March and April, the visibility drops around the islands and seamounts, yet this is the best time for sightings of mantas, Whale Sharks and whales.

GETTING THERE

There are direct flights into La Paz from most of the large hub airports, particularly from Mexico City and Los Angeles.

WATER TEMPERATURES

Cool at 18–21°C (65°–70F).

VISIBILITY

The seal pups are born around June and this coincides with the time of best visibility at the end of the plankton bloom. Around the seamounts visibility usually extends to over 50m (165ft).

QUALITY OF MARINE LIFE

Superb for sightings of large pelagics such as whales and Manta Rays, but also for sea lion encounters.

DEPTH OF DIVES

All depths available on the seamounts, but shallow dives average 15m (50ft).

RECOMPRESSION (HYPERBARIC) CHAMBERS

In La Paz.

SNORKELLING

Superb for sea lions at Los Islotes.

DIVE PRACTICALITIES

All levels catered for.

GOLDEN TRIANGLE

CLIMATE

Galápagos is subtropical with two seasons; the changeover between the seasons is vari-able. The dry, or Garua, season runs from July to December. 'Garua' refers to the fog and mist that often hangs on the higher elevations at this time; air temperatures average 26°C (80°F). The warmer or wet season, when air temperatures often exceed 30°C (86°F), lasts from January through June, with March and April generally being the wettest months.

Cocos and Malpelo are tropical with high rainfall and two seasons. The average rainfall is 2540mm (100 in) at Cocos Island and 1060mm (42 in) at Malpelo. At sea level, land temperatures can reach 32°C (89°F) on the Pacific coast, but the temperatures will be lower at sea. The dry season provides calmer seas for the long boat journey out to the islands and there are more Silky Sharks and Mobula Rays. There are some Scalloped Hammerhead Sharks, but not the large numbers that are encountered during the rainy season. In the rainy season the long boat journey out to the island could be rough.

BEST TIME TO GO

Galápagos: The calmest waters are between December and March/April but it is also wetter. The clearest water is from October till November.

Cocos and Malpelo: November till May for the dry season, June till November for the wet season, July/August for the largest number of Hammerhead Sharks.

GETTING THERE

Galápagos: the boats depart from San Cristobal or Baltra Island, connecting flights are via Quito or Guayaquil.

Cocos and Malpelo: fly to San José, then for Cocos Island transfer by road to Puntarenus to pick up the live-aboard boat. For Malpelo Island fly to Golfito to pick up the live-aboard boat. One live-aboard boat covers both Cocos and Malpelo Islands in one charter.

WATER TEMPERATURE

Galápagos: Warmest from January to May at

22°–28°C (72°–82°F) and coolest from July to November at 16°–22°C (61°–72°–F).

Cocos and Malpelo: 25°–28°C (78°–82°F) at the surface. Below the thermoclines it can drop to 15°C (60°F).

VISIBILITY

9–24m (30–80ft) in the wet season; 20–30m (65–100ft) in the dry season. Variable visibility is possible on the same dive due to strong currents and where currents mix.

QUALITY OF MARINE LIFE

The larger animals are prolific, there is little coral at Cocos or Malpelo so the fish are the major attraction.

DEPTH OF DIVES

Galápagos: 5–24m (15–80ft); Cocos Island: 18–40m (60–130ft); Malpelo: the surface to 40m (surface to 130ft).

RECOMPRESSION (HYPERBARIC) CHAMBER

There are no facilities for recompression, so dive sensibly. For the Galápagos, the nearest chamber is located at the San Eduardo Naval Base in Guayaquil and the Ecuadorian Navy charges a fee for its use. For Cocos and Malpelo the nearest chamber is in Panama City.

SNORKELLING

Galápagos: Possibilities are endless. Penguins, marine iguanas, colourful fish, marine turtles, rays, and sharks are just part of the underwater life you will see while snorkelling.

Cocos and Malpelo: Take care near bait-balls.

DIVE PRACTICALITIES

Best suited to advanced or strong divers. Carry a high visibility delayed deployment surface marker buoy or flag, a power horn or whistle and an old CD for use as a heliograph, to attract the attention of your boat cover. Ear infections are common, so use a suitable ear-drying agent to avoid them. Take warm clothes for use on the boat and non-photographers will find gloves useful for holding on to the rocks in the current and surge. All divers are advised to have a good supply of motion-sickness remedies for the long boat journey out to Cocos and Malpelo, even if they do not normally get seasick.

At all destinations, most walking ashore is over rocky lava terrain.

CARIBBEAN

MEXICO

CLIMATE

Best time is November through June to avoid hurricane season.

BEST TIME TO GO

April to August and December through February are the best months outside the hurricane season.

GETTING THERE

Cancún is serviced directly by all of the major airline carriers from all over the world. Fly direct to Cancún and transfer to Cozumel for Caribbean diving, or fly direct to Cozumel via Miami and Houston.

WATER TEMPERATURE

Rarely drops below 27°C (80°F). Wet suits or full lycra suits are suitable, but you will get chilled after the dive, so warm clothing should be available in the winter months.

VISIBILITY

This shallow bay tends to have an average visibility of around 12–25m (40–80ft).

QUALITY OF MARINE LIFE

Superb sponges at Cozumel and large schools of fish off northern Cancún.

DEPTH OF DIVES

Isla Mujeres Bay is 15m (50ft) maximum and Cozumel is all drift diving off the wall in depths reaching beyond safe diving limits.

RECOMPRESSION (HYPERBARIC) CHAMBERS

On Cozumel.

SNORKELLING

Excellent off the shallow reefs at Chankanaab Marine Park and Xcaret in the Yucatán.

DIVE PRACTICALITIES

Novice divers are more suited to Isla Mujeres Bay and experienced divers for Cozumel due to strong currents.

BELIZE

CLIMATE

With an average temperature of 26°C (80°F) throughout the year and rarely rising above 32°C (90°F), the climate is sub-tropical. November through May are the driest months with the wind predominantly from the east.

BEST TIME TO GO

Best time is November through June to avoid hurricane season, but it can be hot.

GETTING THERE

Continental, Taca and American Airlines all fly regularly from the major US hub airports, such as Houston, Los Angeles and Miami, as well as flights from South America, San Pedro Sula on mainland Honduras and Puerto Rico. Some of the internal flights are on small 16-seaters and there may be a problem with weight allowance, so always pack minimally.

WATER TEMPERATURE

Water temperatures average 26°C (80°F)

VISIBILITY

Generally between 30m (100ft) and 50m (165ft). Most diving is done offshore well away from any rainwater run-off which may spoil the visibility.

QUALITY OF MARINE LIFE

Very good on the outer reefs.

DEPTH OF DIVES

Varied to suit all levels of dive experience, but very deep in the Blue holes to see stalactites.

RECOMPRESSION (HYPERBARIC) CHAMBER

The closest recompression chamber is in Belize City with emergency helicopter service from the outer atolls. Telephone 90 for assistance. In Honduras, the recompression chamber is situated on Roatan and is run by St Luke's Mission. Visiting divers are requested to pay a Dollar a day towards the upkeep of the chamber. Telephone and fax (504) 45-15-15 (DAN) Divers' Alert Network Telephone (919) 648-8111.

SNORKELLING

Good on the shallow reefs within the protected lagoon areas.

DIVE PRACTICALITIES

All levels of diver catered for.

TRAVEL TIPS

Belize City, although not on the ideal tourist map is your starting point to explore many of the ancient Maya ruins which are dotted about the country. The most visually impressive is Lamanai on the shores of the new River lagoon. The closest ruins to Belize City are Altun-Ha at only 62km (38 miles). A large number of nature parks have been created and one or more should be included in any field trip, including the Rio Bravo Conservation area which is the largest in Belize at 100,000 hectares (250,000 acres).

The Roatan Institute for Marine Sciences is located at the Anthony's Key Resort and has a maritime museum and daily dolphin shows (if you like that kind of thing).

Visit the Roatan nature parks with its waterfalls and jungle trails, which can be hot and sticky, but you are able to cool off in the waterfall pools.

CUBA

CLIMATE

Semitropical with two seasons, up to 26°C (80°F) from December to March, rising to 32°C (90°F) in July and August. Humidity and rainfall are highest in September and October. Hurricanes are rare, but possible, between August and November.

BEST TIME TO GO

Diving is possible all year round, though slightly rougher seas are encountered in winter. The Pirate Coast is protected and can be dived even in heavy rain. February to May are among the best months, the wet season is May to October.

GETTING THERE

Direct flights to José Martí International Airport in Havana are available from Europe, Canada, Mexico and nearby South American gateways. Restricted flights operate from Miami (USA). The only scheduled carrier now flying non-stop from London is Air Jamaica. Flights will arrive at the new state-of-the-art International Terminal. Charter flights are often available direct to the larger resort areas from Europe.

A 25-minute flight by turbojet connects Havana's run-down old Domestic Terminal to Rafael Cabrera Mustelier Airport, Nueva Gerona from where it is 40km (25 miles) by road to the El Colony Hotel Diving Complex.

See page 240 for details on American citizens going to Cuba.

WATER TEMPERATURE

Temperatures average 28°C (82°F) in summer, 24°C (75°F) in winter.

VISIBILITY

Generally very clear – more than 30m (100ft).

QUALITY OF MARINE LIFE

Diverse and prolific, tame and approachable.

DEPTH OF DIVES

Usually shallow, generally less than 30m (100ft), but there are some sites that require short decompression and others that descend deeper than sports divers should go, so act responsibly.

RECOMPRESSION (HYPERBARIC) CHAMBERS

Havana

La Habana Hyperbaric Medical Center

Hospital Naval 'Dr Luis Diaz Soto'

Havana del Este,

Telephone 7 973266.

Gerona

Hospital General Docente,

Heroes del Baire

Avenue 39 Nueva Gerona

Isla de la Juventad

Telephone 61 23012

Cárdenas (Near Varadero)

Hospital 'Julio Arietegui'

Centro de Medicina Subacuatica

Carretera de Cardenas, Km 2

Cárdenas

Matanzas

Telephone 5 22114

Santiago de Cuba

Hospital Militar 'Castillo Duany'

Punta Blanca

Santiago de Cuba

Telephone 2 6471

Isla de la Juventud

Hotel El Colony

Carretera de la Siguanea, Km 41

Colony

Isla de la Juventud

Telephone 9 8240

SNORKELLING

With so much shore diving this is a paradise for snorkellers of all standards but the best snorkelling is at the diving sites that are only reached by boat.

DIVE PRACTICALITIES

Cuban diving is mostly relaxed, suitable for all standards of divers except on deeper dives. All operations offer extensive facilities, diving courses and have equipment for hire.

TRAVEL PRACTICALITIES

Most electricity sockets are American style, two flat prong 110 volt/60 cycles. However, some of the newer hotels operate on 220 volts/50 cycles and some hotels have both voltages, so always check with the management before plugging in any electrical equipment.

CAYMAN ISLANDS

CLIMATE

The Cayman Islands are fortunate in having fine weather all year round due entirely to their physical location away from any major land mass and the influence from the sea around them. The summer air temperature averages between 27°C and 32°C (80°F and 90°F) and only drops to the low 20s°C (low 70s°F) during the short winter, can get very stormy in September and October in hurricane season.

BEST TIME TO GO

The Cayman dive operators boast that you can dive every day of the year and, because of the size of the islands, you will always find a lee shore – even during the worst weather – and you will always be able to dive safely. In reality, from May to September are perhaps the best for diving.

GETTING THERE

Eleven scheduled air carriers fly into Grand Cayman. The Islands' national airline is Cayman Airways and, depending on the time of year, it flies three or four times each day from Miami. Other US services connect to most hub airports and other Caribbean islands. For European travellers, British Airways, operated by Caledonian, offer a direct flight to Grand Cayman from London Heathrow and internally, Cayman Airways and Island Air connect daily to Little Cayman Island and Cayman Brac.

WATER TEMPERATURES

Average 27°C (80°F) throughout the year.

VISIBILITY

Average more than 30m (100ft) all year.

QUALITY OF MARINE LIFE

Very good, particularly on night dives for the large variety of invertebrates and, of course, the stingrays!

DEPTH OF DIVES

First dive 30m (100ft), and 18m (60ft) on the second dive of the day.

SNORKELLING

Very good off all shore locations as reef starts directly at the shoreline.

RECOMPRESSION (HYPERBARIC) CHAMBERS

Recompression Chamber,
PO Box 1551G,
George Town,
Grand Cayman, B.W.I.
Telephone 1-345-949-2989.
Emergency: 555 (DAN) Divers' Alert Network
Telephone (919) 648--8111.
  Atlantis Research Submersible, telephone 1-345-949-7700, fax: 1-345-949-8574

DIVE PRACTICALITIES

All levels of diver catered for and strong conservation policies are practiced.

DUTCH ANTILLES

CLIMATE

Sunshine on most days except during the months of December to February. The constant trade winds produce an arid desert climate for the rest of the year with the hottest months being August to October. The lowest temperatures are around 24°C (75°F). The hottest days rarely go above 32°C (90°F) and the average is 28°C (82°F) with a cooling breeze.

BEST TIME TO GO

The protected west coasts of the ABCs allow diving all year. The more exposed sites are best dived in the summer and autumn.

GETTING THERE

KLM Dutch Airways flies direct from Amsterdam with connections all over Europe. There are charter flights to Aruba from London, Gatwick. American Airlines have connections from several North and Latin American gateways to both Aruba and Curaçao with further connections between Aruba and Bonaire. Local airlines connect between Curaçao and Bonaire. American Eagle now has a connection between Puerto Rico's San Juan and Bonaire and Air Jamaica connects with Bonaire and Curaçao. There is now a fast ferry connecting Bonaire and Curaçao twice a day so divers can travel between the two islands without having to wait 24 hours after diving.

WATER TEMPERATURE

24°C (75°F) in the cool season, but the average is 27°C (80°F).

VISIBILITY

Generally very clear – more than 30m (100ft).

QUALITY OF MARINE LIFE

Diverse and prolific, tame and approachable.

DEPTH OF DIVES

Often shallow, generally less than 40m (130ft), but drop-offs and walls may descend deeper.

RECOMPRESSION CHAMBERS

There are no recompression facilities in Aruba – patients are transferred to Curaçao.
Bonaire:
Saint Franciscus (Francisco) Hospital,
Kaya Soeur Bartola, Kralendijk,
Telephone 114.
Curaçao:
The Saint Elisabeth Hospital
(St Elisabeth Gasthuis), located in
Willemstad's Otrobanda district, contains the island's two hyperbaric chambers.
St Elizabeth Hospital,
Telephone 599 9 625100/624900
Recompression Chamber
Telephone 599 9 637457/637288

SNORKELLING

All three islands are a paradise for snorkellers of all standards.

DIVE PRACTICALITIES

Except on their windy north and northeast coasts, diving (other than deep dives) in the ABCs is mostly relaxed and suitable for all abilities. Some dives have moderate currents where intermediate skills are preferable.

All operators offer extensive facilities, diving courses and have equipment for hire. The larger ones offer Nitrox and technical diving.

VIRGIN ISLANDS

CLIMATE

Temperatures are lower than other areas of the Caribbean and averages around 20°–30°C (68°–86°F). There can be cool winds.

BEST TIME TO GO

The Virgin Islands are an ideal holiday location all year round and have a fairly equable climate, sharing the trade winds of the Lesser Antilles. There is a hurricane risk and this can be anywhere from September through to January, but it is rare that this has an adverse effect on your holiday. Summers are hot and humid with temperatures rising above 30°C (86°F) and care should be taken with exposure to the sun, particularly while on the dive boats. A waterproof sunscreen with a high sun protection factor and a hat should be worn at all times.

GETTING THERE

There are regular service jet flights from all the American hub airports such as Miami, Houston, Chicago etc. straight into St Croix and St Thomas. There are also flights from London Gatwick, serviced by Caledonian and operated by British Airways. However, due to the size of the international airport on Beef Island in the British Virgin Islands, all flights are first routed through San Juan in Puerto Rico, with a link by American Eagle.

WATER TEMPERATURES

Average 24°C (75°F), full wet suit and hood recommended.

VISIBILITY

May to September is best for water quality.

QUALITY OF MARINE LIFE

Excellent invertebrate life, particularly squid and octopus.

DEPTH OF DIVES

15–25m (50–80ft).

RECOMPRESSION (HYPERBARIC) CHAMBERS

The region's recompression chamber is located at St Thomas Hospital in Charlotte Amalie.

Telephone (809) 776 8311.

Emergency Telephone 922.

SNORKELLING

Good close to shore, but visibility suffers.

DIVE PRACTICALITIES

All levels of diver catered for, but the water is cooler than in other areas of the Caribbean.

TRAVEL PRACTICALITIES

While on Virgin Gorda, hire a small skiff and motor out to Saba Rock, home of the legendary wreck hunter and latter-day pirate Bert Kilbride.

The Baths on Virgin Gorda are a spectacular clump of simply gigantic granite boulders, which tumble into the sea amid tall palm trees and a gorgeous beach.

On St Croix, visit the Steeple building that houses a superb collection of Indian Artefacts and Wim Great House, which is a curious, moted, former estate building, which has been excellently restored.

Fort Christian on St Thomas dates from the Danes' arrival in the 1660s and houses a superb museum.

St John has great attractions, and is worthy of its National Park.

BAHAMAS

CLIMATE

July to October is the hurricane season and the time of highest rainfall. July and August can nevertheless be particularly busy, though, so book your trip well in advance, especially for the shark dives and dolphin experience.

BEST TIME TO GO

For diving, the best time is from November to June, which are the driest months. Best time is November through June to avoid hurricane season, but can be hot.

GETTING THERE

Nassau is serviced by all of the world's major airlines through any of the hub airports. The majority of divers come from the USA and they will probably route through Miami first. Bahama Air connect the entire Bahamas island chain with Nassau.

WATER TEMPERATURE

Set astride the Gulf Stream, the water stays at an equable temperature all year round with an average of around 27°C (80°F).

VISIBILITY

Generally in the vicinity of over 50m (165ft), but much less on the inshore, shallow dive sites.

QUALITY OF MARINE LIFE

The best location to have encounters with sharks and dolphins in the entire Caribbean.

DEPTH OF DIVES

Average 25m (80ft), but also very deep dives.

RECOMPRESSION CHAMBERS

In New Providence and San Salvadore.

SNORKELLING

Good off the shore, but better off dive boats when they visit the shallow reefs.

DIVE PRACTICALITIES

All levels of diver catered for, water calm and protected.

DIVE ATLAS OF THE WORLD

INDEX

WRECKS

MARINE LIFE

GLOSSARY

Adjustable buoyancy life jacket (ABLJ) – Another name for a jacket style buoyancy compensator device (BCD).

Ahermatypic corals – Corals that do not have symbiotic algae present in the polyp tissue.

Algae – Simple photosynthetic plants.

Aqualung – Underwater breathing apparatus.

Atmosphere – The average pressure of the atmosphere at sea level. A unit of pressure of 14.7psi or 1 bar. The pressure underwater increases by one atmosphere for every 10m (33ft) of depth.

Atmospheres Absolute (ATA) – The sum of the atmospheric pressure and the hydrostatic pressure. In other words, the ATA or atmospheres absolute is the total weight of the water and air above divers.

Atoll – A group of reefs and islands that surround a central lagoon and drop away to deep water on their outer sides.

Bends – Term used for decompression sickness because sufferers bend the affected limb to ease the pain.

Bommie – There is no fixed definition for a bommie, it is mainly an Australian word for an undersea pinnacle, or coral head.

Bora – A strong northerly, squally wind which blows in the northern Adriatic.

Breathing loop (rebreather) – all the internal areas within which the diver's breathing gases flow, including the counterlung, scrubber, breathing hoses and the diver's lungs.

Buoyancy compensator device (BCD) – A device by which divers can adjust their buoyancy underwater or inflate as a life jacket when on the surface. A BCD is usually inflated by a direct-feed, (power-inflator) from the main scuba cylinder by way of the regulator first stage.

However, a BCD may also be inflated by an emergency air cylinder or when on the surface by a cartridge of carbon dioxide, which can be used only once and then has to be replaced.

Buoyant ascent – A rapid emergency ascent following the inflation of a buoyancy compensator device or dry suit.

Caisson Workers Disease – Another name for decompression sickness because caisson workers doing underwater construction work in these watertight chambers suffered from it.

Carbon dioxide cartridge – A small cartridge of carbon dioxide (CO_2) used for one-off inflation of the BCD at the surface.

Cays – Islands formed by the accumulation of sand on a coral reef. These are distinct from islands that do not originate from reefs.

Certification card ('C'-card) – An identification card that provides evidence that at one point the diver has passed certain performance standards of a recognized diving training agency. Some dive operators will also want to see your latest diving logbook to check your experience since qualifying and whether you have had recent diving experience.

Chimney – A steep and narrow, almost perpendicular cleft in a reef-face.

Commensals – Organisms that live together without obvious mutual benefit.

Compressor – A multi-stage pump that is used to fill cylinders or air-banks with compressed air.

Console – A unit that is attached to the submersible pressure gauge to enable a collection of instruments to be mounted together.

Contents gauge – A submersible pressure gauge that indicates the amount of gas in the scuba cylinder by its pressure.

Coriolis Effect – The deflection of the path of a body due to the earth's rotation, to the left in the southern hemisphere and to the right in the northern hemisphere.

Counterlung – the sealed flexible bag that inflates as the diver exhales and deflates as the diver inhales. In acting as a storage area for the diver's breathing gases, the positioning of this bag within the breathing loop can greatly affect the breathing effort.

Cut-through-anything-shears – Shears that will cut through most fishing lines and nets, even thin steel ones.

Decompression dive – A dive which requires one or more decompression stops to release dissolved gases in a controlled fashion.

Decompression sickness (DCS) – A condition caused by the rapid release of pressure on ascent; nitrogen (or helium if used) in the blood and body tissues forms bubbles that can block the circulation.

Decompression stop – One or more pauses during the ascent to allow the excess nitrogen (or helium if used) in the body to dissipate.

Decompression table – A table of times and depths used to calculate the limits of safe diving and any required decompression stops.

Delayed deployment surface marker buoy – A surface marker buoy that is only deployed when required. These include rescue tubes or sausages.

Demand valve (DV) – Another name for a regulator because it only supplies breathing gas on demand.

Depth gauge – An instrument that shows the diver's depth beneath the surface by measuring the water pressure.

Diluent (rebreather) – The gas used in a closed circuit rebreather to make up volume in the breathing loop as the diver proceeds to deeper depths and the gases in the breathing loop are compressed. Depending on the rebreather, and the type of diving, the gas used for diluent could be air, Nitrox, Trimix or even Heliox.

Direct-feed – Also called a power-inflator, a one-way valve connected to a low-pressure hose, which enables a supply of gas from the first stage of the regulator to inflate the buoyancy compensator device or dry suit.

Dive planner – A table of times and depths used to calculate the limits of safe diving, particularly on multiple dives.

Dive timer – A timing device that is activated either manually or when it becomes submerged so that divers know the elapsed time of a particular dive.

Diving logbook – a record of your dives that also acts as proof of what types of dives you have accomplished since qualifying.

Drop-offs – Steep slopes of 60–85°.

Dump valve – A valve used to vent (dump) gases from dry suits or BCDs.

Elapsed time – the time that has elapsed since leaving the surface.

Emergency cylinder – A small cylinder that is fitted to many BCDs for emergency inflation.

Encrusting corals – A coral colony that forms a thin layer over a substrate.

Enriched Air Nitrox (EANx) – Any mixture of oxygen and nitrogen which has more or less oxygen than found in normal air. However, the term usually describes those mixtures with a more than the normal amount of oxygen.

Family – A grouping of related genera with common characteristics.

First stage – The section of the regulator that reduces the pressure of the gases in the scuba cylinder to a pressure that the second stage requires.

Free ascent – A diver surfacing rapidly in an emergency, forcibly breathing out all the way to avoid a burst lung.

Fringing reef – A reef that fringes an island or coast.

Fully-closed circuit rebreather – Refer to Rebreather.

Ghibli – A hot dry southerly/southeasterly wind of north Africa.

Gondwanaland – A supercontinent thought to have existed in the southern hemisphere in Palaeozoic times, comprising the present Africa, South America, Australia, Antarctica, and the Indian peninsula.

Guyot – A seamount with a flat top.

Haboob – A violent and oppressive seasonal wind blowing in Sudan and bringing sand from the desert.

Helictites – Distorted forms of stalactites resembling twigs.

Heliox – A breathing mixture of gases consisting entirely of helium and oxygen. This is used to eliminate Nitrogen narcosis and to control the effects of oxygen toxicity, by eliminating the nitrogen and reducing the amount of oxygen in the breathing mix.

Hermatypic or reef-building corals – Corals with symbiotic algae present in the polyp tissue.

Invertebrate – An animal that does not have a backbone or spinal column.

Khamsin – An oppressive, hot southerly/south-easterly wind, which blows in Egypt at intervals for about 50 days in March, April, and May, and fills the air with sand from the desert (*Khamsin* means 50 in Arabic).

Knot – Unit of speed used in sea and air navigation, equal to one nautical mile per hour.

Latitude (geographical) – The angular distance in degrees, north or south, of any place on the earth's surface from the equator, which is at latitude 0 degrees.

Levanter – A strong easterly wind in the Mediterranean that passes through the Strait of Gibraltar.

Longitude (geographical) – The angular distance of any place on the earth's surface, east or west of the standard meridian of Greenwich (UK), it is measured in degrees up to 180° East or West.

Loraine Smith Effect – see Oxygen Toxicity.

Meridian (geographical) – One of the imaginary lines along the surface of the earth at right angles to the equator, which join the North and South Geographical Poles, designated by degrees of longitude from 0 degrees at Greenwich (UK) to 180 degrees East or West.

Mistral – A strong, cold northwest wind which blows through southern France into the Mediterranean, mainly in winter.

Mollusc – Any animal of the phylum Mollusca, e.g. limpets, snails, cuttlefish, oysters, mussels, etc., members of which have soft bodies and usually have hard shells.

Monofilament cutter – A tool specifically designed to cut through monofilament line or netting.

Mouthpiece – Section of a regulator or snorkel which fits into the diver's mouth.

Nematocysts – stinging cells in jellyfish and other coelenterates that contain a coiled thread, often barbed or poisoned, that is ejected as a defence or to capture prey.

Nitrox – see Enriched Air Nitrox.

Non-decompression stop dive or No stop dive – A dive that does not require any decompression stops.

Normoxic – This is the term used to describe the normal mixture of gases found in the atmosphere.

Nautical mile – The length of one minute of latitude – in practice 1852m (6076ft).

Nitrogen narcosis – A condition affecting divers' mental processes caused by excess nitrogen in their body tissues. The effects of Nitrogen narcosis on divers are similar to being drunk and increase with depth.

Octopus rig – A second regulator second stage that is used for sharing air with another diver.

0-ring – A synthetic rubber ring that fits in a groove and is used to form an airtight or watertight seal.

Oxygen Toxicity – Physiological damage resulting from breathing higher than normal partial pressures of oxygen. There are two primary types. That resulting from long exposures of elevated partial pressures of oxygen is called the

Loraine Smith Effect or Pulmonary Oxygen Toxicity as the primary damage is to the lungs and airways. The other type results from short exposure to high partial pressures of oxygen and is called the Paul Bert effect or Central Nervous System Toxicity (CNS Toxicity) and is characterized by convulsions.

Palaeozoic – Relating to an era of geological time that began 600 million years ago, lasted about 375 million years, and was marked by the development of marine and terrestrial plants and animals.

Partial pressure – The pressure of a particular gas within a mixture of gases. It is commonly represented as 'pp' followed by the atomic symbol of the gas. The partial pressure of oxygen would be written as ppO_2.

Paul Bert Effect – see Oxygen Toxicity.

Pinnacle – A relatively narrow, vertical structure forming a peak.

Pleistocene – Denoting the first epoch of the Quaternary period (the most recent period of geological time), which lasted about 990,000 years and was characterized by widespread glaciation in the northern hemisphere and the evolutionary development of man.

Power-inflator – refer to direct feed.

Rebreather – A self-contained device used to recirculate and regulate breathing gases for the purposes of extended diving times and quiet operation. In a fully closed-circuit rebreather this is accomplished by chemically removing carbon dioxide (scrubbing CO_2), and adding oxygen as necessary to maintain a constant partial pressure of oxygen. This type of rebreather does not release any gases from the unit except under the conditions of ascending from depth. The advantage of this system is the greatest possible use of the oxygen carried, the disadvantage is the added complexity of the electronics and mechanics in the unit. In most semi-closed systems a portion of each breath is released to the water, the carbon dioxide is scrubbed from the remaining gases and a similar portion of new breathing gases are injected into the system.

Regulator – Another name for a demand valve.

A mechanism which reduces the pressure of the gases in the scuba cylinder to the pressure of the water surrounding the body at the level of the diver's lungs so that the gases can be inhaled by the diver.

Rescue tube – A highly-visible surface marker buoy in the shape of a tube or sausage that is only deployed when required.

Residual nitrogen – The amount of absorbed nitrogen that is estimated to remain in the diver's body after a dive.

Sand chute – A sloping channel down a reef which acts as a conduit for falling sand and other debris.

Scrubber or CO₂ scrubber – The part of a rebreather that removes carbon dioxide (CO_2) by passing it through a chemical that absorbs it.

SCUBA – An acronym for Self Contained Underwater Breathing Apparatus.

Scuba cylinder valve – The valve on the scuba cylinder, which is attached either to the regulator or the compressor.

Seamount – A submarine mountain (submerged volcano) rising more than 1000m (3300ft) above the ocean floor. Flat-topped ones are called guyots.

Second stage – The section of the regulator which further reduces the pressure of gases from the first stage to the ambient pressure of water level with the diver's lungs so that the gases can be breathed comfortably through the mouthpiece.

Semi-closed circuit rebreather – see Rebreather.

Shelf – A structure projecting almost horizontally from a reef face.

Shot line – A weighted line marking an object on the seabed or providing a guide for divers during descent or ascent.

Sirocco – A hot, oppressive, and often dusty or rainy wind which blows from the north coast of Africa over the Mediterranean and parts of southern Europe.

Stalactite – A conical or tapering formation that hangs from the roof of a cave, formed of calcite etc. deposited by water droplets that have percolated through the overlying limestone.

Stalagmite – A conical or columnar formation that rises from the floor of a cave, formed of calcite etc. deposited by water droplets falling from the roof or from stalactites.

Spur and groove – The classic formation of alternating spurs and grooves that are formed on an outer reef face by waves of the sea flowing in and then out again. The spur and groove system is formed by erosion.

Stabilizer (stab) jacket – Another name for a jacket-style buoyancy compensator device.

Surface marker buoy (SMB) – A floating buoy used by divers to mark their position.

Swim through – A hole formed by large boulders or eroded coral or rock through which people can swim.

Symbiosis – Two dissimilar organisms living in close physical association, where each benefits the other.

Tectonic Plates – Each of the several nearly rigid pieces of the outer portion of the earth, including the crust and the outermost mantle, thought to make up the earth's surface and to be moving slowly relative to one another. Their boundaries are identified with seismic, volcanic, and tectonic activity.

Tethys Sea – A large sea that lay between Laurasia and Gondwanaland during late Palaeozoic times, i.e. before the continents reached their present positions.

Trimix – A breathing mixture of gases most often composed of oxygen, nitrogen and helium. The proportions of each gas are changed according to the requirements of the particular dive plan.

Vendaval – A strong westerly wind in the Mediterranean that passes through the Strait of Gibraltar.

Walls – A reef wall that is near the vertical and may be either overhanging or undercut.

Zooxanthellae – Any of numerous yellow-brown algae or plants known as dinoflagellates present as symbionts in the cytoplasm of many marine invertebrates.

DIVE ATLAS OF THE WORLD
CONTRIBUTORS

JACK JACKSON

Diver, expedition leader, author and photographer Jack Jackson has been published in most underwater, diving and action-adventure magazines worldwide as well as in major newspapers and in-flight, travel, fashion and social magazines such as *Vogue* and *Harpers & Queen*. He was the second person to be awarded a Fellowship of the Royal Photographic Society in Underwater Nature Photography. He has been a Fellow of the Royal Geographical Society since 1970.

CHARLES ANDERSON

Marine Biologist Dr Charles Anderson has lived and worked in the Maldives since 1983. His profession has taken him to many parts of the world where he dives in pursuit of unusual fish and nudibranchs. He is the author of seven guide books to the marine life of the Maldives, Sri Lanka and Indonesia.

LAWSON WOOD

Lawson Wood has been scuba diving since 1965 and taking photographs underwater for over 30 years. He is a founder member of the Marine Conservation Society and founder and chairman of Scotland's only marine reserve at St Abbs and Eyemouth on Scotland's southeast coast. Lawson is the first person to be awarded a fellowship by both the Royal Photographic Society and the British Institute of Professional Photographers for his underwater photography. He is also a Fellow of the Royal Geographical Society. Lawson is the author of 26 diving related books, including the award-winning *Top Dive Sites of the Caribbean*. He now lives on Cayman Brac with his wife, Lesley.

BOB HALSTEAD

Bob Halstead learned to scuba dive in the Bahamas in 1968, bought his first underwater camera the same year and qualified as a NAUI Diving Instructor in 1970. Moving to Papua New Guinea in 1973 he and his wife, Dinah, formed PNG's first full-time sport diving business based in Port Moresby. In 1986 they started PNG's first live-aboard dive boat operation with the 20m (66ft) dive charter vessel which they had built, the *Telita*. Bob has made over 8000 dives and has discovered several marine species new to science – a fish, *Trichonotus halstead*, was named after them in 1996. Bob Halstead has published numerous articles and books on diving and marine life in PNG.

MICHAEL AW

Michael Aw's work on environmental issues and natural history have been featured in *BBC Wildlife*, *Asian Geographic*, *GEO*, *Underwater GEO-GRAPHIC*, *Nature Focus*, *Action Asia*, *Scuba Diver*, *Ocean Realm (USA)*, *Times*, *Asia Week*, *DIVE*, *Unterwasser*, *Tauchen* and *Aquanaut*. He has won awards for photography from several international organizations, including the Nikon International Photo Contest on three occasions. He has received awards at the BBC Photographer of the Year (Wildlife) competition. He has directed two 24-hour photographic documentaries of coral reefs on the Australian Great Barrier Reef and the Maldives in 1995 and 1999 respectively. These extended sojourns have been encapsulated in books and a video for *National Geographic*. Michael has authored several natural history books about fish, corals and invertebrates, including *Underwater Jungles*, *Celebrate the Sea*, *Beneath Bunaken*, *Dreams from a Rainbow Sea*, *Tropical Reef Fishes*, *Tropical Reef Life* and *Staghorn Corals*.

WADE DOAK

Wade Doak was born in New Zealand in 1940. Discovering treasure prompted him to write *The Elingamite & its Treasure* in 1969. Since then he has concentrated on underwater exploration, documenting the complex social lives of fish and marine ecology. Nineteen more books ensued, including his latest, *New Zealand Sea Fishes*. In 1975 Wade first encountered dolphins. Using gestures, one dolphin taught Wade a new manoeuvre. When he copied, six dolphins reinforced by repeating it in unison. Ever since then, he has sought to know the capacities of the minds of marine creatures and to grasp what sort of relationship cetaceans seek with humans. Four books on cetacean encounters resulted. His three major South Seas underwater and anthropological research expeditions are described in *Sharks & Other Ancestors* and *Islands of Survival*. In these he went from a study of shark behaviour to the lives of a people who worship spirit sharks.

ANDY AND ANGIE BELCHER

Andy and Angie Belcher are freelance photographers and photojournalists specializing in action, adventure and aquatic images of New Zealand and the South Pacific. Their awards include Australasian Underwater Photographer of the Year (twice), firsts at France's Okeanos and Antibes Festivals, a first in the 1997 British Wildlife Photographer of the Year competition and third overall in the Nikon 200/2001 photo contest international which received 34,000 entries. They have their own business, Legend Photography, which supplies underwater, wildlife and adventure images for magazines, books and advertising. They live in Maketu with their children Ben (14) and Ocean (9).

ANN STORRIE

Born 1953 in Perth, Western Australia, Ann Storrie is an animal technologist involved in medical research. She lectures on Animal Care studies at Bentley TAFE College in Perth and is a freelance underwater photojournalist. She started diving in 1982 and, with her husband, Wayne, became engrossed in underwater photography, although nature and marine biology are still her primary interests. Ann founded the Western Australian Underwater Photographic Society (WAUPS) in 1984 and her articles have been published in *Scuba Diver, Sportdiving in Australia and the South Pacific*, and others. She has been guest speaker at various conventions, including the Scuba Expo Congress and Film Festival in Melbourne. She is co-author of several books including the Western Australian Conservation and Land Management publications *Marine life of Ningaloo Marine Park and Coral Bay, Wonders of Western Waters, The Swan River Estuary and Marine Park* and *Beneath Busselton Jetty*. She contributed to the New Holland title *Top Dive Sites of the Indian Ocean*.

ALAN MOUNTAIN

Alan Mountain is a communications and development consultant who was born and educated in South Africa. He has been diving for over 35 years in many parts of the world and has a particular interest in the field of underwater photography as well as in the underwater environment and its conservation. Mountain has a special feeling for Mauritius, having seen it change from an uncertain and underdeveloped country after independence to a trendsetter in the developing world. In the process he has also had the opportunity to explore and enjoy the island's diving diversity and its wonderful hospitality.

BRUCE AND JUDY MANN

Bruce and Judy Mann both completed their Masters degrees in Ichthyology at Rhodes University in Grahamstown, South Africa, in 1992. Since then they have worked for the South African Association for Marine Biological Research in Durban. Judy runs the Education Centre, where she works with a wide range of people. Bruce is a scientist in the research institute where he focuses on fish research and marine protected areas. They are passionate about marine conservation and enjoy outdoor sports including diving, fishing, canoeing and paragliding.

CHRIS AND MONIQUE FALLOWS

Chris and Monique Fallows are marine wildlife photographers specializing in Great White Shark imagery. Chris has been involved with Great White Shark work for over a decade and has worked on over 25 documentaries – for *National Geographic*, BBC, Discovery, CBS and many others. Their focus is on informing the public about the importance of sharks in the eco-system and to show these animals as magnificent apex predators. Chris also runs an eco-tourism business in False Bay, South Africa, that specializes in Great White Shark expeditions as well as Mako and Blue Shark diving.

SAM HARWOOD

Rob Bryning and Sam Harwood have over 14 years of experience operating their live-aboards *MV Sea Spirit* and *MV Sea Queen* in the Maldives. Rob has a passion for underwater video, while Sam's passion is for photography. Together they have acted as guides for BBC wildlife films and many independent media productions. They are authors of Globetrotter's *Dive Guide to the Maldives*, were contributors to New Holland's *Top Dive Sites of the Indian Ocean* and their photography and articles have been used in publications around the world. Bryning and Harwood own Maldives Scuba Tours Ltd and Scuba Tours Worldwide in the UK.

STEFANIA LAMBERTI

Stefania Lamberti was born in Milan, Italy, and educated in South Africa. For the past decade she has been an award-winning wildlife documentary producer, writer and photographer. Her love of Africa has inspired her work on the wildest places of the continent and the Indian Ocean and its islands. Her experience and extensive documentation on these subjects has led to the writing of and contribution to several books and magazines as well as the production of many natural history documentaries in association with *National Geographic* and *Discovery Channel*. Stefania and her husband are based in Johannesburg where they run a television production company The Wildside Aquavision. Stefania continues to pursue her passion for the underwater world.

PAUL LEES

An experienced diving instructor, Paul lees has managed several of Thailand's top diving schools. As writer and photographer he regularly contributes to diving magazines worldwide and has contributed to New Holland's *Top Dive Sites of the Indian Ocean*. Based in Phuket, he runs the diving consultancy service Divelink Thailand.

MARK AND CHARLOTTE DURHAM

Mark and Charlotte Durham were involved in an 11-month sponsored trans-African diving project called 'divethedream.com'. This web site became a live online dive guide which documented sites, centres and marine conservation issues from Cape Town to Northern Kenya. Before Dive The Dream, Mark ran a large watersports store in Central London while undertaking freelance marine contracts as a commercial diver, underwater photographer and hyperbaric chamber assistant. Mark has also worked as a fisheries observer in the South Atlantic aboard a longlining vessel and in the North Atlantic on the Grand Banks. Charlotte, a PADI diving instructor, teamed up with Mark in 1996.

DIVE ATLAS OF THE WORLD

PHOTOGRAPHIC CREDITS

Copyright rests with the following photographers and/or their agents listed below. Key to Locations: t = top; tl = top left; tc = top centre; tr = top right; b = bottom; bl = bottom left; bc = bottom centre; br = bottom right; l = left; r = right; c = centre. (No abbreviation is given for pages with a single image, or pages on which all photographs are by same photographer.)

AB ....Andy Belcher
AM......Alan Mountain
BH.......Bob Halstead
BM......Buddy Mays
CA ......Dr R Charles Anderson
CB.......Chris Butler
CF ....Chris Fallow
DAK ....Danja Kohler
DK ......Dennis King
EI ....Eilat Images.com
ENI......Enlightenment Images

GG......Gary Gentile
GI........Gallo Images / T=Taxi / HL=Harvey Lloyd / S= Stone
GT ......Graham Teague
IB ....Image Bank / GAR=Guide A.Rossi
JJ ....Jack Jackson
JR ....Jeff Rottman
LO.......Lesley Orsen
LP ....Linda Pitkin
LT........Lochman Transparencies / AS=Alex Steffe, CB=Clay Bryce, CR=Col Roberts, EB=Eva Boogard, GT=Geoff Taylor

LW ......Lawson Wood
MA......Micheal Aw
MJF .....Martyn J Farr
OI ....Oceanic Impressions / MS=Mark Strickland
PA ....Photo Access / P =Patrick Wagner
PP ....Peter Pinnock
RG ......Roger Grace
SIL.......Struik Image Library
VD ......Visual Diving / BC=Bert Chauvel
WHS ...Waterhouse Stock / SF=Stephen Frink
WT......World Travel

Page	Loc	Credit	Page	Loc	Credit	Page	Loc	Credit	Page	Loc	Credit	Page	Loc	Credit
1		MA	62	c	DK	110	br	LP	158		VD/BC	220	tr	OI
2–3		OI/MS	62	b	DAK	112	tl	LP	159–160		MA	221	bl	OI
4–5		LW	64	l	DK	112	tr	PP	161		VD/BC	221	br	MA
6		PP	64	r	JJ	114		MA	162–163		MA	222		MA
10		LT/CB	65		DK	116	bl	AM	164–178		JJ	223		LT
13		PP	67	l & r	LP	116	c	MA	180–182		MA	224		LP
18	tl	LP	68–70		JJ	117		MA	185		WHS/SF	227	t	LW
18	tc	LT/EB	72	l&r	JJ	118		OI/MS	186–190		AB	227	b	JJ
18	tr	JJ	73–79		JJ	121	bl&bc	LP	191	t	PP	228		LW
19	bl, bc	JJ	80		PP	121	br	OI/MS	191	b	AB	229	t	MJF
19	br	MA	82	t	MA	122–126		OI/MS	192		OI/MS	229	c & b	LW
20		LP	82	b	PP	128		LT/CR	193	t	OI/MS	230	t	MJF
22		LW	83	t	AM	129		LT/EB	193	b	AB	230	b	LW
24		CF	83	b	OI/MS	130	tl	LT/EB	194–199		BH	231		MJF
26	tl	CF	84–87		PP	130	tr	LT/CB	200	tl	MA	232	tl	GT
26	tc	GG	88	tl	LO	131		LT/CB	200	tr	LT/AS	232	tr	LW
26	tr	LW	88	tr	LW	133		LT/GT	201	t	MA	233	t	GT
27		GG	89 &91		LW	135		BH	201	b	LT/EB	233	b	LW
28	tl	GI/T/HL	92–93	tl	CA	136		LT/AS	203	bl	MA	234		LW
28	tr	IB/GAR	94–95		AM	137	tl&tc	MA	203	br	LT/PN	235		GT
31	t & b	GG	96	tl	PP	137	tr	JJ	204–205		MA	236–239		JJ
32–36		LW	96	tr	SIL	138–141		JJ	207		AB	240		LP
37	t & b	GG	97–99		PP	142	t	MA	208		RG	241	tl	LP
38	l	SIL	100	tl	SIL	142	b	JJ	209–211		AB	241	tc	JJ
38	r	CF	100	tr	PA/PW	145		JJ	212	tl	LW	241	tr	JJ
39–41		CF	101		PP	146	tl	LP	212	tr	BM	242–245		LW
43–55		LW	103	tl	PP	146	tr	JJ	213–214		LW	248–254		JJ
56		DK	103	tr	AM	147		JJ	216	tl	LW	265–259		LW
58		JJ	104	tl	MA	148		LT/CB	216	tr	ENI	260		GT
59	t & b	DK	104	tr	PP	149		JJ	217		LW	261	t	LW
60	l	EI	105–106		PP	151	bl	MA	218	tl	GI/S	261	b	GT
60	r	WT/CB	109		PP	151	br	LP	218	tr	LW	262–264		LW
61		JR	110	bl	LP	152–153		LP	219		LW			
62	t	JR	110	bc	PP	154–157		MA	220	tl	MA			